The New Wind

World Anthropology

General Editor

SOL TAX

Patrons

CLAUDE LÉVI-STRAUSS
MARGARET MEAD
LAILA SHUKRY EL HAMAMSY
M. N. SRINIVAS

MOUTON PUBLISHERS · THE HAGUE · PARIS
DISTRIBUTED IN THE USA AND CANADA BY ALDINE, CHICAGO

The New Wind
Changing Identities in South Asia

Editor

KENNETH DAVID

MOUTON PUBLISHERS · THE HAGUE · PARIS
DISTRIBUTED IN THE USA AND CANADA BY ALDINE, CHICAGO

Distributed in the United States of America and Canada
by Aldine Publishing Company, Chicago, Illinois
ISBN 90-279-7959-6 (Mouton)
ISBN 0-202-90047-9 (Aldine)
Jacket photo by permission of ABC Press, Amsterdam
Photo by F. J. Goodman
Indexes by John Jennings
Cover and jacket design by Jurriaan Schrofer
Printed in Great Britain

General Editor's Preface

This book examines anew one of the large geographic, historical, and cultural areas which has deeply engaged the interest of anthropologists: the Indian subcontinent. In an interdisciplinary arena, the volume exemplifies the method of analysis used by a new generation of social anthropologists in which a basic problem (in this case continuity and change) is informed by a central concept (social identity) and by a methodological conflict (empiricist vs. intellectualist vs. materialist). It also permits a gifted editor to show how the independent work of 17 scholars, and discussion among them and others, can be forged into an intelligible, theoretically significant book. The facts that a majority of these scholars are themselves from South Asia and that the book was generated out of an unusually international Congress suggests why it reflects an interesting tension between "Western" and postcolonial views.

Like most contemporary sciences, anthropology is a product of the European tradition. Some argue that it is a product of colonialism, with one small and self-interested part of the species dominating the study of the whole. If we are to understand the species, our science needs substantial input from scholars who represent a variety of the world's cultures. It was a deliberate purpose of the IXth International Congress of Anthropological and Ethnological Sciences to provide impetus in this direction. The *World Anthropology* volumes, therefore, offer a first glimpse of a human science in which members from all societies have played an active role. Each of the books is designed to be self-contained; each is an attempt to update its particular sector of scientific knowledge and is written by specialists from all parts of the world. Each volume should be read and reviewed individually as a separate volume on its own given subject. The set as a whole will indicate what changes are in store for anthropology as scholars from the developing countries join in studying the species of which we are all a part.

The IXth Congress was planned from the beginning not only to include as many of the scholars from every part of the world as possible, but also with a view toward the eventual publication of the papers in high-quality volumes. At previous Congresses scholars were invited to bring papers which were then read out loud. They were necessarily limited in length; many were only summarized; there was little time for discussion; and the sparse discussion could only be in one language. The IXth Congress as an experiment aimed at changing this. Papers were written with the intention of exchanging them before the Congress, particularly in extensive pre-Congress sessions; they were not intended to be read aloud at the Congress, that time being devoted to discussions — discussions which were simultaneously and professionally translated into five languages. The method for eliciting the papers was structured to make as representative a sample as was allowable when scholarly creativity — hence self-selection — was critically important. Scholars were asked both to propose papers of their own and to suggest topics for sessions of the Congress which they might edit into volumes. All were then informed of the suggestions and encouraged to rethink their own papers and the topics. The process, therefore, was a continuous one of feedback and exchange and it has continued to be so even after the Congress. The some two thousand papers comprising *World Anthropology* certainly then offer a substantial sample of world anthropology. It has been said that anthropology is at a turning point; if this is so, these volumes will be the historical direction-markers.

As might have been foreseen in the first postcolonial generation, the large majority of the Congress papers (82 percent) are the work of scholars identified with the industrialized world which fathered our traditional discipline and the institution of the Congress itself: Eastern Europe (15 percent); Western Europe (16 percent); North America (47 percent); Japan, South Africa, Australia, and New Zealand (4 percent). Only 18 percent of the papers are from developing areas: Africa (4 percent); Asia-Oceania (9 percent); Latin America (5 percent). Aside from the substantial representation from the U.S.S.R. and the nations of Eastern Europe, a significant difference between this corpus of written material and that of other Congresses is the addition of the large proportion of contributions from Africa, Asia, and Latin America. "Only 18 percent" is two to four times as great a proportion as that of other Congresses; moreover, 18 percent of 2,000 papers is 360 papers, 10 times the number of "Third World" papers presented at previous Congresses. In fact, these 360 papers are more than the total of *all* papers published after the last International Congress of Anthropological and Ethnological Sciences which was held in the United States (Philadelphia, 1956).

The significance of the increase is not simply quantitative. The input of scholars from areas which have until recently been no more than subject matter for anthropology represents both feedback and also long-awaited theoretical contributions from the perspectives of very different cultural, social, and historical traditions. Many who attended the IXth Congress were convinced that anthropology would not be the same in the future. The fact that the next Congress (India, 1978) will be our first in the "Third World" may be symbolic of the change. Meanwhile, sober consideration of the present set of books will show how much, and just where and how, our discipline is being revolutionized.

Among the other books in this series which will interest readers of this volume are those on other geographic regions, especially the Himalayas, Southeast Asia, and East Africa; topics concerning urbanization, migration, ethnicity, identity, and social development and change; cultural forms and symbols; and a variety of theoretical and methodological discussions.

Chicago, Illinois   SOL TAX
February 14, 1977

Preface

In the Introduction and in the Epilogue of this volume, I am conscious of writing for a potentially diverse audience. Readers of volumes in the *World Anthropology* series may be undergraduate or graduate students, interested laymen, social scientists from fields other than anthropology, and specialists in world areas other than South Asia. It seems imprudent to ignore the varying degrees of specialized knowledge and expectations of such an audience. Although the various sections of the Introduction and the Epilogue are intended, to a certain extent, to meet the needs of different readers, the sections are complementary rather than mutually exclusive. The first section of the Introduction reviews dilemmas in theoretical approaches found in recent literature on South Asia, dilemmas which yield contrary interpretations of the previously established structure and the emerging structure of identities in South Asia. The second and third sections deal with the responses to these dilemmas found in the papers collected here and in the three conferences that convened to discuss changing identities in South Asia.[1] The final section places these theoretical and methodological developments in a social and scholarly context. Readers seeking a review and

[1] A two-day conference (hereafter, preconference) preceded the IXth International Congress of Anthropological and Ethnological Sciences, which convened at Michigan State University, East Lansing, Michigan, on August 29, 1973. It was chaired by myself and was attended by Professors Steve Barnett, C. von Fürer-Haimendorf, Geraldine Gamburd, Mohan K. Gautam, Ravindra S. Khare, Owen M. Lynch, McKim Marriott, Charles Morrison, William Ross, Syamalakanti Sengupta, and Stanley J. Tambiah. The Congress session convened at the Chicago Hilton Hotel on September 3, 1973, and was chaired by Professors von Fürer-Haimendorf and Stanley J. Tambiah; panelists were Professors Kenneth David, Ravindra S. Khare, Owen M. Lynch, McKim Marriott, and Surajit Sinha. An informal session (hereafter, postconference) convened the following day, chaired by Professor Stanley J. Tambiah; a number of scholars participated vigorously.

discussion of the term *identity* may prefer to skip directly to the Epilogue, where I also summarize the major processes involved in the changing frontiers of South Asian collective identities that have been reported here.

The reader may be surprised to find that half of this volume entitled *Changing identities in South Asia* is devoted to papers addressed to questions — broadly, caste and religious structure — that could have deserved the title of traditional structure. At issue here is a questioning of the kind of explanation best suited to clarify both structure and change, for an author's assumptions in dealing with traditional structure profoundly influence his or her analysis of change. By challenging previous positions, the papers in Part 1, "The Standing and the Moving," may aid this epistemological task. The papers on emerging identities, such as those on ethnicity, agricultural labor unions, and revitalized tribal identities in Part 2, "The Moving and the Standing," provide new information and analytic strategies for dealing with continuities and transformations of the previous structure. Although no finely sculpted, brightly packaged new paradigm (in Kuhn's sense) has been produced here, participants at the conferences were aware that they were not leaving the old dilemmas exactly as they were; in this process, they have put forward new theoretical and methodological approaches which undoubtedly will create new dilemmas. By studying these contrasting approaches collected in one volume, the reader may be able to judge for himself which kind of theoretical framework is best suited to explain structure and change in a new nation.

A long introduction follows, for I have chosen to include excerpts from the transcripts of the preconference and postconference sessions where they are relevant to the discussion of the papers, rather than to append them separately and make dozens of references to them. Tape transcripts, as the United States House of Representatives is currently saying, are not "best evidence," and I apologize for any misstatement of participants' remarks. Much discussion is entirely omitted, as the nonprofessional recordings of these two sessions, where voices sometimes joined in chorus, yielded results which are somewhat better than haphazard. Thanks to the technicians of the International Congress of Anthropological and Ethnological Sciences (ICAES), recordings of the Congress sessions are perfect, and one has been reproduced in this volume.

Inclusion of different kinds of material will require the following reference conventions: a paper included in this volume will be identified with the notation (Lynch, this volume). A conference participant's remarks (in the Introduction and Symposium Remarks) will be indicated by printing the speaker's name in small capitals. References to the literature will be as usual.

Without the generous aid of the Michigan State University College of Social Science, the Center for International Programs, the Department of Anthropology, and the Asian Studies Center, and without the numerous chores ably performed by the staffs of the latter two units, the two-day preconference on changing identities would not have happened.

Many thanks are due to Professors Christof von Fürer-Haimendorf, McKim Marriott, S. J. Tambiah, Owen Lynch, Ravindra S. Khare, Bernard S. Cohn, and Steve Barnett, who participated in the planning, execution, and aftermath of the conference sessions. Members of the International Congress of Anthropological and Ethnological Sciences staff worked overtime to ensure that all the papers selected for discussion were available to the panelists. I am grateful to Ms. Masuma Downie, Ms. Linda Easley, Ms. Patricia Fujimoto, and Mr. Howard Bernstein, who recorded several conference sessions and to Mr. Barry Michie and Ms. Fujimoto, who aided me in transcribing them. Ms. Twila Peck was the critical proofreader during the final stages of this project. While a number of people have responded to these introductory remarks, I must particularly mention Professors Harry Raulet, Ronald Inden, Charles Morrison, and Ms. Emily M. H. Crom.

Thanks is too trivial a word to signify my appreciation to my wife and *śaktī*, Carol, who encouraged me and withstood my changing identities while I was working on this project.

Michigan State University   KENNETH DAVID.
East Lansing, Michigan

Table of Contents

Introduction

KENNETH DAVID

PREVAILING WINDS

As a prelude to the introduction of the papers collected here and of the conference discussions, I first wish to address certain issues, or dilemmas, known to the authors and conference participants, dilemmas concerning the definition of structure in which identities are embedded. I shall be arguing in this section that a number of analysts in what I call the New Wind are now reacting, not to the well-known differences between empiricist and intellectualist interpretations of traditional and modern structure but against the similarities between these two analytic traditions.

As a metaphoric entrée to this novel declaration of similarities between empiricist and intellectualist definitions of structure, I have chosen the indigenous image of the standing and the moving. Parts 1 and 2 of this volume are entitled "The Standing and the Moving" and "The Moving and the Standing" rather than "Traditional Structure" and "Modern Structure" or "Continuity and Change" and "Change and Continuity" for several reasons. These titles refer to new analytic strategies for dealing with transformations and continuities within and between what we usually call the traditional and the modern order. And, consonant with the ethnomethodology used in several papers in this volume, these titles are not based on an image extrinsic to the region; they derive from an indigenous source, a *virasaiva bhaktī* poem, which I now quote:

The temple and the body
The rich
will make temples for Siva.

What will I
a poor man,
do?
My legs are pillars
the body the shrine
the head a cupola
of gold.
Listen, O lord of the meeting rivers,
things standing shall fall,
but the moving ever shall stay (Basavanna 820, quoted in Ramanujan 1973:19).

The central image of the poem, the standing/the moving (an opposition also between the rich/the poor, the temple/the body, and to make/to be (Ramanujan 1973:22), which is resolved in the last two lines in favor of the moving, brings home to me a central point concerning the present state of our study of South Asia: the dynamic diversity of what has been in the past cavalierly referred to as "the tradition." Every researcher in South Asia is struck by the marvelous tendency of the region to provide exceptions to all but nontrivial generalizations. South Asia refuses to display a staid, monolithic, and inflexible tradition, as traditions are supposed to be. Ramanujan's brilliant discussion shows how this genre of *virasaiva bhakti* poems were exceptions to Redfield's (1960) dichotomy of Great and Little Traditions perhaps a thousand years before Redfield wrote. That is, the *virasaiva* saints were consciously denigrating " . . . at least in their intense moods, the 'great' and 'little' traditions. I think it is because the 'great' and 'little' traditions . . . together constitute 'establishment' in the several senses of the word. They are the establishment, the stable, the secure, the (standing) sthāvara, in the social sense" (Ramanujan 1973:29, 30).

This is hardly surprising in view of the fact that the *virasaiva* movement was a protest movement, a "social upheaval by and for the poor, the low-caste and the outcaste against the rich and the privileged; it was a rising of the unlettered against the literate pundit, flesh and blood against stone" (Ramanujan 1973:21). In other words, the concepts of the Great and Little Traditions have been seen as a useful way of describing unity (the Great Tradition) and diversity (the Little Tradition) in Indian civilization. Concepts such as universalization and parochialization, which describe processes of historical exchange between these two levels of tradition (Marriott 1955), make this a dynamic model and not just an exercise in sterile typology. As the *virasaiva* case shows, even this model does not exhaust the dynamics of structures and counterstructures coexisting in the civilization.

This metaphor of the standing and the moving will now be a guide-post for a brief survey of the prevailing winds of method, theory, and interpretation of South Asian caste and religious structure. I shall suggest that the, partially harmonious, song of the New Wind consists in a reaction against certain establishment, or standing, interpretations of traditional structure by intellectualist and empiricist theorists. Further, the New Wind is a reaction against interpretations which tend to distort, to a greater or lesser extent, our object of inquiry by imposing alien (Western scientific) ideologies or synecdochic indigenous ideologies on the data.

One line of evolution concerns the perception of caste and religious structure in terms of unity/diversity. The first stage of research, as Vidyarthi (this volume) suggests, was a descriptive period. Administrators and census takers favored us with lengthy descriptions of the material culture, of anthropometry, of secular and religious customs. These descriptions were atomistic accounts of castes and tribes taken one at a time, a method consonant with the study of low-energy or primitive societies, but not especially suited to the study of societies in the context of a historical civilization. The result is encyclopedic listings of diverse data. Exceptional systematic studies, such as Maine's (1861) study of land tenure systems, were narrowly focused and thus failed to provide a holistic account of societal tradition. During the first half of this century, as Vidyarthi's (this volume) survey documents, with the exception of scholars like Bouglé, Ghurye, Hutton, Hocart, and Wiser, ethnographic research did not generally transcend local systems of action or structures of thought, although the techniques of observation and description became increasingly sophisticated.

To my mind, the period after World War II appears to be a watershed in that analysts lost tolerance for purely descriptive accounts. The notion that "India is a cauldron; and once you get into it, you never get out of it," seems to have been taken seriously, for analysts began to fashion massive analytic handles to cope with the cauldron of diversity. There began a search for the standing structure of traditional South Asia, a search for dominant, establishment, encompassing structures both on the level of social structure and on that of ideology. The rural establishment social structure became characterized in terms of the *jajmāni* system, the dominant landowning caste (Srinivas 1955:17–19), the summation of partial statuses (Bailey 1963; Barth 1960; Béteille 1965), and the nonimitative or qualified-imitative orders of Sanskritization and Kshatriyazation. The establishment religious order, the repository of unity (called the Great Tradition, or Sanskritic Hinduism) was distinguished from the locus of diversity (the Little Traditions). The establishment ideology was defined in terms of hierarchy, separation, interdependence, and holism — all based on the opposition purity/impurity (Bouglé 1958; Dumont and

Pocock 1958). Despite all the polemics between proponents of inductive-empiricist analysis and proponents of hypothetico-deductive analysis concerning the definition of religious and caste structure in the traditional order, there is an astounding similarity in the general analytic strategy of seeking to formulate unified, standing structures of traditional South Asia.

Another line of evolution concerns the perception of traditional caste and religious structure in terms of statics/dynamics. Singer locates the image of static traditional India in the writings of James and John Stuart Mill, Sir Henry Maine, and Karl Marx, who find that

... the decisive evidence of the "traditional" character of South Asian societies and of their stability and even stagnation has been the absence of rapid occupational and technological change. The explanation generally given for the absence of such change is the deep and ramified embeddedness of occupations in the social and cultural systems — in caste and kinship, in ritual and cult, in the organic interdependence of society, and in a theodicy of the social system that was supposed to generate a dread of change and innovation in its believers (Singer 1973:2).

Some very recent accounts still posit an axiomatic opposition between traditional and modern structure. To Hagen (1962), in traditional societies, behavior patterns of each generation replicate those of its antecedents. Social structure is hierarchical and status is usually ascribed rather than achieved. "A traditional society, in short, tends to be custom bound, ascriptive, and unproductive" (Hagen 1962:56). A static, rigid structure is implicit in social structural descriptions of caste society as a noncompetitive order (Leach 1960) or in terms of summation of statuses between castes (Bailey 1963; Barth 1960; Béteille 1965) and, on the ideological level, as a hierarchical, holistic ideology (Dumont 1970).

Unlike these authors, for whom traditional structure is a standing static structure, other authors apparently stress the moving structure, according it more dynamic potential. The Rudolphs note:

The examination of internal variations within traditional and modern societies draws attention to those features of each that are present in the other. If they are dialectically rather than dichotomously related, and if internal variations are attended to and taken seriously, then those sectors of traditional society that contain or express potentialities for change from dominant norms and structures become critical for understanding the nature and process of modernization (Rudolph and Rudolph 1967:10).

Similarly, Singer forwards this view:

Indian civilization has built into it adaptive mechanisms for incorporating new techniques, new ideas, and newcomers with only a gradual displacement of the old (Singer 1968:xi).

Analysis carried on in the name of this revised notion of traditional structure and modern structure yields results which may not be so dissimilar from the first. Analysis of modernizing adaptive strategies by Singer (ed. 1973) for example, proceeds with the latent assumption that the traditional structure (which can handle limited change by means of the South Asian genius for absorbing foreign or novel elements into the tradition) has undergone only one major structural change. VON FÜRER-HAIMENDORF stated this view during the preconference. He cautioned us that we should not expect any single model to fit this situation of change due to the profound confrontation of the endogenous civilization with the exogenous Western civilization, a situation he likened to the hypothetical sociocultural upheaval which would have resulted if medieval Europe had been conquered by the Chinese, Confucian ideas had confronted Christianity, and so forth. The latent assumption of a historically unique, nonrepetitive exogenous/endogenous confrontation resulting in profound sociocultural change underlies many studies which identify changes from the traditional structure under the macrorubrics of modernization, industrialization, Westernization, and the like. The colonial experience has indeed incited profound changes, but use of these terms draws our attention away from previous confrontations and previous structural changes. This assumption has been strongly questioned, as we shall see later.

The point is that the distinction between empiricist and intellectualist interpretations of unity and diversity of statics and dynamics, and of traditional structure appears to be overdrawn. The similarity of the theoretical and methodological problems with which each school of explanation has been charged by the opposite school is equally striking, for both empiricists and intellectualists have been charged with being theoretically reductionist and methodologically centric and synecdochic.

Both schools intend to explain human thought and action, but there is a reductionist tendency for each side to give analytic priority to different aspects of action. For empiricists, hard facts of material resources and control of power are what constrain reality. For intellectualists, a structure of ideas is the hard fact of reality from which the "blooming, buzzing confusion" of economy and polity deviates. The lack of confrontation between these schools is illustrated by debates on caste ranking. Several authors have commented, for example, that Dumont's (1970) intellectualist analysis of local caste ranking explains the extremes of a local system but falters in the middle ranges, where "the politico-economic dragon holds sway" (Tambiah 1972:833); whereas Bailey's analysis (1963), in terms of the summation of stratified relations based on differential control of economic and power resources, explains the middle ranges of the local hierarchy but fails to handle the extremes where the religious ideology of purity and impurity overrules economic and power status discrepancies (David 1974a; see also Madan 1971:10, 11). There has been polemical confrontation between proponents of these two schools of thought, but the presentations have been so mutually reductionist that a meaningful dialogue has not been established.

Theoretical reductionism is rooted in distinctly separate methodological choices, that is, choices of what constitutes the proper source of data and rules for ordering those data into a theoretical explanation. Depending on what choices are made, one's explanation may be charged with verifiability/nonverifiability, inductive/hypothetico-deductive reasoning, analytic sociocentrism/parochialism, comparability/solipsism, atomistic analysis of constitutive units/holistic analysis of the structure of relations between units. The set of choices including the first term in each pair is more typically used, or imputed to be used, by empiricists, the second by intellectualists. The empiricist world view insists that structure be induced from observation and that there be, as Lynch (this volume) says, a constant feedback between observable data and theory. The intellectualist world view holds that structure is not directly observable, but underlies the conscious system of thought and action; the unconscious structure is built up after reality in the mind of the analyst.

Let me illustrate some of the problems and virtues of empiricist and intellectualist methodologies concerning sources of data and ordering of data.

Descriptive concepts based on village studies, such as dominant caste, the *jajmāni* system, status summation, and the Great Tradition/ Little Tradition, have all been criticized for having analyzed units out of context, both in terms of intervillage, state, or colonial socio-political relations and in terms of pan-Indian systems of ideas (Dumont and Pocock 1957a). These same concepts have more recently been viewed as a *synecdochic* stereotype for South Asian village social structure; *the part stands for the whole* in that these concepts are based on studies of rural agricultural villages, excluding fishing and artisan villages (David, this volume). Further, the opposition of Great Tradition/Little Tradition is now seen as not coterminous with the distinction of civilization/village (Dumont and Pocock 1957a; Tambiah 1970:369), the unified peasant religion forming a coherent, meaningful whole which may contradict beliefs and ideas codified in the theological Great Tradition (Gombrich 1971; Leach 1968; Obeyesekere 1963; Tambiah 1970). While the replicable methods of data acquisition and the formulation of concepts suited to the comparative aims of anthropology would be lauded by some, the empiricist method is faulted for a synecdochic restriction of its scope of inquiry for reasons that have to do with the importation of an alien scientific ideology.

The intellectualist method is not free from charges of synecdochism and centrism. The primary focus of Dumont's inquiry, ideology, is not conscious to natives, but an unconscious structure built up by the analyst:

The ideas which they [the people] express are related to each other by more fundamental ideas *even though these are unexpressed.* . . . The caste system for example appears as a perfectly coherent theory once one adds the necessary but implicit links to the principles that the people themselves give (Dumont and Pocock 1957b:12).

I do not claim that the opposition between the pure and the impure is the "foundation" of society other than in the intellectual sense of the term; it is by implicit reference to this opposition that caste society appears rational and coherent to those who live in it (Dumont 1970:44).

To discover the implicit links, Dumont does not restrict his inquiry to traditional ethnographic methods, at which he excels (Dumont 1957a), but seeks them in esoteric sastric texts and in the puranic literature as well. The substantive results of this search have been widely questioned, for example his absolute distinction between the principles of religious status and power and the subordination of the latter by the former (Tambiah 1972; see articles by Singer, Berreman, and Heesterman in Madan 1971). The methodological precedent Dumont draws from this cultural ideology of encompassing of power and economy by religion has also not been taken lightly. He intends to overcome the traditional dualities of Western science, ideas/action and values/fact, by analyzing "non-ideological," that is, empirical, aspects of reality as encompassed by the ideological aspects. While he admits that ideology does not explain everything, his "experiment" in *Homo hierarchicus* is to confront ideological data with observational data.

A major point of Lynch's empiricist reply to this methodology (this volume) is the charge of an ideological distortion of data comparable to the sociocentrism with which Dumont charges empiricists: Dumont's representation of Hindu ideology is synecdochic, the part standing for the whole, in that Dumont reports upper-caste mentality as the traditional mentality. Where this partial ideology confronts reality, where non-Hindus in India and Hindus outside mainland India do have something of caste, where contemporary processes of parliamentary democracy appear to occupy a nonencompassed sphere of influence, etc., then, to Lynch, the ideology is far from explaining everything.

Explanation with a partial or synecdochic ideology is not Dumont's monopoly. Opposite explanations of the *jajmāni* system as a functional system (Orenstein 1962) or as an exploitative system (Beidelman 1959) both take particular structural viewpoints — the dominant caste, the serving castes — in explaining the whole. Tyler (1973) uses cognitive arrangements such as trees, hierarchies, paradigms, and Guttman scales to demonstrate homologies in the structure of *varṇa* categories, *jātī* categories, male life stages, etc. These cognitive arrangements are more easily grasped by many anthropologists than are such terms as "the encompassing" and "the encompassed"; but like Dumont, Tyler moves between two poles of data: precise empirical details and Great Traditional texts. Thus the elegant cognitive arrangements he proposes can be viewed as an abstraction of upper-caste, particularly Brahmanic, mentality. Finally, Beck (1973: xvi, xvii), writing of the coexisting structurings of right- and left-division castes in the Koṅku region of Madras State, explicitly rejects the Western scientistic ideology of arranging chapters of a monograph according to standard anthropological topics such as kinship, social stratification, religion, etc. Chapters in her monograph follow native conceptual structure of the hierarchical levels of categories of territory and kinds of person. As her monograph so excellently documents, this is precisely the conceptual structure of the right-division castes — again, a synecdochic representation.

In his Congress address, Khare said that the papers collected here and the discussions of those papers faced several central, interrelated *dilemmas*. These dilemmas revolve around theoretical, methodological, and sometimes philosophical choices concerning the nature of explanation. The authors of the papers collected here are writing in the context of the opposition between the set of choices made by "Anglo-American empiricists" and that made by "French intellectualists (or structuralists)."

I have attempted to show that the similarities between these two approaches are as striking as the differences. First, both sides have similarly reacted against pre-World War II descriptive accounts, which provided a profusion of diverse details by formulating dominant, establishment, encompassing models of traditional social or ideological structure which emphasize dominant, encompassing features at the expense of subdominant or encompassed features. Second, both sides maintain a static view of traditional structure, although some authors profess otherwise. These stereotypes of traditional structure have been elaborated in entrenched theoretical and methodological stances which have presented dilemmas for understanding both the previously established and the emerging structures of ideas and action in South Asia. Third, even though some authors explicitly reject the imposition of alien scientific ideologies onto the data, they may be questioned for the precedent of representing a synecdochic indigenous ideology or conceptual structure as the traditional ideology.

PART 1: THE STANDING AND THE MOVING

I am not saying that this state of affairs was explicitly enunciated either in the papers or in the discussions. It was clear that a number of analysts are now making two key methodological shifts which amount to at least an implicit recognition. They are attempting to bridge the gap between empiricist and intellectualist analyses by combining symbolic, cognitive, transactional, and material analyses. They are analyzing various levels of symbolic texts without giving priority to any particular level and thus tend to avoid synecdochic representations of the structures of thought.

In the papers on religion and caste in Part 1, there is a tendency to view the previously existing structure as the moving as well as the standing. On the levels of ideology, normative codes, and behavior, there is an opening of the field of inquiry to diversity and dynamics — the moving — as well as a recognition of what is unified and static. With regard to diversity, authors have proposed open-ended sets of ideational features, normative codes, and behavioral structures instead of the prevailing concentration on dominant structures. And they have shown homologies between these systems of thought and systems of action that intend to demonstrate how South Asian society appears coherent and rational to those who live in it. The result is a more exhaustive picture of traditional structure. With regard to dynamics, the exposition of the generativity of the Hindu cognitive system and the fact of coexisting features of thought and action provide more explicit benchmarks for charting continuities and transformations of structure.

One distinct development is a collective methodological choice concerning the use of various levels of symbolic texts and their relation to observable action. Earlier, I spoke of Dumont's charge that certain empiricists were importing an alien, Western ideology which distorted their analyses and the countercharge that Dumont was using a partial indigenous ideology, an upper-caste ideology, which also distorts the data. The point is that Dumont's emphasis on an upper-caste ideology stems from the analytic priority he gives to esoteric texts. Dumont is clear on the priorities. That purity is separate from and superior to power at the global, or encompassing, level of ideology is illustrated with esoteric references such as "the brahman being the source, or rather the womb, from which the *ksatra* [king] springs, is superior"

(Dumont 1962:50). On the other hand, he readily admits that the king and the god are fused at the popular level of religion.

The authors here do not wish to give analytic priority to any level of symbolic texts. This is explicitly stated by Marriott and Inden (this volume):

We here find ourselves restating a cognitive treatment of caste systems that is continuous from the ancient texts of the Vedas, Brahmanas, and Upanishads, . . . through the classical books of moral and medical sciences and the late medieval moral code books of certain castes in Bengal, . . . and on into twentieth-century explanations of their behavior by living peoples. . . . *We combine such diverse materials not because we suppose that one determines or directly influences the other, but simply because we find that they agree on certain major ways of defining the situation* [emphasis mine].

This ethnosociological method drew some fire in the preconference discussions, where LYNCH brought up the reading-in problem: "I wonder how much of it is present there with the Hindus and how much is present because you already know something about it"; and BARNETT questioned the feasibility of directly confronting sastric and village representations. MARRIOTT replied that although further collaboration between Sanskritists, Tamilologists, and ethnographers is necessary to confirm cognitive statements, some results have been remarkably confirmatory. He noted that Wadley (this volume) is working with linguistic anthropology, not from *dharmaśāstra*, and with no texts except three kinds of village texts,

. . . oral texts used by nonliterate peoples in their rituals, ritual texts chanted by priests, and pamphlets that were very popular in current use. These different texts all accord on her finding of six classes of deities, six kinds of transactions between men and gods. And Donald Nelson, the Sanskritist, says that the top three classes are very familiar from Sanskrit literature. Another example is Ronald Inden's material, seventeenth- and eighteenth-century case material of real people and genealogies that tell what people did using *varṇa* terms and terms about *dharma* in a transactional analysis of why they are high or low, how they mix things up or make them more homogeneous.

DAVID added that Wadley's contemporary data on power and Inden's historical data on kinship are just two instances of intermediary texts, texts which mediate the disjunction between ancient texts and village representations:

Tambiah (1970) has already done work on various levels of texts in his study of Thailand. The studies collected here use material from caste origin myths, prayers, ritual chants, and prestations in formulating the structure of Hindu thought. Two other examples of intermediary texts are wedding insult songs sung by women and street plays. Edward Henry has reported insult songs which provide a counterpoint to the formal chants being sung by the priest: while the priest is praising the bridegroom as the son of a king, the women of the bride's party are calling him the son of a whore. Bruce Kaplan has analyzed street plays from Tamilnadu which combine religious and contemporary political messages.

These intermediary texts cannot easily be classified as distinctively Great or Little Tradition. The multivocalic symbolism in these texts includes both esoteric and exoteric meanings. In brief, consideration of all these texts yields a more exhaustive understanding of the Hindu structure of thought.

The refusal to give analytic priority to any privileged level of texts results in a willingness to cope with the diversity of traditional structures on the levels of ideology, normative codes, and action. Dominant structures such as the hierarchical ideology based on purity/impurity or the *jajmāni* system are no longer given a privileged place in analysis, but are set in context with coexisting features on the level of ideology or the level of action. Exposition of diversity yields a picture of tradition with less unified elegance, but there is a gain in another direction, for the analysts proceed to show homologies between these sets of features on the levels of thought and action: it is in these homologies that the unity of structure appears.

Marriott and Inden (this volume) propose to borrow "what now seems to be a repeated empirical finding — the cognitive nonduality of action and actor, code and substance — and use it as a universal axiom for restating what we think we know through deduction about caste systems."

Stated more particularly, they see the nonduality of natural substance and code for conduct as the general principle underlying the ideology of *jāti*s, a nondualist generative system of categories based on subtle or gross substances and transactions between substances. Unlike thought in Western cultures, where the order of culture is differentiated from the order of law and natural substance is differentiated from codes for conduct (Schneider 1968), Hindu thought shows a somewhat Lamarckian cast in that a code for conduct is immanent or embodied and a substance is "also that which passes between bodies — the contents or media of transactions," and therefore transactions "substantialize a code." Like Dumont, Marriott and Inden reject the alien individualist ideology for studying the Hindu cognitive system, but for a different reason. Where Dumont replaces the individual with the notion of the whole, they find the dividual: Hindu cognitive structure is not holistic but particulate. The dividual is composed of mutable particles of coded substances. (This nondual proposition of coded substances has been recognized even by fieldworkers in South Asia who were not looking for it. The research focus of Barry Michie, formerly a graduate student at Michigan State University, was a survey of agricultural production efficiency in Rajasthan. Farmers there generally accurately assessed their economic situation. Members of the dominant farming caste, however, showed great doubt and displeasure when he displayed data proving that one of the most productive farmers in the village was an extraordinary individual from the goldsmith caste. They explained their feelings by saying that only someone with the blood of a farmer could possibly learn to be a good farmer. The proposition of coded substance implies that the potential even to learn a code for conduct — let alone the ability successfully to carry out the behavior — requires the appropriate natural substance.)

Indian specialists will see in this ethnosociological account responses on a number of issues, for example, debates concerning attributional/ interactional ranking (see Marriott 1959, 1968a; Stevenson 1954; Dumont 1970:119-121; Tyler 1973:152-153). The account rejects as "cognitively incomplete" Marriott's previous interactional theory of stratifying transactions between castes. It also rejects attributional ranking theories of either *jāti*s or things transacted because attributes are frequently left undefined. For example, several authors describe raw and cooked food as less or more vulnerable to pollution without defining vulnerability. Marriott and Inden (this volume) are able to define more precisely the cognitive rules underlying exchange of substances: "The substances exchanged are themselves ranked in value according to their greater or lesser capacities for subsequent transformation . . . substances in whole, unmixed, untransformed states may thus be regarded as more productive — more valuable — than nongenerative substances . . . . "

Such ethnosociology does distinguish the logic of raw and cooked food exchange. At the preconference, MORRISON noted that Marriott is not abandoning interactional analysis; rather, the indigenous cognitive structure of substances permits him to analyze more transactions (such as words, money, and honor transacted between individuals and collectivities) than in his previous work.

The principle of nondualism is the central concern of Aiyappan's paper, "Deified men and humanized gods: some folk bases of Hindu theology" (this volume). Aiyappan tests the nondualistic proposition that there is a continuum between gods at intermediate levels and humans (rather than a dualistic distinction between them), with data on ancestral cults and myths of the matrilineal Kurichiya tribals of Wynad District, Kerala. He hypothesizes that ancestral cult worship was characteristic of pre-Nambudiri culture in Kerala, and he has performed a field experiment by studying the Kurichiya, who, "in my view, represent an ancient section of Kerala society from which the matrilineal north Kerala Nayars and the Tiyyar (Izhavas) branched." His analysis shows that while only some ancestral spirits return to guide the living, the line between such spirits and intermediate gods is obliterated in time. Myths record seven deities as deified humans. This study is important in that it may encourage nonindigenous researchers to hold their commonsense categories in abeyance: it is Kurichiya common sense to recognize that gods and humans are not always distinct identities.

Nondualism as a cognitive principle is implicit in other papers which treat purity/power, god/king, temple/palace as inseparable identities rather than as category opposites. Power is treated on a par with purity rather than, as Dumont would have it, as distinct from and encompassed by purity.

In her paper, "Power in Hindu ideology and practice" (this volume), Wadley correlates indigenous paradigms of categories of power, categories of deities, categories of rituals, and categories of transactions between humans and deities. For example, having defined categories of deities into six classes, Wadley is able to show homologies between caste and kinship exchanges and exchanges between humans and different classes of deities. Humans relate to class three deities as *kumin* servants relate to *jajmān* patrons, humans to class two deities as wives to husbands, and humans to class four deities as sisters to brothers. There are no direct transactions between humans and the first, fifth, and sixth classes of deities; a human approaches them through intermediaries such as fire, cows, sun, or another class of deity. Wadley concludes that, "Rather than agreeing that purity or the principle of pure/impure is dominant in Hindu society [as Dumont proposes], I contend that purity and power are two inseparable factors in any ideas of being or action in Hindu thought."

South Asian specialists will note in this study advances in specificity and precision over such previous studies of the structure of a local pantheon as Harper's rather Durkheimian correlation (1959) of the three categories of nonhuman identities (*devaya/dēva/devate* [high, pure, transcendental gods/intermediate, pure and impure, pragmatic gods/low, impure, malevolent gods]) with the three generic identities (Brahman/non-Brahman/untouchable) that exist in Mysore. Wadley's study, which only hints at the complexity of data found in her dissertation (Wadley 1973), is rigorous enough to fulfill Goodenough's program (1965) of analyzing a syntax and grammar of identities and identity relationships between human and divine beings.

The identification of purity and power is evident in the contributions by L. K. Mahapatra and David (this volume). That is, both authors emphasize the identification of god and king and the symbolic and transactional analogies between the temple and the palace. L. K. Mahapatra's historical account shows how "Orissa as a cultural region exemplifies, perhaps in an extreme fashion, the parallelism between the king's court, estates and services, and the state deity."

He goes beyond Hocart's (1970) notion of the caste system as a ritual organization by describing hereditary castes serving both king and god; the similarities in transactions, such as the customs of the pilgrim having an audience with the king before proceeding to the temple and the prohibition of wearing sandals within palace or temple; and the identification of king and god wherein the king is called god-king (*thakur-raja*) and the god dons royal attire during the month of Pousha. The Orissan king is the overseer of the caste order both in the temple and in the society at large: transgression by a hereditary temple servant is punished by the king, acting as an agent of the god; the king preserves the caste order in society by arbitrating caste precedence disputes, legitimizing such changes, and attempting to maintain equivalent rank orders in the several princedoms.

Similarly, I proposed to use the term "exoteric symbolism" to indicate those meanings of multivocalic religious symbols or acts that paralleled the daily life perceptions of contemporary relations between masters and servants, or historical relations between the former Jaffna kings and subjects (David, this volume). Homologies between thought and action become clear when the principles of purity and power are identified rather than kept distinct. It is in the elucidation of such homologies that we begin to demonstrate how social life might appear interconnected and coherent to those who live it, that is, how they might impose a tentative order on daily life perceptions in different spheres of activity.

This concern appears in Khare's paper, "Prestations and prayers: two homologous systems in northern India" (this volume), when he analyzes social prestations and religious prayers as following an essentially homologous set of rules of exchange. Influenced by Mauss's theory of the gift (1967), Khare lists nine characteristics of social prestations in daily life which aptly describe the reciprocity of exchange between men and god in prayer and in response to prayer. His preliminary analysis of forms and functions, of the arrangements of symbolic thoughts, and of the associated linguistic features demonstrates that the prayers are highly effective symbolic systems of exchange, where mythological thoughts and relationships, patterned after the kinship model, predominate.

Another contribution to this revised picture of tradition as ordered homologies between diverse features on the level of thought and features on the level of actions is made in my paper, "Hierarchy and equivalence in Jaffna, north Sri Lanka." First, the paper shows that there is unity in diversity in that there is a common paradigm to the defining features of *jāti* identity: notions of shared natural substance expressed in origin myths, occupations (interpreted, as by Marriott and Inden, as coded substance), and cattle brands. Second, there is an exposition of diverse unities on the level of relations between humans, based on the opposition of hierarchy and equivalence. On the level of ideational features, there is an opposition of the principles of purity and power/mutual satisfaction; on the normative level, an opposition of priestly and aristocratic schemata/mercantile schema; on the level of behavior, an opposition of bound-mode intercaste relations (as followed by landowners and barbers) nonbound-mode intercaste relations (of, for example, artisans and fishermen). Third, there is a certain unity from diversity in that the opposition of hierarchical features/equivalence features is neutralized on the level of relations between humans and the divine: only hierarchical features appear. Humans relate to divinity as do servants to masters. I hinted in the paper that the *bhakti* relation of equivalence between men and the divine posed a problem to this notion of neutralization. Having read Wadley's paper, in which she proposes the twofold action of man to god (faith/service) and the reciprocal relations of god to man (mercy/boons), I believe it more accurate to note the presence of principles of both equivalence and hierarchy in these relations as well. The point is not to dismiss equivalence as a feature "below the level of maximal consciousness" in caste society. Indian specialists will recognize a similarity between this opposition of hierarchy/equivalence and Beck's opposition of right/left. Notwithstanding differences in a number of details between her study of Koṅku Nadu in Tamilnadu and my study of the Jaffna peninsula, Sri Lanka, there are strong similarities between these two oppositions concerning homologies between systems of thought and systems of action in the organization of space, the structure of origin myths, and the structure of intercaste ranking transactions (Beck 1973; David 1974a, 1974b).

Doranne Jacobson's paper is more traditional than the above papers: it is a social structural account couched exclusively in extrinsic analytic categories without reference to indigenous conceptual structure. (This is true of the draft discussed at the Congress. A revised draft does deal with indigenous notions of natural substance. I discuss this further later on in the Introduction.) Jacobson challenges several stereotypes of female social organization in her study, "Flexibility in central Indian kinship and residence." Frequency of a married woman's visits to her natal village have, in the past, been treated as matters of emotion: indulgence of the young bride who has become a stranger in a strange affinal land, who is overworked and kept in seclusion in the new household. To Jacobson, hard economic facts as well as emotion and the cordiality of relations are relevant to the frequency of a woman's visits to her natal village. The young bride is described as a movable labor source, whose presence is desired by both natal and affinal relatives. Her natal family must weigh the expense of travel and food for the visiting woman against her contribution to the family economy. Women do important work in their natal homes, and the request for her return occurs when parents undertake a pilgrimage, are ill, etc., as well as for emotional reasons on both sides. Attention to female networks will help to operationalize Mayer's (1965:4) concept of kindred of recognition, showing how diffuse, enduring relationships are maintained between villages:

... escorting of women back and forth provides occasions for male affines to meet, thus helping to knit the caste together and widening intra- and extra-caste contacts useful for a number of purposes. These visits allow men from distant villages to interact with their affines and the cliques of which their affines are members; such interaction can have important political consequences (as at caste *panchāyat* [council] meetings) and is often of major importance in marriage arrangements. Men who meet each other through such associations may assist each other in financial matters, the obtaining of medical or legal aid, the purchase of land, the finding of employment, and other ways (Jacobson, this volume).

Jacobson's study does then fit with the general emphasis of the papers in Part 1 by helping to revise our picture of traditional structure. Just as my paper is in part a response to a collective methodological bias — the use of data from rural agricultural villages and the exclusion of data from rural fishing and artisan villages in the prevailing characterization of traditional village India — so Jacobson's paper responds to another collective bias, in which male structure stands for the whole of the traditional structure.

Attention to the diversity in structuring is directly related to another trend in these papers, in the conference discussions, and in recent literature: the interpretation of the previously established order as a dynamic structure. The term "traditional period" was criticized as lacking in temporal precision, first, because it can encompass anything up to the moment of fieldwork, its demise varying with the empirical problem being described by the individual researcher; and second, because it can encompass 2,000 years of diverse historical, political, and philosophical variations. It was proposed to speak of the "emerging structure" rather than the "modern structure" because the former term lacks the connotation that present happenings are necessarily novel and disjunct from the previous structure. Interpretation of the previous structure as ordered diversity is thus related to the discussion of dynamics in that the presence of coexisting features of structure permits dynamics with or without the intrusion of exogenous factors.

In this context, TAMBIAH remarked during the preconference that studies of previously unstressed identities and relations, such as Jacobson's discussion of female networks, or David's study of non-bound-mode intercaste relations might provide new benchmarks for charting differences in direction and rate of change in response to factors exogenous to the traditional order. This point was questioned as to whether authors were reading present structures backwards in time. It was noted that Jacobson's paper on rural female networks might be studied in relation to the urban female networks described by Vatuk (1972). DAVID responded with historical data on the differential response of two Sinhalese castes of southern Sri Lanka — Karava fishermen (a nonbound-mode *jāti*) and Goyigama agriculturalists (a bound-mode *jāti*) — to the entrepreneurial opportunities presented by colonialists from the early sixteenth century until 1948.[1] In the Sinhalese case, there is a correlation between different structural positions (positions in the productive process and associated normative codes) and differential responses to entrepreneurial opportunities.

No general statement on structural positions and responses to modernity is possible, as is shown in the contradictory cases collected in *Entrepreneurship and modernization of occupational cultures in South Asia* (Singer, ed. 1973). In Barnett's study (1973) of Koṇṭaik-kaṭṭi Veḷḷāḷars [or KoNTaikaTTI VeLaLars] of Chingleput District, Tamilnadu, these landowners are seen as committed both to a priestly and to a kingly model for conduct; Barnett finds them unwilling to enter many occupations in Madras City and withdrawing from rather than competing in local political fights which might detract from this austere and regal identity. On the other hand, Owens (1973) and Nandy (1973) describe the Bengali Mahaisya landowners as entering modern occupations because of their community spirit, whereas Bengali Brahmans are more restrained. Yet Madras Brahmans have innovated adaptive strategies to permit their industrial activities (Singer 1973). While these studies are not completely commensurate, and a permutation table of structural positions facilitating or retarding entry into nontraditional occupations has yet to be constructed, the more we learn of diversity within the traditional order, the more it is clear that modernization, Westernization, industrialization, etc., have unequal effects on different identities.

Earlier, I discussed the theoretical practice of professing dynamism

[1] Even though low-country Goyigama were in full contact with the colonialists (their villages were situated just a few hundred yards from the coastline), they remained enmeshed in their networks of agricultural relations and did not enter the nonindigenous economic sector until the late nineteenth century. The Karava, on the other hand, had no tradition of intense networks of local ties and were accustomed to mercantile activity (fishing and trading). They entered the colonial economy with alacrity, fighting with the Portuguese against the unsubdued Kandyan kingdom, siding with the Kandyans during the Dutch occupation by running salt through the Dutch blockade, and entering two sectors under the British: carpentry and coffee and tea planting. Roberts (1969) has documented that although the Karava formed only 19 percent of the Sinhalese population in the late nineteenth century, during that period they held 75 percent of native-owned tea plantations in Sri Lanka.

in the traditional order and then proceeding as if dynamic process were truly relevant only after the exogenous colonial powers influenced the system. There is growing awareness that this procedure is not justified, for it rests on an image of a fixed order partially created by British colonial rule. Cohn (1971) has argued that the static picture of castes is partly the result of British censuses, particularly Risley's 1911 census. Galanter (1968) has demonstrated how administrators rigidified local caste laws in an imputed traditional legal system. Beck's account of the Koṅku region in south India shows how certain territorial units were selected from a hierarchical segmentary system of categories of space (related both to segmentary systems of *jāti* organization and to religious organization) and frozen into administrative units. Similarly, *caste* translates but one meaning of the protean term *jāti*. Collaboration between anthropologists, Sanskritists, and historians in the last decade has revised that static image.

Historical accounts of South Asia before the British raj document both positional and ideological changes. L. K. Mahapatra's paper (this volume) documents Barber's point (1968) that the king legitimizes caste mobility movements within the region. Stein (1967) records the eighth-century alliance in south India between Brahmans and peasant landowners against the artisans, which probably led to the division between right and left factions there. Ideological shifts are repetitive processes by peripheral or low-status groups. The Sanskritization of tribals is not just a recent process: centuries ago, the Orissan king incorporated a Hill Bhuiyas deity into the ritual circuit of Orissa state worship (L. K. Mahapatra, this volume).

There are reports of accommodation between religion and society in both directions. Morris (1973) calls attention to repetitive processes of adaptive changes with respect to contemporary ritually neutral activity followed by religious rationalizations of that activity, thus cautioning against the implication of Singer's view that adaptations — such as "compartmentalization," "ritual abbreviation," "vicarious ritualization," and "ritual neutralization" — are but recent processes. This view is supported by Aiyappan's statement (this volume) that the Kurichiya tribals who immigrated to Wynad District in Kerala "brought with them the analogues of several of their deities but modified their roles to meet their needs in Wynad."

Furthermore, anthropologists are drawing attention to properties of the previously established structure of identity categories which accommodated past social changes. The social mobility strategy of opting to have one's identity defined within a different identity domain by adopting a different ideology (for example, the Ambedkar Buddhist movement, which asserts that untouchables are to be defined with the egalitarian Buddhist identity domain) is nothing new, given

Ahmad's report (this volume) of the Islamization of low-caste Hindus over the centuries. Although it has previously been noted that *jāti* identities are a segmentary system of categories (Béteille 1969), the role of the more inclusive identity categories in ordering change is becoming clearer, as, for example, when Ahmad reports that generic identities for Indian Muslims distinguish those of non-Indian ancestry (Ashraf) from those who converted (Ajlaf). Parallels are found in the Hindu system of identities. For example, agriculture has been described as a "caste-irrelevant role" (Silverberg 1959). Although many *jāti*s practice agriculture in addition to their traditional occupation, many instances have been reported of a *jāti* renouncing another occupation and its previous *jāti* identity and taking on an agricultural *jāti* identity.[2]

Then Fox (1969:31, 32) quite reasonably argues that categories such as Maratha in Maharashtra, Veḷḷāḷar in Tamilnadu, and Nayar in Kerala should be considered not as single subcaste identities, but as generic identities which accommodate such changes. Various authors have noted that in towns and urban centers, more inclusive *jāti* categories defined by attributes replace more specific *jāti* categories defined by interactions. These generic identities permit a limited degree of ordered interaction even in the absence of shared cognitive maps of identities (Berreman 1972; Fox 1969; Sebring 1969). It should be noted that Fox's rejection of the *varṇa/jāti* dichotomy in favor of an (admittedly tentative) five-level schema which includes intermediary levels of *jāti* and *varṇa* identities is analogous to a trend reported here: downplaying the Great Tradition/Little Tradition dichotomy and considering intermediary levels of symbolic texts.

Finally, it has been proposed that Hindu cognitive structure facilitates the accommodation of *jāti* identities to repetitive processes of change. Marriott and Inden question Dumont's version of ideology as a single-dimensional hierarchy of purity and impurity that encompasses other hierarchies; instead, they view Hindu cognitive structure as a multidimensional set of hierarchies that crosscut one another: "sex genera, language genera, occupational genera, and kinship genera may and typically do intersect and interbreed in complex ways" (Marriott and Inden, this volume). This line of thought is related to repetitive processes of cognitive dynamics throughout Indian history, for example, the *bhaktī* movements in the Middle Ages. New identity categories (each with a distinct code for conduct) appear when there

[2] In Jaffna, northern Sri Lanka, there are two categories of Veḷḷāḷar strikingly similar to the Ashraf/Ajlaf distinction mentioned above: Big (Periya) Veḷḷāḷar can demonstrate their previous possession of titles, servants, offices, and land in *ola*-leaf records dating back to the last decade of the eighteenth century, while Little (Cinna) Veḷḷāḷar have no such records and are still identifiable as having been Tēvar or Akampatiyar *jāti*s (David 1974b).

are permutations, combinations, deletions, replications — in short, interbreedings — of coded substances. Although Tyler (1973) disagrees on certain fundamental points (e.g. he stresses dualism rather than nondualism as Marriott and Inden do), his exposition of cognitive structure supports their interpretation of the dynamics of the traditional Hindu cognitive system as a generative rather than a static system of categories.

In short, a second revision in the interpretation of the traditional order as the moving as well as the standing is to view it as dynamic, diverse, and generative, as opposed to static, unified, and absorptive. Any notion of a monolithic, inflexible, unchanging traditional structure (to be contrasted with an infinitely variable, profoundly amorphous modern structure) was consistently rejected at the behavioral level of analysis and at the level of cognition and ideology.

I shall now summarize the shifts in methods, theory, and interpretation found in the papers in Part 1.

Most of the authors here explicitly reject the precedent of predominantly emphasizing one source of data (for example, Great Traditional texts) over other levels of texts. The authors consider a wide variety of intermediary texts and symbolic interaction such as the pantheon (Aiyappan and Wadley), prayer (Khare and Wadley), myths (David), and prestations between men and deities and between humans (David, Khare, Marriott and Inden, and Wadley).

Perhaps as a result of this procedure, the authors decline to give analytic priority to any "dominant" feature on the levels of ideology, norms, or behavior. More attention is paid to previously unstressed, or understressed, features.

One development in revising the notion of the traditional structure of religious and caste identity is, in a sense, a reaction to Dumont's prodigious attempt to provide a single encompassing model of Hindu ideology. Dumont, of course, has made pronounced advances in ordering previously encyclopedic collections of diverse materials.[3] But a strain in this model of caste society is noted by Lynch's exegesis (this volume) of the crucial terms used by Dumont. In order to accommodate his model to this complex sociocultural reality, Dumont

---

[3] Noting that nothing less than an encyclopedia of attributes would be necessary to catalogue the male and female deities in popular Tamil religion, Dumont proposes a relational definition. Though the names, icons, rituals, offerings, and priests attending a pair of deities vary from village to village in Tamilnadu, the relation of Lord/Lady between them is constant. This complementary relation is demonstrated with etymological data and with the constant relation they bear to the village: protecting the village from external misfortune/maintaining the internal well-being of the inhabitants (Dumont 1959). Empirical critics are hard put to find an alternative explanation for this coincidence.

uses "hierarchy" and "the whole" in various ways.

A response in several of the papers is to refuse to give priority to any single ideological principle. Dumont states, "The opposition of purity and impurity is the foundation of society only in the intellectual sense of the term; it is by implicit reference to this opposition that caste society appears rational and coherent to those who live in it." In various ways, the papers by Marriott and Inden, L. K. Mahapatra, Wadley, and David are all united in opening the field of inquiry on this point. That is, they emphasize other underlying features, such as nondualism, the dividual, power, and mutual satisfaction, which are also necessary to make caste society appear rational and coherent.[4]

On the level of action, authors have rejected as nonexhaustive, or synecdochic, the prevailing representation of male, agricultural village (dominant caste, *jajmāni* system, etc.) structure; they have highlighted previously understressed features such as nonbound mercantile relations between rural castes and female networks of rural organization.

The previously existing structure of identities, the standing structure that persists and appears unified, is discussed in terms of homologies between diverse features on the levels of ideology, norms, and behavior (or in Marriott and Inden's terms, a nonduality of thought and action) rather than as elegant, but monolithic, structures treated separately by different authors on the level of ideology or on the level of behavior. Thus one theoretical shift is a diminution of reductionist analysis. Both in the papers and at the conferences, we witness the willingness of empiricists to attend to symbolic analyses and the reverse. The authors are here combining symbolic and transactional analyses in order to show homologies between diverse features. (And to note where homologies fail: prayers, as Khare shows in his article [this volume], proceed beyond prestations when they attempt to contradict the institutionalized Hindu principles of social inequality, *karma*, rebirth, and deliverance.)

Once this Pandora's box is opened and the structured diversity of indigenous ideology, normative codes, and behavioral patterns is taken seriously, there are consequences for another theoretical choice. There is a tendency to be more circumspect in the use of certain extrinsic analytic categories. As Khare (this volume) puts it,

Not only is the [logic of] transaction [common to] the majority of social relations, but even what is transacted is not so exclusive to one particular institution. . . . hence, if we regard "economic," "political," "ritual," etc., as specific attributes of social relations (rather than as separate classes of social

---

[4] This trend also appears in recent literature. See, for example, articles in *Contributions to Indian Sociology*, new series 5, where various features such as laterality, good/bad sacred, etc., are discussed.

relations), we are on a more realistic ground to examine them.

In other words, armed with a battery of indigenous ideological, normative, and behavioral features, the analysts are attempting to translate with less sociocentric distortion the structure of domains of thought, the structure of action, and the relations between thought and action.

The explicit attempt to reduce sociocentrism entails the opposite possibility, namely that concentration on indigenous representations might become an analytic solipsism, yielding statements incommensurate with the canons of replicability, comparability, and ordering by analytic techniques derived from outside the region. Clearly, the various authors (Barnett, David, Inden, Marriott, Nicholas, Ostor, and Wadley) who have been using variations of this method are not just ethnosociologists. Although they all have been, or are, associated with the Department of Anthropology or the Department of South Asian Languages and Civilizations of the University of Chicago, and although they all apply Schneider's (1968) culture theory to the study of South Asian materials, they differ widely in their adjunct theoretical interests, which include linguistic, political, structuralist, communications, and Marxist theories. Their responses to the above critique vary as well.

My remark that Wadley's data are susceptible to Goodenough's (1965) formal analysis implies that the potential for rigorous ordering by extrinsic analytic techniques is reached, not by the initial imposition of extrinsic analytic categories such as "pantheon," but by the exegesis of indigenous categories. Ethnosociology, then, need not preclude other forms of analysis: rather, it may further them.

Replicability and cultural comparison (as opposed to Human Relations Areas Files-style social comparison) are also not renounced. For example, Marriott and Inden's treatment of *jāti*s as natural genera closely resembles the Kashmiri Muslim conception of *zāt*: "What does za:t [*zāt*] denote? Apparently it points to birth, as does the well known word jāti elsewhere among Hindus. The Kashmiris use the word za:t in a broader sense, however, to connote essence or inherent nature" (Madan 1972:109). *Zāt*, like *jāti*, is relevant to various systems of classification (Madan 1972: 110) and is defined in a way that parallels the cognitive notion of natural substance and code for conduct: "Both pursuit of hereditary occupation and endogamy are commendable as being inherently right. The word za:t (in its adjectival form of za:ti) is employed in this context also" (Madan 1972: 115). Recourse to homely conceptions of reality rather than ultimate ideological statements about Muslim egalitarianism versus Hindu hierarchy may aid in deciding recalcitrant comparative questions such as, "do castes exist among South Asian Muslims?"

Reanalysis of Jacobson's data (this volume) may serve to illustrate some of the difficulties — but also some heuristic gains — of ethnosociological comparison. Kinship practices in Bengal (Nicholas and Inden 1972); Mysore (Harper 1964); Tamilnadu (Dumont 1957b; Barnett's preconference remarks); Jaffna, Sri Lanka (David 1973); and Madhya Pradesh (Jacobson, this volume) differ markedly when patterns of behavior are compared: patterns of inheritance, or residence, etc. There are, however, striking similarities in the logic of natural substances underlying systems of generic categories for kinsmen and norms for ritual behavior between kinsmen. Underlying the opposition of generic categories, "sharers of natural bodily substance"/"uniters of natural bodily substance," are several indigenous biogenetic propositions, one of which is that a woman's bodily substance becomes identical with that of her husband during the marriage ceremony (Nicholas and Inden 1972; David 1973; Barnett's preconference remarks), although her spiritual substance does not change (Barnett's preconference remarks). As much can be surmised in Jacobson's (this volume) report of the bride's address to the groom, "Oh my Lord, from today I have become like half of your body."

I say "surmise," because these central Indian informants explicitly deny the proposition that a woman's body becomes identical with her husband's body at the time of marriage; they also reject my interpretation of the bride's address to the groom, saying that it is meant figuratively: several pundits told Jacobson that the address means no more than that they are now paired off and thus resembles the American cliché, "My wife is my better half."

The issue becomes clear when we recognize that the ethnosociological assertion is that such indigenous propositions are at least implicitly recognized by natives as causal, tautological, and nonmetaphorical rather than figurative. One general proposition is that a social category, a particular natural substance, a code for conduct, and actual conduct are causally related. The proposition is that the relations among such units as social identity categories and codes for conduct (which social scientists generally assign to the cultural order) and such other units as particular natural substances and actual conduct (which social scientists classify as part of the phenomenal order) are held to be immanent as well as extrinsically learned and shared through processes of socialization. Or, more precisely, learned codes may be learned because of the immanent connections.

Another, more specific, proposition is that certain culturally standardized events simultaneously change a person's constellation of natural substance, identity category, code for conduct, and actual conduct. In peninsular India and Jaffna, Sri Lanka (hereafter, in the

Dravidian cases), the transubstantiation of a woman's substance to that of her husband and her identity from that of the unmarried girl to that of the married woman is held to happen when the groom ties the wedding badge (*tāli*) around the bride's neck; in central and northern India, a comparable event is the custom of knotting together the bride's and groom's clothing and having them circle the holy fire "to seal their union" (Jacobson, this volume). Binding symbolism appears in both cases. This is particularly apt in the Dravidian cases where the ancient word for marriage is *campantam* [literally, binding as one]. Again it must be noted that Jacobson's Madhya Pradesh informants deny the causal nature of this event.

Informants' explicit verbal representations are not, however, the only data relevant to the testing of the presence of such propositions as the transubstantiation proposition. Using the general proposition of the identity of category, substance, code for conduct, and actual conduct as a heuristic guide, it can be seen that the specific proposition of female transubstantiation makes sense of changes in ritual behavior. Before marriage, a woman and her natal kin, that is, all sharers of natural bodily substance (which includes previously transubstantiated, or in-married, women, such as father's brother's wife) are thought to have pollution intrinsically for one another. When someone identical in bodily substance is born or dies, they all become polluted; this is held to happen irrespective of the volition of these persons. Natives contrast having pollution with voluntarily taking on, or observing, pollution. By the same logic, since a married woman no longer shares bodily substance with her natal kin, she does not have pollution for them but may voluntarily observe pollution for them (David 1973: 530; see Dumont 1957b:38; Harper 1964:164-166 for comparative data). Jacobson's ritual data replicate these changing codes for conduct (this volume):

After her marriage, a woman is expected to take on the ritual responsibilities incumbent upon members of her husband's *khandan* [patrilineal lineage]. She must perform the *pūjās* expected of *khandan* members and observe pollution resulting from a birth or death in her husband's lineage. When a death occurs in her husband's *khandan*, a woman is automatically polluted (thirteen days for a deceased man, eleven days for a deceased woman) wherever she may be, and should go immediately to her *susrāl* [conjugal village] to be with the rest of the similarly polluted mourners—the male members of the lineage, their wives, and their unmarried daughters.

The fact of the death itself is said to pollute her (*usko lag gai chhīt*); she is also said to be obliged to "observe pollution" (*sūtak māntī hai*).

In contrast, a married woman need not observe pollution upon the death of any of her natal kin, although she may choose to join the mourners and be polluted by living and eating with them.

And once again, the Madhya Pradesh informants reject the cognitive proposition of changing substances underlying changing codes for conduct, saying that: "She is polluted because of her tie of kinship to the deceased, not because of any notion of putrefaction spreading from the corpse to the kinsmen of the dead" (Jacobson, this volume; cf. David 1973:530).

In the Madhya Pradesh case, then, several kinds of data are contradictory. Informants stoutly deny the proposition of female transubstantiation of any sort of natural substance, be it blood, body, or whatever; the bride's address to the groom to the effect that her body so changes is denied as a causal statement and asserted by informants to be figurative. (In a personal communication following a previous draft of this section, Jacobson assures me that she has extensive documentation of these points.) While not doubting in the least the veracity of these reports, it is possible to note that other data affirm the proposition. The set of kinsfolk for whom an *unmarried* woman becomes polluted (*usko lag gaī chhīt*) and the set of those for whom she may choose to observe pollution (*sūtak māntī hai*) differ from the set of kinsfolk for whom a *married* woman becomes polluted and the set of those for whom she may choose to observe pollution. The definition of these four sets is predictable from the proposition of female transubstantiation. In addition, these two expressions differ grammatically. *Usko lag gaī chhīt* is in the passive voice — the pollution happens to her — while *sūtak māntī hai* is in the active voice — she does it. Does the passive voice index belief in a causal, nonvolitional happening while the active voice indexes belief in an extrinsic, volitional one? If so, there is at least an implicit recognition of the proposition in this grammatical choice. In short, while informants' verbal explanations deny the transubstantiation proposition, both normative codes enjoining specific patterns of ritual action and grammatical choices appear to affirm it.

By denying the transubstantiation proposition, these informants are asserting another proposition: unchanging natural substance. Jacobson connects this latter proposition with the major focus of her paper, the overdue recognition of the extent of the central Indian "married woman's continued participation in affairs in her natal home, even as she finds her niche in her conjugal home" (Jacobson, this volume). That is, the unchanging blood proposition denies the total transfer of a woman to her husband's kin group; this proposition accords with a code for conduct enjoining participation in natal village affairs.

The problem with this statement is that a married woman apparently has a joint appointment: there is really a double code enjoining conduct with both natal kin and affinal kin. Is there no proposition to accord with the code for conduct with affinal kin? With the general proposition of the identity of category, substance, code for conduct, and conduct as a heuristic guide, one might dare to say that there is a double definition of the central Indian married woman's natural substance to accord with the double code. There is a specific analogy: Dravidian informants verbally support the proposition that a woman's bodily substance becomes identical with that of her husband, while her spiritual substance remains the same (Barnett's preconference remarks); spiritual substance is contained in the blood (David 1973). In the central Indian case, despite informants' explicit denials, some evidence suggests an implicit proposition that a woman's bodily substance changes at marriage while her blood remains the same. If this is so (and the evidence is admittedly inconclusive) we have a more cognitively complete counterpart to the double code for her conduct with natal and affinal kin than if we accept the informants' version of unchanging blood alone.

Some readers might react negatively to such cultural comparison on the basis of scanty data; yet they might consider it perfectly legitimate to develop their understanding of an uncharted ethnographic region by tentatively applying such standard social comparative terms as virilocality, uxorilocality, etc. This is common enough practice in cross-social comparative work. Twenty years ago, symbolic studies in anthropology were generally outside the pale; after the structuralist revolution of Lévi-Strauss, less radical symbolic studies have been redefined as legitimate. Provided that indigenous notions defining a cultural domain are thoroughly explored (as suggested by the ethnosociological method), there is potential for rigorous comparison of regional variations in cultural constructs.

We are dealing here with propositions about natural substance, identity categories, codes for conduct, and actual conduct that are not currently stressed in Western culture or scientific theory, and it is no mean methodological task to discern their validity, that is, their presence or absence in indigenous common sense. These ethnosociological propositions are subject to some of the same methodological queries put to structuralist propositions: are they in the minds of the natives or only in the mind of the anthropologist? I am rather uncomfortable with any definitive split between "the anthropologist's unconscious model" versus "the native conscious model" because, as we have just seen, (1) the same proposition may be quite explicitly known by some informants, vaguely known or unknown to others, rejected as figurative by others, or totally rejected by others; (2) in eliciting propositions dissimilar to Western biogenetic notions, there is the possibility that informants underplay their own ideas and beliefs when questioned by a nonindigenous anthropologist in order not to appear "primitive"; (3) whatever the degree of awareness and acceptance of a proposition, the proposition may be otherwise affirmed by grammatical choices, codes for conduct, and secular and ritual action which enact the proposition: these data may amount to implicit recognition of the proposition; and (4) the same proposition may be affirmed by one written text and denied by another, or both affirmed and denied by the same text (see my discussion of *sapinda* rules [David 1973:531, 532]).

Given these methodological problems and the absence of conclusive evidence, I attach little weight to the heuristic foray attempted above except as a call for further comparative research. One such topic, previously mentioned, is Hindu and Muslim propositions about caste. Similarly, while Aryan and Dravidian kinship behavior patterns differ, there is the possibility that Aryan and Dravidian cultural propositions about kinship are not totally dissimilar. Rather, it may be possible to delineate the sets of propositions concerning natural substance that represent ordered variations on the same theme.

Marriott and Inden (this volume) go even further than the others in taking the indigenous conceptual structure as a partial guide to understanding South Asian reality. They follow, *mirabile dictu,* Dumont's theoretical practice of using indigenous cognitive principles to criticize the theoretical contributions of others. Dumont, it will be remembered, criticizes empiricist interpretations that reduce the hierarchical ideology to an epiphenomenon. At various points in the preconference and in his Congress address, MARRIOTT criticized my use of the term "symbol" and Lynch's dualist rebuttal of Dumont's method and theory on the basis of the nonduality of thought and action.

There is, in addition, some similarity between the ethnosociological method and Lévi-Strauss's structuralist method in the treatment of indigenous representations. (They differ, of course, in that for Lévi-Strauss, the conscious native model frequently disguises the true unconscious model.) In "The bear and the barber," Lévi-Strauss notes that because caste societies exchange the products that identify castes and retain the women so identified even though women are "naturally interchangeable," these societies "naturalize fallaciously a true culture" (Lévi-Strauss 1963). Thus, we see that "Classification, for Lévi-Strauss, is mental, arbitrary, and cultural; it is a rendering of the 'natural' world on the native's part, and therefore allegedly a kind of 'science' (the 'science of the concrete') and open to comment (if not criticism) as to the veracity of its distinctions" (Wagner 1973:6). For MARRIOTT, the indigenous cognitive system, elicited through the ethnosociological method, is more than an alleged science; it is a theory comparable to Western systems theories.

A second revision regarding the structure of identities in the previously established order concerns dynamism and generativity of structure. Some previous accounts picture the traditional structure as so static and fixed that contemporary political and economic developments necessarily represent a radical structural change (Béteille 1965; Leach 1960; and others). Other accounts emphasize the flexibility and the adaptiveness of traditional structure (Gould 1963; Rudolph and Rudolph 1967; Singer 1972) yet implicitly posit the equilibrium assumption of teleological functional theory: that profound change requires the confrontation of the endogenous system with exogenous factors, the colonial experience. In addition, this latter view has been criticized for a laxity of definition of traditional structure such that the analyst cannot clearly discriminate those features of traditional structure which have "latent potential for change" from those which do not.

The response in these papers and in the discussions is to stress repetitive processes of positional and ideological changes throughout South Asian history. According to Malik (this volume), these changes are masked by certain stereotypes of the Hindu tradition, such as spirituality and fatalism, which have been retained partly because of the classic writings of certain nineteenth-century writers, such as Weber and Marx, and by British administrators' codifications of native categories of castes, territory, and law. To Marriott and Inden (this volume), dynamism is seen in the underlying generative logic of categories, substances, and transactions. Changing transactions in substances between individuals of the same or different human or non-human *jāti*s are interpreted as constantly redefining the boundaries of different identities all called by that protean term *jāti*. This interpretation is not, as yet, generally accepted; if it is valid, it would go far in explaining (if the system is observed at any one point in time) how South Asian dynamics can give the appearance of arcane stasis, how transformations can give the appearance of continuity, and how the moving can give the appearance of the standing.

PART 2: THE MOVING AND THE STANDING

Discussion of the contributions of these papers and the conferences on the dynamics of tradition leads us to the topic of emerging identities in South Asia. Several approaches underlie the papers and discussion on this topic. As in the divergent interpretations of the previously existing structure, which I labeled the standing and the moving, here there are different interpretations of the emerging structure, the moving and the standing. Depending on one's assumptions about the static or dynamic nature of the previously existing structure, one tends to interpret recent changes either as disjunctions from the previous structure or as continuities and transformations of the previous structure. Although proponents of different approaches might agree in the main with the cognitive definition of identity which I shall outline in the Epilogue, they diverge on the weighting of social and ideological determinants of identity changes in South Asia. There are various levels of analysis, from middle-range theory to broader systemic approaches. There are differences in interpretation between indigenous and nonindigenous anthropologists. Some analysts favor the use of extrinsic, analytic categories, while others advance theories through an interplay of extrinsic and indigenous categories. These distinctions are more frequently crosscutting than mutually exclusive. Theory, method, and interpretation of emerging identities in South Asia are in a state of ferment.

Of the various models presented in papers and in the conference for interpreting identity changes in South Asia, there is greatest perception of change among those analysts who present role theory and symbolic interactionist theories and thus focus on an individual's identities rather than a collectivity's identity.

Rao's paper, "Role analysis and social change: with special reference to India" (this volume), provides, first, an extended review of variations of role theory by Nadel, Merton, Firth, Barth, Goffman, and many others. Rao notes a shift from considering role as a set of expectations ascribed or allocated by society to defining it as a set of expectations applied to a situated activity and a shift from the role-playing or conformity aspect of role analysis to the interactional approach which stresses role taking. It is argued that role analysis facilitates the study of crystallization of new roles and relationships but also helps in tracing, at this low level of abstraction, the specific changes resulting from wider forces such as the factory mode of production, integration into the market economy, and the professionalization of occupations.

As an example of the first shift mentioned above, Rao applies the framework of role relationship, role setting, and role expectation to what may broadly be called the changing occupational culture (see Singer 1973). Thus he discriminates one kind of identity shift, in which an existent role relationship played in a new role setting results in a change in role expectation (when a barber operates in a haircutting salon instead of in the context of a *jajmāni* relationship, he is free to serve anyone who requires his services, and free market conditions operate) from another kind of identity shift in which new role relationships may be played in the previous role setting, with a resultant change in role expectations (Chamars have become contract gardeners; as buyers of the standing crop, they are equal partners in the transaction with Ahirs as sellers, whereas as laborers they were subservient to Ahir peasants).

As an example of the second shift mentioned above, that is, a shift toward the analysis of role taking, Rao applies the framework of role set, role sectors, and role conflict to developments in the urban occupational culture. Role conflict may arise when an individual engages simultaneously in rural, traditional occupations and urban, nontraditional occupations, and thus faces a discrepancy between different norms in different role sectors. On the other hand, role conflict may not arise when the autonomy of different role sectors in a role set permits the existence of logically divergent norms. Such is the case when conduct between workers is defined in terms of skills and experience while their conduct in relation to the employer is governed by norms of patronage. These four examples handled within the framework of role analysis represent but a small sample of the morphological changes in identities observable in contemporary South Asia.

Other analysts also choose a middle-level range of theory to describe changing identities. At the second Congress conference, SINHA opted for a Goffmanesque presentation-of-self approach:

We take the problem of identity to be more complex than ever before in India. People are faced with a radically changing canvas so that all kinds of situational presentations of the self are average. In other words, you have to present yourself on several levels of identity, not only in terms of traditional and so-called modern views, but in terms of where you place yourself. Today in India, living partly in the village, partly in the city, partly perhaps in an industrial complex, an Indian is trying to present himself in many forms. Why? Because of his raw conception of how he would be accepted. It is as simple as that. How, as anthropologists, do we penetrate beyond these various shades of presentations of identity? We can do it by following the general conventions of fieldwork, namely, by observing the person in many contexts and trying to collect the contexts together. Then we will see how he manipulates himself in the various situations. And then we can bring in other shades of inquiry that will perhaps show that there is a broad boundary of an arena in which a person can present himself in a comfortable manner because he is more or less sure as to what his identity is. In other words, there is a conformity between the self and the observer in the arena.

In brief, Sinha stresses the multiplicity of situationally relevant identities borne by individuals.

Another participant at the second Congress conference, S. K. MAHAPATRA, noted the shift from concrete, interactionally based identities in the past to fictional, attributive identities in the present:

In any traditional society, whether tribal or nontribal, the question of identity was a given—a solid and stable thing. It could be taken for granted. Now, as society changes, as political, economic, and technological changes are making inroads into traditional societies, the sense of identity is becoming more fictional, attributive, and adaptive. The socioeconomic aspirations of the individual and the group have to be formulated and transmitted to the sources of authority, so that economic benefits can flow in.

Another direction of changes in identity mentioned at that conference was the fact of cognitive and motivational nonsharing concerning an identity set. PURI stated that he was convinced by the arguments of Wallace (1961) that we cannot demonstrate cognitive or motivational sharing even in very small homogeneous groups, that social interaction within situations does not require the same mental and affective map of these situations for everybody, and different people can interact quite harmoniously and quite successfully without such sharing. The work by Berreman (1972) was cited by several panelists as evidence for this state of affairs in urban India.

In short, one line of thinking on the problem of changing identities in South Asia refers to a wide range of causes of identity shifts — population growth, technological and occupational changes, economic and political aspirations. By means of middle-range theories such as role theory or symbolic interactionist approaches, identity changes are interpreted as a kaleidoscope of multiple, situationally relevant, adaptive, attributive identities in the context of a lessened cognitive sharing of the set of identities. In terms of the dichotomy of the standing and the moving, these middle-range approaches yield the most radically moving interpretation of the South Asian scene. It may be interesting to note that many of the proponents of these approaches are indigenous anthropologists who are thoroughly fluent in nonindigenous, that is, Western, social science theory.

A second line of thought for explaining identity changes which became apparent in some papers and in discussions is similar to the first in that this voluntaristic approach locates the etiology of identity changes in legal, technological, political, and economic changes, particularly in relative political and economic disadvantage; it may be distinguished from the first in that the unit of study is more clearly the collectivity rather than the individual.

VON FÜRER-HAIMENDORF's long experience with various tribal groups provided many insights during the preconference on legal, political, and economic factors affecting changes in their identities. When he first visited the Konyak Nagas some thirty-four years ago, Naga identity could not be said to exist. Persons would identify themselves as members of clans or villages only. It was only after their contact with the wider society — through protest and rebellion — that they became aware of this identity. VON FÜRER-HAIMENDORF likened this new awareness to the experience of an Indian colleague who recognized his Indian identity only when he came to England. Contact has not simply formalized a traditional category but has created something quite new. The replacement of tribal jurisdiction by government courts has undercut traditional ways of dealing with disputes. Further diminution of traditional tribal leadership is seen by comparison of the Gond and the Naga cases. The responses of traditional leaders to the wider societal organization of power differ markedly. Gond leaders have accepted the new channels and have enhanced their power. Naga leaders continue their previous ways of leadership, and their authority is swiftly being undercut by younger Naga men who are becoming bureaucrats and administrators.

It is widely known that the Nagas were among the first tribal group to engage in the politics of protest to their economic advantage; they have been emulated in this tactic by a number of other units (I discuss this further later on in the Introduction). Not so widely known are the unintended, potentially disastrous, consequences of the central government's allocations to the Nagas. There has been a rapid development of the superstructure of the Naga region — schools, administrative and bureaucratic opportunities, etc. — without a corresponding base economic development. Very few self-supporting industries have been built in the region. Administrators are pressured from above to spend their allocations quickly; they do so in ways that, though visible, fail to make the region self-supporting. VON FÜRER-HAIMEN-DORF sees this process, in which material expectations are super-abundantly satisfied in response to political protest, as a stage which will pass when the government finds itself unable to continue the high rate of allocations.

Legislation can also have unintended consequences which incite the mobilization of identities. Mencher's paper, "Agricultural labor unions: some economic and political considerations," shows that in most parts of Kerala there has recently been a significant change in the thrust of peasant agitations as a result of the final passage of the Land Reform (Amendment) Act and the growing pressure on the United Front government to implement it. Previous tenants have benefited from the implementation of this act, but the conditions of landless laborers have worsened. As wage laborers, they have suffered a decrease in real income. The conflict has shifted from landowners versus tenants to the widened category of landowners versus landless laborers.[5] Mencher argues that laborer class consciousness has increased because of the implementation of this act; the laborers are responding by forming agricultural labor unions, whose success in

[5]   See Béteille (1970) for a discussion of the Bengali system of agrarian, class-based identities and the Bengali variant of shifting agrarian relations: struggle between *jamindār*s [intermediaries of various kinds] and *rāyal*s [both owner-cultivators and tenants] is replaced by struggle between *jotdār* landowners and *bargādar* or *ādhiyār* sharecroppers.

various areas is related to labor supply and demand.

Although the point was not stressed in her paper, during the discussion MENCHER clarified that there are two identities emerging in this context: in addition to the laborer identity, there is a coalition of landowners which lobbies for favorable legislation.[6] Because both of these interest groups cross caste lines, we have a situation the inverse of the substantialization process described by Barnett (discussed later in the Introduction); here, the defining feature of landowner or laborer identity is not natural substance but commitment to a code for conduct, opposition to the other party. It would be interesting to know the symbolic tactics used by organizers of landowner or laborer coalitions to neutralize caste ideology. Unfortunately, transcribing such meetings might be rather alarming to the organizers.

Although units such as tribals, low castes, and religious (Muslim) minorities have been distinguished in various typological exercises (see Bailey 1960, 1961; Sinha 1965; Srivastava 1966; and rebuttal by Sachchidananda 1970), it is profitable to discuss them together for various reasons. These units are all marginal with regard to the caste Hindu society in India. Several of the authors in this volume (S. K. Mahapatra, Gautam, and Ahmad) and one panelist (Lynch) have analyzed processes of identity formation with reference group theory. And these units have reacted to a similar structural position — lack of access to regional political power and economic prizes — with a similar process of identity formation — elite emulation followed by rejection of such emulation and choice of an identity outside the Hindu ideology and the Hindu identity domain.

In a paper entitled "Caste elements among the Muslims of Bihar," Ahmad (this volume) traces first the dual process of convergence between Hindus and Muslims: low-caste Hindus convert to Muslim identity; and Muslims of foreign ancestry (Afghans and Persians, who constitute a small percentage of Indian Muslims) assimilate to Hindu religious and caste practices. These processes are cognitively ordered by the system of flexible generic categories for Muslims, which roughly distinguish higher-class Muslims of foreign ancestry from lower-class, converted Muslims. Ahmad then traces a resurgence of the Muslim identity. A series of politico-religious movements beginning in 1826 mobilized Muslims to act according to the egalitarian Shariah ideology. After partition, because of socioeconomic changes

[6] Similar reciprocal identity formation has been reported by Vander Velde in the context of Green Revolution technological changes in the Punjab. Landowners there have, for example, influenced legislators and administrators to have the main spur from a regional irrigation canal cut so as to pass by their fields first. Though democratically allotted an equal time share of irrigation with lower-caste fields, landowner-caste fields receive far more water because most of the water is lost through evaporation or seepage by the time it reaches the more distant fields (Vander Velde, personal communication).

such as the abolition of the *zamindari* land tenure system and the introduction of the parliamentary system, there was a partial neutralization of the categorical class differences among Muslims who remained in India. These changes affected them unequally, the lower-class Muslims benefiting more than the upper-class Muslims. Ahmad concludes that the combination of modernization and Islamization tends to incite rejection of the Hindu hierarchical ideology, a necessary adaptive strategy for this minority community in India.

Like Indian Muslims, both Santal tribals and urban Jatav untouchables lack access to regional political power and economic prizes. And the two-step process of identity formation is identical. In both cases, there was an initial stage of elite emulation, the imitation of upper-caste Hindu life-style, which gained them little. Next, both units opted for an identity outside the Hindu identity domain. Jatavs followed Ambedkar and became, at least nominally, Buddhists, while Santals chose a revitalized Santal identity organized around the Sacred Grove religion and the Jharkhand political party.

An added twist to this emulation-rejection process in identity formation among peripheral (low-caste, tribal, religious minority) units is seen in the comparison of the papers by S. K. Mahapatra and Gautam on the Santals. The revitalization of Santal identity is an innovation. But the success of this innovation, the degree to which Santals are willing to reject Hindu ways and embrace the Santal tradition, differs markedly in two Santal regions according to the relations between the emerging Santal elite — the innovators — and the Santal masses. In my Congress address (see "Symposium," this volume) I summarized S. K. Mahapatra's paper, which outlines contradictions between the elite and the masses and the consequent partial failure of this innovation. Mahapatra's own remarks follow mine and permit a clearer perception of the profound ambivalence of the relations between leaders and followers. By contrast, as seen in Gautam's paper, Santalization has fared well in another region. At the preconference, GAUTAM remarked that leaders in his region tend to underplay life-style differences between themselves and the masses and to distribute more evenly the prizes of political activity.

Cases such as these permit us to reexamine Geertz's (1963) primordial sentiments thesis. Close inspection of the actions of leaders who were exposed to other cultures and then returned to South Asia and began mobilizing identities by appeals to primordial sentiments such as language, religion, shared history, etc., leads to speculation about a possible difference between their public and private images. Several of these leaders may be (or have been) profound innovators in primordial-appealing clothing. Such difference need not affect the movement. What appears to be more crucial, however, in the success or failure of an innovated identity is whether or not the leader acts so as to underplay class and life-style differences between himself or herself and potential followers: whether or not the leader appears to *embody* the ideology and codes for behavior of the innovated identity.[7]

Lynch's refinements of reference group theory with regard to the Indian case in general, and to the urban Jatav caste in particular, appear in his monograph, *The politics of untouchability* (1969). Dissatisfied with culturally bound terms such as Sanskritization, Westernization, Kulinization, etc., which intend to describe reference group processes (Lynch 1969:3–7), Lynch substitutes a structural definition using reference group and status-role theory. He defines three types of reference group: identification, positive reference group, and negative reference group; and two types of status: dominant and salient, which are relevant in identity formation and social mobility (Lynch 1969:8–15).[8] These terms permit a charting of stages in Jatav identity formation. Initially, Jatavs claimed Kshatriya as their dominant status and redefined their origin myth accordingly. They were met by the continued imputation of a salient status of untouchable by upper castes. At this point, they chose two identities in identity domains outside the Hindu domain: *nava* Buddhist and citizen. To further define their identity, they took the Brahmans as a negative reference group, the enemy gatekeepers who were refusing them access to strategic resources.

It may be noted that the analysis of these liminal units (religious minorities, tribals, and low castes) goes beyond previous reference group analyses, such as Orans's analysis of the Santal case (1965:56, 103, 104) with his notion of the emulation/solidarity conflict. The emulation/solidarity conflict is relevant only to the first stage of this process of identity formation.

LYNCH'S position on identity changes was further clarified at the

---

[7] I do not want to imply that an effective leader's *actions* are devoted solely to the interests of one identity. Kidder's interesting study (1974) of urban caste association leaders in Bangalore suggests that diffuse involvements are requisite for influence:

For most of the leaders interviewed, it was difficult to identify any one of their involvements, whether in politics, caste, litigation, business, or particular occupational roles, as being the single identity around which their activities were organized. Each area of involvement tended to lend support to the leader's status and power in other areas (Kidder 1974:185).

Influence [of caste association leaders] does not develop within a single organization or opportunity structure. Instead, it is founded on the individual's continued action as a favor broker between different structures (Kidder 1974:189).

[8] A dominant status is "one which Ego asserts ought to take precedence over all his other statuses in a particular interaction with Alter" (Lynch 1969:13). A salient status is "that one of a number of possible statuses, other than his asserted dominant status, that Alter imputes to Ego." Where Lynch uses *status*, I follow Goodenough's convention and employ the term *identity*.

preconference. To LYNCH, the basic change in South Asia today is the emergence of a competitive political-economic order. Identities coalesce around voting, the politics of protest, and hyperpoliticization. In this view, identity mobilization is a means to an end: access to strategic resources and power. Throughout the preconference, he was a persistent, though sympathetic, critic of the ethnosociological statements with his query, "But what is the practical advantage they see in changing their identity?" Challenged in his turn for regarding identities as epiphenomena, he denied this because "their identity allows them to coalesce in order to satisfy their expectations." Exchanges like these lead me to regard the various aspects of an identity — and the progressive definition of the various aspects of an emerging identity — as arcs of a communications circuit.

There was much discussion at the preconference of the relation between identity changes and expectations in the new political-economic competitive order. Two examples are relations between states and the Indian central government and tendencies to fission at the regional level. KHARE noted that many units are now competing for allocations from the government:

In India, the central government buys off protests from different states. Some states, such as Kerala, Tamilnadu, Kashmir, and Nagaland, are prone to protest chronically. These states produce identities and project them toward the center. This is what chief ministers do in relation to the prime minister and to the appropriation committees. Everyone wants to have the lion's share. See the plight of Uttar Pradesh. It provides three prime ministers but gets nothing. In Uttar Pradesh, there is a fight to divide the state into three parts. First, eastern U.P. would become the East U.P. State. Second, the middle-range people like Lucknow wallahs who are better off than the easterners would become a second state. And the third would be the most affluent area near Punjab, Delhi, and the industrial complex. There is a serious identity crisis in U.P. concerning infrastructure, cultural identity, and power.

VON FÜRER-HAIMENDORF noted similar separatist identity movements in Andhra Pradesh and in Pakistan:

We find the same process in Andhra Pradesh. At one time, they thought that all people speaking Telugu should have the same identity; they should be together. They agitated to break up the old Madras State and Hyderabad and achieved this end. They were thinking only of one facet of identity: language. Once together, they found that though they all speak one language, they were very different. Why should the rich people of the coastal districts support poor Telangana? Why should the grain surplus go there? On the other hand, the people of Telangana found that they had a cultural identity of their own; they had, in Hyderabad, absorbed quite a lot of the Mogul culture. They resented it when dhoti wallahs came barefooted into the secretariat; in Hyderabad they were all properly dressed, etc. These are superficial matters, but they suddenly found that they were not the same. The prime example is Pakistan, originally created on the basis of common religious identity. East

Bengal and West Pakistan are almost all Muslim. Suddenly religion is dropped and language is important. The people of Bangladesh recognize that there are inequalities of representation and allocations.

During the preconference, KHARE took a position similar to those of von Fürer-Haimendorf and Lynch. He responded to Lynch's questions on what caused hyperpoliticization and what legitimized the politics of economic protest with the notion that identity shifts are experimental adaptative strategies to cope with increasing awareness of unmet material expectations. Consciousness by persons is a series of expectations. The rate of expectations in relation to the availability of resources affects identity formation (compare Aberle [1970] on relative deprivation).

A discussion followed in which various panelists mentioned examples of the undercommunication of expectations. KHARE noted corruption in the bank loan system. A person must sign a loan note for double the amount received, the remainder going to the processors of the loan. DAVID noted that the traditional corruption of clerks in Sri Lanka was recognized in the platform of the Sri Lanka Freedom Party during the 1970 elections; when the party assumed power, it set up a system of local party committees to act as mediators. Scattered personal communications assert that while these agents have been effective in uncovering corruption, nepotism, etc., they themselves require bribes. SENGUPTA mentioned the differential development of various sections of a tribe according to access to regional markets. To this, von FÜRER-HAIMENDORF replied that location is relevant in another way: scheduled development blocs receive resources for which recipients are not specified, and caste Hindus profit. Also, though alienation of tribal land is forbidden, file clerks can be bribed and tribals do lose their land. GAUTAM reported that village-level workers are ordered not to report problems to the district inspector so that the latter can produce a report of well-being in the area under his control.

KHARE related these processes of unmet expectations to hyperpoliticization and identity formation. Protest is not new in extent and in reasons; only the strategies have changed. Khare proposed three stages of protest and identity reformulation: (1) strategies to improve material position are attempted through normal legal, bureaucratic, or political channels; (2) the collectivity is alienated on seeing those strategies fail; and (3) the collectivity recognizes that alienation is of no avail and tends to evolve a wholesale alternative identity with different strategies for gaining access to resources and power.

Further discussion followed on the role of the legal system and mass communications in the communication of expectations and in the formation of identities. MORRISON noted that lawyers have a crucial role in that they are frequently the primary link between rural people and urban life. Lawyers, lawyer's assistants, and self-styled village legal experts communicate to the hinterlands strategies of action which may be adopted for collective action. (See Kidder [1974] for the opposite argument that litigation does not have a "tutorial function" for caste associations; see also Galanter [1973], who suggests that politicians are now replacing lawyers as agents of change and intermediaries to government resources.) As everywhere, differential access to and proficiency in legal proceedings tend to further polarize the relatively advantaged and the relatively disadvantaged. DAVID asked Lynch and Barnett:

. . . to describe the relevance of mass communications to protest movements. Lynch has observed the untouchable Jatavs of Agra. Barnett has studied the militant untouchables of Madras City. In some senses, mass communication can muffle the expression of discontent. In Sri Lanka I remember seeing a headline with triple-banner coverage of the Sharon Tate murder next to a very small column describing the troubles faced by Indira Gandhi before the last major election. On the other hand, mass communications can further the formation of identities. Can you chart the various effects of mass communications — the newspapers, the movies, etc. — in disseminating news of protests in other countries and thus mobilizing new identities? In other words, how does mass communication legitimize the politics of protest?

LYNCH replied:

Mass communication is just the mechanism for all this. For instance, the Adi Dravidas I worked with more recently in Bombay were, on the whole, literate. Some of the women were more literate than the men. This was due, in part, to the missionaries, not all of them Christian. There are reading rooms in the slums. They read newspapers day in and day out. They can tell you what is going on. And the south Indian movies are all politicized. But this is just the mechanism for spreading ideas. What I am asking is why do these people, who at one time would not have protested, now feel that they should get out there and do so?

BARNETT replied by relating mass communications to the process of choosing between competing identities and competing ideologies. He gave more weight to communications, for example:

The publication of works by English rational, utilitarian philosophers has provided a tremendous counterbase to feudalism and to caste. Older untouchable leaders still quote John Stuart Mill and Jeremy Bentham. The effect of this has been underplayed. Secondly, the effect of films on untouchables has been quite complex. They are typically politicized in the DMK [Dravida Munnetra Kazhagam] direction, that is, in a Tamil cultural nationalism direction. This has had a consequence unintended by upper-caste filmmakers. That is, the untouchables have tried to take over the Dravidian movement for their own purposes. After all, they are the "original Dravidians." Also, world-wide events do seep down. They are aware of what is going on in South Africa, in America — especially during the Martin Luther King era of protest.

There are, then, differences of opinion on the extent to which law and mass communications transmit local news of unmet expectations, strategies for collective action, etc., and foreign news of collective action upon which local identities can be modeled.

KHARE continued the exposition of his position by discussing identity shifts as adaptive strategies conditioned by the unit's previous structural position (in terms of economics, power, and connections with bureaucrats and politicians). To do this, he considered Apte's paper (this volume), "Region, religion, and language: parameters of identity in the process of acculturation," which I shall now summarize. Apte contrasts the cases of two communities that migrated to Tamilnadu over two centuries ago, Maharashtrian Brahmans who assimilated to a Tamil identity and Maharashtrian tailors who resisted such a shift.

Apte argues:

> . . . that in the South Asian context, groups with high ascribed social status, namely Brahmans, easily adapt to the regional identity because they can readily associate themselves with the Sanskritic Great Tradition shared by most regions in South Asia. Similar opportunities are available to groups with low ascribed social status only if comparable groups exist in the dominant population. If, however, the structural parallels do not exist, or if a group is desirous of upward social mobility and seeks the goal of higher social ranking, then the factors emphasized in ethnic identity may be an affiliation to a broader reference group outside the new region and a continuation of religious practices emanating from the original home region. Thus the available criterion of language for the retention of a distinct identity for a whole community may be superseded by other criteria such as religion, region, or *varṇa* status.

In other words, Apte relates the presence or absence of a reference group structurally analogous to that of the migrating unit and the previous high/low structural position of the migrating unit to the assimilation or rejection of new regional identity.[9] KHARE compared Apte's cases with his own data (1970) on the north Indian migrant Kanya-Kubja Brahmans, among whom a high grade of the caste tends to retain its identity, while the low grades of the caste wish to change theirs. In general, high, middle, and low castes differ in their adaptive strategies of identity formation — even though the object of all is social recognition. KHARE uses "social rather than political or any other specific term because that is the widest term under which various sorts of identity changes can be grouped together." He adds that low-caste shifts are frequently not successful; in these cases there is "negative social recognition" (see also his Congress remarks). Thus

[9] This difference can also be described as local/nonlocal reference group behavior. See also Marriott (1968b) on multiple zones of reference and Fox (1969) on various levels of *jāti* and *varṇa* categories which can be selected in reference group behavior.

Khare complements Lynch's view on the practical consequences of identity change; such change seeks not just social recognition but also material ends; identity shifts are experiments which may be dropped if they do not succeed. In addition, Khare tends to stress the previous structural position of a unit as a partial determinant of identity choices.

In short, various pragmatic approaches emphasize the emergence of a politico-economic ideology, of parliamentary process, and of the perception of relative deprivation as the basic shifts underlying identity changes in South Asia. The formation of new cognitive identity structures is analyzed on the collective level in terms of reference group and adaptive strategy processes. There are variations within this broad pragmatic approach, in that some authors, such as Lynch, emphasize the discontinuities of the competitive order from the past, while others, such as Khare, attend to continuities with the past by analyzing the effect of previous structural positions and the repetitive processes of adaptive changes. These variations are not necessarily contradictory.

I am here using "pragmatic" in its linguistic sense. In this sense pragmatic is not equivalent to practical; rather, a pragmatic meaning denotes the sensitivity of a communication sign to its ethnographic context. A pragmatic meaning replicates, or indexes, information otherwise present in the context (Cicourel 1973:88). A communication sign's pragmatic meaning differs from its semantic meaning: the "arbitrary" meaning that can be defined or "glossed" irrespective of the context of its use.

By analogy, a dichotomy of pragmatic/semantic explanations of identity changes may be of greater utility than the common dichotomy of empiricist/ideationist explanations. Both dichotomies appear at first equally apt, because the main issue separating the (pragmatic) approaches just discussed and the (semantic) approaches shortly to be discussed is the weight given to social, demographic, technological, economic, and political determinants versus normative, cognitive, and ideological determinants of identity changes. (See the Epilogue for further definition of semantics and pragmatics.)

In responding to the former approaches at the preconference, BARNETT agreed with Khare that the structural position of a caste is important in influencing identity choice, adding that regional differences in political culture are also important. For example, untouchables in the south stress their identity as the original Dravidians as part of the emerging Dravidian nationalism movement. Barnett also agrees that practical consequences are relevant. In 1928 the Koṇṭaikkaṭṭi Veḷḷāḷars whom he studied saw the anti-Brahman movement as a chance to replace the Brahmans as a top-ranked category in the region. Their changes (permitting interdistrict marriage, for example) were seen as a move to consolidate their position as a statewide identity to control political process. But he disagrees with Lynch's and Khare's position in that he emphasizes the unintended consequences of identity changes. For example, the Koṇṭaikkaṭṭi Veḷḷāḷars began to underplay their movement when E. V. Ramaswamy, leader of the DMK party in Tamilnadu, strongly reacted against their movement and threatened to attack them once the Brahmans were disposed of. In noting such unintended consequences, BARNETT questions the ability of individual actors to "perceive strategic outcomes and to change their cognitive system accordingly." Thus he denies the deterministic position of perceived practical consequences (material, power, and status interests) in the process of identity formation.

A second line of critique was that while pragmatic analyses of adaptive strategies, relative deprivation, and structural positions do not exactly reduce cultural norms, cognitions, and ideologies to epiphenomenal status, such analyses underemphasize their role in defining who shall take which adaptive strategy with regard to which material interests. BARNETT was the most forceful critic in this direction, saying that the "middle-range explanations such as Singer's notion (1973) of compartmentalization as an adaptive strategy, the Rudolphs' notion (Rudolph and Rudolph 1967) of the interpenetration of tradition and modernity, and other additive [caste plus class] or replacement [class replaces caste] theories fail to attend to the ideologies which give meaning to these supposed processes."

To my mind, Barnett is somewhat overstating the case, as is shown in the papers collected in the volume *Entrepreneurship and modernization of occupational cultures in South Asia* (Singer, ed. 1973). This volume is instructive on the question of social and ideological determinants of identity change because it provides comparative data on structural position, adaptive strategies, and occupational cultures in contemporary India. Several papers (Fox 1973; Mines 1973; Papanek 1973) on the structural position of traditional merchants tend to reject the Weberian hypothesis that something comparable to a Protestant ethic is necessary for modernization.

The papers by Fox, Mines, and Papanek, taken together, show that the behavior of the traditional South Asian merchant is economically rational; given favorable economic opportunities and political conditions, he also draws upon elements of his traditional occupational culture to support a move into industry and to expand his scale of operation. The increase in "organizational rationality," as Fox argues, follows the specific nature of the business activity, new opportunities, and the availability of capital and credit; and it does not depend on the religious ethic and psychology of the traditional merchant. A transformation of the traditional occupational culture is not a condition for modernization (Singer 1973:6).

On the other hand, Owens's (1973) and Nandy's (1973) studies of Mahaisya peasant entrepreneurs and Singer's study (1973) of upper-caste Madras industrialists argue for the presence of an ethic functionally equivalent to the Protestant ethic. Mahaisyas have a "community spirit" and "ethos," while Madras industrialists employ certain "adaptive strategies of compartmentalizing their activities in industry from their traditional ritual and caste obligations, in order to reduce conflict and to work out mutual adjustments in both spheres" (Singer 1973:11). Different structural positions and adaptive strategies are then analyzed in the context of ideology or "occupational culture."

Barnett appears to be on surer ground when he argues that such ideological analysis is incomplete. He objects to the notion of compartmentalization, for example, on the grounds that it is a "partial happening of a much broader ideological process. For, in situations where people attempt to erect compartments, each compartment is ideologically shifting in character."

Papers by Barnett and by Marriott and Inden have given us alternative models for understanding the broader ideological or cognitive processes underlying identity changes. Barnett's study of changing ideology and caste identity is based on the notion that symbols are horizontally integrated within an ideology. That some symbols are more equal than others is argued elsewhere in various usages as dominant symbol (V. Turner 1967), core symbol (Schneider 1968), key symbol (Ortner 1973), or synoptic paradigm (Geertz 1964). (See Nicholas [1973] for a recent review of the topic.)

To Barnett, this volume, ideological shifts can be discerned in the shifts of dominance or centrality of symbols within the ideology, previously stressed symbols becoming less valued and vice versa. He describes the shift from a holistic hierarchical ideology to a non-holistic substantialized ideology in south India. In the previous caste ideology, two codominant features defining caste identity, sharing of natural substance and caste code for conduct, are cognitively nondual: natural substance and code are congruent and mutually defining. Substantialization is the ideological shift from nonduality to duality: the substantialized caste identity (among the Koṇṭaikkaṭṭi V<u>e</u>ḷ<u>ā</u>ḷars studied by Barnett) is defined by natural substance alone, while a wide range of previously proscribed codes for Koṇṭaikkaṭṭi Vḷāḷar conduct is now permitted, codes which are also followed by other castes. The dual dominance or centrality of natural substance and code for conduct in the previous ideology is replaced by an ideology in which natural substance retains dominance while code for conduct becomes peripheral.

This ethnosociological statement of ideological shifts is, to some degree, based upon Dumont's previous work on the subject. For Dumont, substantialization is the transformation from a holistic system of castes to a system of atomistic units (or substances, in Dumont's terms):

The transition from a fluid, structural universe in which the emphasis is on interdependence and in which there is no privileged level, no firm units, to a universe of impenetrable blocks, self-sufficient, essentially identical and in competition with one another, a universe in which the caste appears as a collective *individual* (in the sense we have given to this word), as a substance (Dumont 1970:222).

The two meanings of "substance" must be distinguished. Substance contrasts with the whole as the individual contrasts with the totality, whereas natural substance literally means natural bodily substance.

Barnett sees this ideological shift as underlying a whole panoply of crosscutting identities now emerging in south India: ethnicity, racism, class, and cultural nationalism. Choice among identities becomes the arena for struggle and for increased protest in the context of unmet expectations in the economic sphere.

At the preconference discussion of this thesis, VON FÜRER-HAIMENDORF questioned whether Barnett was using the term "racism" in "the accepted meaning of conflict between groups of different physical makeup" and speculated that racism has never been a dividing factor in the subcontinent (which contains many races) because caste already provided barriers between groups. BARNETT's reply defined this emerging racism as ideological rather than physical; his data on informants' lack of ability to identify castes from photographs showing faces alone argue against physical racism. Ideological racism implies that instead of the holistic continuum of castes under the previous caste ideology, there are now, in south India, two identities, touchable castes and untouchable castes, which are mobilized in certain contexts. The difference between the older nondualistic caste ideology and racism is further illustrated with data in which informants were asked if they could recognize an untouchable who had been raised for twenty years in an upper-caste household. Older and rural informants said the untouchable would be recognized because he would act differently (nondualist caste view), while younger and urban informants said he would be recognized because he would look different (racist, physical-features view). KHARE agreed with Barnett that physical races are difficult to distinguish, especially because the long tradition of concubinage has imparted upper-caste features to low castes, and that north Indians also believe code for conduct to be transmitted through natural substance, but stated that the racist attitude with which he lived as an upper-caste child held that he should not play with untouchable children because he would pick up not only their way of acting but also their looks.

LYNCH, clarifying ideological racism as (1) a shared set of beliefs distinguishing groups on the basis of certain physiological features, and (2) having an action component, argued that the second feature of the definition fits the situation of blacks and whites in America, but not the situation in India. Barnett responded with residential, occupational, and transactional features that demarcate untouchable castes from touchable castes in Madras City; these same features now fail to differentiate between various touchable castes in the city, although they are still operative in rural areas. Urban touchable castes have substantialized into autonomous ethniclike identities: these touchable castes, though differing in natural substance, have crosscutting codes for conduct. But substantialization is not relevant for untouchable castes for whom natural substance still enjoins a code for conduct.

DAVID added that the phenomenon of racism would be a very major footnote to the extent of substantialization because there are about five large untouchable castes in south India. He suggested that substantialization and racism could be defined in terms of communications structure and practical interests. In the previous holistic caste system, there was a communications circuit connecting all castes; if anything, the gaps in communications structure occurred between castes in the agricultural sector and those in the rural mercantile sector. From Barnett's (and Mencher's) data, it appears that two circuits of communication are developing, the first defined by crosscutting codes for conduct which permit entry into more occupations, and the second defined by untouchable occupations (which do not crosscut codes of other castes) and their practical advantage in retaining the scheduled caste classification. In other words, substantialization implies that more articulated communication is developing among touchable castes; racism implies that the gap in communications between touchable and untouchable castes is greater than it was previously.

BARNETT replied that untouchables are taking advantage of both the scheduled caste identity and the substantialized ideology. On the one hand, they take advantage of the benefits of the scheduled caste identity; on the other hand, they recognize that other castes reject the old caste ideology of the influence of acquired characteristics when they engage in occupations previously considered defiling; then they reinterpret their origin myths (in which they are portrayed as Brahmans permanently defiled by an action such as killing a cow) in this light. They assert that natural substance alone is relevant — they were, after all, Brahmans — and that the previous defiling act is irrelevant in the definition of their identity.

A discussion followed on whether or not substantialization represented a discontinuity from the previous structure. TAMBIAH questioned whether the thesis that caste identity is now defined by natural substance, while crosscutting codes for conduct are permitted, is equally applicable to all contexts of action. That is, cross-caste commensal relations fit the thesis because urban castes now interdine in ways proscribed by previous codes, but the nondualism of natural substance and the code enjoining marriage within the caste is still maintained.

A second query introduces us to an alternative model for dealing with ideological shifts underlying identity changes in South Asia, an ethnosociological model explored in Marriott and Inden's paper "Toward an ethnosociology of South Asian caste systems." MARRIOTT questioned Barnett's interpretation of substantialization as discontinuous from the previous cognitive structure. To MARRIOTT, the previous cognitive structure of substance exchange and of *jāti* is not being demolished in the process labeled substantialization; only the level of *jāti* identity that analysts label "caste" has been redefined. The logic by which *jāti*s are defined in terms of exchanges in natural substance is still present. MARRIOTT further applied the ethnosociological method to changing identities by stating that "modernizing movements can create new class, regional, and national genera" by promoting exchanges of food and other substances among people.

In response to LYNCH's query whether such transactions are just a cultural metaphor (compare the controversy over whether kinship is a thing in itself or a reflection of economic and political processes), MARRIOTT stressed that the Hindu cognitive principle of the nonduality of natural substance and code for conduct defines the relation between any *jāti* identity and transactions in substance as nonmetaphorical, tautological, and causal. For example, MARRIOTT has observed the creation of a new identity, an association of pilgrims, by the process of interdining. The pilgrims interpret this act as unifying: "We are one because we eat together, we eat together because we are one." DAVID continued the questioning of the status of metaphor in the ethnosociological method. Certain symbols in Jaffna, such as the tying of the wedding badge (*tāli*), are held to have a nonmetaphorical effect, in this case, the transubstantiation of a woman's natural substance from that of her parents to that of her husband: she becomes physically identical to her husband at the moment the *tāli* is tied. On the other hand, Jaffna Tamil communists use the term *cakōtarar* [sharer of bodily substance; blood relative] when speaking to comrades, yet they are not subject to incest prohibitions as *cakōtarar* should be. MARRIOTT responded that this question is not satisfactorily resolved except that words themselves are a medium that is transacted. They are a subtle substance which can influence others either in their use or, in the case of the *tapasiya* [one who practices austerity], in abstinence from their use.

There was further questioning on operational rules for applying the ethnosociological method to nontraditional identities. It was agreed that trade unions might be a crucial case for testing the applicability of Marriott's continuity thesis versus Barnett's discontinuity thesis regarding the relation of ideology or cognitive system to changing identities.

Two issues are joined here. Several of the preconference panelists (Khare, Marriott, and David) tended to view recent shifts as continuities and transformations of previous structure, while others (Barnett, von Fürer-Haimendorf, and Lynch) emphasized discontinuities. Several panelists (particularly Marriott and Barnett) tended to weight ideological and cognitive features in the discussion of changing identities, while others (von Fürer-Haimendorf, Khare, and Lynch) emphasized economic and political determinants. Tambiah and David suggested strategies for combining these two determinants of identity changes. Having summarized these issues, TAMBIAH said,

As I see it, the truth lies somewhere in between. Let us start with the Dumontian organic picture of traditional society. The notion of hierarchy is that parts perform (unequally) toward the whole. The political-economic domains are encompassed by *dharma*, the realm of morality, ethics, and ritual considerations. That is what makes Indian society so distinctive. This is a noncompetitive model ideologically, although nevertheless a graded one. The *varna* theory, the *puruṣa* theory, and local-level caste transactions are all traditional hierarchical representations. Against this, let us pose another model, which is what we have now been discussing, a model of political economy which is the result of British rule, colonial policy, new ideas, new political developments, and so on. This is essentially a different kind of model, a competitive model. There is a center, the central government, and there are subsidiary member units. The states themselves compete with each other to get the best resources. Linguistic groups are jockeying for power. Again within a particular region or state there are dissident and competing groups. This is the notion of political forces that Lynch has formulated: it is a political process; you compete to gain power and resources.

What is prominent about India today, as Professor Haimendorf has said, is that its bases of social and political affiliation are contextually so shifting. At one stage you invoke one criterion, at another stage, another criterion, and so on. What India is showing today, whether on the level of linguistic, caste, kinship, or any other identity, is a capability of shifting frontiers of identification in relation to this competitive process. This is a key phenomenon that has emerged in our discussions. We can look at it in various ways. Barnett used substantialization à la Dumont. But I think what we see are temporary substantializations. There is no drawing of permanent boundaries of groups, but a capability of forming temporary boundaries of varying sizes and ranges in this political process of competition. I wonder whether this is the essential part of the story of Indian identities today. All these things can be invoked situationally in a political process.

TAMBIAH concluded his synthesizing statement with a tentative link between the above shifts and the positions of Marriott and Barnett:

Whether this process goes back to a fundamental characteristic of Indian culture, that is, the propensity to combine elements and to generate new categories (or new genera, as Marriott would say) and that therefore we should not give a permanence to its manifestations is another matter. We have seen that all sorts of changing frontiers of identities are possible. We are trying to find some underlying formula for this situation at the level of ideological consciousness. Barnett's idea of substantialization — which is really temporary — makes sense in this new model of competition in political economy, not in the old model of caste. Nevertheless, this processual change in identities (within certain parameters) is possible because of an underlying Indian formulation of basic social elements which can be combined and re-combined to form new identities. Is this an underlying propensity of Indian thought which gives us a partial key to why we have this plethora of identities?

Tambiah's position is consistent with his previous studies in which he traced continuities and transformations between the historical Thai Buddhist religion and the contemporary, unified, peasant religion (Tambiah 1970). What is standing, or continuous with the past, is the categorizing propensity. What is moving, or a transformation from the past, is the political-economic order. At the preconference, DAVID said:

Now that Tambiah has stated his position, we should realize we are faced with a model which contrasts sharply with that of Dumont and Leach. Dumont proposes that the pure/impure hierarchical ideology encompasses the political-economic sphere and that all the changes we observe in recent times take place in this latter encompassed sphere. He says that a structure is either present or absent but does not change. Since the changes are in the encom-passed sphere, the hierarchical structure is still present. He would not accept Tambiah's position that there is both continuity and transformation of the structure and that the political-economic model now encompasses the caste model.

Although EDMUND LEACH was not present at the preconference ses-sion, he brought up precisely this point at the post-Congress session:

Anthropologists are of two kinds. There are those ethnographers who are purely concerned in producing descriptions of external empirical facts, and in those terms you can have an infinite number of different ethnographies of India. But as far as the individual Indian is concerned, one must assume . . . — simply from introspection of my relation to my own culture — that the native has an internal representation of that culture which is in itself an un-conscious structure in terms of which he responds to all sorts of situations. This internalized structure on the subconscious level is, at a more conscious level, verbalized in terms of categories which are the signs for the internal structure. The point I am trying to get across is opposite to those who say it is obvious that we all agree that everything is changing. Are we agreeing that everything is changing? It is quite possible that Dumont is right and that by and large the internalized representation of Indian society to members of that society is remaining remarkably constant, and that what is changing is the external attribution of the verbal categories in terms of which this constant structure is represented. That is to say that perhaps you can still represent yourself as being a member of a caste which is a member of a system of castes and which has a particular position in a system of castes. The question is, do you persuade yourself that you are a member of the same society as before? Is the change really taking place at the level of ideas as to how people think of themselves as existing, or not? There are certain social classes in England which have showed an extraordinary ability to maintain their internal representation of what society is like in the face of the most extraordinary external changes and to convince themselves that nothing has changed at all. What I want to know is how far hierarchical man is still a good representation of Indian society.

That the hierarchical representation may be changing, at least for some sectors of South Asian society, was asserted by MENCHER, who replied to Leach that labor unionists in Kerala no longer make the assumption that the state of the world is hierarchical. In the past, landless laborers were not happy with their situation but retained the hierarchical ideology. MENCHER maintained that now that there is

. . . politicization and unionizing activity, you begin to find a change at the underlying level. There is a change not only in people's acceptance of hierarchical position but also in their perception of hierarchy. Among a small but growing percentage of people in Kerala, there is a new image — especially where they have some kind of organization. Their image is usually that of some sort of socialist society, a more egalitarian and less hierarchical society. This, I think, is conscious, because there is a tremendous amount of simple literature in Malayalam which is either read by the laborers or is read aloud to them.

Questioned whether unionists reverted to their caste identities when the chips were down, MENCHER replied that, "although union identity crosscuts caste, it would be wrong to say that caste is gone. There has been no complete and utter breaking of things, but it has lessened and it is strikingly lessened if compared with, let us say, Tamilnadu, where it is much stronger, much more noticeable."

This question of whether to consider changes in internal representations as discontinuities or as continuities and transformations of previous structure is not academic hairsplitting. There are immense consequences for the region. If Barnett's view is correct, the construction of new identities and new nonholistic ideologies implies that knowledge will become more and more socially distributed, that persons will become privy, or interior, to several ideologies and exterior to many more ideologies present within their society (see Barnett, this volume). If Marriott's view is correct and the previous cognitive structures accommodate new identities, a far greater degree of common ideation might be retained throughout the society. In the first case, we would expect an increasing fractionalization of the population into substantialized identities, which begin to resemble atomistic ethnic units, mitigated by the fact that identities and ideologies underlying identities are crosscutting: a coherent structure of identities would not necessarily be constructed by this process. Further, it has been recognized that ideologies (taken in a wide sense with mythic, religious, or other forms of figurative representations) tend to reintegrate individual affect with arbitrary identity categories, codes for conduct, and so forth (see Nicholas 1973; T. Turner 1973); then the proliferation of identity-specific ideologies competing for the allegiance of individuals would militate against any but transitory commitment to any of them. In the latter case, the ancient cognitive nondualist propensity would aid both in constructing a new structure of identities and in integrating individual affect with that new structure.

The question is not just academic for another reason. I have recently heard that some Indian colleagues of Marxist persuasion reject as reactionary views that caste or other structures are adaptive to modern happenings in that they underplay the dynamic role of class antagonisms in South Asia. In light of this discussion, the question becomes whether or not class movements are communicated, at least partially, in terms of the previous cognitive structure of natural substance and transactions in substance (including natural substance, words, power, and money). At the moment, all we have are snippets of data: a man's statement, "I am the wife of the Congress party";[10] the fact that Jaffna Marxists address comrades as *cakōtarar*s [sharers of natural substance]; the fact that Dravida Munnetra Kazhagam party members have been observed walking across a fire pit holding the DMK black flag and shouting "DMK!" instead of holding a red flag and shouting "Amma!" [the mother goddess who spreads her flowing locks over the coals to protect devotees]; and the fact that the Bengali Marxists represent the goddess Kali holding a sickle (without hammer) instead of her more traditional weapons.[11] The point is that even if a political-economic competitive order is coming to the fore, even if productive relations are becoming less opaque, even if class consciousness[12] is fulfilling its transformative course, we must be alert to the possibility that these developments are communicated by means of a

---

[10] McKim Marriott, personal communication.

[11] Ralph W. Nicholas, personal communication.

[12] "Appropriate and rational reactions 'imputed' (*zugerechnet*) to a particular typical position in the process of production" (Lukacs 1971:51).

long-established South Asian cognitive process, to the possibility that the moving does not dispel or dismiss the standing.

THE NEW WIND

"There is a new wind, a *naī havā*, blowing through South Asian anthropology," said OWEN LYNCH while addressing the symposium, "Changing identities in South Asia" (this volume). As another panelist suggested, it remains to be seen whether this New Wind will be a fresh gale, sweeping away misty conceptualization, or just *havā*. It remains to be seen whether this New Wind will emanate from the subcontinent itself, driven by the increased awareness by South Asian anthropologists of the necessity of focusing social science on the practical problems of the region, or whether it will be a new confluence of theoretical and practical interests and a new meeting of Eastern and Western minds. And it remains to be seen whether any New Wind can keep pace with the hurricane of new changes, adjustments, movements, and cognitions happening in South Asia.

As SINHA proclaimed in his address to the Congress symposium, until now, the intellectual exchange has been a prevailing westerly wind from intellectual centers in England, France, Germany, and the United States towards the Orient, and not the reverse. Most of the noted indigenous anthropologists were either trained in the West or were trained by someone who had been. They found themselves scrambling to keep abreast of the latest winds from the West, whether evolutionism, diffusionism, structural-functionalism, culture and personality, or structuralism. To SINHA, indigenous anthropology has been a derived science, practitioners' interests evolving not out of pattern exhaustion and the development of a new Kuhnian paradigm, but out of imitation. The objects of research have also been derivative rather than defined by the pragmatic needs of the region.

It should be remarked that Sinha's position is by no means the most radical statement to be heard on this topic. Several Indian scholars known to have strong, well-articulated views on imperialist, neocolonialist Western social science were invited to the symposium, but communications and, mainly, financial factors intervened. Reactions to the prevailing westerly wind appear at various points in the papers and discussions.

At the preconference, KHARE frequently alluded to potential distortions in theory due to the differences between the external observer's view and the indigenous view. After acknowledging the influence of British and American anthropologists, Vidyarthi suggests (this volume) that "social anthropology in India should [not] overlook what may be termed its 'Indianness'," that is, "a synthetic approach [which] may be conceptualized in terms of our unique cultural milieu, value-attitude system, and heritage and historical experiences." To this end, he recommends our attention to social thinkers such as Mahatma Gandhi and to ancient scripture.

This suggestion that we attend to practical problems has increasingly been put into practice in the last decade. Developmental research in South Asia has not been as concentrated as in Africa or in Latin America, but some notable work has been done by both indigenous and nonindigenous authors. At the preconference, we heard a strong caution concerning the unintended consequences of policy formulated from such research, as in the case of the Green Revolution, which in some areas has sharply increased class differences in the countryside. In South Asia, however, conscious attempts to guide developmental research are being made; an example is the leaflet on priorities of research distributed and discussed by Indianists at the Congress. Given openness to criticism of such plans from at home and abroad, the ensuing research may be of significant aid to governmental policy.

The second suggestion, that we attend to the Indianness, or in general the South Asianness, of our science is being developed through increased use of South Asian textual materials in our formulations. These sources of data have recently been gaining adherents after a long pause due to the antihistoricist bias of British structural-functionalism. Although they were not the first to do so, Dumont, Mandelbaum, Redfield, Singer, Srinivas, and others who have worked on the social and cultural organization of Indian civilization have overcome this bias to some extent.

As was discussed earlier, the diminution of sociocentric and reductionist analysis is closely connected with the methodological questions of whether or not to use texts, and which levels of texts. A number of papers in this volume have chosen to open the field of inquiry to various levels of symbolic texts and their relation to observable action. There is an awareness here that the job of anthropologists who study a society in the context of a civilization is very different from that of anthropologists who study a society in which historical and textual materials are not available. The former requires a longer commitment, a commitment that does not exclude becoming a part-time historian, Dravidianist, Sanskritist, or whatever. It also demands recognition that previous distinctions such as "the analyst's unconscious model" versus "the native conscious model" or "what they say" versus "what they do" are not powerful enough to deal with a society that includes various levels of symbolic texts such as sastra and purana; intermediary texts such as enacted (chanted) ritual texts, prayers, songs sung at weddings by women, caste origin myths, and street plays; and verbal statements by informants of various degrees of initiate and pragmatic knowledge. Several papers in this volume make explicit use of these various levels of texts in the analysis of sociocultural materials.

There are no swift, comfortable correlations to be made between the three broad lines of thought represented here: empiricist-materialist, intellectualist, and ethnosociologist; and positions concerning the relation between the established structure and the emerging structure. Both Dumont, an intellectualist, and Marriott, a critic of Dumont and now a proponent of the ethnosociological method, hold that the established structure of thought is alive and well in contemporary South Asia, although their reasons are entirely different. On the other hand, two strongly empiricist writers, Khare and Lynch, contrast sharply on the question of continuity of tradition, Khare frequently commenting on the repetition of structural change throughout Indian history and Lynch emphasizing the disjunction between the established and the emerging structure.

To conclude, the *naī havā* blowing through the anthropological study of South Asia is a social and academic happening. The recognition that social scientists, as people, are studying a new nation with pressing problems has incited not wholesale applied anthropology, but certain theoretical shifts. There is a growing feeling, among both indigenous and nonindigenous anthropologists concerned with South Asia, that theoretical statements derived either mainly from observational data presented in terminology appropriate to the comparative method of anthropology or from too narrow a range of textual materials may seriously distort our perception of the profoundly changing sociocultural structure. Instead, there has been a certain blurring of the old entrenched lines of materialist and intellectualist analysis, of textual and contextual methods. Finally, and most importantly, a *naī havā* was seen in these conferences where we were able to practice, and not just preach, a more vigorous collaboration between indigenous and nonindigenous students of South Asia.

REFERENCES

ABERLE, DAVID F.
  1970   "A note on relative deprivation theory as applied to millenarian and other cult movements," in *Millennial dreams in action*. Edited by Sylvia L. Thrupp. New York: Schocken Books.
BAILEY, FREDERICK G.
  1960   *Tribe, caste, and nation*. Manchester: Manchester University Press.
  1961   Tribe and caste in India. *Contributions to Indian Sociology* 5:7-19.
  1963   Closed social stratification in India. *Archives Européennes de Sociologie* 4:107-124.

BARBER, BERNARD
1968 "Social mobility in India," in *Social mobility in the caste system in India*. Edited by James Silverberg. Comparative Studies in Society and History, Supplement 3. The Hague: Mouton.

BARNETT, STEVE
1973 "The process of withdrawal in a south Indian caste," in *Entrepreneurship and modernization of occupational cultures in South Asia*. Edited by Milton Singer. Monograph and Occasional Papers Series 12. Chapel Hill, N.C.: Duke University Press.

BARTH, FREDRIK
1960 "The system of social stratification in Swat, north Pakistan," in *Aspects of caste in India, Ceylon, and northwest Pakistan*. Edited by E. R. Leach. Cambridge Papers in Social Anthropology 2. Cambridge: Cambridge University Press.

BECK, BRENDA E. F.
1973 *Peasant society in Koṅku*. Vancouver: University of British Columbia Press.

BEIDELMAN, THOMAS O.
1959 *A comparative analysis of the* jajmāni *system*. Association for Asian Studies Monographs 8. New York: J. J. Augustin.

BERREMAN, GERALD D.
1971 The Brahmanical view of caste. *Contributions to Indian Sociology*, new series 5.
1972 Social identity and social interaction in urban India. *American Anthropologist* 74(3):567-586.

BÉTEILLE, ANDRÉ
1965 *Caste, class, and power*. Berkeley: University of California Press.
1969 "A note on the referents of caste," in *Castes: old and new*. Bombay: Asia Publishing House.
1970 Peasant associations and the agrarian class structure. *Contributions to Indian Sociology*, new series 4:126-139.

BOUGLÉ, C.
1958 The essence and reality of the caste system. *Contributions to Indian Sociology* 2:7-30.

CICOUREL, AARON V.
1973 *Cognitive sociology: language and meaning in social interaction*. Baltimore, Md.: Penguin.

COHN, BERNARD S.
1971 *India: the social anthropology of a civilization*. Englewood Cliffs, N.J.: Prentice Hall.

DAVID, KENNETH
1973 Until marriage do us part: a cultural account of Jaffna Tamil categories for kinsmen. *Man* 8(4):521-535.
1974a "And never the twain shall meet? Mediating the structural approaches to caste ranking," in *Structural approaches to south Indian studies*. Edited by Harry Buck. Chambersburg, Penn.: Wilson College Press.
1974b Spatial organization and normative schemes in Jaffna, northern Sri Lanka. *Modern Ceylon Studies* 3:1.

DUMONT, LOUIS
1957a *Une sous-caste de l'Inde du sud: organisation sociale et religieuse des Pramalai Kallar*. Paris: Mouton.

1957b *Hierarchy and marriage alliance in south Indian kinship.* Occasional Papers of the Royal Anthropological Institute. London: William Clowes.
1959 A structural definition of a folk deity of Tamil Nad: Aiyanar the lord. *Contributions to Indian Sociology* 3:75-87
1962 The conception of kingship in ancient India. *Contributions to Indian Sociology* 6:48-77.
1970 *Homo hierarchicus: an essay on the caste system.* Chicago: University of Chicago Press.

DUMONT, LOUIS, DAVID POCOCK
1957a Village studies. *Contributions to Indian Sociology* 1:23-42.
1957b For a sociology of India. *Contributions to Indian Sociology* 1:7-22.
1958 Commented summary of the first part of Bouglé's *essais. Contributions to Indian Sociology* 2:31-44.

FOX, RICHARD G.
1969 *Varṇa* schemes and ideological integration in Indian society. *Comparative Studies in Society and History* 11:27-45.
1973 "Pariah capitalism and traditional Indian merchants, past and present," in *Entrepreneurship and modernization of occupational cultures in South Asia.* Edited by Milton Singer. Monograph and Occasional Papers Series 12. Chapel Hill, N.C.: Duke University Press.

GALANTER, MARC
1968 The displacement of traditional law in modern India. *Journal of Social Issues* 24:65-91.
1973 "A note on contrasting styles of professional dualism: law and medicine in India," in *Entrepreneurship and modernization of occupational cultures in South Asia.* Edited by Milton Singer. Monograph and Occasional Papers Series 12. Chapel Hill, N.C.: Duke University Press.

GEERTZ, CLIFFORD
1963 "The integrative revolution: primordial sentiments and civil politics in the new states," in *Old societies and new states: the quest for modernity in Asia and Africa.* Edited by Clifford Geertz. New York: Free Press.
1964 "Ideology as a cultural system," in *Ideology and discontent.* Edited by David E. Apter. New York: Free Press.

GOMBRICH, RICHARD F.
1971 *Precept and practice: traditional Buddhism in the rural highlands of Ceylon.* Oxford: Clarendon Press.

GOODENOUGH, WARD H.
1965 "Rethinking 'status' and 'role': toward a general model of the cultural organization of social relationships," in *The relevance of models for social anthropology.* Edited by Michael Banton. A.S.A. Monograph 1. New York: Praeger.

GOULD, HAROLD A.
1963 The adaptive functions of caste in contemporary Indian society. *Asian Survey* 3:427-438.

HAGEN, E. E.
1962 *On the theory of social change.* Homewood, Ill.: Dorsey Press.

HARPER, EDWARD B.
1959 A Hindu village pantheon. *Southwestern Journal of Anthropology* 15:227–234.
HARPER, EDWARD B., *editor*
1964 "Ritual pollution as an integrator of caste and religion," in *Religion of South Asia*. Seattle: University of Washington Press.
HOCART, A. M.
1970 *Kings and councillors* (original edition 1936, Cairo). Edited by Rodney Needham. Chicago: University of Chicago Press.
KHARE, RAVINDRA S.
1970 *Changing Brahmins: associations and elites among the Kanya-Kubjas of north India*. Chicago: University of Chicago Press.
KIDDER, ROBERT L.
1974 Litigation as a strategy for personal mobility: the case of urban caste association leaders. *Journal of Asian Studies* 33(2):177–192.
LEACH, EDMUND R., *editor*
1960 "Introduction: what should we mean by caste?" in *Aspects of caste in south India, Ceylon and north-west Pakistan*. Cambridge Papers in Social Anthropology 2. Cambridge: Cambridge University Press.
1968 *Dialectic in practical religion*. Cambridge Papers in Social Anthropology 5. Cambridge: Cambridge University Press.
LÉVI-STRAUSS, CLAUDE
1963 The bear and the barber. *Journal of the Royal Anthropological Institute of Great Britain and Ireland* 93:1–11.
LUKACS, GEORG
1971 *History and class consciousness*. Translated by Rodney Livingstone. Cambridge, Mass.: MIT Press.
LYNCH, OWEN M.
1969 *The politics of untouchability*. New York: Columbia University Press.
MADAN, T. N.
1971 "Introduction" to *On the nature of caste in India: a review symposium on Louis Dumont's* Homo hierarchicus. *Contributions to Indian Sociology,* new series 5.
1972 Religious ideology in a plural society: the Muslims and Hindus of Kashmir. *Contributions to Indian Sociology*, new series 6:106–141.
MAINE, SIR HENRY
1861 *Village communities in the east and west*, New York: Henry Holt.
MARRIOTT, MC KIM
1955 "Little communities in an indigenous civilization," in *Village India*. Edited by McKim Marriott. Chicago: University of Chicago Press.
1959 Interactional and attributional theories of caste ranking. *Man in India* 39:92–107.
1968a "Caste ranking and food transactions: a matrix analysis," in *Structure and change in Indian society*. Edited by Milton Singer and Bernard S. Cohn. Viking Fund Publications in Anthropology 47. Chicago: Aldine.
1968b "Multiple reference in Indian caste systems," in *Social mobility in the caste system in India*. Edited by James Silverberg. Comparative Studies in Society and History 3. The Hague: Mouton.
MAUSS, MARCEL
1967 *The gift*. Translated by Ian Cunnison. New York: Norton.

MAYER, ADRIAN C.
1965   *Caste and kinship in central India: a village and its region.* Berkeley: University of California Press.

MINES, MATTISON
1973   "Tamil Muslim merchants in India's industrial development," in *Entrepreneurship and modernization of occupational cultures in South Asia.* Edited by Milton Singer. Monograph and Occasional Papers Series 12. Chapel Hill, N.C.: Duke University Press.

MORRIS, MORRIS D.
1973   "Economic change and occupational cultures in South Asia: comments on Ames, Owens, and Singer," in *Entrepreneurship and modernization of occupational cultures in South Asia.* Edited by Milton Singer. Monograph and Occasional Papers Series 12. Chapel Hill, N.C.: Duke University Press.

NANDY, ASHIS
1973   "Need achievement in a Calcutta suburb," in *Entrepreneurship and modernization of occupational cultures in South Asia.* Edited by Milton Singer. Monograph and Occasional Papers Series 12. Chapel Hill, N.C.: Duke University Press.

NICHOLAS, RALPH W.
1973   "Social and political movements," in *Annual review of anthropology, volume two.* Edited by Bernard J. Siegel. Palo Alto, Calif.: Annual Reviews.

NICHOLAS, RALPH W., RONALD INDEN
1972   "The defining features of kinship in Bengali culture." Paper read at the symposium, "New Approaches to Caste and Kinship," American Anthropological Association Meetings, Toronto.

OBEYESEKERE, GANANATH
1963   The Great Tradition and the Little in the perspective of Sinhalese Buddhism. *Journal of Asian Studies* 22(2).

ORANS, MARTIN
1965   *The Santal: a tribe in search of a Great Tradition.* Detroit: Wayne State University Press.

ORENSTEIN, HENRY
1962   Exploitation or function in the interpretation of *jajmāni. Southwestern Journal of Anthropology* 18:302–316.

ORTNER, SHERRY B.
1973   On key symbols. *American Anthropologist* 75(5):1338–1346.

OWENS, RAYMOND
1973   "Peasant entrepreneurs in a north Indian industrial city," in *Entrepreneurship and modernization of occupational cultures in South Asia.* Edited by Milton Singer. Monograph and Occasional Papers Series 12. Chapel Hill, N.C.: Duke University Press.

PAPANEK, HANNAH
1973   "Pakistan's new industrialists and businessmen: focus on the Memons," in *Entrepreneurship and modernization of occupational cultures in South Asia.* Edited by Milton Singer. Monograph and Occasional Papers Series 12. Chapel Hill, N.C.: Duke University Press.

RAMANUJAN, A. K.
1973   *Speaking of Siva.* Baltimore: Penguin Books.

REDFIELD, ROBERT
1960   *The little community/peasant society and culture.* Chicago: University of Chicago Press.

ROBERTS, MICHAEL
1969   *The rise of the Karavas.* Ceylon Studies Seminar 68/69, Series 5. Ceylon: Peradeniya University.

RUDOLPH, LLOYD I., SUZANNE H. RUDOLPH
1967   *The modernity of tradition: political development in India.* Chicago: University of Chicago Press.

SACHCHIDANANDA
1970   Tribe-caste continuum: a case study of the Gond in Bihar. *Anthropos* 65:973–997.

SCHNEIDER, DAVID M.
1968   *American kinship: a cultural account.* Englewood Cliffs, N. J.: Prentice-Hall.

SEBRING, JAMES M.
1969   Caste indicators and caste identification of strangers. *Human Organization* 28(3):199–207.

SILVERBERG, JAMES
1959   Caste-ascribed "status" versus caste-irrelevant roles. *Man in India* 39:148–162.

SINGER, MILTON
1968   "Preface," in *Structure and change in Indian society.* Edited by Milton Singer and Bernard S. Cohn. Viking Fund Publications in Anthropology 47. Chicago: Aldine.
1972   *When a Great Tradition modernizes.* New York: Praeger.
1973   "Introduction: the modernization of occupational cultures in South Asia," in *Entrepreneurship and modernization of occupational cultures in South Asia.* Edited by Milton Singer. Monograph and Occasional Papers Series 12. Chapel Hill, N.C.: Duke University Press.

SINGER, MILTON, *editor*
1973   *Entrepreneurship and modernization of occupational cultures in South Asia.* Monograph and Occasional Papers Series 12. Chapel Hill, N.C.: Duke University Press.

SINHA, SURAJIT
1965   Tribe-caste and tribe-peasant continuum in central India. *Man in India* 45.

SRINIVAS, M. N.
1955   "Social system in a Mysore village," in *Village India.* Edited by McKim Marriott. Chicago: University of Chicago Press.

SRIVASTAVA, R.
1966   "Tribe-caste mobility in India and the case of Kumaon Bhotias," in *Caste and kin in Nepal, India and Ceylon.* Edited by C. von Furer-Haimendorf. Bombay: Asia Publishing House.

STEIN, BURTON
1967   Brahmin and peasant in early south Indian history. *Adyar Library Bulletin* 31:229–269.

STEVENSON, H. N. C.
1954   Status evaluation in the Hindu caste system. *Journal of the Royal Anthropological Institute of Great Britain and Ireland* 84:45–65.

TAMBIAH, STANLEY J.
  1970 *Buddhism and the spirit cults of north-east Thailand.* Cambridge Studies in Social Anthropology 2. Cambridge: Cambridge University Press.
  1972 Review of Louis Dumont, *Homo hierarchicus. American Anthropologist* 74:832-5.

TURNER, TERENCE
  1973 Review of *Structuralism* by Jean Piaget. *American Anthropologist* 75(2):351-373.

TURNER, VICTOR
  1967 *The forest of symbols: aspects of Ndembu ritual.* Ithaca, N.Y.: Cornell University Press.

TYLER, STEPHEN A.
  1973 *India: an anthropological perspective.* Goodyear Regional Anthropology Series. Pacific Palisades, Calif.: Goodyear.

VATUK, SYLVIA
  1972 *Kinship and urbanization: white collar migrants in north India.* Berkeley and Los Angeles: University of California Press.

WADLEY, SUSAN S.
  1973 "Power in the conceptual structure of Karimpur religion." Unpublished doctoral dissertation, University of Chicago.

WAGNER, ROY
  1973 "Distributive hierarchy: a model of ideological encompassing in 'segmentary' societies." Paper read at the symposium, "Analytic Strategies for Mediating the Structuralisms," at the 72nd annual meeting of the American Anthropological Association, New Orleans. 30 November, 1973.

WALLACE, ANTHONY F. C.
  1961 "The psychic unity of human groups," in *Studying personality cross-culturally.* Edited by Bert Kaplan. New York: Harper and Row.

PART ONE

The Standing and the Moving

The Rise of Social Anthropology in India (1774–1972): A Historical Appraisal

L. P. VIDYARTHI

This paper aims to highlight some of the basic factors in the genesis and stages of development of social researches in India. An attempt is made to record and review the researches that have been conducted by social anthropologists on Indian society and culture. In the light of earlier appraisals as well as new facts, three phases in the development of Indian social anthropology are identified. These phases are (1) Formative (1774–1919), (2) Constructive (1920-1949), and (3) Analytical (1950-present). While illustrative materials characterizing each of these phases are given, the more recent trends in Indian social anthropology are especially highlighted. The paper ends by linking the developments of Indian social anthropology to British and then American influences, and concludes with a statement of the need to develop a "synthetic approach" in Indian anthropology.

PREVIOUS REVIEWS OF INDIAN SOCIAL ANTHROPOLOGY

Various attempts to review the researches in social anthropology in India have been made from time to time by scholars such as Roy (1921), Majumdar (1950a, 1956), Ghurye (1956), Dube (1956, 1962), Bose (1963), Vidyarthi (1966a, 1966b), and Sinha (1968). Roy attempted a bibliographical account of the publications on tribal and caste studies as early as 1921. In his paper he referred to the materials published in the form of (1) articles in magazines, (2) compilations in handbooks of

Editor's note: This paper includes several minor changes of phrasing which Professor Vidyarthi has not had an opportunity to approve. The editor of the volume assumes responsibility for all such editorial considerations.

the different regions, and (3) monographs on tribes. Roy's effort, although the first attempt of its kind, recorded fairly systematic information about the early publications in this field, thus documenting the exclusive dominance of the British administrators, foreign missionaries, travelers, etc., in conducting anthropological researches in India. After a lapse of two and a half decades, Majumdar (1947) in a memorial lecture at Nagpur University reviewed the development of anthropology and brought out the impoverished progress of Indian anthropology under the continued efforts of British anthropologists. In the two review papers by Roy and Majumdar, mention of American scholars in any context was conspicuous by its absence.

In another review article of a generalized type, Majumdar (1950b) tried to relate the developing science of anthropology in India (which to him at that time was essentially the study of primitive people) to the theories of culture developed in England as well as in America. He pointed out several areas of research in India in the light of existing theories and he suggested further scope for research.

The most significant review article by Majumdar (1956) was in the form of a supplementary paper to Ghurye's presentation in the UNESCO volume. In this paper he presented a very competent appraisal of teaching and research in anthropology in India in the context of the development of cultural theories elsewhere. One of his comments in this regard deserves to be reproduced here:

Social anthropology in India has not kept pace with the development in England, in the European continent or in America. Although social anthropologists in India are to some extent familiar with the work of important British anthropologists, or of some continental scholars, their knowledge of American social anthropology is not adequate (Majumdar 1956:164).

Ghurye in the same volume evaluated the emergence of Bombay as a center for sociological studies, and of Calcutta and Madras as centers for social anthropological studies, while he looked upon Lucknow as a composite center for economic, social anthropological, and sociological studies. Since both Ghurye and Chattopadhyay received their research degrees under W. H. R. Rivers in 1923 and became the heads of departments in Bombay and Calcutta respectively, Ghurye traced the initial stimuli for the development of sociology and anthropology in India from Cambridge, and made the following observation:

It augurs well for India that if, in Bombay, sociology includes social anthropology, and in Calcutta, social anthropology is extended to include sociology to some extent as perhaps, source of inspiration came from the same teacher (Ghurye 1956:154).

Along with these two review articles which were written and discussed at an international level in 1952, Professor Dube also presented his proposal enumerating "the urgent tasks of anthropology in India" before the Fourth International Congress of Anthropological and Ethnological Sciences held in Vienna in 1952. In his paper (1956:273-275), Dube made a reference to the unfortunate prejudice and distrust of the social workers and popular political leaders toward the anthropologists, and he made a case study of the vanishing tribe, its folklore and art, village studies, caste dynamics, etc. He also suggested an active cooperation among the government, the universities, and individual scholars both Indian and foreign; he presented a proposal for the formation of a central organization at an international level for attacking the basic problems of social anthropological research in India.

Perhaps expanding and revising the same paper in the light of later developments, Dube contributed another paper on social anthropology in India in 1962. In the course of his critical evaluation in the light of the characteristics of the two earlier phases in social anthropology, he highlighted the weaknesses of the contemporary Indian social anthropology as they were reflected in techniques of research and methodology. Here his main concern was with "what ought to be rather than what is," and in view of this he put forward a number of suggestions of theoretical, methodological, and substantive nature (Dube 1962). In the same volume, Bailey (1962:254-256) wrote an exploratory paper. His main concern was to highlight the inadequate researches that had been done in India "in proportion to the richness of social anthropological laboratory situations that demand adequate research in the field of structural explanation of the complex society."

The latest and the most comprehensive publication on this topic was by Bose (1963) in the form of a booklet prepared under the auspices of the Indian Science Congress Association. In this publication, along with a brief reference to earlier researches, Bose reviewed the progress of anthropology in India during the previous half century and presented the materials in three sections: (1) prehistoric archaeology, (2) physical anthropology, and (3) cultural anthropology. Devoting considerable attention to the review of researches in cultural anthropology, he enumerated the major researches done in the fields of (a) village studies and (b) marriage and family, but he leaned heavily toward a discussion of (c) caste. While his attempt to relate the various Indian social anthropologists in terms of prevailing schools was not taken far, his mention of theoretical anthropology remained confined to his own theory of culture. For want of space, unfortunately, other theories of culture and civilization were not mentioned. On the whole, although Bose's appraisal of social anthropology in India was undoubtedly the latest and the most substantive, it tended to remain incomplete insofar as it created an appetite that it could not afford to satisfy.

In his two papers, Vidyarthi reviewed the rise of social anthropological researches in India and highlighted the recent trends in social anthropology. Improving upon earlier classifications, he categorized the history of social anthropology into Formative (1774-1919), Constructive (1920-1949), and Analytical (1950-present) periods, and went on to emphasize in detail the recent trends in village studies, caste studies, studies of leadership and power structure, of religion, of kinship and social organization, of tribal village and applied anthropology. This paper, originally presented during the Seventh International Congress of Anthropological and Ethnological Sciences in Moscow, for the first time made a systematic attempt to review the various phases in the development of Indian anthropology (Vidyarthi 1966a).

In his second paper, published in the same year in the light of similar materials (1966b), Vidyarthi referred to recent trends in Indian social anthropology and pointed out the approaches of anthropologists toward integrating the knowledge of various disciplines for a proper understanding of man and society. He made a special mention of the various efforts of the social scientists to study the problems of tribal and rural communities in India. He also made a plea that Indian social science should not overlook what may be termed its "Indianness." This Indianness in the field of social science referred to India's distinct cultural milieu and value attitude system and to a body of ideas of Indian thinkers reflected in ancient scriptures which are full of social facts and which should be used in the understanding of cultural process and civilizational history of India.

In a paper presented during a conference in New York, Sinha (1968) lent his support to Vidyarthi's threefold division of phases. He also confirmed the imitative nature of social anthropological researches in India and referred to the fact that in general, Indian anthropologists have been prompt in responding to the latest developments in the West without caring to pursue the earlier phases of constructive endeavors that have their logical aims in an Indian context. Acknowledging this craze of imitating the West, Sinha made a search to establish certain Indian traditions in social and cultural anthropology. In the study of the total pattern of Indian civilization he mentioned a few scholars such as Bose (for his contributions to the classification of India into two basic zones of material culture cutting across the linguistic divisions, a pyramidal form of Indian unity in diversity, noncompetitive economic ideology and the Hindu mode of tribal absorption, interrelationship between the villages and supralocal centers), Srinivas (Sanskritization, spread, dominant caste), Karve (agglomerative character of the Hindu society), Sinha (Indian society as evolutionary emergent from a tribal base), and Vidyarthi (study of sacred complex). Continuing his search for India's contribution to research methodology, Sinha observed that Indian anthropologists in general have not paid much systematic attention to devising a special methodology for studying the unique layout of the cultural patterns and processes of the subcontinent. However, he pointed out a few exceptions in this regard: Das (rigorous utilization of genealogical method in the study of Purum social organization), Bose (application of spatial distribution techniques in the dating of Indian temples, utilization of the tools of human geography in studying cultural historical problems, use of family histories in the study of social change in urban centers), Chattopadhyay and Mukherjee (use of statistical techniques in studying social change), Karve (combination of textual analysis with field data in the study of kinship), Vidyarthi (study of sacred complex utilizing such concepts as sacred center, cluster and segment, etc.). In the light of an appraisal of the various phases and trends in Indian anthropology, Sinha made a strong case for pursuing the natural history tradition for completing the basic descriptive outline of the forms of behavior of the Indian people, and for building a superstructure of analytical and incisive studies of specific problems on that base. He further observed that "It is only on the basis of such groundwork that the Indian scholars will be able to effectively participate in the international adventure of expanding the frontiers of knowledge in anthropology" (Sinha 1968).

In addition to these papers written from time to time on the development of social anthropology in India, we come across a few full-length review articles and a number of introductory observations in many books on the different topics of social anthropology in India. Among the authors of review articles, special mention may be made of Dumont and Pocock who, in a series of publications, attempted to highlight significant research areas in Indian social anthropology. Their first publications (1957a, 1957b) reviewed critically the village studies as well as the kinship studies in India. While they reviewed these two sets of studies in a wider context of world literature, the selections from India were from *Village India*, edited by Marriott (1955), and from *Kinship organization in India* by Karve (1953). Similarly, their second volume (Dumont and Pocock 1958) was devoted to a review of literature on caste with special reference to the work of Bouglé (1908) and Hocart (1950). The third volume (Dumont and Pocock 1959) dealt with theoretical discussions of the various concepts of religion in India. Drawing material from the work of Srinivas (1952), Stevenson (1954), Marriott (1955), and Elwin (1955), the two scholars entered into discussion of the concept of purity and pollution, levels of Hinduism in relation to "its ultimate value," and then the institutional function of priests, and so on. In their own ways, each of these three volumes definitely reviewed the contributions to "Indian sociology," but, as has been rightly noted by Bailey (1959), their perspective was too "narrow" and suffered from the "very worst kind of inverted ethnocentrism" on the parts of the editors. However, one finds in these volumes an appraisal of the sociological and social anthropological studies in India in the context of world literature, especially African studies, as they are of significance from the angle of critical comparison.

Finally, the trends of social anthropological studies have been sporadically reviewed here and there in a few prefaces and introductions to specific books on tribal, caste or village studies, and although scattered, they also provide some information and opinions on the trends of social anthropological researches in India. Mention, for example, may be made of Vidyarthi (1964) for tribal studies; Prasad (1957), Srinivas (1962), Mathur (1964) for caste studies; Srinivas (ed. 1955), Majumdar (1956) for village studies; and Dube (1965) for leadership studies. Thus, although sporadic and casual efforts have been made from time to time to review the development of anthropology in India, and although scattered materials by several authors on this topic are available, the efforts in this paper to present a comprehensive and up-to-date appraisal of the course of development of social researches in India are the first of their kind.

THE PHASES OF DEVELOPMENT

Any historical study covering a reasonable span of time needs to be categorized in terms of meaningful chronological phases. While it was too early for Roy (1921) to classify the ethnographic studies in terms of time perspective, he categorized studies in terms of the sources of publication, that is, magazines, handbooks, monographs, and so on, and then in terms of the nationality of the authors. Nor in the more recent writings of Dube and Bose do we find any explicit attempts on their parts to categorize material in terms of meaningful historical sequences. Dube (1962) referred to three phases of development in social anthropology: an earliest phase of compilation and publication of volumes on tribes and castes containing brief and often sketchy accounts of the divergent customs and practices of the various groups, a second phase characterized by detailed monographic studies of individual tribes mostly through personal observations, and the beginning of a third phase after the national independence, marked by considerable quantitative advancement and some qualitative achievement. Bose (1963) also referred to three such phases of writings: (1) encyclopedias of tribes and castes; (2) descriptive monographs; and (3) analytical studies of villages, marriage and family, caste, civilization, and so on. These classifications by far need not be considered to be of much significance since they were not attempted seriously and did not review the anthropological literature in light of trends prevalent in the respective periods. The determination of phases of anthropological trends in terms of theory, methods, and substantive data needs to be attempted in terms of multiplicity of traits so that they may bring out the cumulative as well as the distinctive features of each phase.

An attempt to classify the course of development in terms of the dominant trends of the historical periods was made by Majumdar who cared to suggest landmarks in the course of development of anthropology. Borrowing terms from Penniman (1935), Majumdar (1950a) divided anthropological researches in India into three phases: Formulatory (1774–1911), Constructive (1912–1937), and Critical (1938–present). In determining the beginning of the Formulatory period, the establishment of the Asiatic Society of Bengal was the only obvious choice since it marked the beginning of scientific traditions for the study of "nature and man" in India.

The beginning of Majumdar's second phase was marked by the publication of the first full-length monograph on the Mundas by S. C. Roy (1922), an Indian national who happened to be a great force in molding the anthropological career of Majumdar himself. In recognition of this in a later writing, Majumdar (1959) wrote of Ranchi as a place of pilgrimage for himself. To me the Constructive period seems to begin around 1920, for the department of sociology was opened at Bombay in 1919 with F. Geddes as its head, the department of anthropology at Calcutta began in 1920 with R. Chandra as its head, and the first full-fledged Indian journal of anthropology was begun by the late S. C. Roy in 1921. All these developments in and around 1920 brought a new temper to the development of anthropology in India, and it seems to me that the Constructive period should be dated from that year.

Majumdar conceived of a third phase, a Critical period, beginning in 1938 when the Indian and British anthropologists met together on the occasion of the Silver Jubilee of Indian Science Congress in Lahore and carried out a stocktaking of anthropological developments in India, exchanged notes, and planned jointly for future anthropological researches in India. According to Majumdar, this event marked the beginning of a critical approach. In the same year Majumdar published his own problem-oriented monograph on the Ho tribe (Majumdar 1937). Originally submitted as a doctoral thesis in Cambridge University, in its analysis of cultural dynamics the monograph reflected a departure from traditional descriptive studies. When Majumdar later wrote his essay proposing stages in Indian anthropology, he could not have anticipated the accelerated developments that took place during the two decades following India's independence and owing especially to the new collaboration with and the interests of American anthropologists, particularly in the American initiation of collaboration with Lucknow University and with the Central Ministry of Community Development. American scholars such as Oscar Lewis (as consultant to the Ministry of Community Development) and Morris Opler came to India on a large-scale anthropological mission. Moreover, several Indian anthropologists such as Dube and a few others visited anthropological institutions in the United States. The period also saw the publication of M. N. Srinivas' book, *Religion and society among the Coorgs of south India* (1952), which proved to be of great importance from an analytical perspective. In view of all these considerations it seems relevant to rename this period an Analytical period instead of Critical period as envisaged by Majumdar.

To be precise, then, the course of the development of social anthropology needs to be studied in terms of three phases: Formative period (1774-1919), Constructive period (1920-1947), and Analytical period (1948-present). I do not imply that each phase has completely replaced its predecessor. As a matter of fact, there have been strikingly different rates of development in the different parts of India, and an acquaintance with this fact needs to be emphasized. To clarify this point it may be mentioned that although the formulatory period began in Assam and other northeastern border areas long ago, those areas have just emerged from the constructive phase of descriptive ethnography. Similarly, in contemporary social researches being conducted in different parts of India by various agencies and individuals with different purposes, the coexistence of all three phases is quite evident in the compilation of glossaries about tribes and castes (characteristic of the formulative period), monographic and descriptive studies (constructive period), as well as in theoretically sophisticated researches (analytical period).

THE BEGINNING: THE FORMATIVE PERIOD

We owe the beginning of anthropological investigation in India to the Asiatic Society of Bengal. Credit goes to Sir William Jones who organized the Society in 1774, became its founder president, defined the scope of the Society as the study of "nature and man" in India, and piloted a number of researches and publications on this broad subject.

Since then, British administrators, missionaries, travelers, and a few other anthropologically oriented individuals collected data on tribal and rural groups, and wrote about their life and culture in the *Journal of the Asiatic Society of Bengal* (1784), *Indian Antiquary* (1872), and later in the *Journal of the Bihar and Orissa Research Society* (1915) and *Man in India* (1921). Along with other historical and geographical information, they also collected ethnographic data and published a series of district gazetteers, handbooks on tribes and castes, and then a number of monographs, especially on the tribes of Assam. During censuses, particularly those of 1931 and 1941, some British and Indian anthropologists were associated in the collection of anthropological data on the tribes and castes of different parts of India.

British scholar-administrators posted in different parts of India, such as Risley, Dalton, and O'Malley in east India, Russell in middle India, Thurston in south India, and Crooks in northern India, wrote encyclopedic inventories about the tribes and castes of India which even today provide the basic information about the life and culture of the peoples of the respective regions. The importance of these accounts can be judged from the fact that the Anthropological Survey of India has outlined a plan to reprint some of them with suitable additional notes. In addition to these handbooks, administrators such as Campbell (1856), Lathum (1859), and Risley (1891) published general books on Indian ethnology. The purpose of these volumes was to acquaint government officials and private persons with classified descriptions of tribes and castes with a view to ensuring effective colonial administration.

These generalized works about the land and people were followed by efforts to prepare detailed accounts of specific tribes and in some cases castes in the different regions, as in the studies of Shakespeare (1912), Briggs (1920), Gurdon (1912), Mills (1937), Parry (1932), Grigson (1938). A few missionaries, among them Bodding (1925) and Hoffman (1950), were attracted to ethnographic and linguistic researches. All of these scholars were especially influenced by such early British anthropologists as Rivers (1906), Seligmann and Seligmann (1911), Radcliffe-Brown (1922), and Hutton (1931), who had published monographs based on their work among the tribes of India, Ceylon, and the Andaman Islands.

Early Indian Anthropologists

Under these influences, the first Indian national to write exhaustive monographs on the tribes of India was S. C. Roy, who published his first epoch-making work on the Munda tribe (1912). This was followed by a series of five monographs on the Oraon (1915), the Birhor (1925), Oraon religion and customs (1928), Hill Bhuiyas (1935), and the Kharia (1937). These works by Roy were acknowledged by the British anthropologists of the day as competent studies, and Hutton in his presidential address to the Indian Anthropological Institute in Calcutta on January 5, 1938, described Roy as "the father of Indian ethnology." Under the intellectual inspiration of the British anthropologists and the financial encouragement of the then British governor of Bihar, Sir Edward Gait, Roy did outstanding work in Bihar. After Roy, R. P. Chandra published a book on the Indo-Aryan race in 1916, which evoked great interest in the study of the cultural history of India.

THE CONSTRUCTIVE PERIOD

Social anthropology in India definitely underwent a phenomenal change when it was included in the curricula of the important universities in Bombay, (sociology in 1919) and Calcutta (anthropology in 1921). These two centers for sociological and anthropological researches attracted trained scholars, stimulating them to undertake significant researches. Soon obscure subjects like kinship and social organization were studied by Ghurye (1943, 1952, 1954), K. P. Chattopadhyay (1921, 1926), Srinivas (1942, 1946), Majumdar (1937), Karve (1940); and a few other anthropologists such as P. N. Mishra and L. K. A. Iyer, K. P. Chattopadhyay, T. C. Das, and D. N. Majumdar in east and north India, and G. S. Ghurye, Iravati Karve, L. K. A. Iyer, and A. Aiyappan in west and south India provided the initial stimulus for the organization of scientific anthropological research by conducting field expeditions, by writing books and articles, and by training researchers for anthropological study of tribal and rural cultures.

A big jump came in 1938 when a joint session of the Indian Science Congress Association and the British Association, on the occasion of the Silver Jubilee of the former body, reviewed the progress of anthropology in India. Eminent anthropologists from abroad deliberated with Indian anthropologists and discussed plans for future research in India. During this period a few anthropologists completed their doctoral work and soon provided new theoretical leadership. Critically analyzing their data, for example, Majumdar in his work on the changing Ho of Singhbhum (1950a), Srinivas in his study of marriage and family in Mysore (1942), and N. K. Bose in his publication on "Hindu methods of tribal absorption" (1961[1929]) brought about a certain amount of theoretical sophistication in Indian anthropological research. The appearance of Verrier Elwin's series of problem-oriented publications on the tribes of Madhya Pradesh, Orissa, and then on the religion of the Savara of Orissa (1939, 1942, 1943, 1947) gave further recognition to Indian anthropology, while von Fürer-Haimendorf's publication on the tribes of Hyderabad and other successive publications (1943, 1945a, 1945b, 1946a, 1946b) provided additional refined models for Indian workers.

Indian anthropology, which had been born and brought up under the dominant influence of British anthropology, matured during its Constructive phase also under a British influence. During this period, except for a few studies of Indian institutions such as caste (Briggs 1920; Iyer 1929; Hutton 1946), the tradition of tribal studies which had begun in the work of enlightened British scholars, administrators, and missionaries continued under British and Indian anthropologists until the end of the 1940's. Similar to the anthropology being taught at Cambridge, Oxford, and London, Indian anthropology was characterized by ethnological and monographic studies with a special emphasis on research in kinship and social organization.

THE ANALYTICAL PERIOD

After the second global war and especially following India's independence, contact between American and Indian anthropologists significantly increased. For example, Morris Opler of Cornell University, Oscar Lewis of the University of Illinois, David Mandelbaum of the University of California, and many of their students came and stayed in India with their research teams. The effect of this contact was the creation of an atmosphere (1) for the systematic study of Indian villages with a view to testing certain hypotheses, (2) for refining some of the methodological frameworks developed elsewhere, and then (3) for assisting community development programs in the Indian villages.

Village and Caste Studies

The American scholars not only produced valuable theoretically oriented works on Indian rural cultures, but also inspired both young and old Indian anthropologists to take up similar researches on Indian villages and caste systems. The beginning of this phase may be dated from the publication of Srinivas' book, *Religion and society among the Coorgs of south India* (1952), which was exemplary in making a departure from the descriptive phase to the analytical phase as well as from tribal studies to nontribal community studies. Another marker of the new period was Iravati Karve's book on the Hindu kinship system (1953). During the next decade, others such as Dube and Majumdar took up theoretically sophisticated studies of rural communities, and in a real sense, the literature of Indian anthropology began to be integrated with the world anthropological literature.

Action Research

The tribal and rural community development program of the government of India gave further fillip to the Indian social scientists to study and evaluate the process of change in tribal and rural India. In such development programs, the concepts of action anthropology formulated by Sol Tax partially replaced the principles of applied anthropology which had developed during the British colonial administration. In some of the later writings on tribal policy and programs by Majumdar (1949), Dube (1960), Elwin (1952), Vidyarthi (1957, 1960, 1968, 1969), and Jay (1959), the influence of action anthropology in India has come to be established as an important discipline from theoretical, substantive, and action points of view.

Sociopsychological Research

Under the American influence and under the guidance of B. S. Guha, a graduate of Harvard University, the study of culture and personality found a place in the Anthropological Survey of India. As part of the survey, two psychologists, Uma Choudhury (1955) and P. C. Ray (1951, 1953, 1955, 1957, 1959, 1966), made field studies with a view to establishing racial differences, personality types, and other sociopsychological characteristics among the tribals. Such research received further stimulus when the American anthropologist, G. P. Steed (1955), conducted a study in a Hindu village in Gujarat, and G. M. Carstairs (1957), a British psychiatrist, conducted field research among the different communities of Rajasthan. The work of some of the social psychologists in universities such as Ranchi and Allahabad gave additional impetus to this kind of work.

Folklore Researches

Before the systematic treatments of Verrier Elwin, which were influenced by Franz Boas and Edward Tylor, folklore research took the form of sporadic collections of tribal folk songs and tales appended to monographs on other topics. With the passage of time the social elements hidden in the folklore were also unearthed by a few anthropologists and several scholars of different literatures, especially in Bhojpuri, Assamese, and Marathi. A number of publications began bringing out the social, historical, and behavioral usages of folklore.

Studies of Power Structure and Leadership

The attempt to analyze power structure and decision making in Indian rural society is also of recent origin. Here again the credit goes to the American Oscar Lewis and his Indian collaborator, H. S. Dhillon, who initiated the study of faction and leadership with their two volumes on north Indian (Lewis 1954) and south Indian (Dhillon 1955) villages. Published under the auspices of the Planning Commission, these two widely discussed volumes brought to light the varied roles of kin and caste-oriented factions in decision making. Moreover, these studies inspired a number of American, British, and Indian scholars to take additional studies of rural leadership in different parts of India.

Anthropology of Religion in India

Religion is another field of social anthropology which reflects the British and American influences. An objective study of primitive religion in India was initiated by Majumdar, and his explanation of Bongaism in *Affairs of a tribe* (1950b) paralleled other modern anthropological trends in the study of religion (Sarana 1961). The study of religion in the context of Indian villages was first made by Srinivas, who in his book *Religion and society among the Coorgs of south India* (1952) developed the concept of Sanskritization to explain the process of change in the Hindu village. A full-length study of a tribal religion was published by Elwin (1955) on the Savara tribe of Orissa, in which he supported the concept of "spiritism" suggested earlier by S. C. Roy (1928).

Anthropological interest in the study of religion was focused in the preparation of two volumes, *Aspects of religion in Indian society* (Vidyarthi, editor 1961) and *Religion in South Asia* (Harper 1964). Both volumes included papers based upon original investigations of different aspects of tribal and rural religion. The Majumdar memorial volume appropriately opened with an essay on "Professor Majumdar and the anthropology of Indian religion" by Gopala Sarana, and is dedicated to his memory. Marriott, Aiyappan, Sharma, and Srivastava contributed papers which threw light on some of the dominant and distinguishing characteristics of Indian religion and philosophy. The papers that followed were of more specific nature and the units of study were mostly limited to respective villages. Carstairs and Mathur described the complexes of religious beliefs and practices in three typical villages of Rajasthan and a Malwa village of Madya Pradesh. Singh wrote about religion in a Sikh village; Vidyarthi described the sacred complex of a tribal village. Other papers covered still smaller units, although their theoretical implications were of wider consequence. Madan, Atal, Singh, Chattopadhyay, Sahay, and Sinha analyzed religious features such as festivals, cults and deities in a methodologically significant manner. Thus, as Bose has observed, Vidyarthi's volume covered a wide range — from the analysis of the way religion is practiced by folk in different parts of India to analyses of certain complex beliefs present among tribal peoples, beliefs which have been modified through contact with "Hinduism."

Harper's volume originated in a conference on Religion in South Asia (August, 1961). The subsequent book (1964) consisted of nine papers by Mandelbaum, Ames, Berreman, Kolenda, Opler, Gumperz, Beals, Yalman, and Harper. Publication of the volume brought to light the various approaches of the respective authors, and in general it is bound to stimulate further research in Indian religion.

A work somewhat different in kind from these first two volumes was edited by Singer and Cohn (1958). *Traditional India: structure and change* included papers which dealt with both textual and contextual analyses of oral and recorded traditions. Although the theme of the book was to understand the image of "new India" in the light of her rich and deeply rooted heritage, almost all of the papers had some bearing on religious traditions, which obviously have been a common idiom in Indian history. These papers dealt with the various dimensions of Indian civilization and analyzed aspects of cultural media and cultural performances, including religious ones. A few of the papers, however, dealt exclusively with aspects of religion in specific communities, as in McCormack's paper on the media of communication found among the Lingayat sect and in Raghavan's more general paper on the methods of religious instruction in south India. Other papers examined the Anavils of Gujarat (Naik), the Chamar of Senapur (Cohn), and the Nayar (Gough).

A full-length study of the sacred city of Gaya as a dimension of Indian civilization has been attempted by Vidyarthi (1961b) within a framework of the theories of Redfield and Singer. The study is an aid to the understanding of religion in India in terms of the Great Traditional life of the communities.

Many of the village monographs cited above include materials on religion, and its importance in village life is evident in all these studies. In one such village study, Senapur Planalp did extensive research exclusively on religious life and values as part of his doctoral work at Cornell University, and he subsequently presented a full-length description of religious life in a Hindu village (1956).

Urban Studies

The researches of Robert Redfield, Milton Singer, and McKim Marriott of the University of Chicago provided theoretical and methodological direction toward understanding the folk and peasant communities in India as dimensions of Indian civilization. Their work contributed to a reinterpretation of the Great and Little Traditions of India and led to an anthropological study of "great" and "little" communities of various dimensions. Under the influence of these writings, Indian anthropologists began to study both traditional and modern cities with a view to first understanding them as part of Indian civilization and to then analyzing them in terms of the folk/urban continuum.

Studies of the process of urbanization, industrialization, and city planning have been undertaken as such research schemes have been financed by the National Planning Commission. With Milton Singer's methodological study of Madras, Marriott's study of Wai Town near Poona, and Martin Oran's study of Jamshedpur, the importance of the study of cultural roles of cities came into prominence. With financial assistance from the Planning Commission, some anthropologists took up urban studies, and the scope of anthropology was broadened from the study of isolated primitive tribal communities to rural and then to urban and industrial centers. The studies of Calcutta by Bose (1958), Kanpur by Majumdar (1961), Lucknow by Mukherjee and Singh (1961), and Gaya and Ranchi by Vidyarthi (ed. 1961; 1969) reflect the dual impetus that Indian anthropologists have received from the Chicago anthropologists and from the Planning Commission.

Professional Training and Cooperation

Finally, and also under the American influence (Tax et al. 1953), the universities have realized the need to integrate the various branches of anthropology for the purpose of training and research. In all the Indian universities there is an integration in the teaching of anthropology with of course a bias for specialization in specific branches of anthropology. Additionally, many social scientists have felt the need for collaboration in order to gain a comprehensive understanding of the social and cultural phenomena of Indian communities, and in some recent researches and publications in the areas of village and city studies, religion and leadership, and social change and planning, a trend toward interdisciplinary studies has been conspicuously evident. With the recent constitution of the Indian Council of Social Science Research and with the current efforts of the Ministry of Education to reorganize the Anthropological Survey of India, this trend has been strengthened and is likely to become more so in the future.

CONCLUSION

On the basis of the survey undertaken in this paper, it is apparent that social research in India, which had originated and developed under British influence, is now mainly flourishing under the stimulation received from the United States and other countries. While British social anthropology continues to provide useful models in the study of kinship and marriage, the British functional approach to tribal and rural studies has been supplemented by the American cultural-historical approach. The latter has been necessary as interest in studying India's emergence from its traditional structure has increased. As these newer approaches have developed, the descriptive phase of tribal studies has been replaced by the analytical study of different communities and by the attempt to formulate terms and concepts and to advance theories and methods for the general understanding of Indian society and culture. The administrative anthropology of the colonial pattern has been reorienting toward academic interests and, with this, a new quest for interdisciplinary approaches to understand the complexity of Indian society has become evident. Again following the lead of certain American scholars, there are now more "network studies" and "part-whole" analyses and less "isolate studies," a trend which has led to an emphasis on the similarities rather than the differences among the various Indian communities. As a whole, social anthropology in India has made satisfactory progress during the past two decades and has been recognized by the universities and the government as an important discipline which studies peoples at all levels of cultural development in their wholeness but with precision and empirical orientation.

The journey of Indian anthropology still continues. It has gone ahead under the influence of and in collaboration with British and then American anthropologists. Of course these non-Indians will continue to wield powerful influence in expanding the scope of anthropology in India in the future. Science knows no barriers and the science of man in India has still much to learn in the fields of theory and method from the other scientifically advanced countries of the world. But this does not mean that social anthropology in India should overlook what may be termed its "Indianness." Perhaps to some extent social anthropology has not done so, because it has not progressed under the spell of un-thinking imitation. Because of this salient feature, Professor Kroeber has said that India has listened to England, America, and to herself. The result, we may say, has been a synthetic approach (Majumdar 1959:173). Such a synthetic approach may be conceptualized in terms of India's unique cultural milieu, value-attitude system, and heritage and historical experiences. We have had our own sets of social thinkers who have given thought from time to time to the social problems and who have also given direction in solving them. Among such social thinkers was Mahatma Gandhi, whose teachings and ideals seem to Jaiprakash Narayan (1964) as the submerged part of an iceberg, which the social sciences ought to explore. Social scientists ought also to consider the ancient scriptures such as the Vedas, the Upanishad, the Smritis, the puranas and the epics — all full of social facts and all in need of careful study to help understand the development of the "Indianness" of social anthropology in India as it is especially used in the study of the cultural processes and civilizational history of India.

REFERENCES

AIYAPPAN, A.
 1961 "Thinking about Hindu way of life," in *Aspects of religion in Indian society*. Edited by L. P. Vidyarthi, 38–44. Meerut: Kedarnath Ramnath.
ATAL, YOGESH
 1961 "The cult of Bheru in a Mewar village and its vicinage," in *Aspects of religion in Indian society*. Edited by L. P. Vidyarthi, 140–150. Meerut: Kedarnath Ramnath.
BAILEY, F. G.
 1959 "For a sociology of India," in *Contributions to Indian sociology*. Edited by Louis Dumont and D. Pocock, 101. The Hague: Mouton.
 1962 "The scope of social anthropology in the study of Indian society," in *Indian anthropology: essays in memory of D. N. Majumdar*. Edited by T. N. Madan and Gopala Sarana, 254–256. Bombay: Asia Publishing House.
BODDING, P. O.
 1925 *The Santal medicine*. Memoirs of the Asiatic Society of Bengal 10(2).
BOSE, N. K.
 1958 Social and cultural life of Calcutta. *Geographical Review* 20.
 1961 "Hindu methods of tribal absorption," in *Cultural anthropology*. Bombay: Asia Publishing House. (Originally published in 1929.)
 1963 *Fifty years of science in India: progress of anthropology and archaeology*. Calcutta: Indian Science Congress Association.
 1968 *Calcutta: 1964. A social survey*. Bombay: Asia Publishing House.
BOUGLÉ, C.
 1908 *The essence and reality of caste system*. Paris: Alen.
BRIGGS, W. G.
 1920 *The Chamars*. Calcutta: Association Press.
CAMPBELL, J.
 1856 Ethnography of India. *Journal of the Asiatic Society of Bengal* 35:1–152.
CARSTAIRS, G. M.
 1957 *The twice-born*. London: The Hogarth Press.
 1961 "Pattern of religious observances in three villages of Rajasthan," in *Aspects of religion in Indian society*. Edited by L. P. Vidyarthi, 59–113. Meerut: Kedarnath Ramnath.

CHANDRA, R. P.
1916   *Indo-Aryan races: a study of the origin of Indo-Aryan people and institution.* Calcutta, Rajsahi: Virendra Research Society. (Reprinted in 1969 under Indian Studies.)

CHATTOPADHYAY, G.
1961   "Carak festival in a village in West Bengal," in *Aspects of religion in Indian society.* Edited by L. P. Vidyarthi, 151-165. Meerut: Kedarnath Ramnath.

CHATTOPADHYAY, K. P.
1921   Some Malayalam kinship terms. *Man in India* 1:53-55.
1926   An essay on the history of Newar culture. *Journal and Proceedings of the Asiatic Society of Bengal* n.s. 23(3).

CHOUDHURY, UMA
1955   A comparison of Santal mental test reactions in rural and urban areas. *Bulletin of the Department of Anthropology* 4(1):67-68.

COHN, B. S.
1958   "The Chamar of Senapur," in *Traditional India: structure and change.* Edited by M. Singer and B. S. Cohn, 413-421. Special issue of the *Journal of American Folklore* 78.

DHILLON, H. S.
1955   *Leadership and groups in a south Indian village.* New Delhi: Planning Commission.

DUBE, S. C.
1956   "The urgent task of anthropology in India," in *Proceedings of the Fourth International Congress of Anthropological and Ethnological Sciences* (held at Vienna in 1952), 273-275.

1960   "Approaches to the tribal problems," in *Indian anthropology in action.* Edited by L. P. Vidyarthi. Ranchi: Council of Social and Cultural Research, Bihar.

1962   "Social anthropology in India," in *Indian anthropology: essays in memory of D. N. Majumdar.* Edited by T. N. Madan and Gopala Sarana. Bombay: Asia Publishing House.

DUBE, S. C., *editor*
1965   *Emerging patterns of rural leadership in southern Asia.* Hyderabad: National Institute of Community Development.

DUMONT, L., D. POCOCK
1957a   Village studies. *Contributions to Indian Sociology* 1.
1957b   Kinship. *Contributions to Indian Sociology* 1.
1958   Hocart: on caste relation and power. *Contributions to Indian Sociology* 2.
1959   Religion: critical essays. *Contributions to Indian Sociology* 3.

ELWIN, VERRIER
1939   *The Baiga.* London: John Murray.
1942   *The Agaria.* London: Oxford University Press.
1943   *Muria murder and suicide.* London: Oxford University Press.
1947   *The Muria and their Ghotul.* London: Oxford University Press.
1955   *A philosophy of NEFA* (second edition). Shillong: NEFA Administration.

GHURYE, G. S.
1943 A note on cross cousin marriage and rural organization in Kathia-war. *Journal of the University of Bombay* 5(1):88-90.
1952 Social change in Maharashtra, part one. *Sociological Bulletin.*
1954 Social change in Maharashtra, part two. *Sociological Bulletin.*
1956 "The teaching of sociology, social psychology and social anthropology," in *The teaching of social science in India*, 148-153. UNESCO.

GOUGH, E. KATHLEEN
1958 "Cults of the dead among the Nayar," in *Traditional India: structure and change.* Edited by M. Singer and B. S. Cohn, 446-478. Special issue of the *Journal of American Folklore* 78.

GRIGSON, W. V.
1938 *The Muria Gond of Bastar.* London: Oxford University Press.

GUMPERZ, J. J.
1964 "Religion and social communication in village north India," in *Religion in South Asia.* Edited by E. B. Harper. Seattle: University of Washington Press.

GURDON, P. R. T.
1912 *The Khasi.* London: Macmillan.

HARPER, EDWARD B., *editor*
1964 *Religion in South Asia.* Seattle: University of Washington Press.

HOCART, A. M.
1950 *Caste: a comparative study.* London: Methuen.

HOFFMAN, J.
1950 *Encyclopaedia Mudarica*, volume thirteen. Patna: Government Printing Press.

HUTTON, J. H.
1931 *Census of India*, volume F, India part three B: *Ethnographic notes.* Simla: Government of India.
1946 *Caste in India: its nature and origins.* Cambridge: Cambridge University Press.

IYER, L. K. ANANTAKRISHNA
1929 The Kahars of Mysore. *Man in India* 9:171-172.

JAY, EDWARD
1959 The anthropologist and tribal welfare: Hill-Muria — a case study. *Journal of Social Research* 2:82-89.

KARVE, IRAVATI
1940 Kinship terminology and kinship uses of the Maratha country. *Bulletin of the Deccan College Research Institute* 2-4:327-389.
1953 *Kinship organization in India.* Poona: Deccan College.

KOLENDA, P. M.
1964 "Religious anxiety and Hindu fate," in *Religion in South Asia.* Edited by E. B. Harper. Seattle: University of Washington Press.

LATHUM, R. G.
1859 *Ethnology of India.* London: Van Voorst.

LEWIS, OSCAR
1954 *Group dynamics in a north Indian village.* New Delhi: Planning Commission.

MADAN, T. N.
1961 "Herath: a religious ritual and its secular aspects," in *Aspects of religion in Indian society.* Edited by L. P. Vidyarthi, 129-139. Meerut: Kedarnath Ramnath.

MAJUMDAR, D. N.
1937 *A tribe in transition: a study in culture pattern.* London: Longmans Green.
1947 *The matrix of Indian culture.* Lucknow: Universal. (Sri Mahadeo Hari Bathodkar Foundation lecture delivered in 1946).
1949 The changing canvas of tribal life. *The Eastern Anthropologist* 3:40-47.
1950a Anthropology under glass. *The Journal of the Anthropological Society of Bombay,* special issue (1-16).
1950b *Affairs of a tribe: a study in tribal dynamics.* Lucknow: Universal.
1956 "Special report on the teaching of social anthropology," in *Teaching social science in India,* 161-173. UNESCO Publication.
1958 *Caste and communication in an Indian village.* Bombay: Asia Publishing House.
1959 "The light that failed," in *Anthropology and tribal welfare.* Edited by L. P. Vidyarthi. Ranchi: Council of Social Science Research, Bihar.
1961 *Social contours of an industrial city.* Bombay: Asia Publishing House.

MANDELBAUM, DAVID G.
1964 "Process and structure in South Asian religion," in *Religion in South Asia.* Edited by E. B. Harper. Seattle: University of Washington Press.

MARRIOTT, MC KIM
1955 "Little communities in an indigenous civilization," in *Village India.* Edited by McKim Marriott. Chicago: University of Chicago Press.
1961 "Changing channels of cultural transmission in Indian civilization," in *Aspects of religion in Indian society.* Edited by L. P. Vidyarthi, 15-25. Meerut: Kedarnath Ramnath.

MARRIOTT, MC KIM, *editor*
1955 *Village India.* Chicago: University of Chicago Press.

MATHUR, K. S.
1961 "Meaning of religion in a Malwa village," in *Aspects of religion in Indian society.* Edited by L. P. Vidyarthi, 114-128. Meerut: Kedarnath Ramnath.
1964 *Caste and ritual in a Malwa village.* Bombay: Asia Publishing House.

MC CORMACK, W.
1958 "The forms of communication in Virasaiva religion," in *Traditional India: structure and change.* Edited by M. Singer and B. S. Cohn, 325-335. Special issue of the *Journal of American Folklore* 78.

MILLS, J. P.
1922 *The Lhota Naga.* London: Macmillan.
1937 *The Rengma Naga.* London: Macmillan.

MUKHERJEE, R. K., BALIJIT SINGH
1961 *Social profiles of a metropolis.* Bombay: Asia Publishing House.

NAIK, T. B.
1958 "Religion of the anvil of Surat," in *Traditional India: structure and change.* Edited by M. Singer and B. S. Cohn, 389-396. Special issue of the *Journal of American Folklore* 78.

NARAYAN, JAIPRAKASH
1964 Gandhism and social science. *AVARD, News Letters* 6(5).

OPLER, MORRIS E.
1964 "Particularization and generalization on process in ritual and culture," in *Religion in South Asia*. Edited by E. B. Harper. Seattle: University of Washington Press.

PARRY, N. E.
1932 *The Lakhers*. London: Macmillan.

PENNIMAN, T. K.
1935 *A hundred years of anthropology*. London: Gerald Duckworth.

PLANALP, SENAPUR
1956 "Religious life and values in a Hindu village." Unpublished doctoral dissertation, Cornell University.

PRASAD, N.
1957 *Myth of the caste system*. Patna: Patna University Press.

RADCLIFFE-BROWN, A. R.
1922 *The Andaman Islanders*. Cambridge: Cambridge University Press.

RAGHAVAN, V.
1958 "Methods of popular religious instruction in South Asia," in *Traditional India: structure and change*. Edited by M. Singer and B. S. Cohn. Special issue of the *Journal of American Folklore* 78.

RAY, P. C.
1951 Differences in concrete intelligence among the Jaunsaris. *Journal of the Asiatic Society* 16:45-52.
1953 Maze test performance of the Bhils of central India. *Bulletin of the Department of Anthropology* 2(1):83-90.
1955 The tensional feeling among the Abors and Gallong indicated by the Rorschach. *Indian Journal of Psychology* 30: Part 1-2, 95-103.
1957 Effect of culture-contact on the personality. *Structure of Anthropology* 6(2).
1959 *The children of the Abor and Gallong*. Delhi: Education and Psychology Monograph.
1966 "The Lodha and their spirit-possessed men: psycho-socio-cultural factors in tribal transformation." Paper read before Summer School in Anthropology held at Darjeeling.

RISLEY, H. H.
1891 *Tribes and castes of Bengal*. Calcutta: Bengal Secretariat Press.

RIVERS, W. H. R.
1906 *The Todas*. London: Macmillan.

ROY, S. C.
1912 *Mundas and their country*. Calcutta: City Book Society.
1915 *The Oraons of Chotanagpur*. Ranchi: Bar Library.
1921 Anthropological researches in India. *Man in India* 1:11-56.
1925 *The Birhor: a little known jungle tribe of Chotanagpur*. Ranchi: Man in India Office.
1928 *Oraon religion and customs*. Ranchi: Man in India Office.
1935 *The Hill Bhuiyas of Orissa*. Ranchi: Man in India Office.
1937 *The Kharia*. Ranchi: Man in India Office.

SAHAY, K. N.
1961 "Christianity and cultural processes among the Oraon of Ranchi," in *Aspects of religion in Indian society*. Edited by L. P. Vidyarthi, 323-340. Meerut: Kedarnath Ramnath.

SARANA, GOPALA
1961 "Professor Majumdar and the anthropology of Indian religion," in

Aspects of religion in Indian society. Edited by L. P. Vidyarthi, 1-13. Meerut: Kedarnath Ramnath.

SELIGMANN, C. G., B. SELIGMANN
1911   *The Veddas of Ceylon.* Cambridge: Cambridge University Press.

SHAKESPEARE, J.
1912   *The Lushai Kuki clan.* London: Macmillan.

SHARMA, K. N.
1961   "Hindu sects and food pattern in north India," in *Aspects of religion in Indian society.* Edited by L. P. Vidyarthi, 45-58. Meerut: Kedarnath Ramnath.

SINGER, MILTON, BERNARD S. COHN, *editors*
1958   *Traditional India: structure and change.* Special issue of the *Journal of American Folklore* 78(281).

SINGH, I. P.
1961   "Religion in Daleke: a Sikh village," in *Aspects of religion in Indian society.* Edited by L. P. Vidyarthi, 191-219. Meerut: Kedarnath Ramnath.

SINGH, T. R.
1961   "Hierarchy of deities in an Andhra village," in *Aspects of religion in Indian society.* Edited by L. P. Vidyarthi, 166-171. Meerut: Kedarnath Ramnath.

SINHA, SURAJIT
1961   "Changes in the cycle of festival in the Bhumij village," in *Aspects of religion in Indian society.* Edited by L. P. Vidyarthi, 341-368. Meerut: Kedarnath Ramnath.
1968   "Is there any Indian tradition in social/cultural anthropology: retrospect and prospect." Paper presented during Wenner-Gren conference on The Nature and Function of Anthropological Traditions.

SRINIVAS, M. N.
1942   *Marriage and family in Mysore.* Bombay: Asia Publishing House.
1946   The social organization of south India. *Man, Journal of the Royal Anthropological Institute* 46.
1952   *Religion and society among the Coorgs of south India.* London: Oxford University Press.
1962   *Caste in modern India and other essays.* Bombay: Asia Publishing House.

SRINIVAS, M. N., *editor*
1955   *India's villages.* Bombay: Asia Publishing House.

SRIVASTAVA, R.
1961   "The chief currents of contemporary Indian philosophy," in *Aspects of religion in Indian society.* Edited by L. P. Vidyarthi, 20-37. Meerut: Kedarnath Ramnath.

STEED, GEETAL P.
1955   "Notes on an approach to a study of personality formation in a Hindu village," in *Village India.* Edited by McKim Marriott, 102-144. Chicago: University of Chicago Press.

STEVENSON, H. N. C.
1954   Status evaluation in Hindu caste system. *Journal of the Royal Anthropological Institute* 84:45-65.

TAX, SOL, *et al.*
1953   "Anthropology as a field study," in *An appraisal of anthropology*

today. Edited by Sol Tax, 342-356. Chicago: University of Chicago Press.

VIDYARTHI, L. P.

1957 Anthropology, authority and tribal welfare in India. *Eastern Anthropology* 11(1):14-34.

1961a "Sacred complex in a hill tribe village," in *Aspects of religion in Indian society.* Edited by L. P. Vidyarthi, 241-267. Meerut: Kedarnath Ramnath.

1961b *Sacred complex in Hindu Gaya.* Bombay: Asia Publishing House.

1964 *Cultural contours of tribal Bihar.* Calcutta: Punthi Pustak.

1966a Researches in social science in India: some preliminary observations. *Social Science Information* 5(1). Paris.

1966b Social anthropological researches in India: some preliminary observations. *Journal of Social Research* 9(1):1-74.

1969 *Cultural configuration of Ranchi: study of pre-industrial city of tribal Bihar.* Calcutta: Bookland.

VIDYARTHI, L. P., *editor*

1960 *Indian anthropology in action.* Ranchi: Council of Social and Cultural Research, Bihar.

1961 *Aspects of religion in Indian society.* Meerut: Kedarnath Ramnath.

1968 *Applied anthropology in India.* Allahabad: Kitab Mahal.

VON FÜRER-HAIMENDORF, C.

1943 *The Chenchus: jungle folk of Deccan.* London: Macmillan.

1945a "Tribal populations of Hyderabad yesterday and today," in *Census of India 1941*, volume thirty-one. Hyderabad: Government Central Press.

1945b *The Reddis of the Bison Hills: a study in acculturation.* London: Macmillan.

1946a The agriculture and land tenure among the Apatanis. *Man in India* 26:181-195.

1946b Notes on tribal justice. *Man in India* 26:181-214.

Indian Civilization:
New Images of the Past for a
Developing Nation

S. C. MALIK

Today all developing nations are concerned with the problem of poverty, as well as with social justice, economic equality, and political freedom. India is aiming to transform its traditional society radically, and one of the various means is to change the core structure of values, beliefs, and attitudes so that the nation moves forward into modern times. Of course, we must realize that India ought not to ape the developed nations, and it is not likely to look anything like modern Europe, the United States, Russia, Japan, or even China, since this transformation is possible only if it is within the prevailing indigenous social and cultural traditions. The major problem is to bring about structural changes peacefully, within a democratic framework. It is in this context of creating new forces for a cultural transformation, for implanting new sociocultural values, that the role of the past in creating new images will be discussed in this paper. For instance, some cultural values which we consider to be crucial may be outlined as follows:

1. The commonly accepted dominant philosophy in India is that of *fate*, which has encouraged inertia, apathy, and lethargy, not only preventing progress in practice but also abolishing it in theory. Therefore, the idea that "man's decision is his destiny" needs to become an internalized cultural value if progress is to be made.

2. The first value of progress is closely interlinked with the notion of evolution and change, i.e. that the universe, earth, life, and man are governed by the dynamics of movement and change. This view emphasizes the fact that a radical change of tradition and history through human endeavor and effort is a legitimate possibility; we are not limited to mere internal rearrangements of human societies. However, we must make it clear that there is no inevitability involved in this theme of evolution, progress, and change. All determinist

philosophies — whether materialistic or spiritualistic — have to be rejected since we believe that the fundamentals of a new social and moral order are always renewable and amenable to change.

In short, the basic proposition here is that the political and economic goals of developing nations will be realized sooner if their sociocultural institutions also favor these goals, i.e. the political and economic conditions of a country at any given time are related to the broad social and cultural environment. We know that the mere use of science and modern technology is seldom an indicator of radical change because cultures often adopt material innovations without altering the general structure of society. Therefore, the foremost role of any academic discipline in a policy of cultural transformation is to radically restructure its own philosophic foundations and research goals. To illustrate: in India, many of the research objectives of anthropology, archaeology, and history have, until recently, encouraged elitist and obscurantist interpretations. Scholars concentrated on the rise and fall of kings or studied the history of caste, religion, and race, etc. It is only when intellectuals begin to formulate dynamic concepts which somehow also relate to social and economic development that new value systems will emerge. The general population will then have alternative models available whereby it will be possible for them to perceive the universe in such categories as are in consonance with contemporary knowledge and even our current goals of nation building. To be more specific, the task of a student of Indian history, archaeology, and civilization should primarily be to reconstruct those images of the past which reestablish certain positive and affirmative values of our civilization, rather than the existing negative and life-denying ones. These new images of the past will achieve a sense of clarity for the future, since they may restore idealism and hope for the large majority of citizens who have yet to discover their legal, political, economic, and social rights.

In the history of the study of India's past there is a notable neglect of theoretical developments and interpretative machinery, and even of reexamination of basic premises. There has been a great deal of descriptive research, with frames of reference and models which are by and large implicit. Even today the formulation of explicit models, hypotheses, or theories forms a minor fraction of research work. The study of India's past is still dominated by fieldwork and reports of statistical and taxonomic developments. Theoretical inadequacies have resulted in simplistic methodologies that stress the uniqueness of traits, sites, and cultures, and, in the absence of consciously formulated sophisticated concepts and models, there has been no attempt to develop general patterns and procedural explanations. In short, in order to make the study of Indian civilization — both past and present — socially relevant, an intellectual rejuvenation is an imperative need. All intellectual pursuit is a continuously interacting process between theory and practice, so that no amount of accumulation of empirical evidence in scientific reports can transform a discipline into an intellectual force, and this accumulation is also socially irrelevant from the point of view of contemporary social and cultural transformations which are being planned in India (Malik 1968).

Thus, a study of the past has to be oriented toward the present and future, and not just reinforce tradition; this objective does not conflict with our avowed academic goals of reconstructing generalized patterns of human behavior. In the long run, the goal of understanding past sociocultural and economic processes and patterns is of greater utility than that of mere description and the historiographical pursuit of piecing together the past. For example, many of our researches appear to follow a methodology that seems to be a continuation of the narrative method of myths, legends, and the first epics, and in doing so we seem once again to be emphasizing the ideal norms of Hindu religion and philosophy. Also, Indian history gives one the impression that human beings in all ages and places did little more than struggle for power, fight wars, and the like, that after the sixth century A.D. India rapidly declined from the Golden Age, and that the Indian character structure has been inherently conservative, other-worldly, despondent, etc. There are, therefore, several myths, legends, and prejudices which are present in our so-called objective study of history and archaeology. Below are some of the stereotype interpretations of India's past:

1. "The spirituality of India and its golden past." This concept is contradictory since we were golden because of the accumulation of wealth, business proficiency, and a materialistic nature, rather than because of the "spirit."

2. "India was a melting pot where everything was absorbed into that indefinable, amorphous 'Indianness'." This notion is based on the equilibrium model which suggests a static society, despite many sociocultural, economic, and political upheavals that we know have gone on throughout the past. But even if this is a true statement, it has been explained away in terms of vague spirituality. On the contrary, the melting-pot idea equally suggests the sheer coexistence of several insulated and isolated subunits, while the enduring elements were the result of the development of certain common sociocultural and economic patterns or core elements, rather than the spread of tolerance, nonviolence, and the peaceful nature of the Indian. In fact, the melting-pot theory suggests to us not an equilibrium model, but one which implies continuous change, innovation, and adaptation, since if Indian society was so tradition-bound and rigid it would have gone out of existence long ago rather than survive for several thousands of years.

3. Indians and others often state that the civilization in India is unique, and its antiquity is constantly harped upon. This view of the past appears to be a psychological case of a nation trying to overcome an inferiority complex, or a case of others who are trying to seek in it a utopia — running away from Western "materialism." Such attitudes only act as dead weights and a drag in the nation-building process. However, even if Indian civilization *was* unique, how can its specific evolution as a civilization be rationally explained? Needless to say, in many ways our society and civilization are no more unique and spiritual than many others (Malik 1971).

4. A well-known stereotype, which has been justified by a study of the past, is that those who are poor and suffering materially are in reality somehow spiritually happy, and that they have a remarkable capacity to adjust to this state of affairs. It is an often-quoted value attributed to Indian tradition which implies that materialistic ways, as followed in the West, will not bring about any happiness. This is not just a commonsense view, it is one which is built into the implicit models of Indian historical and social sciences. There is a powerful lobby of the "status quo" people today who wish to keep a majority of the underdeveloped population in a state of utter poverty and degradation, by constantly reminding them that materialism will ruin their treasured contentment! Empirical facts seriously contradict these notions that in the past Indians were ever so spiritual, and many examples may be cited to support this argument. To give only one instance, it is suggested that Indians were constantly thinking and writing about metaphysics, moral ideals, and other themes of a very serious nature. But this lopsided viewpoint overlooks another set of values which represent Indian literature no less; these are the works of drama, lyrical poetry, and the numerous tales of romance, etc, which delight in the sheer act of living, in artistic sensitivity, and praise the rewards of prosperity. It is conveniently forgotten that the notion of sorrow and suffering ought to be seen more as theological presupposition and dogma than as representing reality. Therefore, we might say that if the highest moral order present in Indian thinking is considered to be enduring, then the real and immediate experiences of the ordinary mundane joy of daily living were equally contributing to this way of life.

It is worthwhile to note here that this stereotype of the spirituality of Indians is comparatively recent in origin. It began with the Orientalists whose interpretations tended to fossilize and reinforce the "sacred" and the traditional social and economic class divisions. These and the other views propagated by British administrators and missionaries became a part of Indian scholarship and have been blindly adhered to. But recent studies of the past reveal that Indians were a very practical and down-to-earth people; travelers from the West and other parts of the world who visited India from the thirteenth century onwards have clearly made it a point to mention the mundane aspects of Indian civilization, suggesting that the Indian character structure was especially materialistic and acquisitive in nature!

An examination of research publications in the study of Indian history and civilization indicates the major current objectives of research, as follows:

1. Techno-economic models that have a classificatory, descriptive, chronological, or aesthetic orientation. These models have helped to increase the accumulation of data quantitatively, whether in pre-history, archaeology, or history. Often, past research concentrated on locating evidence which would verify or support religious textual material, oral traditions, mythology, linguistic models, and racial beliefs. Examples are the model of Aryan waves, Aryan (north)/ Dravidian (south) dichotomy, tracing Ramayana and Mahabharta sites, etc. But these researches are based on nineteenth-century models of unilinear evolution, type concept, diffusion, migration, and replacement which seek external factors in order to explain change, thereby implying an inherent conservatism of Indians, as well as the self-sufficiency of their villages. Underlying this theme is the basic "status quo" idea that after each change Indian society returns to a familiar state of equilibrium.

2. Environmental reconstructions which are based on a simple identification and listing of geological and biological evidence, without any explanation of ecological processes.

3. Racial-cultural correlations which identify given historical and archaeological sites with a race, tribe, or community, and even identify specific traits as indicators of some cohesive sociocultural units — even though these units may be spread over hundreds of miles on the subcontinent.

The above brief aims and objectives are clearly based on models which are static, mechanical, and formalistic reconstructions that have given only piecemeal explanations. These have led — not very sur-prisingly — to dead ends in seeking solutions to many of the problems which researchers have continued to study during the last fifty years. This has happened despite the great accumulation of data by the ever-increasing use of very modern scientific techniques. But in the absense of a sophisticated theoretical base, the objectives of acquiring more empirical data without employing dynamic concepts of sociocultural and economic systems have remained limited. At any rate, fieldwork for the sake of mere discovery is really a sophisticated form of dilettante activity.

The following are a number of brief questions and problems — based on current researches, irrespective of the regions where they have originated or have been employed — which may help us in India to build newer models, and this exercise might serve to illustrate an integrated dynamic approach to the study of the past (Malik 1972):

1. What are the units of our study, and how and why do these change? In human systems, what is changing has little meaning unless one knows *how* and *why* it is changing (e.g. these units may be ethnographic, historical [*Janapadas*], ecological, cultural, or even a sampling statistical unit).

2. Do different environments lead to similar technological and cultural levels? Or, do similar techno-economic levels lead to similar sociocultural levels? Or, will not similar sociocultural levels lead to identical techno-economic stages?

3. Do social and/or cultural changes produce needs? Or, do needs create the potential for sociocultural and technological changes? If, however, there are multiple interacting variables involved, how is this multivariate process to be identified?

4. How and why do we identify and define a cultural stage, a phase, a period, etc., in greater depth than the mere mechanical following of the geological principle of stratification which we have transplanted wholesale to sociocultural systems? Have we worked out a time scale to judge the rates of sociocultural and techno-economic changes, or do we even know about how long it takes for a society to adopt or adapt to innovations and newer ideas?

5. It may be simple — relatively speaking — to formulate techno-economic reconstructions, given the material nature of our evidence. But what models do we have which are multivariate in character that will explain the interrelationships of technology and economics and culture, or even the role of technology and economics in social systems? Do we have models for recovering the evidence of land use, trade patterns, population density, social life, etc.?

6. Is preindustrial society inherently conservative, as we seem to believe, or does that depend on its level, simple or complex? Is Indian society — especially in the village — conservative, and if so, what is the empirical evidence for it? And if we suppose it is not, will we not need to look at our evidence afresh since all our interpretations are based on the conservative nature of human society? What conditions are required for the creation of innovations and/or inventions? Depending upon the culture and society, one or many of the variables may be amenable to change, such as technology, economics, social life, ideology; alternatively, any one aspect may tend to remain constant and be conservative. How does one identify these processes?

7. Even with regard to diffusion-migration models that are used so

often, we have not taken into account the following questions which must be carefully examined in the Indian context:

a. Under what conditions and how do people migrate, and who in this sociocultural group migrates? Does migration always lead to replacement and not acculturation?

b. How and why do ideas spread singly and not in complexes? (e.g. the "Megalithic" ideas most probably spread alone, to be adopted by different cultural groups).

c. Under what conditions do ideas and/or trait complexes diffuse?

d. When do traits or trait complexes spread and diffuse? (e.g. ceramic designs often show similarity because of some common aesthetic sense, while ceramic technique may spread independently without involving large-scale migrations, indicating contact only).

e. Does the role of convergent and parallel evolution, as well as of invention and innovation, have no place in diffusion and migration? If so, these processes must be carefully considered before rejecting them outright.

f. Under what conditions do people borrow, replace, or adopt alien technology, and/or culture, economic systems, ideology, etc.? In order to answer this, we must also pose the question: how do we seek inner differentiation and change within a given cultural unit — a boundary system — instead of invoking external cultural factors as a cause for change? Do we not have to take into account certain inner compulsions, indigenous — local and regional — needs of a society?

8. A holistic study of Indian civilization may have to be viewed not in terms of equilibrium models, but from the point of view of "change, conflict, and tension" models. Moreover, we will have to see the past not by seeking meaning in the contents alone, but in terms of contemporary meaning and intelligibility. It is these frames of reference which will enable us to explore the enduring content of Indian civilization and to see how it has been transmitted to its various parts. It will also help us to find out the rates of change, the kinds of changes, and the agencies of change, etc. For this kind of study we need a new kind of theoretical premise:

It is a commonly accepted fact that the present is based upon the foundations of the past, which has a great bearing not only upon man's present activity but also upon his future. This statement is often misconstrued to mean that we are determined by the past. However, this is not the same thing as being conditioned by it, since the past also enables man to follow his many potentialities. Each fresh day creates a new climate of existence, albeit in doing so many past values have to be destroyed. We must visualize that the states of existence, the past, present and future, — within the relative notion of time — are not static entities as we seem to think, and there is no movement through the passage of time from fixed positions, A to B to C. Therefore, these states of existence are really qualities of activity processes which have their relationship to present existence alone. The so-called static movement, from one entity to another, in fact represents the passage of time from one present to another present, so that each present produces both the past and the future. If we accept this concept, then it suggests that man's existence is always within the framework of a dynamic and creative present.

In the context of this proposition, Indian civilization will no longer be seen as a result of cause and effect or as one which is *determined* by a linear historical process. Instead, it will be analyzed in terms of the development of specific modes of particular networks of structural relationships of the social, cultural, economic, political, and ideological systems which have existed in space and time. That is, it would be an attempt to show how structural transformations from one configuration to another have taken place, by looking at the structures behind deep empirical evidence rather than considering the contents as the basic stuff of history. Thus, this view of Indian civilization will not base its analysis merely on the contents, chronology, or other narrative descriptions of historical and archaeological evidence, but on its structure and change.

A nation's models of the past are crucial in bringing about any radical changes — structural changes — in its present outlook, especially in a developing society. But our earlier concepts and models have acted as constraints both on providing more information and on our predictive capabilities. Moreover, our interpretations cannot be based on the so-called description of "objective" facts, on vagueness, on a nostalgia for the past, or even on mere historiography. The past will only help us if we learn from its regularities, its patterns and processes *how* and *why* rather than *where*, *what* and *when*, because the latter questions are essentially subsumed under the former. Therefore, changing our goals in theory and research methodology is part of the social, cultural, and economic revolution which all developing nations are aiming to bring about. It may be objected that research of academics is being mixed up with some political ideology. But the counterargument is that in the search of our past, selectivity and value orientation have always played their parts. For example, even when we try to encourage in India today national integration and the concept of Indian unity, we try to support it by citing empirical evidence from the past. This again is an interpretation based on those sociocultural values which we consider to be essential for our national survival. But justified though this may be for us as a national policy, is it being objective and value-free? There must, however, be a caution stated about the suggestions made here; our approach is likely to be misconstrued as a closed system, or as offering State versions of our past, or some other kind of dogmatism. But this is far from the truth. Nevertheless, if we do not wish our goals to change, we will indeed be following "colonial" research values and dogmas, especially the view of a peaceful, harmonious past development of Indian society.

Moreover, an integrated view of the past is only possible through a reorientation of our academic concepts and models as well as the development of a humanistic, scientific, and rational world view that must come about through an internalization of new sociocultural and politico-economic values. In other words, the new approach to a study of the past will have to be related to one's general approach to life and world view. Today, this cannot any longer be a traditional one because it is not in keeping with the contemporary scientific and humanistic ideas about life and the universe. Furthermore, the task of each one of us, finally, as intellectuals and academics, is to contribute to an understanding of the sum total of human existence and human society, and not just to an understanding of the minutiae of human interaction.

However, it may be questioned, for instance, why we need to consider newer concepts such as that of "change, conflict, and tension" at all to view the past and the present and the future. For one thing, the fact is that change and continuity are twin fundamentals of the dynamics of human societies, whereas we have concentrated on the continuity aspect of tradition in India. But the other broader reason lies in the argument that the cosmos is governed (as we know today) by the dynamic laws of change, and earth and life are very much part of it. This is an accepted scientific view of the universe today albeit without any inevitability, and it provides the rationale for accepting change as a model; in the same way the rationale for accepting "status quo" or equilibrium models lies in the earlier "harmony" and "equilibrium" view of the universe.

In the ultimate analysis, models are ideal type referents against which individual cases can be compared. In fact, any model represents a structured set of concepts and ideas. But this does not necessarily mean that human sociocultural systems may be equated and expected to behave like natural systems of inorganic or other organic matter. Furthermore, concepts and models are not only heuristic devices which help to put into order our complex data and observations, they also have a self-fulfilling prophetic value through the building up of an image of the past. It is only through this image that it is possible to realize the vision of a new society, because every society necessarily has to relate itself to its past not only in order to explain to itself its present state of existence but also to project and predict the future directions it is likely to follow.

REFERENCES

MALIK, S. C.
1968   *Indian civilization: the formative period (a study of archaeology as anthropology).* Simla: Indian Institute of Advanced Study.
1972   "Indian archaeology: models and social relevance," in *Proceedings of Carbon-14 and Indian Archaeology Conference.* Edited by D. P. Agrawal. Bombay: Tata Institute of Fundamental Research.
MALIK, S. C., *editor*
1971   *Indian civilization: the first phase (problems of a sourcebook).* Simla: Indian Institute of Advanced Study.

Deified Men and Humanized Gods: Some Folk Bases of Hindu Theology

A. AIYAPPAN

Whether the gods and human spirits are a continuum or two distinct though interacting categories seems to have been a matter of some interest to formulators of world views. In the part of India to which this article relates, namely Kerala State, the subject is occasionally discussed by rural philosophers, but the question is phrased differently. It is asked this way: Is the god X a man who became a god or was he a real god? Was Rama a good king elevated to the rank of a god or was he an incarnation of Vishnu?

Except for the extreme rationalists, no one questions the ranking of Vishnu, Shiva, etc. as high gods, but the question arises about deities at the intermediate levels. The most ancient Vedic tradition seems to have been *dualist* insofar as it kept the gods and ancestral spirits in two categories. Later, Ramanuja, the dualist philosopher, also maintained the separation of the human soul from God. Hindu myths contain dozens of stories of human beings aspiring through the performance of austerities (*tapas*) to the position of Indra, the leader of gods in the Hindu heaven. Likewise, in the stories and beliefs about yoga, humans gain superhuman power (*siddhis*) annihilating the distance between man and the Supreme Being. The underlying "mood and motivation" (Geertz 1966:4) in all these mythical and ritual activities seem to be an assertion of man's will to power in contrast to the absolute surrender (*sarana:gati*) of the dualists.

Shankara, the chief protagonist of the *advaita* [nondualist or monistic Hindu theology], viewed the human spirit and the divine as identical — as a unity. Shorn of his dialectics, Shankara would appear to an anthropologist almost Tylorean! Shankara was a Nambudiri Brahman of Kerala in the eighth to ninth century A.D. A student of

Kerala society cannot but be interested in Shankara's catholicity of view which gave ready acceptance to folk religions and their rites as stages in man's spiritual development.

One of the things I have attempted in this paper is to give some hints about the probable nature of popular religion in Kerala in the centuries preceding Shankara. Such a reconstruction as I have attempted is necessary, as Kerala has no history or literature worth the name until after the tenth century A.D. Even a rough idea of the sociocultural milieu in which Shankara's basic personality structure was laid out would be of interest to a wide range of scholars.

The concept of *avatar* [the incarnation of gods as human beings or animals] is the second aspect of the man-god continuum which is central and crucial in Hindu religion and mythology. I refer to this transformation as the process of humanization of gods. In order to deal properly and adequately with spiritual beings they have to be given forms. Hence the term *mu:rti* [that which has taken or been given a shape] for spiritual beings and also for their icons.

The Upanishads and mythologies (*pura:na*) of the Hindus are works of the elite, mostly Brahmans, and they are in the Sanskrit language. Through Brahman propagandists and through translations into other languages the ideas concerning their ancestor cults, gods, *avatar*, and yogic practices have spread widely among the upper non-Brahman castes, but only in an extremely vague, diluted form among the lower castes and least among the tribal communities of India.

I propose to examine the nature of the spiritual beings, but more particularly ancestral spirits among a tribal community of Kerala. On the basis of this examination, I present the hypothesis that the germ of the idea of monism, namely the continuity of man with god, is likely to be found among the primitive substratum of India's population.[1]

---

[1]   After this paper was drafted, I came across the following paragraph in which Dr. Pauline Kolenda discusses a possible line of evolution of monistic thought among the sweepers of Khalapur: "Another category are all those supernaturals who have gained a measure of autonomous power from God through mortifications, or devotion either to him, or to another of these same autonomous creatures. Supposedly, during the *Satyug* [ancient age of pure morality], the important mother goddesses and male godlings were devout mystics who died in religious trance. Through their austerities and closeness to God, they gained power from him, but power independent of his will. Thus, it is explained, there is monism in supernatural power. All power is God's, but nevertheless these creatures who take their power from him are independent of him" (Kolenda 1964:76-77).

The Gond of Mandla have a collective ceremony to *unite* the life spirits of their dead with Baradeo, their supreme god. The expression "unite" which they use in this context is significant. It may be incipient monism. The object of the ceremony is to get rid of the spirits effectively and forever. There is no thought of helping them in their postmortem life as in the Indo-Aryan *shra:ddha*. The Gonds erect cairns in honor of their distinguished dead and it is considered an act of merit to add a stone to the cairn (Fuchs 1960:343-354).

Anyway, the idea could not have been a sudden discovery of the Upanishadic philosopher but should have been vaguely in the popular mind at its sensitive, creative, myth-making level.

The same broad spectrum of religious beliefs and practices is found in Kerala as in other regions of southern India, with slight local variations matching with the specialities in the social structure and history of the Hindus of the state. The Brahmans of Kerala — the Nambudiri Brahmans — being more exclusive in religious matters than their counterparts elsewhere share very little of their Vedic specialities with the non-Brahmans. The result of this Brahman attitude is that most of the non-Brahman transition and calendric rites have been more or less without the intervention of Brahman ritualists. The number of Shiva or Vishnu temples are few in Kerala compared to the large number of those dedicated to the Mother Goddess Bhadrakali.

The worship of Sasta or Ayyappan at Sabarimala, of Subrahmanya at Palni in Tamilnadu, of Vishnu at Guruvayur and of Bhadrakali at Kodungallur is of statewide importance. The worship of ancestral spirits and the propitiation of spirits concerned in sorcery and diseases are extensively practiced, though their popularity is declining among the educated sections of Keralites who are exposed to the neo-Vedantism popularized by Swami Vivekananda. Like all people burdened with a syncretic growth of religion, mostly Keralites have now to divide their attention between different and occasionally contradictory worlds of faith and thought.

Until about the fourth century A.D. (on a rough estimate) ancestral cults associated with urn burials and megaliths such as cists played a very great part in the religious life of Kerala. The evidence for this is found in the very large number of urn burials, cists, etc. found all over Kerala (Aiyappan 1933:299-314). When the Nambudiri Brahmans, with their very great and superior prestige, began their cultural conquest of Kerala, their impact influenced first the chieftains and the ruling classes. The degree of Sanskritization of rituals, modes of worship and of spoken Malayalam was closely correlated with the closeness of the local people to the prestigious Brahman immigrants.

As adequate historical research has not been made into the dynamics of Sanskritization in Kerala, we are not in a position to get a correct picture of the manner in which pre-Nambudiri culture, and more particularly the religious institutions, was changed by the Brahmans. There is no doubt that massive changes took place and during the process the Nambudiris themselves made several adaptations, some of a radical nature.

Of all the local rituals, those connected with the treatment of the dead and ancestral spirits by the non-Brahmans underwent the maximum amount of change. The honoring of the dead by urn burial and the construction of megalithic cists gave place to the Brahmanical type of funeral and *shra:ddha* ceremonies. An example of a cult which the Brahmans took over from the pre-Aryan culture of Kerala is the cult of serpents. They not only accepted it but became high priests of the cult at two centers in Kerala while the non-Brahman specialists, reduced to untouchable status, continued their serpent rituals in their own style.

As regards the cult of ancestors, the Nambudiri Brahmans, naturally, and the highly Sanskritized clans of ruling chieftains such as the Zamorin Raja and the Rajas of Cochin follow the Indo-Aryan practices *in toto*. Except for the *shra:ddha* ceremonies, they do nothing else for their ancestors. The non-Brahman castes led by the Nayars, however, have not become Sanskritized to such an extent as to be able to give up their old practice of making shrines for their ancestral spirits and worshiping them as though they were minor gods and communicating with them through mediums. In northern Kerala the shrines for ancestral spirits are called *kottam*. Anyone who is not able to build a special shrine uses a room in his dwelling to keep the symbols of the ancestral spirit — a stool or an image. Or he keeps a piece of stone under a tree as the symbol of the departed to be worshiped on prescribed occasions. The same shrine room or open tree-shaded shrine may be used as a shrine for family gods by the non-Brahman castes from the high-ranking Nayars down to the low-caste Pulayas.

For a social anthropologist who has set for himself the difficult task of analyzing the belief and religious systems of a complex society with a population of over twenty million, the study of tribal communities of the region offers some tactical assistance. He can contrive an experimental field situation with fewer variables to be handled at a time.

In Kerala I have had the good fortune to study an intensely traditional, religious-minded tribal community, the Kurichiyas of Wynad, who have been isolated in a hilly tribal pocket of the Kerala State with minimal contacts and communication with the plains people until recent times. The Kurichiyas number now about 11,000 and are believed to have migrated to their present habitat as farmers. Though it is not possible to date their migration exactly, the probabilities are that it was prior to the fourth or fifth century A.D., when the influence of the Brahmans was slight or even absent, the caste structure and economic differentiation had not assumed their present morphology and the basic matrilineality of Kerala society was strong.

The Kurichiyas consider themselves equal in status to the Nayars, yet they tap palm wine, which is at present the diacritical occupation of an inferior caste, the Izhavas (Aiyappan 1944), who are now untouchable to both the Nayars and Kurichiyas. The social distance between the Nayars and Izhavas has been growing over the centuries, the initial impulse for this having come, in all likelihood, through the intervention of the Brahmans.

The Kurichiyas, in my view, represent an ancient section of Kerala society from which the matrilineal northern Kerala Nayars and the Tiyyar (Izhavas) branched off. The Nayars, as a matter of fact, are not one caste, but a cluster of castes set apart to perform various services for the Brahmans and the ruling families, the services ranging from administration and fighting to various forms of ceremonial assistance and menial work.

The religion of the Kurichiyas may also be taken to represent a broadly archaic form of the faith and practices of the pre-Nambudiri Keralites, more specifically the Nayars and Izhavas. Several centuries of peripheral contacts with advanced groups, Brahmans and Nayars, who came later to Wynad have had some impact on the Kurichiyas, but their effect is indeed slight. Shiva, Vishnu, Rama, Krishna and other gods and goddesses of the Puranic Hindu pantheon mean almost nothing to the Kurichiyas. In none of their shrines do they have any icons.

The Kurichiyas believe that they had 108 named matrilineal sibs of which the names of only sixty-six are remembered and of these nine became extinct within living memory. The fifty-seven clans are grouped into two exogamous phratries, marriage within the phratry being strictly prohibited and sanctioned. They live in large matrilineages of the type described for the northern Malabar coast Nayars by Gough (1962:385-404).

The Kurichiyas believe in a Creator who in their prayers is referred to as I:svara or Peruma:l'. He created the various gods, goddesses and innumerable evil spirits. Ranking just below Peruma:l are the Four Mothers or great Mother Goddesses to whose world the dead are believed to go. The most pervasive and active god of the Kurichiyas is Malaka:ri.[2] Their myths describe him as a great hunter armed with bow and arrows. He established his supremacy over Wynad by subduing another god Pul'l'aya:ran and a ferocious bloodthirsty goddess Karimpili whom he reduced to a pacific character, placed in charge of the welfare of women and children, and also made the goddess of graveyards. Vadakkatti is the Kurichiya goddess of dry farming;

---

[2] The word Malaka:ri means "Kari of the Hills." Kari is a very old Dravidian personal name surviving now in backward areas as a personal name of lower-caste men in Kerala. The Malayalam word for cairns which represents the seat of Malaka:ri and other Kurichiya gods is *tad'angay* [a structure which retains (things)]. Hill gods in backward areas of central Kerala have cairns, to add a pebble or piece of rock to which is considered to be an act of merit. As cairns are associated in prehistoric southern India with funerary rites, I wonder if Malaka:ri may, after all, be a deified culture-hero. This question requires far more probing than I have been able to undertake. For the present, in the absence of other cultural clues, I have desisted from discussing this matter and accept the views of my Kurichiya informants.

Vet't'aka:l'an of hunting, fishing, and the making of bridges and rafts; Gul'ikan of the threshing floors and cattle. A male deity, Atira:l'an, also called the Mediator god (*Mu:nna:n teyyam*) looks after the interpersonal relationships in the large Kurichiya lineages and is the main channel of communication between men and gods. Atira:l'an is a close spiritual equivalent of the secular functionary, Mu:nna:n.[3] Each sib has a tutelary god or goddess (some of whom are major gods) as its special guardian. No segment of a sib can attain independent social status without a shrine established for its tutelary deity. True to their matrilineal organization, twenty-seven out of their total number of forty-six deities are female.

The Kurichiyas build small temples for their mother goddesses about whom they share cults and beliefs with the rest of the Kerala Hindus. However, for Malaka:ri, Atira:l'an, Vet't'aka:l'an, etc., they build only cairns, which is a very old Dravidian tribal practice (Fuchs 1960:343-354). Each sib may have shrines and cairns for three to seven gods in a special enclosure not far from the cluster of dwelling houses. In a room in the best of these houses, the ancestral shades of the clan have their place. A lighted lamp or a simple low stool of wood is the material symbol for the shade. When new households are established, the presence of a shade is essential before it can be called a house. A house without an ancestral shade is regarded as only a shed (*pandal*). In the kitchen block a female ancestor spirit (*pe:na*) is believed to be present. She is symbolized there at the time of ceremonies by a lighted lamp.

The Kurichiyas call their male ancestral spirits *nizhal*, a word which literally means "shadow." The Kurichiyas have a simple burial ceremony with none of the elaborations noticed among the nontribal Keralites. After the burial, care is taken to observe ritual pollution and then to remove it. The dead are believed to go to the world of the Four Mothers. Only a very small number of outstanding men who were considered able and efficient during their lifetime are, on request, permitted by the Creator and the Four Mothers to return to the earth and be with their kin.[4]

The living have to seek the help of the old shades of the clan, the Mediator god and Malaka:ri to bring them down from the spirit world and conduct elaborate rites spread over two to three years. When a shade comes down, its medium, now possessed, rolls down on the

[3] The Mediator god, or Mu:nna:n god, is sociologically speaking a most interesting deity providing a Durkheimian proof for Kurichiya religion as a projection of society. For details about the equivalent of this social functionary among the Nayars and Izhavas, see Gough (1962:327). Her "Enangar" is spelled as "Inangar" by me (Aiyappan 1944).

[4] Persons who have died of smallpox may become shades and have to be ritually disposed of.

ground. This is characteristic of this class of superhumans. In the final act of the drama, while the shade's medium is still in trance, the shaman of the senior shade requests the shaman of the Mediator god to lead the new shade to the shrine room of the household. The Mediator god leads the new shade by the hand to the room where he remains forever or until transferred to another branch household.

The position of the shades in the hierarchy of superhumans is at the lowest level, but their functions are more numerous and diverse than those of any other member of the superhuman group, except perhaps the Mediator god. Though the shades are housed separately, offerings of food, etc. are given to them side by side with other superhumans at the time of the New Rice ceremony. The shade is believed to make the seeds germinate properly and the plants thrive, to discipline the members of the household, to receive fines from the head of the household if he is guilty in any respect and to watch the storage bins of cereals against pilferage.

When the head of a lineage goes out on important business, he formally seeks the permission of the shade. Instances are known of the shade punishing failure on the part of heads of families to observe this rule. In all respects the shade acts as a superior family head. The shade of a sib with administrative functions for a village, in like fashion, exercises control over other sibs in the territory.

The spirits of ancestresses, less numerous than those of male ancestors, are called *pe:na*. (This is an old Dravidian word used extensively among the Gond tribe for their goddesses.) For the rest of the Malayalis, *pe:na* means "ghost," "spirit," or "devil." The Kurichiyas refer to her respectfully as *pe:na mutta:chi* [spirit grandmother]. It is interesting to find that the Kurichiyas use this word in its old Dravidian sense. The place for the *pe:na* is a corner of the "northern" house which is used as the kitchen and dining hall of the household. When offerings are to be made to the *pe:na*, she is represented by a lighted brass oil lamp. She is believed to be concerned with the affairs of the women of the household. When the women quarrel, the Mediator god is believed to appeal to the *pe:na* to intervene and punish the guilty. Punishment usually takes the form of sickness.

Gough (1959:240-272) has described in detail the way in which the cult of the dead is organized among the Nayars and I have described the same for the Izhavas (Aiyappan 1944). The role of the ancestor spirits in the affairs of the living has been routinized and narrowed down in the case of the Nayars and the Izhavas while the funeral ceremonies involving the services of priests and specialists have grown enormously. Unlike the punitive Nayar ghost, the Kurichiya shade is a constant presence, generally beneficent and used as an important channel of communication with the gods.

The Nayars, Izhavas and Kurichiyas agree, however, in making very little difference between the gods and shades. The Nayars and Izhavas regard the shades of some sorcerers to be as powerful as some of the minor gods. It is, however, difficult to generalize about the Nayars and Izhavas, as their culture and social structure are heterogeneous and complex compared to the homogeneity and simplicity of the Kurichiya social structure and culture. The Kurichiyas are more egalitarian and less authoritarian than the Nayars, and the differences in the roles of their respective ancestor spirits have to be seen against this background.

The Nayars and Izhavas who perform *shra:ddha* ceremonies of the Indo-Aryan pattern primarily as a filial duty to assist the *preta* [ghost] in its progress further away from the earth and only marginally for the benefit of the living are not conscious of the contradiction in the continued practice of their ancestor worship which, unlike the *shra:ddha*, is a response to the wish, in the ritual drama, of the spirit to return to the earth. The Kurichiyas are clear in their minds about what they are doing. They have no categories corresponding to the *preta* and *pitris* and a still higher category of gods. The Kurichiya ancestral spirits and their gods are alike in being denizens of the world of the Four Mothers.

Kurichiya experts in mythological lore are agreed that seven of their deities are humans who became gods. My best informant went to the extent of claiming the Bhagavati of Vallu:rka:vu as an ancestress of the Kurichiyas who was unjustly killed by her mother's brother. In the light of this claim, the legends about this temple and its rituals require close study. The deities with legendary human origin are: (1) Pra:ntan Pul'l'a Teyyam, (2) Cha:ntampili, (3) Da:rampili, (4) Vel'anilattu Bhagavati, (5) Kal'l'amvet't'i Bhagavati, (6) Atiral'ichi and (7) Kalliyot Mutta:chi. The first of these is believed to have been a weaver attached to the temple of Teytal Amma. I have been able to collect very little information about the second and third. The fourth is said to have been a Kurichiya girl, a flawless person or "full person," as the Kurichiyas believe, and was selected for a foundation sacrifice but was miraculously saved by Vet't'aka:l'an. The fifth, Kallamvetti Bhagavati, was a Kurichiya woman who guided the god Pul'l'aya:ran in the Vemom area. The sixth, Atiral'ichi, was a Kshatriya woman stolen by the god Pul'l'aya:ran and given away to the Kannolan sib. Kalliyot Mutta:chi was a young woman whose honor was miraculously saved by a rock splitting and engulfing her. An eighth god, Vet't'aka:l'an, stands on a somewhat different plane. What is of interest to us here is the firm belief of the Kurichiyas that men and women are potential gods and goddesses.

To say definitely which of the Kurichiya deities are their cultural inventions and which are adaptations from the general Kerala types will be a worthwhile task which I wish to attempt later in my full-length study of the Kurichiyas. It is obvious that they brought with them the analogues of several of their deities but modified their roles to meet their needs in Wynad. Earlier I have mentioned their god Vet't'aka:l'an This is the god of hunting and of war in Kerala, but the Kurichiyas have given him an additional role as the god of public works. The myth about this god worked out by Kurichiya myth makers gives Vet't'-aka:l'an a new incarnation as a Kurichiya youth and then as a somewhat different god. The story in bare outline is as follows: A good Kurichiya was working under a Nambiar chieftain. As he was overworked, the chief gave him his young daughter and niece as assistants. The niece became pregnant and asked her Kurichiya lover for palm wine and meat. Malaka:ri at this time wanted the god Vet't'aka:l'an to remain in Wynad to help the Kurichiyas. So he asked that the pregnant woman be given the palm wine and meat sacralized by having been offered to him. The baby boy she gave birth to had miraculous powers and vanished in various forms: as a bird, butterfly, etc. Ultimately, he attached himself as the divine manager of the goddess, Bhagavati, of the Tondernad temple. The motif of the miraculous generative powers of sacralized food in this story is found elsewhere in Kerala, but its incorporation in a myth to transform the role of Vet't'aka:l'an appears to me suggestive of a germinal theory of *avatar* [incarnation of gods], crude though it may be.

The Kurichiyas are generally illiterate. They refused to go to schools, because it meant getting polluted. They are more pollution-purity conscious than even the Nambudiri Brahmans of Kerala. Only now do we get a few of the first generation to attend school. The concepts I have been talking about — monism, dualism, man-god continuum, incarnation of gods, etc. — would all be strange to them. The distinguishing feature about them is their strong commitment to their gods and rituals and to the values which keep their matrilineages, clans and community well knit and integrated. While modernity confuses and confounds them, their tradition is clear to them. If I were to tell them in monistic language, "You are that," they might not understand me, but if I put the idea in another way, "Your shades are as good as your gods," they would all agree. About *avatar*s in the Kurichiya belief system, I am not sure; nor are they.

REFERENCES

AIYAPPAN, A.
1933   Rock-cut cave-tombs of Feroke, S. Malabar. *Quarterly Journal of the Mythic Society, Bangalore* 33:219-314.
1944   *Iravas and culture change.* Bulletin of the Madras Government Museum. Madras: Government Press.

FUCHS, S.
1960 *The Gond and Bhumia of eastern Mandla.* Bombay: Asia Publishing House.

GEERTZ, C.
1966 "Religion as a cultural system," in *Anthropological approaches to the study of religion.* Edited by M. Banton, 1-46. London: Tavistock.

GOUGH, KATHLEEN
1959 "Cults of the dead among the Nayars," in *Traditional India: structure and change.* Edited by M. Singer and B. S. Cohn. Special issue of the *Journal of American Folklore* 78: 240-272.

1962 "Nayar: north Kerala," in *Matrilineal kinship.* Edited by David M. Schneider and Kathleen Gough, 384-404. Berkeley: University of California Press.

KOLENDA, PAULINE MAHAR
1964 "Religious anxiety and Hindu fate," in *Religion in South Asia.* Edited by Edward B. Harper, 71-81. Seattle: University of Washington Press.

Prestations and Prayers: Two Homologous Systems in Northern India

R. S. KHARE

Prestations and prayers, both as a system of relationships and as separate systems of parallel significance, require more systematic attention than they have received thus far in South Asian anthropology. If prestations help regulate the sphere of social relations, prayers signify the major relationships that the members of the society posit with regard to the supernatural, the society, and the individual. However, prayers, like prestations, present a wide variety of relationships of the religious sphere and they require systematization in terms of some common logical relationships.

The argument in this essay is that prayers essentially follow a logical paradigm that is characteristic of social prestations, and that this is particularly true for the devotional prayers of Hinduism so widely circulated in contemporary India. These prayers, it is further proposed, are essentially based on the premise of give-and-take, with an explicit idea of both the "quality and quantity of exchange" between the deity and the devotee. The point that the "deities practice exchange" should hardly surprise those who, being acquainted with modern legal practice, know that the deities can formally fight court cases either to retain or to augment the property that their temples hold.

In a more real sense, as we readily understand, a deity's "delegates" (like priests and trustees in a temple) practice exchange and litigate on the deity's behalf. But our treatment will emphasize not only the exchange of *things* (for which at least two individuals are necessary) but also of *ideas*, where sometimes only the devotee may do the job — "he" may answer himself on behalf of the deity. In the latter cases, the thought that the exchange has occurred is most significant, and it is a *fact* with the devotee. Let us now finish with the preliminaries to reach such a stage of discussion.

In our following discussion, prestations will provide, often only implicitly, a yardstick against which to assess the relative nature, position, and function of prayers. Since the latter are virtually an unexplored field of study in recent social anthropology, we shall concentrate a good deal on their nature under the Hindu tradition of devotion (*bhaktī*). We will first establish some general homologous points between prestations and prayers to help channel our later discussion of the nature of devotional prayers among the Hindus. We will discuss in some detail forms, functions, and meanings of such prayers, and then return to the underlying idea of exchange in prayers and in prestations. It will be argued that both the structure of contents and the language of expression in prayers are developed to highlight this characteristic. Finally, we will indicate that what prayers display (in thought patterns) is a replica of the entire *bhaktī* movement and that they contain several important contradictions.

PRESTATIONS AND PRAYERS:
SIMILARITIES IN STRUCTURE

Mauss, with his celebrated *Essai sur le don, forme archaïque de l'échange* (translation, 1967), and his *La prière et les rites oraux* (in Mauss 1968), remains a pioneer in the field of sociological thinking.[1] Many more recent attempts have appeared that have discussed the topics of gifting and exchange to illustrate further their forms, functions, and cultural meanings under different ceremonial and social situations. However, as Ian Cunnison remarked in his "translative note" to *The gift* (Mauss 1967:xi), the French word *prestation* may be used to mean "any thing or series of things given freely or obligatorily as a gift or in exchange; and includes services, entertainments, etc., as well as material things."[2]

The point is important for our present discussion because the broader scope of the term "prestations" will facilitate our task of examining forms, functions, and meanings of prayers. If what is exchanged is not rigidly tied down to only selected things, relationships, and manners, the field of this study widens considerably, opening up the way for us to

---

[1] While his first work, originally issued in 1925, has been available in English, his writing on prayer, published in 1909, is available only in French.

[2] The scope of this word is more clearly evident in French usage. Coming from the Latin *praestatio*, the meaning of the word varies from *action de fournir* [applying, furnishing, stocking] to *allocation donnée aux militaires* [military pay], to *allocation de maternité* [maternity benefits] (Robert 1972).

analyze certain logical structures that may cut across the usual distinctions inherent in such categories as the religious, the economic, and the political. Certain ideas and actions of give-and-take, to put it as a crude simplification, may run through all the three categories of social relationships, and even what is given and taken — and how, and what for, it is given and taken — may not, after all, differ so fundamentally as we are led to believe under the established classification of social relations.

On closer inspection one finds that not only is the transaction a normal process in the majority of social relations, but even what is transacted is not so exclusive to one particular institution. One usual instance given is that of power or influence which may be, either in fact or in essence, transacted through diverse economic, political, religious, and ritual relations, and not only (or exclusively) through the political situations. Hence, if we regard "economic," "political," "ritual," etc., as specific attributes of social relations (rather than as separate classes of social relations), we are on a more realistic ground to examine them.

Ceremonial and ritual prestations, it follows from the above, are also essentially those social relations that carry some distinguishing attributes of their own but these attributes, either in form or function, are not exclusive to them. Prayers, as we shall presently see, may have a basic structure corresponding (and similar) to that of ceremonial and ritual prestations. If prestations do not transfer only goods and commodities but also ideas, then this is even more true of prayers.

Prayers follow a paradigm of social exchange; they are a homologue of social prestations. If prestations keep the social relations alive and connect people with people, then prayers do the same — and more, for they help consolidate a social group around a more symbolic idea — the presence of God. This resemblance between the structure and function of prestations and prayers is neither superficial nor spurious, because it runs through both thought and action patterns — a point that should be more than evident from the following considerations, which essentially deal with the Hindu case.

The basic structure of Hindu prestations, concisely stated here, emphasizes nine major characteristics: (1) giver-receiver dichotomy, (2) reciprocity, (3) directionality, (4) "ultimate" idea of equivalence, (5) an idea of relative ranks, (6) an idea of "things" transacted, (7) direct/indirect reciprocity, (8) long-range (circulation)/short-range reciprocity, and (9) an idea of part (individual) and whole (collective).

If we examine prayers with respect to these features, we may discover strong similarities. Prayers, like prestations, have inherent giving/receiving ends: the person who says prayers offers "something" to his deity, which, in return, reciprocates. One static view is that the deity always gives and the devotee always receives. However, on closer inspection, the feature of reciprocity comes to the fore; a deity does not "give" without receiving "something" from the devotee. Further, while in a religious sense, a direction is built into prayers (God always gives more than a human can hope to reciprocate), in actuality, the reverse is more true, where a devotee prays, whether his deity immediately "answers" him or not. (As we shall see below, there are reasons for this attitude, which, as a matter of fact, are sustained by the reciprocity built into prayers.) But this is true only to an extent. According to a priest of the temple of Rāma at Adyodhya in Uttar Pradesh: "Who will pray if it is not answered at all, or more accurately, if there is no idea (or hope) that it is to be answered, even in the remotest way, in the remotest time?"

Here, therefore, once we recognize that the principle of reciprocity is at work in prayers, we should also note its specialized nature. The reciprocity, in a short-range perspective, may here appear to be incomplete, for only one dimension of the action (from devotee to deity) is empirically testable, leaving the other one, the deity's reciprocation, largely an experience of the devotee. Unlike in gifting and exchange, here one often has to depend on the attestation of the devotee to know whether his particular prayer has been answered or not. However, at the same time, it is an equally true social fact that prayers get "answered," and that the belief in this reciprocal dimension is invariably held by members of the society as a mental fact.

However, for a careful social anthropologist, there is another way (at least many a time, if not all the time) to ascertain that the "prayers get answered." Prayers, as acts at a particular time and by particular members of a society, often ventilate needs, anxieties, crises, and calamities. And though they are directed "to the One seated up there" and it is He who is supposed to respond, in fact it is the surrounding individuals and social groups who often answer the prayer. (But for the faithful it, of course, is always his deity.)

In terms of a Hindu's life-aims, prayers offered to obtain something that relates to *dharma, artha,* and *kāma* (three out of the four aims) are actually such that the "society must respond to them." It is of course not just a hypothetical postulation but one that can often be verified in the field. While the prayers related to *artha* and *kāma* get answered with the help of those who have these things (which are "gifts" of God, and not simply fruits of one's past *karma*), the prayers for the maintenance of one's *dharma* get answered in a different way — it is protected with the help of others. If *dharma* is essentially a preoccupation of the individual, its protection and maintenance are a societal concern.

It is in the same *extended way* that the fourth aim — *moksha* — is also ultimately sustained by the social reality, and the prayers connected with this aim, at least in some sense, depend on the society for being appropriately answered. (As we shall discuss below, this classical scheme of ideas is subject to exceptional forces of the *bhaktī* movement.)

The above should be sufficient to indicate that in prayers reciprocity is a fundamental idea, once we are able to include in this concept the direct and the indirect, the short-range and the long-range notions of reciprocity. It is also important in the context of prayers, which, being as diverse in purposes as they are, are mostly neither directly nor immediately answered. Some prayers of the Hindus are not meant to be answered "either in this life or in this world," others are not meant to be answered at all in the regular sense of the term reciprocity. However, as argued here (and later on), this is not to deny the idea of reciprocity but only to postpone the use of it for a more appropriate occasion.

The ideas of relative rank and of equivalence between what is given and what is received by way of prayers appear together. While no devotee either expects or hopes for exact equivalence between what he does during the prayers and what his deity does in response, there is some definite idea of quantity (as well as quality) attached to prayers. More prayers (usually counted by number) are supposed to accrue more rewards, although beyond this general notion it is hard to specify the measure in any exact manner. Besides, there are notions about the quality and quantity of response that a prayer might invoke from a deity.

Leaving aside some specific considerations until a little later, we might observe here a basic assumption; a devout person's prayers never remain unanswered and God always determines how (and how much) the devotee's wishes should be met at any particular time, "for God always determines only what is in the supreme interest of the devotee." Under the prevalent notions of the *bhaktī* sect, one's deity is always generous in his response to one's prayers; if however he seems miserly it is because of the limited — the myopic — view of one's own spiritual interest.

Hence, from God's end, this view continues, prayers are always amply and appropriately answered; only our human interpretation varies "because of the short-sightedness and ignorance of mortals." However, from the human end, prayers do seem to be randomly answered, for the skeptics may sometimes complain that they pray more and receive less (in terms of what they prayed for). In brief, therefore, while exact equivalence (in any quantitative sense) in prayer transactions is unobtainable, there are wide maximum and minimum limits along which the response to prayers may vary.

The idea of rank and the response to one's prayers are also closely related in several different ways, once we do not limit the idea of ranking to caste-systemic relations alone (even when such a relevance is not denied). The "politics of prayer" is, if we may make here an association that is not as absurd as it may look at first sight, that one ranking higher can always give as well as receive more, without being accountable to the one who ranks lower. (The relevance of such an observation with regard to the traditional caste system remains obvious.) It follows from the above that the one of highest rank — God — is responsible only to himself. Beside this obvious aspect of ranking between God and his devotee, there are, as we shall see below, numerous rank distinctions recognized within the categories of prayers and devotees that ultimately have an influence on the effectiveness of prayers — or so it is thought.

Finally comes the basic distinction of the part and the whole — of the individual and the collective in current sociological terminology. Prestations and prayers make use of this distinction — or rather it is this distinction that fundamentally necessitates such practices as prestations and prayers. If prestations help link one individual with the other (and one group with another), the prayers help endure human failures and unavoidable crises at one level and link the individual and the group with a supernatural force at another. For the devout, the prayers forge a "living link" with his article of faith. Further, individuals who pray get linked together more because they share their faith rather than other social characteristics. Individuals drawn from different caste groups are known to forge and maintain such a cohesiveness over an extended period of time.

Prestations socially, and prayers philosophically, help a Hindu to announce his identity in relation to a greater totality. It is with the help of prayers that he demonstrates his correct alignment with ultimate values of the culture; and it is with prestations that he correctly recognizes the presence of social collectivities that surround him. The analytical significance of studying such relationships is that they allow us to enter an area of inquiry (individuality *vis-à-vis* collectivity) that has hardly been sociologically investigated in terms of Hindu thought. The interrelationships between the part and the whole, it is here suggested, could be more concretely (and accurately) investigated with the help of an appropriate selection of prestations and prayers.

Elsewhere (Khare 1975) I have discussed some issues and perspectives connected with such an inquiry that suggest the usefulness of the material obtainable from prestations and prayers. Furthermore, they help illustrate criteria that guide the formulation, separation, and merger of the identity of the individual. The point that prayers are a potent means for expressing such urges is well known, but their underlying structure of thought needs to be studied before they can yield those shared criteria that *persistently regulate* the expression of interrelationships between the part (devotee) and the whole (the deity, or God) across situations.

Prestations, when intensively studied in terms of kinship, marriage, and death, afford similar possibilities, for they offer occasions when the individuality is successively developed, differentiated, and lost. In the interim, in various ways they demonstrate the relationships that are forged and maintained (or altered) between the individual and the social collective. This much should be sufficient for making the point that the question of the part and the whole is inherent in the basic structure of both prestations and prayers.

ON THE NATURE OF HINDU PRAYERS

The preceding section, devoted mainly to establishing a linkage between prayers and prestations, prepares us to see some vital resemblances that make prayers an important topic for social anthropological study. Two levels of analysis should be evident in my discussions: one at the level of thought — its structure and its relevance in the Hindu system of ideologies and values (here a direct reference to its sociological significance may not be made beyond the obvious, because I regard its study as rewarding in itself, and for what will be more directly sociological in nature a little bit later); and the other at the level of social reality, either as alleged in the past or as at present.

From now on, prayers will constitute our main focus of inquiry, though we will often draw implicit parallels to prestations; and in prayers, as I see them, thought structures (and their linguistic expressions) are far more significant than the ritual acts (as "technologies") that attend them. A study of the latter is significant (or more informative) in the context of the thought that prompts them. However, we must first suitably channel our inquiry by intensifying our analysis of prayers.

We have so far considered the concept of prayer from a distance, keeping its contents, functions, and varieties constant. Now before we can go any further, we must examine these variations. The term "prayer," as used here, has of course the obvious disadvantage that it carries with it certain traces of Judeo-Christian traditions, and it may be impossible to fully disown these "meanings at the fringe," and maybe this is not necessary as long as the major thrust of the Hindu idea is clearly kept in the forefront during the discussion. (Most desirable would be to use the appropriate Sanskrit and Hindi lexicon, but I shall refrain from it in this attempt to facilitate reading.)

Very briefly, in contemporary *popular* usage and in my usage here, the lexical entries that are included under the label "prayer" are: *stotra, stuti, vintī (vinaya,* m) *prārthanā,* and *ārādhanā.* These entries, as explained in any good Sanskrit-English or Hindi-English dictionary, variously emphasize the following minimal dimensions: (a) that something is asked for, (b) that some power or force is being invoked, apologized to, and eulogized, and (c) that an attitude of humility and submission (by the one who prays) is being inculcated.

If the first two dimensions bring out the content and function of prayers, the third one states a necessary value precondition for it. By implication, therefore, all those attitudes where either a confrontation or a contest or a conflict is espoused with some power or force fall outside the scope of prayers. So one should note here the point that while invocation, exhortation, and activation of power or forces are included within the scope of Hindu prayers, any coercion and contestation, devoid of the spirit of submission, is held outside it. Further, it should be obvious that the idea of prayer is not confined to supernatural forces; it also applies to the inhabitants of the mundane world in a very real sense but again, only the powerful are prayed to, for they alone can answer prayers. (Collectivities of the weak may appear powerful under the democratic system, and they may accordingly be "prayed to" by politicians to derive power to answer the prayers, in turn, of the individually weak.)

However, our concerns here will be quite limited: we shall restrict our attention to religious prayers, primarily directed toward that composite idea in Hindu belief called "God." Although we might occasionally take the liberty to benefit from the width of such a universe, it is still unmanageable. We will therefore further restrict ourselves to the prayers of the *bhaktī* tradition, especially because they are more directly relevant to the majority of the contemporary Hindus, whether of the north or the south.

But even so, we will remain at a sufficiently general level to allow us to observe some features of a broad framework that characterizes such prayers. We will therefore, for example, not specify either the deities or the philosophical systems, or the prominent devotees, in terms of whom the structure of these prayers might have originated and developed with time. We will be, instead, content with the criterion that the categories of features discussed below remain a part of the written and/or oral living tradition and knowledge of the Hindus over wide regions. (Such a demarcation of the field of study should greatly allay fears of those who might argue that prayers are too illusive a subject for social anthropological research.)

The General Conception

Once we move into the religious field that is dominated by the idea — and tenets — of devotion (*bhaktī*), it becomes easier to exclude those formulas and prescriptions from consideration here (e.g. such *yantra, mantra,* and *tantra*), that coerce a supernatural god or deity to action, not out of humility and submission but by either threat or command. Such a distinction cannot allow one to dismiss out of hand any specific sect, deity, or body of literature; given the complexity of development of thought about the Hindu pantheon, one has to be more circumspect. Yet the criterion of distinction is neither blurred nor confused in this complexity, as a close study of the material should reveal. However, by the same criterion, there is an enormous body of literature (in Sanskrit and in regional languages), almost with every significant sect, that may not strictly fall in the category of prayers but that goes best with them by criteria of affinity. This body of cognate literature may lay out explanatory schemes in relation to those ultimate values that are clearly spelled out time and again in actual prayers. As a learned devotee recently summarized it to me at Rae Bareli (Uttar Pradesh): "Prayers, as composed by saints after hard and long meditation, encapsulate all those major strands of thought that have taken centuries to develop under exposition and commentary of the learned. But let us not forget: prayers are real power, while commentaries and philosophical expositions are mere words, for the former are directed to God under the influence of true devotion."

This connection, as it exists today in the minds of the devotees, is useful to note here because, while the philosophical literature may be seen to furnish categories and concepts for prayers, the latter are evidently something more real and potent, and they do not depend on such a literature for their effectiveness and survival. Prayers are supposed to be halos of God.

Finally, the majority of medieval and modern literature that is written to expound directly the virtues (*guṇa*), forms (*rupa*), divine sports (*līlā*), etc., of God (in his numerous incarnations) falls under the category of prayers — some directly and some indirectly. Thus, the contemporary body of literature called *bhajan*s and *keertan*s (for one systematic study of these in Madras, see Singer 1966, 1972), with the help of a devotee's specified purpose and attitude, becomes a powerful and diverse repository of prayers. (It should be more evident a little later in this article why this is so.)

Now let us come to the shared conception of prayers today. Prayers, to be sure once again, chiefly underline the themes of spiritual humility, invocation, eulogy, verecundity, and doxology. (Although the English language carries a number of words that vary in emphasis, there are no easy equivalents to what Sanskrit and Hindi or other regional languages have in India.) Actually, even the current Hindi lexical categories are a poor label for what they are supposed to cover, unless one is prepared to go to numerous prevalent (even if only regionally valid) terms that the *sādhu*s have used to denote and classify shades of devotional attitudes (more correctly called *bhāva*) toward one's deity of worship. Thus appear, for example, in Hindi, such categories of prayers as ones dealing with either union (*milan*) or separation (*virah*) or admonition (*chétāvanī*) or bliss of realization (*darshanānanda*) or renunciation (*sanyāsa*) or divine sports (*līlā*). A systematic study of linguistic categories in this context should be useful, particularly since much regional vocabulary seems to be on the wane, or at least narrowly used.

Here we of course must also recall the basic classification of sentimental "attitudes" (*bhāva*) towards the deity, ranging from that of a servant (*dāsya*) to a beloved (*mādhurya*), for they help classify prayers according to the dominant sentiment of the deity-devotee relationship, and they may facilitate comprehension of a set of values that a devotee of a particular *bhāva* can follow in his prayers. Beyond these indications about the formal categories of devotional prayers, the task must be deferred to a more intensive study; here I must now pass on to a more popular conception of prayers.

Prayers are a popular, and yet powerful, avenue to God, open, ideally, to all, even in the face of the exhaustive ranking of individuals and groups in Hindu society. As the preachers these days endlessly argue, they are especially potent for the hopeless, the downtrodden, the meek, and the pure of heart and mind. Sincere prayers, again under the ideal conception, never fail: "When all hopes are lost, prayers do miracles." (Hereinafter, unless otherwise specified, sentences within quotes are taken from the actual religious lectures — *pravacan* — of the contemporary holy men, saints, and priests, which were recorded in substance in 1962 in Lucknow on the premises of the Ramakrishna, Gauranga, and Geeta-Bhawan organizations.)

"Prayers of the helpless are especially effective in the *darbār* [hall of audience] of God, because the devotee has then lost all other mundane props and they become truly sincere and desperate like those of the Gaja."[3] For the devotee who is not under the influence of a specifically acute crisis, the preachers do not forget to make the point that prayers done halfheartedly and without intense concentration remain unanswered. Since praying with heart and soul is everybody's birthright, unvitiated by one's caste, creed, wealth, and learning, the argument is made for its widest practice "in an age when the wants, the sorrows,

---

[3]   It is quite frequent that the religious preachers draw upon mythological characters (like Gaja — an elephant who successfully prayed to God [Vishnu] while in distress) for driving home the point. That the preachers advise recitation of such prayers (either in Sanskrit or in one of their regional renderings) to the devotees with some specific purpose in mind is also quite common. Given the scope of our discussion here, however, we shall refrain from drawing in all mythological evidence, for it would invariably draw us to footnote explanations and hence inordinately prolong the discussion. But the ensuing discussion could be easily backed by such data.

and the ailments engulf all." Most of such prayers remain unrecorded, and what we find recorded is only the tip of the iceberg.

Beyond their immediate curative use, prayers, as the Hindu devotional thought makes clear, are *natural* to any soul yearning for God. "It is neither flattering nor bribing the Supreme Being; it is, however, an important indication about the proper journey of one's soul, for prayers are both necessary and sufficient for attaining *bhaktī* as well as, if desired, *moksha*. The glory of God is not an artificial attribute that a mortal can invent at will, and one's participation in it is both natural and inescapable — sooner or later." This is what we may call the long-range view of prayers that is more preventive than curative in function. All ills, whether physical (*daihik*), or material or "this-worldly" (*bhautik*), or supernatural or "other-worldly" (*daivik*), are always curable through earnest prayers, and hence the latter constitute a very powerful preventive step *before* such ills have fettered a soul. Mythologies again provide perfect examples to emphasize the point. Thus, in whatever way we look at the general function of prayers, they are *restorative* in both their short-range and long-range functions. This statement must be further qualified to assert that prayers, when directed towards mundane crises, do not lose their long-range benefits to the soul.

Prayers, it is argued, cannot be divested of their spiritual benefits. As a related thought: Whether a devotee prays with a specific purpose in mind or not, prayers automatically bring divine blessings. "The true devotees never ask for results, for they know this fact: 'you get more without asking'." (Consider here the relation between prestation and prayers for the fundamental principle of reciprocation and the maximization of what one can get.)

The above concept may seem to rather unduly exaggerate the utilitarian motive underlying prayers, unless it is also emphasized that prayers, in principle, cannot always be expected to yield immediate results, because even if praying is within human possibilities, its "fruits lie in the hands of God, and if he does not answer them, it is his will." But of course it does not mean the devotee should be disheartened or dejected, "because who knows when God may answer, making up for his past silence all at once." This structure of thought should prompt the devotee to pray again and again, "without losing either patience or faith." It is through such a silence that God tests the faith of his devotee, and in order to avoid frustration during such periods, one should learn to pray without attaching specific desires, i.e. in *nishkāma bhāva*, for the sole purpose of pleasing one's deity of devotion. Alternatively, "he should resign himself to the will of God (*Hari-ékshā*), but without either diminishing his faith or reducing the duration and number of his prayers." Therefore, we may summarize: Successful or unsuccessful, praying with faith must go on undaunted, for it is in contemporary India a major foundation for the *dharma* of the Hindu. The devotional prayer is held to be above the fetters of ritual rules, and of *karma* and *dharma*.

Forms, Functions, and Meanings

Before we continue to discuss other related aspects of the devotional prayer, we must here discuss the structure of prayers — in terms of discernible thought arrangements and of social relationships. The social structure of prayers may differ widely according to the purpose, occasion, and duration of the prayers, as well as varying as a result of the participants. However, the basic distinction is that between the individual and the collective.

Some prayers may be exclusively meant for personal, exclusive use, and the most common, yet forceful, example of this category is provided by one's *guru-mantra*, which only two persons know in this world — the guru and his disciple, who received it as a whisper in his ear when he took *guru-dikshā*, i.e. when he became initiated, for his spiritual welfare. A similar rite may take place during the sacred-thread ceremony of the twice-born, but it can become quite an elaborate separate affair, for a spiritual *guru* is approached once in a lifetime and the *mantra* given by him remains the deepest secret with the disciple; the latter never imparts it to anybody else because it is suited only to "his soul's needs."

Counting the Holy Name [*Nāma japa*] or a phrase eulogizing a deity are other examples of prayers that may be conducted alone while meditating before one's deity. The severity of a crisis may also force a devotee to pray in seclusion, for this way one can really give vent to his feelings and emotions "before the deity whom one adores and who, after all, can help most in distress." Beside these prayers that are meant to be prayed alone, one can of course find many other prayers for either individual or group praying.

As for accompaniments of praying, worshiping remains the most closely associated activity. Very often, while the prayers *per se* may not require a certain ritual state of purity and certain arrangements of objects and accessories of worship, the deities, to whom the prayers are, after all, directed, may invariably require them. Hence, to be able to pray (in a formal sense), a devotee has first to invoke a deity by proper worship (and offerings). These requirements, as the priests and the householders argue, also depend on the nature of the deity. If he is benevolent and omnipotent like Rāma and Krishna, *no* bars apply — they can be prayed to always in any state of ritual purity.

Numerous mythological examples are provided to support this injunction. "One can pray to them even in a most impure state, and they do not need an invocation every time you pray. However, if you worship them daily, it strengthens your faith anyway, and it is, at least indirectly, a help in the prayers." However, one has to be very scrupulous with lesser gods and deities, "for they are temperamental, fussy, and more demanding." They require exact preparations every time — all the time — before starting prayers. If it is not done in appropriate sequence, the effect of the prayer may be either nil or even negative, i.e. instead of granting the wish, the deities may cast their wrath and punish the erratic devotee. Examples usually given (at least in northern India, excluding the benign transformations inculcated in, and exported from, Bengal) are those of the goddesses of *navagraha*, astrological stars — as deified in the Hindu thought, and of Hanumān. Localized gods usually fall in this same category and require preparations for "proper prestation and invocation" before they can be fruitfully prayed to. Do such gods, as a consequence, fall into disfavor? The answer is "no," because these deities work for quite specified purposes (ailments, crops, efforts, etc.) and, as the people repeatedly argue, "what will a sword [i.e. a bigger deity] do where only a needle [i.e. a lesser deity] is required?" As a result, devotees in search of specific help repeatedly come to these deities, and they remain popular in their own right, despite the deeper urge to be a *bhakta* of the omnipotent Rāma and Krishna "to get away from it all" (*samsāra*).

Further, some deities work slower and some faster — some only after the accumulation of prayers from the devotees. Some act fast but only after an initial delay, while some slowly guard and supervise all the time during a specific endeavor, if once invoked in the beginning (e.g. the god Ganesha). However, all deities, so to speak, reserve the right to deny a prayer, despite the best human care for their invocation and worship. Such denials may mean either their disposition (at that occasion they may be regarded as displeased) or a signal for further demands, which of course a priest will normally suggest the next time around. Some deities — like goddesses, who are supposed to have awesome control over human affairs — should be prayed to at least twice a year (normally during days set apart for them during the months of October and March) irrespective of any specific purpose. The rich may assign this duty to their priests for a fee, while the poor may do it themselves by setting apart more time for their worshiping hour. This observation should indicate that the nature of deities and their relationship to their devotees are important factors that influence the social and ritual arrangements attending prayers, whether said individually or collectively.

The prayers also can be said directly or indirectly. Under the latter provision, the principle of substitution works with wide latitudes. The rich, the invalid, the diseased, the busy, and the impure may take recourse to it to a considerable extent. A substitution of the actor may be most frequent, but depending upon the necessity and the situation, the substitution may extend to ritual acts, ingredients, contents (of worship and of the prayer) and even gods.

If a certain god is being worshiped but one more effective is later on suggested "by a person who knows about such things," he may be substituted for assuring success in the endeavor. Obviously, such substitutions, as we can readily see, can occur only within the ranks of lesser gods; the supreme ones are kept above such a shuffle. Although "prayers by proxy" may be quite common with many in these times of change, they are left behind in favor of the direct approach if the crisis really deepens, or if it relates to one's near and dear ones. In this ultimate context "everybody knows how to pray, to implore, to beseech the Almighty."

All the above distinctions assume a *basic* two-way relationship between the deity and the devotee. The transaction is completed, in thought at least, when the deity has "answered" his devotee's prayers, or even when the deity has "received and accepted" them. When concerned with the thought structure, there is another interesting dimension. Prayers, very often, especially those in Sanskrit and originated by a renowned saint, or commentator, or philosopher, are a tradition in themselves, and to them are attached, normally as legends and tales, the names of some well-known saints and devotees from various parts of India as an evidence of attestation towards the efficacy and potency of such prayers.

When saying such a prayer, a contemporary devotee feels as if great souls stand behind his prayer because it was their prayer. He then does not feel alone and derives faith and support from the glorious passage of the prayer through time. This diachronic perspective behind certain famous prayers is neither a whim of the few nor is it hard to discover in the field. The devout cite their experiences to claim that such a diachronic company (to invent a bit of sociological slang) is not only real but truly helpful in making their prayers work. Symbolically, therefore, if Po was the original person who invented a particular prayer centuries ago, his following over time could conceivably refer to Po — when praying towards the same deity who was originally addressed. Unless there is some specific reason for somebody to keep such prayers a secret, they are openly shared, advocated, and expounded in detail, leading to a following at any one time.

The same basic phenomenon may be observed in an encapsulated form in another way. Whatever the prayer — if it comes from a famous sage of the past, so much the better — one's *gurū* may agree to work as a "catalyzer" (from the viewpoint of the devotee), standing between him and his deity. "One's real *guru* supervises all that transpires between his disciple and the god, and obviously, the former does not do anything without the consent of his spiritual teacher." So, often a *guru* may act to obtain appropriate results for his disciple from the deity. This is of course an act of kindness and piety on the part of the *guru*, which also enhances his spiritual powers.

Another alternative arrangement is that, in an extreme crisis, a *guru* may be moved to grant a prayer directly without apparently going to the deity — or so at least may be the thinking of a devout disciple. It continues to be commonplace knowledge that the *genuine gurus* (who are admittedly considered to be rare) carry enormous spiritual powers and that there is *nothing* beyond them: "Actually, they produce miracles."

Still another arrangement is that where the devotee and the deity are interpolated by an additional temperamentally complementary deity to advance the chances of success of the devotee's prayer. Obviously, the intermediary deity should be "heard" by the main deity. The famous examples of such arrangements, the devotees say, come from such teams as Sita-Rama, Hanuman-Rama, Bharat-Rama, and Radha-Krishna. The link evidently can get longer and more complicated in some cases.

Collective praying, let us note here, does not exclude any of the above arrangements as far as the deity-devotee relationship is concerned. Although it cannot be denied that collective praying does produce, in the Durkheimian sense, a feeling of exuberance and solidarity among the members of the group, the identity of the individual, we must emphasize, is not lost under normal circumstances. Only the exceptionally devout are known to be able to do that. The example is of course given of saints like Chaitanya Mahaprabhu in this regard. "Those who claim that they can dissolve their identity frequently and freely [in their devotion to God] are very often fakes who intend to impress the congregation by their artificially induced emotional states," argued a Sangh-Keertan leader of renown from Vrindaban. But, of course, to be able to submerge one's identity while praying is a most desirable goal for the devotee. It is by reaching this state, the devotees argue, that a soul truly stands in communion with the Whole, of which it is, after all, a part. Prayers, therefore help the parts to stand in appropriate relationship to the Whole, according to the *bhakti* idioms.

Collective praying, following essentially the explanation set forth by powerful saints like Chaitanya, is considered to be helpful in many different ways. It draws in the lukewarm and the doubting (who would not pray if they were left alone) to participate in and to realize the significance of praying. The emotional charge that collective participation produces helps shake off the doubts of the devotees on the fringe. The collective enterprise, at least in modern times, allows for sharing of time, expense, and energy; and the entire *keertan* event is not a burden of a single individual anymore. (Earlier, the *rājās* and the *talukdārs* used to do that, given the conveniences they had at their command.) For the devout, the collective praying (done loudly, even with the help of loudspeakers these days) disseminates the Holy Name to the idle of a whole *mohallā* [neighborhood], or even farther. Also an active role in collective praying can easily intimate that one is very *dhārmika* — hence "a pious soul in the community." (In most of the towns and villages today such a characterization is helpful; it may have even certain pragmatic advantages in the locality — at least, such a person may wield some extra influence over his *keertan* mates.) The collective efforts can also pull in (or buy in) renowned saints, career-*keertan*ists and expert musicians who adorn and glorify the group's activities at least on such special occasions as Krishna *Janamāstamī*. The size of the crowd, the religious aura created on the podium, and the many hours spent in prayers — either sung, recited, or advocated — combine to make the event a success. The common man in the congregation, then, feels more elated. He gets *darshan* of the holy persons, who can truly, by their mere presence, help him in his spiritual journey. If, however, he has some vexing illness in the family (or the *kula*), he may try to obtain an audience with a holy man, who, in turn may tell him about a special prayer for the purpose. Some may even prescribe certain herbs for the purpose.

The collective prayers may also follow a recognizable sequence of steps to honor the deities and gods of all kinds. For example, a prayer session may begin with an invocation to the god Ganesha (who will protect the sacred event from any accident or disruption), moving next to numerous gods and goddesses that surround Shiva and Vishnu, including astrological stars, mythological figures, and natural elements like earth, sky, water, and fire. The third phase may be to move to chosen devotees of the chief deity. For example, Hanumān for Rāma and Arjun for Krishna may be "invited." An invocation to one's *gurūs*, famous saints of the sect, and other *siddhas* must immediately follow. All of this "introductory" invocation of course helps the congregation to "get in touch with" the chief deity, who is finally prayed to and extolled in a number of ways, mostly by recalling his benevolent deeds towards his devotees. This is, of course, the climax of the event. Once this phase is over, the invoked gods must be appropriately requested to "return in peace" to their abodes. Usually appropriate prayers drawn from a scripture like *Ramacharitamānas* help do it when accompanied by worshiping activities. Once all deities return in peace, their *prasād* [blessed food] is obtained and the group may disperse soon after to join "the world that they had left behind for a while to seek a brief respite."

It may also be mentioned here that recitals of sacred texts, when undertaken for an explicit purpose, work like one long prayer that has to be finished during a specified period (e.g. in twenty-four hours, a week, a fortnight, or even a month) by observing some rules of austerity, ritual purity, and seclusion. These recitals may also be undertaken either singly or collectively.

Even *mohallā* committees exist today in towns for such undertakings — some composed only of women (since they have free afternoons) and some mixed. Thus one may volunteer to participate in a sacred recital to help his neighbor in seeking divine intervention in an ongoing litigation or sickness. As a related variation, some prayers may actually be so long that they cannot be recited in a day, but may have to be done in several days to coincide with some auspicious days. An important example of this kind is provided by *Sri Durgāsaptasati Stotra*, which is divided into thirteen chapters with a text of seven hundred verses in Sanskrit. However, since this must be recited during the nine-day period occurring twice every year devoted to the goddess Durgā, the task can be suitably divided either by the devotee or by the substitute whom the devotee may appoint to perform on his behalf. Only the men do it; hence the women cannot be of much help here. Further, since the prayer has to be done with required religious formalities, the task is much more extensive.

Again, these formalities (called *sāngopānga* in Sanskrit) follow a standardized pattern where, besides the regular worship of the deity, a number of preparatory and concluding steps are carried out, called *dhyāna* [invocation by sacred incantations and meditation of the form of the deity], and *nayāsa* [certain ritual steps through which the devotee prepares himself to undertake the actual recital], etc. An idea of such elaborations may be obtained from a Sanskrit-Hindi book published by a well-known press for religious books in northern India (Gita Press, Gorakhpur). While the Sanskrit text of the prayer to the goddess (with special meditation instructions at the beginning of every chapter) occupies 118 pages, the introductory and the concluding material occupies approximately 122 pages. These latter categories of pages are there of course "to enhance the effect of the prayer." This same prayer, as the book states towards its end (on page 233), helps one attain all the four major goals of a Hindu's life — *dharma, artha, kāma,* and *moksha.*

Besides, the compiler has produced some thirty incantations that, when singly recited with every verse of the main prayer, grant blessings of the goddess that could work toward anything from collective welfare and easing world crises or controlling an epidemic, to predicting one's future through one's dreams. The book also lists thirty specific "works" that the prayer can perform when it is recited with a specified incantation. Despite these specific assignments, however, the fact that the prayer helps attain devotion to the deity is endlessly emphasized, as it is held to be the most noble aim to work for.[4]

Given the diversity and complexity of the Hindu prayers in different sects, the observations of this section naturally do not exhaust either variety or detail. However, the do bring together some major general features of the prayers, which may be easily comparable at an intercultural level.

PRAYERS AS A "LANGUAGE OF EXCHANGE"

Our aim of accounting for functions and meanings of prayers will be similar in this section as well, but with an altered emphasis.

Varieties

We have so far taken it for granted that all prayers originate in the Sanskritic tradition, and that they may only gradually get translated into regional dialects, keeping their essential cultural elements intact. Obviously it is one side of the coin — and incomplete at that. For example, translations, however well done, do alter the cultural content of the original, especially when the translator brings with him the values of the regional subculture. Further, if deities vary regionally (as they do in India) in significance, in form, and in disposition, the prayers associated with them, wherever translated, should also reflect these differences.

More precise studies of such changes need to be done, and prayers offer a very sensitive piece of thought and writing, where major

---

[4]   I compared a publication in English from southern India for the same prayer (Shankaranarayanan 1968). The results were not much different. The prayer, discussed in greater philosophical detail, has an introductory section of 129 pages, giving the significance of the prayer and all the ritual preparations that are required. The English translation of 700 verses takes 138 pages with spaces for special meditations at the beginning of each chapter. Finally, the concluding section of 47 pages, again given to specialized prayers (for the goddess) that would enhance an appreciation of the glory of the main prayer, also presents appropriate "secrets" about how to use the prayer as a "practical manual" and as a "purposive science." The "works" assigned to the prayer in this book generally conform to those given by the book considered earlier. One could count them over 30 here. One specialized usage: If one wants to remove somebody's wrath, this prayer, in 13 chapters, should be read in the following sequence: chapters 13,1; 12,2; 11,3; 10,4; 9,5; 8,6; and 7,7. The underlying Hindu principle is that sequence of ritual activity determines its meaning and consequence. A reversed order may mean the opposite consequence.

changes, whenever consciously brought about by a translator or a saint or a commentator, can normally be explained after an intensive inquiry. If prayers tend to resist change to preserve their authenticity and efficacy, there is also a contradictory tendency — prayers are profusely translated in numerous regional languages and local dialects, for it is both religiously desirable and actually essential for wider dispersal. It means that for major prayers in Sanskrit there may be found vernacular translations or renderings for wider understanding, presenting two distinct levels which can be compared for a study.

Popular versions of the Sanskrit original are often obtainable, and they do not have to be either less authoritative or less effective *if* the persons responsible for producing such versions are renowned saints and devotees of God. *Ramacharitamānas* in the north is cited as an outstanding example (and, we know, the south, the east and the west have also produced similar regional authorities in India). This rule applies even today with such renowned contemporary saints as Anandmai Mā and Sai Bābā, among several others. Such religious personages are supposed to originate as well as translate prayers, while adding "more special spiritual force" to them. Actually, the devotees may develop a body of prayers just around the miracles of these saints, which append to those meant for deities.

However, such prayers remain secondary in the larger context; they remain group-specific, carrying lore of a religious personage fixed around the enduring values of renunciation, piety, true devotion, spiritual miracles, etc. In popularization of prayers, the language of expression and the religious personage both have very significant parts to play; they reinforce each other, but the role of the latter personage is more crucial, "because prayers, in essence, work through the force of one's faith in, and intensity for, the *bhaktī* of the Lord. Even if a devotee does not understand the meaning of a prayer, and he is not learned enough to keep its linguistic niceties in their proper places, his faith and spiritual intensity help carry the message to God. Hence the true language of any prayer is the faith that links the devotee to the deity." These observations come from a renowned Sanskritist from an Ayodhyā-based Sanskrit school, who was recently honored in New Delhi for his scholarship in grammar.

However, popular renderings of Sanskrit prayers are constantly made, because not all people can become attracted towards something which they cannot comprehend. If a popular version has a stamp of authority from a spiritual leader, so much the better for the common man; but if it does not, many may settle for something that they can make some sense out of. Once this fact is accepted it is not difficult to realize that even popular versions may belong to different categories of cultural legitimacy. At the top of course stand such works which, as we have already indicated, come from renowned saints like Tulsidās, Meerā, Sūrdās, Kabīr, and Chaitanya (primarily for northern India). The prayers that they produced are already recognized as *mantra* of immense potency. They are as good as — or even better than — some in Sanskrit. One reason is that not only did these personages produce what illustrates, and even refines, the cherished values of the Sanskrit literature, but they, by their actions, had set an example of the *bhakta* lifeways. This cardinal principle keeps guiding the product that appeared since then, and even today. Higher cultural legitimacy is awarded to those prayers that are backed by an exemplary instance of the *bhaktī* behavior. These are "tested" prayers and hence most effective in the time of need.

Next come the prayers that are popular because they have been examples of either scholarship, musical composition, or prolific — and freely understandable — expression, or all of these. Again, while these features become the carrying force for such prayers, the basic principle of keeping and honoring the sets of ultimate values is assiduously maintained. These may be widely used, but their spiritual test may be often provided by some devotee other than the author. Such a prayer is spread by word of mouth and in this way it gains further popularity. (In Uttar Pradesh, an example of this kind of work is provided by Rādhey Shyāma Rāmāyana and Binduji's *keertan*s.) Other such prayers, if they remain untested for long, may disappear after the initial fascination wears off. They become only a ripple in the pond of popular literature. Since the latter is a very large category, several layers of quality become immediately apparent, at the top of which may stand the acknowledged poets and writers (who are chiefly — or only — appreciated for their literary skill, even when they are writing or composing a "prayer").

The component of faith may be totally lacking here, leaving a question whether they are prayers at all. On the other extreme may appear village bards who compose a devotional prayer to catch the ear of the devout to invoke the sentiment of piety and charity in him. These may snatch a line from a popular film song to weave other parts of the composition around it; but whatever the improvisation, a mention of some ultimate cultural values, an echo of the reflective words of a regionally renowned saint, and a distant image of the *bhaktī-bhakta-bhagvān* trilogy is almost invariably required to gain attention. Sources of borrowings do not matter if these criteria are satisfied.

The rural devout and the rural literati remain two major sources for either producing or bringing in appropriate prayers for the deities of concern. If, however, the rural devotee is also of the rural literati, the effect of his prayers is similar to what we have described earlier for the urban class. Villagers know very well how to retain and incorporate such valuable rural products in their rural ethos for a long time to come. The specific contents may get altered or added to over time, but this is not of much concern, as long as the personage is remembered in terms of some tangible objects (a temple, a hut, a mud platform, or even a place where such-and-such a tree stood before) and the prayers that he asked to be recited in happiness and triumph, and tragedy and failure get recited.

Related to these general prayers is another category. These prayers, mostly event-describing, rather than reflective, are generally more direct in their purpose. Folk deities here would like simple, undisguised, and specific statements from these devotees; if there are some circumlocutions, there must be some evident purpose behind it — for example, making the deity understand some implicit matters that cannot be publicly stated for the fear of offending the violators of specific moral or ethical codes. Such prayers are evidently quite topical and localized, for they are tied to the episodes of one village or several that are situated close together.

In between these two poles of popular prayers, represented by scholars and village literati, there are again several discernible categories which need a more detailed study than I can here provide. But I must refer to them because they constitute a very sizable and significant body. The upper layer here is represented by priests and scholars of traditional style, and the lower one by the women folk who devoutly observe numerous feasts, festivals, and ceremonies the year round.

The priests, and even some religious-minded young university graduates (mostly studying Hindi, Sanskrit, ancient Indian culture, etc.), now increasingly write about the domain that in practice almost exclusively belonged to the women observing *teej* and *teuhār*, following oral traditions and familial practices. Examples from the scores of such titles that I recently came across in Uttar Pradesh, Delhi, and Rajasthan are: *Complete fasts and festivals for all the twelve months* (n.d.) by Bharatiya and Brahmachari (Mathura); same title (n.d.) by Hiramani Singh "Sathi," M.A. (Allahabad); and *Customs and practices of Rajasthan* (1966) by Sukhvir Singh Gahlot (Block Development Officer, Ratangarh, Jaipur).

All of these books provide at least four types of prayers — original in Sanskrit (at least one in every volume that I have seen), original prayers by renowned saints, new prayers written either by authors or by the *gurū*s of authors, and prayers that were until recently orally transmitted by women but are now written down, as known to the authors, after "some consultation" with old women and old priests. The last category of prayers, let us note, often end by saying "As the deity [name given here] blessed so-and-so [a character of the folk tale or a story] with such-and-such things [e.g. progeny, riches, health, wifehood, divine grace, *bhaktī*, etc.], the deity may do the same to all [implicitly to those who are praying at that time]." The published books, however, sometimes drop it, but they always add a paragraph on the significance of a fast or a festival in modern times.

To summarize, in terms of the language of prayers, it could be Sanskrit, Hindi, or a regional language — or any of the dialects of these. But prayers in Sanskrit stand at the top; this language has recognizable cultural legitimacy of its own. It is the ideal language for prayers, as it were, despite its limited popularity at present. Hindi for the north (and southern regional languages) stands as the next most employed medium for Hindu prayers, scores of which have become as — or even more — legitimate as those in Sanskrit. Prayers in these languages cater to the majority with or without interpretation, but they do *not* (for they cannot) replace the ideas inherent in Sanskrit literature.

There is, then, a fairly clear rule-of-thumb about translations: originals are always better and more effective, and they rank higher than their translations. If the language of the original version cannot be understood, the translations serve the purpose. But classics like *Ramacharitamānas*, I was repeatedly told, stand beyond this characterization, "for it is really not a translation of Valmiks' work." Reflective language is more extolled (appreciation of it is another matter) than the descriptive and illustrative, and the emotional over the tersely argumentative.

Then, the standard vehicle of prayers has always been poetry rather than prose. The former can be sung and can be illusively cryptic, leading to alternative interpretations for decades and centuries to come.

Language and the Structure of Thought

Let us now turn to an interesting related problem: how, and how effectively it seems, does the language of prayers convey the idea of exchange lying behind words, and what are some general characteristics in this regard that stand out in the Hindu devotional prayers? To be sure, all prayers are not uniform as far as the moods and the attitudes of the devotees that they inevitably reflect are concerned. Not only are the trials and tribulations of a devotee's spiritual life reflected there, the closeness to and distance from the deity are also evident.

Thoughts are freely "exchanged" with one's deity, mostly in the form of a dialogue, even if the prayers may not often be written in that way. There are certain general notions that guide such expressions. A true devotee is supposed to stand very close to his deity. This closeness brings spiritual power according to those who surround him, but it brings informality for him that is often expressed in prayers. The devotee, then, may fret and frown over his "deity's behavior." He may complain about his deity's "heartlessness" and also about his "indifference and delay"; and he may, when he sees fit, gibe the deity to goad him to action.

In the most intimate hours of the *bhakti bhāva*, a devotee, I was repeatedly told by the devout, may even rebuke his deity — "a rebuke that arises out of fathomless love for Him." Instances were cited of devotees "who took to rebuking their most loved one as a regular mode of prayer, at least in public, although these same persons might have lavished adoration on their *ārādhya-deva* [deity of worship] in secret." Sometimes these are mere façades to conceal the real depth of one's devotion from the surrounding people. Here the culturally valued principle is: if one keeps one's actual depth of devotion a secret from the common crowd, the "fruits" of devotion are obtained faster, as there are few interruptions from the outside.

These intimacies of the devotee are reciprocated by the deity. He "speaks" back in prayers. He settles the position of such devotees in most unambiguous terms: he regards them as the nearest and the dearest ones in his whole creation. He speaks about the influence and the hold that these devotees have on him. In fact, he would do anything for them; he bars nothing from them; and there is nothing that he cannot offer in return to them for their unflinching devotion and dependence. The deity even forsakes his vow to honor his devotee's, as a famous song of Surdas says. Briefly, therefore, a devotee's sincere and complete dependence on his deity brings out a reciprocal response: "the deity feels dependent on his devotee."

Like begets like even at this level, and not only in the social world, allowing us to assert that the basic idea and logic of exchange are squarely (and very often consistently) met in the structure of prayers. They are not merely one-way movements of thought and action, as a hasty look at them might initially suggest. Further, there is graduation of both thought and action that flows back and forth between the deity and the devotee. Prayers record these movements in all their gusto and frustrations. Nothing, as in the social world, is given that is free of the idea of reciprocation sooner or later. The same rule of social relationships applies to the entire world of prayers.

The structure of devotional thought, to be sure, closely reflects the paradigm of social relations. It is actually patterned after it, as we demonstrated above, and not beyond or beside it. If one decides to establish a relationship with God, either as child or friend or servant or beloved, how is one going to behave toward him, except by establishing a homology with the social world. Thus, if the *bhakti* movement abolishes (at least ideally) caste, creed, and rank distinctions, it maintains and glorifies the most essential social relationships. The joys, emotions, and depressions of these social relationships enchant the devotee and the deity in an equal measure; they both love, reciprocate, and cherish these infatuations "that are beyond the erosion of time." Hence sang Meera about her "eternal" lover and husband (Krishna), mocking the one her parents gave to her for this world (Rānā). The true *bhaktī*, the saint sings, transforms the transient of the social world into permanent bliss.

The above homology has had some pervasive influence on the character and social organization of the entire *bhaktī* movement. Numerous temples, sects of *sādhus*, their numerous prayers every morning and evening, and the attending congregations endlessly repeat the paradigms of social relationships during every period of worship. They seek the deity either as a child or a parent or a beloved; and while they of course lament that it is not easy, they are almost endlessly bent upon making it true. They draw courage in this task from their saints who proved that it can be done.

Deities in temples and *sādhus* in sects live, as it were, to reach the same goal. The deities, although immortal, live like mortals (they eat, sleep, and dress), while the *sādhus* renounce the same family bonds that they are going to seek in the changed, divine, context. (Further similar points can be made on closer inspection.) Although most of such prayers of the millions of Hindus remain unrecorded, they obviously represent (and repeat) a model set by their devout leaders. In this sense, devotional prayers follow an essentially similar structure of thought, the major arrangements of which can be clearly understood through a study of the prayers of saints.

Although the scope of the present attempt precludes a more formal analysis of the thought structure of chosen prayers, it seems perfectly possible — much like Lévi-Strauss' *Structural study of myth* and his other recent studies of mythology. Such an approach can help one check some of the observations made above, particularly with regard to the internal consistency of prayers in expressing primary social relationships and cultural values and in evolving and arranging specified mythological personages and relationships to convey specified meanings and functions. (Moreover, the same approach can also help one observe the underlying "grammatical rules," some of which are restricted to prayers and some of which in general hold for any mythical narrative).

Under the prayer-specific category may appear the usage of, for example, Hindi second-person pronouns — *aap*, *tum*, and *tū*. Normally, as we proceed from the first to the third, increasing emotional nearness and informality is indicated. But then, there are other usages as well, where they may begin to reflect increasing grudge, reproach, and insult. Prayers may reflect these — and other — meanings. Prayers, as an index of humility, on the other hand, may play down the *frequent* (chaste) use of first-person pronouns. This may be particularly true of the prayers written under *dāsya bhāva* (see above).

While answering prayers, the deity may demonstrate the reverse order of the usage of, or preference for, first- and second-person pronouns. His "I" and *tū* (endearing "you") are quite consistent, while for the devotee this sequence will mean hurling an insult at the deity. More such "cross-usages" can be plotted by studying specific prayers. In terms of the gender, prayers, as an offshoot of *bhaktī* (and like it), are characterized as "female." The characteristics of surrender, soft speech, emotionalism (including loud wailing), and abjuring coercion and command — all conform to the Hindu view of femininity.

If mythological material is carefully studied, it also yields clear arrangements that follow syntactic rules of correspondence and concatenation. For the initiated, mythological figures like Yashodā, Hanumān, Rādhā, and Sudāmā stand for such specified kinds of devotional relationships as *vātsalyā, dāsya, madhur,* and *sakhya*, respectively. Similarly, one could prepare a catalogue of mythological events and personages that illustrate how social inequality, impiety, villainy, depravity, and vice are eroded and removed through the grace of God.

Another catalogue could be prepared of the famous devotees who really "conjugate" the divine for the good of the mundane. These catalogues, read as separate columns, illustrate primary categories out of which the content of a devotional prayer is most commonly composed. If the entries in columns are switched, they produce cultural anomalies. For example, if *bhakta* Hanumān is used (instead of Rādhā) in the context of lover-beloved expressions in prayers, the problem becomes obvious. "Even the novice does not make such a mistake." More aspects of such an approach need to be separately considered.

CONCLUDING REMARKS

Prayers, as considered above, reflect only some of the essential features which are contained in the devotional context. As almost a virgin field of study, their many preliminary dimensions need to be charted out in the context of the traditional domains of social anthropological inquiry. We may here remark only on one general aspect.

Prayers, like the entire *bhaktī* movement, point out contradictions that have lingered on without being resolved. Here they move beyond the domain of social prestations. They, for example, espouse social equality in the face of institutionalized inequalities of the caste system, and they have, as yet, not won on any lasting basis. But the ideal lingers on, getting an occasional fillip from religious personages on a regional basis. Prayers, as a part of sincere devotion, decry and aim to cut through the cobwebs of ritualism that pervade all of Hinduism. Thoughts, and not techniques, are important before God, one is repeatedly told in devotional songs; and while rituals become redundant for those who have achieved the *bhaktī*, they are meant to be only minimally followed by the beginners.

More serious philosophical contradictions are brought forth when the prayers repeatedly declare that with God's blessing, one can cut through the bondages of *karma* [action] and *punarjanma* [rebirth]. Mythology provides strong illustrations to support the claim. Not only are the devout members of the lowest caste (and even tribals) accepted by God, but even prostitutes, bandits, and destitutes. And if bondages of *karma* cease to operate in such instances, hope exists for all. When this "rebellious" thought is further pushed, it is logical to find that a devotee does not care for the fourth ideal of the traditional life — *moksha*. Instead, he craves for the eternal company of his deity (i.e. of the form of God that he fervently worships). Briefly, therefore, *bhaktī* prayers, standing close to the social order, produce a *total*, alternative system of thought that exerts increasing influence on the social as well as the philosophical framework of the Hindu society. And the recent political movements toward egalitarianism discover here — often by chance — a strong parallel force that may be popularly tapped in one form or another.

REFERENCES

BHARATIYA, ROOPKISHORE, KRISHNA R. BRAHMACHARI
    n.d.   *Vrat aur teuhār* (in Hindi, second edition). Mathura, India: Govardhan Pustkālaya.
GAHLOT, SUKHVIR SINGH
    1966   *Rajasthān ké reet-rivāz* (in Hindi). Jaipur, India: Roshan Lal Jain and Sons.
KHARE, R. S.
    1975   "Hindu social inequality and some ideological entailments," in *Culture and society*. Edited by B. N. Nair. Delhi: Thompson Press.
MAUSS, MARCEL
    1967   *The gift* (Norton edition). Translated by Ian Cunnison. New York: Norton.
    1968   "Oeuvres I: Les fonctions sociales du sacré," in *Marcel Mauss oeuvres. Edition critique et présentation de Victor Karady*. Paris: Les Editions du Minuit.
PANDIT RAMNARAYANDUTTA SHĀSTRI, *translator*
    1960   *Durgāsptasatī stotra* (in Hindi and Sanskrit, eleventh edition). Gorakhpur, India: Gita Press.
ROBERT, PAUL
    1972   *Dictionnaire alphabétique et analogique de la langue française.* Paris: Société du Nouveau Littré.

SHANKARANARAYANAN, S.
1968   *Glory of the divine mother: devi māhātmayam.* Pondicherry, India: Dipti Publications.

SINGER, M.
1966   "The Radha-Krishna bhajans of Madras City," in *Krishna: myths, rites and attitudes.* Edited by M. Singer. Honolulu: East-West Press.
1972   *When a Great Tradition modernizes: studies in Madras.* New York: Praeger.

SINGH, HIRAMANI
n.d.   *Vrat aur teuhār* (Hindi). Allahabad, India: Durga Pustak Bhandar.

Power in Hindu Ideology and Practice

SUSAN WADLEY

The utility of power as an analytical concept has long been recognized by anthropologists, whether dealing with South Asia or with other areas. The term "power" as it has been used traditionally by South Asian anthropologists, however, reflects a Western, ethnocentric, materialist bias. Consequently, their discussions of dominant caste, kinship relations, the *jajmāni* system, etc., though perhaps descriptively correct, do ultimate injustice to the phenomena themselves. Alternatively, if we look at power in South Asian terms, a very different understanding of the same phenomena (dominant castes, *jajmāni* system, kinship relations) emerges. I hope this new understanding will aid the correction of imbalances in the weights given to intellectualist ideas focusing on the principle of pure/impure and to a materialist, behaviorist methodology.

The aim of this paper is thus twofold, creating a new duality out of a methodological point and a substantive one. I aim to show the methodological value of paying close attention to what our informants say, whether informal comments, songs, stories, myths, or prayers. I wish to develop the substantive role played by and importance of the concept *shakti* [also *śaktī*] [power] in South Asian society. The reader may wonder at the conjunction of dominant castes, *jajmāni* system, and kinship relations with *shakti*, a well-known religious term. Comprehending power in Hindu rather than Western terms, however, leads to an awareness of a related Western imposition on Indian society, a truncated view of religion, which must also be redefined in terms of native Hindu concepts.

METHODOLOGICAL ORIENTATION

In the longer study on which this paper is based,[1] my primary consideration was with comprehending rural Hindu religious behavior by analyzing the structure of the verbalized beliefs of its practitioners. There has been little previous work on the structure of the concepts of Hindu villagers. Furthermore, in the work that has been done, almost no attention has been paid to Little Traditional or local-level texts. Yet despite the visible complexity and apparent chaos of village religious behavior, the conceptual system of the practitioner is systematically organized and provides a conceptual reality for his ritual activity. By analyzing the oral traditions of a north Indian village, we can identify the principal conceptual categories in which religious action takes place. One of these conceptual categories is that of power.

Studies of religious traditions in India have been primarily concerned with the doctrines of the Sanskritic traditions, the Great Traditions of Hinduism. Anthropologists have countered this tendency to discuss Hinduism in terms of theology and philosophy by, for the most part, merely acknowledging formalized religious doctrine and, perhaps more importantly, disavowing any Little Tradition doctrine.[2] A notable exception is the work of Louis Dumont (1970); his concern with shastric and esoteric Sanskritic texts leads, however, to a Brahmanic, elite orientation which may be as misleading as not dealing with texts at all. Yet to a large extent the nature of the anthropological discipline demands little more than lip service to the religious doctrines of the Great Traditions. Anthropology has historically been concerned with the relations among religious practices and practitioners and, to some extent, doctrinal ideas. Moreover, the lack of context for the texts expounding the Great Traditional doctrines does not allow the anthropologist to comprehend these relationships, although recent advances in textual analysis and social history may partially remove this hindrance.

There is yet another problem related to the anthropologists' lack of concern with the ideas of religious traditions. Modern anthropology, beginning at least with Durkheim, is based on the primacy of behavior. It maintains that ideologies must be subordinated to actual, preferably visible (and thus empirically controlled) behavior. This viewpoint is increasingly under attack, as the influence of French anthropology

---

[1] The discussion which follows may appear at times sketchy; it is based on and adapted from a much longer work (see Wadley 1973), and a full discussion of analytic principles and results is not possible here.

[2] It appears, in fact, that many anthropologists have denied either the possibility of local-level doctrine (or primitive doctrine, see Radcliffe-Brown 1965:156) or the possibility of its being systematized.

(Lévi-Strauss and Dumont) and the development of folklore studies toward a structural semantic approach (see Maranda and Köngäs Maranda 1971) illustrate. In recent years, anthropologists have thus become increasingly aware of the need to examine the verbal components of religious behavior, both in statements about religious belief and in ritual itself (see Freedman 1967; Gombrich 1971; Goody 1962; Tambiah 1968). Gombrich, in *Precept and practice* (1971), for example, relies heavily upon the verbal statements of his Sinhalese informants (statements about religion and statements used in ritual) in his analysis of the relations between Pali doctrine and present-day ritual behavior in Sri Lanka. In a similar fashion, but with no concern for comparison with Sanskritic texts, this study examines what a north Indian villager says about and to his deities in relation to how he behaves toward them.

Yet the anthropological behavioral bias continues and is notable in the realm of Indian studies: while studies of Hindu doctrine by the philosopher and theologian are based almost totally on textual materials which are usually Sanskritic, studies of the Little Traditions of Hinduism are almost never concerned with textual materials, for which context is available. One result is that the standard texts of the north Indian villager are seldom even translated.[3] Clearly, studies of Little Tradition religious doctrines are lacking.

The purpose of this paper is to begin narrowing this conceptual gap in our knowledge about Indian religion; that is, to outline one segment of the conceptual belief system of a north Indian Hindu villager. My concern here is to present one idea which gives meaning to north Indian peasants' religiosity. In particular, I focus on that aspect of the conceptual system which concerns the natives' beliefs about the nature of their deities and the deities' relationships to men. Two basic questions become readily apparent: "What is the nature of those many beings to whom and for whom rituals are enacted?" and "What is there in the belief system of the Hindu villager that makes necessary the performance of rituals?" These two questions, essentially who and why, interlock at the level of social action, where both are used to define situations and lead to certain courses of action.[4] In the discussion which follows, I shall sketch the answers to these two questions, focusing on the ordering principle of power in Karimpur belief.

[3] Some authors have used or mentioned conceptual material in substantiating their theses; until recently, however, none have attempted to explore the possibilities of using non-Great Traditional texts in understanding village religious behavior.

[4] A secondary aim is to relate these two questions, dealing specifically with the belief system, to actual ritual behavior; that is, to define the ideas which organize and give meaning to ritual behavior and to demonstrate the points at which religious categories of thought and categories of action interact (see Wadley 1973: Chapter 8 for such an attempt).

RESEARCH SETTING

I conducted research for this paper in Karimpur, Uttar Pradesh, India.[5] Karimpur is a Brahman-dominated village of 1,380 people belonging to twenty-two castes. (For previous works on this village see Wiser 1933, 1958; Wiser and Wiser 1971.) It is a village of farmers in a semiremote area and remains relatively untouched by modern agricultural methods. Throughout the past forty years, the *jajmāni* system described by Wiser (1958) has changed, with a noticeable decline in participation by some castes. The Brahmans dominate economically (they control 54 percent of the land), numerically (they comprise 22.4 percent of the population), and politically (pre- and post-Independence headmen have all been Brahman). The literacy rate is low, especially among women and the lower castes, and the primary mode of transmission of religious themes is the oral traditions of the area: songs, myths, stories, ritual sayings, etc. These oral traditions form the corpus of data for the major part of the following analysis. The remainder of the analysis is based upon the religious observances and social actions which occurred during my fifteen-month stay in Karimpur during 1967-1969. The aim of the following analysis is to explore one of the basic principles by which people in Karimpur order their religious thoughts and actions, the principle of *shakti*, power.

THE NATURE OF KARIMPUR SUPERNATURALS

One of the first problems facing any investigator of Hindu religion is, "With what objects is it concerned?" This critical question has been largely ignored by most Indian anthropologists, although Indologists seem to be more aware of the problem. This question is particularly important because, in any discussion of a Hindu pantheon of gods, godlings, demons, ghosts, etc., we may feel that we should be able to define the boundaries of that pantheon or to enumerate its members.

The nature and classification of Hindu deities, demons, ghosts, etc., is a recurring theme in the literature on South Asia. Unfortunately, most authors do not provide information regarding their definitions of the supernatural, nor do they specify the boundaries of the pantheons

[5] Karimpur is a pseudonym given this village by Wiser (1933, 1958); for the sake of continuity in the literature, I have retained it. The fieldwork on which this study is based was carried out between December 1967 and April 1969. The research was supported by a grant from the National Science Foundation and by the South Asia Committee of the University of Chicago; their support is gratefully acknowledged. My mentors at the University of Chicago, particularly McKim Marriott, Milton Singer, Paul Friedrich, and Ronald Inden, guided and aided me in my attempt to understand Karimpur religion; their help and comments have been invaluable.

discussed. For example, Harper (1959:227) has attempted "to order and classify the supernaturals affecting the inhabitants of the village of Totagadde." If one is going to deal with the order of a Hindu village pantheon as Harper does, a necessary first step is to define what is meant by "Hindu supernatural" and what are the characteristics of beings who are supernaturals. Without this first step, without knowing the limits of the pantheon, any ordering becomes meaningless. This bias in the literature has resulted in narrow, circumscribed discussions of Hindu pantheons, discussions which do injustice to the notion of power or force and which are not related to the reality of the pantheons of deities and demons in the villages of India. We must know with which objects we are dealing before we can comprehend their nature. This essential task presents several problems.

The first difficulty in enumerating the members of a Hindu pantheon for village Hinduism is that there is much inconsistency between the lists of objects that any two Hindus consider as belonging to the realm of religion. It is impossible, then, to define the members of the pantheon for a given area, village, or family without interviewing every last man, woman, and child, constantly hoping that they have not forgotten someone, that some minor deity who can aid or hurt them in some relatively unimportant aspect of their lives has not been temporarily mislaid. Moreover, I would not consider this a worthwhile task. Potentially, all beings can be members of a Hindu pantheon; any being with powers over other beings could be, for the individual concerned, a member of his pantheon. It is possible, however, to make statements about the potential characteristics of that pantheon, about the relationships believed to exist among some members of it, and also about the ways in which members of that pantheon will be treated by men on earth.

Second, there is no bounded supernatural spatial domain. Concepts of "heavenly world" or "underworld" do not define objects of worship, because Hindu deities exist in any or all of the three worlds of the universe. Certainly the idea of "heavenly" does not define Hindu deities, whether good or bad; while valid to some extent, at least for good gods and goddesses, it does not include the yogi, still on earth, or the snakes and others of the underworld. Three worlds are commonly recognized in Karimpur: *svarg lok*, the heaven world, the world above; *majhlī lok*, the middle world (earth); and *pātāl lok*, the lower world. Good and bad deities exist in all three worlds, and movement back and forth among them is considered plausible and natural. For example, Arjuna goes from *majhlī lok*, his home, to *pātāl lok* for the right kind of wood for a sacrifice. Later in the same story he goes to *svarg lok* after a girl. Basuk Dev, the snake king, comes from *pātāl lok* to Karimpur to possess his oracle, while the goddess Devi comes from *svarg lok* to Karimpur to possess hers. Ravana, the evil ruler of Lanka, is a demon who exists in the middle world, as does his antagonist, Rama, the incarnation of Vishnu on earth, representative of good divine power. Only living men and women cannot travel between the worlds, although some claim to do so while asleep. All beings are thus intertwined in an all-encompassing whole. And all these beings are able to aid or hurt others because of internalized (embodied) extraordinary power.

A third difficulty is that there is no noun in Hindi which corresponds to the idea of supernatural, meaning beings with superhuman power. The only noun in Hindi which comes close to including all possible powerful beings is *dēva*, which is defined as both demons and good deities, but not the most evil beings, ghosts, and other spirits of the dead.[6] Fortunately there is an adjectival phrase which refers to all gods, ghosts, demons, etc.: *shakti-sanpann* [literally, power-filled]. Hindu deities are power-filled; all have the power to move in more than one of the three worlds, to assume various bodily forms, and to aid or hurt other beings. Thus the basic characteristic of any god, demon, or ghost is the power which it controls and represents, the fact that it is, in essence, power. Those beings filled with power are the supernaturals, and they constitute the village pantheon.

This conception of Karimpur supernaturals (using the definition "powerful being" for "supernatural") leads to further complications. Other authors have recently introduced us to the idea that every being of the universe embodies its share of *shakti*, a share originating "from a single, all-powerful, perfect, undifferentiated substance, commonly called *brahman* by Hindus" (Marriott and Inden, this volume). The resulting implication is that the Hindu pantheon includes all beings in the universe, and data from Karimpur substantiate this claim.

Since the one common characteristic of all Karimpur deities, both good and bad, is *shakti*, the concepts implied by *shakti* are important. Probably the most widely known connotation is that of the goddesses, of the Goddess Shakti. In this sense, *shakti* implies the female energy of the universe, the energizing principle of the universe without which there would be no motion. But *shakti* does not mean just female power or the representative of female power, but power in general. *Shakti* carries the concepts of strength, energy, and vigor, but strength based on a spiritual embodied force, not merely on physical force. In accord with the South Asian "cognitive nonduality of action and substance"

---

[6] The following dictionary definition corresponds to the Karimpur usage of *dēva*: "*daitya* [demon]; danav [demon]; *bhīmkāy manushya* [fierce men]; *svarg me vicaraN karnewālā divya shakti-sanpann amara prāNī* [animate immortals filled with divine power who "stroll" in heaven]; *devatā* [gods]" (Prasad et al. n.d.). In addition, *dēva* can be contrasted to *devatā*, which definitely refers only to good or goodish supernaturals.

(Marriott and Inden, this volume), a similar nonduality functions in the concept of *shakti*. *Shakti* is neither moral power nor physical power, but both. *Shakti* is a result of morality or right action which is transformed into an embodied *shakti*, which results in a transformed physical state (bodily substance). A being is, at one and the same time, spiritually powerful and physically powerful, and these two facets of his identity are not separate but always coexistent.[7]

Each item of the universe has its share of *shakti*. As Marriott and Inden note, "Every genus of living beings shares from the moment of its generation its defining qualities (*guṇa*), power (*śaktī* [*shakti*]), and actions (*karma*)" (this volume). Every being of the universe thus embodies its share of *shakti*, a share, as noted above, originating from *brahman*. Some beings have more power than others, however; these beings are the powerful beings or supernaturals for those with lesser powers. Moreover, because every being in the universe embodies some power by definition, every being in the universe is potentially a powerful being. Some of the power-filled beings recognized in Karimpur are the normally acknowledged deities such as Shiva, Krishna, Parvati, Ram, Lakshmi, Ganesh, etc. In addition, we find Khan Bahadur, the village guardian deity (he began life as a mere Muslim raja, but because he once aided the village, he is believed to continue to do so); the wheat seeds which are planted on *nāg pānchme* [Snake's Fifth] are allowed to grow for two weeks, and are worshiped and discarded — but which nevertheless must be worshiped in order to insure the year's crops; the yogi who because of his asceticism has extraordinary powers; a bride and groom during their wedding festivities;[8] the plow, worshiped before the sugar cane is sown, and the bullocks, also worshiped, who draw it; husbands at *karva chauth* [Pitcher Fourth], when women worship them; the snake during the summer monsoon; and the woman who died in childbirth and comes back to wreak havoc among those still on earth; these are all *shakti-sanpann* or power-filled.

---

[7] Note the distinction between this concept of power and the Western physical one. The Hindi term closest in meaning to *shakti* is *bal*; but *bal* implies a physical strength, while *shakti* implies a spiritual power — although that spiritual power can be manifested physically. Thus the village wrestler is said to have *bal* but not necessarily *shakti* (of an extraordinary sort), and the gods have *shakti* but not necessarily *bal*.

[8] The bride and groom are recognized for the period of the marriage ceremonies as god and goddess. In Karimpur they are usually considered to be Ram and Sita, so much so that their feet are touched by their elders, including at times elders from higher-ranking castes (an acknowledgment of superiority comparable to the eating of leftover food). There are limits, however, to this physical acknowledgment of powerful status: my "mother," a proper Brahman lady, refused to touch the feet of a Thakur bride and groom, although she did give them money. She could and did call them god and goddess, but her rank was so high that her touching their feet was out of the question.

The preceding examples make it clear that gods, ghosts, and demons have powers of varying kinds, with the primary characteristic being their possible control over human conditions. The wheat seed is power-filled because if it does not grow, men will starve. The plow is power-filled because if it does not turn the soil correctly, there will be no sugar cane. A bride and groom are power-filled because they represent fertility and prosperity, the future growth of the family. A snake is power-filled because it can kill. All that exists in the universe contains some power and can be part of a Hindu pantheon. It is this potential allness which we must recognize in attempting to discuss a Hindu pantheon, particularly in attempting to set limits to it. We must thus recognize the inclusive nature of such a pantheon and avoid setting arbitrary limits; we must recognize that there is no native Hindu conception of a bounded domain of religion or of the spiritual.

This perception of the Hindu idea of the supernatural provides insight into the religiosity of the Hindu villager. All actions toward other beings on the basis of their power and man's potential benefit from it are religious actions, whether that other being is a new bride, a plow, or Shiva. Since all beings have some share of power, all action could be based on this power, all action could be religious; the oft-repeated "Hinduism is a way of life" is no figment of some British administrator's imagination. This stance is especially plausible if we accept Spiro's[9] (1966:66) definition of religion as "an institution consisting of culturally patterned interaction with culturally postulated superhuman beings," in which superhuman beings are "any beings believed to possess power greater than man" (1966:97). Clearly, to Hindus, power-filled beings ("superhumans" in Spiro's terms) are also other men, wheat seeds, the plow, etc. What is important is that everything is considered to have *shakti* and that all interaction on the basis of that *shakti* is religious behavior. The definitive characteristic of Karimpur supernaturals is that they are power-filled. But human and other earthly things are also power-filled. The pantheon of the village of Karimpur is potentially without boundaries. Interaction with supernaturals thus can be and is frequent and does indeed affect all aspects of life, including those generally considered secular by Western-oriented interpreters of South Asian culture. There is, as stated before, no native conception of a bounded domain of religion or the spiritual, and no separation of sacred and profane.

Those beings for whom rituals are enacted are thus those who are believed to have powers which could affect the life of the performer of the ritual. These beings range from Bhagvān, the most inclusive, most

---

[9]   Other definitions of religion could be used to make this point. I chose to use this one because it is, by comparison to Geertz, for example, a relatively limiting one.

powerful god normally recognized in Karimpur, to Krishna, to the bride and groom at a wedding, to one's brother on Brother's Second, etc. To recall a persistent question in the literature, man and god are not disparate beings, locked into different continua, but rather exist along one continuum, based on their recognized powers and qualities.

THE PERFORMANCE OF RITUALS

I have said that the only defining characteristic that applies to all normally recognized Hindu supernaturals is their nature as powerful beings. Yet it is legitimate to ask if, in fact, various gods, godlings, demons, etc., are worshiped because of their powers.[10] Evidence from various verbal traditions in Karimpur gives a definite affirmative answer to this question. Rituals are performed because of a recognition of the powers of another being and one's desire to receive the benefits of that power (birth of a son, curing of illness, *moksha*, etc.) or to avoid the malevolent effects of that power (attack by a ghost, smallpox, death, etc.). Elsewhere I have examined the relationships between perceived powers and the corresponding ritual actions in detail. A brief summary of parts of this analysis should substantiate the claim that men worship their deities because of those deities' potential actions based on their powers.

This analysis is based on the religious literature of Karimpur. The religious literary traditions of Karimpur are not easily categorized into levels or units such as all-India, regional, Sanskritic, vernacular, etc. Likewise, Karimpur deities and rituals are only with difficulty and injustice so categorized. Myths told in Karimpur in the village dialect[11] are found in Sanskritic traditions, while other myths are read in the regional dialect from bazaar pamphlets. The mantras for one ritual are in the village dialect and invoke Sanskritic deities, regional deities, and Mohammed. The corpus of data used in this study was thus any verbal tradition found in Karimpur regardless of its language or the potential origin of its content.

In Karimpur a series of myths are told in connection with rituals. Although rituals are often described in the literature, and although the importance of the physical transaction, the transfer of food which

[10] Note that they are worshiped because of their powers. The manner of this worship, including frequency and types of offerings, depends upon their qualities, including state of purity and share of power.

[11] Karimpur is in a Hindi language area, with a village dialect that can be described as part Braj and part Kanauji based on the discussion of these two regional dialects in Kellogg (1965). Many women, some men, and most young children lack a command of standard Hindi or a broader regional dialect.

occurs in *pūjā*, has been noted (see Babb 1970), the nature of the ultimate transaction, the fact that worship returns benefits, is not specified. Harper (1964:151) states at one point, "Gods are superior to men and thus must be worshipped by men; in return, gods bestow benefits on men." Yet he never explains the exact nature of this superiority and never accounts for his "and thus must be worshipped." Moreover, Harper never tells us what the relationship is between men and the gods which mandates, as he states it, that men should be and are given benefits by the gods. Clearly there is a transaction of some sort occurring: men worship, gods give. Yet aside from the fact of the gods' superiority, the literature offers little which is relevant to this transaction and its underlying principles. In order to give meaning to the ritual idiom, it is necessary to examine the conceptual system to discover the related belief transaction, in this case to discover the exact nature of the opposition worship/benefit.

A structural analysis of the myths told in conjunction with certain rituals (following Lévi-Strauss in spirit if not in detail) allows us to further penetrate the meaning of people's dealings with their varieties of deities. This analysis is summarized here. These myths, called *kathā*, form a category of Karimpur verbal traditions and are prescribed as a part of a ritual called *vrat*. *Vrat* requires that the *kathā* be read or told, that the participants fast, and that worship (*pūjā*) be done to the presiding deity. *Vrat* is a major category of Karimpur ritual activity, and the *kathā* are the primary village exegesis for this ritual. The following is one of the *kathā*:

The kathā *of Tuesday*[12]

A Brahman named Dampati had no son and for this reason both husband and wife were very sad. The Brahman went to the forest in order to do Hanuman's *pūjā*. Along with *pūjā*, he made known to Mahavir his desire for a son. At the house his wife did Tuesday's *vrat* for the gain of a son. On Tuesday after making food and offering it to Hanumān, she ended her fast and began to eat. One time there was a fast for which the Brahman woman could not prepare food and then could not offer it to Hanuman. Making herself a promise that after giving the offering to Hanuman on the next Tuesday, she would eat grain and water, she slept. She remained hungry and thirsty for six days. On Tuesday she fainted. Seeing her great love and faith, Hanuman then became very happy. Giving his *darshan*, he made her conscious and said, "I am very pleased with you. I am giving to you a handsome boy who will do all of your service." Then giving his *darshan* in the form of a boy, Hanuman vanished. The Brahman woman was very happy at getting a handsome boy and she named him Mangal.

At sunset, the Brahman man returned from the forest. Seeing the handsome

---

[12] Tuesday is the day of Hanuman worship and called *mangalvār*. The *kathā* presented here is translated from *saptvār vrat kathā* printed in Delhi by Anand Prakashan and read in Karimpur.

boy happily playing in the house, the Brahman asked his wife, "Who is this boy?" His wife replied, "Hanuman gave his *darshan* and this boy because he was happy with my fast on Tuesdays." Knowing his wife's story full of deception, he thought that she was a bad person who made up the story in order to hide bad habits.

One day the husband went to the well for water. His wife said, "Take Mangal with you." He went with Mangal and after dumping Mangal in the well, he obtained water and returned. Then the wife asked, "Where is Mangal?" Some time later Mangal, smiling, returned to the house. Upon seeing him, the husband was very astonished. That night, Hanuman said to the husband in a dream, "I gave this boy. You understood it a fault of your wife." Knowing this the husband was happy. Then the husband and wife observed Tuesday's fast and began to spend their life in happiness. Any man who reads or listens to the story of Tuesday's fast and keeps the fast by the rules will have all troubles removed and many happy gains, due to the kindness [*krpā*] of Hanuman.

Initial narrative (syntagmatic) analysis of the myths reveals that men worship their gods because of a desire to obtain happiness in this life, as the last line so clearly states. But more important is the insight into the nature of man/god relationships to be gained by a paradigmatic analysis. Faith and service (*bhaktī* and *sevā*) on the part of the worshiper are reciprocated on the part of the deity by mercy and boons (*krpā* and *vardān*). (In the myth above, the woman's worship and fast conducted with great faith and love result in the deity's happiness and the gift of a son.) The transactions represented by these two sets of terms mediate between man and the gods, as do the opposite transactions represented by disrespect or wrong acts by men and anger or revenge by the gods. That is, the paradigmatic message (structural in Lévi-Straussian terms)[13] of these myths is that the relationship between man and god is built on the transformations of faith to mercy and service to boons. Likewise the reciprocal transformation holds: mercy by the gods leads to men's faith; the gods' boons result in men's service. In the *kathā* for Monday, a statement by Parvati to Shiva emphasizes this point:

One time Parvati, seeing his feeling of devotion, said to Shivaji, "This Sahukar is your great devotee and always does your *vrat* and *pūjā* with great trust. You have to make his mind's desires full.". . . Parvati said with persistence, "Maharaj, when your devotee is such a one and he has this kind of sorrow, then you must without doubt make them far because you are always generous to your devotees. You make their sorrows far. If you will not do so, then why will men do your service, *vrat* and *pūjā*?"[14]

[13] Structural analysis includes both syntagmatic and paradigmatic analysis in Saussurian terms. Lévi-Strauss, however, deals almost totally with paradigmatic analysis when discussing his version of the structural analysis of myth.

[14] From the *kathā* of the fast of Monday, translated from *saptvār vrat kathā*, Anand Prakashan, Delhi (see Wadley 1973:89-94 for the complete myth).

Because the gods are power-filled beings and men recognize their powers, men and gods are connected by transactions in these two sets of terms.

At the same time, looking again at the myths syntagmatically (in terms of narrative structure), these same two sets of terms (faith/service and mercy/boons) represent the transformation from sorrow to happiness. Moreover, the myths demonstrate the importance of man's transformation from sinner to devotee, that is, from one who does not have faith and who does not follow the rules of *dharma* to one who follows *dharma* and has faith in more powerful beings. Men worship their gods to avoid sin and to find happiness. They must honor their deities with faith and service, and in return they receive mercy and boons.

The boons which a particular deity can give are a clear illustration of his power, both the amount of power and its potential application. Thus, although a particular god's power is internalized, is embodied, it is materially manifested in the boons which he is able to grant. Men choose the god they worship on the basis of the boon desired, a clear acknowledgment of that deity's power. Yet at all times a god's granting of a boon must be motivated by his feeling of mercy, a feeling motivated by the devotee's faith.[15]

Men's concern for the protection and boons of various deities is also continually reiterated in songs in Karimpur. Singing is a popular recreational activity and a major way of showing devotion (*bhaktī*) to the gods; religious songs (e.g. *bhajan* and *kirtān*) often proclaim the praises of the gods and call upon them to demonstrate their skills. Here are some examples:

I

Bhagvān,[16] a servant came begging at your door;
Prabhu, give your sight to the beggar.
My boat is in the middle of a whirlpool:[17]
Prabhu, without you who is the boatman?
I am standing at the door. I will pray.
Prabhu, ferry me across.
I do not want grain or riches. The house left [behind]
　　is no concern.
From the world this heart is troubled:
This servant comes into shelter.
Bhagvān, a servant came begging for your sight (*darshan*).

15　See Wadley (1973: Chapter 4) for a fuller and more explicit analysis.

16　Bhagvān and Prabhu are generic terms for a good male deity.

17　Many Karimpur devotional songs use the whirlpool analogy for a crisis situation, along with other nautical imagery (the ocean of existence, boatman, ferry across, the far side, etc.).

II

Oh my Bhagvān, tell me where to search for you.
In the whole world I searched and I never found you.
Take me and my unworthy boat across existence, oh Prabhu.
Because you hear a sad voice, come and rescue me.
You came, I heard, and rescued Prahlad:
This is a true story, or false? Tell me.
You did the same to Ganka and Ajamil and Gautam Silmani.
Tell me the path, Prabhu, the stairs by which you can be reached.
Prabhu, now open all the windows of knowledge.

III

My boat of life is in the middle, Kanhaiya,[18]
    Take me across.
Loaded with sins, the boat sinks: without you there is
    no boatman.
Enough. You are my boatman, Kanhaiya: Take me across.
The poet Winod with folded hands is praying.
Fulfill my hopes, Prabhu.
Now take me up, Kanhaiya, take me across.

IV

Bhagvān, when will you save me?
Bhagvān, you saved Dropadi, giving the excuse of a sari;[19]
When will you save me?
Bhagvān, you saved Mira, giving the pretence of a cup;
When will you save me?
Bhagvān, you saved Shivji, giving the excuse of a *thamru*;[20]
When will you save me?
Bhagvān, you saved Arjuna, giving the pretence of an arrow;
When will you save me?

These songs illustrate the devotee's concern for some action by a god in his life, that he be rescued, saved, ferried across, taken across, given knowledge, given shelter, etc. The deity is felt to be the boatman who will row the boat of the devotee through life, aiding him when there is a crisis, as he aided Mira, Dropadi, Arjuna, Prahlad, etc. The deity is a powerful being whose primary function in life is to provide comfort

---

[18] Kanhaiya is another name for Krishna.

[19] This song is concerned with episodes from the legends of Krishna in which he saves various figures: Dropadi is being stripped of her sari in the court of her in-laws when Krishna provides her with an endless sari, thus relieving her shame; Mira refers to Mirabai, a famous devotional poet who is given a cup of poison by Krishna when her family torments her; Arjuna, well known from the Bhagavad Gita, is given an arrow by Krishna to fulfill his warrior *dharma*.

[20] *Thamru* is the drum used by Shiva in beating out his cosmic dance. The association here with Krishna is unclear.

and aid for his devotee.[21] But as the *kathā* discussed earlier tell us, the god will not come to man's aid without first receiving faith and service. Men therefore do *pūjā*, fast, recite tales of the gods, and sing their praises, hoping to show their devotion adequately and thereby receive their rewards, the god's mercy and his boons.

The essence of those beings, whether husband, bride, snake, or Krishna, whom men worship is in their possession of *shakti*, their embodiment of power. And because of the specifically Hindu (or Karimpur) comprehension of the relationship between men and gods, a relationship built on the dual transformations of faith and service to mercy and boons and of mercy and boons to faith and service, men are able to obtain the benefits of this *shakti*.

POWER AS AN ORDERING PRINCIPLE IN KARIMPUR

There are two areas of Karimpur life in which power in the sense developed here is an ordering principle of social action. The first is in relation to the pantheon itself, including human beings, and the second in relation to human beings *per se*.[22]

Most discussions of Hindu village pantheons and the ordering relations within them use analytical constructs such as all-India, regional, local (Srinivas); Sanskritic/non-Sanskritic (Dumont, Harper, Babb); Great Traditional/Little Traditional (Singer, Marriott). In answering some questions about the nature of Hindu religion in South Asia, these tools may be valuable. For comprehending the natives' perceptions of powerful beings and their corresponding ritual actions, however, these constructs are inadequate. Evidence from Karimpur suggests rather that the villager's primary consideration is with that kind and amount of power controlled by a particular being.

Three categories of possible actions (powers) by other beings are dominant in the stories, songs, mantras, etc., of Karimpur. These are (1) the ability to give *moksha* [freedom from the bondage of the chain of life, death, and rebirth]; (2) the ability to give shelter, implying removal of sins (usually in this life), removal of sorrows (*dukh*), and continuing long-term protection of the devotee from the vicissitudes of life; (3) rescue, implying immediate aid in times of distress (*kashT*).

---

[21] The fact of a deity's giving his devotee shelter, long-term protection, is a highly meaningful element of the Karimpur conceptual system. The deity makes a commitment to give life-long comfort and aid to his devotee as asked; in return, he expects continuing worship. Less powerful deities are not asked for shelter; from them men desire only irregular aid, and they are worshiped only when their aid is required.

[22] It is probable that there are not two areas, but only one. For analytic and explanatory purposes, however, I will make the distinction.

Shelter, *śaraṇ*, is an important recurring theme in Karimpur verbal traditions. Shelter means literally "place of safety" and to say, "I came into your shelter" means more fully, "I came into the place of safety made by you." There is also an implication of extreme humility and humbleness, of "I place myself completely in your hands." The prerequisite for obtaining shelter is that the individual be a devotee, that he honor and trust the deity concerned. Once in the deity's shelter, the devotee can expect the deity to act in those ways most necessary for his happiness and welfare, to be his lifelong boatman to aid him in the whirlpools of life and across the ocean of existence. A long-term commitment on both sides is required; the devotee will continue his acknowledgment through prayer, song, and worship of the deity's powers, and the deity will aid the devotee as called upon.

Shelter, as understood in Karimpur, presents a series of ideas vastly different from the implications of the English gloss, in which a common usage could be, "I obtained shelter from the rain for the night." The implications of the meaning of shelter to the north Indian Hindi-speaking villager are fundamental to the discussion which follows. A person obtains the shelter of his chosen deity by acknowledging the power of that deity through worship and prayer. The deity in turn can remove conditions of sorrow, remove the sins of this life, and fulfill his devotee's mind's desires. In opposition to the implications of rescue, the giving of shelter becomes even more focused. Rescue is a short-term act, the immediate removal of physical distress. Worship of the rescuing deity is implied, but the long-term devotion which is a prerequisite for shelter is not required. When an individual asks for rescue, he invokes a short-term relationship between himself and the concerned god. When a person asks for shelter, he mandates an enduring relationship based on devotion and service. This distinction between short-term and enduring relationships is the basis of much ritual action in Karimpur.

Deities who are felt to have the power to give shelter versus those who are felt only to be able to rescue men on particular occasions can be further distinguished through the implications of the Hindi lexemes *dukh* [sorrow] and *kashT* [distress]. There is an important difference between "to remove all sorrows" (*sab dukh dūr karnā*) and "to remove conditions of distress" (*dash kī kashT dūr karnā*). *KashT* implies that the physical well-being of the individual is in danger, while *dukh* tends to emphasize his mental well-being. Moreover, in *kashT* there is an emphasis on an outside inflicting agent, while *dukh* tends to emphasize some lack or wrong action on the part of the one who is sorrowful. Last, *kashT* is brief, immediate, occurring now; *dukh* can be long-lasting, extending over a period of time, timeless.

The removal of sorrows (*dukh*) and the removal of conditions of distress (*kashT*) are thus very different acts. *KashT*, associated with outside influence and intervention and with brief physical danger, is opposed to *dukh*, associated with one's own fortunes and sins and mental, not physical, anguish. Action to remove sorrows is greater than action to remove distress; the deity removing sorrow must be shown that the devotee is serious, that he will become a keeper of fasts and a follower of *dharma*. In most cases the plaintiff must have asked and sought the deity's shelter before that deity will remove his sorrows. Those actions implied by rescuing through the removal of distress can be of various sorts: curing snakebite, removing eye trouble, etc. Likewise, the removal of sorrows can be made even more specific; that is, the gods can give sons, wealth, knowledge, sovereignty, etc. Again, some gods cannot perform all of these actions: some can give only sons, others only wealth; some can cure only smallpox, others only snakebite.

The above discussion of categories of divine action in Karimpur has been concerned with positive divine action. Not all divine actions are good, not all aid the individual on his journey through existence; some indeed make his journey more troublesome. We must acknowledge that these negative acts are as definitive a factor as positive ones in comprehending the nature of divine action in north India. The actions of malevolent powerful beings in Karimpur represent role behavior which is, with some limitations, the inverse of benevolent roles. Malevolent powerfuls are able to cause illness, not to cure it; they can be enemies, not remove them.

Expanding upon the categories of divine action recognized in Karimpur, we obtain both malevolent and benevolent classes of powerful beings, defined by their possible actions, presented in Table 1.

A few comments must be made to clarify the implications of this chart. These again relate to the possible actions which deities may perform. First, a "0" indicates neutrality: no action of the defined sort is possible by that kind of god. Second, a "−" indicates oppositeness to the stated category, so that the opposite of "to give nonexistence" is "to take away nonexistence" and the opposite of "to remove sins" is "to give sins." And "to fulfill one's mind's desires" becomes "to take away one's mind's desires." Logically, each of the above actions could be so reversed, but logic and culture do not always form a one-to-one relationship. The reader may note that no negative actions are attributed to any kind of deity for actions classified under categories A and B. In north Indian village Hinduism (and probably in Hinduism in general) none are possible; the state of nonexistence cannot be taken away and existence reimposed; the

Table 1. The structural roles of Karimpur powerful beings: a model for divine action

Class of powerful being	A Salvation	B Shelter	C Rescue
1	+	+	+
2	+	+	+ (−)
3	0	+	+ (−)
4	0	0	+ (−)
5	0	0	— (+)
6	0	0	—

Key: + = can act positively in this category.
  0 = cannot act in this category.
  − = can act negatively in this category.
  () = can possibly act but action is unlikely.

gods may remove sins as a boon, but they cannot give sins;[23] desires cannot be taken away, only filled. On the other hand, opposites of category C are possible: a deity can cause distress and can create, or be an enemy. The culturally defined logic must be recognized. It overrides etic logic.

Third, it is necessary to recognize that the actions I have indicated are only possible; any deity need not act, either positively or negatively. In the cases of those divine beings who act negatively, the victim obviously wishes that they would not act. Likewise, men also wish that those who can act positively would do so.

Table 1, then, represents the broad outlines of action by powerful beings in Karimpur. It is based on the roles of deities as perceived by a member of this culture; all more specific roles can be categorized as the type of either A, B, or C. In the table, the general type of

[23] In an earlier attempt to understand the role-playing possibilities of Hindu deities I included "giving of merit," only to realize much later that Hindu gods do not give merit. Merit accrues only through the actions of a man or god without the outside intervention of another individual. Merit (*puṇya*), though not given by the gods, is rewarded by them in both this life and the next. Merit's complementary quality is sin (*pāp*). Man sins, powerful beings do not cause or force him to. The Satan/devil paradigm of Christianity in which man is urged or compelled to sin is lacking in Hindu belief systems. This is not to say, however, that disaster does not occur; it does, but it is not tied to a desire to cause man to sin. Recently, when I discussed this matter with a north Indian Hindu, he said that people who have acted in an apparently wrong way will say, "A demon is sitting in me." The idea of one being sitting in another is, in north India, tied to the idea of possession; essentially it means that the being who possesses me acted thus, I myself did not; that being sinned, I did not. As I understand the texts and these ideas, this only substantiates the idea of no being causing another to sin.

powerful being (vertical column) is defined by the roles which he can fulfill (horizontal column). Thus a deity of class one can give salvation, can provide aid as defined by shelter, and can provide physical aid as defined by rescue. And a deity of class four cannot give salvation, cannot give shelter, can rescue individuals, and can also cause them physical distress. A class six powerful being can only harm men; he cannot even, by himself, undo his harm.

It is in relation to the classes of powerful beings, classes based on the perceived powers of these beings, that the residents of Karimpur act. Those beings who are thought to be able to give shelter to remove sorrows are ritually treated in a manner different from those who can only cause distress. The villagers' perception of a given deity's power thus provides them with the conceptual reality for ritual action. It is this perception of power, of ability to affect the lives of men, that gives meaning to village religion, not a recognition of Sanskritic or non-Sanskritic deity, etc.[24]

Let me now turn to power as an ordering principle in man/man relationships in Karimpur. One major area of concern in anthropological studies of Hinduism has been the interrelationships of religion and social behavior. Yet the above analysis has shown that there is no separate realm of the sacred in Karimpur belief. Finding that power is a fundamental idea in Hindu religion, I thereby contend that conceptions of power also operate in man/man relationships in Karimpur.

It cannot be denied that men are also powerful beings of one sort or another. They too are born with their share of the powers of the universe; they too can alter their substance and thereby their powers through various means.

The ritual specialists of Karimpur provide some human examples. The Brahman priests, and Brahmans in general, obtain their powers by birth (actions in previous lives), although they must continue to maintain and increase these powers by correct action in this life. The Brahman priests serve as intermediaries between men and some gods; Brahmans in general are also intermediaries in some instances: for example, men feed them so that the offerings will reach either Bhagvān or their ancestors. In contrast, the village oracles (bhagat [literally "devotee"]) obtain their powers because of their actions in this life. Because they are extraordinarily devoted to their chosen deity, that deity rewards them with the boon of manifesting the deity, of becoming possessed.[25] Likewise, the village exorcist is taught mantras by his gurū; when sanctified by repeating them while im-

---

[24] See Wadley (1973: Chapter 8) for details on the relationships between these classes of powerful beings and ritual action.
[25] Not all possession, however, is a boon. Possession by malevolent spirits is definitely inauspicious.

mersed in the Ganges, the exorcist obtains the power to call upon more powerful gods for their aid in crisis situations. Men call upon these various specialists when their particular extraordinary powers are needed. The individual faced with a crisis may not be able, because of his lack of devotion, to coerce a given deity to aid him; but by approaching that deity through an intermediary whom the deity recognizes as a devotee, he can obtain the diety's aid.

Actions based on perceptions of power are found elsewhere in Karimpur social life. The worshiper's devotional attitude (*bhaktī*) reciprocated by the deity's mercy (*krpā*), as found in the *kathā*, is remarkably similar to the *kamin*'s attitude towards his *jajmān*. In the hereditary patron/client (*jajmān/kamin*) relationship, the client (*kamin* or *kām karne wālā*) has a duty to serve his patron, in return for which he receives foodstuffs, a house plot, firewood, cowdung, fodder for cattle, etc. The songs and *kathā* tell us that some deities can give shelter, which symbolizes a long-term commitment to their devotees. The hereditary patron/client relationship is recognized twice yearly on the threshing floor of the patron, when the client is given his yearly share of that harvest. Moreover, deities with enduring, sheltering relationships with men have commitments to aid men when they are in danger, as the gods in the songs above help men out of whirlpools. Likewise, the patron has a commitment to aid his worker in times of crisis, whether by giving milk for an infant, giving grain when the crops have failed, or providing wood for a new house. The patron/client ties are also reiterated on festival days, when the client is able to claim food from his patron, who of course wishes to give him food and thus clearly establish his superiority. In return for physical aid and symbolic shelter, the client provides services for his patron, the same type of service which men often provide for their deities in *pūjā*, primarily concerned with the removal of the deities' polluting substances. *Kamins* in Karimpur include the washerman, the sweeper, and the barber (whose wife comes on festival days to decorate the feet of the women in her *jajmān*'s household, just as the women themselves adorn the god or goddess whom they worship that day). Other services are performed by *kamins*, but it is noteworthy that in the changes which have occurred in the past forty years, the *kamins* most concerned with the bodily welfare of their clients have continued in service, while those more concerned with general welfare (e.g. the goldsmith and the oilpresser) have tended to lose their hereditary jobs.[26] On major festival days, however, present and past *kamins* are

[26]   I do not wish to suggest that treating the *jajmān* as a god is the only factor in these changes; obviously, other economic factors are important. Further research needs to be done both on attitudes involved in the *jamāni* system, particularly various groups' perceptions of the necessity of shelter, and on the economic positions and benefits of the various groups.

expected to claim food from their *jajmāns*. The *jajmāns*, like the gods, give food; the *kamins*, like the devotees, receive it. From the viewpoint of the *jajmān*, the *kamin* is a lesser, inauspicious being (though the degrees of lesser and inauspicious of course vary); from the *kamin*'s viewpoint, the *jajmān* is an auspicious being who provides shelter.

If we recognize that men think of and act toward their gods on the basis of the gods' powers and that men likewise have powers and are treated in various ways because of these powers, some of the apparent inconsistencies in caste ranking in the villages of India can be understood. An example from Karimpur is relevant here. Over forty years ago, a poor *mahājan* woman (a caste of shopkeepers who have very lowly status in many places) came to Karimpur with her sons. By the mid-1960's, these sons and their sons had prospered. They now own a large shop by the roadside, run a mill for grinding grain, and have bought land. In addition, they are moneylenders. As a symbol of their increased prosperity, they built a large brick house, and at the opening of their house they gave a feast to the whole village. There was much consternation over this event because the Brahmans of Karimpur had never before taken cooked food from this group or eaten in their houses. Given the idiom of Hindu transactions, the Brahmans would be admitting some kind of increased status for the shopkeepers by taking food from them. Eventually the Brahmans did decide to eat in the new house, and the shopkeepers gained points in the ranking system of Karimpur. In explaining these events to me, the Brahmans were explicit about the fact that they had to eat in the shopkeepers' house because of their new wealth. We have known that in the caste-ranking game, individuals and castes could buy, through increased material prosperity and political clout, a higher rank, symbolized in food transactions marking increased purity (see Marriott 1969:114–115). Adding the dimension of *shakti* to our conceptual apparatus for comprehending the caste-ranking game, in which wealth is important, makes the rules of the game clearer.

Material prosperity is closely tied to people's perceptions of someone's powers. The deities of heaven and the underworld need not have visible manifestations of their embodied powers, although it is relevant to note that if a god does not grant boons, he is assumed to have lost his power. That material wealth signifies power should not be surprising, because the attainment of *artha* [wealth] is a justifiable pursuit under most codes for conduct as long as that wealth is used correctly. Wealth, then, appears to be interpreted as an indication of that family's or person's correct actions, indicating that their embodied powers have increased. The case of a Brahman family whose wealth and position in Karimpur had been drastically cut in recent years represents the opposite situation. As the grandson of this family explained to me, "My father and grandfather and uncles have acted badly. Because of this we have no money now and it will be very hard to find wives for my brothers because our family does not act right and people think we are bad. People were glad to marry a daughter to me [three years previously]."

Power relationships are also expressed among kin. The wives' worship of their husbands has already been mentioned; in addition, wives daily eat their husbands' leftovers. A wife, even though incorporated into her husband's lineage at the time of marriage, continues to be subordinate to him. During the marriage ceremony the new husband and wife exchange food, but all later transactions mark the woman's inferiority. Moreover, the wife's membership in her husband's lineage is continually restated in a variety of ways, suggesting some of the ambiguity of her position. The first meal served by her in her husband's home is *besan-bhāt*, symbolizing her rise in status to that of her husband's lineage.[27] This same meal is served whenever a wife returns to her husband's home after a long absence, thus reiterating her solidarity with her affines through meaningful transactions of food.

Other affinal relationships are marked by equally meaningful food transactions. A woman's husband, who has by birth greater powers than his wife's family, must be fed honorific foods whenever he visits his wife's village, and, naturally, he is fed first. In addition, all of his male affines are required to touch his feet in respect (foot touching, taking bodily substance from the lowest part of the other's body, is a sign of extreme humility, devotion, and lesser status). In contrast, a woman's parents should never accept food from her husband's family, particularly in his village.

There are many other instances of similar behavior: a wife touches the feet of her husband's mother, as well as of his older brothers' wives, his sisters, and his brothers. A son touches the feet of his parents and older relatives. Sisters eat before sisters-in-law; mothers before their sons' wives, etc. These transactions, like those of the *kamin/jajmān* relationship, are evidence that there is no bounded domain of the religious or spiritual in Karimpur, given the definition of "supernatural" developed in this paper. Any behavior toward any being which is based on the fact that that being has power is thus religious behavior.

I find myself continuously returning to the question of power. If men think about their deities in terms of power, and if cultural principles for relationships among gods/gods, men/gods, and men/men

---

[27] Only members of the family share this meal.

are based upon perceptions of power, then surely power and the principles by which it is understood are fundamental to Hindu society.

Power, although a fundamental concept in the ideology of Hindu society, is not generally considered a dominant theme. Yet power underlies two of the most important concepts which aid Hindus in defining action: *dharma* and *karma*. Right action, *dharma*, guarantees that an individual's fate, *karma*, will be good and that his status in the next life will be higher than in this one. With a higher status, perhaps even that of a *devatā*, comes an increase in power, the ability to control, to command, the lives of other beings.

It is in his perception of power that I disagree most strongly with Dumont (1970). Rather than agreeing that purity or the principle of pure/impure is dominant in Hindu society, I contend that purity and power are two inseparable factors of any ideas of being or action in Hindu thought. Power in human affairs is always embodied and is a characteristic of the state of any being. In addition, all being is in some state of purity. An individual's quantum of power in this life and his quantum of purity are both based upon his actions, that is, his fate as derived from the correct or incorrect following of his *dharma* or code for conduct in previous lives. Thus Brahmans are both the most powerful beings and the most pure. Likewise, in Karimpur at least, sweepers are the least powerful and the most impure. Moreover, in this life, as an individual's bodily substance changes through various transformations and transactions, his or her power and purity likewise change. The Brahman male after the sacred thread ceremony has an increase in both power and purity and a corresponding new code for conduct. The woman at marriage receives the power and purity of her husband's family; she becomes one with them in terms of bodily substance and has a new code for conduct. The shopkeepers mentioned earlier illustrate an increase in both power and purity; the Brahmans, in deciding to take food from them, were also making a judgment in terms of purity and were careful to take only the most honorific foods, those least contaminated by the shopkeepers' lesser purity. Even the gods' powers are connected with their purity: those with the most influence tend to be the most pure. Both power and purity are used jointly in determining hierarchical relationships. Thus any being is at one and the same time purity and power, and action changes both purity and power.

Dumont's contention, then, that the principle of purity encompasses the political-economic sphere is erroneous. Political and economic clout, material manifestations of an individual's embodied powers, are of the same order as purity. Just as men know which gods are powerful (have *shakti*) by what and how many boons they can grant, so men know which men are powerful by noting what they can do for other men on earth. *Shakti* is obtained through right actions, it is a part of an individual's being and identity, but it is known to other men only through what it can do. You act badly, you lose power, you become poor. You act properly, you gain power, you become rich. As you gain power through right actions, you also transform your embodied purity; your bodily substance is altered.

Previous works in village Hinduism have been largely concerned with behavior as manifested in ritual action, with the physical transactions between man and deity, but insufficiently with the meanings of the transactions which that ritual represents. I suspect that the tendency to overemphasize purity as the dominant theme in South Asia is due in part to our lack of attention to the meaning of the transactions. Ideas about purity are more readily seen in ritual actions; ideas about power are not so easily seen but instead must be listened to. Moreover, we can apply our own Western concept of power to much South Asian behavior, to economics, politics, kinship. The fact was missed that South Asian economic relationships, kinship relationships, etc., although in many ways visibly the same, are based on a completely different notion of the meaning of power.

Modern anthropology with its apparent fixation on actual, preferably visible, behavior, like materialist anthropology with its attention to nonhuman substance, has created unnatural biases in our studies and has led to culturally erroneous interpretations of native societies. The trend is beginning to change: functionalism and materialism no longer have exclusive sway. I hope that this paper, in focusing on the role played by and the importance of the concept *shakti* in South Asian society, has demonstrated the necessity of attending to the words used in ritual and myth to gain a more complete understanding of all behavior.

REFERENCES

BABB, LAWRENCE A.
1970   The food of the gods in Chhattisgarh: some structural features of Hindu ritual. *Southwestern Journal of Anthropology* 26:287-304.

DUMONT, LOUIS
1970   *Homo hierarchicus: the caste system and its implications.* Translated by Mark Sainsbury. Chicago: University of Chicago Press.

FREEDMAN, MAURICE
1967   *Rites and duties of Chinese marriage.* London: G. Bell.

GOMBRICH, RICHARD F.
1971   *Precept and practice: traditional Buddhism in the rural highlands of Ceylon.* Oxford: Clarendon.

GOODY, JACK
1962   *Death, property and the ancestors.* London: Tavistock.

HARPER, EDWARD B.
1959   A Hindu village pantheon. *Southwestern Journal of Anthropology* 15:227-234.

1964   "Ritual pollution as an integrator of caste and religion," in *Religion in South Asia.* Edited by Edward B. Harper. Seattle: University of Washington Press.

KELLOGG, REV. S. H.
1965   *A grammar of the Hindi language.* London: Routledge and Kegan Paul.

MARANDA, PIERRE, E. K. KÖNGÄS MARANDA, *editors*
1971   *Structural analysis of oral tradition.* Philadelphia: University of Pennsylvania Press.

MARRIOTT, MC KIM
1969   "Caste ranking and food transactions: a matrix analysis," in *Structure and change in Indian society.* Edited by Milton Singer and B. S. Cohn. Chicago: Aldine.

PRASAD, K., R. SAHAY, M. SHRIVASTAVA
n.d.   *Brihat Hindi kosh.* Varanasi: Gyanmandal.

RADCLIFFE-BROWN, A. R.
1965   *Structure and function in primitive society.* New York: Macmillan.

SPIRO, MELFORD
1966   "Religion: problems of definition and explanation," in *Approaches to the anthropological study of religion.* Edited by M. Banton. London: Tavistock.

TAMBIAH, S. J.
1968   The magical power of words. *Man,* new series 3:175-208.

WADLEY, SUSAN S.
1973   "Power in the conceptual structure of Karimpur religion." Unpublished doctoral dissertation, University of Chicago.

WISER, WILLIAM H.

1933 "Social institutions of a Hindu village of north India." Unpublished doctoral dissertation, Cornell University.

1958 *The Hindu* jajmāni *system*. Lucknow: Lucknow Publishing House.

WISER, WILLIAM H., CHARLOTTE V. WISER

1971 *Behind mud walls: 1930-1960*, with a sequel: *The village in 1970*. Berkeley: University of California Press.

Gods, Kings, and the Caste System in India

L. K. MAHAPATRA

That the caste system in India is not purely a secular social order, but that religious values, rites, gods, and goddesses are important in it, has been known for a long time. We need only mention the well-known fact that cults of specific deities are associated with specific castes irrespective of status in the caste hierarchy. Hocart's view of a new caste emerging along with a new cult is derived from this (Hocart 1950:59). Among others, Bouglé has stressed the importance of the sacrifice and the concepts of purity and pollution as distinctive characteristics of the caste order (Bouglé 1908:81-82; 1958:24-26). Hocart conceives of the caste system as a ritual organization, within which the individual castes have been assigned ritual duties or services to perform; the polluting services are relegated to the vassals or serfs (Hocart 1950:17-18), who do not have a share in the public or state sacrifices and thus do not have communion with the Aryan gods. This viewpoint of Hocart has certain relevance to our theme, and we shall revert to him later. But, incidentally, it is important to note that Hocart has been neglected for various reasons (compare Dumont and Pocock 1958:3ff.).

Of late, Marriott has referred to Hocart, while probing the link between the caste hierarchies of little communities and the Great Tradition of the greater community (1955:189-190). Marriott notes the process of filtering down from great to little communities since later Vedic times, when there were two classes of sacrifices, simpler ones of the householders with the assistance of kinsmen and elaborate ones conducted only by kings with the help of professional ritual specialists. The royal sacrifices grew more elaborate, involving greater specialization of the ritualists. Similarly, he thinks that the villagers today practice more elaborate household sacrifices and employ a larger number of specialists. He leans directly upon Hocart to trace the kinds of ritual relationships among castes in villages from those once prevalent in the royal palace among royal retainers. Hocart points out that "royal ways filter down to the common people, sometimes slowly, sometimes with astonishing rapidity, but naturally shorn of their pomp" (1950:155). Even a poor householder of Kishan Garhi, according to Marriott, today retains six or seven servants of different castes "mainly to serve him in ceremonial ways demonstrative of his own caste rank." Marriott adds some other facts throwing light on such royal association:

Householders and their servants formally address each other by courtly titles. Thus the Brahman priest is called "Great King" (*Maharaj*) or "Learned Man" (*Panditji*), the Potter is called "Ruler of the People" (*Prajapat*), the Barber "Lord Barber" (*Nau Thakur*), the carpenter "Master Craftsman" (*Mistri*), the Sweeper "Headman" (*Mehtar*) or "Sergeant" (*Jamadar*), etc. About half of the twenty-four castes of Kishan Garhi also identify themselves with one or another of the three higher *Varṇa*, thus symbolizing their claims to certain ritual statuses in relation to the sacrifice or the sacrificer of Sanskrit literary form. "Thus the apparent degradation of the royal style becomes a step in social evolution" [Hocart 1950:155] (Marriott 1955:190).

However, the role of the Hindu kings in the evolution, functioning, and maintenance of the caste system has been very rarely considered (Datta 1968; Bose 1949; Hutton 1951; Srinivas 1952, 1955, 1966; Maynard 1972; Sinha 1972). Hocart has given extensive thought to it, but he carries the analysis further when he considers the kings as gods, having priestly functions and working with the Brahman to form a sacerdotal pair, upholding the sacrificial organization for the good life on earth, that he makes the state appear as a ritual organization, and the king's palace, court, and complement of functional castes are duplicated in the god's temple, court, and ritual functionaries (Hocart 1927:10–11; 1970:93, 105). In fact, according to Hocart, "the Church and the State are one in India. The head of this Church-State is the king" (Hocart 1950:67). "The temple and the palace are indistinguishable, for the king represents the Gods" (Hocart 1950:68). ". . . everyone likes to imitate his betters, the big feudal nobles the king, the small nobles the big ones, and so on . . ." (Hocart 1950:155). We shall have to examine Hocart's insightful ideas in some detail in the light of some empirical data from Orissa.

Although implicit in Hocart's writings, the temple organization of ritual and other services based on a caste division of labor and the relation between the state deity, the divine kings, and the vassal kings, on the one hand, and the caste system at various levels, on the other, have not been expressly analyzed in terms of the relevant empirical data. We shall attempt to do that here within the limitations of space and data. However, it is felt that in analyzing the caste system of India, it is methodologically feasible and substantially profitable to begin with a particular cultural region because there is much truth in the statement that there is hardly a single caste system, but several, each specific to a linguistic-cultural region (compare Ghurye 1961). Orissa as a cultural region exemplifies, perhaps in an extreme fashion, the parallelism between the king's court, estates, and services, and those of the state deity. On the basis of this regional empirical study, further implications for understanding the interaction and interdependence between the gods, kings, and temples, on the one hand, and the caste system at the levels of the region as a whole, the princedoms, and the villages, on the other, can be identified and analyzed for India as a whole later on.

GOD-KING IN ORISSA

Perhaps a little introduction to Orissa as a cultural region in this context is in order. Orissa had a checkered political history, although paradoxically its cultural continuity over a wide area in the ancient Kalinga or Utkal is significant. The cornerstone of this cultural continuity in the pre-Islamic past has been the cult of Lord Jagannath, the Lord of the Universe, identified as the penultimate incarnation of Vishnu in the form of Buddha, at Puri, Shrikshetra, one of the four most sacred centers of pilgrimage (*chaturdhama*) for the Hindus. Lord Jagannath is looked upon as the protector and even the sovereign of Orissa, and the Raja of Puri (formerly, of Orissa at Khurdha) officiates as his earthly deputy. The king is himself conceived as Vishnu, or Mobile Vishnu (*Chalanti Vishnu*). The institution of a state deity is perhaps as old as urban civilization itself, and we learn of it in the civilizations of Babylonia and Egypt. The Pharaohs were notably the Children of the Sun. So are many Rajput chiefs, as are also the chiefs in Orissa, who are "descended" from the gods, the sun, the moon, the ritual fire god, Agni, and even from the serpent god, Naga. Such a conception of divine kingship was also quite widely prevalent for a long time in Southeast Asia, where Shiva, Vishnu, Harihara, Shiva-Buddha, Bodhisatva Lokéswara of Mount Meru, or Indra were represented in the king on earth, his palace being the sacred microcosm of the kingdom (Heine-Geldern 1942:22ff.). In ancient Cambodia, the king was an incarnation of the God-King Devaraja, who was Lord Shiva himself (Heine-Geldern 1942:22ff.). Similarly, the Raja of Puri, the descendant of the paramount sovereign of Orissa, is called *Thakur-Raja* [God-King], so much so that pilgrims used to have a *darshan* [audience] of the king before proceeding to the lord's temple. As such, he also functioned as the head ritual functionary of the Jagannath temple; "in the absence of other functionaries in cases of emergencies, [he can] . . . perform all

ritual services except cooking and offering food to the Images"
(Patnaik 1970:88). Patnaik also refers to the similarities between the
rituals of the temple and those of the palace. The palace was considered
as a sacred place, the abode of the God-King and Mobile Vishnu; because of this none were allowed to enter the palace with leather foot-
wear as is also the case in a temple (Patnaik 1970). In the painted reliefs
on the wall of the temple the king is seen performing the twelve important festivals in the manner that Lord Jagannath's are conducted
(Mishra 1971:114-115).

The king and the god underwent similar rituals at the time of waking
up, bathing, receiving presents, eating breakfast, putting on clothes,
giving audience, making offerings, and other daily rituals. Besides, the
king had many special privileges, similar or homologous to those of
Lord Jagannath himself, when he went to have an audience with the
god. The king had vassal chiefs performing several services at the time
of royal installation, coronation, and at the time of the temple visit. In
the palace, the king's establishment had a vegetarian cuisine, and the
queen was subject to no fewer ritual austerities (Mishra 1971:114-115).
Only Lord Jagannath and the king were addressed with the reverential
terms, *Manima* or *Mahaprabhu*, not only at Puri, but also in the
feudal princedoms, because feudal princes are conceived as minor gods
in the image of the paramount king. The paramount Raja of Orissa, at
least since the days of the Ganga dynasty in about the twelfth century,
has made the Jagannath cult a state cult. It may be that this was
gradually superimposed on the prevailing state cults of the feudal chiefdoms, where usually some form of *shakti* [tribal goddess] was the *ishta-
devata* [patron-deity] of the royal dynasty (Bhattarika in Baramba,
Samaleshwari in Sambalpur, Kila Munda in Ranpur, and Hingula in
Talcher, etc.) (compare Kulke i.p.).

Lord Shiva has been worshiped almost everywhere in Orissa as
Mahadeva [Great God] from time immemorial, and the Pashupat cult
was in the ascendancy from the times of the fifth and sixth centuries.
We may, therefore, visualize that Lord Lingaraj, the King of the
Phallus, at Bhubaneswar Ekamra-Kshetra, was the state deity of Orissa
by the seventh century, when the temple is said to have been constructed at Bhubaneswar by Yayati Keshari (Panigrahi 1961). But by the
time of Shri Shankaracharya of the eighth century, who had visited
Puri and whose monastery was established there to campaign in favor
of the revival of Hinduism, the worship of Lord Jagannath and the cult
center of Puri must have attained all-India importance and all-Orissa
supremacy in the spiritual realm.

STATE DEITY AND TEMPLE ORGANIZATION

At any rate, there is evidence that after the days of the Ganga paramount king Aniyankabhima III (who had completed construction of the present temple of Lord Jagannath), the worship of Jagannath in Orissa was more intensified than during the previous kings' times. Traditionally, thirty-six functional castes were deployed to render services in the temple. It was this king who expressly regarded Purushottama [Lord Jagannath] as the real Emperor of Orissa, he himself ruling as his representative. Thus, by the early thirteenth century Lord Jagannath might have been well established as the state deity (*rashtradevata*) although according to Mishra (1971:38), Purushottama [Jagannath] and Balabhadra were already regarded as *rashtradevatas* of Kongada and Toshali under the later Vaishnav Bhaumas by about the eighth century. Lord Jagannath was believed in so strongly as the lord and protector of Kalinga and Utkal, kingdoms of ancient Orissa (Mishra 1971:43–44), that during the reign of Purushottama Gajapati, both Lord Jagannath and Lord Balabhadra rode horses and led the Orissa soldiers to victory, according to a popular legend painted on the temple walls. This identification of the god with the king of Orissa and the king's empire as the god's realm under his protective arms must have persuaded the feudal chiefs — in addition to the fact of military or political subjugation — to become willing tributaries of a divine King-God-State polity. In fact, there is an inscription in the temple of Lord Jagannath by the paramount king Purushottama Deva that enjoins the vassal kings of Orissa to obey his orders on proper attitude and approach toward Brahmans; transgression of these orders constitutes a great sacrilege and sin (*mahapataka*) against Lord Jagannath himself (S. N. Dash 1966:264). At any rate, we find perhaps no princedoms in Orissa under British occupation where we do not come across the worship of Lord Jagannath, usually with his brother, Balabhadra, and sister, Subhadra, and where a complement of functional castes does not serve in the temple as they do in the palace nearby. There is some evidence that in order to legitimize their occupation of territory and curry favor with the Gajapati kings of Orissa, the vassal kings, like the king of Bolangir-Patna, constructed temples of Jagannath, Balabhadra, and Subhadra (S. P. Dash 1962:253). Therefore, we may note that the Jagannath cult has been used for political purposes both by the emperor and the vassal kings, at least since the thirteenth century. Again, with political purposes of espionage and public propaganda in view, the *Panda* system was introduced by Aniyankabhima Deva III to court pilgrims from various parts of India, by learning their language and visiting them (Mishra 1971:44). Lord Jagannath is invoked for permission to punish rebellious vassals (Mishra

1971:49). In another inscription in the temple, the paramount king threatens, presumably on the authority of Lord Jagannath, that if the people do not work for the good of the sovereign and avoid the evil path, they will be expelled from the kingdom and all their properties will be confiscated (Mishra 1971:50).

Let us now briefly consider the types of services and the number of functional castes engaged in serving in the two most important temples of Orissa, those of Lord Jagannath at Puri and of Lord Lingaraj at Bhubaneswar. The world-famous Sun Temple of Konarak (Konerka), now in ruins and with no record of organized worship, need not concern us. Although it has been noted that the ritual and other services in the temple of Lord Jagannath were systematically organized in the thirteenth century, there is no justification to infer therefrom that the functional castes were not associated with the temple services much earlier, perhaps from the beginning of the temple worship in the legendary days of King Indradyumna, who, according to Skanda Purana, constructed the first temple of Puri. Even in the days of Indradyumna, as the legend goes (Mishra 1971:82), the descendants of Savara chief Visvavasu, known as Daita, the descendants of Savara girl, Lalita, and the Brahman emissary, Vidyapati, known as Suara (Supakara), and third, the descendants of Vidyapati (by a Brahman wife?) were to serve as decorators and ministrants, as cooks, and as priests, respectively. Previous to the organization of services by Aniyankabhima Deva III, the local tradition has it that there were nine *sevak*s [servants]: (1) *Charu Hota*, (2) *Patra Hota*, (3) *Brahma*, (4) *Acharya*, (5) *Pratihari*, (6) *Puspalaka*, (7 and 8) *Dyata*s [the washerman and the barber], and (9) *Dvarapalaka* (Mishra 1971:12-121).[1] It is highly probable that every time the temple was rebuilt, it became more complex and bigger, and the ritual services were further elaborated; the latter occurred also when dynasties changed. Again, just because there is a close parallel in the temple services in the Puri and Bhubaneswar temples, there is no valid reason to suspect that the services are wholly a carry-over from the temple at Puri to the Bhubaneswar temple. First, the Lord Lingaraj temple is probably 600 years older (compare Panigrahi 1961) and the cult center Ekamra-Kshetra is perhaps even older. King Indradyumna is said to have worshiped Lord Shiva there before Lord Jagannath in his present form appeared at Puri. Second, both Lord Jagannath and Lord Lingaraj are, as the legends run, gods of the Savara autochthones who had been recognized as some categories of temple functionaries. King

---

[1]   Some of the names of these nine *sevak*s cannot be translated exactly because they are proper names. Possible meanings are: (1) *Charu Hota* [the handsome headpriest], (2) *Patra Hota* [the priest in charge of vessels], (3) *Brahma* [the demiurge Brahma], (4) *Acharya* [preceptor], (5) *Pratihara* [garland arranger], (6) *Puspalaka* [flower arranger], (7 and 8) *Dyata*s [washerman and barber], and (9) *Dvarapalaka* [gatekeeper].

Yayati Keshari, alleged to be a founder of the Lord Lingaraj temple, is said to have brought some Dravidian Brahmans (Kama Brahman) (Bose et al. 1958) as temple priests because, presumably, the local Brahmans were not well versed in Shaivism at that time, and he had to elevate the temple services from the tribal rites to Sanskritic ones.

The temple of Lord Jagannath engages temple servants performing 101 services or roles with their respective names, rights, duties, and perquisites (Mishra 1971). However, the actual number of castes is not ascertained from this, although castes from Brahmans to some untouchables, even to some descendants from tribal worshipers are known to be involved. Similarly, at the temple of Lord Lingaraj, somewhat less elaborately, in 1958 forty-one types of services were recorded (Bose et al. 1958), involving twenty-two separate castes, ranging over almost the same ethnic spectrum. This has also been largely confirmed by M. Mahapatra (1972), who, however, gives a tally of thirty types of services. There is no doubt that there has been wide fluctuation in the total number of ritual services (roles), at least in the temple of Lord Jagannath. These ritual services were recorded by British officers in 1807, soon after their occupation of Orissa after the Marathas, and the number was 219; apart from this there were 139 types of services connected with the management of the temple. In the 1950's the Orissa government compiled a record of ritual rites, which gave the number of ritual services as 140. Again the number of castes involved is not given, and it is seen that many of the priestly and other castes perform several roles at the same time. The fact that specific Rajas and even temple managers have been known to have introduced or discontinued specific services, offerings, and even fairs, etc., points to the prevalence of caste-centered core services in spite of the periodic fluctuations in the elaboration or proliferation of services. This is very clear from the stereotypical reference to *Chhatisha Nijoga* [thirty-six caste-centered ritual servants].

That almost all of the caste-centered ritual services performed in the temple of Lord Jagannath were duplicated in the palace of the king of Orissa may not be far from the truth, as indicated by Patnaik (1970) or by Mishra (1971:44). Similarly, one may refer to the royal installation, attended by vassal chiefs in various roles, as bearing close similarity to the divine installation at Poushabhisheka in the month of Pousha when Lord Jagannath assumes *Rajavesha* [royal attire] in a series of king-worthy rituals (*raja niti*). There is another divine installation in the month of Jyestha, known as *Rajendra-bhiseka*, auguring the proposal of marriage with Rukmini, as in the *Mahabharat*. Lord Jagannath assumes *Rajavesha* again on the day of the full moon in the month of Phalgun. Not only that, the Lord holds his royal court on Sunian day in the month of Bhadra, when his servants and subjects (temple servants and peasants and other holders of temple lands) offer him loyalty and tribute. This Sunian is celebrated also in the Lingaraj temple, and this had been introduced by a former paramount king of Orissa, marking the beginning of an indigenous royal calendar of Orissa. But this should not lead us to expect absolute conformity of the royal services with temple services or vice versa. Each system of services has its own pattern of proliferation and development, although basically the same complement of castes renders more or less similar secular and ritual services in the temple as well as in the palace. With this limitation, we may properly appreciate the concept of *temple community* developed by M. Mahapatra (1972) under this author's guidance, wherein Lord Lingaraj is seen wielding both ritual and secular authority and performing other roles through kinship, kingship, and property institutions among gods and men in his Ekamra-Kshetra. The temple servants here, as at Puri, invite the god on the occasion of auspicious ceremonies in their families; the funeral pyre is ignited with fire from the temple, at least in the case of Brahman *sevak*s; and the *Daitapati* [descendants of Savara, worshiper of Lord Jagannath] perform "funeral rites" of the Lord when a new set of images is made every twelve years. Besides, the *Daitapati*, *sevak*s take charge of the Lord's decoration, worship, and offering of fruits, etc. from the day the Lord falls ill until the end of the *Car* festival. As the *Daitapati* are considered to be family members of Lord Jagannath, they share the familial (*gyantisara*) dishes (Mishra 1971:93–96). All of this very much corroborates Hocart's view that in India the Church and the State are one (1950:67).

STRUCTURAL CONSEQUENCES OF GOD-KING AND TEMPLE-STATE IDENTITIES

If we accept the implications of the observations made so far, we may broadly agree with Hocart on the essential identity of the caste organization as mediated through the temple organization and through the organization of services to the king's establishment. Our assertion is that such identity is all the more pronounced in the case of state deities of a kingdom, like Orissa, in which the deity is not monopolistically owned (as, for example, the Brahman priestly families monopolize Lord Pandurang of Maharashtra) and in which tribesmen abound, among whom the caste system has yet to take strong roots. That the two acclaimed tribal deities came to be elevated as state deities, one after the other, opens up a new field of promising research into the building of the Hindu state, empire, and society on Orissa, much of which was part of the Dandakaranya forests of the Ramayana era or of Jharkhand jungles of medieval times; but this is not within the scope of our discussion.

At any rate, we may still consider the major structural consequences of god-king and temple-state (or palace) identities. First, the caste system became well differentiated; rights and duties as well as hierarchical relative positions became established with reference ultimately to their ritual relevance and importance; caste regulations were not only backed by state authority but also acquired the character of divine dispensation. This last development can be well documented from the temple inscriptions or *Sanad* grants by various paramount kings wherein the caste and other regulations were enjoined upon all including the vassal chiefs and Brahmans, and which could be transgressed only at the cost of committing a sin against Lord Jagannath. In this connection, we may bring in here the supreme council of Brahman scholars at Lord Jagannath's temple (*Mukti Mandap Pandit Sabha*), which sat in judgment on caste matters and rituals, among other things. The present building for this *Pandit Sabha* was constructed in 1578. But the institution appears to be much older than the buildings.

Second, the caste system, in its supposedly ideal differentiation and elaboration at the temple of the state deity and the palace of the paramount king, became the model for emulation at the temples and palaces of the vassal princes, with a *Pandit Sabha* of some sort to adjudicate on caste matters. Everything was not necessarily an exact replica of the model at the state capital and state temple. Actually, the roots go deep into the Hindu society and polity, where the king is looked upon as the authority in caste matters and is advised by Brahman scholars, who together constitute the supreme authority on caste matters in a princedom. Appeals from the level of the vassal chiefs lay before the *Mukti Mandap Pandit Sabha*, which had derived royal authority and divine ordination from the paramount king and the paramount god, respectively.

Third, the superposition of the state deity, the paramount king, and the paramount council of *pandit*s on caste matters thus signified the spiritual, political, and social leadership of the Vishnu-Mobile Vishnu or god-king combination at the heart of the state and society in Orissa. That the paramount kings derived political sustenance from this trinity is without question, but that is outside the scope of the present paper. However, we have seen how the state deity cult was used for political purposes for achieving subjugation and integration of vassal princedoms into an empire.

CASTE IN PRINCEDOMS

Although the above structural consequences have been cast in a static, timeless frame, this is not at all the case objectively. Let us take the second situation for a closer view, the one in which the caste order, political setup, and the ritual organization at the level of the princedom are shown as more or less modeled after the system evolved at the political and religious centers of the state in Orissa. This author has tried to throw some light in one of his national lectures (L. K. Mahapatra 1970) on the dual role of the Hindu king as the preserver of, and also as the catalytic agent for change in, the caste order within his domain. It can be argued, as Maynard (1972) has done, that in his original role of maintaining the traditional order, the Raja gradually also, driven by logic and pragmatism, became the authority to accord recognition to the relative interactional status attained, in addition to keeping the relative ascribed status of the castes (apparently) fixed. This transition from fixity to flux gave the essential leverage to the caste system insofar as individual castes or their sections could be recognized or not recognized as having this or that ritual or caste status in a specific politically autonomous domain. It has also been this author's thesis that in India, as in Orissa, such politically autonomous entities tended to behave as economically and socially autonomous units. This, at any rate, has been the situation in most of the former princely states and *zamindari*s of Orissa, where the political, economic, and social (caste interactions and status equivalence and hierarchy) boundaries tended to coincide in the recent past. If a caste or its subgroup attains a higher relative status in one princedom, perhaps because of its political or economic power or ritual purity or because of its value to the state or the king himself, this becomes the signal for the same caste or subcaste in other princedoms to claim such higher status. That the *Pandit Sabha* was not always obliging to the king or the castes in their claims is not very important. That this avenue was open to the castes, by going to the local king and *Pandit Sabha*, or by going over their heads to the *Mukti Mandap Sabha* for final judgment in matters of caste rituals and status determination, added an element of dynamism to the caste order. This is not so clearly evident from the traditional model of the caste system, whether in the Hindu scriptures or in early Western "scriptures" on Hindu society. This author has even come across cases of flouting of the decision of the *Mukti Mandap Pandit Sabha* in one or two princedoms. This happened during the late British regime, when the political hold of the descendant of the paramount king of Orissa was nonexistent and the local princes or their people did not need to fear any social or divine retribution, because of the prevalence of overwhelming secular trends toward social and economic freedoms in a countrywide democratic and capitalistic order.

CASTE DUTIES AS RITUAL SERVICES

It is necessary now to point out two important things. First, in the temples and palaces of princedoms the caste organization did not exhibit as much differentiation and specialization as evidenced in the state deity's temple organization, where services were highly elaborate and sophisticated. In the variety and elaboration of caste-based services, the paramount king's palace and establishment appear to parallel closely the local Jagannath temple.

Second, the tasks allotted to particular families of particular castes in the temple, as well as in the palace, on a hereditary basis came to be invested with sanctity and privilege. It was one's religious duty as well as a privilege to perform the hereditary job, much as the "calling" was a religious duty in Christian medieval Europe. Hence the well-known Sanskrit saying *Swadharme nidhanam shreyah, parodharmah bhayavahah* [one's own duty is the best to perform, others' duties are bound to give fear]. This elevated caste duties to what one might call ritual services. Therefore, transgression of caste duties in general came to be looked upon as sacrilege, not merely an act of criminality, to be punished by the king, the preserver of the social order. According to Hocart, these caste services were born of the sacrifices, especially the public or state sacrifices, whose elaborate, ritual requirements were functionally differentiated, coordinated, and mediated through the caste system. He says,

. . . the caste system is a sacrificial organization, . . . the aristocracy are feudal lords constantly involved in rites which require vassals or serfs, because some of these services involve pollution from which the lord must remain free (Hocart 1950:17).

Again, ". . . the worthy or excellent castes are those which alone are admitted to share in the sacrifice, with whom alone the gods hold converse" (Hocart 1950:18).

It is very difficult to pronounce on Hocart's theory of origin of caste. The only positive comment one may offer is on its plausibility. The state sacrifice to which he explicitly refers is a king's consecration or priests' installation ceremony. From what is known of such rituals in the palace of the present descendants of the paramount kings of Orissa, it appears that the services are not so elaborate or differentiated as in the temple of Lord Jagannath, although there is close resemblance. Apart from that, there are many vassal Rajas of the former princedoms who had been assigned services in the royal procession and other state ceremonies (Patnaik 1970:62). One vassal chief was to hold a betel leaf container, another to hold a spittoon, and still others to hold swords, golden canes, or daggers as insignia of royal authority. Such services did not always conform to the royal roles, which the godlike Kshatriya Rajas were supposed to perform, had these services any caste nexus. On the other hand, in the daily and periodic ritual services at the state deity's temple, all the castes from the very low untouchable castes to the Veda-knowing Brahman had their assigned tasks and status inside or outside the temple. Hocart might not have attached importance to the temple organization; at the most important Temple of the Tooth in Sri Lanka (which he cites as an empirical source of his theory), he notes how all who officiated inside the sanctuary were Buddhist farmers. But inside the temples at Puri and Bhubaneswar several castes have ritual duties. Therefore, even if we do not accept his theory of origin of the caste from public sacrifices because there is a lack of adequate empirical evidence to support it, at least the continuing organization of temple services in Orissa and elsewhere may supply an important basis for his assertion that caste is born of ritual, or caste is a ritual organization. Further, we may, on the basis of the facets of equivalence of the palace and the temple, agree largely with him that,

. . . the temple and the palace are indistinguishable, for the king represents the gods. Therefore, there is only one word in Sinhalese and in Tamil for both (S. *maligava*; T. *maligai*). The god in his temple has his court, like the king in his palace: smiths, carpenters, potters all work for him (Hocart 1950:68).

Again, we may also go along with him (quite a bit) when he asserts:

. . . just as each clan has a chieftain, and the whole tribe a chief, so each clan has a temple and the whole tribe a state temple of the chief god. Thus as usual, the human organization reflects the divine, and vice versa, since the two are one. . . (Hocart 1927:105).

Hocart, however, goes too far when he says that in India, "every occupation is a priesthood" (Hocart 1950:16) because all craftsmen, including the dancing girl, worship the objects with which they earn their livelihood. While priesthood is meaningful in the context of a community, and family rituals are far from public ceremonies, we may concede that a degree of sanctity is ascribed thereby to the caste duties, to be performed with reference to their respective religio-ethical norms. But this is true of each caste taken *individually*; there is no clue as to how *a system of castes* can be viably organized, put into execution, and maintained over a long period in a particular region.

CASTES IN VILLAGES

Hocart, however, becomes very effective — as much as a true seer — when it comes to the functioning of caste at the village or inter-village level:

The king's state is reproduced in miniature by his vassals; a farmer has his court, consisting of the personages most essential to the ritual, and so present even in the smallest community, the barber, the washerman, the drummers and so forth (Hocart 1950:68).

Hocart identified the farmers, with much logic, with "feudal lords to whom the others owe certain services, each according to his caste" (Hocart 1950:8). If we find fault with him over his ill-chosen epithet, "feudal," what he actually means is clear from the following:

The gods of the farmers, the Maruts, act as Indra's bodyguard. Since divine society is a replica of human society, we must conclude that the farmers are the king's mainstay in battle. They are just as military then as the nobles (Hocart 1950:39).

But Hocart uses a back door to induct the farmers into the sacrificial organization thus: "The farmers . . . are the support on which the monarch and the priesthood rest, and their duty is to feed the sacrifice from their lands and cattle" (Hocart 1950:39). In the state, which is a ritual organization, the others have other duties and if they cultivate, they do so only to feed themselves (Hocart 1950:41). We may not agree with him wholeheartedly on the place of the sacrificial organization at the base of the caste system and especially on the role of the farmers *vis-à-vis* the sacrificial organization. For, this role of the farmer also agrees well with the view of the society as a military organization, which he himself pointed out.

However, there is substantive truth in what he says below:

This ritual organization has spread downward to such an extent that the poor cultivators in the jungle have their retainers to play the part which they alone are qualified by heredity to play at births, weddings, and funerals, but these are retainers of the community, the village, not of one lord (Hocart 1950:68).

We must again warn against absolute identities or replicas. The model is set by the court of the paramount king and the temple of the state deity, and the vassal chiefs and the temples, especially the Jagannath temple, in the princedoms largely follow suit. When we come to the village and intervillage level, this model is still valid and is looked upon as ideal, although the circumstances at the operational, interactional level do not allow for a 100 percent compliance. We shall discuss this below. But let us just recall how at the princedom level, representing the subregional organization of castes, the element of dynamism and flux has been as clearly evident in the variations of circumstances of each caste as in the variations between princedoms. The caste organization at the state deity's temple and the king's palace seems immutable and sets the standard by which the caste status, activities, and norms are to be tested when in doubt or dispute. Thus, this apparent immutability and stability is an important structural aspect of the regional caste system of Orissa.

Let us examine briefly the social structure of villages in Orissa, in the first instance. A large multicaste village usually has a complement of functional castes: blacksmiths, carpenters, barbers, washermen, and Brahmans, with or without potters and astrologers, who have remained, in most cases until recently, in *jajmāni* relationships with the clean castes. In most villages of Orissa the cultivating caste (*Chasa*) or the militia-cum-cultivator caste *Khandavat* [the wielders of swords] were the landowning and economically powerful castes, which were served by all the functional castes. They conform to the significant features of *dominant castes*. The *Khandavat*s especially behaved like lords and held in many cases military service *jagir*s, although there are some villages whose owners and/or dominant castes were Brahman, braziers (*Kansari*), *Teli* [oilmen], or even fishermen, etc. The dominant castes or at least their representative, the headman of the village, who was appointed by and represented the king, exercised authority over the organization of caste-based services within the microcosm of the village. In many princely states or *zamindari*s in Orissa, the headman had the power to appoint or evict the village servants of functional castes, and he often took the initiative to bring a washerman or a barber to be settled on some *jagir* land under his control. He, or vicariously his (dominant) caste members, saw to it that the ritual services and other services, performed by the various resident and peripatetic members of other castes serving the village, were attended to properly, without conflict and disruption, and without intruding upon the privileges of other castes. He thus secured what is called by Srinivas *vertical solidarity* in the village. We need not go into all the facets beyond pointing out the phenomenon. He also saw to it that all the important agricultural and related rituals and crisis rites for village welfare were performed and each section played its assigned role. In this sense, the headman and the dominant caste ensured the functioning of the village as a ritual, economic, and social organization. Hocart would give preeminence to ritual organization and derive the other facets from it. We may not grant him that; but this is not very important.

Although there may be a temple of the village goddess or other minor gods, the rituals are not elaborate and one or two castes (usually a non-Brahman, sometimes even a tribal priest) may be involved in the temple services. Thus, the services of the castes in the area cannot be readily invested with sanctity from their ritual relevance in the temple organization, and no public sacrifices are normally held on a large scale in the villages. But the chief deity is drawn into the caste disputes and into the village organization and well-being because the village assembly and the caste councils usually sit near the abode of the deity. Thus, the deity's blessings are easily invoked to seal the decisions that are made, or the deity acts as divine witness to the oaths and contracts. There is a belief that the deity will punish a transgressor if norms are violated. Therefore, although the caste services have their ritual character derived primarily from the temple-palace ritual network, this is also locally reinforced by the involvement of the main deity of the village. The close parallel between this situation at the village level and that at the state level with the state deity and king may easily be perceived.

The question as to why the functional castes are looked upon as village servants and not as servants attached to temporal or spiritual lords can be resolved simply. In the villages there are no such powerful or affluent lords as are available at the capitals of the state or of the princedoms. Basically the peasants have a subsistence economy and do not grow much beyond their needs; hence they have to pool their common resources, village land, or their individual resources to support the members of the functional castes (compare Hocart 1950:155).

We may also briefly note that the caste headmen in a princedom in Orissa were invested with royal authority by the kings, who formally appointed them. Thus, we find how even at the village and intervillage levels, the gods and the kings have lent their authority and sanctity to the caste organization. It is not meant by this that there is only a filtering down of the Great Tradition from upper layers of the society or from their acknowledged centers. The very fact that minor gods, caste gods, various local cults and fairs, village headmen or Pargana-heads are of crucial importance in village India indicates that the vitality and importance of local traditions are not to be belittled.

KING AND HINDUIZATION OF TRIBES

In fact, there is some evidence to show how the king has been instrumental in integrating tribal traditions (Little Traditions) and cults with the higher traditions and cults (Great Traditions) in a process identified by Marriott (1955) as *universalization*. Thereby the king has often taken some steps to make it easier for a hill tribe to become gradually accepted as a clean Hindu caste. We may consider one case from Orissa as an illustration.

A Hill Bhuiyas priest was worshiping Kanta-Kuanri, a goddess allegedly represented by a *tantrik yantra* found by chance in the area. The Raja of the Benai princely state came to learn of its importance in the Hill Bhuiyan lore and belief, and arranged the annual circuit of the goddess up to the palace temple of the state deity and back to the hill sanctuary. On the way the goddess was worshiped by all castes and tribes inhabiting the villages, where the ritual procession came to scheduled halts. Gradually the tribal goddess became allied to, and even identified with, a form of Durga, a Sanskritic goddess of the Great Tradition, and the Bhuiyan and other low priests of the goddess thus gained higher ritual and social status from the viewpoint of the Hindu society (compare Roy 1935:104-117).

In the Hindu society of Orissa, there is a hierarchy of gods and goddesses, with the state deity, Lord Jagannath, at the top, and the tribal minor gods and spirits at the bottom. The recognition of this hierarchy, as well as the several grades of purity and pollution attached to different occupations and ethnic communities, belongs to an initial phase of the process of Hinduization. To this we may add the other concessions granted by the king in his anxiety to woo the politically dominant tribal group in the region, the Hill Bhuiyas. Prominent among the concessions were that water from them was acceptable to Brahman and all other castes, as if the Bhuiyas were a clean Hindu caste and not *Mlechha*, and that the washermen might serve them at their life-cycle rituals, as in the case of clean Hindu castes. With this background and anchorage on the fringe of the Hindu society, it did not take long for the landholding, dominant, and long-settled cultivators among the Hill Bhuiyas, inhabiting the open plateaus in Bonai and other parts of Sundargarh, who sometimes owned *zamindari*s as vassals of the Rajas of princely states, to become accepted as a clean Hindu caste of cultivators. They sometimes even claimed status equivalent with the militia-cultivator caste of *Khandavat* (compare Khandavit Bhuiyas, Paik Bhuiyas, Praja Bhuiyas; Roy 1935: Appendix B, XI-XXIV). It is also not without significance that some Bhuiyas families continue to worship the local gods and goddesses as the only appropriate priests for the welfare of all castes. A similar process might have been at work in Bastar in elevating the goddess Danteswary beyond the tribal pale (compare Sinha 1962).

Therefore, the interaction between Little Traditions and Great Traditions is a two-way process and is very complicated. This hierarchy of gods in the Hindu pantheon, the hierarchy of "feudal" lords in princely states in Orissa, and the locally dominant political power of tribal groups and their locally popular and — in the local imagination — also powerful cults of minor gods and goddesses have conjoined to open the avenues to integration with the Hindu castes and Hindu religion. (The Raja of Sambalpur had adopted the tribal goddess, Samalai, worshiped by the local Sahara [Savara], as the state deity, who came to the aid of the state during crisis [S. P. Dash 1962:301, 303-304, 307-308, 342].) As we have seen above, the Rajas have played a significant role in the creation of new castes not only from among Hindus themselves, but also out of the tribal communities.

Sinha in his brilliant analysis of the state formation and Rajput myth in tribal areas of central India (1962) has thrown significant light on the role of the tribal Rajas and feudal overlords in the spread and intensification of Brahmanical tradition in tribal areas. The induction of ritual specialists and service castes was necessitated by the urge to follow the model of Rajput or Kshatriya rulers. This, in turn, resulted in the introduction of Hindu gods, rituals, festivals, ideas, beliefs, and values (Sinha 1958), besides effecting internal stratification based on grades of assimilation into higher Hindu caste culture and of interaction with higher Hindu castes (Sinha 1962). These processes must have gone on not only in Chhatisgarh and the former Gond states of Madhya Pradesh and in Manbhum areas among the Gond, Bhumij, and allied tribes, but must also have taken place in Orissa princedoms, where most of the princes were either themselves of tribal origin or adopted by the dominant tribal groups or heavily dependent on their tribal supporters.

To sum up, the state deity and the paramount divine king were served by a complement of castes, who attended to various ritual and secular tasks. But, because these tasks were performed for divinities, whether in temples or palaces, caste duties acquired the characteristics of ritual obligations. In this sense, the caste system may be conceived as a ritual organization. As the vassal kings also assumed divinity in the image of the paramount king and as the cult of the state deity spread to the princedoms, caste duties at the level of princedoms were similarly invested with ritual values. At the village levels we find the end point in the progressive decrease in elaboration of caste services, which nevertheless retained ritual character after the model of the paramount king and the vassal princes. The vassal chiefs often played a vital role in integrating the tribal peoples in the caste system by helping to "universalize" some local Little Traditions centering around local gods and cults. These developments in Orissa have parallels elsewhere in India; Hocart's theoretical insights probably have been largely borne out by our empirical study in one cultural region of India.

Let me finish with an attempt to answer the question as to why it is that in the Orissa region, as perhaps nowhere else, the state deity has developed such an elaborate, sophisticated, and differentiated organization of caste-based services. Orissa, known in ancient times as Kalinga, was famous as a center of Jainism and Buddhism, and some merchants of Orissa were among the first disciples of Lord Gautama. It is well known how these two puritanical religions strove to usher in a caste-free (without *varṇa* and four *ashramas*) society. There must have been widespread, long-standing confusion of castes, anarchy in the performance of traditional duties, and economic disruptions, as pointed out by Maynard (1972), which brought, as a reaction, stiff, standardized norms and regulations to be enforced by the king. The *Kautilyashastra* recites the conventional form of duties of the four *varṇa* and then goes on to assert, "The observance of duty leads a man to bliss. When it is violated the world will come to an end owing to the confusion of castes and duties. Hence the king shall never allow people to swerve from their duties" (Maynard 1972:90). This enhancement of royal responsibility to bring back the caste order to its normal efficacy is a plausible guess on the part of Maynard. In Orissa, well known all over India at least since Ashoka's days, it must have been felt that the tribal component of the population would become overpowering if allowed to remain too long outside the Hindu fold. And this could not be allowed because Orissa forms a continuous link with northern, eastern, southern, and central India. In this context it is not surprising suddenly to find Indradyumna, the legendary king of north India, with whom all the gods are pleased and who can go to *Brahmaloka* in his mortal body, coming to Orissa to elevate an unknown tribal god of the local Savara to the status of a supreme deity of the Hindus of India. Similar might have been the attempt by some other king to elevate the local Shiva Linga, worshiped by the Savara, to the status of a deity (Lord Lingaraj) of all-India importance. It is also significant that the great anti-Buddhist saint Shankaracharya is said to have visited Purushottama-Kshetra (Puri), one of the foremost sacred pilgrimage centers in the eighth century, and to have composed the famous *Jagannathashtakam*. A monastery (*math*) established by him was shifted to Puri in the ninth century where it assumed tremendous importance in the management of temple ritual (Mishra 1971:151-152). The Shaiva king Yayati Keshari, perhaps the same as Mahashivagupta Yayati II of south Koshala, the doyen of the Somavamshi emperors of Orissa, is reputed to have built the Lord Jagannath temple at Puri and the Lord Lingaraj temple at Bhubaneswar, brought Veda-knowing Brahmans from north India, held a famous public horse sacrifice, and to have reestablished Brahmanism in Orissa in the tenth century. As a result, he is popularly designated Indradyumna II (Mishra 1971:30-32).

The resurrection of Brahmanism was aided by the process of universalization which, it appears, must have been a very ancient and recurrent process in the orthogenetic growth of Indian civilization. But this was especially imperative and expedient in the region known as Dandakaranya or Jharkhand, which was the hinterland of the Orissa coast, where the spread of the Jagannath cult in the interior came in handy for holding up the caste services as ritual obligations, sacred and inviolable. To aid in this process, the Rajas, many of whom were tribal in origin, founded numerous Brahman villages in their princedoms. No wonder, therefore, that "in the Protected States of India few chiefs have retained their position as the paramount caste authority to such an extent as the chief of the Feudatory States of Orissa, a tract long isolated and untouched by modernizing influences" (O'Malley 1932:64-65). Whether this speculation is valid or not, the fact remains that most of the numerous and powerful tribes inhabiting the northern, western, and southern hills and plateaus, the Bhuiyas, the Bathudi, the Gond, the Binjhal or Binjhwar, large sections of the Kond and Savara, the Bhumia, and the Amanatya, have come to be more or less assimilated to the Hindu peasantry, often considered equivalent in status to a clean caste. For once, Elwin (1943) has been proved wrong, because Hinduization has not left the tribesmen in the dungeon of low menial status in Hindu society.

REFERENCES

BOSE, N. K.
1949   *Hindu Samajer Gadau.* Calcutta: Viswa-Bharati.
BOSE, N. K., *et al.*
1958   Organization of services in Lingaraj Temple, Bhubaneswar. *Journal of Royal Asiatic Society* 24:2.
BOUGLÉ, C.
1908   *Essais sur le régime des castes.* Paris: Alen.
1958   "The essence and reality of the caste system." Introduction to *Contributions to Indian sociology*, volume two. Translated and edited by Louis Dumont and D. F. Pocock. The Hague: Mouton.
DASH, S. N.
1966   *Jagannatha Mandira O Jagannatha Tattwa.* Cuttack: Friends.
DASH, S. P.
1962   *Sambalapura Itihasa.* Sambalpur: S. P. Dash.
DATTA, N. K.
1968   *Origin and growth of caste in India,* volume one (second edition). Calcutta: K. L. Mukhopadhyay.
DUMONT, L., D. F. POCOCK
1958   A. M. Hocart on caste. *Contributions to Indian Sociology* 2.
ELWIN, VERRIER
1943   *The aboriginals.* Oxford: Oxford University Press.
GHURYE, G. S.
1961   *Caste, class and occupation.* Bombay: Popular Prakashan.
HEINE-GELDERN, R.
1942   Conceptions of state and kingship in South East Asia. *Far Eastern Quarterly* 2:1, 15-30.
HOCART, A. M.
1927   *Kingship.* Oxford: Oxford University Press.
1950   *Caste: a comparative study.* London: Methuen.
1970   *Kings and councillors.* Chicago: University of Chicago Press.
HUTTON, J. H.
1951   *Caste in India.* Oxford: Oxford University Press.
KULKE, HERMANN
i.p.   *Some remarks about the Jagannath trinity.* Heidelberg: South Asian Institute.
MAHAPATRA, L. K.
1970   "The role of the Hindu princes in the caste system in India." National lecture delivered at Ravishankar University, Raipur.

MAHAPATRA, M.
1972 "Lingaraj Temple: its structure and change, circa 1900-1962."
      Unpublished doctoral dissertation, Utkal University.
MARRIOTT, MC KIM
1955 "Little communities in an indigenous civilization," in *Village India*. Edited by McKim Marriott. Chicago: University of Chicago Press.
MAYNARD, H. J.
1972 Influence of the Indian king upon the growth of caste. *Journal of the Punjab Historical Society* 6:88-100.
MISHRA, K. C.
1971 *The cult of Jagannatha*. Calcutta: K. L. Mukhopadhyay.
O'MALLEY, L. S. S.
1932 *Indian caste customs*. Cambridge: Cambridge University Press.
PANIGRAHI, K. C.
1961 *Archaeological remains at Bhubaneswar*. Bombay: Orient Longmans.
PATNAIK, N.
1970 The recent Rajas of Puri: a study in secularization. *Journal of the Indian Anthropological Society* 5:1-2, 87-114.
ROY, S. C.
1935 *The Hill Bhuiyas of Orissa*. Ranchi: Man in India Office.
SINHA, S. C.
1958 Changes in the cycle of festivals in the Bhumij village. *Journal of Social Research* 1:1.
1962 State formation and Rajput myth in tribal central India. *Man in India* 42:1, 35-80.
1972 *A survey of research in caste*. New Delhi: Indian Council of Social Science Research.
SRINIVAS, M. N.
1952 *Religion and society among the Coorgs of south India*. Oxford: Oxford University Press.
1955 "The social system of a Mysore village," in *Village India*. Edited by McKim Marriott. Chicago: University of Chicago Press.
1966 *Social change in modern India*. New Delhi: Allied.

Hierarchy and Equivalence in Jaffna, North Sri Lanka: Normative Codes as Mediator

KENNETH DAVID

1: *Introduction*

In a Jai myth, a boy is stranded in a treetop (Lévi-Strauss 1970). In a Hidatsa myth, an eagle, swooping down after a bloody bait, is caught in midair by a hunter who rises from a subterranean trap (Lévi-Strauss 1966). A structure common to these two myths is the resolution of the separation between heaven and earth. The boy and the hunter ascend and the eagle descends to the middle air; middle air mediates heaven and earth.

The hiatus, frequently found in explanations of human action, between analysts who emphasize structures of thought and analysts who stress hard facts of control of power and resources, is certainly present in anthropological studies of South Asia. After a spirited exchange between Dumont and Bailey, proponents of the two schools, Bailey finally proposed that their differences might lie beyond the pale of academic discourse (Bailey 1959:88).

Must this analytic opposition of structuralism and structural-functionalism remain unresolved? A mediator, as used in the mythic analysis above, means a symbol which has attributes of each of a pair of contraries. Heaven and earth are mutually exclusive but the middle air is part of both. Structures of thought and patterns of behavior, the subjects of structuralist and structural-functional analyses, are mutually exclusive. But cultural norms, codes for conduct in a society, epistemologically mediate these contraries.

Cultural norms are form to the content of behavior, structuring, for actors, the complexities of social happenings. And cultural norms are content with respect to the form of thought structures such as the opposition purity/impurity, since such features of thought are the conceptual foci structuring the interconnected systems of normative symbols which I call normative schemata (see section 8). Thus I contend that normative analysis, like the middle air, mediates the stratosphere of structuralist analysis and on-the-ground behavioral analysis.

As a vehicle for this theoretical issue, I address the substantive question of unity versus diversity in rural South Asia. Of the numerous authors who have characterized Hindu civilization in terms of unity and diversity, Dumont, a structuralist, and Karve, a behavioral positivist, stand near the end points of the continuum. Unity, to Dumont, derives from the principle of hierarchy which encompasses Hindu society by pervading many contexts of human action[1] and providing a general structure of action which can be modified only by the encompassed nonideological features of power and wealth (Dumont and Pocock 1957a; Dumont 1966a:28). To Karve, diversity derives from the syncretistic process of societal formation: individual caste cultures and mores become aggregated into village confederations. The unique identities of a plurality of castes resist the integrating effect of the Great Traditional heritage, the principles of hierarchy, pollution, and *karma*. Compared with intense intercaste interaction, interdependence among castes is "tangential and peripheral" (Karve 1961:16). Normative analysis, a level of analysis treated tangentially by both Dumont and Karve, helps clarify an important aspect of the unity/diversity question. In the three parts of this paper, I ask the question: is there unity/diversity in symbolic and normative orientations at the level of the caste, at the level of intercaste interrelations, and at the level of man/god relations?

Part I rejects certain aspects of Karve's diversity model. It is clear that different castes have different versions of pan-Indian principles; e.g. in the Uttar Pradesh untouchable's interpretation of *karma*, retribution for wrong action occurs in the present life, rather than influencing the state of future reincarnations as in classic exegesis (Kolenda 1964). Castes do not, however, have idiosyncratic cultures, for there exists a regular paradigm of defining features of caste identity. Individual caste categories are defined as a symbolism of sharing: shared natural substance within each caste, caste occupation, caste cattle brands, and caste origin myths. The common symbolism which defines the diverse caste identities implies a certain uniformity in diversity.

---

[1]   Marriott (1969:1166), reviewing Dumont's notion of hierarchy in the latter's book (Dumont 1966a), notes that

[Hierarchy] expresses itself positively in the existence of a caste system, in rules of contact and food, in a ritualized division of labor, in ranked structures of marriage, and so on, and negatively in the opposed ideas of the world renouncing Hindu sects.

Part II is more inclusive than Part I since it considers normative codes for intercaste conduct. Contrary, that is, hierarchical and non-hierarchical, codes coexist in Jaffna, north Sri Lanka. These variations in normative structure, which correspond to variations in actual patterns of intercaste behavior, indicate that neither Karve's diversity model nor Dumont's unity model is strictly applicable in this context; instead, there are diverse unities of normative orientations.

Part III moves to a still more inclusive set of relations, namely those between man and god. An analysis of ritual relations in Jaffna shows how diversity of normative orientations resolves to unity. The opposition of hierarchic/nonhierarchic normative codes present on the level of relations between castes is neutralized on the level of relations between man and god; only the hierarchic norms appear. Thus, an unmarked/marked category model from structural linguistics (Greenberg 1966) is used to explain the structuring of contrary normative schemata within the traditional order.

In Part IV I summarize the substantive question of unity/diversity in symbolic and normative orientations. Then I return to the theoretical question posed at the beginning. Using Piaget's notion of the nesting of form and content (Piaget 1970), I show first, that norms structure patterns of behavior, from the analyst's viewpoint, in that norms are an indigenous, fictional representation of reality; and second, that norms are themselves structured, again from the analyst's viewpoint in that deep structures of thought are conceptual foci for systems of norms. Explicit norms (those consciously used by natives) mediate implicit structures of thought (those formulated by the analyst) and patterns of behavior observable both by natives and by the analyst. So normative analysis is said to mediate the opposition of structuralist/structural-functional analyses, an opposition which yields such disparate substantive generalizations as in the unity/diversity problem.

I: DEFINING FEATURES OF CASTE: THE ORDERING OF DIVERSITY

The Jaffna peninsula is the northernmost area in Sri Lanka. Except for Sinhalese members of the administrative, banking, police, and military corps, the 612,000 residents are Tamil-speaking Hindus. As in Geertz's (1959) study of Bali, there is no standard village spatial organization; space in agricultural, fishing, and artisan villages is organized differently according to the differential orientations of the inhabitants to the principles of purity/pollution, commanding/being commanded, and mercantile enterprise (David 1974b).

Present inhabitants recognize twenty-four named, endogamous caste (*cāti*; Sanskrit *jāti*) categories in Jaffna.[2] This hierarchical social differentiation is coded by a symbolism of sharing; each caste category is defined by four attributes: shared natural substance, shared traditional occupation, shared cattle brands, and shared origin myth. That this paradigm of identity symbols is common to all castes denies Karve's assertion that caste cultures resist the integrating effect of the wider culture.

2: *Shared Natural Substance: Blood and Spirit*

"Why is it that heroes in the Mahabharata or in the Skanda purana could be shot full of arrows and yet not die at once?" a village theologian asked me. "I shall tell you," he said immediately:

In the golden age of the Krita Yuga, the animating spirit (*uyir*) resided in the marrow. In the silver age of the Dvapara Yuga, the spirit resided in the bones. This was the age of the great battles recorded in the puranas. Arrows would not reach the bones. Therefore, the heroes would not die from that cause alone. In the bronze age of the Treta Yuga, the spirit resided in the flesh. In the iron age of the Kali Yuga, the spirit resides in the blood.

Villagers quite unfamiliar with this elegant schema are, nevertheless, quite aware of the connection between blood and spirit. The spirit resides in the blood. Since all members of a caste share the same origin myth and thus the same ancestor, they all distantly share the same blood, the same natural substance, and the same spirit.[3]

In the indigenous theory, blood-and-spirit is a hierarchical concept. A caste's blood-and-spirit is either good (*nālla*) or bad (*kutāta*), high (*mēle*) or low (*kīre*). Note that the classificatory term for high castes (*uyirnda cātihul*) derives from the term for spirit (*uyir*). Since each caste is considered to have a unique level (*patinilai*) of blood purity/impurity (*cuttam/tittu*) relative to every other caste, natural substance is a defining feature of caste identity.

3: *Substantial Sharing of Traditional Caste Occupation*

At first glance, the traditional occupations identified with castes appear to be codes for conduct rather than defining features of caste

---

[2]   See Table 2 for a list of castes and their traditional occupations. Transliteration follows the *Tamiḷ lexicon* (1936) conventions.

[3]   There are grades of purity within each caste. But there are also more specific origin myths of a quasi-historical nature, those related to various migrations to Sri Lanka from India.

identity. Jobs are, after all, learned by the individual. This outside, objective viewpoint misses the villagers' representation of the learning process. Learning any traditional occupation, be it that of priest, fisherman, or devil dancer, requires initiation. Initiations are formal only for spiritual roles, but any initiatory learning demands an inner sympathy between teacher and student to further the required inner propensity of the student to cut through his or her ignorance and participate in the knowledge of the teacher. The propensity to perform the caste occupation is held to be substantially transmitted from parents to children;[4] parents are considered the best teachers of the caste occupation because they share natural substance with the child. Similarly, since the spiritual master (*kuru*) does not share natural substance with the spiritual pupil (*sisya*), mantras which unite their bodies must be said before the *kuru* can cut the ignorance of the *sisya*. In cultural analysis, caste occupations are more than standard patterns of social relations, more that diacritical markers; since they relate directly to the caste's shared natural substance, they are a feature defining inclusion in or exclusion from caste categories.

4: *Caste Cattle Brands*

If the above argument is accepted, caste cattle brands also are defining features of caste identity since these are iconic symbols of the caste's traditional occupations. As depicted in Figure 1, Brahmin priests brand their cattle with a trident (*sulam*), a symbol of Siva. Saiva Chettiyar, traders and moneylenders, use a moneybag with a long string. Vellālar cultivators have a two-leaved lotus (*ērilaitamarai*); the stems of the two leaves join in a circle in which the man's initial is branded. Fishermen/traders use a crescent-shaped boat (*toni*) with a rudder; Cantar oilpressers and -mongers have an oilmill (*chekku*); washermen use a bundle of clothes (*pottali*); barbers have a shaving knife (*savarakaṭṭi*); Pallar agricultural workers use a double yoke for bulls; Nalavar toddy tappers use a climbing strap (*talarār*), which is looped behind the tree and around both feet, as their brand; and Koviar herders use an inverted omega sign which resembles a bull's horns.

---

[4] The notion of aptitude for behavior transmitted in natural substance appeared in a questionnaire administered to a high non-Brahmin caste in Madras City. Most older respondents stated they would be able to identify a Paraiyar untouchable by caste-bound etiquette even if he had been brought up for the first twenty-one years by high-caste parents (Barnett 1972).

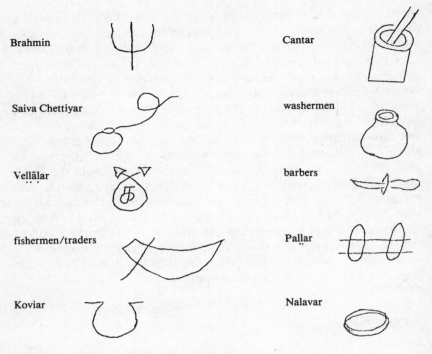

Brahmin

Saiva Chettiyar

Vellālar

fishermen/traders

Koviar

Cantar

washermen

barbers

Pallar

Nalavar

Figure 1: Caste cattle brands (*kuripatti*)

5: *Caste Origin Myths*

Various origin myths must be presented in some detail (each myth is the translation of an entire text) since these documents of self-definition are the data I will use to show the differential commitment of the different castes to the three normative schemata, the priestly, the aristocratic, and the mercantile, which I outline in part II. In that section no clear classification of the myths is given because, in most myths, references are made to more than one schema's normative symbols. To foreshadow the exegesis in part II, some myths have action referring to norms of the priestly and the aristocratic schemata, other myths refer to the priestly and the mercantile schemata, but no myth refers to all three; this pattern of pairing denotes a dichotomy of hierarchic/nonhierarchic value orientations.

5.1: BRAHMIN MYTHS

Origin Myth. Brahmins relate various versions of the birth of 48,000 *ṛṣi*s [seers] from the face of Brahma, the god of creation. Each of these *ṛsis* was the progenitor of a *kotiram* (Sanskrit *gotra*). The myth focuses on a feature of kinship distinguishing Brahmins from all other castes, exogamous *kotirams*.

Emigration Myth. A Cola princess named Marutappiravikavalli was endowed with a horse's face. She heard of the healing properties of the spring at Keerimalai on the north coast of the Jaffna peninsula, two miles west of Kankesanturai, and when she bathed in its waters, her face became human and beautiful. The name of her campsite, Kōvil Kadavai, was changed to Maviddapuram (*ma* [horse], *vidda* [left off], *puram* [city]) in memory of the event. She asked her father, King Tisai Yukkira Colam, to build a Kandasamy (Murukan, Subramaniyam) temple at Maviddapuram. It was built according to Agamic scriptures by a famed architect from Maturai. But the king could not persuade Brahmins to cross the sea (that is, the Palk Strait). They felt they would lose caste if they did so. The chief Brahmin, Periyamanath Tullar, fasted and saw a vision which incited him to go to Maviddapuram: as the narrow strait could be crossed in several hours, the Brahmins would not lose caste, because they could perform their morning *pūjā* on Indian soil and the evening *pūjā* in Sri Lanka. This marked the entry of Brahmins into Sri Lanka.

5.2: VEḶḶĀḶAR [LANDOWNER] ORIGIN MYTH. Although many Vellālar, the dominant landowning caste, were asked to relate their origin myth, I was unable to elicit anything more explicit than the myth recorded by Arunachalam (1964):

A branch of Vellālas, the old ruling caste of Tamil land, claimed to have received grain and instruction on its cultivation from the Earth Goddess, Parvathi, hence Vellālas were called *pillais* [children of Parvathi]; kings also drove the plow.

Vellālars would elaborate by saying that they were both the creators of life (in that they created food) and the rulers of the land.

5.3: KAMMALAN [ARTISAN] MYTHS

Origin Myth. One day Sivaperumal was leaving Kailas mountain in the company of the artisan of the gods, Visvabrahma. Siva became angry when his consort, Umatevi, bowed to Visvabrahma but not to him. Fire flashed from his *netti kaṇ* [third eye] and the five-headed Kammalan was born. Later, Siva sent Viravar with a sword to cut off the heads of the Kammalan. Brahma, the five-headed god, was accidentally struck by Viravar and lost one of his heads. Kammalan took the sword of Viravar and separated himself into five bodies, each with a head. The five men are the ancestral carpenter, blacksmith, brass-worker, sculptor, and goldsmith.

Inspiration Myth. Siva and Kamacciamma were renowned dancers. Kamacciamma, full of pride, boasted about her ability. When word of her egoism (*ahamkaram*) reached Siva, he arranged a dancing contest. Siva and Kamacciamma danced superbly for a while. None of the gods could decide which was the better dancer. Siva assumed the Nataraja pose, with his leg raised in the air. As soon as Kamacciamma imitated this pose, Parvatiamma, Siva's consort, protested that Kamacciamma had lost, since it is immodest for a woman to raise her leg while dancing. When the other gods agreed, Kamacciamma became furious. She caused a fire to break out which threatened to destroy all the created (manifested) universe.

Siva and all the gods were helpless until Visvabrahma, the artisan of the gods, conceived a plan. He made a pair of tongs out of Brahma, Visnu, and (U)rudra. Brahma and Visnu became the two handles and (U)rudra became the connecting pin. With these divine tongs, Visvabrahma seized Kamacciamma by the neck and subdued her.

When she became calm, it was decided that she should turn her power (*śakti*) to the service of man. She would aid the five descendants of Visvabrahma (the goldsmith, the stonesmith, the coppersmith, the carpenter, and the blacksmith) in their work. As a living sign of her aid, she is present in the fire of the blacksmith's forge.

5.4: KARAIYAR [FISHERMAN] MYTHS: THE KURUKULAM

Origin Myth. A celestial nymph (*apsara*) was flying over the sea. An ovary (*vintu*) dropped from her into the water. A fish swallowed the ovary, and a child was born to the fish. The child came to shore, where she was found and raised by Karaiyar fishermen. As she smelled of fish, she was called Matchakanti [fish smell]. The girl grew up and took the trade of her foster parents, who were ferrymen.

One day Pararajasekaram *munivar*, a Brahmin *kuru*, was ferried across the river by Matchakanti. The *munivar* realized that if he copulated with her at that moment, a great *kuru* would be born. She consented to his astrological persuasions, but her smell repulsed him. Before uniting with her, the *munivar* sang a mantra which changed her into the sweet-smelling one, Paramalakanti. The son born to her was Viyāsar (the author of the Mahabharata). As both Pararajasekaram and Viyāsar were *kuru*s, their descendants were called the Kuru clan, or Kurukulam.

The sweet-smelling Paramalakanti attracted the attention of King Santanu; they married and had three sons. The sons married but had no children. After Santanu died, Paramalakanti wanted the royal line to continue and asked the fierce-looking, bearded Viyāsar to sleep with his stepbrothers' wives, the princesses. Since the first princess shut her eyes when Viyāsar entered her, her son, Tirutarasyiran, was born blind. Since the second princess was frightened when Viyāsar slept with her, her son, Pantu, was born nervous. The third princess was also afraid of Viyāsar and required her maid to sleep with him. Being a courageous woman, the maid united fearlessly with Viyāsar, and her son, Vituran, was quite bold and healthy. The first son, Tirutarasyiran, had 101 sons named Kaurava, the combatants in the Mahabharata war and the ancestors of the Karāva or Karaiyar.

When I questioned the Karaiyar about the intriguing incident of Viyāsar's affairs with the three fearful princesses and the courageous maid, they responded with another myth:

Unmelting Heart Myth. Kurukulam was the sailor (*patakoti*) and trader (*sampanotti*) for Siva. One day, God (Katavul or Siva), his consort Parvati, and the lesser gods (*tēvarhul*) were walking by a river when Kurukulam, a Karaiyar, passed down the river in his boat. The foremost of the lesser gods asked Kurukulam to take them all into his boat. Kurukulam said he would take only Siva and Parvati. The lesser gods agreed. Kurukulam helped Siva and Parvati into the boat, but then the lesser gods asked Kurukulam to take them also. Kurukulam said he was the servant only of God (*katavulukku kattupātu*) and that he would not touch the other gods with the same hands with which he had touched Siva and Parvati. Kurukulam then agreed to bring the boat close to shore and tip it to one side in order that the gods could enter without his touching them. As the gods were thus entering the boat, Siva said, *"Ullamum Karaiyān, Yukattilum Karaiyar"* ["The heart will not melt, in the whole period of creation (*yukam*) it will not melt (or dissolve)"][5] The root of the verb "to dissolve" (*karai*) is exactly the same as the root of the proper name of the Karaiyar people, that is, the people, *ār*, of the shore, *karai* (*Tamil lexicon* 1936:767).

5.5: KAIKULAR [SILK WEAVER] ORIGIN MYTH.[6] At the time of the creation of Murukan, nine virgins became pregnant by the look of Siva after

---

[5]   There are two variants of this myth. In the first, Siva, Parvati, and the other gods are fleeing from the destruction of the evolved universe. Otherwise the myth is no different. In the second, the Karaiyar boast of their superiority over the other two fishing castes in Jaffna. Instead of gods accompanying Siva and Parvati, a Mukkiyar man and a Timilar man are with them. Kurukulam will not touch them after he has helped Siva and Parvati into the boat, etc. In these variants, the refrain remains unchanged: "The heart will not melt, in the whole period of creation it will not melt."

[6]   This is straight from the Skanda purana.

Parvati refused his embrace. Amman (Parvati) cursed them and the children were not born for ten years. Finally Siva begged Śakti (Parvati) to allow the children to be born. When she granted her permission, the nine virgins delivered nine children, each with a full head of hair. Later, these nine children, who were called the nine heroes or Nava Vēravan (from *vēran* or *viran* [hero]), assisted Murukan (Skanda) in the battle against the demon Suran. Vērapahu Tevar, the foremost among them, slew Tarakan, the younger brother of Suran. The Senkuntar Mutaliyar (Kaikular) descend from Vērapahu Tevar. In the olden days, the Senkuntar in India were warriors and were given the title Mutaliyar for their bravery.

5.6: KUSAVAR [POTTER] ORIGIN MYTH. A Brahmin was living in the kingdom of Vikkiramattiran in Mysore. He was married to a Brahmin woman. Having calculated that sexual union on a certain day would be astrologically auspicious for the birth of a ruler, he left the village in order not to cohabit with his wife and impregnate her before the proper time. On the appropriate day he was trying to return to his village but found himself stranded on the wrong side of a river in flood. One of the Kusavar ancestors belonging to the Bakttar family (*bakti* [devotional worship]) asked him what he wanted, and the Brahmin explained. The Bakttar replied that it was certainly impossible to cross such a turbulent river and invited the Brahmin to his house. The Bakttar's daughter had attained age and the Bakttar permitted the Brahmin to sleep with her. The Brahmin then went on a pilgrimage to Kāsi (Banaras). The girl became pregnant and bore a son.

This Bakttar made pots for King Vikkiramattiran. When the child was ten years old, he told his grandfather that he should not demean himself by delivering pots to the king. The king's servants should come to the Bakttar's house and take them away.

The child made many elephants, horses, camels, lions, and other animals out of clay. One day he circumambulated the house carrying some of the animals, one of which was a lion, the vehicle of Kali. As soon as he finished the circumambulation, Chamundeswary Kali appeared to the boy in the form of a woman. She gave him a pot of water and a cane and told him that the last days of Vikkiramattiran had come. She told him to sprinkle the water on the clay animals and they would come to life. With these animals and the cane he could fight the king.

The king was angered by the Bakttar's demand that the king's servants fetch the pots. The king and his soldiers fought against the boy with his cane and his animals. The king died in the battle, and the boy began to rule the kingdom. The Kusavar are his descendants. In the king's palace in Mysore you still find the *cakkaram* [wheel] of the Potter. It is made of gold. In September during the Navarattiri [nine nights] Festival (the north Indian Dashara festival), they turn the golden *cakkaram* while performing the *pūjā* to tools and weapons (*Ayuta pūjā*).

5.7: VANNAR [WASHERMAN] ORIGIN MYTH. Parameswaran (Siva) left the house and was gone so long that Parvati, his consort, became annoyed. She sat inside the house, closed the door, and held it closed with stiffened legs. Siva knocked at the door. No answer. She was strong and had the courage to hold out. To reduce her strength, Siva made her menstruate. Her strength gone, her legs became limp, and Siva was able to enter the house. Parvati asked Siva who was going to wash her clothes. Siva raised his hand and a boy (*podien*) appeared. Parvati told the boy to wash her clothes. The boy told her that washing alone would not suffice; he would have to strike the clothes on a stone. The boy asked Siva for a pond and a stone; Siva raised his hand and a pond and a stone appeared. The boy washed the clothes. The Vannar are the descendants of this boy.

5.8: AMPATTAR [BARBER] ORIGIN MYTH. Barbers came to Jaffna as servants of the warriors. Since they came without their wives, they were given unchaste Vellālar women for their wives. Subsequently these women refused to take food from the leftovers of their husbands in commemoration of their former high position. They are permitted a very intimate duty, delivering to the Vellālar women a razor with which to shave their pubic hair from the time of their marriage until widowhood. But they are ashamed to appear on festive occasions as do the wives of other servants.

5.9: PALLAR [AGRICULTURAL LABORER] ORIGIN MYTH. Pallan and Vellālan, both farmers, were *annan* and *tampi* [older and younger brother]. Pallan had many children; Vellālan had four children. There was a horrible thunderstorm and a cyclone which destroyed Pallan's land, tools, cattle, and crop but left Vellālan's possessions intact. Pallan had no food and had to ask his younger brother for something to eat.

Vellālan felt sorry for his elder brother, but Vellālan's wife was a bad woman. He was afraid of her. Vellālan asked his wife to give Pallan and his family shelter and food. For two days she obeyed, although she did not wish to do so. On the third day Vellālan's wife scolded Pallan and told him to go away. Vellālan was so sad that he died of shock (*mar padaippu* or *atircci*).

Vellālan's wife became the owner of the property[7] and Pallan and his family had to take food from her hands. She soon told them to go away. They started crying, and she then made them work for her. She made her husband's elder brother plow, sow, harvest, draw water, and do other menial work; Pallan's wife had to cook for her; Pallan's children had to look after the cattle. Having kept an account of all the food she gave them, she bought all the land once held in Pallan's name. After acquiring all the land, she said, "You must sharecrop[8] on your own land. You must cut and plow." She added sarcastically, "Pallan is the rightful owner of milk and rice." Vellālan's wife continued to live on the raised land (*mētu*). Pallan lived on the low land (*pallam*), which was more suitable for irrigation and cultivation. The name Pallan derives from the term for low land.

5.10: NALAVAR ORIGIN MYTH. There is no Nalavar caste. The Nalavar are the Deventera caste, called Nampi in India. The Nampi were the trusted regiment (*nambi pattalan*) of the king. Their main duty was to keep watch from the highest watchtower. When they saw a foreign army coming, they would blow their war conch and alert the regiments on the ground for the attack. If their king went to war, the Nampi were charged with protecting the seven wives and the treasure of the king. They were the "life" of the king.

Their Indian king went to fight the king of Sri Lanka. The Indian king lost the first battle but won the second. Having lost the second battle, the Sri Lankan king used a ruse. He forged the handwriting of the Indian king and wrote the Nampi to bring the king's wives to Sri Lanka. The Nampi prepared a ship and set sail for Sri Lanka. In mid-passage the king's wives became suspicious of the letter and of the Nampi. They wanted to return to India. The Nampi told them that they had received the king's order and would continue until the order was rescinded. The wives, deciding that the Nampi were going to rape them, threw themselves overboard to save their chastity, crying, "The Nampi have broken [or spoiled] faith [*Nampikkai ketta nampi*]."

How could the Nampi return to India? What could they say to the king's kinsmen? They decided to continue to Sri Lanka. Landing at Manār, the closest landing place from India, they sought shelter in a village of tree-climbers called Cantar. The Cantar were frightened because the Nampi were wearing the king's uniforms. The Nampi told them not to be frightened. They explained they were not kings but

---

[7]   This is contrary to the law of inheritance, by which Vellālan's sons or close agnates would own the property.

[8]   *Vāram* is the term for the giving of a sharecrop holding. It implies a hierarchical arrangement between lessor and lessee. The same term denotes the granting of supernatural power by Siva (or another high deity) to a properly austere ascetic.

were in danger and wanted shelter. They destroyed their uniforms and ate and relaxed for two or three days. When their money ran out, they were forced to ask the Cantar if they could take up Cantar work. The Cantar agreed, and the Nampi began to climb trees for coconuts and toddy, repair fences, and do agricultural labor. When the king's envoys came searching for the Nampi, the Cantar replied that the Nampi were kinsmen. The Nampi eventually married Cantar women.

A variant of this myth connects the Nampi with the Vanniar, land-owners in the Vanni section south of the Jaffna peninsula. There is an inversion: one of the Nampi wives is raped instead of the Nampi being suspected of rape. The one addition is that they were called Nalavar because they slipped away from their caste (*naluval* [slip away]; *nalavar* [tree-climbers (who descend the tree in a slippery fashion)]) (Sivaratnam 1968:148, 149).

5.11: PARAIYAR ORIGIN MYTHS

First Variant. Two brothers were the *pusaris* [priests] in a Mariam-mam[9] temple. The elder brother decided to fast and to observe a vow of silence. He wanted his younger brother to watch over the temple. So he said to the people, "*Nān parrayan, tampi pārpār*" ["I will be silent (*parrayan*), my younger brother will watch."]. But the people misunderstood him and thought he said, "*Nān paraiyan, tampi pārpār* ["I am the drum person (*parai* [funeral drum], *an* [person]), younger brother is the priest" (*tampi* [younger brother], *pārpār* (from *pār* [to see]) [seer, wise one, priest]).].

Second Variant: Paraiyar as "Nanthanar." In former times, Viru-pasikai slept with Kasipa *munivar*.[10] Twenty-seven girls were born. The *munivar* gave the twenty-seven girls in marriage to Sukkira Bhavan. The sixteenth girl was Kāti. She and her children went to live in the forest. They had no work at first, then began to weave, slaughter goats and cows, and deliver messages for others. They were ignorant of God (*tēva valli pātu illai*). They were not clean (*tupira-vullāmal*). The Nanthanar (Paraiyar) caste originated from this girl.

At this time, Viyāpāhar *munivar* was doing penance (*tāvam*) with seven other *munivars* in Vatam Meru Malai. One evening there was a beam of light crossing the sky from the south to the north. Seeing the light, Viyāpahar *munivar* worshiped it. The other *munivars* asked him why he had done so. He replied, "Kāti and Sukkira Bhavan had

---

[9] Mariammam is a fierce goddess who spreads smallpox and is "cooled" by animal sacrifices. She also cools the earth by bringing rain for the crops.

[10] Kasipa Gotra is the largest Brahmin *gotra* in the Jaffna peninsula.

children. They are now at the crossroads [that is, not in a civilized society]. A son named Nanthan was born to them to bring up their state. The light signaled the event. That is why I worshiped it. The light is the light from Siva's third eye. The light has Siva's power [*śakti*]. This light created Nanthan. Therefore I worshiped the light."

Nanthan became a young man and worshiped Siva daily. He decided to go to Sithamparam, the site of a famous temple to Siva. As was seen by others in Sithamparam, he became one with Siva in a burst of light. He stepped on fire, became God, and disappeared.

While Nanthan was living with Kāti and her children, the Paraiyar or Nanthanar [people of Nanthan] progressed. They moved out of the forest to a settlement between the forest and the village, the *ceṛi*. After Nanthan appeared, they learned how to keep themselves pure.

6: *Summary and Conclusion: Ordering of Diversity*

Part I has shown that castes are categories differentiated by a regular paradigm of defining features: natural substance, occupation, cattle brands, and origin myths. Symbols defining diversity are not themselves diverse. That is, the system of symbols used to define caste identity does not vary from caste to caste. This point does not support Karve's (1961) position that each caste has a separate caste culture because it was formerly a separate tribal society.

II: NORMATIVE CODES FOR INTERCASTE CONDUCT: DIVERSE UNITIES

Part II will discuss the contrary normative codes by which different castes orient their intercaste conduct. I label this second variation on the theme of unity/diversity as diverse unities (of intercaste relations). This view again contrasts with Karve (1961), who holds that intercaste relations are "tangential and peripheral" as compared with the intensity of intracaste relations.

First, a *social structural* analysis will detail two contrary modes of intercaste relationships. Castes in the agricultural sphere (priests, landowners, barbers, laborers) are engaged in *status* or *bound*-mode intercaste relationships. Castes in the fishing, artisan, and merchant sectors are engaged in *contractual* or nonbound-mode intercaste relations. *Bound* and *nonbound* are emic distinctions.

Second, three normative schemata will be detailed in a *normative* analysis. The *hierarchic priestly* schema enjoins a code for conduct of hierarchic separation between castes. The *hierarchic aristocratic* schema enjoins a code for conduct of enduring, diffuse, hierarchic, solidary intercaste relations. The *nonhierarchic mercantile* schema enjoins a code for conduct of temporary, specific, equivalent, manipulative relations between castes. This analysis is based on exegesis of native symbols.

Third, a *value orientation* analysis will prove certain correlations between the first two analyses. The test of correlation is the thematic content analysis of origin myths of *bound* and *nonbound* castes in which mythic action incorporates norms of the above normative schemata. Castes engaged in *bound*-mode relationships are committed to the *priestly* and *aristocratic* schemata. Castes engaged in nonbound relationships are committed to the *priestly* and *mercantile* schemata.

7: *Modes of Intercaste Relations: Bound and Nonbound Relations*

Present views on South Asian rural social structure are synecdochic, the part standing for the whole, in that most studies are of multicaste agricultural villages dominated by landowning castes (Bailey 1960; Cohn 1955; Gough 1960; Majumdar 1958; Marriott 1960; Mathur 1964; Mayer 1970; Opler and Singh 1952). A stereotype of rural social and cultural structure has emerged from this inexhaustive sample: the locus of organization in agricultural villages is typically a dominant landowning caste of fairly high religious status. The dominant caste in an agricultural village has diffuse or multicontextual relationships with each of its traditional serving castes. Roles of hierarchical reciprocity are played in the contexts which analysts label economic exchanges, ritual exchanges, and political exchanges:

These economic relations were, however, only one aspect of the multiple relations which linked the different caste households in the Indian village. For instance, the hereditary relationship between a Peasant master and his Untouchable labourers operated not only in the economic but also in the political and ritual spheres. If an Untouchable was involved in a dispute with another, whether Untouchable or not, his Peasant master had to come to his support. Similarly, the Untouchable allied himself with his Peasant master in disputes. He was expected to fight for the latter, even against Untouchables aligned with other Peasants in conflict with his own master. Perhaps even more important, the Untouchable had to perform a number of ritual services for his Peasant master, such as carrying a torch ahead of a funeral procession from his master's household. These different types of relations—political, economic, and ritual — reinforced each other and in turn helped to insure the stability of the Indian peasant economies (Epstein 1967:232, 233).

This type of intercaste relationship, which has been reported from many regions in South Asia, is often called the *jajmāni* relationship.

In addition to noting the *jajmāni* relationship, authors have called attention to the more particularistic, contractual relations between

194   KENNETH DAVID

artisan and fishing castes and all other castes. Epstein (1967:232) classifies two types of intercaste relationships in terms of mode of reward, duration of service, and regularity of demand:

Thus in Mysore in south India I found two types of hereditary link in the villages: one between Peasant masters and their Untouchable labourers, the other between Peasants and certain functionary castes, such as washerman, barber, and blacksmith, whose services were continually required. Village craftsmen, such as the goldsmith and potter, whose services were not in regular demand, had no hereditary relationship with Peasant caste households; they were not rewarded annually, but rather on the occasions when their services were required.

Wiser (1936) distinguishes intercaste relationships in terms of recruitment: "those who serve some" and "those who serve all;" in the former, the religious status of the other caste is relevant to recruitment: "those who serve some" and "those who serve all"; in the other caste is irrelevant. Pocock (1962) elaborates on Wiser's distinction in terms of the purity/impurity dichotomy. The occupations of some, "those who provide a service," such as barber and washerman, are a direct reflection of the underlying value of purity/impurity. Occupations of others, "those who provide a commodity," are but an extension of the same value.[11]

Certainly, to try to determine the variations in the structural positions of the various castes in a region, the variations even within one village locality, is an empirical question. In Part II, I report two polar modalities of intercaste relationships and mixed modes, that is, deviations from the two modes. Each mode comprises a set of options from seven pattern variables. A mixed mode is an ordered transformation, in that the set of pattern variables includes some options from the opposite mode.[12] That is, the Vellālar landowner, the Brahmin priest, the barber, and the untouchable all have intercaste relationships of the status mode; the alocal artisans such as the goldsmith, the temple carver, the weaver, and the oilpresser, and fishing castes such as the Mukkiyar and the Timilar have intercaste relationships of the opposite polar mode, the contractual mode. Local artisans such as blacksmiths, carpenters, potters, and the dominant fishing caste, the Karaiyar, have relationships which combine options from both modes.

7.1: STRUCTURE OF RELATIONS BETWEEN CASTES IN AN AGRICULTURAL VILLAGE: THE BOUND MODE. In Jaffna agricultural villages there is a highly uni-

[11] Pocock's "those who provide a service" is similar to Wiser's "those who serve some"; "those who provide a commodity" is similar to Wiser's "those who serve all."
[12] Let pattern variables A, B, and C each have options 1 and 2. Then one mode is defined as A_1, B_1, and C_1 while the opposite mode is defined as A_2, B_2, and C_2. A mixed mode might be defined as A_1, B_1, and C_2.

form structure of intercaste relations between the dominant[13] land-owner (Vellālar) caste and the serving castes. I follow the local category and call this mode of relations the bound mode (*kattupātu* from *kattu* [to tie, to bind]). The Jaffna equivalent of the north Indian *jajmāni/kumin* distinction is *nainar/kutimākkal*. *Nainar* is a Telugu word adopted for master or lord. *Kutimākkal* means people (*mākkal*) of the house (*kuti*). Individuals are referred to as son or daughter of the house (*kutimakan* or *kutimakal*); they are addressed as younger brother or younger sister (*tampi* or *tankacci*). This usage is telling: a master is engaged in bound-mode relations with both his children and his people of the house.

In the agricultural village the landowner caste is *nainar*. The *kutimākkal* are the Brahmin [priest], Koviar [domestic servant, factotum], Ampattar [barber], Vannar [washerman], Pallar and Nalavar [agricultural laborer], and Paraiyar [drummer, remover of excrement].

I shall now give a brief account of the empirical characteristics of the bound mode of relationships observed between the dominant land-owning caste and the serving castes with the following seven pattern variables:

A. *Recruitment.* Recruitment to a bound relationship is perhaps a misnomer. The relationship exists due to the relative social categories with which individuals are identified at birth. One man is born to land-owner parents, another to barber parents; the relationship exists between them without voluntary contract.

B. *Time.* The relationship is long-lasting, frequently hereditary.

C. *Space.* The relationship is restricted in locality. Most relations take place in one's hamlet or village and in adjacent villages. Spatial defini-tion implies both proximity and categorical restriction, that is, wards within a village (David 1974b).

D. *Clientele.* The relationship is *restricted to certain categories of people*, that is, landowners of a specific status grade who occupy a spe-cific ward. The specifications are honor-*cum*-dominance and purity/impurity.

[13] "Dominance" is a descriptive, not an analytic, term. Srinivas' various definitions include factors of numbers, economic and political power, relative religious status, and land ownership (Srinivas 1955 and 1966:10). Dumont and Pocock (1957b) emphasize the dominant caste's influence in regulating life-styles of other castes. By excluding the land ownership requirement, this descriptive term aptly covers cases of locally dominant fisher and artisan castes.

E. *Pricing Mechanism: Traditional Price — Mode or Media of Exchange.* The relationship is compensated by a traditional pricing mechanism. Harper (1959) wishes to distinguish between payment in produce and payment in cash. I would argue that the price-fixing mechanism is more relevant than the media of exchange. There is no bargaining between the dominant caste and the serving castes. The major payments, whether in produce or in kind, are observably related to the agricultural cycle, payments occurring with some small ceremony between employer and employee. Unit jobs with unit compensations can also occur without ceremony. In my view, price fixing for service by fiat (without bargaining), redistribution, and cyclical, ceremonialized compensation are the important indices of the traditional price mechanism rather than payment in produce versus payment in cash.

F. *Context of Relationship.* The relationship, although localized in the village, is *multicontextual.* Although actors would not necessarily make the distinction (they tend to think of roles played in economic, political, and ritual contexts as part of one undifferentiated relationship) the observer notes roles played in analytically separable *contexts.*[14]

G. *Vector of Relationship.* The exchange between two castes in a bound relationship is asymmetrical within each context of the multicontextual relationship. A landowner will *require* the Brahmin and the barber to support his faction; the Brahmin and the barber *petition* the landowner to intervene for them in time of trouble. The Brahmin gives cooked food to the landowner and the barber; the Brahmin will not accept cooked food from either. Similarly, the landowner gives cooked food to the barber but will not accept cooked food from him. The landowner receives and pays for the services of the Brahmin and the barber, but he will neither work for nor accept pay from either. Thus there is asymmetry in each exchange context.

Barth (1960) uses the term *status summation* to characterize the involute structure of relationships in a caste system. In most cases there is a constant direction of asymmetry of exchanges between the landowner and his serving castes. The landowner is superior to the barber in ritual, economic, and political exchanges. This situation may be termed *status summation.* But between the landowner and the Brahmin priest, the direction of asymmetry is not constant: the landowner is inferior to the Brahmin in ritual exchanges but superior in other respects. Since the two pattern variables cover more cases, I thus use two terms (bound relationship as multicontextual and bound relation-

---

[14]   See the quote from Epstein in section 7.

ship as asymmetrical within each context) in preference to the previously used single term "status summation."

Terminology: Bound Relationships. Although averse to throwing yet another term into the cauldron of neologisms, I will call the above set of characteristics *bound relationships*. Since the term *jajmāni* relationships encourages a view from the top, a sort of superordinate centrism, it will not do. The term *bound relations* is an emic distinction: *kaṭṭupāṭu totarpu.*

7.2: NONBOUND RELATIONSHIPS: EMPIRICAL GENERALIZATIONS. The data that I collected in an agricultural village in northern Sri Lanka agree well with the above empirical model. Northern Sri Lanka, like the rest of rural South Asia, is composed not only of agricultural villages but also of fishing villages, artisan villages, and rural towns. A strongly contrasting mode of traditional intercaste relationships obtains between artisans and fishermen on the one hand and the other castes on the other hand: nonbound relationships (*ishtamāna totarpu*). Using the same pattern variables as above, the empirical characteristics of the *nonbound relationship* are as follows:

A. *Recruitment.* Recruitment to a nonbound relationship is voluntary between individuals.

B. *Time.* The nonbound relationship is of no set duration. Each transaction (for example, buying fish or cloth) lasts but a few minutes. A man may trade with many fishsellers or become friendly with a particular fishseller and buy only from him. He is not bound to buy from any of them.

C. *Space.* A nonbound relationship is *not restricted or defined* in terms of locality. Market centers may be within a man's village of residence, but many items are available only beyond the village. Availability of items and their relative prices, rather than any categorical restriction, determine the locality in which they will be bought.

D. *Clientele.* The nonbound relationship is *not restricted to certain categories of people.* Wiser (1936) distinguishes between castes which serve only some other castes (in my terminology, bound relationships, such as the barber who will not cut the hair of an untouchable) and those who serve all (nonbound relationships, such as the potter who sells pots to all customers). I accept Wiser's formula, except I would not say that the potter serves all but rather that he trades with all. (Service and work have a particular inferior connotation not current to the same degree in the West.) In any case, one index of the nonbound relationship is that the client's ability to pay is the relevant criterion for the occurrence or nonoccurrence of the transaction, not any hierarchical values.

E. *Pricing Mechanism.* Commodity transaction is governed by a *contingent* (supply-and-demand) pricing mechanism rather than by any *fixed* (traditional) compensation. Prices may fluctuate irrespective of the medium. (Barter was rare in 1968, but some people still exchanged rice for fish. When fish were scarce, more rice was given for the same amount of fish.) Further, payments are made at the time of the exchange; there is no periodic large-scale payment as occurs in *jajmāni* (bound) relationships. Finally, payment is not the occasion for any ceremony.

F. *Context of Relationship.* The nonbound relationship is *mainly unicontextual.* Buyer and seller meet only in the economic context.[15] This economic transaction does not imply interaction in ritual or political contexts. (There is some ambiguity on this point concerning service of an artisan to a temple and in life-cycle rituals.) Note, however, that in the limiting case, the nonbound relationship is zero-contextual, as it is in the case where goods are sold through a middleman and producer and consumer have no contact at all.

G. *Vector of Relationship.* With nonbound relationships, each exchange is symmetrical. Normally, buyer and seller meet on neutral ground, the market. A buyer of higher rank than the seller cannot command the seller, nor can the buyer of lower rank than the seller be commanded by the seller in the market place. Bargaining is antithetical to hierarchy.

7.3: SUMMARY: MODES OF INTERCASTE RELATIONS AND TRANSFORMATION OF MODES. The differences between bound and nonbound relationships are summarized in Table 1.

---

[15] Artisans may have jobs in ritual context; for example, a goldsmith melts gold for the wedding *tāli* on an auspicious occasion. But this is a unit job — the goldsmith would not be invited to the wedding for which he made the *tāli*.

Table 1. Summary of characteristics of bound and nonbound relationships

Pattern variables	Bound relationships	Nonbound relationships
Recruitment	No real recruitment; from birth	Voluntary between individuals
Time	Long-lasting, often hereditary	No set duration
Space	Restricted or defined in terms of locality	Not restricted or defined in terms of locality
Clientele	Restricted to certain categories of people	Client's ability to pay for the commodity is the only criterion
Pricing mechanism	"Traditional" (fixed) pricing; periodic payments with ceremony	Supply-and-demand (contingent) pricing; payment on delivery of commodity; no ceremony
Context	Multicontextual: roles played between a given dyad in economic, ritual, and political contexts	Mainly unicontextual: only economic transactions between a given dyad
Vector	Asymmetrical exchanges; hierarchical reciprocity	Symmetrical exchanges; nonhierarchical reciprocity

Although castes engaged primarily in bound-mode relations are sometimes called bound castes (*kattupāṭu cāti*), and castes primarily engaged in nonbound-mode relations are sometimes called free-willing castes (*ishtamāna cāti*), there is no neat classification of bound-mode castes versus nonbound-mode castes. That is, artisans are always engaged (allocating their time and resources) in nonbound (*ishtamāna*) relationships. Agriculturalists and their serving castes are only predominantly engaged in bound (*kattupāṭu*) relationships, since they must interact frequently with artisans and fishermen in nonbound relationships.

In sum, bound and nonbound relationships are variations in social structure occurring within one society, rural Tamil, Sri Lanka. I speak of the variations as polar modalities. Each mode is a cluster of interrelated empirical characteristics.

In the agricultural sphere there are deviations from the bound mode: the relationships *between* serving castes are not as systematically asymmetrical nor multicontextual as those between the dominant landowner and each of the serving castes. In the mercantile sphere, some artisan castes[16] have relationships more conditioned by locality, expectation of duration, and tendency toward a fixed clientele than other artisans. Note that the deviations from the bound mode are in the direction of the options of the nonbound mode; and deviations from the nonbound mode are in the direction of the bound mode. The variant modes of intercaste relations are complemented by variants in normative structure, to which I now turn.

---

[16] Local artisans: blacksmiths, carpenters, and potters. See Table 2 (p. 203).

8: *Normative Analysis*

Every cultural symbol is an indigenous theory of reality for members of that society: regularities in phenomena are codified by symbols, and orientations for action are provided by symbols. For actors, a cultural symbol is both a descriptive theory (code of conduct) and a prescriptive theory (code for conduct) of the *phenomena* it is arbitrarily identified with by the culture. Bound- and nonbound-mode relationships are two contrary modes of *behavioral phenomena*. Previous sociological descriptions of types of intercaste behavior by Epstein (1967), Wiser (1936), and Pocock (1962), among others, did not explore the possibility that the modes of intercaste relations might be prescribed by distinct, contrary codes for intercaste conduct. That is, the two modes of relations might result from different value orientations, the implementation of different norms into action.

After months of interviews and observations of disputes concerning actors engaged in the two modes of relationship, I induced two separate indigenous theories, two contrary normative schemata by means of which actors oriented themselves to the action of others (code of conduct) and with which they guided their own action (code for conduct). Each schema is composed of a discrete set of indigenous symbols. The meanings of the symbols in each set are integrated: the code prescribed by each symbol in the set is compatible with the codes prescribed by the other symbols in the set; each set yields an internally consistent orientation to action. The meanings of symbols in one set, however, are not compatible with the meanings of symbols in the other set; the meanings are contrary. An actor cannot follow both schemata in the same transaction.

Space does not permit me to relate anecdotes of disputes which illustrate that actors follow the code for conduct prescribed by the aristocratic schema when engaged in the bound mode of relationships and the code of conduct prescribed by the mercantile schema when engaged in the nonbound mode of relationships;[17] nor have I space to describe ranking data showing that the third normative schema, the priestly, is compatible with the aristocratic and the mercantile schemata (David 1974a). The priestly schema is a code for conduct for actors engaged in both bound-mode and nonbound-mode relationships.

8.1: NORMATIVE SCHEMATA. The aristocratic schema enjoins a code for conduct of enduring, diffuse, hierarchical, solidary relationships between units (castes).[18] The set of symbols comprising the *aristocratic schema* are *paṭṭam* [titles], *urimai* [nonnegotiable right of master and

---

17 Re choice of codes, see section 8.2.
18 This description builds from Schneider's (1968) notion of the code for conduct between kinsmen in American culture: enduring, diffuse solidarity.

servant to service and remuneration], *kauravam* [honor], *maraiyātai* [respect and limitation, that is, preserving honor], *vāram* [command, in the specific sense of the giving of a power to a subordinate], *anumati* [command, in the sense of giving permission for action to take place], *ātaram* [mutual support], and *varicai* [mutual definition of status].

The *mercantile schema* enjoins a code for conduct of temporary, specific, equivalent, mutually manipulative relationships between units (individuals). The set of symbols comprising the mercantile schema are *ulaippu* [profit and manipulation], *cantōcam* [mutual satisfaction], *nītam* [fair dealing], *keṭṭikkārar* [individual skill, cleverness, and achievement], and *upakāram* [specific aid].

The priestly schema enjoins a code for conduct of hierarchical separation between units (castes). Separation should be hierarchically ordered in terms of the religious principles pure/impure: a place for everyone and everyone in his place. The symbols of this set are *ācaram* [purity] and *tiṭṭu* [pollution].

In the aristocratic schema, an intercaste relationship *tōtarpu* is strongly conditioned by the category of birth of the actors. The category of birth (*jāti* [caste]) provides the limits (*maraiyātaikuḷ*) for potential interaction, and the general rules (*murai*) for the interaction. The hierarchical aspect of relationships in the aristocratic schema is described by villagers as respect (*maraiyātai*), the deference shown the superior by the inferior. In many gestures of etiquette between the superior and the inferior, the superior always gives (food, money, and so forth), while the inferior always receives and serves. The superior is held always to command and to give permission for action to take place (*anumati*). In fact, the inferior is not without some power (to withdraw from stratifying interaction), but the inferior never directly commands activity to take place.

The mutual, or solidary, aspect of relationships in the aristocratic schema is further exemplified by the norms of *varicai* [symbol of status] and *ātaram* [mutual support]. The term *varicai* is a cognitive shorthand for a social phenomenon: intracaste ranks of bound-mode castes are, in part, defined by the existence of relationships between master and servant and by the intracaste rank and behavior of the other party.[19] The term *ātaram* refers to the right to expect aid from the other in happy times and support from the other in troubled times. In sum, the aristocratic schema is used by villagers to describe conduct of and prescribe conduct for bound relationships.

---

[19] In eighteenth-century English comedies of manners, the butler of a highly placed lord scorns the butler of a lord of lower state. In Jaffna, the barber of a titled landowner will neither dine with nor marry a barber of an untitled, albeit wealthy, landowner.

The norms emphasized in the mercantile schema are the code of conduct and the code for conduct of nonbound relationships. In this schema the relationship is not strongly conditioned by the category of birth of the actors. Given the customary symbolic value of many commodities, every Tamil buys gold, cloth, and oil at some time during his life. Trading of these commodities is guided by nonhierarchical norms, *nītam* [fair play] and *cantōcam* [mutual satisfaction]. Nonhierarchy does not exactly mean equality, but rather balance, equilibrium, lack of inequality or partiality; these latter meanings are connotations of the terms *nītam* and *cantōcam*. These notions have no place in the aristocratic schema, where the superior rules by fiat and the inferior's satisfaction is obligatory. Furthermore, in place of the absolute, ascriptive, categorical value of respect (*maraiyātai*), the mercantile schema emphasizes the prestige of cleverness (*keṭṭikkārar*). A *keṭṭikkārar* is a man who is clever and is able to prove it; for example that he is a skillful craftsman or an adroit fisherman. This aspect of individual achievement is also seen in the emphasis on effort and industry (*uḷaippu*). Finally, in place of the aristocratic norm of diffuse mutual aid (*ātaram*), this mercantile normative schema enjoins specific unit acts of help (*upakāram*).

Put another way, the code for conduct embodied in the *aristocratic* schema is that of *hierarchical amity*: diffuse, enduring, hierarchical solidarity. The *mercantile* code for conduct is exactly the opposite, *nonhierarchical instrumentality*: nondiffuse, nonenduring, nonhierarchical nonsolidarity. Since relations between castes are usually characterized in terms of ritual distance, the notion of castes behaving toward each other with hierarchical amity gives a different focus to the relationship. True, relative purity of different castes is a feature of the system, but this difference in terms of ritual purity does not prevent an intense (diffuse, enduring, solidary) relationship. Hierarchical amity is a foreign notion in Western class society, where ranked classes are seen (in Marxist theory) as being in antagonistic relation. In Jaffna caste society, the antagonistic or, at least, manipulative relation (euphemized as the *cantōcam* [mutual-satisfaction] relation) is associated with the nonhierarchical relation in the mercantile schema. Specific, temporary, manipulative dealing is associated with equivalent position between the transacting parties.

8.2: ACTORS' CHOICE OF APPROPRIATE NORMATIVE SCHEMATA. By means of terms for classifying social relations, the villagers do know when to follow the code for conduct prescribed by the aristocratic schema and when to follow that prescribed by the mercantile schema. Castes engaged in bound-mode relations (*kaṭṭupāṭu totarpu*) are either high caste (*uyirnda cāti*) or low caste (*korenja cāti*); castes engaged in nonbound-mode relations (*ishtamāna totarpu*) are good caste (*nallā cāti*) (see Table 2). When the aristocratic schema is in effect, actors say that they are connected, that there is *kontāttam* between the units (my description of the bound relation details what they mean by *kontāttam*). When the mercantile schema is in effect, actors say that there is no connection (*kontāttam illai*) between the units (my description of the nonbound relation details what they mean by *kontāttam illai*). These indigenous classifications of units (castes) and modes of relations between units permit consistent *value orientations* to the different normative schemata, that is, *translation of norms into action*.

Table 2. Castes of Jaffna: traditional designations, traditional occupation, and mode (bound/ nonbound) of intercaste relationship

Type	Caste name	Other designation		Traditional occupation
		Aryan	Dravidian	
Bound-mode castes: priests and castes of the agricultural sector (see section 7.1)	Brahmin[a]	Brahman	Pārpār, Antanar	Temple priest
	Saiva Kurukkal[a]		Pārpār, Antanar	Temple priest
	Vellālar[a]	Sudra	Marutam	Landowner
	Koviar[b]		Idaiyar, Mullai	Herder, domestic servant
	Vannar[c]		Kattati [exorcist: sergeant-at-arms]	Washerman
	Ampattar[c]		Parikari [surgeon]	Barber
	Pallar[c]			Agricultural laborer
	Nalavar[c]			Agricultural and fishing laborer, toddy tapper
	Paraiyar[c]		Muppar, Valluvan	Funeral drummer, weaver, sanitation man
	Tirumpar[c]			Washerman for Pallar and Nalavar
Nonbound-mode castes: merchants and alocal artisans (see section 7.2)	Saiva Chetty[a]	Vaisya		Merchant
	Acari[b]		Visvabrahman	Temple carver
	Tattar[b]		Visvabrahman	Goldsmith
	Kaikular[b]	Vaisya	Cenkuntar Mutaliyar	Silk weaver
	Ceniar[b]	Vaisya	Vanikar	Cotton weaver
	Cantar[b]	Vaisya	Vanikar	Oilpresser
	Mukkiyar[b]		Neytal	Fisherman
	Timilar[b]		Neytal	Fisherman
Mixed-mode castes: primarily bound mode	Pantaram[b]	Lingayat		Temple cook and assistant to priest
	Nattuvar[b]		Isai [music] Vellālar	Auspicious musician
Mixed-mode castes: primarily nonbound mode (fishermen and local artisans)	Karaiyar[b]	Kshatriya	Neytal, Kurukulam	Trader, fisherman, landowner
	Tachar[b]		Visvabrahman	Carpenter
	Kollar[b]		Visvabrahman	Blacksmith
	Kusavar[b]	Brahma		Potter

[a] *Uyirnda cāti* [high caste].
[b] *Nallā cāti* [good caste].
[c] *Korenja cāti* [low caste].

9: *Value Orientation Analysis*[20]

The previous assertion, that bound-mode castes are committed to the priestly and aristocratic normative schemata and that nonbound-mode castes are committed to the priestly and mercantile schemata, will now be substantiated by thematic analysis of caste origin myths. The contention is that mythic action is consciously related by villagers to the normative schemata to which they are oriented.

9.1: BOUND-MODE CASTES. The priestly aristocratic references of the Vellālar landowner myth (section 5.2) are based on a pun. The Vellālar are children (*pillai*) of the goddess Parvati. Their high, pure parentage is essential for the prosperity of the territory under their command; their purity brings forth the crops from the earth.[21] But *pillai* is also a lordly title held by the landowning castes in southern Tamilnadu, where most Vellālar probably came from.

The aristocratic notions of command (*vāram*) and hierarchical rights and obligations (*urimai*) are closely defined in the washerman myth (section 5.7). Recall that when the master (Siva) commanded the servant to clean Parvati's polluted clothing, the washerboy demanded a pond and a stone. The servant can command the master in that he can require the proper equipment to carry out his task. This norm of nonnegotiable rights and obligations (*urimai*) of masters and servants is again illustrated in the Pallar (untouchable agricultural laborer) myth of the fall of a landowner to a worker (section 5.9). Having taken advantage of Pallan's misfortune to reduce him to becoming her worker, the wife of Vellālan sarcastically tells Pallan that he is now the "owner of rice and milk." Even Vellālar informants, who were displeased with the picture of the Vellālar woman, nevertheless approved the insight of the myth: to have an undeniable right (*urimai*) to a portion of the harvest, as all servants do, is, in a sense, to be a parcener of the estate. Note that these mythic definitions of the related norms of command (*vāram*) and nonnegotiable rights (*urimai*) yield a code for conduct similar to the notion of *noblesse oblige*, that is, hierarchical reciprocity.

Servants' ability to influence their master is greater than is generally noted; they enforce aristocratic norms. Is it gratuitous that the washerman, whose alternate name is Kaṭṭati [literally, the one who binds or ties], enforces norms which govern the bound relationship (*kaṭṭupāṭu*

---

[20] The identification of mythic themes with priestly, aristocratic, or mercantile norms was made largely with the help of informants. The use of a tape recorder during the myth-telling sessions permitted me to catch side comments which were as valuable as or more valuable than direct questioning after the telling of the myth.

[21] This theme is found elsewhere in India (see Barnett 1970:164; Nicholas 1967).

totarpu)? He investigates the honor and purity of his master's prospective marriage allies. He partitions the row of eating mats by tying a white cloth in order that distant relations (*tūratte contakkārar*) or nonkin (*paratuvar*) within the same caste may each have a separate eating place (*panti*). Before a wedding feast begins, the Kattati is traditionally asked whether any improper guests are present. Anyone pointed out by the washerman, even a landowner, is expelled. The Kattati sets the limits (*maraiyātai*); he watches over proper social distinctions and thus guards his master's respect (*maraiyātai*) and honor (*kauravam*). Given the norm of mutual definition of status, the servant is protecting his own honor as well. These norms are also seen in the barber myth: sexually indiscreet Vellālar women become the wives of the low-caste barbers (section 5.8).

The Nalavar myth (section 5.10) about the king's trusted regiment wrongly suspected of rape is an account of a fall from an aristocratic position. All these myths not only make reference to norms of the aristocratic schema (titles, command, honor, respect, guarding against loss of honor, mutual rights) but also give subtle interpretations of the norms which differ from Western definitions of the same norms: the superordinate commanded by the subordinate, the superordinate's honor guarded by the subordinate, and so forth.

The priestly schema (pure/impure hierarchy) is emphasized in the origin myths of two other castes engaged in bound relationships: the Brahmin priest and the Paraiyar untouchable. The Brahmin myth (section 5.1) concerns the preservation of purity in the face of a violation of scripture — crossing the sea. Their mythic sophism is that they remained pure since they did the morning *pūjā* and the evening *pūjā* on dry land, having crossed the sea in the interim.

In caste society, according to Dumont (1966a:65ff.), the principle of hierarchy is defined by the opposition of the pure and the impure, the opposition of the Brahmin and the Paraiyar. One Paraiyar myth (section 5.11), of the elder brother who decides to remain silent (*parrayan*) and becomes the Paraiyar, while the younger brother is told to watch (*pārpār*) the temple and becomes the Pārpār or Brahmin, certainly supports this view. Originally higher in the hierarchical older brother/younger brother opposition, the Paraiyar/older brother becomes the lowest of the hierarchy, while the Brahmin/younger brother becomes the highest; the Paraiyar is an inverted Brahmin.

Hierarchy is further defined as a human/extrahuman continuum[22]

---

[22] In the West, social stratification entails ranked relations only between different categories of humans. The South Asian conception of hierarchy includes, in addition, categories of gods, demons, and animals. Inden (1969:12) notes this more extensive definition of hierarchy in the progressive distribution of god's food (*prasadam*) to the whole hierarchy; first the priest, then clean castes, then untouchable castes, and finally animals and impure spirits are fed. Ostor (1971:28) makes a similar point for Bengal:

in the second Paraiyar myth, the tale in which the Paraiyar saint, Nanthan, civilizes the wood-dwelling Paraiyars (section 5.11). The pure Brahmin and the impure Paraiyar, the human limits of a hierarchy which extends beyond humans, mediate between the human and the extrahuman. Brahmins of course mediate between all men and god, between the human and the suprahuman or divine; they are known in Jaffna, as elsewhere in South Asia, as *piritivar* [god's representatives on earth]. That Paraiyar are also mediators — a point not noted in the literature — is the thrust of the Paraiyar exegesis of their Nanthan myth:

The twenty-seven sisters who wedded Sukkira Bhavan had five kinds of children: (1) herbs and plants; (2) animals and reptiles; (3) ordinary men; (4) saints, seers, and gods (*munivar, rsi,* and *tevar*); and (5) ghosts and people between earth and heaven (*pey* and *kintheruvar*). In the course of the myth, the Paraiyar moved from barbarism to a position between animals and men, between the lowly spirits (ghosts and people between earth and heaven) and men. Even today there is evidence of this position because in India Paraiyar live in a *ceri,* [settlement between the forest and settled communities].

While other castes describe the *ceri* as a hamlet removed from the main village because of the Paraiyar's pollution, Paraiyar describe the *ceri*'s location as a spatial symbol of their role as mediators between men and the infrahuman:[23] they live in an area between the forest, where ghosts and other spirits dwell, and the settled village.

In summary, myths of two castes involved in bound-mode relations, Brahmin and Paraiyar, incorporate the themes of purity and impurity, the conceptual focus of the priestly normative schema. Again, we note that these ideas of purity/pollution and hierarchy are defined in ways which differ from Western notions of hierarchy, just as the previous myths elaborated the notion of command.

9.2: MYTHS OF NONBOUND-MODE CASTES. Unlike the hierarchical mythic themes of bound-mode castes, the origin myths of nonbound-mode castes (artisans, fishermen) incorporate nonhierarchical mercantile norms such as *cantōcam* [mutual satisfaction, impartiality to status

---

There is no fundamental cleavage between men (*manus*) and deities (*debota*) but the line is drawn repeatedly on a continuum, and the series of gradations are more extensive than a mere opposition would allow.

[23] Elaboration of the second proposition exceeds the scope of this paper. Two points: first, Paraiyar (and other low castes) are the black magicians dealing with ghosts and demons. Second, there is an extension above and below the human hierarchy in the opposition saint/demon (*munivar/muni*). The saint can escape from the cycle of creation. The demon is permanently bound to creation. The *muni*, in Jaffna theory, is a *munivar* who either renounced his renunciation or successfully pursued his asceticism, received supernatural power from god (*vāram*), and misused his power. The *munivar* is, in both cases, punished by god: he is transformed into a demon.

difference], *keṭṭikkārar* [cleverness, individual autonomy, and achievement], and *ishtamāna vēle* [work commanded and inspired by the divine rather than commanded by humans].

I was discussing Jaffna castes with four Karaiyar fishermen, one of whom regaled us all with his biting, incisive impressions. When he came to the Karaiyar, he said, "Karaiyar? *Virakkarar* [brave man]! When he goes to sea he does not think of his wife and children! Karaiyar's heart will not melt! He fights with a cutlass against a man with a rifle [an incident I observed]. Karaiyar's heart will not melt! He sells fish to a Brahmin or to an untouchable at the same price. Karaiyar's heart will not melt!"

With this statement, the mythic images (section 5.4) of the princess's undaunted maid who sleeps with the horrifying Viyāsar and the obstinate boatman who refuses to touch minor gods after touching Siva and Parvati come into focus with norms for daily social relations. The unmelting heart refers not only to bravery (the martial ethic characteristic of the Kshatriya ruler) (Hitchcock 1959) and puritan obstinacy (refusal to touch inferior beings after having touched the highest beings); the unmelting heart is also a symbol of the mercantile ethic of impersonal attitudes (toward kin and clients) and impartiality regarding religious status differences in business dealings. To "forget about wife and children" and to deal with all castes on the same footing are strong statements in a hierarchical caste society, where the individual ordinarily acts as a member of a category following a traditional customary exchange with a representative of another social category. Against this background of categorically defined exchanges, making an individual contract is like sailing through uncharted waters. A compassionate trader goes out of business. An obstinate trader who is impartial to status differences between himself and the buyer and who is also willing to sell for a just (*nītamāna*) price will be likely to find himself and the buyer satisfied with each other (*cantōcam*). In a trading context, the unmelting heart, which implies mutual satisfaction through obstinacy and impartiality, is a prerequisite to profits (*uḷaippu*). The unmelting heart is thus a central symbol of the mercantile schema, a set of symbols enjoining a code of nonhierarchical, manipulative relations between castes.

These same norms are seen to be valued in the origin myth of the Kusavar [potter] (section 5.6), another caste engaged in nonbound relations. The potter boy does not oppose his grandfather's trading with the king Vikkiramattiran; he bridles only when his grandfather is submissive to the king. To go to someone's house or palace is a sign of respect. Trading goods at the neutral marketplace yields no superiority to buyer or to seller. The potter boy's request is that the relationship be evened off; he does not demand that the king himself come to pick up the pots, which would put the king in an inferior position, but only that the king's servants pick up the pots at the potter's house. The boy is trying to implement the mercantile principle of *cantōcam*, mutual satisfaction, equal dealing between buyer and seller. The king rejects this mercantile solution and selects a martial (aristocratic schema) code for action. With the aid of Chamundeswary Kali, the king is then beaten at his own game.

Action in other myths implies that mercantile norms are divinely oriented or inspired. The definition of work in fisher and artisan myths relates to the priestly and mercantile normative schemata: to work (*vēle*) for another man is demeaning. Artisans and fishermen say, in life and in their myths, that they are autonomous and free-willing (*ishtamāna*) with respect to men. Such was the boatman Kurukulam's reply to god's ministers when they wanted him to serve them by lifting them into the boat. Kurukulam was willing to serve god but no one else (section 5.4). Artisans are willing to be bound in service to god (*katavulukku kaṭṭupāṭu*) because their skill is divinely inspired. In the Kammalan artisan myth, divine skill is ensured by Kamacciamma's vow to live in the blacksmith's fire after Visvabrahma tamed her with the divine tongs made from Brahma, Vishnu, and (U)rudra (section 5.3). Skill is irrelevant in the aristocratic schema: a bad barber still has his right (*urimai*) to remuneration. But in the mercantile schema the skill (*keṭṭikkārar*) of the artisan, held to be divinely inspired, is rewarded by men; a maladroit artisan (*mutal* [fool]) is not.

10: *Summary and Conclusions: Diverse Unities*

The two contrasting modes of intercaste relations, the bound and the nonbound, have been described, as have deviations from these modes. The three normative schemata relevant to intercaste relations, the hierarchical priestly and aristocratic schemata and the nonhierarchical mercantile schema, have been outlined. It was then proposed that castes primarily engaged in bound relations with other castes would have a value orientation to the priestly and to the aristocratic schemata, while castes primarily engaged in nonbound relations with other castes would have a value orientation to the priestly and to the mercantile schemata.

The projective test available in caste origin myths demonstrated these hypotheses. In these cultural documents of self-definition, castes engaged in bound relationships[24] value the norms of the aristocratic

[24]   That is, Brahmin, landowner, washerman, barber, untouchable laborer, and Paraiyar castes.

schema: *paṭṭam* [titles], *urimai* [nonnegotiable right of master and servant to service and remuneration], *kauravam* [honor], *maraiyātai* [respect and limitation, that is, preserving honor], *vāram* [command in the specific sense of the giving of a power to a subordinate], and *aṇumati* [command in the sense of giving permission for action to take place]. On the other hand, origin myths of castes engaged in nonbound relations[25] value the norms of the mercantile schema: *uḷaippu* [profit and manipulation], *cantōcam* [mutual satisfaction], *nītam* [fair dealing], and *keṭṭikkārar* [individual skill, cleverness, and achievement].

All castes in Jaffna know the various normative codes prescribed by the discrete sets of symbols which I have labeled the priestly, the aristocratic, and the mercantile schemata. Knowledge is, of course, not a sufficient cause of human action. Translating the aristocratic norms into social relations requires expenditure. The landowner pays for the ritual services which maintain his honor (*kauravam*). Similarly, resources are mustered by castes committed to the mercantile norms; a goldsmith who, unlike the serving castes, refuses to take food from the landowner, must pay for his autonomy (*ishtamānadu*). Nonrelational forms of commitment, such as incorporating priestly, aristocratic, or mercantile ideas into the caste origin myth, require no material expenditure.

Whether in relational or in nonrelational contexts, castes in Jaffna are committed to a finite number of normative codes, some castes stressing the feudal order, other castes stressing the enterprise order. Although many castes have some unique ideas about behavior, they are not solipsistic, that is, each committed to a unique set of ideas. Rather, there are diverse unities of intercaste symbolic orientations: contrary, hierarchical/nonhierarchical, codes for intercaste conduct. I conclude that Karve's (1961) emphasis on diversity, her notion of idiosyncratic caste cultures, has several limitations. Conversely, in the context of relations between castes, Dumont's (Dumont and Pocock 1957b, 1959) stress on ideational unity, that is, the primacy of the hierarchical principle of purity/impurity, is not exhaustive, for castes are also strongly oriented toward the hierarchical principle of commanding/being commanded and the nonhierarchical principle of mutual satisfaction.

III: THE HUMAN/DIVINE CODE FOR CONDUCT: UNITY FROM DIVERSITY

This article has proceeded in reverse-Chinese-box fashion; starting with the individual unit, the caste, and proceeding to relations between

---

[25]   That is, Kammalan artisan, Karaiyar or Kurukulam fisherman, and potter castes.

castes, it will now consider a still more inclusive set of relations, those of all castes with the divine. This third part completes the variations on the theme of unity/diversity; symbolic orientations were described in Part I as ordered diversity and in Part II as diverse unities. Now, the final variation will be unity from diversity; for, irrespective of the diverse normative codes with which castes orient their interrelations, all castes follow a unified normative code, a hierarchical servant/ master code, for conduct with the divine.

11: *Exoteric Symbolism*

Space forbids a full exposition of the symbolic structure of relations between humans and the divine. It should be stressed that all villagers relate to ritual symbols because these symbols have exoteric meanings. Religious symbols, whether they fit the attributes of Great Tradition or of Little Tradition (Redfield 1960), have both esoteric and exoteric meanings.

Apicēkam [the act of pouring liquids] has the arcane, or esoteric, meanings of dissolution of cravings, separation of the spirit from the body, and purification of the spirit and the body. These inner meanings (*ūl karuttu*) are known and shared by initiates but not by much of the rural populace. *Apicēkam* also has a popular, or exoteric, meaning, that of a rite capable of increasing the sacrificer's wealth. This meaning derives from the identification of *apicēkam* with the anointing of kings at their coronations and present-day aristocrats at their lavish *rites de passage*. The Jaffna exoteric reasoning is that the kings were anointed and they were wealthy; if you are anointed you will be wealthy. Thus the ritual symbol of *apicēkam* has both esoteric and exoteric meanings. It is only the exoteric meanings of ritual symbols, however, representations referring to normal sensations and perceptions (*koṇṭāṭṭam*) of village life, that are known and shared by the uninitiated and the initiated, by members of every caste.[26] Therein lies a unity of symbolic orientations.

12: *Men/God as Servants/Master*

Many ritual symbols have an exoteric component of their meaning which identifies the human/divine relation as the servant/master rela-

---

[26]   Turner (1967) holds that ritual symbols are polysemic; he demarcates as the sensory and normative poles the two clusters of meanings usually associated with ritual symbols. In my definition of exoteric meanings, I am expanding his notion of the sensory pole to include perceptions of social events as well as sensations.

tion. God is treated as a king in one episode of the *pūjā*: the priest displays *varicai* [symbols of status such as miniature flags, whisks, mirrors, or umbrellas] before the icon; villagers readily identify with this episode since they frequently witness servants displaying the same *varicai* at the *rites de passage* of a dominant caste. *Apicēkam* is the anointing of a king. The annual festival of a deity is not complete without the procession around the temple in the *tēr*, or king's chariot. The very name of the temple is *kōvil*, the king's palace (*kō* [king], *il* [place]) (Subrahmanian 1966:66). The minor god Viravar guards temples to pure gods from impure or evil influences for the duration of the festival; he is bound as a servant to god (*katavuḷukku kaṭṭupāṭu*) for the duration and is rewarded "like a servant" with food offerings when the festival is finished. The worshipers also consider themselves bound as servants to god for the duration of the ritual, ceremony, or festival: volunteer ritual workers are called slaves (*atimai* or *tontar*) during the occasion and wear armbands to signify their temporary bondage.

Do all castes follow this servant/master code for human/divine conduct irrespective of the codes to which they are committed in their daily intercaste relations? Discussion of ritual division of labor suggests that they do. Dumont's arguments are sometimes rejected too quickly by canons of verifiability. For example, his definition of caste society as holistic determines his definition of the division of labor in caste society. Thus he revises Marriott's (1960) nonholistic statement, "An occupation is a sort of behavior which constitutes a service rendered to a caste by another caste," into his holistic statement, "It is a service rendered to the whole by the intervention of its castes" (Dumont 1966a:120). This view will never be verified by analyzing daily dealings between men. It is only at the level of relations between men and god that Dumont's statement — that each caste has a duty with respect to the whole — can be verified.

Participation of all castes is essential at the deity's annual festival. Each caste is hierarchically bound in service to god (*katavuḷukku kaṭṭupāṭu*), like servants to the master in the bound mode of relationship, at least once during the year, at the annual temple festival (*tiruvilā*). A simple list of caste duties, as shown in Table 3, should suffice to illustrate this statement. If the giver of a festival is rich, then the services or products contributed by each caste are more than each would have given on its own. The silk weaver not only is commissioned to provide a certain amount of silk cloth but also provides a certain amount not paid for by the giver of the festival. In literal terms, it is this little bit that makes all the difference.

Consider an expression of *homo aequalis*, of the atomistic, equalitarian ideology of Western industrial societies: Leeds Football Club

Table 3. Duties of castes to the whole: caste services or products contributed to a deity's annual festival

Caste	Duty
Brahmin [priest]	Officiant
Saiva Kurukkal [priest]	Officiant
Saiva Chettiyar [merchant]	Giver of the festival (*upayakkārar*)
Vellālar [landowner]	Giver of the festival (*upayakkārar*)
Pantaram [templar]	Assistant to the officiating priest during ritual; cook of offering to god (*prasadam*); decorates the temple, ties garlands, etc.
Koviar (Kovilar: *kōvil* [temple]) [domestic]	Cook of offering to god (*prasadam*); cleans and decorates the inner courtyards
Sippacari [icon carver]	Sculptor of stone and wooden icons; builder of the temple
Kannar [brass worker]	Maker of brass vessels for ritual use
Tachar [carpenter]	Builder of platforms, arches, etc. for ritual use
Kollar [blacksmith]	Maker of ritual brazier, knives for cutting coconuts, and other metal utensils for ritual use
Tattar [goldsmith]	Maker of golden icons and ornaments for the icon; maker of the ritual fan, flag, whisk, etc.
Kaikular [silk weaver]	Maker of silk garments for the icon; maker of the temple flag essential in Agamic ceremony
Ceniar [cotton weaver]	Maker of the cotton draping hung during the festival
Nattuvar [musician]	Festival musician
Kusavar [potter]	Maker of the water pots which represent deities, the cardinal directions, etc. in the ritual
Karaiyar [fisherman/trader]	Importers of ritual objects unobtainable locally, such as the yak tail whisk, deer skin mat, sacred wood for the Homa fire, etc.
Cantar [oilpresser]	Provider of oil for the Homa fire lighting, torches, etc.
Vannar [washerman]	Ties cotton cloth in drapings around the temple
Ampattar [barber]	Aids in purifying the priest (ritual shave); pours oil on torches during processions
Untouchable	Cleans outer courtyard of temple; collects firewood

had narrowly beaten Manchester United, and the Manchester partisans were rallying for the traditional postgame fight with Leeds. I heard one man yell, "Every man for himself and God for us all!" Sectarianism aside, in Western societies, "All for God, and God for all!"

would be an eccentric thought. But in caste society, all men are for god in the same way, in that all Jaffna castes follow the same code for human/divine conduct, the master/servant relation of the priestly and aristocratic normative schemata described earlier.

Both hierarchic schemata are amalgamated in ritual participation, the act of temporary renunciation of daily roles. The worshiper must provide a service or a commodity proper to his caste. For his service or commodity, he receives from god a nontangible, traditional reward: merit (*punya*). Thus the code for conduct resembles the aristocratic schema. In addition, the worshiper must be in a state of extreme purity when he approaches god. He must abstain from meat, liquor, and sexual intercourse. He must bathe and don ritually pure clothing. He must separate himself from impure influences such as demons by tying a sacred thread around his arm. He is protected from impure influences by a portal guardian deity, in Sri Lanka usually the fierce Viravar (Sanskrit Bhairava). A longer list could be given, but the relevance of the priestly (pure/impure) code for conduct between man (qua worshipers at the annual festival) and god is obvious.

13: *Conclusion: Unity from Diversity*

To show how diversity of symbolic orientations resolves to unity, I will now discuss the formal structure of the three normative schemata. It was argued earlier that the category of "relationship" (*koṇṭāṭṭam*) is held by villagers to refer only to bound relations (*kaṭṭupāṭu totarpu*), for which the hierarchic priestly and aristocratic schemata are the code for conduct. In contrast, the category of "no relationship" (*koṇṭāṭṭam illai*) is held by villagers to refer only to nonbound relations (*ishtamāna totarpu*), relations for which the nonhierarchic (equivalent) mercantile schema is the code for conduct (section 8.2). The opposition *koṇṭāṭṭam/koṇṭāṭṭam illai* is isomorphic with the opposition work/business (*vēle/viyāparam*). For example, a landowner and a barber have a relationship, since the barber is bound in service to the landowner and must work for him; the landowner and the goldsmith have no relationship, since they are not bound in master/servant relation but have only business dealings with each other. On the level of relations between castes, there is a contradiction between the two hierarchic normative schemata (the priestly and the aristocratic) and the schema of equivalence (the mercantile), an opposition of hierarchy/equivalence.

This contradiction is only resolved on the more inclusive level of relations between men and gods. During the annual festivals, all men temporarily take on the servant position with respect to god and are bound in service to god (*katavuḷukku kaṭṭupāṭu*). Such is the lot of ordinary men in the world, the undeniable duty (*urimai*) of house-holders (*grhastas*): the "path of the servant" (*dāsya marga*). All men temporarily renounce their normal roles, whether the hierarchical roles of master or servant or the nonhierarchical roles of artisan, fisherman, or trader, in favor of the servant role with respect to god: they all do temple work (*kōvil vēle*) for god during the festival.

This opposition man/god may be relevant in many parts of India. For example, in Chhattisgarh, Madhya Pradesh, India,

. . . food is offered to the deity and then retrieved from the altar for con-sumption by participants in the ritual. The transaction allows the deity to be paid for divine favors and at the same time establishes a hierarchical rela-tionship between the deity and the worshippers as a group. Differentiation within the congregation is obscured by the wider opposition between divinity and the worshipping group as a whole (Babb 1970:287).

Thus, in relations between men and god, the opposition hierarchy/equivalence is resolved in favor of the hierarchical term. Since this normative code is followed by all castes, we may speak of a unity of symbolic orientations.

This same analysis too briefly indicates what kind of symbols struc-ture diversity into unity, a question requisite for an anthropologist working with a peasant society. Are the abstract, refined, codified symbols called the Great Tradition solely representative of the men-tality of the Hindu villager? Are the concrete, homespun, locally known symbols of the Little Tradition an exhaustive representation? Obeyesekere (1963) argues that peasant villagers have traditions which integrate religious figures and religious action otherwise segregated by the analyst's rubrics Great Tradition (GT) and Little Tradition (LT). For example, the Lord Buddha (GT), gods (GT and LT), and demons (LT) are all part of a hierarchy ordered by the principles of purity, merit, and command.

Following his lead, I argue that a more appropriate dichotomy than that of the Great/Little Traditions is that of esoteric/exoteric tradi-tions, that is, the structuring of symbolic diversity as analyzed in terms of a popular, exoteric symbolism which ordinary villagers relate to perceptions and sensations of daily life.

This issue, which will be studied in another paper, must be men-tioned here, since I have here been using an exoteric definition of hierarchy which differs from Dumont's (1962) textually based, eso-teric definition. Dumont might deny that the priestly and aristocratic schemata are both hierarchical schemata. In his definition, the priestly schema alone is hierarchical since, to him, hierarchy entails the abso-lute separation of the spiritual principle (purity/impurity) from the temporal principle (power: commanding/being commanded); as the spiritual principle encompasses the temporal principle, the spiritual principle alone is a hierarchical, holistic principle. Elsewhere (David 1972:474-503) I contend that the more popular, exoteric definition of hierarchy entails the conjoining of the two principles and the lack of encompassing/encompassed relation between them, both principles being holistic and segmentary.

IV: CONCLUSION

14: *The Substantive Question: Normative Analysis as Guide to Unity/ Diversity Characterizations of Rural South Asia*

Unity/diversity characterizations depend upon the various authors' theoretical positions: how are a multiplicity of normative codes for conduct and a multiplicity of types of behavior handled in the literature? Bailey (1960:6) deals with diversity on the social structural level of analysis by distinguishing conflict from contradiction. Conflict can be resolved within the framework of the structure; contradiction cannot:

It was very obvious in Bisipara that the ritual sub-structure in which the Warriors [caste] and the Untouchables interacted was in many respects inconsistent with their political and economic relationships. There was an irresolvable contradiction between these two sub-structures, and, taken together, they did not add up to one consistent structure.

Conflict, which can be resolved within the framework of the structure, threatens neither equilibrium nor homogeneity; contradiction, which cannot be so resolved, implies both disequilibrium and diversity. Bailey's (1960:7-8) response to the presence of contradiction is to posit the presence of more than one structure:

The presence in any situation of irresolvable contradiction between different roles indicates that the total situation cannot be understood within the framework of a single omnicompetent structure. If the analysis is to be continued within the framework of one structure, then one or the other side of the contradiction must be ignored. This is not satisfactory since it removes the analysis further from reality. Alternatively, it may be assumed that there is not one structure to be analyzed, but there are two or more structures operating in a single social field.

Whereas Bailey does not offer suggestions on how to deal with the presence of more than one structure operating in a single social field, Moore (1960:815) opts for a methodology of dialectic between ideal types:

The literature of sociology abounds with dichotomous classifications, ranging from culture-types through forms of social cohesion or relationship, to paired normative alternatives. Although such modes of classification are "primitive" in the sense that they attempt analysis in terms of attributes rather than variables, they are not useless. It is the beginning of wisdom to identify the dichotomies as polar extremes on a range of variation, and the pursuit of wisdom to note that "pure" types do not concretely exist. A very considerable gain in wisdom results, however, from *recognizing the paired alternatives as conflicting principles of social organization, both of which are persistent in the system. Predominant institutionalization of one alternative does not dispel or dismiss its counterpart. . . . Sociologists have noted, for example, that "achieved" status systems retain elements of ascription, and conversely* [emphasis mine].

Dumont posits a rather different relation between polar opposites in his analysis of Hindu society. To Dumont, there is no relation of dialectic between hierarchy and individualism. Rather, hierarchy "encompasses" individualism:

L. Dumont's Homo Hierarchicus raises most provocatively the issues of comparing cultures given a structural analysis of the symbolic domain. He suggests that anthropological understanding derives from the mediation of systems real for the people themselves (stressed by them) [i.e. the encompassing feature] and systems singled out by the anthropologist because of his antecedent mindset (unstressed by the people themselves) [i.e. the encompassed feature]. Generalization involves locating features common to all cultures and seeing them in their stressed or unstressed aspect in any particular culture; that is, generalization must start with two cultures and the stressed/unstressed features might not be applicable to a third culture. Dumont has concentrated on the question of hierarchy and stratification, individualism and holism in India (Anonymous 1971:20).

To Dumont (1966b:30-31), hierarchy is the feature on the level of maximal consciousness of ideology which underlies caste society. Equality and individualism are marginal features in caste society, expressed only in the ideal of the renouncer.

On one hand, Bailey's notion of contradictory structure within one society eschews cultural analysis but includes a strict empirical test[27] to determine the presence of contradictory behavioral structures in a social setting.[28] Since he offers no suggestion on how to analyze the

---

[27] "Every conflict needs to be examined to see how far it brings into play redressive mechanisms and how far it is contained within one structure. It is clearly a mistake to leap at once to the conclusion that every conflict is evidence of irresolvable contradiction and therefore of change. Some conflicts are temporary disturbances of a structure which has its own means of finding a way back to equilibrium. It is only after this question has been asked that one is justified in concluding that the analysis can only be saved from undue 'unreality' by postulating the presence in the social field of more than one structure" (Bailey 1960:10).

[28] My use of *contrary* must not be confused with Bailey's use of *contradictory*. Bailey's definition of *contradictory* follows from his interest in equilibrium structures

formal relations between such contradictory structures, the final account is of an unordered collection of structures, of diversity, although different from Karve's (1961) view that diversity results from the amalgamation of individual caste cultures in village communities. On the other hand, Dumont's (Dumont and Pocock 1957a:13) analysis, which concentrates on abstract ideological features such as purity and impurity, is not easily amenable to empirical verification. But his constant attention to the relations between units rather than to the units themselves, to relations whose form is constant due to the encompassing ideological feature, ends with a picture of unity.

Normative analysis, specifically the structuring of contrary normative schemata provides a middle way between these theoretical and substantive contributions. In this article, the review of a substantive problem, unity/diversity in South Asian society, has focused upon patterns of commitment/noncommitment to symbol systems in Jaffna, Sri Lanka. The picture of diversity of symbolic orientations in caste society in Part I was limited by discussing individual caste identity; each caste defines itself with a culturally shared system of symbols: ideas about natural substance, occupations, cattle brands, and origin myths. Each caste defines itself not by a unique set of symbols but by a paradigm of symbols known and shared by all castes. This section thus rejects certain aspects of Karve's diversity characterization in which individual caste cultures dominate wider societal principles.

Like ideas defining social differentiation, ideas defining social inter-relations are also shared by all castes. In Part II, codes for intercaste relations were described as diverse unities of symbolic orientations. Jaffna castes have distinct modes of intercaste relations and distinct systems of normative symbols which prescribe contrary normative codes for intercaste conduct. Since Dumont's unity model emphasizes hierarchy as the encompassing ideology in Hindu South Asia, egalitarianism and individualism not being stressed in the culture, Part II modifies his position. The mercantile schema emphasizes equivalence and individual skill if not, strictly speaking, egalitarianism and individualism. This nonhierarchic schema coexists with the hierarchic aristocratic and priestly normative schemata in rural Jaffna. Similarly, nonbound-mode and bound-mode intercaste relations are variant social structures in rural Jaffna.

In Part III, which considered ritual relations between men and god,

---

(cohesion/lack of cohesion, conflict/resolution of conflict, etc.): he uses *contradictory* in the sense of irresolvable conflict between roles in different substructures. In using *contrary* to describe modes of behavior or normative codes, I follow the etymological sense: elements are in contrary relation when there is a contrast of opposition in the logical sense and not opposition in the behavioral (i.e. conflict, confrontation) sense.

an analysis of exoteric ritual symbolism was used to describe unity of symbolic orientations.

The structuring of contrary normative schemata at different levels (diversity on the level of relations between castes and unity on the level of relations between men and god) may be stated more formally with a descriptive model. Following Black's (1962) definition, a model has nothing to do with data. The logical connections of terms of a well-developed theory are borrowed for use on a domain of data with underdeveloped theory. A new theory is thus modeled on an existing theory. To understand the structuring of contrary normative schemata, I shall borrow unmarked/marked category theory from structural linguistics.

Although Greenberg (1966) attempts to show the relevance of un-marked/marked category analysis to the phonemic, morphophonemic, and semantic levels of language, I shall use an example from the semantic level only. The term *man*, meaning mankind as opposed to animals or to nature, is on a higher taxonomic level than the terms *man* and *woman*, the two genders of mankind. *Woman* is a category further specified, or semantically *marked*, in relation to the *unmarked* category *man*. Conversely, the opposition *man/woman* is neutralized at the higher taxonomic level. There exists the opposition man/nature but not woman/nature.

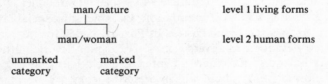

man/nature		level 1 living forms
man/woman		level 2 human forms
unmarked category	marked category	

In this study, the more inclusive taxonomic level is the opposition man/god (in Tamil, *maṇisan/katavuḷ*) and the lower level is the kinds of man, or castes, that is, intercaste relations. Then the opposition existing at the lower level between hierarchic normative codes for conduct (unmarked category) and the nonhierarchic code for conduct (marked category) is neutralized at the higher level of relations and only the unmarked category appears.

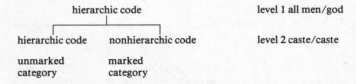

hierarchic code		level 1 all men/god
hierarchic code	nonhierarchic code	level 2 caste/caste
unmarked category	marked category	

Similarly, the opposition between two modes of intercaste relation-ships, which, following indigenous categories, I label bound and unbound relationships, is neutralized at the higher level of relations. That is, some castes are involved in bound relationships with some other castes; different castes are involved in nonbound relationships with other castes; but members of all castes are involved in a bound relationship with god.

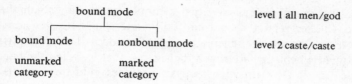

Another neutralization concerns labor. Work (*vēle*) is a hierarchical concept since to do work is inferiorizing: the barber works for the landowner. Business (*viyāparam*) is a concept of equivalence since marketing connotes the superiority of neither seller nor buyer: the goldsmith and the landowner have business relations with each other. Temple work (*kōvil vēle*) is a hierarchical concept since man is working for god as a member of a serving caste works for the master: Brahmin priests and Sippicari icon carvers, for example, do nothing but *kōvil vēle*, but *all* castes do temple work during the annual festival.

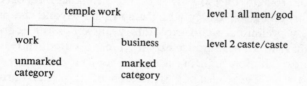

The formal relation of unmarked and marked categories is intended to resemble Dumont's usage of the encompassing and the encompassed. The opposition of unmarked/marked categories, one of the several notions used in ethnographic semantics to describe hierarchical arrangements of lexical units, may be of wide utility in analyzing patterns of thought in hierarchical societies. Here it was demonstrated that all castes, regardless of their normative orientations in intercaste conduct, both share and are committed to a single system of exoteric symbols prescribing a hierarchical servant/master code for human conduct toward the divine. Unlike the level of relations between castes, the opposition of hierarchic (priestly and aristocratic) normative schemata/nonhierarchic (mercantile) schema is here neutralized: only hierarchic schemata are relevant in ritual relations between men and god. The unmarked category, hierarchy, and the marked category, equivalence, are both present on the lower level of relations. The unmarked category alone appears at the structurally higher level of relations. Thus the analogy with unmarked/marked categories of structural linguistics is fulfilled.

This model clarifies the question of unity/diversity of symbolic orientations. Unity in symbolic orientations in Jaffna caste society is incited by exoteric meanings of ritual symbols, meanings which the uninitiated villager relates to normal daily experiences. Castes committed to diverse normative schemata on profane occasions are united in commitment when they approach the sacred, that is, when they act as a whole. In short, normative analysis provides guidelines to disentangle the question of unity/diversity in symbolic orientations in caste society at three levels: within the caste, between castes, and between men and god.

15: *Normative Analysis as Mediator*

As indicated in the introduction, using normative analysis to clarify a major aspect of the unity/diversity puzzle was a vehicle for a more general theoretical question. Social structural analysts and structuralist analysts were viewed as talking past each other on this puzzle. Must the hiatus between these two important perspectives of explaining human action remain unresolved? Do the differences between two eminent anthropologists, Bailey and Dumont, lie beyond the pale of discourse? My preliminary and exploratory answer is the following: social structural and structuralist explanations are frequently reductionist, each explanation reducing to epiphenomena the object of the opposite analysis. Yet conscious structures of thought, normative codes, mediate in a cognitive sense between actual networks of relationships and unconscious structures of thought. That is, the object of normative analysis mediates the objects of social structural and structuralist analyses. A nonreductionist strategy of analysis would thus be to reject any notion of a one-to-one correspondence between these levels of analysis and to delineate the relations between normative symbols and behavior patterns and between conscious normative symbols and unconscious structures of thought.

Different brands of theoretical reductionism have influenced Bailey's and Dumont's views, not only on the unity/diversity problem but on other empirical questions, such as local caste ranking. Bailey reduces cultural ideas to social structure, to hard facts of resources and power. For example, he notes that, in the middle ranges of a village hierarchy, the ritual ranks of castes correspond to their politico-economic ranks. When he dismisses the lack of correspondence concerning Brahmins and untouchables as a "peculiar rigidity . . . at the extremes of the hierarchy" (Bailey 1964), he incurs Dumont's (1966b:19) charge of reducing the whole ideology of purity and impurity to an epiphenomenon.

In turn, Bailey, Marriott, and others have criticized Dumont's brand of structuralism as reductionist and unverifiable. His analysis jumps from empirical detail directly to "intellectualist" formulations on the structural level. In explaining the central data of Bailey's analysis, correspondences between social and ritual ranks, Dumont (1966b:28) assigns empirical factors, politics and economics, to an "encompassed" secondary position relative to the "encompassing" position of the hierarchical ideology. These analytic "residues" are reduced to epiphenomena in a novel way; they condition human action only within the limits imposed by the hierarchical ideology.

The analytic strategy used in this article to cope with these opposing forms of reductionism is to attend to the level of analysis stressed by neither Dumont nor Bailey; normative analysis can give equal time to both material and ideational features, the subjects of social structural and structuralist analyses, because cultural norms mediate, in a logical and cognitive sense, between the two factors.

Put otherwise, Piaget's (1970) idea of the relativity of form and content helps to describe the relations between behavior patterns, cultural norms, and the underlying features of ideology. To Piaget, no absolute opposition exists between form and content. Rather, what is form with respect to a cognitively inferior level is content with respect to a cognitively superior level: real objects are content ordered by numbers, numbers are content with respect to algebra, algebra with respect to calculus, and so forth.

First, how do cultural norms give form to the content of patterns of behavior? Cultural norms are an indigenous "fictional" theory of real phenomena, including real patterns of behavior. As Leach (1965:ix) puts it, symbols bear an "as if" relation to reality, both for anthropologists and for natives.

In brief, my argument is that although historical facts are never, in any sense, in equilibrium, we can gain genuine insights if, for the purpose of analysis, we force these facts within a constraining mould of an *as if* system of ideas, composed of concepts which are treated *as if* they were part of an equilibrium system. Furthermore, I claim to demonstrate that this fictional procedure is not merely an analytical device of the social anthropologist, it also corresponds to the way the Kachins themselves apprehend their own system through the medium of the verbal categories of their own language.

De jure, norms are what actors ought to do or ought not to do. *De facto*, they are fictional representations of reality used by actors to simplify their perceptions of complex patterns of behavior; to render to ambivalent or ambiguous psychic phenomena a coherent, psychologically reassuring form; to euphemize indiscreet behavior or base motivations; to provide a clear cognitive frame for coordinated action when the motivations of individual actors are disparate or antithetical or antipathetic. Shared norms are conditioned by reality (they are a code of reality) in that they are fictions manipulated by actors to bring them in line with *faits accomplis* or with proposed action; and reality is conditioned by norms (code for reality) in that the norms provide both positive guides for proposed action and cognitive frames to differentiate "acceptable" behavior from "unacceptable" behavior and then to eliminate from consideration what is judged to be "unacceptable."[29]

Given all these relations between the normative level and action, an apposite comparison is the relation of an analyst's theory to his data. The normative level is an indigenous, culturally coded theory of reality; the normative level abstracts from blooming, buzzing reality complex behavioral and psychic phenomena. Complexity is reduced for the sake of order (Lévi-Strauss 1966:22). Analogous to the normative level as a model of and for reality are the analytic processes in which, respectively, acquisition of data conditions the formulation of a theory and theoretical formulation conditions the perception of a domain of data. In brief, to recognize cultural norms as an indigenous, fictional theory of reality is to insist that norms provide form for the content of behavioral phenomena while reducing neither ideas nor action to epiphenomenal status. With attention to the normative level, politico-economic factors are not reduced to a secondary encompassed status.

Continuing with Piaget's idea about the relativity of form and content, how are ideational features the form ordering the content of cultural norms? Ideational features are the analyst's abstraction from the meanings of the normative symbols of normative schemata. Verifying that symbols of each normative schema express different ideational features is not a metaphysical but a simple exegetical task. Informants, by their words and actions, define the meanings of symbols. I began to group symbols into normative schemata when I recognized recurring themes in native exegeses of different sets of symbols. For example, the theme of commanding/being commanded appeared as informants defined (1) nonnegotiable rights (*urimai*), (2) honor (*kauravam*), and (3) work (*vēle*). In the first case, "the master does not have unlimited command for he must heed the rights of his servants"; in the second, "many *varicai* define the honor of the master, his pure ancestry, his wealth, his command of all the serving

---

[29] Compare "double-think" in George Orwell's *1984*.

castes''; in the third, work is inferiorizing because ''when you work for a man you are commanded by him.'' The exegeses of these symbols, *urimai, kauravam, varicai, vēle*, appeared as variations on the theme of commanding/being commanded.

Turner (1967:50, 52) has said that symbols are multivocalic, that is, polysemic. Commanding/being commanded is a voice heard in all the symbols of the aristocratic normative schema. Put more formally, commanding/being commanded is a conceptual focus for the symbols of the aristocratic normative schema, a general idea elaborated in the meanings of the symbols composing the schema. Similarly, the opposition purity/impurity underlies the meanings of the symbols composing the priestly schema, and the term ''mutual satisfaction'' underlies the mercantile schema.[30]

Dumont (1966a:66) allows for this direction of inquiry when he says,

We do not pretend that the opposition pure/impure underlies (*fonde*) society other than in the intellectual sense of the term; to those who live in it, caste society appears coherent and rational by implicit reference to this opposition.

Norms, of course, are referred to in actuality, not implicitly. To the extent that norms can be shown to be expressions of structural oppositions, actors are then making implicit reference to the structural oppositions.

An Indian student of mine, having read the debates in *Contributions to Indian Sociology*, said, ''Bailey is Bailey and Dumont is Dumont. And never the twain shall meet.'' He is wrong. The gulf between behavioral analysis and structuralist analysis seems unbridgeable only as long as we fail to attend to normative analysis. Cultural norms give a ''fictional'' form to the content of actual behavior. And the concepts or meanings identified with normative symbols are content with respect to ideological features; ideological features are conceptual foci for sets of symbols composing normative schemata. Thus, in the idiom of relativity of form and content, cultural norms relate both to behavior and to ideological features. As the middle air mediates heaven and earth, normative analysis mediates structuralist and social structural analyses. Such a detailed argument is necessary if one chooses the analytic strategy of delimiting the relations among three separate levels of analysis. As in the story of the Hidatsa eagle hunter, it takes some effort to keep one's feet planted on the earth while reaching for the sky.

---

[30] This point was demonstrated by an exegesis of transactional ranking symbols of Jaffna, Sri Lanka. The opposition purity/impurity is part of ranking symbols such as food giving/food taking, proximity behavior, and permission to use a well. The opposition commanding/being commanded is part of the meaning of ranking symbols such as giving/receiving an object with one/two hands, removal of shawl and turban, and pronouns of address (David 1974a).

REFERENCES

ANONYMOUS
   1971   Prospectus for seminar entitled "Institute: Homo Hierarchicus, comparison and generalization." Preliminary Program, 70th Annual Meeting. *American Anthropological Association Bulletin* 5:20.

ARUNACHALAM, P.
   1964   *Sketches of Ceylonese history*. Colombo: M. D. Gunasena.

BABB, LAWRENCE
   1970   The food of the gods in Chhattisgarh: some structural features of Hindu ritual. *Southwestern Journal of Anthropology* 26.

BAILEY, F. G.
   1959   For a sociology of India? *Contributions to Indian Sociology* 3.
   1960   *Tribe, caste and nation*. Manchester: Manchester University Press.
   1964   *Caste and the economic frontier*. Manchester: Manchester University Press.

BARNETT, STEVE
   1970   "The structural position of a caste in south India: Koṇṭaikkaṭṭi Vellālars." Unpublished Ph.D. dissertation, University of Chicago.
   1972   "Lineages in the context of alliance." Unpublished manuscript read at the seminar of the Anthropology and South Asian Faculties at the University of Chicago.

BARTH, FREDRIK
   1960   "The system of social stratification in Swat, north Pakistan," in *Aspects of caste in India, Ceylon, and northwest Pakistan*. Edited by E. R. Leach. Cambridge Papers in Social Anthropology 2. Cambridge: Cambridge University Press.

BLACK, MAX
   1962   *Models and metaphors*. Ithaca, N.Y.: Cornell University Press.

COHN, BERNARD S.
   1955   "The changing status of a depressed caste," in *Village India*. Edited by McKim Marriott. Chicago: University of Chicago Press.

DAVID, KENNETH
   1972   "The bound and the nonbound: variations in social and cultural structure in rural Jaffna, Ceylon." Unpublished Ph.D. dissertation, University of Chicago.
   1974a "And never the twain shall meet? Mediating the structural approaches to caste ranking," in *Structural approaches to south Indian studies*. Edited by Harry Buck. Chambersburg: Wilson College Press.
   1974b Spatial organization and normative schemes in Jaffna, north Ceylon. *Modern Ceylon Studies* 3(1).

DUMONT, LOUIS
   1962   The conception of kinship in ancient India. *Contributions to Indian Sociology* 6.
   1966a *Homo hierarchicus*. Paris: Gallimard.
   1966b A fundamental problem in the sociology of caste. *Contributions to Indian Sociology* 9.

DUMONT, LOUIS, DAVID POCOCK
   1957a For a sociology of India. *Contributions to Indian Sociology* 1.
   1957b Village studies. *Contributions to Indian Sociology* 1.
   1959   Pure and impure. *Contributions to Indian Sociology* 3.

EPSTEIN, T. SCARLETT
  1967 "Productive efficiency and customary systems of reward in rural south India," in *Themes in economic anthropology*. Edited by Raymond Firth. Association of Social Anthropologists Monograph 6. London: Tavistock.

GEERTZ, CLIFFORD
  1959 Form and variation in Balinese village structure. *American Anthropologist* 61.

GOUGH, E. KATHLEEN
  1960 "Caste in a Tanjore village," in *Aspects of caste in India, Ceylon, and northwest Pakistan*. Edited by E. R. Leach. Cambridge Papers in Social Anthropology 2. Cambridge: Cambridge University Press.

GREENBERG, JOSEPH H.
  1966 *Language universals*. Paris, The Hague: Mouton.

HARPER, EDWARD B.
  1959 Two systems of economic exchange in village India. *American Anthropologist* 61.

HITCHCOCK, JOHN T.
  1959 "The idea of the martial Rajput," in *Traditional India, structure and change*. Edited by M. Singer. American Folklore Society Bibliographic and Special Series 10. Austin: University of Texas Press.

INDEN, RONALD
  1969 "Exchange, sacrifice, and hierarchy in early India." Unpublished manuscript.

KARVE, IRAWATI
  1961 *Hindu society—an interpretation*. Poona: Deccan College.

KOLENDA, PAULINE MAHAR
  1964 Religious anxiety and Hindu fate. *Journal of Asian Studies* 23.

LEACH, EDMUND
  1965 *Political systems of highland Burma*. Boston: Beacon.

LÉVI-STRAUSS, CLAUDE
  1966 *The savage mind*. Chicago: University of Chicago Press.
  1970 *The raw and the cooked*. Translated by John and Doreen Weightman. New York: Harper and Row.

MAJUMDAR, D. N.
  1958 *Caste and communication in an Indian village*. Bombay: Asia Publishing House.

MARRIOTT, MC KIM
  1960 *Caste ranking and community structure in five regions of India and Pakistan*. Deccan College Monograph Series 23. Poona: Deccan College.
  1969 Review of Louis Dumont's *Homo hierarchicus*. *American Anthropologist* 71.

MATHUR, K. S.
  1964 *Caste and ritual in a Malwa village*. Bombay: Asia Publishing House.

MAYER, ADRIAN C.
  1970 *Caste and kinship in central India*. Berkeley: University of California Press.

MOORE, WILBUR E.
  1960 A reconsideration of theories of social change. *American Sociological Review* 25.

NICHOLAS, RALPH W.
  1967 Ritual hierarchy and social relations in rural Bengal. *Contributions to Indian Sociology*, new series 1.
OBEYESEKERE, GANANATH
  1963 The Great Tradition and the Little in the perspective of Sinhalese Buddhism. *Journal of Asian Studies* 22.
OPLER, M. E., R. D. SINGH
  1952 Two villages in eastern Uttar Pradesh (U.P.), India. *American Anthropologist* 54.
OSTOR, AKOS
  1971 "The play of the gods among men." Unpublished Ph.D. dissertation, University of Chicago.
PIAGET, JEAN
  1970 *Structuralism.* New York: Basic Books.
POCOCK, DAVID
  1962 Notes on *jajmāni* relationships. *Contributions to Indian Sociology* 6.
REDFIELD, ROBERT
  1960 *The little community/peasant society and culture.* Chicago: University of Chicago Press.
SCHNEIDER, DAVID
  1968 *American kinship: a cultural account.* Englewood Cliffs, N.J.: Prentice-Hall.
SIVARATNAM, C.
  1968 *The Tamils in early Ceylon.* Colombo: United Merchants.
SRINIVAS, M. N.
  1955 "Social system in a Mysore village," in *Village India.* Edited by McKim Marriott. Chicago: University of Chicago Press.
  1966 *Social change in modern India.* Berkeley: University of California Press.
SUBRAHMANIAN, N.
  1966 *Sangam polity.* Bombay: Asia Publishing House.
Tamil lexicon
  1936 *Tamil lexicon.* Madras: University of Madras Press.
TURNER, VICTOR
  1967 *The forest of symbols: aspects of Ndembu ritual.* Ithaca, N.Y.: Cornell University Press.
WISER, WILLIAM H.
  1936 *The Hindu* jajmāni *system.* Lucknow: Lucknow Publishing House.

Toward an Ethnosociology of South Asian Caste Systems

McKIM MARRIOTT and RONALD B. INDEN

This paper, with its companion (Marriott and Inden 1974), aims to make some valid statements about caste systems in all of South Asia in cognitive and ethnosociological terms. In other words, it aims to offer some parts of a cultural analysis of caste systems, using concepts that are believed to be understood and accepted by all sorts of South Asians in discussing their own social systems. It does not exclude, on grounds of ideology, the caste systems of Buddhists in Sri Lanka or those of Muslims in Pakistan and Bangladesh (as does Dumont 1966, 1970), nor does it include them for their behavioral similarities to Hindu systems while minimizing the consequences of their religious differences (as do Marriott 1960 and Mandelbaum 1970). It aims rather to state some cognitive elements that accompany the various and changing caste systems of all South Asians and to describe how these elements are differently arranged in some of the main variant systems.

THE NONDUALITY OF SOUTH ASIAN SOCIAL THOUGHT

The aims of this paper are inspired by the results of a cultural style of analysis exemplified in Schneider's book *American kinship* (1968). Schneider finds that all kinds of Americans understand their varied kinship ties as consisting ultimately of pairs of things. One constituent they conceive of as "nature," that is, linkages through natural acts, especially love or sexual intercourse. The other constituent, something that Americans often think of as transcending nature, is "law" — codes for the conduct of persons who have made linkages with each other. Schneider suggests that Europeans in general

— Christians and Jews — and possibly peoples of other areas are similar to Americans in using such dual categories to define both kinship and concepts like "religion," "race," "ethnicity," and "nation."

At the first glance of a Euro-American, South Asians appear to possess the same sort of dual categories. South Asian analogies for the concepts of "law" or "code for conduct" seem to be highly developed in the treatments given to caste and kinship by the classical Hindu moral code books (*dharmaśāstra*). Conceptions of morality (*dharma*) have been extensively researched by generations of Indologists (e.g. Kane 1930-1962) and, more recently, ethnographers. South Asian concepts analogous to but different from American notions of kinship in nature — blood and genetic substances, for example — are discussed in great detail in classical South Asian medical books (e.g. Caraka 1949; Sushruta 1963) and have been reported, after field investigations, by Carstairs (1957:77-88) and Yalman (1967:136-142).

It has long been disturbingly evident to Westerners in many small ways, however, that South Asians do not insist on drawing a line between what Westerners call "natural" and what they call "moral" things; the Hindu moral code books are thus filled with discussions of bodily things, while the medical books at many points deal with moral qualities (*guṇas* [the three primal qualities or attributes of matter], etc.). Using Schneider's American kinship categories as analytic concepts, Barnett (1970) has detailed some close connections between the beliefs of one south Indian group about its morality and its beliefs about its purity of blood.

A similar critical finding for understanding of South Asian caste — that the code for conduct of living persons is not regarded as transcendent over bodily substance, but as immanent within it — was developed by Inden and Nicholas (i.p.) from an investigation of the cognitive categories of kinship among Bengali Hindus and Muslims in both India and Bangladesh. Inden and Nicholas find that when a Bengali woman marries, her body is thought to be transformed, as is her inborn code for conduct. This striking finding mirrors the widespread and familiar but equally striking observation that a South Asian's moral qualities are thought to be altered by the changes in his body resulting from eating certain foods, engaging in certain kinds of sexual intercourse, taking part in certain ceremonies, or falling under certain other kinds of influence. Bodily substance and code for conduct are thus thought to be not fixed but malleable, and to be not separated but mutually immanent features: the coded substance moves and changes as one thing throughout the life of each person and group. Actions enjoined by these embodied codes are thought of as transforming the substances in which they are embodied.

The present paper borrows what now seems to be a repeated empirical finding — the cognitive nonduality of action and actor, code and substance — and uses it as a universal axiom for restating, through deduction, what we think we know about caste systems. We intend what Barth (1966) calls a "generative" model.

We here find ourselves restating a cognitive treatment of caste systems that is continuous from the ancient texts of the Vedas, Brahmanas, and Upanishads (explored in some relevant aspects by Heesterman 1964 and Inden 1969), through the classical books of moral and medical sciences and the late medieval moral code books of certain castes in Bengal (Inden 1976), and on into twentieth-century explanations of their behavior by living peoples (as reported, for example, in the cognitively incomplete study of village transactions by Marriott 1968). We combine such diverse materials not because we suppose that one determines or directly influences the other, but simply because we find that they agree on certain major ways of defining the situation.

The combination of authoritative texts with field observations has commonly been deplored by anthropologists as an unwarranted muddling of prescriptive and descriptive materials. Our use of remote texts here, however, is neither as prescriptive nor as descriptive documents but as cognitive statements of categories and their relationships. We use them as analytical sociological models, comparable to the theoretical generalized social systems of Max Weber or Talcott Parsons (as suggested tentatively by Singh 1970). We take such texts seriously, as we would informants' statements, preferring to read them literally rather than symbolically, since our aim is to understand the cognitive categories of the world from which they come. We do not wish to dissolve those indigenous categories for instant translation into the very different categories of our own ethnosociology or common sense. Nor do we wish to assume, *a priori*, that the indigenous store of categories and principles of arrangement is the same as that of Western thought (as suggested by Dumont 1966). Once we have understood the message of the texts in their own terms, we have all the more reason to heed them and not to worry about their being unrealistically prescriptive, since they assume that "prescription" and "description" are merely two aspects of a single reality. Whether we look at codes or at behavior, we should expect to find ordered phenomena.

GENUS: *JĀTI* AND "CASTE"

Having defined our aims and our peculiar methods at such length, we must now state that we cannot talk precisely about what is commonly meant by "caste" in the terms of Indian ethnosociology. "Caste," generally understood as the institution of ranked, hereditary, endogamous occupational groups, is a foreign concept. There is no indigenous word or idea which means just that.

"What about the word *jāti*?" one may ask. Mandelbaum (1970) has made good use of this word in discussions of South Asian caste systems. But he has taken the indigenous word *jāti* and trimmed its meaning down to what sociologists of the Western tradition want to mean when they say "caste." The South Asian word *jāti*, like the word *varṇa*, refers to a great many kinds of things other than those we mean by the word "caste." It refers to all sorts of categories of things — sets of colors and sounds, for example; it includes living creatures generated from seeds, from moisture, from eggs, and from wombs. *Jāti* means the whole range of earthly populations that we call families, kin groups, genders, occupational categories, speakers of the same language, regional populations, religious communities, nations, races; it encompasses the categories of gods in their heavens, demons, etc. It means "genera" or "species" in the broadest sense.

The English (and Latin, and international biological) term "genus" seems as close a synonym as can be found for the South Asian *jāti* or *varṇa*. "Genus" and *jāti* have the good fortune to share the same Indo-European etymology, both deriving from and still carrying a root meaning of "categories due to a common origin, genesis, or birth" (Sanskrit *jan*).

Terms like "genus," "species," "breed," etc., are useful for approximating South Asian concepts like *jāti*, but they cannot be regarded as perfect translations. For one thing, there is in the South Asian view of generic order no Linnaean assumption of an exclusively differentiating, branching, taxonomic pattern; instead, sex genera, language genera, occupational genera, and kinship genera may and typically do intersect and interact in complex ways. Such intersections of generic substances can be conceived of by means of the South Asian theory of particles: particles may be shared and exchanged with other genera across the boundaries of any given generic category.

IMMANENT CODES FOR CONDUCT

Every genus of living beings shares from the moment of its genera-tion its defining qualities (*guṇa*), powers (*śaktī* [also *shakti*]), and actions (*karma*). These together make up its corporate code for con-duct, or *dharma*, which, when realized through actual appropriate conduct (*ācāra*), nourishes and sustains the genus. Codes are pre-sumed to be inherent in all generic categories — there is a *varṇa-dharma* and a *jātidharma* and so on — right down to the single person. The single person has an embodied moral code for this world (San-skrit *svadharma*) as well as an enduring, encoded subtle body (*sūkṣma-śarīra*, *jīva*, etc.).

South Asian thought does not oppose "matter" to "spirit" or separate "nature" from "morality" or "law." South Asians think that human genera (including occupational "castes") are, to use Western terms, at once the "natural" and the "moral" units of society. There is thus in indigenous South Asian theories of cosmic origin no prior, transcendental, divine Word in the Biblical sense; rather, there is an ordered diversity of animal, human, and other forms, all emanating from a single, all-powerful, perfect, undif-ferentiated substance or principle. Words, like full codes, are thought to be from the beginning embodied in ether, minds, bodies, ears, mouths, etc. — in substances that may have physical attributes, such as sound, shape, matter, force, etc. Bodies are likewise always en-coded with their own proprieties; there is no form of living human flesh that lacks inherent morality.

The codes of South Asian genera are internal formulas for uplift-ing conduct, and not imposed imperatives. Also, unlike some inter-pretations of the idea of "genetic codes" in the West, they are not necessarily thought of as determinants of conduct. A genus may cling to its code because that way of ordering its behavior is proper and congenial to its nature and yields good results (*phala*). The *dharma* of a *jāti* is thus somewhat different from the character of a "race" in Western racist doctrine: it appears to be optative rather than abso-lutely limiting or binding upon the conduct of a genus, and it may be modified by action in time.

These South Asian monistic conceptions of society also do not easily accommodate Dumont's (1966) interpretation of Hindu society, which holds that a polarity of ultimate moral values regarding purity-impurity "encompasses" an inner sphere of amoral politico-economic action. The "encompassing-encompassed" distinction that places the "sacred" on a plane of superior influence and authority above the "profane" appears to be more typical of dualistic thought in the Judeo-Christian West.

FLOWING SUBSTANCE: PARTICLES AND DIVIDUALS

We have already illustrated an important feature of cognitive analysis by looking closely at the wide-ranging concept of *jāti*, or genus. Schneider (1968) advises us to look especially to the irreducible elements and units of any cultural system, since the way they are conceived of as being bounded and defined is likely to reveal the general dimensions of the whole world view, in terms of which action takes place.

In looking for irreducible units in South Asian culture, as we have already seen, we cannot rest after discovering that all genera and their component units, down to the level of the single person, have their particular substances with their proper natures or particular codes. We must go further, and note that genera and persons in South Asia are "particularized" in two senses: they are particular because they are peculiar, unique parts of a highly differentiated, "particularistic" (see Parsons 1951) order of intersecting natural categories; and they may also be called "particular" because they are thought to be constituted of coded components, parts, or particles (Sanskrit *piṇḍa*s, etc.) of substance.

At this point there is apparent convergence between the present ethnosociological view and the assertion by Dumont (1970:8-9) that "individuals" do not exist in South Asia as ultimate valorized units of society. The reasons for this convergence are somewhat different, however. Dumont holds that South Asian individuals are not primarily valued as such, because they are submerged in the larger, encompassing, whole society that bears primary value. The indigenous ethnosociology also holds that single persons are not ultimately individual units; instead, persons are "dividuals," or unique composites of diverse subtle and gross substances derived ultimately from one source; and they are also divisible into separate particles that may be shared or exchanged with others. Perhaps beginning from the medieval European Scholastic devaluation of materialism and thinking of Leibnizian philosophic monads or of Hobbesian political men, Dumont denies the relevance of unordered, Western, individualistic "atomism" to his perception of the spiritual orderliness of South Asian social thought. But thinking from its own assumptions of a monistic genetic order — an order more like the orders conceived of by modern linguistics or physics — South Asian thought embraces a positively valued subindividual atomism as a means of systematizing moral or social complexity.

The coded bodily atoms of South Asian social thought are acquired by transfers from various sources and are disposed of by transfers toward various destinations. Some substances are acquired originally from the seed and food provided by the parents before birth; others are acquired by later addition through ingestion of food, sexual intercourse, and other means of reception, including sensation. Particles separable from the body (hair, sweat, semen, etc.) are disposed of through excretion and reproduction by the living, and later through dissemination of the gross and subtle remains of the dead.

Persons and genera are thus conceived of as channeling and transforming heterogeneous, ever-flowing, changing substances. Living beings naturally and properly may seek to acquire the most appropriate substances for themselves through right eating, right marriage, and other right exchanges and actions. Existing bodily substance may be improved by selective additions, by "polishings" (*saṃskāras*), and by sorting out and selecting from among the existing mixtures of particles through physiological distillation and other processes. Less desirable or appropriate particles may be rejected by internal sedimentation, by right excretion, or by external removal, often aided by persons of suitably lower genera.

This indigenous scientific view of flowing substance and striving persons as the normal state of affairs contrasts with previous Western characterizations of South Asian thought as concerned largely with maintaining static "compartments," "closed classes," and "boundaries." (The interpretations of Hindu ritual by Douglas [1970: 147–152] are an example.)

The ethnosociological attention to actors seeking for appropriate substance also balances and corrects the commonly one-sided, rather negative emphasis that has seemed to posit avoidance of pollution, misunderstood as avoidance of involvement in life processes, as almost the sole motivation for action relevant to caste systems (Stevenson 1954; Orenstein 1970). On the contrary, life processes are valued and used as major means for improvement.

Heat is catalytic in many of these internal processes and external exchanges; it creates an instability that facilitates either separation or combination among particles of different kinds of substances. Processes like digestion and sexual intercourse require heat to separate, to distill, and to mix different substances. One is always likely to become what he eats, and he may also be atomically involved in what he feeds to others, especially if and when the food is hot. Hence the cooking and serving and eating of warm foods like boiled rice and ordinary fresh, unleavened bread are liminal processes in which bodily and nutritive substances must be very carefully managed.

THE SYNTAX OF RANK: VALUE IN
TRANSFORMATION AND EXCHANGE

The basic syntactic code for relations between gods and men dates at least from the Vedas (Inden 1969, 1976). All genera of men that are bodily descended from the original cosmic *Puruṣa* [Code Man] of the Rig Veda are thought to share this code. It endures through time and throughout South Asia, generating and regenerating actual social relations.

Giving is ranked over receiving in the Vedic sacrificial syntax of exchange among the original genera (*varṇas*); consistency (i.e. homogeneity of action) in the direction of giving can maintain such rank. Higher rank inheres in the Brahman genus, since it maintains asymmetrical relations with other genera, giving greater value than it receives. Lower rank inheres in those genera that can return only substances or services of lower value. The more differentiated exchanges occurring in post-Vedic worship (*pūjā*) similarly yield ranks among the plethora of later, regional genera.

As in linguistic structure, the syntagmatic and paradigmatic orderings of South Asian social thought are mutually translatable and mutually supportive (cf. Lyons 1968:73–76). Thus the ranks of the Vedic genera as derived paradigmatically from their higher and lower places in the body of "Code Man" agree with their ranks as derived syntagmatically from their exchanges connected with the Vedic sacrifice. Further, the ranks of the many later genera can be stated with identical effect either paradigmatically by their qualities or syntagmatically by their mutual transactions. The inborn qualitative ranks of the later genera are in turn thought to derive from the syntax by which they originated — first, by the syntagm of consistency (whether or not the intergeneric and intersexual ranks of the parents are harmonious, i.e. positively correlated), and second, by the syntagm of homogeneity (whether differences of rank or qualities between parental genera are small or great) (*Manu* 1886:8, 3–67).

The substances exchanged are themselves ranked in value according to their greater or lesser capacities for subsequent transformation and transfer. Powers, essences, generative substances, and substances in whole, unmixed, untransformed states may thus be regarded as more productive — more valuable — than nongenerative substances, processed or mixed substances, and residues of substances that have lost their original integrities.

In an exchange, the values of such substances vary according to the ranks of those who produce and exchange them. The residues or other less valuable substances of a superior may thus be regarded as more valuable than the essences or other more valuable substances of an inferior. As substances pass from hand to hand between ranked exchangers, they are thus often transvalued—raised or lowered in value.

A term like "substance" (usually thought of as particles of substance) is a desirable term in our analysis because of its neutrality. Thinking of substance as itself neutral permits us to see more clearly the transformations and transvaluations that are constantly happening to substances as they are exchanged and to actors as they make exchanges. The terms "purity" and "impurity" are awkward terms to use for things transferred, since they have fixed values; things can be "pure" or "impure" from the relative point of view of only one actor or one process at a time, while what we need are terms that make it easy for us to comprehend and distinguish the processes of exchange, transformation, and valuation relative to two or more actors at once. Orenstein's (1970) ethnosociological treatment of birth and death as constants to which differing caste values are applied is an analytic step responding to the same need.

The term "substance," which in Schneider's American usage (1968) refers only to the natural substance contained in the bodies of persons, refers in South Asian usage also to that which passes between bodies — the contents or media of transactions. Notice also that "code for conduct," which in Schneider's American usage refers only to norms of interaction, in South Asian usage refers also to ways of being — to the inner qualities or values of substances attained through actions by actors. We may therefore speak of norms of action as being "embodied" or of transactions as "substantiating" a code, just as we spoke earlier of the mutual translatability of paradigmatic and syntactic analyses. According to indigenous social thought, rank may be read either from the qualities of the coded substance in the actors or from their exchanges of substance. Interactional and attributional perspectives ("two aspects of the same thing," according to Marriott 1959:106) are thus ultimately to be reconciled and identified.

COGNITION IN VARIATION AND CHANGE

So much for the bare outline of a South Asian ethnosociology of caste. Anthropologists will readily recognize its resemblance to some other things that they have commonly observed about caste systems (and also about cooking, dietetics, ethics, genetics, marriage, physiology, worship, etc.) in Hindu villages. But they may wonder what it can do for the understanding of regional differences in caste systems and of changes such as those wrought by Buddhism and Islam (generally seen as counterstructures — radical breaks in South Asian tradition), what it can add to the understanding of caste in the Hindu devotional movements (sometimes characterized as antistructural), and what it can tell us about modern changes in caste systems (often seen as structural disintegration or entropy).

Briefly applied to these problems, an ethnosociology of this sort can be said to offer an understanding of variants or changes in caste systems as replications and deletions, as permutations and combinations, as negative and reciprocal transformations of coded substance in accord with the preceding cognitive repertory of kinds of nondual units, relationships, and processes. Deletion and replication are perhaps the commonest devices, as most of these variants either subtract or add (extrapolate or interpolate) features patterned on the same basic cognitive template that is already largely attested to in Vedic texts. Marriott and Inden (1974) sketch regional, religious, and historical variants of these kinds.

Hindu devotionalism (including Viraśaivism and Sikhism) manipulates divine substance, often reciprocally, so as to initiate humans into the higher genus of gods while they retain participation in their original, lower genera. Tantric movements do much the same thing but temporarily detach persons from their original genera and transform them through negative inversions of the proper movement of bodily substance. Buddhism and Islam both cut the two-way circulation of food substance at the highest level in order to set that level apart, Buddhism countenancing only upward flow, Islam only downward flow. Both Buddhism and Islam institute higher moral orders comprising new voluntary categories among which contractual exchanges follow the most common South Asian syntax of rank, while the lower orders of natural genera and their exchanges also continue. Modernizing movements strive, often effectively, to create new class, associational, regional, and national genera by promoting inverse and reciprocal, ultimately diffuse, exchanges of divine and human substance among persons previously of different genera.

CONCLUSION

By redefining old data in indigenous cognitive terms, we have tried to understand South Asian caste systems in a fresh way, as part of what South Asian thought sees as a structured flow of coded substance. We believe that variety and change in South Asian caste systems may also be understood as permutations that continue to assume the inseparability of what is termed "nature" and "law" along with many homologous pairs — elements whose fundamental distinction and contingent associations are so vital to the ethnosociologies of the West.

REFERENCES

BARNETT, STEVE
1970 "The structural position of a south Indian caste." Unpublished Ph.D. dissertation, University of Chicago.
BARTH, FREDRIK
1966 *Models of social organization*. London: Royal Anthropological Institute.
Caraka
1949 *The Caraka saṁhita*, six volumes. Jamnagar: Shree Gulab Kunverba Ayurvedic Society.
CARSTAIRS, G. MORRIS
1957 *The twice-born*. London: Hogarth.
DOUGLAS, MARY
1970 *Purity and danger*. Harmondsworth, Middlesex: Pelican.
DUMONT, LOUIS
1966 A fundamental problem in the sociology of caste. *Contributions to Indian Sociology* 9:17-32.
1970 *Homo hierarchicus: the caste system and its implications*. Translated by Mark Sainsbury. Chicago: University of Chicago Press.
HEESTERMAN, J. C.
1964 Brahmin, ritual and renouncer. *Wiener Zeitschrift für die Kunde Süd- und Ostasiens* 8:1-31.
INDEN, RONALD B.
1969 "Exchange, sacrifice, and hierarchy in early India." Mimeographed.
1976 *Marriage and rank in Bengali culture: a social history of caste and clan in middle period Bengal*. Berkeley: University of California Press.
INDEN, RONALD B., RALPH W. NICHOLAS
i.p. *Kinship in Bengali culture*. Chicago: University of Chicago Press.
KANE, PANDURANG VAMAN
1930-1962 *History of dharmaśāstra*, five volumes. Poona: Bhandarkar Oriental Research Institute.
LYONS, JOHN
1968 *Introduction to theoretical linguistics*. Cambridge: Cambridge University Press.
MANDELBAUM, DAVID G.
1970 *Society in India*, two volumes. Berkeley: University of California Press.
Manu
1886 *The laws of Manu*. Sacred Books of the East 25. Translated by G. Bühler. Oxford: Clarendon.
MARRIOTT, MC KIM
1959 Interactional and attributional theories of caste ranking. *Man in India* 39:92-107.
1960 *Caste ranking and community structure in five regions of India and Pakistan*. Poona: Deccan College.
1968 "Caste ranking and food transactions: a matrix analysis," in *Structure and change in Indian society*. Edited by M. Singer and B. S. Cohn. Chicago: University of Chicago Press.

MARRIOTT, MC KIM, RONALD B. INDEN
  1974   "Caste systems," in *Encyclopaedia Britannica* (third edition), *Macropaedia* 3:982–991. Chicago: Helen Hemingway Benton.
ORENSTEIN, HENRY
  1970   Logical congruence in Hindu sacred law: another interpretation. *Contributions to Indian Sociology*, new series 4:22–35.
PARSONS, TALCOTT
  1951   *The social system.* Glencoe, Ill.: Free Press.
SCHNEIDER, DAVID M.
  1968   *American kinship: a cultural account.* Englewood Cliffs, N.J.: Prentice-Hall.
SINGH, YOGENDRA
  1970   For a sociology of India. *Contributions to Indian Sociology*, new series 4:140–143.
STEVENSON, H. N. C.
  1954   Status evaluation in the Hindu caste system. *Journal of the Royal Anthropological Institute* 84:45–65.
Sushruta
  1963   *An English translation of the Sushruta samhita,* three volumes (second edition). The Chowkamba Sanskrit Studies 30. Varanasi: The Chowkamba Sanskrit Series Office.
YALMAN, N.
  1967   *Under the bo tree: studies in caste, kinship and marriage in the interior of Ceylon.* Berkeley: University of California Press.

Method and Theory in the Sociology of Louis Dumont: A Reply

OWEN M. LYNCH

In his book *Homo hierarchicus* (1970) Louis Dumont has presented us with what is perhaps the most stimulating, challenging, and at times irritating sociological interpretation of India in this century. Dumont's explicit purpose in writing the book is to present an understanding of "the traditional [and pan-Indian] social organization of India from the point of view of theoretical comparison" (1970:xv). Central to this purpose is an exposition of hierarchy, an idea which we in the West fail to understand, according to Dumont. The book's viewpoint is intellectualist; the attempt is to "grasp other values intellectually" (1970:2).

The implicit purpose of the book is to present an example, if not an outline, of sociological explanation and method which is radically different from that of empiricist, Anglo-American social anthropology. Indeed, the book is a direct attack on what Dumont considers the inadequacies, ethnocentricity, and distortions of Anglo-American anthropology. These faults arise from two sources. First, the empiricist approach devalues ideology and attempts to build up a model of society inductively. Second, Anglo-American anthropology uses concepts derived from modern values and, therefore, fails to see the fullness of other societies through their own more adequate ideas about themselves.

In this essay, I wish to consider the implicit purpose of *Homo hierarchicus*, which has heretofore been given less attention than its

In writing this paper I am grateful for the comments and suggestions of my colleagues Gerald Berreman, Robert Crane, Suzanne Hanchett, Doranne Jacobson, David Mandelbaum, and McKim Marriott. Any mistakes in interpretation, however, are strictly my own.

interpretation of India. I will, therefore, outline Dumont's socio-logical method, its assumptions, and its goals. This part of the paper is purposely extended in order to answer Dumont's objection that reviewers have not given a reasonable outline of the theory as they understand it before criticizing it (1971:59). Then I will critically evaluate the method and its results. From this viewpoint India is only an example of the method and a test of its adequacy and fruitfulness.

THEORY, METHOD, AND GOALS

Dumont's basic approach to sociology (and India) is through what he calls theoretical comparison. What does this mean, what are the assumptions made, and what are the methods and procedures followed? There are three basic assumptions:

1. "Men do not behave; they act with an idea in their heads" (1970:6). This is *social*; it is men, not a man, who act with this idea in mind. This idea is *constitutive*; it does not merely reflect reality; on the contrary, it orients and directs action (1970:37). This idea is *meaningful*; men do not behave, they act through a conceived and perceived system of ideas. Such ideas Dumont calls values.

Corollary: Because such values are constitutive, they embody a model of the society and are prior to concrete social reality.

Corollary: Because such values are social, men act in a coherent and rational way (cf. 1970:37).

Corollary: Because these ideas are social, they are independent of the men who think them, they have a separate ontological status. They are a whole *sui generis*. This whole is called society.

2. All societies are wholes constructed from the same set of universal components or values, but the arrangement or patterning may be different. Therefore types of society are unique transforms of the same universal components (1970:186; 232-34; 330, fn. 107b; 340, fn. 118d; 1966:31).

Corollary: Because societies are transforms of the same set of universal components, it is the study of the *relations* which form wholes from the components that is important and not the study of individual parts. The systemic whole is one of relations, not one of parts (1970:40).

3. "In every society one aspect of social life receives primary value stress and simultaneously is made to encompass all others and to express them as far as it can" (1967:33; 1970:77, 213, 237, 263, 340, fn. 118d). This means that the patterning of different societies is organized around a single dominant value. The dominant value is conscious, or overtly expressed in the ideology. Unstressed values are

less conscious, below the threshold, and nonconscious or nonideological, but still in the framework of ideas.

According to Dumont, the basic method of sociology built on these
assumptions is twofold. First, because ideas are prior to, and constitutive of, action, and because action is behavior plus meaning (valorized), then the study of values is primary or central (1970:263, fn. 1a).
Moreover, the arrangement of these values is unique and particular
to a society and can only be understood on its own terms. This
implies that to study behavior without values is to study a society
through ethnocentric ideas derived from one's own society and value
system. According to Dumont, we have direct access to a society's
values or ideology, presumably through its literature, its encoded
tradition (1970:3, 263-64; 1957:7-22):

The alternative must be clearly stated: one may either start from conscious
ideas and move from the whole to the parts, . . . or else one starts from
behavior, in which case one can neither account for the whole nor finally
build a bridge between Indian concepts and our own (1970:76).

At this point Dumont's comparative method comes in. A researcher
in a society other than his own will have observed many things during
the course of his stay. Following Dumont's method, he will be able
to relate many of these observations to the ideology and find that it
accounts for and explains them. But there will remain a set of observations which are not directly accounted for in the ideology. These
Dumont calls residual facts (1970:38); they are known to us not
directly through the indigenous ideology but indirectly through concepts developed in our own society. Dumont, therefore, calls them
comparative concomitants of ideology (1970:38). In the case of India
these residual facts turn out to be phenomena of territory, force,
power, property, etc. When known through the concepts of the researcher's own society, these phenomena become devalorized and
distorted from the cultural context in which they appear and in which
they have meaning. Thus they, too, must "be set in their place and
related to the ideology which they accompany in fact, it being understood that *it is only in relation to the totality thus reconstructed that
the ideology takes on its true sociological significance*" (1970:38). In
effect, the residual facts, though not immediately accounted for in the
ideology, are in some way related to it and are accounted for by it,
as implied in the first assumption. This relation of the ideological and
nonideological is what the book attempts to explain, through the
concept of hierarchy, a relation of encompassed values to encompassing values (cf. 1966:21, 32).

When Dumont speaks of ideology, he means first global or pan-
societal ideology, in this case pan-Indian ideology (1970:271, fn. 21c;

1966:31). Second, the ideology may consciously touch on or recognize other values, but the dominant values form the core, nucleus, or encompassing structure of the system and its social expression (1970: 273–274, fn. 22c). Thus, *artha* [gain, power], though touched on in the Hindu texts, is really secondary. Of primary importance is *dharma* [law, religion]; it encompasses all other values, including *artha*.

It must be understood that the nonideological or nonconscious aspects of a society are strictly matters of mind, but, as it were, unconscious or nonvalorized. This seems evident from Dumont's methodology of using ideas from our own society to discover them in others; from his defining the distinction between the ideological and the nonideological as relative, not absolute (1970:273, fn. 22c); from his models of Indian and Western societies (1970:232 ff.); and from his metaphor of an iceberg to describe the relationship of the ideological to the nonideological (1970:38). Thus, when Dumont occasionally seems to refer in an ambiguous way to the nonideological as empirical aspects (1970:xviii, 37, 201, 212, and *passim*), he really seems to mean that the empirical facts of power, division of labor, etc., are accounted for within the nonconscious or encompassed part of the ideology, just as the empirical fact of ranked castes is accounted for in the conscious or encompassing part of the ideology (1970:308, fn. 71a). There is a similar ambiguity in the concept of "the whole," a term which constantly and vaguely occurs throughout the book. At times it seems to mean the whole of the ideology only, and at other times it seems to mean the whole of the ideology plus the empirical facts. It really seems to mean that the whole of the ideology accounts for and explains the whole of the empirical reality; the one is coordinate to or isomorphic with the other. The whole is, therefore, a total society with its unique configuration of the universal ideological components present in all societies.

Since it is possible for the universal components to be arranged into uniquely different structures, it is minimally possible to have two types of value systems or mentalities. Dumont isolates two, modern mentality and traditional mentality. In modern mentality, system as such does not exist; men think in terms of elements and objects each with its own essence; a whole is at best the sum of its parts; and both philosophically and sociologically the individual is primary and the unit of society. It is unnatural because it is "unaware of itself as a hierarchized whole" (1970:253). Traditional mentality is dominant in societies preceding our own. In this type of mentality it is not the individual but the whole, or society, which is important; the whole is more than the sum of its parts (1970:76), the "elements in themselves of which the system seems to be composed are disregarded, and only considered as the product of the network of relations; this network would then constitute the system," in this case the social system (1970:40). It follows that there are two possible types of society constituted by these mentalities. They are traditional society, that of Plato's *Republic*, of "collective man," "of hierarchy"; and modern society, that of "elementary man," in which the individual is the measure of all things (1970:9–10). The ghost of Levy-Bruhl and "mystical participation" seems to lurk in the shadow of traditionally minded man. Traditional man knows little or nothing of himself as an individual but only as part of society. He lives in a society where "collective man" (1970:9), not individual man, is valorized.

The goal of sociology following these assumptions and this method is twofold. First is the attempt to understand other societies on their own terms, from within. This can be done best by understanding a society's most fundamental and consciously expressed values in relation to its unconscious values. A society is best explained and understood through its own ideology and categories, through the model it has of itself. Such a model, according to Dumont, accounts for the total society because its ideology is constitutive and therefore isomorphic with its concrete manifestation. This follows from his first assumption.

The second goal of sociology is to set in mutual perspective the various types of societies (1970:258). To accomplish this, sociological theory must be built upon "concepts which take into account the values that different societies have chosen for themselves" (1970:258). The sociologist must not invent concepts for comparison and analysis but must take them from those societies which have developed them fully (cf. 1970:36):

Thus, the sociologist can *name* without arbitrariness in a given society features which it neglects, because he has learnt their names from another society. For instance, the India of caste and varna teaches us hierarchy, and this is no little lesson (1966:30; original emphasis).

The meta- or universal language of sociology (1966:24) would, then, be a United Nations of concepts for Dumont.

Because all societies are made up of the same universal features, we can best discover them in those societies which have consciously elaborated them in their purest and clearest form (1970:330, fn. 107b). Thus the justification for the Durkheimian single-case method:

In sociological studies the universal can only be attained through the particular characteristics, different in each case, of each type of society. Why should we travel to India if not to try to discover how and in what respects Indian society or civilization, by its very particularity, represents a form of the universal? (1970:3).

INDIA AND THE CASTE SYSTEM

The type case in which the traditional mentality of collective man is found is India and its caste system. Caste, according to Dumont, has been misunderstood by men of modern-type societies because they lack understanding of hierarchy and because they have an inadequate empirical methodology, derived from their own society and its individualistic value orientation. A better approach to the study of caste is through the Hindu ideology using the comparative method outlined above. Dumont clearly states his point of view that "caste is a state of mind, a state of mind which is expressed by the emergence, in various situations of groups of various orders generally called castes" (1970:34). Moreover, this state of mind is ordered, it is a system in which parts are interrelated into a whole according to certain principles. There are three analytically separable principles of the caste system:

1. Hierarchy: ordering or ranking according to status.

2. Separation: rules of marriage and contact maintaining distinctions of status.

3. Interdependence: division of labor resulting from hierarchy and separation.

Underlying these three principles is the single structural opposition of pure and impure. This opposition makes caste society consistent and rational to Hindus and is the basis upon which distinctions of rank are expressed in actual castes. Insofar as superiority and superior purity are the same, the "ideological distinction of purity is the foundation of status" (1970:56). The opposition of pure and impure had its experiential origin in impurities of personal life such as fecal material, blood, hair and nails, saliva, etc. Groups of people specializing in tasks connected with these, for example sweepers, barbers, etc., partook of this impurity and were therefore of low or impure status. Thus, the original and fundamental expression of the system in the phenomenological world was the opposition of pure Brahman and impure Untouchable.

Intermediate rankings in the system are also based on the opposition of pure and impure. This is because the fundamental opposition is capable of generating secondary, tertiary, and n . . . number of distinctions of status, which find concrete expression in symbols involved with various types of food, water, or polluting substances (1970:27, 56-57). For example, vegetarianism is purer and higher than meat eating, and so is food cooked in clarified butter as opposed to food cooked in water. On the basis of these distinctions, specific castes or groups of castes can unite in opposition to other castes. What is important is not these kinds of food or these substances in themselves but rather the basic opposition underlying and generating them. In other words, the symbols (food, etc.) are a code whose semantic content is different castes. Moreover, the basic grammatical principle of opposition which structures the code can be applied to other channels, such as pure and impure women who can symbolize in a flexible way isogamous, hypergamous, and endogamous groups. The fundamental opposition can operate, then, as a principle of segmentation which can expand or contract the boundaries of specific groups through the use of symbolic distinctions based on itself. The various symbols are irrelevant or arbitrary as long as the basic opposition can be maintained in concrete situations. "Brahmans probably eat meat where competition from vegetarians did [*sic*] not make itself felt" (1970:141). From this point of view, then, it is senseless to look for and try to isolate the concrete unit of the system, the caste group. Such diverse elements as endogamy, caste council rules of commensality, specific customs, etc., which are often used to identify the specific groups, are not in fact restricted to one group at a unique level of segmentation but to groups at different levels of segmentation (1970:63).

It can now be understood what Dumont means when he says that the caste system is a state of mind. Specific castes and concrete caste systems are merely an arrangement of fluid and fluctuating elements; what is stable, what is fixed, and what is in the minds of all Indians is the intellectual principle which generates these systems and gives them their sociological meaning. "The fundamental opposition is [not] the cause of all the distinctions of caste . . . it is their form . . . [it] is constitutive" (1970:45). In this sense, too, Dumont demonstrates some of the basis for his postulate that India is one (1957:9). Moreover, it can be seen how Dumont, like Lévi-Strauss, sees structure as being in the mind, as a principle which orders, explains, and legitimizes reality for human beings of a particular society.

The fundamental opposition of pure and impure is also hierarchical in nature. This means, first, that hierarchy is a principle by which the elements of the whole are ranked in relation to the whole (1970:66). "A hierarchical relation is a relation between larger and smaller, or more precisely between that which encompasses and that which is encompassed" (1970:xii). Second, hierarchy is a religious way of seeing things; it is "purely a matter of religious values" (1970:66). (Dumont in one place [1970:65–66] admits that hierarchy need not be religious but he proceeds as though it must be.)

For an ideal hierarchy to arise, as it has in India, two conditions are necessary. First, there must be an absolute distinction between status (religious values) and power (political values). Second, power must be inferior to or encompassed by status or a religious world view. It is here that Dumont turns to the traditional theory of the *varṇa*s for an explanation of how these conditions were fulfilled. In his interpretation the *varṇa* theory is one of power and its ideological devaluation and legitimation (1970:53, 67). It is also a theory explaining the historical conditions for the origin of the Indian caste system. The *varṇa* theory, according to Dumont, is distinct from the theory of pure and impure and is constructed on different principles (1970:72). Nevertheless, it is both complementary and subordinate to purity. Dumont argues that in the *varṇa*s an absolute distinction was made between the category of Brahman (purity and priesthood) and Kshatriya (power and royalty). Thus the semantic universe of religious values was completely distinguished from the semantic realm of power. Once this separation had taken place, India made a "choice" (1970:213) of value orientation toward the religious; and with this choice the religious value of purity/impurity became primary and stressed. Purity came to encompass, suffuse, and subordinate to itself all others in the Indian world view. Today in India both dominant and dependent castes live under the sway of a system in which ideas of politico-economic relations are encompassed by and subordinated to those of religion.

Within the Indian conceptual universe there is a concept for power, *artha*, but it is not part of the dominant ideology, it is a sort of non-valorized concept. Nevertheless, according to Dumont, it unites with purity in opposition to all other values which constitute the society (1970:77, 212). In concrete terms this seems to mean that Brahmans and Kshatriyas unite against all other castes.

Dumont then goes on to note that the ideological relationship of status to power is often reversed when one observes actual situations. Non-Brahmans in situations of power, wealth, and control often seem to lord it over Brahmans; non-Brahmans, too, seem to be in control of the division of labor (*jajmāni* system), a system which is not directly accounted for in the ideology of pure and impure. To look at India this way, however, is to see it from a modern point of view using Western concepts of the individual, politics, and economics. Indians, following Dumont's second assumption, have a world view different from our own and patterned in a different way. Theirs is a traditional mentality and world view in which "everything is directed to the whole, to the 'village community', . . . as part and parcel of the necessary order. This view of an ordered whole, in which each is assigned his place, is fundamentally religious" (1970:107). The unity of this whole, of society, consists "in the conscious expression of the whole in *one* language. This is the language of priests," of purity (1966:28). This orientation not only legitimizes one's position in the whole society, it also motivates conforming action within it because "the principle of hierarchy . . . is among the most constraining facts of political and moral life" (1970:3). The psychological correlate is that within the caste system the dominant and overriding motive to act is not power or wealth but the desire to preserve status and the relations based on it (1970:113, 179–180).

From the above discussion it becomes clear how Dumont can assert that he has "made a first step out of the dualism of the 'religious' and the 'politico-economic' " (1970:78–79). In the Hindu conceptual order, power is a virtually meaningless concept. The dominant religious values devalue it, give it no meaning, and encompass it. Dumont goes on to assert that this is also a first step out of the dualism of "idealism and materialism, of form and content" (1970:79), because no matter what causal independence material factors may have, they are always perceived, interpreted, and encompassed by a society's ideology, which is decisively oriented by its fundamental value. Yet such a claim is possible *only if* one accepts the assumptions of Dumont's method and its goals. Only then does the Hindu ideology become an "objective" and accurate account or explanation of Indian society and the Anglo-American empiricist view a "subjective" and sociocentric view of that same society. Empiricists, working under different assumptions, would assert that Dumont has only accounted for an ideological view of reality, one of form but not of content. Whether or not this is also the real world of conception, experience, and motivation in which Indians, except perhaps Brahmans, live is open to doubt and examination.

Other things follow from Dumont's interpretation of the Hindu ideology, though they may not be directly and overtly expressed in it at the conscious level. First of all there is interdependence, the division of labor in the *jajmāni* system. In it, goods and services are exchanged. "This takes place within the prescribed order, the religious order. The needs of each are conceived to be different depending upon caste, or hierarchy, but this fact should not disguise the entire system's *orientation to the whole*" (1970:105). It is an embedded system, at least at the ideological level. In it conscious religious values encompass the non-conscious element of politics, and politics encompass economics; these are not separate institutional spheres as in modern societies (1970:165). What Western or modern man might call exploitation is not really so for those who live in this system, according to Dumont. This is because Indians live under the sway of a system of ideas which legitimizes the system and their position within it (1970:107). Dumont can then conclude, "In short, the caste system should be seen as less 'exploitative' than democratic society. If modern man does not see it this way, it is because he no longer conceives justice other than as equality" (1970:105). Just as in the case of power, hierarchy, confronted with exploitation (if it exists in our terms) "is obliged to close its eyes to this point on pain of destroying itself" (1970:77). Considerable evidence has been collected, however, by Berreman, Cohn, and this author, that lower castes often do see their position as an exploited rather than as a legitimate and proper one within Indian society. This once again seems to point out that Dumont's analysis does not account for the concrete facts even from the viewpoint of many Indians themselves. His view of Indian social reality is really an upper-caste point of view, as often noted by Berreman.

A second item included in hierarchy as a system of ideas is justice and authority. Once again, in the world of caste mentality, there is a recognition of higher authority both within castes and between them. *Panchāyats* [caste councils] exist not only to settle cases between members of the same caste; but also castes (and probably, according to Dumont) frequently have recourse to members of higher castes to settle both intra- and intercaste conflicts. This is submission to authority:

If force becomes legitimate by submitting to Brahmanic ideals, and thus becomes power, then . . . power is invested with judicial authority by those who are subjected to it. Thus, acknowledged, and in some way interiorized by its subjects, power becomes equal in a specific sphere, to authority *par excellence*, i.e., religious authority (1970:167).

Dumont then makes the interesting observation that *panchāyats* seem weakest when dealing with internal caste conflict between men of equal status. This leads to an emphasis on conciliation. On the other hand, *panchāyats* seem strongest when dealing with caste conflict between castes of unequal status. This is because conflict then becomes at root a matter of preserving group status, that is, a matter of hierarchy (1970:179–183). (The empiricist sociologist considers this an interesting hypothesis worthy of investigation rather than an established sociological fact.)

Dumont goes on to consider other things which are implicit in the ideology, such as territory, the sects and the renouncer, social fission and mobility, etc. These, too, are included in a similar way in the ideology, though like power and authority they are below the threshold of conscious ideas. For want of space, they cannot be discussed here. There are, however, two other questions Dumont treats which must be mentioned. The first is the question of whether or not there are castes among the non-Hindus in India and whether or not caste exists outside India. The second is the problem of change.

As regards the question of caste outside India, Dumont does not say that this is impossible. His position is that caste may exist outside India where there are permanent and closed status groups and when two conditions are fulfilled. First, the entire society must be made up of castes. He excludes the Eta of Japan on these grounds, though it is hard to see why, since all of Japan is made up of two groups, Eta and non-Eta. Second there must be a disjunction of status and power, similar to the Brahman-Kshatriya relationship in the *varṇa* ideology, because religious values must be dominant in order for hierarchy to manifest itself in its pure form, the caste system. "The opposition of purity is thus the *necessary* ideological form of the ideal type of Hierarchy" (1970:213). But this is a Hindu value. Thus, in effect, a caste system cannot and does not exist outside India because the Hindu value system is present only in India.

Concerning the problem of castes among non-Hindus in India, such as the Lingayats, the Christians, and the Muslims, Dumont feels that "these communities have at the very least *something of caste despite the modification in their ideas or values.* Caste is weakened or incomplete, but not lacking altogether" (1970:210). What precisely does having "something of caste" mean? While these communities overtly adopt other value systems, they covertly share in the Hindu value system because of the pervasive influence of the Hindu environment in which they live. Thus, while the Muslims have a value system completely opposed to that of the Hindus, they have nevertheless learned to live together in some sort of association in which "lying beneath the ultimate or Islamic values are other values presupposed by actual behavior" (1970:211). This seems to mean that Muslims have their own conscious plus nonconscious value complex as well as an unconscious value complex which is generative of actual behavior. In this sense, elements in their own value system would be pathological, just as racism, according to Dumont, is a pathological resurgence of hierarchy in the individualistic value system of the United States.

According to Dumont, the state of tension in which Muslims, Christians, and Lingayats live because of their opposed value systems within the Hindu environment could have been avoided if these religions "had offered or imposed an alternative system to the caste system" (1970:211). Just what Dumont means here is unclear. If value systems are primary and constitute social action and society, then how could Islam and Christianity have offered or *imposed* an alternative social system not already contained in the value system to which these people have converted? Can it be that Dumont himself is "surreptitiously" forced to admit that the concrete social system can be seen as primary and generative of social reality, that a social system can be "imposed" upon others without a corresponding change of value system?

As regards change in India, Dumont admits the empirical facts of the emergence and development of modern professions and cities; the unification of the nation state and increased spatial mobility; and the development of markets and industry. But as accounted for in the Hindu ideology, these are only changes at a secondary, politico-economic level. Such changes amount to changes *in* the society but not *of* the society. There have been no changes "*in relation to* the caste system" (1970:219). "Everything happens as if the system tolerated change only within one of its secondary spheres . . . we would conclude that the facts they [Bailey, Srinivas, Ghurye, and other empiricists] adduce display neither reinforcement nor any essential transformation of the system, but only a change involving its minor areas" (1970:228). The traditional system is even able to incorporate Western individualistic values, but these are neutralized in their assimilation to the idea of the renouncer of society (*sannyasin*) and the various sects based on the idea of renunciation. The renouncer and the sects were the areas in traditional society where the idea of individual man could and did exist in a relatively neutralized form. Thus, the Westerner "appeared not only as a heathen prince, but also as a sort of *sannyasin* of an unusual type" (1970:236).

What, then, of the introduction of parliamentary and democratic principles of government, of the ideas enshrined in the Indian constitution and the Hindu Codes bills, of the ideas behind the five-year plans, and of modern industry and medicine? Dumont with his Shiva-like eye reduces these to "an insertion of an egalitarian sub-set at the juridical and political level without a corresponding voluntary modification of the overall hierarchical framework" (1970:228-229). In effect they have been swallowed up in, encompassed by, the traditional religious hierarchical principle of purity and pollution. The Western empiricist might agree that there is much truth to this interpretation but would be forced to demur that it is not as simple as Dumont makes it appear. At this point, one comes to suspect that the power of hierarchy is so great that it can "encompass" and demote anything and everything to a secondary, unimportant level whenever Dumont so wills it.

DISCUSSION AND CRITIQUE

The kind of theory and method which Dumont has outlined is radical both for its conception of sociology and for its interpretation of India. These two topics must now be discussed and subjected to scrutiny.

Sociology

Dumont's outline of sociology as discussed above operates within a different framework and set of assumptions than that of most Anglo-American empirical social anthropologists. One source of his difference from the empiricists lies in conflicting opinions about what an adequate explanation consists of.

Dumont is an ideological reductionist and a rationalist. He seeks an explanation which is reduced to a single idea or principle (1970:77; 276, fn. 24e). For him, reason is a sufficient source of knowledge and is superior to an empirical test or source. This belief appears on two interconnected levels: the level of explanation of a single society such as India, and the level of universal sociological theory.

A society such as India can best be understood or explained through its own conscious ideology and through placing in the perspective of the conscious ideology facts not consciously expressed. But a society's ideology is an adequate explanation of itself because, and *only because*, of the assumptions of Dumont's method, particularly those which state that ideology is constitutive and that men act in a coherent and rational way because of the ideology. Do such assumptions meet the test of human experience and common sense? Are they contrary to fact? In the case of India, are we to believe that all the empirical facts of the changes, which have occurred there, and which Dumont admits, have in no way disturbed Indians? Do they demote them to a secondary and unimportant ideological level as easily as does Dumont (1970:217–238; 331, fn. 111b). This is contrary to the expressed experience of many Indians. Sweeping these empirical facts under an ideological rug is no more than ignoring and being blind to them. This is sacrificing reality on the altar of reification to save ideology. It is hardly a satisfactory explanation of what has been and is occurring in India. It is, moreover, straining common sense to the point of incredulity, as well as ignoring the real experiences of many Indians, when Dumont asserts that Western empirical scientists see these things as change and as disturbing only because of their own ideological biases and world view.

On a more general and powerful level of explanation, particular ideologies are adequate and true in Dumont's theory because they express the universal. Since ideology is assumed to be prior, the ultimate explanation of particular ideologies lies in different arrangements of the same set of universal components or ideas. Societies are different manifestations of universal forms. It is easy, then, to understand how Dumont can begin his explanation of caste with Hegel (1970:42). ˙

When Dumont tells us that he can pass from the particular to the universal in the study of caste in India, he is talking of the logically, not the empirically, universal. Nowhere is his rationalism clearer than in the statement criticizing the empiricists who "can only ever achieve the general, as opposed to the universal" (1970:3). Though the question of the ontological status of ideology, and therefore of the universal, is left open, Dumont methodologically must assume it to exist (1970:263, fn. 1a). Dumont, in effect, assumes a realist position on the existence of the universal; indeed, he often talks of reaching the *essence* of institutions. An important implicit assumption lies in this sociological theory, namely that there are innate ideas which are limited in number. This is Cartesian anthropology in its clearest form.

There are a number of problems with this type of explanation. First, "things good to think" are not necessarily "things good to be." That Dumont can think all things in terms of purity and hierarchy and demote anything that can be called politics or economics to a secondary encompassed level does not necessarily mean that this is the way things are, even for Indians. This is rationalistic reification masquerading as explanation.

The second problem concerns the number of elements in the universal social whole and how they are related. It is sociologically meaningless to say, as Dumont does, that a structure exists "when the interdependence of the elements of a system is so great that they disappear without residue if an inventory is made of the relations between them; a system of relations, in short, not a system of elements" (1970:40). That a relation exists is meaningless unless we also know what is related to what. Dumont does this in practice, as when he says that power is encompassed by religion in India. The importance of hierarchy is, presumably, that it pulls together into one system a great many values which would otherwise be disparate and discrete. The problems are, thus, what and how many are the components or values or universals in the universal social whole and how do men come to agree upon what they are? Either we know them beforehand and there is therefore no reason to try to discover them, or they are known to us subconsciously and the study of other societies makes them known to us consciously. If we know them subconsciously, how are we to recognize them when we see them, how are we to distinguish them from nonuniversal elements? Dumont gives us no epistemological or methodological criteria.

Evidently there are as many universals as there are societies with different ideologies, difference being defined by the universal which is "stressed" and encompasses all the rest. But what is a different ideology and what criteria do we use for defining and delimiting it? Are Russia and the United States to be equated because of their common philosophical heritage from Plato to Marx?

In practice, Dumont comes perilously close to committing the error he most severely castigates the empiricists for, namely substantialization, or the error of analyzing the parts of a system rather than a whole of relations. This Dumont does when he concentrates on the "stressed" value of a society or when he tries to reduce all to a single principle of explanation. Indeed, hierarchy comes to be much like a monistic principle of *brahman*,

. . . in this model [of hierarchy] nothing can happen in the dialectical manner, there can be no development in dialectical terms, for what the dialectical movement should produce was already there from the outset, and everything is forever contained within it (1971:78).

The third problem with explanation through the universal is that explanation by reference to the universal contradicts his proposed method, which seeks explanation through ideology. What Dumont has really given us, then, is an etic theory of the universal, but he has concealed it in an emic discussion of the ideology of pure and impure.

Dumont's program for the development of the universal language of sociology suffers from his ambiguity about what a universal is, and how to know one. On the one hand, these concepts appear to be unique and confined to one society. Hierarchy, in the case of India, is reduced to "one fundamental conception and a single true principle, the opposition of pure and impure" (1970:43; cf. 252). But pure and impure is a Hindu value unique to India. How then can hierarchy be a universal when it is reducible to the unique and particular (cf. 1970:330, fn. 107b; 3)?

On the other hand, hierarchy, which India can teach us, is a universal and appears in some form in all societies. Thus, we find hierarchy manifesting itself in India in the form of the caste system (1970:3) and in the United States in the form of racism (1970:16, 237, 239–258). Indian caste and American racism are both forms of the same universal. If this is so, could not one start from racism and move to the universal of hierarchy? Need one go to India to ratiocinate to the Platonic heights of hierarchy as a universal? This deductive classifying of racism and caste as forms of the same universal is formally equivalent to the generalizing typologies of the empiricists who follow the social-stratification approach. This is especially so when Dumont leaves ontological status of the universals an open question.

Dumont, therefore, tries to have it both ways; the unique is also the universal. Those who accept the law of contradiction will find it difficult to follow him here. Moreover, such an approach for the development of the universal language of sociology would result not in a United Nations of concepts but rather in a Tower of Babel. Sociological theory would then indeed be a miscellaneous collection of concepts, a thing of shreds and patches.

Most Anglo-American empiricists do not accept Dumont's assumption that ideology is prior and constitutive. Indeed, Dumont himself says that this assumption is contradicted by the facts (1970:264, fn. 1a). To construct a sociology on the basis of an assumption which is contrary to fact seems at the very least odd, if not unscientific. Nor do empiricists take a realist position on the existence of universals. Anglo-American empiricists assume that phenomena of power or material conditions and phenomena of ideology or mind are cybernetically or dialectically related and that one influences the other. Of the two, however, the former is assumed to be the more likely source of influence. Moreover, they seek universals not through the unique, but rather through induction and comparison of similarities. Such an approach, Dumont argues, can achieve only the general and not the universal. This is an unwarranted assumption on his part, since we have neither empirical nor philosophical proof of the universal or of universals (cf. Staniland 1972).

His claim that his method can overcome the duality of the religious and the politico-economic while that of the empiricists cannot is once again only because of his second assumption. Because of this assumption, Dumont's method is limited in the questions it can ask and in the conclusions it can give. The empiricists would make the assumption into a hypothesis for testing and would then have much more to tell us about what actually happens rather than what must happen in men's minds because of methodological assumption.

Incidentally, Dumont must here be cleared of the charge which is often made against him, that he is an idealist, interested only in ideas. Both he and the empiricists have the common goal of deriving a theory capable of describing and explaining the societies they study. Both theories are in conceptual form. But once again Dumont is an epistemological rationalist; his explanatory framework is deductive. The source of the concepts he uses must be in the ideologies of the societies studied. The empiricists would go a step further and would attempt to account for ideologies in more general language and with a more general explanation. Dumont's conceptual phenomenology is open to the objection all such approaches are subject to: ultimately they give us the investigator's own standpoint or interpretation of a society. More cannot be established beyond a doubt (Goldstein 1968:103). The result is to throw us back not merely to a form of conceptual relativism but also to a form of conceptual solipsism.[1]

Perhaps the most drastic consequence of following Dumont's method is that it reverses the meanings of objectivity and subjectivity held by Anglo-American empiricists. The empiricists try to abstract

[1]   Some have applied Thomas Kuhn's ideas of the nature of scientific knowledge to that of sociological knowledge. The question is too complex to go into here at length. Briefly, however, it is argued that our understanding of the world is given *only* in the scientific paradigms which we hold. If these paradigms change in a scientific revolution, then our understanding of the world too undergoes a revolution into something completely other than it was. Such an interpretation emphasizes revolution only and neglects the significance of anomaly in Kuhn's theory. Anomaly appears precisely because it is difficult or impossible to account for it within the current paradigm. Yet it can be recognized and to some extent dealt with. So too with many sociological phenomena. Much of the discussion of Benjamin Lee Whorf's theories would also seem applicable here.

from the subjective emic worlds of the societies they study to an etic set of categories applicable to all societies. What is observed through these categories is held to be more objective than the categories and the possibly subjective observations of native informants. The empiricists accept that there *may* be congruence between ideological categories and the society in which they exist as well as cultural lag. But they also assume that ideology may be a rationale for and/or a rationalization of a society or a group in it. This is precisely the issue for them. To what extent is this so, for whom is it so, and what conditions create and maintain such a situation? These questions are outside Dumont's method because of the assumptions he works under. Yet even he cannot help hinting at their significance and importance. He talks of societies making a "choice" of value orientation (1970:77, 213) or conceiving of themselves in a fashion contrary to that of holistic man (1970:237). These are problems of emergence, choice, and change. They imply that men can change their value systems, that one group in a society may hold one value system and another group another value system, that value systems may not be constitutive or isomorphic with concrete social structures, and finally that man as a choice-making creature can be prior to the value systems he chooses and *uses*. Dumont needs "choice" to begin, but his static theory must ignore it, to the detriment of the kinds of question his sociology can deal with and the understanding it can give us.

Another consequence which follows from Dumont's deductions from his assumptions and from this reversal of objectivity and subjectivity is that traditional societies characterized by traditional mentality have a better sociology and therefore better sociologists than modern societies with a modern mentality. (I do not think that these two types of mentality need necessarily be derived from the assumptions, but since Dumont does so, we follow him.) This is because traditional societies still retain a concept of the whole, of collective man, of hierarchical man. They have a direct perception of the whole, of society. On the other hand, modern man has merely a residual sociological apperception. In modern society, sociology emerges "as a special discipline, replacing an idea that was common to all in traditional society" (1970:11). But because it emerges in modern society and derives its concepts from individualistic values, sociology will continue to be sociocentric until it learns from traditional society. Dumont is clear about this. He says, "A society as conceived by individualism has never existed anywhere [because] . . . the individual lives on social ideas" (1970:10). In effect, what Dumont has done is to open up one more new area for the interminable debates surrounding cultural and linguistic relativity; we now have a form of sociological relativity, at least as far as the development of concepts is concerned. Indeed, the resemblance of traditional-minded Indian sociologists to Whorf's physicist-minded Hopi is more than striking.

Unfortunately, some contradictions do seem to arise in Dumont's discussion here. If a society as conceived by individualism never existed, then either we must reject Dumont's assumptions and method when applied to modern societies or we must interpret this statement otherwise. It must mean that the real ideology of modern society is at the nonconscious level and individualism is nothing but a rationalization. Modern man, then, is really deluded man. "The ideal of equality . . . is artificial . . . it represents a deliberate denial of a universal phenomenon [hierarchy?] in a restricted domain [society?]" (1970:20). The choice seems clear; modern society should admit to hierarchy, and better yet to hierarchy in its pure form, the purity-pollution concept, and accept its concrete expression, the caste system.

Dumont's view of society seems to have three sources. The first source of his model for the whole, for society, is explicit and comes from Lévi-Strauss and Gestalt psychology. This modern source for his concepts does seem to contradict the program and method he has outlined, but it seems to bother Dumont only when the empiricists do it. The basic notion he makes use of here is that of structural opposition. "It is the whole which governs the parts, and this whole is very rigorously conceived as based on an opposition. Moreover, there is no other way of defining a whole as distinct from a simple collection" (1970:43-44). It is this notion, according to Dumont, which transports us from 'a world built up of basic elements to a world of structure in which we are interested in a system of relations. The notion of oppositions is, however, just one kind of relation, and a limited one, at that, for building a model of society. Using the notion of oppositions, Dumont is able to account for many criteria or signs whereby castes distinguish themselves on the basis of a single principle, the pure/impure opposition. But this does not account for why these oppositions are necessary in the first place and for the concrete conditions underlying caste segmentation or fusion. Dumont can only give us results and form, not processes and causes. In practice, Dumont himself cannot work with a single notion, and oppositions get mixed with many other notions under the cover term of hierarchy which I discuss below.

The second source is implicit and is based on one of the two types of society he isolates, that is, the traditional society, a society of collective man which recognizes hierarchy. The archetype of this society is India, and the model for the archetype is found in the Hindu ideology. The generalization process from India to traditional society, to society in general, is, if not explicit, clearly implied in the book, though I doubt if this was intended by the author. Society in this model is a whole, wherein everything is perfectly balanced and all is oriented toward the good of and maintenance of the whole. In effect, Dumont's model is a perfect interdependent (eufunctional?) system. Thus, in the caste system:

The needs of each are conceived to be different, depending on caste, on hierarchy, but this fact should not disguise the entire system's *orientation towards the whole.* . . . If we look closely and see the farmer part with a significant portion of his crop for the benefit of a whole series of different people, we shall feel in the end that we are not in the world of the modern economic individual but in a sort of co-operative where the main aim is to ensure the subsistence of everyone in accordance with his social function (1970:105).

This view of cooperative interdependence, of hierarchy, must be a model of all societies, since India manifests to us in a clear form the universal aspect of hierarchy which modern man does not see (1970:237). In these days of change, revolution, and attacks on the functional paradigm, it is difficult to accept such a model "Out of Utopia" (Dahrendorf 1968:107–128). If empirical sociology is, as Dumont says, a short circuit, then a sociology based on this model is a dead end.

The third source of Dumont's model of society is implicit and is the notion of the collective man. This is society anthropomorphized and reified. In this notion, society has a conscious level and a nonconscious level, it *acts* as a whole (1970:11), it gives place to power and closes its eyes (1970:77), and it wills itself to be (1970:254). The values which constitute Indian society can be seen doing many of the same things as when *artha* is held in check by *dharma* (1970:196). It is also interesting to note at this point that voluntarism, which Dumont so much deplores in any account of caste origins through the actions or choices of individuals or groups (1970:23–24), is here given permission to express itself freely at the level of collective man.

Dumont does not explicitly distinguish these three sources of his notion or, better yet, notions of society. This makes for puzzling reading with an illusion of consistency. With society, or its, at times, almost mystical equivalent, "the whole," as a cover term, Dumont is able to cover many disparate topics and yet make them appear a unified subject of discourse. His interpretation of India, therefore, is no longer singular, but multiple. This makes for heated polemic when one tries to find out what Dumont is "really" saying, but it also makes for frozen understanding of sociology and of India.

Implicit in Dumont's sociology is a view of man who, as a social being, acts out of conformity to his society's values. He does so not because of habit but because he must; values constrain social action (1970:3), and men "live under the sway of a system of ideas" (1970:107). "Man acts as a function of what he thinks, and while he has, up to a certain point, the ability to arrange his thoughts in his own way, to construct new categories, he does so starting from the categories which are given by society'' (1970:6). Dumont in practice ignores man's constructive intellectual abilities and concentrates on the categories given by society. Indeed, his whole method requires it. The Indian, therefore, must act in order to preserve his status; the modern man must act to preserve his individuality and freedom. "Roughly, our own society obliges us to be free" (1970:8). In effect, when Dumont says "the individual is a value" (1970:9), he relativizes man as well as sociology. Just as, in Dumont's view, society no longer exists ontologically for the empiricists, so, too, the individual no longer exists ontologically for Dumont. Only collective man or society exists. The individual is merely a concept homologous to the concept of society (1970:10). Man in this theory is absolutely socialized man (cf. Wrong 1961). In a post-Freudian world, this view of man is as difficult to accept as are the theories and conclusions based on it. As for the individual being nothing more than a value without ontological status or foundation, *solvitur ambulando*. It would appear that a sociology based on some idea of a choice-making individual has a firmer, more immediately recognizable ontological status than that based on a whole of mystical participation, of collective man, or of society.

India

The key to Dumont's interpretation of India and the lesson which comparative sociology can learn from it is the true nature of hierarchy. This concept is also the major problem of the book. Just what does this concept mean and why is Dumont able to do so many things with it? It is puzzling to note that Dumont gives credit for this notion to a doctoral thesis by Raymond Apthorpe at Oxford University; puzzling because, as in the case of the notion of structural oppositions, it apparently gives credit to a modern Western source for the key to understanding India. This would seem to go against Dumont's own canons for the source of sociological concepts and theory. In any case, what is hierarchy?

If one reads Dumont closely, hierarchy is many things. On the one hand we learn that it is the conscious form of reference of parts to the whole in India, that is, a value (1970:65; 282, fn. 31a); that it is reducible to the principle of pure and impure (1970:43); that the *necessary* ideological form of the ideal type of hierarchy is the opposition of pure and impure; and that hierarchy cannot exist outside India without the opposition of pure and impure and the absolute distinction of power from status. On the other hand, we also learn that hierarchy is a universal and necessary fact present in all societies (1970:237); that it is a principle whereby "elements of a whole are ranked in relation to the whole" (1970:66); and that it is a relation of encompassing to encompassed (1970:xii; 1967:33). In a more schematic way, what are the meanings of hierarchy? They are:

1. a value unique to India (1970:43, 251);
2. a universal component of all societies (1970:237);
3. an ideal type (1970:74, 213, 252);
4. a logical principle of thought. This last is perhaps most important, but it too confuses four types of logical relation: (a) a relation of inclusion (encompassing and encompassed) (1970:xii, 67); (b) a relation of rank ordering (expressed in caste status) (1970:57, 65, 91, 251); (c) a relation of complementation (structural opposition) (1970:39 ff.). This is neither simply a relation of contradiction, that is, of consideration of one of two classes and its logical relation with the other (1971:70); nor is it a relation of complementarity, that is, of consideration of "the universe of discourse and its constitution" (1971:70). Hierarchy subsumes complementarity, and complementarity subsumes contradiction. Hierarchy, then, is "an indispensable adjunct to the longer recognized 'distinctive opposition' or relation of complementarity, in strictly structural thinking" (1971:78); and (d) a relation of conjunction (interdependence) (1970:92, 105). This relation does at times seem to be separate from hierarchy (1970:92-93; 308, fn. 71a), but at other times it seems to be reducible to hierarchy or purity (1970:105, 43). Dumont is unclear about the exact status of this relation in his theory; and it, therefore, should perhaps not be included on this list.

Hierarchy is thus an equivocal concept in the theory; it is not perfectly univocal as Dumont says (1970:251). Not only is the concept equivocal, it has virtually been defined away into an inclusive *all* as indicated in 4(c) above. It is uninformative and nonstructural.

Dumont is least clear in defining what is most fundamental. At times he tells us that hierarchy is reducible to the opposition of pure and impure; at other times that it is a fundamental conscious value or universal principle in itself. The confusions and contradictions that arise in the theory because of these multiple meanings are too many to recount here. Indeed, Dumont himself says that the linear order of castes is only one by-product of hierarchy (1970:57). It is because of these multiple meanings that Dumont is able to do so many things with the concept and make his interpretation of India seem unitary and consistent when it is not.

Let me outline one of the possible kinds of interpretation which exist in or result from this theory. Following Dumont's method, we go to India to understand what hierarchy really is. We find it and recognize it in its expressed conscious form, the theory of pure and impure (hierarchy as a cultural value). Thereafter we can look for it in the nonconscious part of our own ideology, and we find it in the pathological form of racism in the United States. But what is racism?

The simplest hypothesis . . . is to assume that racism fulfills an old function under a new form. It is as if it were representing in an egalitarian society a resurgence of what was differently and more directly and naturally expressed in a hierarchical society. Make distinction illegitimate, and you get discrimination; suppress the former modes of distinction and you have a racist ideology (1970:254).

What are Americans to make of this? On the one hand, they notice that racism is really hierarchy made illegitimate. It is an illegitimate value whereby rank orders of status are made in an egalitarian society. This leaves them on the horns of a dilemma. Either they consciously admit their racist values, make them "legitimate" and "natural," accept the Hindu values of purity and pollution which are "necessary" in order to see racism in its clearest form, and thereby accept a caste situation in the United States; or they reject these values and continue to live with racism as a pathology. On the other hand, they can see racism merely as a principle of thought, equivalent to hierarchy, whereby distinctions are made. In this case, they must accept that they have second-rate intellects, since hierarchy in its ideal form can exist only in India, or that their egalitarian values have led them logically to the pathology of racism. These are not choices mentioned by Dumont in his book, but they do follow from the statements he has made.

Racism or delusion seem to be the only alternatives Dumont offers for the untouchables to get out of their situation. On the one hand, he says "untouchability will not truly disappear until the purity of the Brahman is itself radically devalued" (1970:54). If it is devalorized, then it must go down below the threshold to the nonconscious part of the ideology, and we get racism or some form equivalent to it. On the other hand, he says that the road to the abolition of untouchability

. . . is likely to lie in caste actions, and that only the content of a caste action indicates whether it militates for or against caste. Not to recognize this is to remain within the traditional Indian way of thinking . . . it is clear today, contrary to Gandhi's opinion, that the Untouchables will not be finally emancipated save by themselves: *the good will* of their politician superiors cannot be enough (1970:223).

If the untouchables are to militate against caste, they will have to change their ideology and accept some form of egalitarian ideology. But they will be deluding themselves, because a society as conceived of by egalitarian ideology has never existed. Moreover, in the Indian environment, they probably will not be able to rid themselves of the dominant ideology, as is the case with the Christians and the Muslims.

The quote above (1970:223) is, however, very important. It implicitly contains the ideas that ideologies can change and that politics are a force in changing them. Does this not mean, then, that politics or power may be primary and constitutive? It would seem at times that Dumont's values and humanitarian concerns in the pragmatic world do not allow him to follow his own theories.

The meaning of hierarchy to which Dumont gives greatest importance is that of a relation of inclusion; it is a relation between that which encompasses and that which is encompassed. Because of this relation, Dumont claims that he is able to interpret Indian society in a more complete, more satisfactory, and more consistent way than heretofore. This occurs because everything is encompassed by the religious value of purity. Moreover, it is this term which allows Dumont to overstep the strict boundaries of his own method, that of understanding India on its own terms through its own ideology. Because of *his assumption* that each society has one value which encompasses all others, Dumont is able to interpret purity as a value encompassing all others. This makes his interpretation of India look encyclopedic and complete. But is this true of the facts of the ideology as expressed in the Great Tradition of India? We can never be sure, and in fact, have cause to doubt, because of the problem of *indirectly contained* ideology. Dumont continually makes the assertion that anything that is *not directly* contained in the ideology is encompassed by it at a secondary or nonconscious level. But this assertion is valid only because of his methodological assumption. This problem sits uneasy with Dumont's whole method as well as with *his* interpretation of Indian ideology.

Of what, then, does this important relation, "to encompass," consist, and what are its boundaries? At first glance, the universe it defines would seem to be without bounds, or infinite. If this were so, it would be so broad as to be meaningless; it would explain nothing by including everything. At second glance, Dumont seems to put some boundaries to this relation, though he does not specifically tell us what they are. We do get some clues from the way in which he uses and describes the relation. He tells us that it means to become blind or to close one's eyes to (1970:77); it means to cloak differences (1970:78); it means to be surreptitiously assimilated to (1970:212 and *passim*); and it means to demote to a secondary level (1970:78 and *passim*). In other words, the content and boundaries of the concept are set by the extent to which the anthropomorphic analogy can be exploited. This may be good literature, but it is poor social science. If we reject this meaning of "to encompass" as it is described in the theory, then the only other limits that can be put on the term are those of authority, and authority in this case is Louis Dumont. This is fine for a *guru/chela* relationship, but once again it is not good social science. Moreover, one gets the impression at times from this theory that anything that Dumont is uneasy with or finds difficult to deal with, or that is not directly contained in the ideology, must be demoted to a secondary, unimportant, encompassed level. Just as hierarchy, like "the Mantle of Our Lady of Mercy[,] shelters sinners of every kind in its voluminous folds" (1970:78) so, too, it shelters Dumont from many unsolved and knotty problems. Once again, imprecision and the equivocal meanings of concepts make not only heated polemics but also frozen intellectual progress.

In summary, we are led to the conclusion that Dumont has offered us neither a productive paradigm for sociological research nor a particularly enlightening interpretation of India. His interpretations are only as good as the equivocal concepts he has used to make them.

REFERENCES

DAHRENDORF, RALF
   1968   "Out of Utopia: toward a reorientation of sociological analysis," in
           Essays in the theory of society, 107-128. Stanford: Stanford University Press.
DUMONT, LOUIS
   1957   For a sociology of India. Contributions to Indian Sociology 1:7-22.
   1966   A fundamental problem in the sociology of caste. Contributions to
           Indian Sociology 9:17-32.
   1967   "Caste: a phenomenon of social structure or an aspect of Indian
           culture," in Caste and race: comparative approaches. Edited by
           Anthony deReuck and Julie Knight, 28-38. A Ciba Foundation
           Volume. London: J. and A. Churchill.
   1970   Homo hierarchicus: the caste system and its implications. Trans-
           lated by Mark Sainsbury. Chicago: University of Chicago Press.
   1971   On putative hierarchy and some allergies to it. Contributions to
           Indian Sociology, new series 5:58-81.
GOLDSTEIN, LEON
   1968   "The phenomenological and naturalistic approaches to sociology,"
           in Theory in anthropology: a sourcebook. Edited by Robert A.
           Manners and David Kaplan, 97-104. Chicago: Aldine.
HANCHETT, SUZANNE
   n.d.   "Reflections and oppositions: on structuralism." Unpublished paper
           presented to the Society for South Indian Studies.
STANILAND, HILARY
   1972   Universals. Garden City, New York: Doubleday.
WRONG, DENNIS
   1961   The oversocialized conception of man. American Sociological
           Review 26:183-192.

Flexibility in Central Indian Kinship and Residence

DORANNE JACOBSON

Until recent years, many scholars viewed Indian culture as characterized by relatively rigid structural features. Permanence, formality, and little flexibility have been attributed to caste hierarchies, caste and occupational relationships, pollution ideologies, systems of kinship, marriage, and residence, patron-client relationships, male-female relationships, and many other aspects of Indian society and culture. An important trend of current scholarship in India, however, is to concentrate on the mutability of much of the culture. A high proportion of recent publications pertaining to India include the word "change" in their titles. Additionally, there is increasing recognition of a flexibility long extant within traditional Indian institutions.

Discussions of stability versus change and rigidity versus flexibility are significant to the development of ethnographic procedures and to anthropological theory in general. Essential to enhancing the understanding of change and flexibility is full cognizance of differences between the ideal and the actual. All too often failure to distinguish between what people say they do and what they actually do has led to

The data on which this paper is based were collected by the author during approximately three years of anthropological fieldwork in "Nimkhera" (Madhya Pradesh), 1965–1967 and 1973–1974. I am very grateful to the residents of Nimkhera for their hospitality and cooperation and to my research assistant, Miss Sunalini Nayudu, for her valuable insights and aid. I am indebted to numerous state and district government officers in Bhopal and Raisen for the many courtesies they extended. My husband, Jerome Jacobson, provided essential assistance, advice, and moral support.

The field research was supported by a predoctoral fellowship and grant from the National Institute of Mental Health, United States Public Health Service, and by a Senior Research Fellowship from the American Institute of Indian Studies. Preparation of this paper was in part made possible by the Ogden Mills Fellowship, awarded by the American Museum of Natural History, New York, of which I am most appreciative.

difficulty and inaccuracy in collecting and analyzing anthropological data.

With reference to most parts of the world, it has long been usual to classify systems of kinship and residence according to ideal typologies, for example "patrilocal," "virilocal," "patrilineal," "matrilineal." Anthropologists have of course recognized that everyone in a given society does not adhere to the stated kinship and residence ideals of the society, but cases of nonnormative behavior in these areas are often treated in the literature as deviant or insignificant. As Harris (1971:333–335) has indicated, to enhance our understanding of cultural phenomena in these areas, we should not focus on descent rules and ideal residence patterns but should concentrate on actual on-the-ground spacing of people.

This paper discusses kinship and residence in the Bhopal region of central India where, as in north India, Hindus are said by both social scientists and members of the culture to be patrilineal and patrilocal. Data pertaining to actual residence units, however, indicate the existence of a variety of residence possibilities. Further, careful observation of the movements and behavior of women and their kinsmen reveals that, even among those coresident groups which are ostensibly patrilocal and patrilineal, there exists a pattern of residence and kinship obligation which is much more complex than the labels "patrilocal" and "patrilineal" would suggest. This pattern and its relationships with other aspects of the culture are the primary foci of this paper.

PATRILINEALITY AND PATRILOCALITY IN NORTH AND CENTRAL INDIA

The ideology of patrilineality and patrilocality is very strong in north and central India (in this paper, India north of the Narbada River). A common theme in Indian folklore and song is the unhappiness of the Hindu bride uprooted from the beloved home of her childhood and sent to live in the home of strangers — her husband and his kinsmen. Throughout much of north and central India, the birth of a daughter brings less joy than the birth of a son, for a daughter is expected to leave her natal home, while it is anticipated that a son will remain in his parental home all his life. At the same time, many parents view their daughters sentimentally and treasure them in anticipation of their departure for their husbands' homes. Some parents say they do not punish a daughter, "because she belongs not to us but to others." In many villages across the land, girls are often told they should learn their lessons in housekeeping and proper conduct well, for they will soon live among critical strangers.

In north and central India, almost every Hindu considers himself a member of a shallow patrilineage, the *khāndān* or *kuṭumb*, and of a patrilineal clan, usually called the *gotra*, as well as of a caste, or *jāti*. The caste is endogamous, but the clan and the lineage are typically strictly exogamous. Among most groups, also excluded as possible marriage partners are persons known to be consanguineally related to ego through females, at least for a certain number of generations. Additionally, throughout most of north India the village is exogamous, and in some regions even whole groups of villages are exogamous. In central India, while marriages within the same village occur, marriages linking residents of different villages are preferred. The bride is usually expected to make her official residence with her husband and his parents — usually strangers to her — in a village which may be many miles distant from her natal home.

One scholar has referred to Hindu marriage as "the transfer of a female from one family to another" (Mandelbaum 1970:97), and several other authors have stressed the completeness of this transfer (e.g. Dube 1955:151; Gough 1956:841-842; Mathur 1964:43; Orenstein 1965:60, 73-74; 1970:1366). Indeed, in much of north India and parts of south India, a bride is clearly shifted from her parental household to the household and lineage of her husband. After the wedding, or at the *gaunā* [consummation ceremony, usually from one to three years after the wedding], a north Indian bride is carried off to her husband's home to begin a new life. Most young brides are allowed visits to their parental homes, but the frequency of such visits varies among different groups. Typically, a north Indian bride remains in her husband's home for a year or more, sometimes until she has produced a child, before she visits her parents. For example, in Senapur village, near Varanasi (Banaras) in the Gangetic valley, among a sample of sixteen Thakur women, five had remained with their in-laws for between seven and eleven years before visiting their own parents' homes. Four had never returned to their parents' villages because their parents had died (Luschinsky 1962:350-351). Such an abrupt transition from being a daughter cherished by indulgent and loving parents to being the wife and daughter-in-law of strangers ready to criticize the slightest deviation from dutiful and subservient behavior is difficult indeed. Furthermore, a young north Indian wife is expected to veil her face and remain inside her husband's house most of the time — purdah [seclusion and veiling] restrictions to which she was not subject in her parents' home. Most young women succeed in making the adjustment, but some brides are troubled by psychosomatic physical and mental illness (Freed and Freed 1964). In Senapur, many young wives visit shamans, where they are possessed by spirits (Luschinsky 1962:694-709). Some brides commit suicide, typically by jumping into a well.

Most north Indian women retain some affiliation with their natal homes after marriage. Although a north Indian wife may have to wait years between visits, each sojourn in her parental home may last several months or a year. Her brother may also visit her in her marital home, particularly on certain ceremonial occasions, when he brings gifts to her and her husband's family. Ideally, a north Indian woman always retains an affectionate bond with her brother, and her children are fond of their mother's indulgent brother. Nevertheless, the distance between their villages and the lengthy periods between visits may gradually weaken these ties.

WOMEN IN TWO HOUSEHOLDS: CENTRAL INDIA

As in north India, village parents in the Bhopal-Raisen area of central India say they prefer the birth of a boy to the birth of a girl, "because boys stay with us forever, but girls go away." Some central Indian rituals and most overt statements of norms clearly indicate that a girl is formally transferred to her husband's household and becomes a member of his patrilineage at marriage. Some other ideals and ritual observances, however, point to the existence of a permanent tie between a married woman and her natal kinsmen. Indeed, observation of what women actually do and analysis of disputes between affines show that a woman's natal kinsmen do not give up their claim on her company and her services at her marriage. In this region, for many years after marriage most village women act as important members of both their natal and their conjugal households (respectively *māīkā* and *susrāl* or *sāsre*). To the ethnographer, a most striking feature of village life is the constant procession of women coming and going on visits to their two homes. Many women also spend significant amounts of time in their mother's brother's homes (*mamehāro*), particularly in their childhood and young adult years. The female population of a village is never constant in size and never composed of the same individuals for more than a few days at a time. Women's *de facto* membership in two kin groups appears to be related to the economic importance of women's activities, to inheritance rules, and to the seclusion and veiling of women. Whether and to what extent a woman ceases to be a member of her own patrilineage and becomes a fully participating member of her husband's patrilineage at marriage is somewhat ambiguous in the Bhopal region. The exact relationship of a married woman to the two patrilineages in which she has rights and obligations is an area of flexibility in the kinship system which allows a woman to respond to her own needs and to the varying needs of her kinsmen. The flexibility of the married woman's position as a member of two households seems to fulfill important functions in the family, the lineage, and the caste as a whole.

The significance of women's participation in the activities of two households may be better understood by examining the activities and movements of the Hindu daughters and wives of a village in central India.

The Village

Nīmkherā, a small village in Raisen District, Madhya Pradesh, is similar in many respects to hundreds of settlements in central India.[1] The 621 villagers, of whom 80 percent are Hindu and 20 percent are Muslim, belong to twenty-one castes and five Muslim groups. They live in low whitewashed earth-and-stone houses clustered on a hillside overlooking their fertile fields on the plain below. The village is forty-five miles from Bhopal, the capital of Madhya Pradesh, India's largest state, and few men work at urban jobs. Most villagers are farmers, laborers, and craftsmen, supported by the abundant wheat crop grown on the village fields. Rice, gram (*chanā*), pulses, maize, millet, linseed, and several varieties of vegetables and fruits are also grown.

That the district, once part of Muslim-ruled Bhopal State, includes much uncultivated forest land is reflected in the low district population density of 170 per square mile (compared with 471 for all of India). The district is almost completely rural: 95 percent of the district population lives in villages, of which 81 percent have fewer than 500 inhabitants. As in many other parts of India, there are fewer females than males (900 to 1000) (Pandya 1974).

The Hindu residents of Nimkhera currently have affinal ties with residents of 131 other villages, towns, and cities, many of which are situated in neighboring districts, particularly Vidisha District to the north. Hindu daughters-in-law of the village come from eighty settlements, and daughters of the village are married to men from seventy-seven settlements.

Residence

About four-fifths of the village Hindus reside patrilocally or virilocally,

[1] The pseudonym "Nimkhera" refers to a large *nīm* tree in the center of the village, whose leaves are used by all the villagers for making soothing medications.

The data presented in this paper refer only to the village Hindus, not to the Muslims, whose system of kinship and marriage differs significantly from that of the Hindus.

The language spoken in Nimkhera is a variety of Hindi. In this paper Hindi words are written with diacritics only at the first appearance of each word.

and about one-fifth live uxorilocally or neolocally (see Table 1). Since land and houses are inherited by males patrilineally, a man must usually live in or near his father's home to claim and use these assets. Although there is a strong feeling that patrilocal residence is best and virilocal residence an acceptable substitute, there is no prohibition on other forms of residence, and persons who do not follow the ideal pattern are not generally criticized. The necessary paramountcy of "lucri-locality" — living where one has access to strategic resources (Buchler and Selby 1968:56; Bick and Ebihara 1972:3–4) — is recognized by most villagers.

Fifteen of the Hindu women now living in Nimkhera who have ever been married (12.5 percent of 120 women) are daughters of the village living permanently in the village of their birth, ten with their husbands and the rest as divorcees and widows. Nineteen of the women who have married into or out of Nimkhera (9 percent of 210 women) live permanently in their natal villages. In most cases, the availability of land or employment in the woman's village has encouraged such residence. For example, two men living uxorilocally are Thakurs whose wives have no brothers and were willed land by their fathers. Landless widows and divorcees weigh both sentimental and economic factors and frequently opt for residence with natal kinsmen or a daughter and her husband. (Landed widows normally reside patrilocally in order to safeguard the patrimony of their offspring and their own interests in their husbands' lands.)

The Ideals of Patrilineality, Patrilocality, and Women's Ties to Natal Kin

Much of the ritual and ideology of the village Hindus stresses patri-lineality, patrilocality, and the transfer of a woman to membership in her husband's kin group at marriage. Existing in tandem with these ideals are ritual and ideational insistence that a woman's ties to her natal kin cannot and should not be severed.

BLOOD AND PROCREATION. Most of the village Hindus believe that a child is formed solely of two drops of semen, derived from the father's blood, deposited in the mother's womb. "The mother gives nothing to the child's substance — she only provides the place for it to grow. Just as we plant a seed in a field, so the child is formed of the seed planted by the father," explained one informant. Several informants stressed that a child is always said to be its father's offspring and never its mother's. One woman complained, "The mother bears the burden of the child inside her for nine months, suffers the pain of its birth, nurses and feeds it, and cleans up its dirt; still the child is said to be the

Table 1. Residence in Nimkhera

	Patrilocal†	Virilocal	Uxorilocal	Neolocal‡	Total
Percent of couples*	70.0%	9.7%	9.0%	11.2%	99.9%
Number	94	13	12	15	134

* Units include married couples currently living together, as well as couple-remnants (once-married adults, now widowed or divorced).
† This category includes couples and couple-remnants residing in or immediately adjacent to the husband's father's house. Of couples living patrilocally, only 23.6 percent have living fathers, and only 19.3 percent are actually residing with the husband's father in the same household. (Four men — 4.3 percent of those living patrilocally — have living fathers to whom they live immediately adjacent.)
‡ This category includes nine couples and couple-remnants residing in the household or village of the spouse of a mother, sister, daughter, or son. Also included are a couple who were both residents of Nimkhera before marriage but live separately from the kinsmen of both.

father's. And if a man divorces his wife, he has the right to claim his children, because they are of his blood."

Despite this notion of a unilateral contribution to procreation, the child of a Brahman father and a lower-caste mother would not be considered a Brahman. First, the child would be irremediably polluted by drinking its mother's milk, and second, the child of *any* improper union, whether intra- or intercaste, cannot be fully accepted as a Brahman.[2] The children of rare intercaste marriages are usually accepted as members of the lower-ranking parent's caste.

Another theory of conception is held by a few learned village Brahmans. They consider a child to be formed of a mixture of semen (*vīr* or *bīr*) and uterine blood (*raj*). The child's teeth, hair, and bones derive from the semen, and his blood, flesh, and skin from the mother's blood.[3] The pandits stated that those who believe that only the father contributes to a child's substance are merely ignorant of the facts.[4] All

[2] An intercaste union is inherently irregular, but even a marriage contracted within the caste may be improper. Several informants pointed to the example of a local Jijotiya Brahman man married to his dead elder brother's wife. Jijotiya Brahmans consider this union illegitimate on two counts: Brahman widows should not remarry, and although acceptable in other castes, the union of a Jijotiya Brahman man and his brother's wife (*bhābhī*) is scandalous because she is supposed to be "like his mother." The children of this couple will not find mates in the Jijotiya Brahman caste but may be accepted in a lower-ranking Brahman caste. None of the Jijotiya Brahmans accept food touched by this errant couple or their children.
[3] From a feminist point of view, the definitions of *raj* and *vīryā* (standard Hindi for semen) as given in a Hindi-English dictionary (Pathak 1973) are quite revealing:
raj: n. mas. menstrual excretion in women, sin, water, pollen of flowers, dirt, dust, night, light, the second of the three constituent qualities of living beings which produce worldly desires and passions and is the cause of vice.
vīryā: n. mas. sperm, semen, virile, fortitude, power, strength, valour, splendour, seed.
[4] Villagers similarly disagree on the extent to which blood is shared by kinsmen beyond the nuclear family. One informant stated that all members of the same caste can be said to be of the same blood, and that at the same time all persons born into one patrilineage

informants agreed that a child receives its spirit from neither parent, but from God.

WOMEN AND PATRILINEAGE MEMBERSHIP

Childhood. Despite their heritage of blood and body from their father (and mother), all girls in the Bhopal area are told that they are but temporary members of their natal household and patrilineage, destined to join the household and patrilineage of their husbands. At the annual worship of the family goddess (*Bījāsan Mātā pūjā*), oil lamps are lit and special fried cakes (*khũt*) are offered to the goddess. Males of the *khandan* and their wives partake of the offerings, but daughters, married and unmarried, do not. They are told that they will eat such cakes in their husbands' homes. It is said that in the past daughters were not even allowed to see the flames of the *puja* lamps.

A girl also knows that the lands and house of her natal family will be inherited by her brothers, and that except in unusual circumstances she will have no share.[5] A girl is told that her brother represents security to her parents, but that she does not. Few parents would feel comfortable accepting food or lodging from a married daughter, to whom they are expected to be donors, not recipients of her gifts or hospitality.[6] In contrast, a married son is expected to support his aged parents.

Marriage. As much as her parents may wish to keep her with them, they must arrange her marriage, for no girl can remain single past puberty without arousing much negative comment. In fact, most village Hindu girls of the area are married before puberty, and all are married before age sixteen.

At her wedding, a girl is veiled for the first time in her life and carried out of her house to sit among the strange men who comprise her groom's wedding party. They fill her lap with gifts of clothing and expensive silver jewelry. There later follows the *Bhãwre* ceremony, in

---

share the same blood, in contrast to members of other patrilineages, whose blood is different. This segmentary notion of shared blood is similar to the segmentary theory of natural substance observed among Jaffna Tamiḷs (David 1973:522). Others, however, denied that even the offspring of two brothers share the same blood. "The children of different fathers, even if they are of the same patrilineage, definitely do not have the same blood," one Brahman stated adamantly. Another said, "Well, in a way we can say that all human beings are of the same blood and bones, but then all people are different too."

[5]   Modern Indian legislation provides for daughters as well as sons to inherit shares in land. Some village women have begun to avail themselves of these legal rights, but most villagers condemn such action. "When our parents have married us off and given us rights in another household, why should we take from our brothers?" said one woman, summarizing the prevailing sentiment among village women.

[6]   For a detailed discussion of the donor-recipient relationship between bride-givers and bride-takers in Uttar Pradesh, see Vatuk (1973).

which the officiating Brahman reads texts outlining some of the mutual obligations of the bride and groom:

The girl addresses the groom and requests,

"Oh my Lord, from today I have become like half of your body, so please keep in mind always these things I am telling you.

Making a religious sacrifice, or conducting a sacred fire ceremony, keeping a fast, going to a forest, garden, park, fair, market, place of pilgrimage, or on a journey, etc., saving and spending money, buying and selling cows, bullocks, buffaloes, horses, etc., should be done with my permission in all seasons of the year.

And if I commit any offense, then please do not punish me when I am sitting among a group of my friends, so that I will not be embarrassed in front of my friends."

The groom should follow these seven vows until the end of his life.

The groom addresses the bride and requests,

"Women should never go into a forestlike garden alone. You should not become friendly with or even talk to drunkards. You should not go to your father's house or anywhere without a reason, without an invitation, and without my permission. You should always pay heed to my admonitions. You should never laugh for improper reasons. You should cover your body properly before appearing before elders and men. You should never discuss family matters with outsiders."

The girl should keep in mind until the end of her life these seven vows sought by the boy.

Then in a moving ritual, the "Gift of the Maiden" (*Kanyā Dān*), the bride is formally bestowed upon the groom. As watching women softly sing, the bride's parents together cradle in their hands a ball of wheat-flour dough mixed with turmeric, containing one-and-a-quarter rupee and a whole *supārī* nut (*sankalap kā golā*). The Brahman chants a prayer and, with a betel leaf, sprinkles the ball with drops of water to render it ritually pure and to drive away all evil influences. The bride's parents transfer the sacred ball into the upturned hand of the groom. The bride is now officially his. To seal their union, the couple walk together seven times around the embers of the sacred wedding fire with their clothes knotted together.

The next day at the concluding ceremony of the wedding, spokesmen for the bride and groom deliver speeches. Through his Brahman, the bride's kinsman says,

I am merely giving you a maiden for washing the dishes and plastering the hearth. I am not capable of giving any more than this.

The groom's kinsman replies,

You have given us a boundless gift, the maiden of your soul, a beautiful daughter-in-law who is called Lakshmi [the Goddess of Wealth]. When you have given Lakshmi, then there is no need for anything else to be given. Amen.

In a longer version of the farewell speech, the groom's spokesman says,

Oh relative, having seen your wealth and your perfect lotuslike garden, we are very much pleased. Our lives have been completely gratified by receiving a very virtuous daughter-in-law exactly like Goddess Ramā [Lakshmi], whose flamelike brilliance completely destroys the darkness.

We have received the utmost happiness, such as one would receive upon having wisdom as bright as the sun, bringing joy for millions and billions of births. Our honor has risen to the fullest heights. We have received everything.

What was lacking in what you have given us? Absolutely nothing. We have profited in every respect.[7]

Although delicately couched in flattering phrases, the clear implication of these speeches is that the bride has been given to her husband and his kin group; she can visit her own only when allowed to do so by her husband. After witnessing a wedding, the mother of several daughters said wistfully, "After the *Kanya Dan*, the girl is no longer ours. We have no right to her; she belongs to them now." Another woman said, "After she marries, a daughter becomes *parāyī* [not of us, belonging to others]."

At the same time, it is recognized in these ritual orations that the bride has a right to expect considerate treatment from her husband, and that, when proper arrangements have been made, she will be allowed to visit her natal home. In fact, the vital roles of matron-of-honor and best man (*Sawāsan* and *Sawāsā*) for a bride or groom are specifically reserved for a married sister or father's sister and her husband.

The participation of a sister or a father's sister is also prescribed in other rituals. For example, it is the father's sister who should bless a new infant in the *Chauk* ceremony, a rite held ten days after a birth.

It is considered best for a child's first word to be either "*māmā*" [mother's brother] or "*būā*" [father's sister], and infants are actively taught to utter these sounds first, clearly implying the desirability of retaining a link between an adult woman and her natal kinsmen.

Susral *Ritual Obligations*. After her marriage, a woman is expected to take on the ritual responsibilities incumbent upon members of her husband's *khandan*. She must perform the *puja*s expected of *khandan*

---

[7] Likening the bride to Lakshmi is in accordance with the villagers' belief that it is the bride's fate which determines the amount of wealth and material prosperity which comes into her conjugal home. To some women is attributed the power of increasing food stores by mere touch, while others of less happy fate bring depletion of family resources. On the other hand, the number of living children a man has is said to be dependent upon his fate, not upon his wife's.

members[8] and observe pollution resulting from a birth or death in her husband's lineage. When a death occurs in her husband's *khandan*, a woman is automatically polluted (thirteen days for a deceased man, eleven days for a deceased woman), wherever she may be, and should go immediately to her *susral* to be with the rest of the similarly polluted mourners — the male members of the lineage, their wives, and their unmarried daughters.[9]

In contrast, a married woman need not observe pollution upon the death of any of her natal kin, although she may choose to join the mourners and be polluted by living and eating with them.

When she dies, her husband and his kinsmen will be polluted for eleven days and will mourn for her. They will give a small death feast after three days (*Tij* or *Din*) and a large death feast (*Rasoi*) after eleven days.

If she dies in her *susral*, her natal kin observe no pollution and give no feast. But if she dies in her natal home, in recognition of their ties to her, attenuated though they are, her natal kin observe a three-day pollution period and give a small death feast.[10]

Every year for sixteen days in the month of Kuar, men offer water and food to deceased ancestors, and their wives offer flowers and "touch the feet" of the ancestors. Sons, but not daughters, may participate in the rites. Interestingly, however, the ancestors for whom these offerings are made include not only those of the patriline but fourteen generations of ancestors on all sides — the forebears of the man's father, mother, father's father and mother, mother's father and mother, etc. Thus, although a woman does not make offerings for her parents, her son may do so. On pilgrimages, married couples together offer sacred water to wash away the sins of all ancestors of both the husband and the wife.

---

[8] In the village headman's (*patel*'s) family, the head of the household and his wife are expected to make substantial offerings to Matabai, the village protectress, on particular occasions. After the death of the old *patel*, responsibility shifted to the eldest son and his wife, who were somewhat lax in their observances. The goddess possessed the wife, punished her by temporarily depriving her of the power of speech, and then spoke through her in a whisper of her displeasure. The goddess specifically mentioned that the wife had failed to offer her *ghi* and sweets as she should have. The new *patel* rushed the missing offerings to the goddess's shrine and then his wife regained her senses and full power of speech.

[9] The fact of the death itself is said to pollute her (*usko lag gai chhit*); she is also said to be obliged to "observe pollution" (*sutak manti hai*). She is polluted because of her tie of kinship to the deceased, not because of any notion of putrefaction spreading from the corpse to the kinsmen of the dead (cf. David 1973).

[10] All other death pollution strictly follows the patriline and is restricted to members of the *khandan*. For example, a man observes no pollution for a deceased mother's brother, mother's brother's son, father's sister's son, etc.

Property Rights. A married woman and her children have a right to food, clothing, and shelter in her husband's home. One mother, dissatisfied with the paucity of material care her daughter was receiving in her conjugal home, remarked, "She has rights in that household. She didn't force her way in." A widow is entitled to the use of her husband's share of the family lands as long as she does not remarry, but traditionally has not had the right of absolute ownership of the land, as a man does. If she divorces her husband and remarries outside his *khandan*, a woman gives up all rights in his land and is expected to return the jewelry received from his family. Only jewelry received as gifts from her own natal kinsmen is hers to keep and dispose of completely as she wishes.

Unchanging Blood. That the bride does not actually become a full member of her husband's *khandan* at marriage is indicated by the fact that, despite the existence of a rule of strict *khandan* exogamy, in most castes leviratic remarriage of widows is allowed. In fact, it is recognized that although a woman is formally transferred to membership in her husband's kin group, her ties of blood are always with her natal kin. All informants unequivocally rejected the thought that a woman's blood could change at her marriage (cf. David 1973; Nicholas and Inden 1972). As one woman said, "No matter where you send her, a woman's blood cannot change. When my brother comes to visit me he sometimes says, 'You have a sharp mind.' I say, 'You do too,' and he says, 'Well, we're of the same blood, aren't we?' "

Thus, patrilineality, patrilocality, and the transfer of a married woman to her husband's kin group are distinctly emphasized in beliefs about the nature of procreation and shared blood, in wedding ritual, in the observation of death pollution, and in the rules of women's property rights. At the same time, particular features of these beliefs, rituals, and rules, in addition to other aspects of ideology, deny the complete and total transfer of a woman to her husband's kin group, thus reflecting — and reinforcing — the possibility of a married woman's continued participation in affairs in her natal home, even as she finds her niche in her conjugal home.

Life in Two Households

Although she has been formally given to her groom and his family, the young bride usually remains at home with her parents for about three years, until she has reached puberty, after which the *gauna* is held. Then, departing for her conjugal home, the veiled bride clings to each of her relatives in turn and cries most bitterly. Her relatives, too, weep as they see her borne away by her husband and his kinsmen.

In her new home the bride is treated and acts like a different person. She remains veiled and shyly submits to scrutiny by her mother-in-law and other women. There she is addressed not by her personal name but by a name derived from the name of her natal village (e.g. *"Nīmkherāwālī"* [Woman from Nimkhera]). Although she does not take her husband's name, she may be referred to as her husband's wife (e.g. *Rūp Singh kī dulhen*).[11] Her situation is not as it is in her natal village, where as a daughter she is free to move about with uncovered face and to attend the village social functions that interest her; as a wife in her conjugal home she is expected to observe purdah. She veils her face in the presence of elder affines and residents of her husband's village and also veils before her husband when others are present. She may not move about as she wishes but stays inside the courtyard except for a few essential outings sanctioned by her mother-in-law. Brides of high-ranking families normally leave the courtyard only to eliminate, but after a few years they begin making brief trips to the well to fetch water and to attend important rituals. Young wives in lower-ranking families veil as do women of higher status, but they observe stringent seclusion for a shorter period of time. Within a few months they may go out to fetch water and work beside their kinswomen in the fields.[12]

After a week the bride is called for by a party of her kinsmen and is taken home, where she stays for some time, usually about a year. The next time her husband's family send for her may be for her to participate in the worship of the family goddess, at which ceremony she will eat one of the communion cakes shared only by members of the lineage. But within a month she will again be at her parents' home to stay for six months or so. Thus begins a cycle of visits back and forth between conjugal and natal homes that in most cases continues for many years.

There are some occasions when it is deemed essential for a woman to visit her natal home. She should be at home for the *Rākhī* and *Bhujariyā* festivals in the rainy season, and for any wedding, *gauna*, or other important rite performed for close natal kinsmen. A daughter should be at her parents' house when they are away on pilgrimage. Ideally, a daughter should be at home to celebrate the *Holī* festival and to witness the annual *Havan* [sacred fire] ceremony in honor of the village mother goddess, Matabai.[13] A daughter-in-law should also attend the *Havan* in her *susral* village and be there for important life-cycle celebrations involving her husband's kinsmen. It is mandatory for her to give birth to her first child in her husband's home and preferable that she give birth to all her children there.

---

[11] In her natal home she continues to be known by her personal name.
[12] For details of purdah observances in the Bhopal area, see Jacobson (1970, 1974).
[13] In this region some villages organize annual *Havan* ceremonies but most do not.

Beyond these minimal requirements, the length and frequency of a woman's visits to her natal and marital homes vary according to a number of interrelated factors: age, caste, the strength of bonds of affection between the woman and her various kinsmen, wealth, distance between natal and conjugal villages, size and composition of the household units, the work expected of a woman in the two households, the nature of the purdah she observes, and the health of the woman and her relatives.

Table 2. Visits to natal home by age

Age group	Extensive	Moderate	Slight	Number
15-24	82.6%	17.4%	0.0%	46
25-39	26.7	63.3	9.8	71
40-75	17.2	52.7	30.1	93
				210

Source: Based on data obtained in 1965-1967, pertaining to 210 Hindu women who are or have been married and who are wives and daughters of Nimkhera village. Of these women, 9 percent live permanently in their natal homes.
Key: Extensive: From permanent residence in natal home to two or three visits, a month or more each, annually (25 to 100 percent of time in natal home).
Moderate: From two or three visits, a day to a month each, annually, to a visit approximately every two years.
Slight: From a visit every three to five years to no visits.

Age and Caste. Generally, young women spend long months in their *maika*s, while middle-aged women may restrict themselves to visits of a week or a month once or twice annually[14] (see Table 2). There is a slight tendency within each age group for women of the higher-ranking castes to spend more time in their natal homes than do women of the lower castes.

Affection. Women often state that they prefer the warmth and freedom of their natal homes to the restrictions and onerous chores they must endure under the watchful eye of the mother-in-law in their conjugal homes. They say the love they have for their parents can never be equaled by any affection for husband or in-laws. Young women particularly welcome any excuse which might justify a long visit at home, since it is not considered appropriate for a woman to visit her parents merely because she desires to do so. A woman's affines must give permission for the visit, and her natal kinsmen must send an escort and pay her travel expenses. The frequency and duration of a woman's *maika*

---

[14] When a young woman refers to her "home" (*merā ghar*), she usually means her natal home; an older woman's "home" is more likely to be her conjugal residence. Because the reference is not always clear, a woman ordinarily clarifies her meaning by indicating whether she is speaking of her *susral* or *maika* home. There is no such ambiguity in a man's reference to his home.

visits are usually decided by a mutual give-and-take between her natal and conjugal relatives. Both parties feel they have rights in the woman, even though the husband's relatives usually have final say. One woman explained, "My son-in-law can't demand to take my daughter. It's not as if we have sold her to someone. She is ours to send." But some affines are resentful of a woman's ties to her natal kinsmen and even threaten to divorce the wife if she is not sent immediately upon demand. In such cases, persuasion and subterfuge sometimes win the woman a few extra days in her natal home or entice her back to her marital home. In-laws who refuse to allow a woman appropriate visits to her natal home arouse much antagonism and are the subjects of nasty gossip. Bhopal newspapers sometimes describe murders and violence resulting from *maika-susral* disputes over women.[15]

As the years pass, a woman gradually develops emotional attachments to the people in her conjugal home — especially her husband, children, and grandchildren — and she slowly weans herself away from her natal kin and friends, many of whom have died. Even so, many older women maintain at least moderate ties with their original homes, particularly if a brother or brother's children remain there. (As in other parts of India, a brother and sister ideally maintain a lifelong relationship of affection and concern for each other, and a brother should visit his sister and present gifts to her and her conjugal family on appropriate occasions.)

A woman desiring a divorce may use a trip to her parents' home to achieve it; she simply refuses to return to her husband and eventually goes away with another man. Similarly, a man may neglect to call for a wife he wishes to be rid of.

A woman who has contracted a second marriage unacceptable to her

---

[15] The most popular song in India in 1973-1974 was from the film "Bobby." In dialogue, a couple sing:

F: If you tell a lie, a crow will bite you;
    Be afraid of the black crow.
    I'll go to my *maika*, you just watch. . . .
M: If you go to your *maika*, I'll come with a stick.
F: If you come with a stick, I'll jump into a well. . . .
M: I'll pull you out with a rope.
F: I'll climb up a tree.
M: I'll saw it down.
F: You love me and you'd saw it down?
    Beware of such a lover!
    I'll go to my *maika*, you just watch. . . .
M: If you go to your *maika*, I'll get married again. . . .
F: If you get married again, oh! You'll bring a rival wife —
    I won't go to my *maika*, I won't go to my *maika*. . . .
    I'll sacrifice myself for you. I won't go to my *maika*.
    I'll observe the seven wedding vows forever.
M: . . . I'll bring a rival wife, you just watch. . . .
F: I won't go to my *maika*, you just watch.

kinsmen may not be welcome in her *maika* and consequently may never visit there.

Wealth and Distance. The wealth of a woman's natal kinsmen may affect the frequency and length of her visits with them. In addition to paying travel expenses, the natal kin must feed the woman and her children during their visit and should buy her gifts of clothing or even jewelry. Some parents cannot often afford these expenses. On the other hand, daughters of poor families may be welcome at home for long periods because they contribute to the household income or provide valuable help in agricultural operations. Relatives of a woman whose two villages are within easy walking distance have no travel expenses to consider, and such a woman may enjoy short but frequent visits with her parents.[16]

Household Composition. Women who live with their husbands in nuclear families tend to visit their parents less than women who live with their husbands in joint families. A woman in a nuclear family has no need to escape her mother-in-law or quarrelsome sisters-in-law and she may develop strong feelings of affection for her husband. Additionally, she is responsible for all women's work in her husband's household, unless her husband's sister should visit during her absence. A woman in a nuclear family soon gains a sense of proprietorship in her husband's home and property and may be reluctant to leave them improperly attended. Even so, many women living in nuclear families do stay away for several weeks at a time, and their husbands must cook and fetch water for themselves. When asked whether her husband objected to cooking for himself during her lengthy absences, one young nuclear-family wife in Nimkhera replied, "Shall I stay away from my *maika* just because of his food?" She made this remark in the presence of her husband, who made no retort.

A woman whose natal household lacks any other adult woman may spend much of her time there, particularly if she is needed to help care for children.

Work. Young women burdened with chores in their marital homes look forward to visits to their parental homes, where they say they can rest

---

[16]   The average distance between Nimkhera and the villages with which the Hindu villagers have marital ties is 20.9 miles (84 percent of such villages are within 40 miles). This is greater than the 11.37 miles reported by Mayer for the Dewas area of Madhya Pradesh (1960:210), but comparable to Lewis's figures for a village in the Delhi area ("average distances falling between 12 and 24 miles" [1965:161]). Luschinsky reports that 93 percent of brides married into Senapur in the Varanasi area have come from a distance of 28 miles or less (1962:322).

and relax. In fact, visiting daughters usually perform important household and agricultural work in their parental homes. Both *maika* and *susral* kin, when fetching a woman, commonly state that they need her for work — household work because of the illness or absence of another woman, cooking or fieldwork during sowing and harvest seasons, or cooking and performing other tasks at weddings, funerals, and other ceremonies. At times of peak demand for labor, especially at sowing and harvest, both sets of kinsmen vie for a woman's services. Married women thus comprise to some extent a shifting labor supply which moves to the place where the demand is greatest. If both kin groups seem to need a woman equally urgently, the claim of the *susral* usually takes precedence.

Purdah. Women who observe strict purdah in their husbands' homes tend to crave visits to their parental homes, where they can enjoy relative freedom of movement and behavior. Such women, usually young high-caste wives, use all their powers of persuasion and resistance to ensure long *maika* visits for themselves.

Health. When a woman falls ill in her conjugal home, a trip to her parents' home is usually recommended as likely to benefit her. A woman typically reports feeling much better after visiting her *maika*, and it is sometimes thought that the health of her children is improved by their visiting their mother's brother's house. Indulgent parents sometimes pay for medical care denied a woman by her husband's parents. Illness or confinement of a member of either household is considered a valid reason for calling a woman to assist until the crisis passes. In fact, a new baby's father's sister should be in her *maika* to take her prescribed role in the *Chauk*.

DISCUSSION

The lengthy and frequent visits of rural women of the Bhopal-Raisen region to their natal homes appear to serve a number of functions.

Long visits by a young wife to her parents' home help her to adjust to married life gradually and without severe difficulty. Periods of freedom from purdah and other *susral* tensions refresh a woman mentally and physically and allow her to return to life and labor in her husband's home with increased contentment and efficiency. Although a small percentage of young wives in the Bhopal region do suffer from emotional disturbances, few women consult shamans, and severe problems of adjustment to married life appear to be much less common here than in the Gangetic valley. The tensions of joint family living may also be reduced considerably by the periodic absences of quarreling coresident females.

A woman may use her trips home as a means of gaining concessions or bettering her material position. A woman sometimes refuses to return to her husband until he promises to treat her better, to live separately from his family, or to give her more jewelry. The woman's position in such a situation is strengthened by the fact that women are in short supply. Living without a wife is very difficult for a man, and finding a new wife is expensive and frequently impossible.

Some women secretly convey cash and other goods from their conjugal homes to their natal homes. These items may be given to the natal kin for their own use or may be converted into jewelry and clothing which a woman keeps for herself and displays as having been presented to her by her natal kin. Such "gifts" increase a woman's prestige in her *susral* and also improve her position in a very tangible way, since the only property over which a woman has absolute and unlimited rights of ownership and disposal is that given her by her natal kinsmen.

Some women live with their husbands permanently in their natal homes because they have no living brothers and were willed land by their fathers.

A woman's *maika* visits ensure that her feminine skills can be shared by at least two households in a region where women are relatively scarce. For any family, a kinswoman can provide important assistance at a time of crisis or at sowing and harvest time. Poor agriculturalists particularly benefit from extra pairs of hands at peak agricultural seasons, since the need to hire laborers is thus reduced.[17] Also, since a Hindu woman does not observe purdah in her natal home, she can be more productive there than in her husband's home. A daughter is able to work at a wide variety of tasks both inside and outside the home, including sowing, harvesting, and threshing, whereas many young wives, particularly those of high caste, are able to work only within the house and courtyard.

The Raisen area of central India is relatively sparsely populated, yet the fertile fields yield a surplus. Sowing and harvesting seasons occur at the same time in neighboring villages but differ between more distant villages, particularly if different crops are grown. In at least some instances, women move from harvesting in their *maika*s to harvesting in their *susral*s or vice versa. It is probable that a mobile labor force of

[17] I do not, of course, mean that a low female : male ratio is the reason or even a necessary condition for women to retain strong ties to their natal homes after marriage. My data are not adequate to permit such an interpretation, nor to explain why such ties are not found in all parts of India where women are scarce. I am suggesting, rather, that in the Bhopal region, given the low sex ratio, women's extensive *maika* visits serve economically important functions for many families, and that this probably tends to encourage such visits.

women who can be called upon to work where the demand is greatest is an advantage in exploiting the environment of this region, given the low density and relatively small average size of settlements in the area. Further, the opportunity to take part in the harvests in two different areas can provide valuable extra income for women of limited means.

Finally, women's visits back and forth help to mark the social boundaries between a woman's two affinally related kin groups and at the same time to stimulate important social interaction between members of these groups. The distinctiveness and opposition of affinally related Hindu kin groups are an important feature of social structure in this region.[18] A woman weeps as she leaves her *maika*, but she is joyous as she departs from her *susral*. Loud and quiet struggles occur between a woman's two households for her presence and services, and affines frequently speak ill of each other. In most castes, female members of a woman's two households never meet. The woman who travels back and forth behaves quite differently in each household — in one the apparently dutiful, faceless, and hearthbound daughter-in-law, and in the other the happy, open-faced, and sociable daughter. Many other features of etiquette and ethos point up the distinctions between the two households and kin groups and the individual woman's roles within them.

On the other hand, the escorting of women back and forth provides occasions for male affines to meet, thus helping to knit the caste together and widening intra- and extracaste contacts useful for a number of purposes. These visits allow men from distant villages to interact with their affines and the cliques of which their affines are members; such interaction can have important political consequences (as at caste *panchāyat* [council] meetings) and is often of major importance in marriage arrangements. Men who meet each other through such association may assist each other in financial matters, the obtaining of medical or legal aid, the purchase of land, the finding of employment, and other ways.

A woman's visits to her natal home are also vital in maintaining and enhancing the tie between her natal kinsmen and her own children. Proper maintenance of this bond helps to ensure her children of a wide group of kinsmen on whom they can call in time of need and to secure other advantages. For example, a Brahman woman dissatisfied with the rustic life in Nimkhera spends a significant amount of time in her *maika*. She plans to send her son to live with her brothers so he can attend high school and college in her natal town.

We see then that in the Bhopal region of central India the ostensible transfer of a woman to her husband's kin group at marriage is in fact

---

[18]   For a detailed discussion of the opposition between affinally related Hindu kin groups in the Bhopal region, see Jacobson 1970.

only a partial transfer, in which the husband's kin group is given rights in the woman which may take precedence over those of her natal kin but do not replace them. The relative rights of natal and conjugal kin in the woman are not clearly defined, and this ambiguity provides flexibility to the system. A few specific rules and practical considerations interact with several varying personal, social, and economic factors to affect the woman's travels so that some of her own needs and the needs of her two sets of kinsmen are at least partially met.

Women's visits, and the attendant movements of men, are also important in the diffusion of ideas and technology, both traditional and modern. Through the exchange of visits between them and their affines in other villages, residents of a village obtain information about rituals, notions of proper conduct, dress, house construction, agricultural technique, and a host of other features of life in those villages. This can lead to both the reaffirmation of traditional patterns and the spread of new culture traits within a region. For example, on a visit to his cousin's city *susral* to invite her to his home, a Nimkhera youth learned that it is acceptable for his cousin to speak to her husband in the presence of elders and even to appear before her father-in-law with her face unveiled. "If it were up to me, that's the way it would be in my home," he said wistfully. In the not-too-distant future it may well be up to him — and to his wife, who may bring with her from her natal home other standards of correct behavior. Thus, the travels of women and their escorting kinsmen are a vital element in the intracaste and intervillage communications network of the region.

REFERENCES

BICK, MARIO, MAY EBIHARA
    1972   "Residence reconsidered." Paper presented at the Annual Meeting of the American Anthropological Association, Toronto.
BUCHLER, IRA, H. A. SELBY
    1968   *Kinship and social organization: an introduction to theory and method.* New York: Macmillan.
DAVID, KENNETH
    1973   Until marriage do us part: a cultural account of Jaffna Tamil categories for kinsmen. *Man* 8 (4).
DUBE, S. C.
    1955   *Indian village.* London: Routledge and Kegan Paul.
FREED, STANLEY A., RUTH S. FREED
    1964   Spirit possession as illness in a north Indian village. *Ethnology* 3:152-171.
GOUGH, E. KATHLEEN
    1956   Brahman kinship in a Tamil village. *American Anthropologist* 58:826-853.

HARRIS, MARVIN
1971 *Culture, man, and nature.* New York: Thomas Y. Crowell.
JACOBSON, DORANNE
1970 "Hidden faces: Hindu and Muslim purdah in a central Indian village." Unpublished Ph.D. dissertation, Columbia University, New York.
1974 "Purdah and the Hindu family in central India." Paper presented at the Annual Meeting of the Association for Asian Studies, Boston.
LEWIS, OSCAR
1965 *Village life in northern India.* New York: Random House.
LUSCHINSKY, MILDRED STROOP
1962 "The life of women in a village of north India." Unpublished Ph.D. dissertation, Cornell University, Ithaca, New York.
MANDELBAUM, DAVID G.
1970 *Society in India,* two volumes. Berkeley: University of California Press.
MATHUR, K. S.
1964 *Caste and ritual in a Malwa village.* Bombay: Asia Publishing House.
MAYER, ADRIAN C.
1960 *Caste and kinship in central India.* London: Routledge and Kegan Paul.
NICHOLAS, RALPH W., RONALD INDEN
1972 "The defining features of kinship in Bengali culture." Paper read at the symposium on "New Approaches to Caste and Kinship," Annual Meeting of the American Anthropological Association, Toronto.
ORENSTEIN, HENRY
1965 *Gaon: conflict and tension in an Indian village.* Princeton: Princeton University Press.
1970 Death and kinship in Hinduism: structural and functional interpretations. *American Anthropologist* 72:1357-1377.
PANDYA, A. K.
1974 *Raisen District: district census handbook.* Census of India 1971, Madhya Pradesh: Government of Madhya Pradesh.
PATHAK, R. C., *editor*
1973 *Bhargava's standard illustrated dictionary of the Hindi language.* Varanasi: Bhargava Book Depot.
VATUK, SYLVIA
1973 "Gifts and affines in north India." Paper presented at the 29th International Congress of Orientalists, Paris.

PART TWO

The Moving and the Standing

Role Analysis and Social Change: With Special Reference to India

M. S. A. RAO

While role theory in its varied aspects has undergone significant refinements, its value in understanding social change has not been sufficiently stressed. This paper aims to illustrate, with reference to examples from India, the utility of role analysis in coping with problems of studying social change. Before I attempt to do this it will be necessary to review briefly two interrelated trends — structural and interactional — in the development of role theory with a view to pointing out their relevance to the analysis of social change.

ROLE AND SOCIAL STRUCTURE

Linton (1936) was one of the earliest to have clearly formulated the concepts of status and role. He defined status as a collection of rights and duties, and role as representing the dynamic aspect of status. Later (1945:50-52), he elaborated the concept of role by using it to designate the sum total of the cultural patterns associated with a particular social status, including not only the attitudes, values and behavior ascribed by the society to any and all persons occupying this status, but also the legitimate expectations of such persons with respect to the behavior toward them of persons in other statuses within the same system. Thus the interrelation between the actor and alter was already envisaged by Linton. However, his concern was with the relation between individuals, which he thought was a useful way of looking at social structure. He showed (1945:37) how individuals as members of society are

The author wishes to thank Professor A. C. Mayer for his valuable comments and Drs. B. S. Baviskar and A. Chakravarti for some useful suggestions on an earlier draft of this paper. His thanks are also due to Dr. Glynn Cochrane for useful clarifications.

assigned their roles in the corporate existence of the society, thus relating status and role of individuals to social structure.

Following Linton's formulation, Parsons made a significant contribution to the refinement of the role concept. He conceived role as actualization of status (1951). In his scheme of analysis, role and status are related to values and norms of society (culture) on the one hand, and to internalization of these norms by the individual (personality) on the other. He further related the paired concepts of role and status to his scheme of institutions, modes of orientation of actors (pattern variables), and functional imperatives of the social system. The basis of his analysis, however, was the theory of social action, and against this theoretical setting, role analysis gained clarity of meaning and purpose (Parsons and Shils 1951: 23-27, 208-230). Parsons perceived the operation of feedback mechanism in role interaction and outlined the conditions for meaningful *role playing*. Although Parsons combined the structural analysis with the interactional,[1] the emphasis was on the former, relating role to the normative and social systems.

Marion J. Levy, Jr. (1952), following Parsons, pursued the structural analysis of role further and pointed out that the concrete social structure requires a differentiation and assignment of the roles of its members. He systematically analyzed the structure of role differentiation in terms of structures of distribution of the members of the system among the various positions and activities distinguished in the system. He considered role differentiation as a structural requisite of any society and of role assignments. Thus, Levy's concern was also with structural analysis of role, at a formal level, conceiving role as a mere *allocation* made by society.

Another significant attempt to see role in relation to social structure (system) was made by Nadel (1957). He built up his concept of social structure on the basis of roles played by actors relative to one another. He also conceived of roles as allocated by society which individuals filled, and distinguished between recruitment and achievement roles. While the individual has no choice in the assumption of the former, in the latter there is an element of selection. However, conformity to the norms or role expectations was an essential feature of role for Nadel. In fact, he made it the necessary condition of role playing, where feedback mechanisms could effectively operate.

Another aspect of Nadel's role analysis was the interconnection of roles forming a network or social structure. Here Nadel concluded that the social structure cannot be spoken of in the singular as there are

[1] Parsons' analysis of status role stimulated the interest of several sociologists on the interactional aspect. For instance, Bales (1950, 1953: Chapters 4, 5) in his analysis of small group research made extensive use of role theory in explaining the problem of equilibrium and the process of differentiation.

logical cleavages, factual dissociations and enclaves in the emergence of a single network of roles. The three mechanisms — mutual inclusiveness of roles in a single person, specialized actor-public relationships, and dichotomization — only contribute to minimizing the three limitations respectively; but these cannot be completely eliminated at the empirical level. Hence, in order to arrive at the positional picture of society, or social structure, Nadel maintained, it was necessary to empty the roles and relations of their qualitative content and indulge in abstraction. He suggested two command criteria (command over action of persons and command over resources and benefits of society) to derive the positional picture, and rightly insisted that it was in the process of *arriving* at the positional picture that invaluable insights into the working of the society would be gained.

While Nadel advanced our understanding of the internal structure of roles and their interrelations, he tended to conceive of role as an allocation made by the society as a whole. He failed to perceive the multiplicity of norms characteristic of complex societies. Further, he sought to work out a unitary system of roles and came to a negative conclusion. This exercise of Nadel has demonstrated that role as an analytical concept can be advantageously made use of in perceiving linkages of roles and relations within a particular range; but stretched beyond this point to arrive at a *coherent network* (social structure), it is not feasible.

ROLE AND INTERACTION PROCESS

Major and more promising developments in role analysis have taken place in the investigation of interaction processes rather than in relating role to overall social structure. First, there is a shift in the emphasis from considering role as a set of expectations ascribed or allocated by society to a consideration of it as a set of expectations applied to a situated activity. Secondly, while structural analysis emphasizes the role-playing (conformity) aspect, the interactional approach stresses the role-taking dimension. These developments have enabled handling of two situations which the structural focus overlooked, viz., the dichotomy between role behavior and role expectation, and the analysis of moment-to-moment behavior in the interaction process.

To take the second first, Goffman's analysis (1961) emphasizes role as the typical response of individuals in particular positions. He points out that when one studies a role one usually limits the interest to the situation of a person in a place and time, i.e. in a situated activity system. He argues that the individual does not embrace the situated role by holding all his other selves in abeyance but he constantly twists and turns, even allowing himself to be carried along by the controlling definition of the situation. The typical aspect of role for Goffman is *role distance*, which refers to actions that effectively convey some disdainful detachment of the performer from the role he is performing in a situated system. The process of maintaining his role position is one of skewed communication; overcommunicating that which confirms the relevant status position and undercommunicating that which is discrepant. Such behavior Goffman calls *impression management* (1959). The advantages of Goffman's analysis lie first in seeing role behavior as not being specified in the rights and obligations comprising the status, and in viewing different areas of social life as interpenetrating one another in a defined activity situation.

A major focus in role analysis relates to the approach of the symbolic interaction theory. This approach tends to select behaviors, influences, structures, and variables from everyday life. It emphasizes the element of continual flux of human behavior and social life, i.e. the processual aspect. A basic assumption here is that man lives in a symbolic environment and he is selecting and interpreting the environment toward which he guides or directs his behavior in a given social setting. The term *role* is used to refer to a cluster of such related meanings and values that guide and direct individuals' behavior.

Turner (1962, also 1969) developed the notion of *role taking* on the basis of Meadian role theory. While Linton conceived of role as a cultural given, Mead (1934) treated role chiefly as the perspective or vantage point of the relevant "other." Following Mead, Turner emphasized the role-taking aspects in the interaction process. Role taking consists of the process of discovering and creating consistent wholes out of behavior. There is an internal validation criterion in role taking which insures a constant modification, creation, or rejection of the content of specific roles. Role taking is also affected by external validation. It is based upon others' judgment which has some claim to correctness and legitimacy. Turner's conception of role taking further emphasizes the interactive aspect of role relations rather than merely conformity to perceived expectations in role playing.

Neal Gross and his colleagues (1958) similarly treated role as a set of evaluative standards applied to an incumbent of a particular position by some role definer or definers. The emphasis of the dynamic aspect of role analysis in the context of interaction process has been to isolate a *sector* or social situation from daily life and to see role not as something ascribed or allotted to individuals by society to which they then must conform, but as role taking and as an arena of impression management. These aspects of *role behavior* do not always form part of prescriptions, expectations, rights, and obligations of roles.

Individual variation in both role playing and taking is evident in the context/of role relationships. Southall (1959) made an important distinction between role and *role relationship*. For instance, a person may be a teacher (role) and, being one, enter into a relationship with each one of his several students. His role behavior in all the role relationships is not necessarily uniform, as he might have some pet students. Thus there is scope for manipulation of "obligations" of roles. Still another kind of differentiation in the concepts of role and status was suggested by Goodenough (1965), who stressed the need to include the cultural context of roles, on the lines of vocabularies and the syntax.

Closely connected with the concepts of role sector and role relationship is the notion of *role set* as developed by Merton (1957). While multiple roles refer to several roles played by an individual, role set applies to several interacting situations in the performance of a single role. Thus a doctor's role set consists of his relations with the hospital administration, with the nurses, and with patients. Each interacting relationship is a *role sector*, which in turn includes several *role others* and hence several role relationships. For example, doctor-nurses is a role sector which includes several role others, i.e. nurses. Insofar as a doctor interacts with several nurses separately, there are different role relationships in a role sector.

It may be noted in this connection that Bates (1956) has emphasized the normative component of a role which for him is part of social position consisting of more or less integrated or related subsets of social norms. A norm being a patterned or commonly held behavior expectation or a learned response, held in common by members of a group, Bates shows that there is a strain toward consistency among the norms forming a single role. The question of strain is very important in role performance and role taking, for it is the basis of conflict, the resolution of which involves change. *Role strain* and *role conflict* as key notions in understanding social change have been pointed out by Etzioni (1961, 1968) and Goode (1960a, 1960b). The latter rightly maintains that dissensions and role strain, the difficulty in fulfilling role demands, should be considered normal.

SOCIAL CHANGE: STRUCTURAL AND ORGANIZATIONAL

We may now see role analysis in relation to social change. Two levels of analysis of social change have been current in sociological theory, structural and organizational. Firth (1951, 1959), who distinguished between the two, meant by the former a change in the forms of social realignment. For example, a change in the authority pattern in a household from mother's brother to father of children means an alteration in the character of the social system, or more specifically in the principles on which a society operates and the framework upon which its social relations are constructed. This kind of social change is different from another aspect of social change where the position of individuals or groups in the social system has altered but the character of the system as such is not affected. Processes of "social replacement" and "social multiplication" belong to the realm of organizational changes.

Firth further recognized the intimate relationship between social structure and social organization, and between structural and organizational changes. He argued that social organization is the working out of the social structure and organizational changes lead to structural changes as in the case of Tikopia. In his study of rank and religion in Tikopia (1970), Firth has richly documented the changes in the roles that have occurred as a result of structural changes in the religion of Tikopia, i.e. the conversion of the pagan Tikopia to Christianity. For instance, the chiefs and elders are divested of their traditional priestly roles. This illustrates the way in which structural changes are reflected in organizational changes.

Firth (1954) had earlier pointed out that social organization was concerned with roles, involving more spontaneous activities. While Radcliffe-Brown (1952) rightly associated roles with organization, he tended to consider roles as forming a system where a person does only what is assigned for him to do by his social position within an organization. Firth, however, laid stress on the analysis of social organization in understanding social change, i.e. a closer study of roles, the setting, and results of individual choices and decisions as they affect activity and social relations.

Barth (1966) developed the analysis of social organization for a more fruitful investigation of the process of social change. He formulated models of social organization on the basis of the analysis of process, to explain how the observable frequency patterns or regularities are generated. The argument is that an aggregate of people exercise choice while being influenced by certain constraints and incentives, canalize choice and determine the probable interdependence governing the course of events and the formation of patterns. Thus a model of social organization describes and discovers the processes that generate the form; it provides the means to describe and study change in social forms as changes in the basic variables that generate the forms, facilitating comparative analysis.

The concept of status role, no doubt, equips one to analyze the fundamental social process whereby binding rights and obligations are made relevant in particular social situations. Barth's emphasis on institutionalization led him to construct a model whereby complex and comprehensive patterns of behavior (roles) may be generated from a simpler specification of right (statuses), according to the set of rules (to

Goffman, the requirements of impression management). Barth formulated the notion of transaction as an analytical isolate in the field of social organization in order to understand institutionalization. It is in transaction that the systems of evaluation are revealed as maintained. It should be noted that transaction is only one of the interactional situations which is helpful in understanding the process of social change through role analysis.

A concept which defines, or is amenable for defining, social situations in relatively unstructured terms is social network in the conceptual realm of social organization. Complex societies abound in social situations which are dynamic and less structured. Clyde Mitchell (1969) has recently summarized the development and use of the concept of social networks.[2] It is sufficient for our purpose to discuss here the use of social network in relation to role. As Mitchell (1969:46) points out, the concept of role becomes relevant at the level of abstraction involving partial network. It should, however, be noted that the concept of network also enables the analysis of dynamic interaction of role relationships rather than mere abstraction of isolated dyadic relations.

Mitchell (1966) earlier pointed out the significance of using network in relation to role. In a network, which is a relatively unstructured situation, the actor is able to draw on several definitions of what his role ought to be. In an African town, one may interact with a person as a fellow tribesman, as a person of equal status, as a kinsman in the flexible kinship system in the town, or as a personal friend. Choice in such a situational context provides the locus of change, as there is scope for manipulation, turning, and skewing by the individuals.

The distinct advantage of network analysis in terms of roles, as I see it, consists of tracing the presence or absence of feedback between and among different interaction isolates, which involve roles, rather than merely preparing a chart of chained contacts, which is morphological. For example, when a person, as a subordinate, is interacting with his boss, his wife's relation with his boss or boss's wife may affect the interaction situation. The feedback of such extrainteractional relation-

---

[2] The concept of network was formulated by Barnes (1954) in an attempt to distinguish different kinds of social fields. He maintained that each individual tends to have a different audience for each of the roles he plays. While Barnes emphasized the open-ended character of network, Bott (1957) distinguished between close-knit networks and analyzed conjugal role behavior in terms of these. Srinivas and Béteille (1964) distinguished between the *"subjective"* network of the actor and the *"objective"* network of the observer. However, the essential feature of personal network is that it does not constitute a group, but consists of several categories of relations such as caste, religious, ethnic, linguistic, territorial and kinship ties. P. Mayer (1961) and A. Epstein (1961) have also used the notion of personal networks although in varying ways. A. C. Mayer (1966) has attempted to characterize a less structured social situation in terms of action set. In complex societies it is difficult to identify areas of social relations in terms of groups. Hence network and action sets form effective situational contexts for role analysis.

ships has to be distinguished from what Nadel called dichotomization. The third party of Nadel is the general social norm and not specific interactional situations. These interconnections (or lack of them) are best worked out in the context of personal network situations. A certain element of flexibility is provided by relatively unstructured situations where an individual is free to assume the kind of role that he wants to play and also the manner in which he wants to execute it.

ROLE ANALYSIS AND ECONOMIC CHANGE AND DEVELOPMENT IN INDIA

Against the foregoing account of the trends of development in role analysis, I shall attempt to demonstrate the application of role analysis in studying economic change and development in India.[3]

Economic change or development implies differentiation of occupations and specialization of minute, task-oriented roles. The process of differentiation and innovation is, however, a continuous one found in both economically developed and developing countries, although the level, scale and nature of the processes are different. Thus, if spaceman or moonwalker emerges as a role in the United States, netboss may be a new role among the fisher folk of Norway. Emergence or assumption of new occupational roles is not a mechanical process. It involves changes in the value system and crystallization of new modes of behavior backed by acceptance of new norms. It also involves changes in the activities and role relationships.

In Yadavpur, a village on the metropolitan fringe of Delhi, the Ahirs, who were peasants cultivating food crops for their own consumption, have assumed a new role of market gardeners (Rao 1970). It meant for them learning new skills and undertaking new tasks, and entering into relationships with wholesale auctioneers in the city vegetable market and the contractors who buy standing crops in the village. The process also involved changes in the value system because Ahirs previously considered vegetable gardening to be degrading. It was only when a sufficient number of Ahir peasants became aware of the economic benefits of growing vegetables that market gardening became an established practice and crystallized into a role with appropriate norms and relationships.[4]

---

[3]   Application of role analysis in the study of social change may be illustrated with reference to different areas of social life such as kinship, family and marriage, religion, politics, and formal organizations and management. Here I have concentrated only on economic change and development. By economic change I mean a change in the structure of economic relationships and organization of economic activities. Economic development also implies change especially on the level of organization and scale.
[4]   Changes in the values underlying the role have been stressed by Banton (1965:57-64).

It is, however, important to recognize the prevalence of different levels of organizing new activities and acceptance of new norms of market mechanisms. For instance, while Ahirs accepted the new role of market gardening, they did not take to it on an extensive scale as did some of the Jat farmers in a few villages of south Delhi, who grow vegetables on large plots and transport them in trucks to the urban market. Many of the large estate holders in Yadavpur sell the standing vegetable crops to local contractors. Thus the level at which they have sought to reorganize their material and human resources has given the Chamars (leather workers), who were formerly agricultural laborers, an opportunity to become contract gardeners. They purchase standing vegetable crops from the landowners, and this has meant that those who were hitherto agricultural laborers have assumed a new role, and this has altered their traditional relationship with the Ahir peasants.

One of the implications of the assumptions of new occupational roles where the same sets of individuals are involved, is the change in the quality and meaning of relationships between them. The rights and obligations governing the two interaction situations are different. Chamars, as buyers of the standing crop, are equal partners in the transaction with Ahirs as sellers, whereas as laborers they were subservient to the Ahir peasants.

The distinction between the two social situations of interaction is no doubt easily identified where the two occupational roles are different, e.g. agricultural laborer and contract gardener. But it is not often recognized when the occupation remains the same but the social setting varies. For example a barber in an Indian village may serve others either in the context of institutionalized service relations [*jajmāni*], or in a barber shop opened by him. The nature of the services performed by him in the two situations is similar; however, if he works in the setting of the *jajmāni* system he is required not to serve the untouchable castes, whereas if he opens a barber shop and thus opts out of the *jajmāni* system, he is free to serve anyone who requires his services under free market conditions. In the context of economic development, a difference in what may be called *role setting* makes all the change in one and the same occupational role.

He remarks that just as goods are profaned when their value is determined by the market in accordance with the law of supply and demand, roles are profaned when their importance is decided by the current demands of the social organization without regard to the pattern of expectations that individuals have learned and invested with moral significance. Barth (1966) has shown the process of the emergence of role as netboss among the fisher folk of Norway. With increased capital investments, echo and asdic equipment, the role of the netboss emerged as a kind of logical opposite to the skipper. He also shows how simple contracts about a few basic rights come first and role stereotypes emerge afterwards. Belshaw (1965:71-73) has also described the differentiation of roles and establishment of new relationships following the introduction of marketing in peasant societies.

It should be noted here that even within the traditional rural service relationships, there were variations in the setting of a single service role, and a lack of appreciation of these variations in roles and their settings has led to a misunderstanding of the nature of the *jajmāni* system and the trends of change in it. For instance, a Chamar repairs or prepares leather buckets used in drawing water from irrigation wells. Here a part of his occupational activities forms part of the *jajmāni* system. He may also be a cobbler or a casual agricultural laborer or a cowherd outside the *jajmāni* system. Apart from these occupational activities, there are certain customary services which a Chamar is expected to render. He removes the carcasses of dead cattle. He beats the tom-tom on the occasion of the birth of a child in his patron's house. Hence there is distinction between the occupational, ritual or ceremonial, and customary services, which is not often recognized.

Beidelman (1959), for instance, takes the whole caste as the unit of *jajmāni* system and includes all these activities in it. Pocock (1962) promoted our understanding of the nature of *jajmāni* relationships by distinguishing three categories: (1) specialists providing religious service; (2) specialists who provide a commodity (artisans); and (3) unskilled laborers. Even in this scheme the unit of relationship is a person belonging to a particular caste. I suggest that we should treat role and its setting as the unit of relationship between individuals. This helps identify different settings in which the same person is involved, such as institutionalized exchange relations, occupational activity involving piecework, ceremonial service relations, and customary service relations. It also serves to identify different processes of change. Thus, while under the influence of Arya Samaj, Chamars in many parts of northern India have abandoned the customary service of removing the carcasses of dead cattle, they continue to remain in the *jajmāni* system only in regard to a part of their occupational activity, viz., preparing or repairing leather buckets for irrigation purposes. Similarly, in the case of barbers, while they have opted out of the *jajmāni* system by opening barber shops, they continue to render the customary service of acting as messengers at weddings or other ceremonial occasions. Again, potters may not supply pots and pans as part of *jajmāni* relations, but they continue to render the ceremonial service of supplying decorated pots needed for the wedding ceremony, for which they receive customary payment in kind. Thus differentiation of roles and their role settings is essential in understanding the processes of both continuity and change.

Lynch (1969:32–65) analyzes the emergence of new occupational roles of Jatavs in the city of Agra. Jatavs (a caste of Chamars) in the 1880's followed several occupations such as stonecutting, scavenging, leather tanning, and shoemaking. After World Wars I and II a modern shoe industry began to grow. There was not only a national market for Agra shoes but also an international one. Most Jatavs moved into the shoe industry, some as owners of factories and many as craftsmen.

Two kinds of shift in occupations occurred. For those who were not connected with shoemaking earlier and now took up shoemaking, it meant new roles; for those who continued in shoemaking, it meant learning of new skills — making modern-style shoes instead of country-style shoes. Both groups picked up the new skills by working as apprentices, and worked in the framework of factory methods of production for daily wages.

Further there was specialization of tasks such as cutter, fitter, soler, heeler, completer, and finisher. Each worker, as a wage earner, performed one task, unlike the traditional shoemaker, who, as a self-employed man, worked a pair of shoes from start to finish. The modern factory worker, also unlike the traditional shoemaker, is far removed from the customers. Thus the emergence of new roles will have to be seen in the situational context of different degrees of organization of the factory mode of production and market economy, where there are new interactional situations and also a different set of norms governing role relationships.

In considering the changes that have occurred in an occupational role of an artisan, a further distinction has to be noted in respect to changes in both the nature of commodities manufactured and marketing skills. For instance, a village potter (in Yadavpur) manufactures water jugs and sells them in the city by hawking. He carries the load on a donkey. This is no doubt a departure from the traditional activities of supplying, on demand, pots and pans to the villagers, for payment in kind. An even more skilled and enterprising Yadavpur potter has moved to Delhi, where he manufactures flower pots of modern designs and sells them to foreign embassies, making huge profits. Here there is not only a change in the products that are manufactured but also a change in the skills of marketing, showing entrepreneurial ability. A differentiation of these levels in the pursuit of the same occupational role is of great significance in understanding the process of economic development in general and occupational mobility in particular.

Occupational mobility is generally seen in relation to intergenerational and intragenerational variations. Often, in the context of availability of new employment opportunities, villagers do not totally discard their traditional occupations. This results in a situation where an individual follows more occupations than one, i.e. he combines in himself diverse occupational roles. Let me cite an example: a barber (by caste) in Yadavpur is employed as an office boy in a factory in Delhi. He follows his traditional occupation on weekends in the village. During his off-hours in the week, he undertakes the repairing of sofas in the city. Many Ahir commuters are weekend cultivators and in the urban context they follow the practice of taking part-time jobs. The part-time job may be the same as the main job or a different one. If it is different, it means that the individual is equipped with several skills, which he exploits to economic advantage. In such circumstances, the question of the compatability of the several occupational roles which he plays simultaneously during his workaday life becomes relevant. If the norm of dignity of labor operates effectively, the individual is able to follow both manual and nonmanual jobs. However, in the absence of such a favorable norm, and where jobs are sharply distinguished on the basis of prestige, it leads to role conflict which may be resolved by eliminating the job which is considered incompatible. This is, however, only one way of resolving conflict where one adjusts himself to prevailing social norms instead of attempting to change the norms.

In analyzing changes in an occupational role, the notion of role set is highly significant. With the growth of economic differentiation and organizational complexities, the role set in professional roles has become complicated and more role sectors have been added. For instance, with the growth of trade union activities among the teachers, a new role sector[5] has emerged, viz., teacher and teachers' union. At any rate, it is clear that a person entering the profession of teacher does not acquire different dimensions (role sectors) all at once.[6]

There is a sequence in the unfolding of roles. M. Karlekar (1970) has analyzed the process of career orientation and commitment of women school teachers in terms of sequential development of different role sectors and their interconnections. It is seen that a woman entering the teaching profession concentrates first on the sectors of teacher/student and colleagues. After gaining some experience, she is drawn into authority roles or may develop interest in professional associations.

It is necessary to emphasize that there is an interaction or a feedback between role sectors. Karlekar (1970) shows the interconnection between several role sectors. In a Delhi women's higher secondary school, a closer association of a teacher with the administration affects her relations with her colleagues adversely, for she is dubbed as a person of the establishment.

The distinction between several role sectors of a role set has an important consequence of questioning the assumption of *consensus* on role. In defining roles, some may include only a few sectors and others

[5]   Goffman (1961) has rightly indicated that social changes in a role can be traced by the loss or gain of the role set or types of role other.

[6]   Neal Gross et al. in their studies of the school superintendency role found that some expectations may be learned prior to and others during position of incumbency. The concept of role sector allowed them to investigate the set of expectations as applied to the relationships of a focal position to a single counterposition (1958:62).

may emphasize all of them. B. V. Shah (1967), in his analysis of the role of the secondary teacher in terms of different role sectors, has stressed the relativity of norms in role definitions. The expectations of parents were different from those of the educationists. A discrepancy may also exist between the specific and general value systems behind the definition of the same role. Incongruence between the goals as postulated by the norm-setters in the wider society and the perceptions of goals by the practitioners at the grass roots was pointed out in the context of analyzing the status and role of worker-leader in a trade union by N. R. Sheth and S. P. Jain (1968).

Role perception is an important criterion in the definition and performance of roles. T. N. Madan (1971) illustrates this point with reference to doctors' roles in an urban context. Doctors have adopted the Western cognitive model and this defines elaboration of their role and its performance in relation to the patients. There is a differentiation in role performance of the doctors working in a hospital and private practitioners. However, in both cases, the doctor-patient relationship remains an encounter, which is typical of urbanism. Madan's study also shows that different sets of norms are associated with different role sectors. Thus while doctor-patient role sector is based on a sense of duty, doctor-doctor role sector is based on professional jealousies. Since one doctor looks upon another as a competitor, he depends more on the medical representative for learning the latest developments in medicine.

Autonomy of the different role sectors in a role set permits the existence of logically divergent norms between different sectors. N. R. Sheth (1968) shows that in a factory, while the roles of the workers in their work situation were clearly defined in terms of their skills and experience, their role sector involving their relations with the employer was not governed by impersonal norms. The workers looked upon the employer as a patron. They thus participated in interactions of dual norms and values without envisaging the conflict which is logically perceived by some sociologists.

In the context of modern management functions a leader tends to occupy authority roles in several economic organizations and committees, and there exists a complementary linkage between them. This situation of complementary linkages between roles is pointed out by Baviskar (1970) in his study of a cooperative sugar factory in Maharashtra. Baviskar tells how there are two factions competing for positions of power in the management of the factory, and in this attempt the leaders of the factions also seek to be elected to the office of chairman of the district cooperative bank and the membership of other relevant organizations. These different authority roles mutually supplement one another, and help the leaders of respective factions to build up a following. Further, if the chairman of the factory is also the chairman of the district cooperative bank, it will help him overcome an economic crisis in the factory. These two committee roles will be further reinforced by his leadership role in the Congress Party.

It is necessary to note that only the persons who belong to one's faction consider such different roles as complementary whereas those belonging to the opposing faction consider them conflicting. The latter criticize the chairman of the district cooperative bank for being partial to the members of his faction in the factory in sanctioning loans. However, when the leader of the opposing faction gains control of the management of the factory, his mode of operation will be exactly the same. Then it would be the chance of the leaders of the losing faction to point out the incompatibility in the norms governing the behavior of the chairman in the two different roles. The norms involved in role playing and role taking are relative to group membership.

Relativity of norms to specific situated activity systems throws further light on the nature of linkages of different areas of social life. It is argued that economic change and development in underdeveloped countries, involving differentiation of role and acceptance of a new value system, will necessarily affect other areas of social life such as family organization and religious activities. In terms of roles it means that changes in the occupational role of an individual will necessarily bring about changes in the interpersonal relations in the family and in the religious activities of the person. However, it is facile to assume such necessary linkages between roles covering different areas of social life; it can only be a matter for investigation.

In Yadavpur (Rao 1972:104-117) while Ahir peasants changed their occupational roles by becoming farmers and by exploiting urban employment, they continue to adhere to norms of joint family organization in their kinship roles. From the point of view of role analysis, it means that an individual validates his behavior pertaining to occupational roles in terms of modern norms, whereas he continues to enact his kinship roles according to the traditional constraints with some modifications. Thus the continuance of performance of kinship roles in the context of traditional constraints coexists with the change in the occupational role with its new norms.

Another illustration of such a dichotomization of role norms in different areas of social life comes from T. S. Epstein's study (1962:235-238) of the role of women in Dalena, a village in Mysore, where there has been an appreciable degree of economic differentiation. While men have taken to diversified occupational roles, women have remained tradition-bound. There has been no change in their domestic or economic roles, and they have remained submissive. This means that while occupational roles of men have undergone changes, the norms of the domestic wife continue to derive their legitimacy from the traditional values.

The linkage between different role areas need not necessarily be one of harmonious coexistence. In fact, conflicts do arise. In his analysis of role conflict among nurses, Rajagopalan (1963) points out the basic conflict between the occupational role of nurses and the desire on their part to get married. There is a social stigma attached to their jobs which comes in the way of their marriage. The cultural norms of society have not changed to combine the role of a nurse with that of a wife or mother. Hence the conflict continues to be dominant.

The point is that the different areas of social life do not necessarily constitute a functionally integrated whole. There is discreteness, and a plurality of value systems coexist in a situation of rapid social change. It is possible for an individual to enact his occupational roles in accordance with the changed set of constraints and perform or take his role in another area of social life within the traditional constraints. Thus if the notion of role sector is helpful in analyzing the differentiation within a role set, I suggest that the idea of *role area* guides our understanding of linkages or dichotomization of role norms between several areas of social life such as economics, the kinship system, politics and religion.

Distinction of role areas also helps in investigating the feedback processes of change without always treating changes in the economic area as the loci of changes in the other areas of social life. For instance, the Chamars in many parts of northern India have come under the influence of Arya Samaj, a reformatory religious movement, and this has adversely affected their occupational role of tanning.[7] Similarly, many

---

[7]   Specific investigations of linkages of roles in different areas of social life have yielded valuable insights into the processes of social change. Neil J. Smelser's study (1959, also 1963) of changes in the Lancashire cotton industry is a case in point. He has worked out, with some measure of success, role differentiation as a theory of social change, by demonstrating how a social role or organization which has become archaic differentiates into two or more roles or organizations which function more effectively under changed circumstances. The changes in the family and community life of the British working classes in the early 19th century are seen, among other things, in the context of re-organization of economic roles. Smelser considers in detail the differentiation of two sub-sectors of the family economy — the division of labor and family consumption — and finds that the worker and his family could no longer work on the old basis, which fused the family economy with other functions such as rearing of children. The changed conditions of urbanization and industrialization pressed for a reorganization of roles and family relationships. Similarly, the changes in the family consumption were reflected in the emergence of savings banks, cooperative stores, and other measures of economic welfare.

Although Smelser tried to analyze structural differentiation in terms of roles, this has not been as successful as he wanted it to be, because of the paucity of data on the inter-personal and interactional behavior of persons. Role analysis is fruitful and also more meaningful in the context of microstudies rather than macrostudies tracing the trends of differentiation and change in social history.

Izhavas, a caste of toddy tappers in Kerala, gave up their occupation under the influence of Sri Narayana Suru Swamy movement (Rao 1957:49).

ROLE TYPE AND SOCIAL CHANGE

We have considered thus far the utility of role analysis in understanding the processes of economic change and development in terms of formation of new occupational roles (role innovation); differentiation in scale; nature of organization in the social setting; emergence of new role sectors within a role set; linkage or dichotomy of role sectors and role areas. In the end we may consider the notion of role type or pattern that has been used in characterizing social change in general.

Southall (1959) observed that the passage from rural to urban conditions is marked by a rise in the density of role texture, i.e., role relationships are more narrowly defined and hence there are more roles. Frankenberg (1966:242, 290) adapts Goffman's distinction between role embracement and role commitment to characterize rural-urban distinctions. While people in a rural community tend to accept their role pertaining to an ascribed status enthusiastically, people in an urban community may be merely attached to roles. They may show this by discordant displays of role distance. Frankenberg also associates "locals" and "cosmopolitans" (cf. Merton 1963:398-406) with rural and urban communities respectively. Thus changes from rural to urban are sought in terms of movement of people from one type of role structure to another.

It is, however, necessary to point out that an analysis of the processes underlying the changing role patterns would yield better insights rather than the positional pictures such as "local" and "cosmopolitan." For this purpose the importance of studying the situational contexts of role playing or role taking needs to be emphasized. For example, in the present urban context in India there has been a loosening of multiplex ties which characterized role relationships in the framework of traditional institutions of caste, kinship, religion, and local community. The point of contrast should be traditional urbanism before the introduction of modern urbanism during British rule, rather than the rural context. India has had a well-developed urban culture which differed from the traditional rural style of life. Participation of people in the new structural and organizational framework with a different set of values (under British rule) led to different levels of role reorganization. Let me illustrate the point with reference to my fieldwork in a caste ward in Delhi.

Before the turn of the present century, Ahirs, the resident caste of the ward, were employed as transport contractors to Mogul emperors and later to the British. Each contractor had a fleet of bullock carts under his control, and he executed government contracts for transporting men and material from one place to another. Thus, first, the urban Ahirs differed in their occupational roles from their counterparts in villages, who were mostly peasant cultivators. Second, there was a differentiation between the roles of contractors (leaders) and members of the team. The personal network of the contractor included relationships with members of different religious and caste groups and with officers in the administration. Comparatively, contractors were cosmopolitans and member carters were locals in terms of their respective personal networks.

Today the situational context has undergone a drastic change which has altered the nature of personal networks and the cultural contents of role patterns. The Ahirs lost their trade as transport men with the growth of modern means of transport and communication. Some Ahirs who received an English education have secured good jobs in the Delhi administration. One such officer has moved out of the ward into the accommodation provided by the government. He is a member of a fashionable club and moves in a highly diversified social circle consisting of persons from different occupations, religions, and nations. His role pattern approximates the image of a modern cosmopolitan, the situational context here being different from the one in traditional urbanism. Further, the officer has not ceased to be a local in the sense that he has no role *vis-à-vis* his castemen and the local community. He participates in the community activities of the ward; he is one of the leaders of the Delhi Yadav Sevak Samaj, a voluntary association for the welfare of Ahirs (Yadavs) in Delhi; and he is the vice-president of the All-India Backward Classes Federation, an association of the Backward Classes including the Yadavs.

It is necessary to note that the nature of caste itself has changed in the urban context. While formerly Ahirs had a well-organized caste council in the ward, they have now an association to organize community activities. The sanctions of the traditional caste council have ceased to be effective. The associational activities[8] of a voluntary nature are gaining precedence, and caste as a category, rather than as a group, is emerging as a more meaningful area of personal network. These changes in the situational context are important in understanding the processes of shifts in the role patterns from "local" to "cosmopolitan." Not only the network of relationships varies from one situa-

[8] Gutkind (1965) made a useful distinction between kin-based network and association-based network. While the former is designed to meet the demands of reciprocal roles, the latter is designed to meet flexibly new situations to which role responses are yet uncertain.

tional context to another but also the norms underlying either role playing or role taking.

The types of role structure such as local and cosmopolitan only have a heuristic value, and they can be seen in operation in different situational contexts within the urban milieu, not necessarily between rural and urban as Frankenberg (1966) thinks. The value of role analysis lies essentially in working out the processes of change. The positional pictures by themselves tend to be tautological. It is only by analyzing the processes in defined situational contexts that we gain insights into their meaning and achieve a deeper understanding of the mechanisms that direct change.

CONCLUSION

Role analysis has its main focus on the activities with which social organization is concerned. The activities include alternatives, choices (decisions), incentives, and constraints. Social activities in a defined social situation consist of a network of interaction isolates involving roles. Role analysis provides a technique of analyzing social processes which are dynamic. As Southall (1959) has rightly pointed out, role analysis is operational. I would add that it is also explanatory insofar as it helps explain why activities tend to follow the direction they do, thereby identifying patterns of change.

First, it shows that choices of a particular kind help crystallization of new roles and relationships with appropriate norms and provide an insight into the mechanisms which direct choices in one direction rather than in another.

Second, it helps trace the changes, at the level of roles, that are brought about by general forces. For instance, a factory mode of production, integration into the market economy, and professionalization of occupational roles will have to be traced to the changes in the traditional occupational roles and role situations if we are to understand what they mean to the individuals who are involved in these processes and how they would handle problems of qualitative changes in relationships and the values underlying them. There seems to be a great deal of variation in terms of the equipment of actors, specific nature of relationships of the actor to the role other, cultural content of relationships, the social setting in which interaction takes place, the personal network relations of which an interaction isolate is a part, and the norms that govern different interaction processes.

It is necessary to emphasize that role analysis becomes meaningful only in the context of defined (not structured) social situations of both activities and interactions. The empirical material presented here in regard to some aspects of economic change and development illustrates the importance of roles and their situational context (which I have called role setting involving notions of rights and obligations, expectations, and norms with their sources of legitimacy) in understanding processes of continuity and change.

In complex traditional societies many occupations that are considered modern would already be present. An individual may continue to follow the same occupation but a variation in the social setting makes all the difference in his role playing. Similarly, acquisition of new skills by artisans and farmers, changes in the commodities they manufacture or the produce they raise, and alterations in their marketing skills will make their roles different from the ones in the traditional setting. Such changes in the occupational roles either imply or have consequences for the traditional multiplex and unequal relationships which were structured on the basis of different norms.

One of the ways in which professionalization of occupations takes place is the emergence of new role sectors within a role set, which is best worked out in the situational context of personal network. A consideration of the linkages (or their absence) between role sectors throws light on the nature of role development. It also brings to light the problem of relativity in role consensus and role perception.

Finally, the empirical material presented here illustrates that just as one can speak of interrelations between role sectors in a role set, one can study interrelations between different role areas in the situational context of personal networks involving roles in different areas of social life, such as the economic, kinship, religious, and political. In the context of social and cultural change in India it is seen that different traditional and modern sources of legitimacy operate at the same time in different areas without necessarily producing conflicts. There is a great autonomy of role areas, and the presence of multiple, diverse, and divergent norms gives a wide scope for manipulation to the individual in both role playing and role taking.

REFERENCES

BALES, R. F.
  1950 *Interaction process analysis.* Cambridge, Mass.: Addison Wesley.
  1953 "The equilibrium problem in small groups," in *Working papers in the theory of action.* Edited by T. Parsons, R. F. Bales and E. A. Shils. New York: The Free Press.
BANTON, MICHAEL
  1965 *Roles: an introduction to the study of social relations.* London: Tavistock.

BARNES, J. A.
   1954   Class and committees in a Norwegian island parish. *Human Relations* 7.1:39-58.
BARTH, F.
   1966   *Models of social organization.* London: Royal Anthropological Institute.
   1967   On the study of social change. *American Anthropologist* 69:661-669.
BATES, F. L.
   1956   Position, role and status: a reformulation of concepts. *Social Forces* 34:313-321.
BAVISKAR, B. S.
   1970   "A sociological study of a cooperative sugar factory in Maharashtra." Unpublished Ph.D. thesis, University of Delhi.
BEIDELMAN, T. O.
   1959   *A comparative analysis of the* jajmāni *system.* New York: Association for Asian Studies.
BELSHAW, C. S.
   1965   *Traditional exchange and modern markets.* Englewood Cliffs: Prentice-Hall.
BOTT, E.
   1957   *Family and social network.* London: Tavistock.
EPSTEIN, A. L.
   1961   The network and urban social organization. *Rhodes-Livingstone Papers* 29:29-62.
EPSTEIN, T. S.
   1962   *Economic development and social change.* Manchester: Manchester University Press.
ETZIONI, A.
   1961   *A comparative analysis of complex organizations.* New York: The Free Press.
   1968   *The active society.* New York: The Free Press.
FIRTH, R.
   1951   *Elements of social organization.* London: Watts.
   1954   Social organization and social change. *Journal of the Royal Anthropological Institute* 84:1-20.
   1959   *Social change in Tikopia.* London: George Allen and Unwin.
   1970   *Rank and religion in Tikopia.* Boston: Beacon Press.
FRANKENBERG, R.
   1966   *Communities in Britain.* Harmondsworth: Penguin.
GOFFMAN, ERVING
   1959   *The presentation of self in everyday life.* New York: Doubleday Anchor Books.
   1961   *Encounters: two studies in the sociology of interaction.* Indianapolis: Bobbs-Merrill.
GOODE, W. J.
   1960a   A theory of role strain. *American Sociological Review* 25:483-496.
   1960b   Norm commitment and conformity to role-status obligations. *American Journal of Sociology* 66:246-258.
GOODENOUGH, W. H.
   1965   "Rethinking 'status' and 'role': toward a general model of the cultural organization of social relationships," in *The relevance of models for social anthropology.* Association of Social Anthropologists Monographs 1. London: Tavistock.

GROSS, NEAL, WARD W. MASON, ALEXANDER W. MC EACHERN
  1958 *Explorations in role analysis: studies of the school superintendency role.* New York: John Wiley and Sons.
GUTKIND, C. W. PETER
  1965 African urbanism, mobility and the social network. *International Journal of Comparative Sociology* 6:48-60.
KARLEKAR, M. (née Malvika Chanda)
  1970 "Career orientation and commitment of school teachers: a study in the sociology of professions among women teachers in secondary Delhi schools." Unpublished M.Litt. dissertation, University of Delhi.
LEVY, MARION J., JR.
  1952 *The structure of society.* Princeton: Princeton University Press.
LINTON, RALPH
  1936 *The study of man.* New York: Appleton-Century.
  1945 *The cultural background of personality.* New York: Appleton-Century.
LYNCH, O. M.
  1969 *The politics of untouchability.* New York: Columbia University Press.
MADAN, T. N.
  1971 "Doctors in a north Indian city: recruitment, role perception and role performance," in *Beyond the village: sociological explorations.* Edited by Satish Saberwal (unpublished).
MAYER, A. C.
  1966 "The significance of quasi-groups in the study of complex societies," in *The social anthropology of complex societies.* Association of Social Anthropologists Monographs 4. London: Tavistock.
MAYER, P.
  1961 *Townsmen or tribesmen.* Cape Town: Oxford University Press on behalf of the Institute of Social and Economic Research, Rhodes University.
MEAD, G. H.
  1934 *Mind, self, and society.* Chicago: University of Chicago Press.
MERTON, R. K.
  1957 The role-set: problems in sociological theory. *British Journal of Sociology* 8:106-120.
  1963 *Social theory and social structure.* Glencoe, Illinois: The Free Press.
MITCHELL, J. C.
  1966 "Theoretical orientations on African urban studies," in *The social anthropology of complex societies.* London: Tavistock.
  1969 *The concept and use of social networks in urban situations: analysis of personal relationship in central African towns.* Edited by J. C. Mitchell. Manchester: Manchester University Press.
NADEL, S. F.
  1957 *The theory of social structure.* London: Cohen and West.
PARSONS, TALCOTT
  1951 *The social system.* Glencoe, Illinois: The Free Press.
PARSONS, T., R. F. BALES, E. A. SHILS, *editors*
  1953 *Working papers in the theory of action.* New York: The Free Press.
PARSONS, T., E. A. SHILS, *editors*
  1951 *Toward a general theory of action.* New York: Harper and Row.

POCOCK, D. F.
  1962   "Notes on *jajmāni* relationships," in *Contributions to Indian sociology*. The Hague and Paris: Mouton.
RADCLIFFE-BROWN, A. R.
  1952   *Structure and function in primitive society*. London: Cohen and West.
RAJAGOPALAN, C.
  1963   Social change: an analysis of role conflict and deviation. *The Indian Journal of Social Work* 26:11-18.
RAO, M. S. A.
  1957   *Social change in Malabar*. Bombay: Popular Book Depot.
  1970   *Urbanization and social change*. Delhi: Orient Longmans.
  1972   *Tradition, rationality and change: essays in sociology of economic development and social change*. Bombay: Popular Prakashan.
SHAH, B. V.
  1967   "The role of [the] secondary teacher." Mimeographed manuscript, Sadar Patel University, Vallabh Vidyanagar.
SHETH, N. R.
  1968   *The social framework of an Indian factory*. Bombay: Oxford University Press.
SHETH, N. R., S. P. JAIN
  1968   The status and role of local union leaders. *Indian Journal of Industrial Relations* 4:70-88.
SMELSER, N. J.
  1959   *Social change in the industrial revolution*. Chicago: University of Chicago Press.
  1963   "Mechanisms of change and adjustment to change," in *Industrialization and society*. Edited by B. F. Hoselitz and W. E. Moore. The Hague and Paris: UNESCO-Mouton.
SOUTHALL, A.
  1959   An operational theory of role. *Human Relations* 12:17-34.
SRINIVAS, M. N., A. BÉTEILLE
  1964   Networks in Indian social structure. *Man* 212:165-168.
TURNER, R. H.
  1962   "Role-taking: process versus conformity," in *Human behaviour and social processes: an interactionist approach*. Edited by A. M. Rose. London: Routledge and Kegan Paul.
  1969   "Role: sociological aspects," in *International encyclopedia of the social sciences*. New York: Macmillan and Free Press.

Agricultural Labor Unions: Some Socioeconomic and Political Considerations

JOAN P. MENCHER

An examination of the development of agricultural labor unions in Kerala shows that in most parts of the state there has recently been a significant change in the thrust of peasant agitations, with profound implications for the position of agricultural laborers. With the major exception of the Kuttanad region of the former state of Travancore, peasant agitations have been directed until recently toward tenancy reform and land ceilings, with the laborers and tenants uniting against the former landowners (both large and small). With the final passage of the Land Reform (Amendment) Act and the growing pressure on the United Front government to show its sincerity by implementing it, there is a change in the thrust of the movement. It is now clear that the landless laborers have not benefited much from land reform, and the thrust of new movements is primarily toward establishing agricultural labor unions (apart from "land-grab" movements, which are mostly serving to pressure the state government into more rapid settlement of land ceiling cases).

The data which provide the basis for this study were collected incidentally as part of a comparative study of structural constraints to development in Kerala and Madras. Though the data are limited, they

The author has worked in Kerala in 1958-1960, 1962, and again in 1970-1971. The present paper is based on research done under a joint Columbia University-Delhi School of Planning and Architecture project funded by a grant to Columbia University from the National Science Foundation. Data for Trichur and Palghat Districts come from the project, data for North Malabar from the author's work there in 1958-1959 and from more recent reports by friends in the area, data for Kottayam from Mr C. Fuller (see note 4), and data from Kuttanad from written reports and conversations with Professor P. G. K. Panikar. The author is grateful to Professors F. C. Southworth, K. R. Unni, and P. G. K. Panikar for their many useful suggestions. The views here expressed, however, are solely the responsibility of the author.

nevertheless provide a basis for a preliminary examination of important structural changes going on in Kerala today. After examining the background of labor union activities in different parts of Kerala, I will attempt to identify some of the reasons why unions started earlier and have done better in Kuttanad than elsewhere. I will also discuss a number of factors which may be expected to hasten or impede their development elsewhere.

The discussion which follows will focus on the latent and manifest areas of social conflict in relation to the broader Kerala socioeconomic system, employing a dialectical model which treats conflict as a basic process in the germination of social change. A model of this type postulates change as a process of transformation through resolution of conflicts. This type of model is exceedingly useful in trying to explain the differential development of agricultural labor unions in a number of different places in Kerala, as well as the efflorescence of such unions starting in 1971.

It is currently being predicted that by 1985 the percentage of the total labor force involved in agriculture will be reduced to less than 3 percent in "developed" countries like the United States. In the "centrally planned economies," the figure is expected not to exceed 43.8 percent of the labor force. By contrast,

. . . the developing market economies are expected to witness considerable increases in the agricultural labor force. . . . Although the relative importance of farming in these countries will decline, in 1985 it will still be the principal source of employment (*Ceres* 1972:13).

If this prediction turns out to be true, we can expect that the problems of agricultural laborers will also continue to multiply. As Patnaik (1972:22) has noted,

. . . in the peasant-holding family labour is employed for a certain number of days annually; if it could find employment for the same number of days on a daily wage basis, the total income from labouring for wages would be higher than the income (after meeting all other costs of cultivation) from cultivation on own account. Why then does the peasant family not sell its land and start working as agricultural labourers? Clearly, because it is not certain of finding employment for the same number of days which is ensured by the possession of land. The explicit unemployment among full-time agricultural labourers, the lower quantum of employment they obtain on average and their consequent lower incomes, makes them the poorest class in the entire population.

On the other hand, in examining the decade 1960-1970, two Indian economists have shown clearly how the lot of the poor has become increasingly worse; they are poorer — if that is possible to conceive of (Dandekar and Rath 1971). It is clear at present that, barring radical social change, the formation of unions to help agitate on their behalf is one of the few courses of action open to rural laborers. An understanding of the process of formation of such organizations is thus extremely relevant at the present time.

Classical anthropological and sociological research in India has not concerned itself primarily with the emergence of new forms of social organization. Rather, there has tended to be an emphasis on the study of the traditional (whatever that may be).[1] To a large extent, we have left the discussion and analysis of current movements and problems to our sister disciplines of economics and political science. Nevertheless, there is something that we can contribute to the analysis of current socioeconomic processes because of our emphasis on the collection of detailed data from specific locales (including data from people on all levels of the socioeconomic system), especially if we then try to relate our detailed data to the larger scene of which it is a part. Social anthropology can also contribute to the understanding of what is actually going on in a given social system because of the nature of the questions we ask. Some of these questions, though obviously cast in synchronic perspective, derive from the early functionalist approach and attempt to go beyond the description and analysis of what linguistics calls the surface structure. Thus, we ask questions like these: What function does it serve for change A to occur in area X but not in area Y? What are the explanations given by the people, and what do we, as observers, postulate to be the underlying reasons? Who serves to benefit from the system as it is and from changes going on, and why? Economists looking at such systems have tended to look only at the so-called economic dimensions, and political scientists primarily at the political ones. It has been the tradition of social anthropology to try to include both with the social structure, in order to develop a more integrative view of what is going on. (Nonetheless, I draw heavily on the work of colleagues in other disciplines in the present analysis. See Table 1 for distribution of agricultural workers in India.)

There is a considerable literature on peasant movements, including agricultural labor union activity, for the Latin American region. That rural union activity has perhaps a longer history in that part of the world than in India derives in part from the particular pattern of colonial administration set up in the New World, which tended to encourage the setting up of large estates which generally remained intact after the independence of most Latin American countries. It has therefore to some extent been easier for agricultural labor union activity to develop there than in India. Another relevant factor is that the Latin American countries have been independent longer, despite

[1] What has often passed as the traditional has been the picture of India presented in early British or other European sources and occasionally the idealized picture shown in the Brahmanical scriptures. This has in part been inevitable because of the limited data from other sources, but it is quite dangerous to generalize from such a picture.

Table 1.   1971 census

	Total cultivators	Total agricultural laborers	Total other workers
Kerala	1,067,000 (20%)	1,795,000 (34%)	2,358,000 (45%)
Cannanore	126,000 (20%)	229,000 (37%)	262,000 (42%)
Kozhikode	76,000 (18%)	137,000 (32%)	204,000 (49%)
Malappuram	92,000 (19.5%)	190,000 (41%)	186,000 (39.5%)
Palghat	92,000 (17%)	278,000 (52%)	168,000 (31%)
Trichur	81,000 (15%)	195,000 (34%)	268,000 (49%)
Ernakulam	96,000 (19%)	142,000 (28%)	266,000 (53%)
Kottayam	145,000 (26%)	152,000 (27%)	262,000 (47%)
Alleppey	91,000 (19%)	169,000 (35%)	217,000 (45%)
Quilon	183,000 (29%)	133,000 (21%)	311,000 (50%)
Trivandrum	83,000 (18%)	169,000 (36%)	213,000 (46%)

Source: Census of India supplement: provisional population totals 1971:106–109.
Note: According to Modernizing Indian agriculture: fourth report on the Intensive Agriculture District Programme (1960-1968) 2, 56 percent of the agricultural population of Kuttanad was agricultural laborers.

their continuing lack of economic independence from the United States. It is not my intention to present a full comparison of Latin America and India here, but it is useful to look at some of the generalizations that have come out of Latin American studies in this field in recent years and see to what extent they are relevant to the Kerala situation.

In an analysis of peasant movements in Latin America, Landsberger (1969) has suggested a number of hypotheses concerning the nature of such movements:

1. They are most likely to develop in changing societies and to achieve success only in modernized societies.

2. The better-off sectors of the peasantry are most susceptible to organization, with the most likely participants being those whose traditional values have been modified through education or exposure to outside influences.

3. Leadership and allies tend to be drawn from elements outside the peasantry, particularly middle-class intellectuals, lawyers, etc.

4. The goals of peasant movements vary but are primarily grievance oriented.

5. Ideologies, especially radical ones, are introduced from outside.

It is certainly true that Kerala today is undergoing rapid and extensive changes, and that these changes are the result of the early involvement of this region first with European mercantile traders and later with the British colonial power. Gough (1961:6) has shown how the effect of 150 years of British control on the west coast clearly upset traditional socioeconomic relations. Indeed, as one writer has shown, 60 to 80 percent of the rural population in Kerala could be considered by 1950 to be rural proletariat or semiproletariat: "This is the result of the combined exploitation of imperialism, feudal and semi-feudal land-lordism, and usury'' (Namboodiripad 1952:92).

One of the ways in which Kerala has been distinguished from other parts of India has been its relatively high rural literacy rate, varying in 1971 from a high of 75 percent (Alleppey District) to a low of 53 percent (Palghat District) for males.[2] Not only is the literacy level high, but so is the extent of newspaper reading. Even back in 1958, I was struck by the fact that in remote villages daily newspapers (both Congress and Communist oriented) were read aloud to small groups of people. Thus, within a few hours after the papers had arrived in the village, important political news could reach most of the people in the widely dispersed village area where I was working. In partial contrast to the Latin American situation described by Landsberger (1969), while the dominant radical (Communist) ideology operative in Kerala was drawn from the outside, by now, after more than thirty years of Marxist education, it is very much a part of the Kerala scene.

In Kerala, the better-off sectors of the villages have not been the most susceptible to organization. Rather, the Marxists have tended to focus on two related groups: small landowners and tenants, and landless laborers. It is clear that the original party leadership, at least on the district level, was, as in Latin America, drawn mostly from the middle classes, primarily higher-caste, middle-class intellectuals. This has not always been true on the village level, however, though leaders have usually had at least some small amount of economic security or have been somewhat less dependent on village employers.[3]

The change which has taken place in the labor union movements in this area (see introductory paragraph) represents, among other things, a new focus on the growth of what has sometimes been called proletarian consciousness. Greaves (1968:1), in a paper on the development of

---

[2]   Kerala has the highest literacy rate in all of India. This is true for females as well as for males. The lowest literacy rate is 36.97 percent for females in rural parts of Palghat District, but if one were to examine the figures for each age group, for example data for people under thirty-five, the literacy percentages are much higher than revealed by the gross statistics currently available (the detailed volumes of the 1971 census are not yet published). It is also true, however, that within the lower age groups, those people who are illiterate are all from the poorest strata of society. This is abundantly clear from our project's house-to-house census data.

[3]   Pandey (1971:41) notes for Unnao District, Uttar Pradesh:

The somewhat better-off sectors of the peasantry played a key role in organizing the peasantry in Unnao, and the most depressed classes of the peasantry, i.e., landless agricultural workers, were always under-represented. Further, those individuals who were socially, culturally, and economically better off, as compared to other groups of people, furnished leadership and active workers to the movement.

Though partly true in Kerala, in that leaders came from the better-off classes, it is clear that the Communists had a better mass base in Kerala than in Unnao.

proletarian consciousness among Peruvian peasants, notes that when this emerges, two things happen:

. . . their major locus of identity and affiliation changes from a locality to a class, cross-cutting locality boundaries. A second change concerns relationships with those who control power and access to wealth. . . . As proletarian consciousness emerges, this interactional domain increasingly becomes one of contract.

It is clear that in upper Kuttanad, where this occurred many years ago, contractual relations now dominate completely. It seems likely that during the next few years we shall witness an increasing breakdown in traditional feudal ties and a greater stress on contractual arrangements in the rest of the state. It is striking that many former landlords bemoan the ending of these feudal relations and speak sentimentally about the past. They often mention that the attached laborers could count on their landlord for loans and help in times of crisis or when there were family problems. The laborers were mostly paid in kind by the landlords. The landlords gave them protection and looked after their general welfare. According to Pillai and Panikar (1965:120),

Labourers . . . used to look upon the landlord not in the modern sense of an employer but as their sovereign and benefactor. There was a personal bond of allegiance to the landlord and his family which was passed down in the hereditary manner from one generation to another. The labourers shared in the joys and sorrows of the landlord and his family and vice versa. . . . Liberal advances of money or paddy were given when they ran into difficulties by exhausting their stock of paddy before the next harvest. These commitments bound these families so strongly to their masters that it was difficult for them to extricate themselves from these bonds. Nor was there any desire to do so, as the bonds of personal devotion were so great. . . . Custom and tradition held such an unshakable sway over the scheme of things that a "disloyal" labourer could not hope to get employment anywhere.

Though this passage refers to Kuttanad, similar comments have been made for other parts of Kerala. An article in *The Hindu* (1971) about Alleppey District depicts the feelings of many landlords nowadays:

The farmers would recall the times when the harvest season went off like a festival, when the workers spent their leisure time during night, singing and dancing, young men courting their would-be brides and eventually celebrating their unions in wedlock. The ryots blessed the couples and gave them presents and all were happy. With the change that has come over in the outlook and attitude of the workers towards landlords, their relationship has been strained, and now, harvest time is an occasion for collective bargaining and continuous confrontation.

What has impressed me greatly in the villages where I worked in central Kerala is that while former landlords might speak of the security offered to the laborers in the old days, I have never heard a villager belonging to one of the traditional laboring castes speak of the security he used to feel or express any preference for being a tied laborer. Nor have I ever heard any speak with affection of the "good old days" (Mencher 1975).

Our data for the analysis of the development of agricultural labor unions in Kerala are drawn from a number of sources. For north Kerala, I rely primarily on data from one village area about sixteen miles inland from Cannanore town, where I worked in 1958-1959, and where a research assistant collected new data during the summer of 1972. For central Kerala and selected parts of Palghat District, I rely primarily on data collected in 1970-1972. For Kuttanad I have used published reports, and for Kottayam I have had the benefit of personal communication from Fuller.[4]

Before I proceed to examine the data from the different regions, it is useful to comment briefly on some of the important changes which took place in the land tenure system in Travancore, Cochin, and British Malabar in the period prior to the formation of Kerala State in 1956.[5] According to Varghese (1970:75-97), important changes took place in the land tenures of Travancore, Cochin, and Malabar during the period when they were separate political units: by the end of the nineteenth century, Travancore had almost become a region of peasant proprietors (that is, the state had control, directly or indirectly, of 80 percent of the cultivated lands and almost all of the arable and uncultivated waste); Cochin had become a tract of peasant proprietors plus absentee landlords (with less than half of the cultivated area being listed as government lands); and Malabar had remained primarily an area of absentee or at least noncultivating landlords (*jenmis*) under the traditional complex system of subinfeudation.

One result of state control over land in Travancore was the attractiveness of that region for British investors:

. . . here the planters were able to lease-in lands on favourable terms directly from the State whereas, in Malabar, they would have had to take them from private jenmis, which was relatively insecure and costlier than the direct State leases. . . . The influx of foreign capital into plantations opened up new opportunities for agricultural and non-agricultural economic expansion (Varghese 1970:116).

---

[4] Christopher Fuller is a doctoral student from Cambridge University who was working in rural parts of Kottayam District in 1971-1972. His study included work in both a Christian-dominated and a Hindu-dominated area. At present his material is being written up for his dissertation.

[5] The present state of Kerala consists of the former British Malabar and the former princely states of Cochin and Travancore. The state was formed as a politico-linguistic unit in 1956. Before independence, when the British ruled directly in Malabar, their presence was also felt very forcefully in Cochin and Travancore. Furthermore, they had political control of a small part of the land in Cochin harbor. This helped British capital to make an important thrust into the Cochin and Travancore economies.

Varghese notes that in 1949-1950 the eastern highlands of Travancore had 268,600 acres given over to plantation crops (1970:118), whereas in Malabar in 1956 plantation cultivation extended over an area of about 60,000 acres (1970:121). It is worth noting that agricultural labor union activity in Travancore started in the high ranges, in the tea estates where the incredibly miserable conditions of the laborers prompted a number of early organizers to do something.[6] The resemblance between employment on the estates and factory employment helped in part to make organizing easier. We do not at present have enough data to show directly the influence of agricultural labor unions in the high ranges on workers in the Kuttanad, but there is no question that such a relationship exists.

By the mid-1950's, when Varghese did his research, the three regions were strikingly different, as shown by the following figures:

In Travancore, about one-eighth of the surveyed households has been reported as landless, and . . . more than one-half gets classified on the above criterion as owner-cultivators, one-fourth as tenants, and the rest under other categories. The Malabar sample shows roughly the same proportion of landless households, but the share of owner-cultivators is only one-tenth while that of tenant households is as high as three-fourths. . . . Cochin occupies an intermediate position between Travancore and Malabar, more than one-fourth of the households reporting as owner-cultivators and one-half as tenants. . . . The proportion of landless households is the highest in Cochin (being one-fifth of the total). . . . In Kuttanad pocket [in Travancore], about two-fifths of the surveyed households are landless, one-third are tenants, one-fifth are owner-cultivators, and the rest are rent-receiving households (Varghese 1970:161-162).

Table 1 lists the proportions of landless laborers for each district from the provisional tables of the 1971 census. Unfortunately, the figures for Kottayam and Alleppey Districts do not differentiate between Kuttanad villages and other parts of each district. According to the Fourth Report on the Intensive Agricultural District Program for the years 1960-1968, in Palghat District agricultural laborers account for 32 percent of the population in 1968, and in the Kuttanad, for 56 percent

---

[6] In his excellent novel, *Red tea*, P. H. Daniel gives a clear picture of the tremendous abuses suffered by the plantation workers in the high ranges during the early part of the twentieth century. Indeed, in many ways their working conditions resembled a kind of debt slavery, as the law itself provided that:

When an estate manager complained in writing to a magistrate that a worker had run away, the magistrate should arrange for the production of the worker before him, by issue of summons or warrant of arrest. And . . . any worker who ran away during the period of contract would be liable to pay a fine of Rs. 50/- or suffer imprisonment up to one month or both (1969:v).

During the period between 1940 and 1960 the trade union movement grew in the plantation area and undoubtedly influenced more accessible workers in other sectors who were also experiencing various types of oppression.

(Varghese 1970:371, 421). I suspect that the percentage of agricultural labor listed for Palghat is on the low side since, prior to 1971, people who were primarily landless laborers were not classed as such if they owned even a tiny plot of land. In other words, it looks as if both these areas have high concentrations of landless agricultural labor. What is striking is that labor union activity has had a much longer history in Kuttanad. (We will return to a discussion of this.) It should be kept in mind through the following discussion that in each of the regions to be discussed the vast majority of landless laborers are now and have for a long time been active supporters of the Communist Party (now the CPM).

The thrust of movements in north Malabar, as in south Malabar and Cochin, has until the past two or three years been focused on tenancy reform. This is not to say that wages have not come up from time to time as an important issue, but in general the focus of attention has been on tenancy reform and land ceilings rather than on agricultural wages. This began to change only after the 1970 Land Reform (Amendment) Act was passed and actual steps were started to implement it. Thus, in many parts of Kerala, it is not surprising that *Karshaka Thozhilali* [agricultural labor] unions have either been formed or finally started to function only since the end of 1970 or early in 1971.

NORTH MALABAR

The first *Karshaka* [agricultural] movement in north Kerala was in the mid-1930's. At first it was run by members of the Congress Party. It focused on relief for tenants, whose situation was clearly a major grievance of the people of the region at that time. One result of this movement was to ease the situation for tenants in years when the crop was bad or failed altogether (though the latter happened rarely in Kerala). Thus, payment of rent was reduced in bad years, and landlords were no longer allowed to attach a tenant's property if he failed to pay the full amount because of a poor harvest. But evictions continued, and in 1940 a Tenancy Committee was constituted to investigate the situation in both north and south Malabar. This committee came to the conclusion that "fixity of tenure, both heritable and alienable, should be granted to all classes of tenants, present and future, holding land of any class whatsoever, but not to certain kanamdars who are really mortgagees. . . ." The report suggested restoration of the scope for resumption by landlords, and also reduction in the rent and renewal fee payable by the tenants (Varghese 1970:231) In the early 1940's there was a strong Communist movement in north Malabar which focused on two things: permanency of tenure and distribution of forest and other uncultivated land to landless families. When the Soviet Union was attacked by Germany, the Communist Party gave its support to the joint British-Soviet forces; this temporarily lost them some of their support among the rank and file who felt that they were siding with the imperial masters. But in the years immediately following the end of the war (1946-1948), the Communists were again active among the agricultural workers and tenants. At this time both the army and the Malabar Special Police were called in by the government to crush them. Temporarily the Communist Party was ruled illegal and many of the leaders were forced to go underground. Although this did not reduce the power of the party in electoral politics, it was certainly one of the factors leading to a lessening of activity in strikes and local unionizing in the years that followed.

At the present time in the village area where I worked, there are two unions in existence (the *Karshaka Thozhilali* Union and the Weavers' Union), and a brick-quarry workers' union is in the process of being formed. The *Karshaka Thozhilali* Union was formed at the end of 1970 by a man who has land of his own but also works for some of the bigger landowners. So far, there has been very little benefit from this union because there is very little paddy land in the village. Thus if the laborers strike for higher wages, the landlords can decide not to cultivate their fields or just to ignore the crop and wait until the laborers return. For crops like coconut, cashew, and pepper (the three main crops in the village) it is possible to wait; if the landlord does a minimal amount of work himself, the trees or vines continue to flourish and not much is lost. For other crops, if laborers strike, the landowners often either ignore the work that could be done or, in some cases, bring in pump sets and do everything themselves. Local people say that if the land-owners lose one or two crops of paddy, their families can still eat, whereas if a laborer does not work, his family could starve. Nonetheless, after a strike in the spring of 1971 the daily wages for workers did increase slightly. For a half day's work, the wage for men went up from 2 rupees to 2.5 rupees, and for women from 1 rupee to 1.5 rupees. For a full day's work, the wage for men went up to 4.5 rupees plus lunch, and for women to 2.25 rupees plus lunch. (Previously it was 3.5 to 4 rupees and 1.5 to 2 rupees.) There has not been any change in the harvest wage, however: harvesters still receive one bundle in twelve for the first harvest and one *edanazhis* in ten for the second (where the work also includes threshing and winnowing the paddy).

It is clear that the reason the *Karshaka Thozhilali* Union is not very successful in this area is that there are too many workers and not enough jobs. In addition, there are a few large landowning families (all belonging to two or three traditional *taravad*s) and a large number of small landowning families who do not employ much labor except under special circumstances. Furthermore, there is only a small amount of land given over to paddy cultivation in the village area. And finally, there are only limited possibilities for employment in the nonagricultural sector.

There are a number of weavers in the village who do piecework for a weaving factory near Cannanore (weaving is a general feature of this region). The Weavers' Union has had some success in obtaining concessions from the companies that field out the yarn, but workers who do piecework in their villages do not have the same kind of organization as workers in the main factories. Indeed, this has been one of the incentives to owners to continue this type of work. Another, of course, has been that it requires much less capital outlay for space and other facilities.

In this region, because of its lateritic soil, it is possible to dig excellent laterite bricks from the ground for use in house construction. This work, which is exceedingly arduous, is well paid, but the workers do not have any protection if they are injured, nor do they get bonuses or retirement funds or any of the benefits which other organized workers get. At long last they are also starting to organize.

According to village informants, in areas close to Cannanore or Tellicherry town where there are other jobs available, such as making *beedies* [whole-leaf cigarettes], or working in the large weaving factories, agricultural laborers can make better use of their union than inland, where laborers are more dependent on agricultural jobs.

CENTRAL KERALA

The situation in central Kerala (apart from the extreme eastern *taluks* of Palghat District, which lie outside our project area) in many ways resembles that in north Kerala, except that there was no strong peasant movement in this region in the 1930's and 1940's, though there was certainly considerable agitation for tenancy reform. This area has remained extremely traditional in many ways until recently and very much dominated by well-to-do Namboodiri Brahman families, Sthani Nayars, and large temples. Fewer cash crops are raised here than in either north Kerala or Travancore, and in many ways this region has maintained more feudal ties (as opposed to capitalistic types of relations) until quite recently. In the 1920's and 1930's, central Kerala was the center for movements to permit the partition of the property of Namboodiri Brahmans and Nayars. There was also agitation on the part of middle-class Nayars and other caste people for fixity of tenure for *kanam* tenants of Namboodiri landlords. In more recent years, as in the north, land legislation has been the main focus of attention of most of the political parties, and there has been relatively little labor organizing.

With the breakup of the large holdings of the Namboodiris and Nayars, there have been major changes in the agricultural setup in this general area. To begin with, certain cash crops have been introduced during the past twenty-odd years, such as rubber (which still remains exempt from the land ceiling), pineapple, areca nut, etc. Workers on these estates receive a fixed wage. As estate workers have begun to organize, the agricultural laborers have been affected as well.

With the abolition of prohibition, the toddy tappers have also begun to organize. Indeed, in this region, the toddy tappers' unions have been perhaps the most successful in holding their own and increasing their wages, because of two related factors: (1) There is one main group of shopowners who purchase the toddy. If they did not get their supply regularly they would be forced to go out of business, so they can be pressured into paying more. (2) The majority of tappers belong to the same caste (the Izhavas, a traditional toddy-tapping community).

Our project concentrated on four villages in Talappilly *taluk* (Trichur District), two in Ottapalam *taluk* (Palghat District), and two in Alathur *taluk* (Palghat District). In one of these villages there was a really active *Karshaka Thozhilali* union at the time of the project, though in most villages, one was in the process of formation, despite considerable variation in the wages paid for agricultural operations (Mencher 1974). These differences seem to correlate primarily with the extent to which alternative employment exists. If laborers can get jobs in a nearby factory or are free to go far and wide to seek employment (because of the breaking of traditional bonds), wages are higher; if they have no alternative source of employment, wages are lower.

Until recently, the major organizational activity in the area has been agitating for land reform. Today in this area there are in few villages families owning over the land ceiling.[7] Thus land legislation, while of benefit to tenants, has not particularly benefited the landless, the people who never were fortunate enough to be tenants (such as the untouchables), or those who lost any tenancy rights many years ago when landowners saw tenancy reform in the offing. Yet, although the

---

[7]   Previously there were many large landowners in the area. One result of land legislation has been to take away all tenanted land from big landlords. In practice, this occurred as soon as it was clear that land legislation would be enacted, so that many of the former large landowners have received very little or no payment from tenants for the past five to ten years. The real sufferers from land legislation have been certain high-caste small landowners who had given land to tenants because they could not cultivate it themselves, such as old people, widows with small children, etc. The only parts of Palghat District where there are still any really large landowners are in the extreme eastern irrigated development blocks and parts of the Kole lands of Trichur District.

laborers in this region are solidly Marxist,[8] it is only very recently that there has been any sign of labor union activity.

In part, the slowness in organizing the agricultural laborers in this region can be related to the fact that many of the Marxist leaders in the villages are themselves small landowners of high or middle castes who are at least partly dependent on agricultural labor. The ambivalence of such "leaders" and the effect of their ambivalence on the nature of their leadership are reflected in the following quote from one of the more active leaders in a village in Talappilly *taluk*:

> . . . in K [village name] . . . the people don't know. They are not interested. They are not well educated for the union, or what is their unity — or nothing. We are teaching, every day. . . . Next year, rainy season, we will have to make it [i.e. get an effective union organization and agitate for higher wages]. That is when we are catching all these people. . . . So we are arranging now to make it, organizing and giving membership and everything. We will also be telling them they can make demands. Otherwise, simply they will be sitting in their house waiting for the owner to call. . . . I am telling them to demand more wages. Even my own workers. We are giving in a standard rate. We are paying the same as everyone else. But I tell my workers they should demand more from the owners.

According to one student assistant who worked in three villages in Talappilly *taluk*, the agricultural laborers' union is not active in any of the three. He was surprised to find it so "different from my own place [in Quilon District], where we have several competing unions operating in the village." Another assistant, from a village near the town of Trichur (about twenty-two miles away by road), noted the absence of strong union activity in the project area. It is clear, however, that this situation is now changing. Thus, in one of our villages in Ottapalam *taluk*, it was recently reported by the investigator that there is now a union forming, and members are starting to agitate for wage increases.

KUTTANAD

When we turn to Kuttanad, we find a totally different situation. Here, agricultural labor unions were started even before independence (prior to 1947). Several explanations have been given for this, including the influence of the nearby coir (coconut fiber) and other industries, as well as by the union activities on the tea estates in the high ranges of Travancore. Other factors often cited include the high literacy level in this area

---

[8] Our project area was the one part of Kerala where Marxist members of Parliament won in 1971 (Ponnani constituency, which included Talappilly *taluk* of Trichur District, and Palghat constituency, which included Ottapalam and Alathur *taluks*).

(70 percent) as compared to other areas.[9] In any case, none of these factors is sufficient to explain the rapid development of the labor movement in Kuttanad as compared, for example, to the area around Kottayam town, where agricultural labor unions are just now in the process of forming (see next section).

The area known as Kuttanad consists of seven *taluks* of Alleppey District and three *taluks* of Kottayam District. It makes up 4.2 percent of the land area of the state but 8.0 percent of the population, with a density of 2,688 people per square mile (*Report of the Kuttanad Enquiry Commission* 1971-1972:37). The general consensus is that the entire region has emerged as a result of reclamation activities over several centuries. (Much of the area lies below sea level.) According to Pillai and Panikar (1965:14), records show that since 1833 reclamation has been going on, and they suggest that it probably has a much longer history. During the 1880's the increasing need for more paddy lands led to a rapid increase in reclamation programs, however. The social background is described by Pillai and Panikar in the following terms (1965:118-120):

Reclamation-cum-farming developed in the Kuttanad area against a predominantly feudal background. Both . . . demanded the services of large numbers of labourers. The landowners who in earlier days were mostly caste Hindus were loath to work in the fields and employed hired labour. The tenant class which arose in the course of time was also drawn from the rich capitalist farmers who grew richer with the fruits of this enterprise. . . . The divorce between proprietorship of land and work in the fields was as complete as it could be. . . . From early days these labourers were drawn from the lowest stratum of society — the "untouchables". . . . The relations between the attached labourers and the landed proprietors in Kuttanad . . . were of a semi-feudal nature. It was not the labourer alone but his whole family which was attached to the landlord.

In recent times, the tremendous expansion of the cultivable area has brought an enormous increase in the demand for labor. This demand is, however, highly seasonal and therefore very intense during a short period of time:

Agricultural labourers from surrounding districts regularly migrate to this area and live there for periods extending from 4 to 6 weeks. Thus there is a large floating population of agricultural labourers in this area whose number is estimated at about 2 lakhs [200,000] during the agricultural season (Pillai and Panikar 1965:122).

Reflecting the feelings of many observers of this area, Panikar has

---

[9] I am not altogether certain that the agricultural laborers are really so literate. I strongly suspect that the majority of the 30 percent illiterate comes from landless laboring households. Still, it is true that general literacy in the area may play a part in union activity.

suggested that it was almost inevitable that the situation in Kuttanad would lead to union activity:

> . . . labouring under unfair institutional set-up for generations, and acute competition for employment, unionism is the only bulwark against employers driving wages below the subsistence level. Agricultural labour, it must also be borne in mind, compares very unfavourably with other classes of workers, like civil servants and factory workers; they have no leave with salary, pensions, gratuity, provident fund, bonus, etc., which are the normal benefits of other categories of workers; they have no regular employment or income during their normal working life; they have no compensation in the event of death in harness. . . . Naturally, they try to grab the available work and drive a hard bargain on wages. Demands for wage increase must be appreciated as a desperate effort to ensure a minimum annual income for their family where employment is so limited and uncertain (1972:37–38).

Previously Pillai and Panikar (1965:127) had noted some of the other factors influencing the development of trade unionism among the workers in this region:

> . . . the rise of unionism in this sector was the natural corollary of the growth of trade unions in the industrial sector. The proximity of Kuttanad to Alleppey which is an important industrial and trading center was one of the factors which facilitated the spread of unionism in the agricultural sector also. The essentially capitalistic nature of the enterprise and the scale of operations in kayal cultivation which demanded large numbers of labourers were other factors. The need for the speedy execution of seasonal agricultural operations placed the employer at a disadvantage in bargaining and the labourers found that they could drive home their advantage only if they were organized. The wide prevalence of literacy among the working class in this region made organization easier. . . . The labourers . . . were mostly attached, were at the mercy of the landlords because alternative employment was almost nil. . . . The socialistic ideologies soon penetrated into the innermost recesses of waterlogged Kuttanad and gradually the attached labourers also came under its influence.

Some of the details of the history of agricultural union formation in Kuttanad are given in the following passages quoted from Oommen (1971:246–247):

> The first agricultural labour union in Kuttanad was formed in 1939, as a branch of the Travancore Karshaka Thozhilali (agricultural labour) Union (TKTU). The activities of the union, in its early phase, were confined to Alleppey town and the surrounding rural areas. Although the union was conceived as an instrument to secure the demands of agricultural workers, it was as much an agent for the mobilization of rural people against the British rule. . . .
> The TKTU was by and large an organization of the Communists. In order to make its presence felt on the agricultural labour front, the Indian National Congress organized the Travancore-Cochin Karshaka Thozhilali Sangam (TCKTS) in 1954. At present, the membership of the TCKTS consists mainly of lower middle class workers such as engine drivers, poultry farmers, or those who carry headloads. It is important to note that while its membership is

equally drawn from Christians, Nairs, and Ezhavas, the number of Harijans is very small. At present, this union claims a membership of 6,000 in Alleppey District, although other unions contest this figure. Consequent upon the split of Communist Party of India in 1964, the TKTU too was split into two: The Kerala Karshaka Thozhilali Federation (KKTF) organized by C.P.I. and the Kerala State Karshaka Thozhilali Union (KSKTU) led by C.P.(M). Both these unions draw most of their members from the Pulayas and the Ezhavas, the traditional agricultural labourers of the district. . . . The KKTF claims a membership of 5,000 while the KSKTU claims 14,400 members in Alleppey District.

Another active agrarian association is the Kuttanad Karshaka Thozhilali Union (KKTU), although its influence is confined to a few pockets. The KKTU came into existence only in 1968 and is led by the Revolutionary Socialist Party (R.S.P.). It claims a membership of 1,200.

In 1965 (127-128) Pillai and Panikar list the following as "leading trade unions" in Kuttanad: (1) the Travancore Karshaka Thozhilali Union, Moncombu (registered in 1953); (2) the Thiru-Cochi Thozhilali Sangam, Alleppey (established in 1954); (3) the Thiru-Cochi Karshaka Thozhilali Sangam, Moncombu (registered in 1954); and (4) the Karthikappally Taluk Karshaka Thozhilali Union, Haripad (registered in 1955). The first three are affiliated with the Indian National Trade Union Congress (Communist Party), and the last with the All India Trade Union Congress (Congress Party). Though the last-named was the largest in the area at that time (3,561 members), the first was the most active in the recently reclaimed *kayal* areas and had led large and successful strikes in 1954 and 1961.

Oommen (1971:248) suggests that all this political rivalry and competition among the unions has not always been necessarily beneficial for the workers. He reports that the union officials he contacted agreed that they were often working at cross-purposes:

In their attempt to project themselves as "progressive," each union is trying to out-do the others by demanding more and more for agricultural labourers. . . . We have been told that agricultural labourers, said to be Marxists, are willing to work for lower wages in certain areas where non-Marxist unions are strong in order to discredit the rival unions. The non-Marxist labourers indulge in precisely the same kind of activity elsewhere.

While this is no doubt true in some areas, the competition has nevertheless had the effect of forcing the unions to produce some tangible results. It is clear that without the unions the plight of the laborers in this area would be even more desperate.

The Kuttanad Karshaka Sangam (KKS), one of the two important farmers' associations in Alleppey District, came into existence in 1939. According to Oommen (1971:248-249), its membership was originally confined to the top landowners in the area, and it was at first viewed as merely an association for economic benefits such as debt relief, irrigation facilities, etc. Oommen points out that in 1957 this group, realizing its numerical weakness and its inability to resist the demands of labor unions of leftist orientation, invited small and medium landowners to join the association, which has in the 1970's become very strong.

Oommen indicates, however, that it has been less successful in lower Kuttanad, where the middle-class population is very small and the few rich families rarely cooperate with each other. I was told by one of the CPM legislators that strikes in this area have been the most successful in helping the landless laborers. He explained that the reason for this success was that with only a few large landowners in the area, it was more like organizing a strike in a factory. It was much easier to mobilize total support for the workers here.

In upper Kuttanad the KKS is much more firmly entrenched, in part because there is a larger number of middle-class landowners there. The Sangam is dominated by Christians, especially Syrian Christians (75 percent of the membership, according to Oommen). Of the remainder, 18 percent are Nayars and the rest Brahmans and Izhavas. The Sangam also has associate members, mostly low-caste Christians (generally attached workers of the well-to-do Christians). According to Oommen (1971:249), though the KKS disclaims any official connection with party politics, most of its active workers are also in the Kerala Congress (an offshoot of the Congress Party that is somewhat rightist in orientation).

There is one other farmers' organization, led by the CPM. This group, the Kerala Karshaka Sangam, is affiliated with the All India Kisan Sabha (Oommen 1971:249-250). Its activities have been limited to date, though it did lead one agitation in Trivandrum City during the summer of 1972.

Pillai and Panikar (1965:129) note that there have been a large number of disputes about wages and conditions of work between unions and individual cultivators during the last decade, but that the majority arose before the fixing of minimum wages in July 1957, when a tripartite committee consisting of representatives of the government, farmers, and agricultural laborers was established by the government of Kerala. One of the first decisions of that committee (known as the IRC) was to examine all problems relating to agricultural labor in Kuttanad. According to Oommen (1971:250-253):

In 1958, the Committee recommended Rs. 1.25 for men and Rs. 0.87 for women for an eight-hour working day. This wage rate was recommended for "ordinary operations". . . . The rate of payment recommended for harvesting and threshing was two-nineteenths of the produce, in addition to the erpu, wherever it was in vogue. . . . The wage rate of agricultural laborers was revised by the IRC. In October 1967, the Committee recommended a daily wage of Rs. 4.85 for men and Rs. 2.88 for women which was further raised to

Rs. 3.40 in September 1969. . . . It is wrong to assume that the workers are always paid at the rate recommended by the Committee.

According to Pillai and Panikar (1965:129-131), in actual practice conciliation has been the method most often employed in Kuttanad as a result of the peculiar nature of agriculture in the area. Since a large percentage of the workers are migratory, they want quick decisions on disputes. Being able to make use of the labor officer, who usually acts as a mediator, has often led to rapid settling of disputes. They note that the major strikes in 1954 and 1961 were ended and settlements arrived at by the Labor Commissioner.

What is striking, however, is that, despite all the labor union activity in Kuttanad, because of the decline in the coir industry in Alleppey and the rapid increase in population, there has been a steady increase in the number of available workers. This has resulted in a decline in the number of days of work available per person per year. Furthermore, Panikar notes (1972:35):

. . . it is clearly brought out that there is a steady decline in the real wages of agricultural labour from 1944-45 to 1967-68; the paddy equivalent of daily wage of a male worker in Kuttanad which was 5.7 kilograms in 1944-45 came down to 3.0 kilograms in 1967-68. . . . It only went up to 4.1 kilograms in 1968-69 and 5.1 kilograms in 1969-70. Thus as late as 1969-70, the paddy equivalent of the daily money wage of a male agricultural labourer in Kuttanad was below the level of 1944-45 and the same for last year, viz., 6.2 kilograms, was just 8.7% above the 1944-45 level.

He goes on to state (1972:37) that the situation would appear even more striking if one looked at what the money could buy of other commodities (such as clothes, food, or other items). Today in Kuttanad, the average male worker gets about 100 to 120 days of work per year, the average female, 80 to 100. Thus the average male worker can only hope to earn between 600 and 720 rupees per year. In September 1972, there was new agitation among the workers in Kuttanad. They were asking for 8 rupees for men and 5 rupees for women, as opposed to the 1971-1972 rates of 6 and 3.75 rupees respectively. According to some of the people I spoke to, however, it seems likely that they will settle for 6 to 7 rupees for men and 4.50 rupees for women. This would bring the workers more than 10 percent above the 1944-1945 level for the first time in terms of real money.

AREA NEAR KOTTAYAM

When Fuller first did his survey of labor relations in October 1971, most people said that there could never be a strike in this area. But between then and March 1972, things changed considerably. Fuller notes that in early January the Marxists from a neighboring village staged a demonstration for membership in his village, demanding that the payment for the paddy and the tapioca harvest be raised to one-eighth, that the minimum wages act should apply to all landlords, and that all hutment dwellers be given their ten cents of land immediately. At that time the reaction of the landlords, especially the big ones, was to form a branch of the Kerala Karshaka Sangam. They tried to convince the public that the Communists were leading the workers astray, and they also began firing workers who joined the Karshaka Thozhilali Union. (It should be noted that the actual union organized in his village was mostly controlled by the CPI, not by the CPM.)

By the end of February, a real change had begun. The workers started demanding one-eighth of the harvest, and when the first landlord's harvest was done and he refused to pay it, the workers struck and staged a *satyagraha* at his threshing ground. The landlords in this village retaliated by organizing and doing the work of the other big landlords themselves. Many of the small holders joined the landlords' association and, with a few loyal workers and their wives, actually did the harvesting. This broke the morale of many of the union members, who then worked on other lands for one-tenth. Only the most militant stuck it out. But eventually even they had to give in, as the union had no money to pay them, and after two weeks they had no food. So they too settled for one-tenth.

In 1972 the workers stated that they would refuse to work again for less than the minimum wage. Fuller reported that at the next harvest the landlords did pay one-eighth, though they refused to employ union members. One of their aims was apparently to show the workers that it does not pay to join a union.

This conflict showed clearly how the small landholders, especially small Christian landholders, will react if forced, and it also demonstrated that the union has failed to wean the small holders away from the landlords' association. It is difficult to say why they are on the side of the big landlords, but probably it is a mixture of kin ties, debts to the big landlords, caste feeling (most of them are Syrian Christians), and anti-Communist sentiment.

It is interesting that in the Nayar village nearby the owners immediately paid the workers more. Not all of them were asked to pay one-eighth, because the union is not so strong there yet. But in the localities where the union is strong, the owners paid one-eighth, arguing that it made no difference since they stopped all gifts to workers at the same time. The Christians knew this too but refused to change, under pressure, although this might account for their change the following harvest season. Some of the Nayars have told Fuller that they would rather pay the workers any amount than do the work themselves.

It is hard to tell whether the setback to the union will result in its immediate decline, or whether it will learn from its mistakes and build up its strength. The basic error was in starting the strike too soon, before the union had the total support of all workers. (All of this information comes from personal communication with Christopher Fuller [see note 4].)

UNNAO DISTRICT, UTTAR PRADESH: SOME POINTS OF COMPARISON

Though a general comparison of agricultural labor unions in Kerala and those in other parts of India would be a major study in itself, it may be useful to note that the possibility of conflict between the interests of tenants and those of laborers is not confined to Kerala. In an analysis of the situation in Unnao District in Uttar Pradesh, Pandey provides some details about the Kisan Sabha [farmers' society] and some of its internal problems:

. . . on the eve of the second general elections . . . the Kisan Sabha was in a dilemma. On the one hand, it did not want, and perhaps could not afford, to neglect the problems of adhivasis whose main demand was the conferment of sirdari rights of tenure. On the other hand, it could not launch a district-wide agitation on the issue since many of its active workers were actually trying to retain their lands from the adhivasi cultivators. . . . In places where Communist workers were to lose their land, the pace of the movement was quite slow. But wherever the adhivasis constituted a significant membership of the Kisan Sabha and Communist Party, the movement was quite strong and the leadership of the Kisan Sabha concentrated their activities in those areas (1971:32).

Since its inception, the Kisan Sabha had been engaged mainly in seeking redressal of the problems of the farmers having some land under their possession. The problems of landless agricultural workers were always a secondary consideration. . . . While the farmers' fight has been directed mainly against the government and the big landlords, the landless workers' demands such as higher wages, better treatment, and greater share in produce in case the land was given to them on share-crop basis, had a direct bearing on the farmers who were deeply entrenched in the Kisan Sabha. . . .
   The formation of a separate organization solely for landless agricultural workers seemed to be the only solution to the organizational dilemma before the Communists. . . . 30 September 1959, when the Khet Mazdoor Sabha was formed . . . with a view to minimizing the possibility of any direct confrontation between the landless workers and the farmers, both under the control of the same political party, the major demand on which the organization campaign for the Khet Mazdoor Sabha was to be launched at local level was distribution of surplus and fallow land to the landless agricultural workers. . . .
   The Khet Mazdoor Sabha . . . could not make much headway for want of

effective leadership and, consequently, the landless agricultural workers continued to be represented by the Kisan Sabha till 1966 (1971:37–39).

Pandey points out that even this Khet Mazdoor Sabha never agitated for higher wages or ownership rights on the lands which they were cultivating (but which belonged to other farmers) because it would have resulted in the withdrawal of support by many farmers from the Kisan Sabha. What is striking in Kerala is that while there was no agitation for higher wages (except in Kuttanad) until the late 1960's, tenants were free to agitate for permanency of tenure. On the other hand, Pandey notes (1971:39),

The movement for the distribution of land to landless persons was launched in January 1970 . . . in areas where the village panchayats were either controlled by the Communists or were sympathetic towards them, the landless persons were directed to gradually and peacefully start cultivating waste and surplus lands.

In Kerala, there has not been any waste land or surplus land in the north Indian sense, since all land has been owned by individual families at least since the end of the eighteenth century and probably earlier as well. By that time, the only unoccupied land was forest land owned by aristocratic Nayars and a few Izhava and Muslim families. In Travancore, however, as well as in some parts of Cochin and Malabar, some of this unoccupied land has been settled by low-caste Christian migrants from the Travancore coastal belt. Thus in the 1970's the only surplus land included some forests which have remained under individual or corporate ownership. In 1971, the Kerala government passed a law confiscating the privately owned forest land both in order to settle some of the landless and to maintain the land as government forests. Parts of the bill were struck down by the Supreme Court, however, and at present (September 1972) the government is in the process of trying to find a way to get around the legal objections to the bill.

Thus land-grabs occurred mostly on land held by people who had more than the ceiling. In 1972, the CPM led a movement to occupy all such land. In an attempt to keep them from getting the credit, however, the CPI-led United Front claimed that it was taking action against all holders of excess land. The problems had not been completely settled as of the end of August 1972, and some influential people have reported that they personally know people who have managed to get away with holding more than they are allowed — indeed, a great deal more than they are allowed. Nonetheless, it is likely that eventually all large holdings will be confiscated.

CONCLUSION

One point that emerges clearly from this discussion is that, except in Kuttanad, agricultural labor unions in Kerala have only just begun to form. It seems that the main reason for the change that we are observing is the 1970 decision by the government to implement land legislation. In many ways, the Kerala land reform measures far outstrip any other such legislation passed so far elsewhere in India. In comparison with other parts of India, in Kerala the new legislation has actually made the tenants into the owners of the land on which they worked.[10] A series of methods of payment for the land was prescribed in the law, but in practice most tenants are simply not bothering to pay, thus leaving it up to the former landowner to appeal to the land tribunal. (There have even been some cases of hardship because of this, for example in the cases of owners of three or four acres who are elderly, or widows with small children, who have no alternative sources of income. But it is interesting to note that most of the large landowners anticipated the situation and have managed to find alternative sources of income.)

Until the land reform bill was passed and upheld (except for some minor provisions) by the Supreme Court, it was easy to mobilize tenant votes by focusing on tenancy reform and to mobilize laborers' votes by concentrating on land ceilings and redistribution (again, except in Kuttanad). The legislation also set fixed land ceilings, but there has not so far been much land recovered for redistribution as a result. While there are still some landowners in some areas whose holdings are far in excess of the ceiling, there has been considerable pressure by the CPM on the CPI United Front government to do something about confiscating such land and giving it to the landless. Even assuming, however, that they will be successful (and there is some expectation that the government may succeed because of its desire to be reelected), it will not mean much for the majority of landless laborers. It is clear that in Kerala today, with a population of over twenty-two million and a high rural population density, even with the present land ceiling (the lowest in all of India) only a small amount of land will be available for the landless. A family may get its plot of land for a house, but most of the landless will still have to work for wages in order to eat. Therefore, we now see arising in the countryside a new conflict which was only latent

[10]   In early November 1969, the minifront government declared that the Kerala Land Reform (Amendment) Act, 1969, would be implemented from January 1, 1970. It has taken a considerable amount of time, however, for land tribunals to be set up and for the government (reelected in 1971) to begin implementation. It is true that some of the large owners still have not given up any of their land (indeed, they have tried making all sorts of *benami* transfers or paying all political parties, especially the two Marxist parties, to keep off their land), but it is not possible that they will be able to keep really large holdings much longer. Most such holdings can be found in Kuttanad and surrounding regions and in the irrigated parts of Palghat District.

before (except in Kuttanad): that between laborers and employers. More precisely, the split is between those who labor for others (including both those who are truly landless and those who own tiny plots and cannot survive from their own produce alone), and those who employ laborers but do not labor for others. This latter group ranges from owners having land up to the ceiling (clearly middle class in their orientation) to smaller landholders who own paddy land and also have other sources of income (often from white-collar jobs). It is not possible at this point to draw a simple diagram based on the size of landholdings alone, but it is obvious that there is a group of landowners who stand in clear opposition to the demands of the agricultural laborers. These two opposing forces are buttressed by another group of landowners (all small, and primarily holders of garden land rather than paddy land) who neither work for others nor employ outside laborers.

What is beginning to happen today is that the landless, realizing that they are not going to benefit in many areas from land legislation, are now starting in increasing numbers to take to the new strategy of unionizing. It can be expected that they will be given the silent support of the self-employed small landowners. It is clear that land reform

. . . will not be complete simply by an imposition of family ceilings and the distribution of surplus land to the tillers. That is, of course, the condition precedent for a higher reform which means organization of voluntary cooperatives . . . for the purpose of creating an upsurge of agricultural production. . . . Experience of the socialist countries has revealed that small peasants can be brought into cooperatives only if the state gives them extraordinary facilities for scientific agriculture by supplying them with improved machineries, electricity, irrigation, seeds, and other amenities. . . . To achieve all these objectives, a powerful united peasant movement and a mass kisan sabha are indispensable (*Mainstream* 1972:10).

Today the peasant movement in Kerala has moved into the same stage that existed earlier in Kuttanad, namely that of conflict between laborers and managers or employers. As one of the agricultural officers put it to me:

Now that the tenants have the land, they, too, will experience problems. Now they will have to cope with the labor problems because the laborers will be thinking, "It is not theirs by heredity, so why shouldn't we also be getting something more?" And they will begin striking for higher wages all over, not only in the Kuttanad. In some places they will succeed, in others they won't.

It is clear that unionizing is more likely to succeed in places where laborers feel that they have something to gain from a strike. The places where this is true are primarily places where:

1. There are alternative sources of employment for villagers within commuting distance;
2. For one reason or another there is a labor shortage;

3. The laborers have for one reason or another broken from their former feudal attachments and are willing to go far afield (sometimes sizable distances) in search of work. It may be noted that often two neighboring villages differ in this regard;

4. It is imperative that paddy be harvested during a relatively short period of time. If the landowners are not willing to harvest the paddy themselves, strike actions are more likely to succeed. This point is well illustrated in the Kottayam area reported on by Fuller;

5. There are several agricultural labor unions all competing for members and trying to show that they can do more for their members than any other union. (For a fuller discussion of strikes, see Mencher 1975.)

In conclusion it should be pointed out that, rather than abating as a result of land reform, class consciousness is beginning to emerge as a vital force for change within the Kerala context. At the present time it is taking the form of the development of agricultural labor unions which agitate for higher wages and other rights for their members. These union organizations, though drawing their membership primarily from lower castes (who have always been lower in the economic hierarchy), do override traditional caste distinctions and can be said to represent a step in the conscious articulation of social classes (Mencher 1974).

REFERENCES

AIYAPPAN, A.
  1965   *Social revolution in a Kerala village.* New York: Asia Publishing House.
BÉTEILLE, A.
  1971   "Class Structure in an agrarian society: the case of the Jotadars." Mimeographed paper, University of Delhi.
  1972   Agrarian relations in Tanjore District, south India. *Sociological Bulletin* 21:122–151.
BÉTEILLE, A., *editor*
  1969   *Social inequality, selected readings.* Harmondsworth: Penguin Books.
CENSUS OF INDIA
  1971   *Census of India supplement: provisional population totals.* Delhi: Government of India Press.
Ceres
  1972   *Ceres.* Food and Agriculture Organization of the United Nations. May-June: 13.
DANDEKAR, V. M., N. RATH
  1971   Poverty in India 1. *Economic and Political Weekly.* January 2: 25–48.

DANIEL, P. H.
  1969   *Red tea*. Madras: Higgenbotham.
FIC, VICTOR
  1970   *Kerala: Yenan of India*. Bombay: Nachiketa.
GOPALAN, A. K.
  1959   *Kerala past and present*. London: Lawrence and Wishart.
GOUGH, KATHLEEN
  1961   "Nayar: central Kerala"; "Nayar: north Kerala"; "Tiyyar: north
          Kerala"; "Mappilla: north Kerala," in *Matrilineal kinship*. Edited
          by D. M. Schneider and Kathleen Gough. Berkeley: University of
          California Press.
  1965a Politics in Kerala. *Peace News*. January.
  1965b Village politics in Kerala. *The Economic Weekly*. February 20:27.
  1969   Communist rural councillors in Kerala. *Journal of Asian and
          African Studies*.
GREAVES, THOMAS C.
  1968   "Proletarians, patrons and clients in Viru." Paper presented at the
          70th Annual Meeting of the American Anthropological Association.
HJEJLE, B.
  1967   Slavery and agricultural bondage in south India in the nineteenth
          century. *Scandinavian Economic Review* 15 (1,2):71-126.
KUMAR, D.
  1962   Caste and landlessness in south India. *Comparative Studies in
          Society and History* 4 (3):337-363.
  1965   *Land and caste in south India*. Cambridge: Cambridge University
          Press.
KURIAN, GEORGE
  1961   *The Indian family in transition: a case study of Kerala Christians*.
          The Hague: Mouton.
LANDSBERGER, HENRY A., *editor*
  1969   *Latin American peasant movements*. Ithaca, N. Y.: Cornell Uni-
          versity Press.
Mainstream
  1972   Article in *Mainstream*. July 22:10.
Malabar land tenures
  1882   *Malabar land tenures* 2. Malabar Special Commission 1881-1882.
          Madras: Government Press.
MENCHER, JOAN
  1965   Social and economic change in India: the Namboodiri Brahmans.
          American Philosophical Society Yearbook 1964:398-402.
  1966   Kerala and Madras: a comparative study of ecology and social
          structure. *Ethnology* 5:135-171.
  1970   Change agents and villagers: an analysis of their relationships and
          the role of class values. *Economic and Political Weekly* 5. July.
  1974   "Group and self-identification: the view from the bottom." Indian
          Council of Social Science Research Bulletin. May.
  1975   "Agricultural labour movements in their socio-political and eco-
          logical context: Madras and Kerala," in *Festschrift in honour of
          Professor Aiyappan*. Edited by B. N. Nair.
MENON, A. S.
  1962-1965   *Kerala District gazetteers*. Trivandrum: Government Press.

Modernizing Indian agriculture
1960-1968 *Modernizing Indian agriculture: fourth report on the Intensive Agriculture District Programme* 2. Published by Ministry of Food and Agriculture, Community Development and Cooperation.

NAMBOODIRIPAD, E. M. S.
1949 "Occupational and employment structure of some Malabar villages." Unpublished Ph.D. thesis, Bombay University.
1952 *The national question in Kerala.* Bombay: People's Publishing House.

OOMMEN, T. K.
1971 Agrarian tension in a Kerala district: an analysis. *Indian Journal of Industrial Relations.* Reprint 15. Shri Ram Centre for Industrial Relations, New Delhi.

PANDEY, S. M.
1971 The emergence of peasant movements in India. *Indian Journal of Industrial Relations.* Reprint 14. Shri Ram Centre for Industrial Relations, New Delhi.

PANIKAR, P. G. K.
1972 *Dissension to report of the Kuttanad Enquiry Commission.* Trivandrum: Government Press.

PATNAIK, UTSA
1972 Development of capitalism in agriculture. *Social Scientist* 1(2): 15-31.

PILLAI, V. R., P. G. K. PANIKAR
1965 *Land reclamation in Kerala.* Bombay: Asia Publishing House.

RAO, M. S. A.
1957 *Social change in Malabar.* Bombay: Popular Book Depot.
1970 "Caste and joint family in Kerala," in *Essays on sociology of economic development and social change.* Bombay: Popular Prakasam.

Report of the Committee on Unemployment in Kerala
1971 *Report of the Committee on Unemployment in Kerala* 1. Trivandrum: Government Press.

Report of the Kuttanad Enquiry Commission
1971-1972 *Report of the Kuttanad Enquiry Commission.* Trivandrum: Government Press.

SHAH, S. A.
1969 *Structural obstacles to economic development.* New Delhi: People's Publishing House.

SINGH, JITENDRA
1959 *Communist rule in Kerala.* New Delhi: Diwan Chand Indian Information Center.

SLATER, GILBERT, *editor*
1918 *Some south Indian villages.* Madras: Oxford University Press.

THOMAS, P. J., K. C. RAMAKRISHNA
1940 *Some south Indian villages: a re-survey.* Madras University Economics Series 4. Madras: Madras University Press.

THORNER, DANIEL
1956 *The agrarian prospect in India.* Delhi: Delhi University Press.

THORNER, DANIEL, ALICE THORNER
1962 *Land and labor in India.* Bombay: Asia Publishing House.

VARGHESE, T. C.
1970 *Agrarian change and economic consequences: land tenures in Kerala 1850-1960.* Bombay: Allied Publishers.

WOLF, ERIC
  1969   *Peasant wars of the 20th century.* New York: Harper and Row.
ZAGORIA, DONALD S.
  1971   The ecology of peasant communism in India. *American Political Science Review* 65 (1):144–160.

Caste Elements
Among the Muslims of Bihar

ZEYAUDDIN AHMAD

The state of Bihar is in the eastern side of the Indian Union with a population of over 50 million. It is situated between 22° and 27° North, and 83.5° and 88° East. To the north and south of Bihar lie the Himalayan kingdom of Nepal and the state of Orissa, respectively. The states of Uttar Pradesh and Madhya Pradesh fall in the west, while West Bengal is situated in the east. It had been a part of Bengal during a long period of British rule in India, and it was only in the year 1912 that it was administratively separated, and a lieutenant governor was appointed there. The river Ganges flowing down from the Himalayas divides the state into northern and southern regions. The northern part is composed of the fertile plain of the Ganges and its tributaries, while most of the southern portion is hilly and covered by the Chotanagpur plateau, famous for its mineral deposits and traditional abode of the aboriginal tribes of Bihar, numbering 2.2 million.

This state contains the highest Muslim population in India, after Uttar Pradesh. According to the census figures of 1971, there are roughly 7.6 million Muslims, i.e. 13.48 percent of its total population, residing in the state. The greatest concentration of the Muslim population lies in the Purnea district (adjacent to West Bengal), followed by Darbhanga and Champaran. Bakhtiyar Khilji in 1195 established the first Muslim rule in Bihar. However, only in the days of Sultan Mohammed Tughlak (1325-1351), was it brought under full control of the Delhi administration. Thereafter, a band of Muslim merchants, *sufis*, and saints made regular contacts with the local population and preached the teachings of Islam vigorously among them, with the result that mass conversion of the local people became a common phenomenon. Mention may be made of the efforts made by Shaikh Yahya Maneri (fourteenth century A.D.), Hazrat Makhdoom Sharfuddin Yahya Bihari, Qazi Shahabuddin Pir Jagiot, Sharfuddin Tawana, Maulana Nizam Maula, Qazi Ola Shuttari, and others, who did a commendable job in this connection.

It is now a well-known fact that the existence of Arabian, Persian, or Afghan strains in the present Muslim community of Bihar is negligible in comparison to the local population. The *Census of India* (1921:I(1), 227) reports: "The great majority of Muslims in this subcontinent are the descendants of the Hindu converts. In 1911 it was estimated that 85 percent of the Punjab Muslims were of native stock. In the rest of India the proportion must have been greater." The more we proceed to the eastern side of India, the more the percentage of the progeny of the converted Hindus goes on increasing.

Further, for the small minority in Uttar Pradesh, Bihar or Bengal, it was neither practicable nor desirable to keep themselves aloof from the local population. The Muslims of foreign origin therefore settled down, and started developing relations — social, cultural, commercial, etc. — with the local people. As a result of this longstanding cultural contact both communities were mutually influenced by each other. Tarachand (1946:137) observes:

The Muslems who came to India made it their home. They lived surrounded by the Hindu people and a state of perennial hostility with them was impossible. Mutual intercourse led to mutual understanding. . . . Thus, after the first shock of conquest was over, the Hindus and Muslims preferred to find a *via media* whereby to live as neighbors.

The effort to seek a new life led to the development of a new culture which was neither exclusively Hindu nor purely Muslim. It was indeed a Muslem-Hindu culture. Not only did Hindu religion, Hindu art, Hindu literature and Hindu science absorb Muslem elements but the very spirit of Hindu culture and the very stuff of the Hindu mind were altered and the Muslems reciprocated by responding to the change in every department of life.

The Hindu masses were groaning under the tyranny of the caste system. Low-caste Hindus, and especially the Shudras and the out-caste people, had to suffer a lot. Analyzing the causes of mass-scale conversion of the local people to Islam, Ram Gopal remarks:

The so-called low-caste Hindus lived under many social disabilities. As a knife goes into a melon without much effort, so did Islam penetrate into these castes with little persuasion. Many came forward to free themselves from degrading oppressions and raise themselves and their descendants in the social scale. Islamic equality coupled with the powerful influence of Muslim merchants made conversion a daily occurrence (1964:2).

It is an established fact that the missionaries flourished more on the evils of Hindu society than under the patronage of Muslim rulers, for they won a far larger number of converts in those parts of the country where low-caste and outcaste Hindus abounded than in the centers of the Muslim government.

The position of Hindu women in general and the widows in particular had been far from satisfactory. Young widows were compelled to lead a wretched life. The supreme religious duty that they could perform was to burn themselves on the funeral pyres of their husbands. They were excluded from religious and other social ceremonies because of being considered ill-fated. On the other hand, the priesthood among the Hindus, which had degenerated into debauchery, allowed its members to have any number of wives. The result was that there existed a seething discontent among women and the general Hindu masses.

Young widows, wherever Muslim missionaries happened to meet them, were told that they had committed no sin to deprive them of the pleasures of this world, and that Islam showed liberation to those in distress. A widow became a bride once again; an untouchable drew water from a common well to which he had been denied access when he was a Hindu, such was the power of Islam (Ram Gopal 1964:7).

The low-caste Hindus had a deep-seated aversion to the caste system and its tyrannical rules. In accepting Islam they not only got rid of the degrading treatment at the hands of the caste Hindus, but they also were convinced that they would be treated as equals by their foreign coreligionists and share their political power and style of life. In order to attain their lifelong ambition they had to imitate foreign ways and even to abjure their ancestral patterns of livelihood.

The Hindu religion had a wide exit but no entrance, whereas the doors of Islam have been always open to incoming Hindus, who for one reason or other, had been made outcastes.

The spread of Islam in Bihar and Bengal had been a gradual process. As the number of people of foreign descent was not particularly high, it was all the more necessary to win over the support of the local people, either by converting them or by pacifying them. This necessity implied some sort of compromise with the local customs and beliefs. Therefore, on the one hand, the Muslims, because of sociocultural compulsions and partly because of their present strategy, adopted local rituals and practices, while allowing the converts to retain most of their habits and customs.

Granted the well-known absorptive power of Hinduism, it is not surprising that many of the nominal converts retained much of their former religion, and that indeed Islam underwent considerable Hinduization in India. Because of conversion and because of interbreeding between Muslim men and Hindu women, the Muslims became racially indistinguishable from the Hindu population. Even the Muslim rulers were in many cases descendants of Hindus, having Hindu mothers and grandmothers (Davis 1951:192).

All these facts led to large-scale Hinduization of the Muslims in this country. Complete Islamization of the converts was neither possible nor practicable. The impact of the idolatrous surroundings upon them was great. Moreover, their neighbors and many of their relatives were still Hindus. It is little wonder, therefore, that the worship of the village godlings was sometimes performed as before, that in places animistic beliefs continued, and that Brahman priests were still employed and Hindu festivals observed. The wonder is not that these hereditary customs and beliefs were adhered to but that some of the teachings of Islam were strictly observed. "It is natural therefore that the caste system should permeate Muslim society. The mere switch of religious alliance . . . could hardly incur a complete change of social life" (Davis 1951:164).

Blunt gives a detailed account of the Malkhana community in Uttar Pradesh:

There are converted Hindus of various castes belonging to Agra and adjoining districts. . . . They are reluctant to describe themselves as Muslims and generally give their caste names. . . . These names are mostly Hindu. They mostly worship at Hindu temples. They use the form of salutation *Ram Ram* and intermarry mostly among themselves only. On the other hand, they sometimes frequent a mosque, practice circumcision, bury their dead, and they eat with the Muslims. . . . They admit they are neither Hindus nor Muslims, but a mixture of both (Blunt 1911:118).

There are numerous such communities, particularly in the eastern region, where we notice survival of Hindu rituals centering around birth, marriage, and death; worship of many gods and goddesses, as, for example, Krishna and Durga; and retention of the Hindu manner in the singing of songs, playing music, shaving of hair, observance of unclean periods, ceremonial feeding of pregnant women (*sada vakshan*), wearing of conch shells and bangles, fasting during lunar eclipse, abstinence from eating fish and meat after a death, chewing of betel leaves, engagement ceremony (*mangani*), applying *sendur* [red powder, i.e. vermilion], observation of *sharadh* [death ritual], *Diwali* [festival of lights], *Holi* [color festival], consultation of Brahmans for fixation of auspicious days, etc.

Islam aims at the establishment of an egalitarian society in which there should be no distinction among men on the basis of family, birth, or caste. The philosophy of Islam centers around two basic principles: the oneness of God, and brotherhood among men. Islam considers Allah as the single and personal God, and all Muslims are equal in the sight of Allah. The Koran (sura 49,13) explicitly declares: "O ye men! Verily, we have created ye, of male and female . . . verily the most honorable of ye in the sight of God is one who feareth him most."

But in actual practice gradations among Muslims existed even from the days of the Caliphs. When Islam came to stay in India in the twelfth century, its social organization had already changed. Although the concept of equality and brotherhood remained as an ideal — as an ideal it still exists, even to this day — in practice there had been social grades within Muslim society. Twelfth-century Muslim society in India was distinctly divided into priests, nobility, and all the others, such as soldiers, merchants, artisans, etc.

The Hindu society, on the other hand, had the very old and organized social institution of the caste system. Hutton (1961:2) considers it to be an essential part of Hindu society, with a history of growth of some three thousand years or more. To do away with caste would mean to jettison the whole structure of their society. Srinivas considers caste to be "the structural basis of Hindu society" (1970:212). This system broadly divided Hindu society into four major castes — Brahmans, Kshatriya, Vaishya and Sudra — while each of these was further subdivided into a number of subcastes. Hutton says that there are some 3,000 castes in India and it would need an encyclopedia to deal with them all (1961:12). Every individual was born into a caste, with a definite name, occupation, status, and social function, and the obligation to obey the caste restrictions. As Ghurye (1961:4) observes, ". . . castes are small and complete social worlds in themselves, marked off definitely from one another, though subsisting within the larger society." He enumerates (1961:2) the characteristic features of caste society as follows:

1. segmental division of society,
2. hierarchy,
3. restrictions on feeding and social intercourse,
4. civil and religious disabilities and privileges of the different sections,
5. lack of unrestricted choice of occupations,
6. restrictions on marriage.

This caste organization depends upon distinctions among men, the extreme case being the observance of untouchability and the procedure of declaring individuals as outcastes on the basis of their violation of the rules of food or intercourse.

It was thus partly the direct age-old contacts with the Hindu community and partly the large-scale conversion of Hindus, especially from the lower castes, which resulted in the development of certain aspects of the caste system among the Muslims. The new converts, though they accepted the theoretical foundations of Islam, could not erase the deep-rooted customs and traditions of their original caste society. The Muslims, after long cultural contact, acquired them from the Hindus. Thus, after emphasizing the democratic nature of the teachings of Islam, the *Imperial Gazetteer of India* (1908:329) observes, "In India, however, caste is in the air; its contagion has spread even to Mohammedans and we find its evolution proceeding characteristically on Hindu lines." We thus find that there are groups and classes of people among the Muslim population in Bengal, Bihar and Uttar Pradesh — as in the rest of India — who are organized in groups more or less like the Hindu castes.

They are similar in many respects to the Hindu castes, with the only difference being that they are less rigid, because of the influence of the teachings of brotherhood preached by Islam.

. . . in spite of the influence of Hinduism on Islam in India, there has always been a greater mobility and flexibility in the Islamic system. But, at the same time, the Hindu caste organization left its mark on the Indian Muslem social system in spite of the contrary effort of Muslem reformer priests (Karim 1956:123).

In his article "Islam in Bengal," John Talke makes the following observations about the Muslim community: "Socially, the community has had the misfortune to inherit the traits of both Hindu and Muslim forebears. Caste prejudices have left their mark upon many. There are about thirty-five Muslim castes in Bengal" (1914:12).

In this way we find that through contacts and conversion the Muslim society borrowed caste elements. But a caste system just like that of the Hindus could never evolve in their community. The concept of caste pollution and thereby the institution of untouchability is alien to Islam. It was a peculiar blend, on one side, of an egalitarian society believing in the universal brotherhood of mankind and, on the other, of a caste-ridden society torn by internal differentiation. Crooks is quite correct when he holds (1921:9):

Islam in its orthodox type does not permit the differentiation of its followers into castes. In theory, at least, all Mohammedans are brethren and can eat together and, though endogamy is the rule among certain tribes and castes, particularly in the case of those families which claim Arabic or Persian lineage, there is nothing to prevent intermarriage with strangers. But among the class of converts from Hinduism the laws of endogamy and exogamy still have force, and the rules prohibiting eating with a stranger to the group are observed.

Blunt (1931:189) differs with part of this observation on the ground that a Muslim may marry any woman outside the prohibited degree, and therefore "the Hindu caste system is entirely incompatible with the tenets of Islam." Again, according to him, Sayyid, Shaikh, Pathan and Moghul are not castes; though usually spoken of as such, they are not even tribes. "They are merely names given to groups of tribes that are supposed to be of similar blood."

The *Census of India* (1901:I (1), 543–544) listed 133 castes wholly or partially Mohammedan. The present-day Muslim society in India is broadly divided into four major groups. These are: (1) the Ashraf who trace their origin to foreign lands such as Arabia, Iran, Turkestan or Afghanistan, (2) the Hindus of higher birth who were converted to Islam, (3) the clean, occupational castes, and (4) the converts from the untouchable castes: Bhangi [scavengers], Mehtar [sweepers], Chamar [tanners], etc.

These four groups fall into two sections, Ashraf and Ajlaf (or Atraf). The first, meaning noble or of high family, includes all Muslims of foreign blood and converts from higher Hindu castes. Ajlaf, meaning degraded or unholy, embraces the remaining low-ranking converts. In Bihar, as in Uttar Pradesh and Bengal, Sayyids, Shaikhs, Moghuls, and Pathans constitute the upper-caste Muslims, i.e. the Ashraf, while the Ajlaf are carpenters, painters, artisans, glaziers, tanners, milkmen, etc.

According to the *Census of India* (1901), "In some places a third class, called Arzal or 'lowest of all' is added. It consists of the very lowest castes, such as the Halalkhor, Lalbegi, Abdal, and Bediya, with whom no other Mohammedan would associate, and who are forbidden to enter the mosque or to use the public burial ground." There are Arzals in Bihar but untouchability does not extend to their not being allowed to enter religious places. We find here some sort of discrimination against them in social gatherings and wedding feasts. Once these people wash themselves they are considered clean, and without hesitation they can go to a mosque and pray with their coreligionists.

The weekly gatherings of *Jumā* [Friday] and the annual prayers of Id and Bakrid bring Muslims of different occupations and classes together, where if anyone shows even the slightest evidence of hatred, i.e. untouchability, towards another person he is to be condemned. Therefore I do not find, at least in Bihar, any instance when Halalkhors or Lalbegis are refused admission to religious places, particularly mosques. But so far as social gatherings, festivals or dinner parties are concerned, such distinctions are observable. Personally, I feel that even this is mainly due to the existence of class consciousness and is certainly not the result of caste or professional hatred.

The Ashraf castes are to be taken as an integral part of the Muslim society in Bihar as elsewhere in northern India. They definitely rank highest and enjoy the greatest position and prestige in the community. The moment we accept the fact that the Muslims in India have a caste system, however modified, we must come to the conclusion that the Ashraf constitute the highest strata in that hierarchy. Their position in the Muslim community corresponds broadly with that which the Brahmans and Kshatriyas, grouped together, enjoy in the Hindu community. Thus, Sayyids and Shaikhs are the priestly caste like the Brahmans, and the Moghuls and Pathans, famous for their chivalry, are equal to the Kshatriyas. In Bihar, we have the Mullick caste instead of Moghuls. The term *mullick* means "chief" or "king." The Mullicks claim to be the descendants of Mullick Mohammed Ibrahim, the respected commander-in-chief in the days of Sultan Mohammed Tughlak, and Sayyid by caste. Once the king called him, adding Mullick to his name, and thereafter he was generally called Mullick. Sayyid Ibrahim, after conquering Bihar in 1334, was murdered here (Khajapuri 1935).

Then there are occupational castes who are considered lower castes in the hierarchy. Among these people there are different grades and classes who maintain a hierarchical relationship on the basis of their occupations, which are often hereditary. These castes have hereditary names based on their occupations and there is a definite tendency among them to practice endogamy. These castes constitute the bulk of the Muslim population in Bihar. They are descendants of members of the Hindu clean castes who have been converted to Islam either in groups from the different castes or as whole castes. Now there are castes which are wholly Muslims; others in which the population is predominantly Muslim, and again others in which the population is overwhelmingly Hindu.

Castes which have 100 percent Muslim population are: Atishbaz [fireworks maker], Bhand [jester], Bhatiyara [innkeeper], Julaha [weaver], Mirasi [musician], Qassab [butcher], Faqir [beggar], Nanbai [baker], Bhishti [water transporter] and Mir Shikar. The following are the castes which have predominantly Muslim population: Darzi [tailor], Dhuniya [cotton carder], Kunjra [greengrocer], Manihar [bracelet maker], Saiqalgar [metal sharpener], Rangrez [cloth printer], Chunihara [bangle keeper] and Kalal [brewer]. Castes with larger Hindu population than Muslim are: Dhobi [washerman], Kumhar [potter], Nai [barber], Gaddi [glazier], Guala [milkman], Halwai [sweetmaker], Kaber [palanquin bearer], Sonar [goldsmith], Teli [oilpresser].

Besides these two classes mentioned above, there is a third section of the Muslim in Bihar (also in Uttar Pradesh and Bengal), i.e. Arzal [lowest of all]. The members of the Arzal class normally cannot associate with the Ashraf class. They pursue the meanest and most degrading occupations and are called Bhangi, Mehtar, Halalkhor, Lalbegi, etc. Thus there are roughly thirty-one caste-like groups among the Muslim community in Bihar.

The upper-caste Muslims — Shaikh, Sayyid, Mullick and Pathan — are to a very great extent endogamous, but there have been instances when they have married among one another. But as far as the lower castes are concerned, upper-caste Muslims have married their daughters off and on, but they have never married their own daughters to lower-caste men. The *Census of India* (1901) comments that "in spite of the theoretical equality in Islam of these classes with one another and with fellow-Mohammedans of native origin, the influence of the Hindu caste system has brought certain distinctions of its own, and the so-called hypergamous system is in vogue amongst the Ashraf." To maintain their purity of blood as well as class distinctions, endogamy was adopted by the Ashraf group.

To me it appears that Ashraf and Ajlaf, representing two different sets of castes, are factually two different classes among the Muslims. Besides their claim of foreign descent, the Ashraf group enjoyed maximum economic advantage. Mainly big landlords, *jagirdar*s, and *nawab*s constituted this class. Education was also to a very great extent confined to them. The result was that the Ajlaf were not only people converted from the local Hindus, but in most cases they were economically poor and educationally backward too. The Julahas, Dhuniyas, Qassabs and such other occupational castes which formed the bulk of the Muslim community all had a very low standard of living. Political power, economic advantages and social privileges centered around the Ashraf castes.

The Ashrafs in Bihar maintained their purity of blood by being endogamous. But, in most of the Ashraf families, it had become an established practice for a man to keep one or two women from the lower-caste people or even from the low-caste Hindus. Neither these wives nor their children enjoyed positions of equality with the children of the first wife, who belonged to a high-caste family. Thus in all the well-to-do Ashraf families there were two lines of descent: one line constituted the children of the high-caste wife, while the other line of descent originated through the wives of low castes. Such children were always given lower positions in society than the children of the high-caste wives. Such women were married on the payment of a very low amount of *mehr* [dowry], and their children were never given shares equal to the children of the high-caste wife. Out of such hypergamy and through concubines a new caste in Bihar developed called Malzada, the progeny of low-caste women. They were always considered a second line of descent, much inferior in status and privileges to the children of the first wife. With the abolition of the *zamindari* system, however, this practice has also come to a halt.

The upper-caste Muslims tried to maintain their caste pride by practicing a sort of endogamy among themselves and by abstaining from interding or mixing on equal terms with the lower-caste Muslims. Nesfield (1885:123) also held that "they can intermarry with each other . . . whatever the tribe of the woman may be, her children take the rank of the father." Thus, in view of the facts observed in the Muslim community in Bihar, I fail to agree with the observations made by Ghaus Ansari (1960:139) when he says that "the rules of endogamy among Ashraf castes are far more strict than those observed by the lower strata. The tendency for preserving the purity of blood among Ashraf castes has been predominant." I think that his conclusions are wrong, at least in the case of Bihari Muslims, where there are numerous examples of intercaste marriages among Ashraf castes. There is no doubt about the fact that the first preference has always been, by and large, their own caste. However, as far as lower castes were concerned the Ashraf had practically no marital relations with them.

I also differ from the views of Hutton (1961:52-54) as well as Blunt (1931:201) when they assert that among the Ashraf castes rules of hypergamy were observed. The fact is that in Bihar when intercaste marriages took place, daughters of Shaikhs, Sayyids, Pathans and Mullicks were married without discrimination of caste. Practically, it was education, income and property that usually determined the relative status of the castes in a particular area. Hence there are cases where Sayyid girls were married to Shaikh or Mullick boys. There are also numerous instances of marriage between Shaikhs and Pathans.

As far as the lower-caste Muslims are concerned, the practice of endogamy is strictly observed among them. In this connection the statement made by Blunt is very correct even for the Bihari Muslims:

The marriage customs of groups descended from Hindu converts to Islam often exhibit a curious mixture of Hindu and Muslem rites. Contrary to Muslem customs almost all of these groups are strictly endogamous, and many are split into smaller sections that are also endogamous. Some castes restrict the Muslem custom of cousin marriage, and many preserve more or less completely the Hindu wedding rites. The Bhat goes further still; he carries out first a Hindu wedding in its fullest form, and then follows it up by a Mohammedan ceremony. Rules of adoption, inheritance, divorce, and remarriage are often more Hindu than Muslem. In fact, most of those castes of Hindu converts preserve some trace of their former marriage customs; and many preserve a great deal (1931:201-202).

Among lower-caste Muslims, except for the ceremony of *Nikah* [consent by boy and girl], the lengthy process of marriage is replete with Hindu rituals. At some places Hindu gods and goddesses are prayed to for the welfare of the wedding couple. I feel that it is in the marriage rituals that the maximum influence of Hinduism is to be noticed. Singing of songs, use of vermilion on the forehead of the girl, typical dresses used, joking with the in-laws, display of fireworks, participation in *Holi* and *Diwali* festivals and the like, are all Hindu impacts upon Muslim marriage and society which are obviously most common among the Muslims of Bihar.

A sort of social survey was conducted by the author regarding social stratification among the Muslims of Bihar with the help of some post-graduate students preparing for their masters' theses in 1971. The research was done through a well-designed questionnaire administered to 800 Muslim respondents, selected on a random basis, living in a few Muslim localities in the city of Patna, the capital of Bihar.

It was found that 85 percent of the Muslims of higher castes married within their own castes. Out of the 15 percent of respondents who married into castes other than their own, it was found that Shaikhs have married amongst the Sayyids or vice versa, i.e. upper-caste Muslims have married to some extent among themselves. But there was not a single case where a high-caste Muslim married into a low-caste family. The low-caste Muslims were 100 percent endogamous, i.e. all of them married within their own caste groups.

Those respondents in the younger age groups (under fifty years) expressed the desirability and benefit of intercaste marriage among Muslims. About 50 percent of the respondents expressed their willingness to marry off their own daughters and sons without the least caste consideration. Old people, above fifty years, were totally against intercaste marriage, though they themselves declared that Islam does prohibit such segregation and endogamous marriages. Generally among people in the younger group of Muslims, caste-mindedness in marriage and in social life has much less appeal.

Again, the respondents were given some qualifications of a prospective bride and groom, and they were asked to select three of them. It was found that 75 percent were inclined to consider factors other than caste. For example, education, income and personal qualities of a boy were considered more important than his caste. In the same way they considered education, family background, beauty and dutifulness as desirable qualities in a girl. Only 25 percent of the people mentioned caste as one of the three desirable qualities. This indicates that in the younger generation there is a growing class consciousness, and caste considerations are proportionately receding into the background.

Another question put to the respondents was related to the caste stereotypes which one caste group ascribes to other caste people. The result shows that among the high-caste Muslims there is little tension, as, on the whole, they ascribed good traits to each other. But up to 30 to 50 percent attributed unfavorable traits to the low-caste Muslims. Surprisingly enough, the low-caste groups have largely — 60 to 75 percent — ascribed bad traits to each other, while a very low percentage, 15 to 25 percent, ascribed bad traits to the high-caste Muslims.

This means that high-caste Muslims are on the whole held in high esteem, and they enjoy a better social position even in the eyes of lower-caste Muslims. But among the lower-caste Muslims there exists some sort of psychological tension, which may be due to a feeling of growing competition for the achievement of higher social prestige and position.

The present-day Muslim community in Bihar, more than any other region in India, stands at a three-way junction of modernity, Islam, and Hinduism. It is in an amorphous stage now. What final shape will come about depends upon the interaction of numerous forces at work. However, my own impression is that the impact of Hinduism, and particularly of caste characteristics, is getting weaker with the passage of time. There are political, economic, religious, and other reasons for this.

In the first place, the process of large-scale conversion from Hinduism to Islam has practically stopped for the last fifty years. The emergence of the Muslim League and the development of communal feelings among the Hindus, urged by Hindu Mahasabha and Arya Samaj, are primarily responsible for this. No doubt the policy of divide and rule adopted by the British government also is to be blamed for this. The advocacy of a two-nation theory propounded by the Muslim League created a gulf between Hindus and Muslims, which culminated in the division of British India into present-day India and Pakistan. The leadership of the Muslim League was provided by the feudal landlords, aristocrats, lawyers, and men of big business, who had little knowledge of the socioeconomic life of the people. This political conflict manifested itself in the economic, social, and religious spheres, with the result not only that the Hindu masses were kept aloof from the Muslims in general, but that there was also a complete alienation of the Hindus from Islam. Islam, instead of being considered the bearer of a dynamic ideology, has created a sense of inferiority among the Muslims of India, and we may consider the establishment of Pakistan as the acceptance of final defeat on the part of the Muslims. Kipling Davis (1951:191) rightly maintains that "the partition of the region into Pakistan and the Union of India was the admission of final defeat so far as the Muslim conquest of India is concerned." Thus, on the one hand, the exodus of Hindus to Islam was completely checked and, on the other hand, there was an increasing feeling of community consciousness among the Muslim masses. They drifted away more and more from the Hindu social life. Being cut off from day-to-day contacts with the majority community, the Muslim masses gradually were reduced to a position of cultural minority. Analyzing the tension and distance which developed because of this communal feeling, Mujeeb (1967:554) remarks, "Muslem participation in Holi and Diwali, as well as Hindu participation in Moharram and the anniversaries of saints was gradually reduced owing to communal tension.''

Coupled with this there had been movements for the revival of Islam raising their heads every now and then. The fall of the Mogul empire and the ascendancy of the British were taken to be the punishment given to the Muslims by God because of their deviation from the right path and indifference to Islam. In Uttar Pradesh and Bihar a number of Muslim *Ulemas* [religious heads] established institutions of learning and training for the purification of Muslims from the Hindu and Western impacts.

The Wahabi movement launched by Syed Ahmad Barailvi in 1826 was a politico-religious movement. On the one hand, it aimed at throwing out the British rule from India and, on the other, it tried to purify the day-to-day life of an average Muslim to the pattern and standards of Islamic faith, as practiced and preached by the Prophet Mohammed. Thousands of Muslims were attracted toward this movement and people, particularly from the lower castes such as the Momins [weavers] and Kunjra [grocers], joined it in large numbers, partly because of its political motivations and partly because of their inner desire to be treated on equal terms with the higher-caste Muslims. After producing a great stir in the sociopolitical and religious life of the Muslims, it did succeed in getting the Muslim community to shed quickly Western as well as Hindu customs and rituals from their social life.

In 1867 there were the Deobandi and Barailvi movements which simultaneously, but in different ways, attempted to make the masses into good Muslims. They did the least to convert the non-Muslims to Islam but confined their activities to reforming Muslim society from within. A new sect of Qadiani Muslims was developed by Mirza Gholam Ahmad (1839-1908). Apart from some of his controversial principles, he succeeded in establishing the most active missionary body among the Muslims with branches in many parts of the world.

Then, towards the middle of the twentieth century, two other religious movements came to the fore — the Jamaat-e-Islami, founded by Maulana Abul Ala Maudoodi (1941), and the Tablighi Jamaat (1920-1930), a group of preachers organized by Maulana Mohammed Ilyas of Mewat (Uttar Pradesh). These two created a religious stir among the Muslims, and even after the creation of Pakistan their activities continued in both India and Pakistan. Maulana Maudoodi, now the head of the Pakistani Jamaat-e-Islami, organized a team of dedicated workers and writers for the cause of Islam. He is a prolific writer with forceful language and a very logical and coherent style of writing. He preached that the establishment of *Deen-e-Ilahi* [the divine system] in the world was the basic purpose of the existence of Muslims. He produced a vast literature on Islam which has had a powerful appeal for the Muslims, especially the intelligentsia.

The Tablighi Jamaat confined itself mostly to oral preachings and has a great following among the masses. I feel that the Jamaat-e-Islami and the Tablighi Jamaat are complementary in this respect, as both of them teach purification of life to Islamic ideals and have a band of dedicated workers. The former is much more organized, with branches in different parts of the country.

The cumulative impact of these religious movements has been a great revival of Islam, and they have all succeeded in mobilizing Muslims to act according to the Shariah, or Islamic way of life. In India, after the creation of Pakistan, the religious movements made a vast appeal to the Muslims, and lots of changes started taking place in their social life. Even the young men could not remain indifferent to the impact of this transition. Thousands of educational institutions, where religious teachings were imparted to youngsters, were opened throughout northern India, and particularly in Bihar and Uttar Pradesh.

It may be called a period of Islamic renaissance in India. My impression is that during the last twenty-five years or so the Muslims have been more religious-minded. They are offering prayers more regularly and punctually, observing the Ramadan fasts and trying to act upon the teachings of Islam very meticulously.

In this process of Islamization, on the one hand, Muslims remained aloof from the impact of modernization as much as practicable and, on the other hand, the general masses purified themselves more and more from the influences of Hinduization or Indianization. The entire gamut of social life was put under serious scrutiny and an attempt was made to screen out the non-Islamic practices systematically. In customs, rituals, festivals, ceremonies, and social life in general, the Islamic way of life started gradually replacing the Hindu traits, including the caste elements.

On the economic front there were great and far-reaching changes taking place in India. In Uttar Pradesh and Bihar the Muslims were a minority, while they enjoyed a majority in Punjab and Bengal. In Uttar Pradesh and Bihar, however, they had been given many privileges by the British government. There were large numbers of Muslim landlords, *jagirdar*s and *nawab*s in these provinces, the educated Muslims were being given good positions in the administration, and Persian and Urdu were the favorite court languages.

After the partition of the country and independence of India a number of changes took place. Many Muslims migrated to Pakistan, particularly to East Pakistan, thereby creating an intellectual and economic vacuum in the Muslim communities of Bihar and eastern Uttar Pradesh.

Moreover, the national government in India abolished the *zamindari* system, which broke the backbone of the aristocracy in general and that of the Muslims in particular. Now the Muslims found themselves economically crippled. They were never good cultivators or business-men. In services, too, the Hindus got preference partly due to feelings engendered by the partition and mainly because of their superior educa-tion and training. This created a sense of utter frustration and help-lessness among the Muslim masses in India.

These politico-economic changes influenced the Muslim community profoundly. The lower-caste Muslims, hitherto neglected and to some extent despised by the upper-caste Muslims, were in a much better posi-tion in every respect. They were professional groups and were not much concerned about the Hindu-Muslim politics. They continued to live in this country even after the partition and, by and large, stuck to their hereditary occupations. Therefore, even by the abolition of *zamindari* they could not be affected in the least.

On the other hand, the national government started paying more and more attention to the depressed castes and classes. In educational insti-tutions and welfare schemes they were given preference and special consideration. These people had rather a better socioeconomic position in the changed political setup in Bihar. The weavers of Bhagalpur and Biharsherif, and the *bidi*-makers of Jhajha and Monghyr were getting good dividends for their past loyalty to the Indian National Congress and their opposition to the two-nation theory of the Muslim League. Now, economically and educationally, the balance was tilted in favor of the lower-caste Muslims, and the so-called high-caste people were lag-ging far behind them. Any socioeconomic survey can show this glaring difference between these two sections.

The introduction of a democratic constitution in India also helped the lower-caste Muslims a great deal. By virtue of their numbers they were being elected to the local bodies, assemblies, and Parliament more than the upper-caste Muslims. Thus, politically, economically, and socially they are much better off than they were in the days of the British government or even during Muslim rule. This equality in their status brought them on a par with, if not higher than, the high-caste Muslims.

Another factor, which contributed to the reduction of caste barriers and feelings of superiority and inferiority among the different sections of Muslims, was the socioeconomic life of the people in Pakistan, par-ticularly in East Pakistan. As a result of partition there was a large exodus of Hindus from East Pakistan and vice versa, and a great emigration to that country of Muslims from Bihar and eastern Uttar Pradesh.

Pakistan, being a new theocratic state, provided opportunities in services and business to the new Muslim immigrants, who were all termed "Biharis." These so-called Biharis in the erstwhile East Pakistan (now Bangladesh) enjoyed the highest positions in services and very preferential treatment in business and industries. The result was that young people earned much more than their qualifications, experience, or labor justified. It was one reason why a lot of young men, graduates, doctors, engineers, and others migrated there every year in large numbers. Their income was definitely much better than that of their counterparts in Bihar or anywhere else in India. The young migrants of lower-caste groups, eager to be called Ashraf, high-caste family men, declared themselves Shaikhs and Sayyids after attaining a better life economically. That they have already started changing their caste names and adopting higher-caste nomenclature may be evident from this proverb which was quoted in the *Census of India* (1901): "Last year I was a Julaha; now I am a Sheik, next year if prices rise I shall be Sayid." Partly through lack of knowledge and partly through deliberate connivance on the part of high-caste Muslims there, many of these boys managed to marry into Ashraf families, and the number of such undeclared but approved intercaste marriages went on increasing by leaps and bounds with the passage of time. At first this produced some resentment among Muslims living in Bihar and Uttar Pradesh, but gradually they became reconciled to such marriages. Many of them also contracted such marriages, though the number of these is still not very high. But once the ice was broken it was not uncommon to find high-caste girls being married to low-caste boys, provided they were well educated and had a good earning capacity.

Over and above these factors, the forces of modernization have also influenced the Muslim community in Bihar, as elsewhere in India, very profoundly. The growing pace of industrialization in Bihar, the expansion of urban centers, the spread of modern education, expanding knowledge of science and technology, and the opening of new avenues of employment have changed the Muslim community a great deal.

Gradually the Muslims are getting modern education in large numbers. Even the girls are going to educational institutions on buses, trams, and other vehicles. Muslims are getting jobs in factories and firms. Hundreds of young men are going to foreign countries every year and bringing new ideas and modes of living back with them. These forces are leveling the socioeconomic disparities which once existed between high-caste and low-caste Muslims.

As far as the impact of Hinduism is concerned, the forces of both Islamization and modernization are lessening it rapidly, and though these two forces have different ideological backgrounds, in this respect they have helped the Muslim community in Bihar to get rid of caste traits. Also, with the opening of new avenues of employment and the increasing tempo of caste mobility, differences between different castes are already being blurred, and in the case of the Muslim community particularly, social distance between them is fast disappearing.

Given the tempo of modern forces and the growing consciousness of the Indian Muslims of the evils of caste differentiation, we may well expect that twenty-five years hence different caste groups may exist with different names, but the system of endogamy and feelings of superiority and inferiority will gradually fade out of this community. The Muslim community in Bihar is in a stage of transition.

The religious movements launched among Muslims during the last 100 years, and the political, economic, and social changes, together with modern forces, are continually weakening caste barriers among Muslims. The caste system is, of course, a negation of the basic teachings of Islam. As such, caste elements had always had a sort of uneasy adjustment in the body politic of the Muslim community. Hence, in the case of Muslims, unlike Hindus, religion has helped in shedding caste traits to a very great extent.

We must also keep under consideration the fact that, of late, there has been a growing tendency on the part of the low-caste Muslims to imitate the mode of life and practices of the upper-caste Muslims, especially the Shaikhs and Sayyids. They have already started changing their caste names and, with increasing income and education, many are calling themselves by Persian names and tracing their ancestry from the West. Julahas are Ansaris, Kunjaras are Rains, and so forth. Not only have they changed the caste nomenclatures but they are also tracing their origin from Arabian or Persian heritage. Having a better socioeconomic position in the modern setup, they are in the very comfortable position of fulfilling their long-cherished desire — they have started living just like the Shaikhs and Sayyids, so far as their mode of life, dress styles, and practices are concerned. On the other hand, the higher-caste Muslims are tending more and more toward a modern way of life. They are becoming increasingly Westernized. Among them the twin processes of Islamization and Westernization are at work, just like the process of Sanskritization and Westernization operating in the Hindu community as envisaged by Srinivas (1970:1-46). We may take the practice of *Purdah* [remaining within the four walls], for example. Twenty years ago, upper-caste women observed *Purdah*, but now this practice has been increasingly adopted by the low-caste Muslims, while the upper-class Muslim women, under the impact of modernity, are coming out of their homes, doing marketing, and sometimes not wearing veils as they walk in the streets of big towns. The time is fast approaching when the low-caste

Muslims will also adopt modern ways of life in large numbers. That will further erase the differences not only between the high- and low-caste Muslims, but also between different communities living in India.

Among the Hindus the caste system still persists because of its religious sanction. In this democratic socialistic pattern of society, in which vast technological and scientific changes are taking place, the caste system has no place. The practice of untouchability has already been declared a punishable offense according to the Indian constitution. Among the Muslims, religion does not support any sort of distinction between different groups of the community. Therefore, any sociological analysis, based on the above-mentioned trends, will not fail to notice the declining influence of caste in the Muslim community.

By experience, the community has learned that now there are only two alternatives before it — modernize or perish. No doubt, the forces of modernity are, in every way, overwhelming, and have already made deep inroads in every sphere of life. But traditions die hard. Islam has proved its vitality in spite of many odds. It depends now upon the forces of modernity and religion to prove their relative acceptability in the community.

A sociological study of tradition and modernity among the Muslims of Bihar is long overdue. We have yet to decide whether there is a basic antagonism between modernity and Islam. Islam being a world religion, this question is relevant everywhere on the globe. Is Islam a negation of modernity? If not, should the community find a way out to reconcile the tenets of Islam with the postulates of modernity? Then, how is Islam to be modernized, or in other words, into what type of social structure should the modern Muslim community evolve? Let the social scientists, thinkers, and religious teachers come forward to solve this burning problem and suggest a practicable approach.

REFERENCES

ANSARI, G.
1960   *Muslim castes in Uttar Pradesh.* Lucknow, India: Ethnographic and Folk Culture Society.
BLUNT, E. A. H.
1931   *The caste system of northern India.* London: Oxford University Press.

CENSUS OF INDIA
   1901   Volume 1, part 1:543–544.
   1911   Volume 1, part 1:118.
   1921   Volume 1, part 1:227.
CROOKS, W.
   1921   "Introduction" to *The Qanune Islame* by J. Sherif. London: Oxford University Press.
DAVIS, K.
   1951   *Population of India and Pakistan.* Princeton, New Jersey: Princeton University Press.
GHURYE, G. S.
   1961   *Caste, class and occupations.* Bombay: Popular Book Depot.
GOPAL, R.
   1964   *Indian Muslims.* Bombay: Asia Publishing House.
HUTTON, J. H.
   1961   *Caste in India.* London: Oxford University Press.
IMPERIAL GAZETTEER OF INDIA
   1908   Volume II.
KARIM, N. A. K.
   1956   *Changing society in India and Pakistan.* London: Oxford University Press.
KHAJAPURI, A. H.
   1935   *Tarikhe Mullick* [History of the Mullicks]. Patna.
KORAN, THE
   n.d.   Sura 49, 13.
MUJEEB, M.
   1967   *The Indian Muslims.* London: Oxford University Press.
NESFIELD, J. C.
   1885   *Brief view of the caste system.* Allahabad: Indian Press.
SRINIVAS, M. N.
   1966   *Social change in modern India.* Bombay: Asia Publishing House.
   1970   *Caste in modern India.* Bombay: Asia Publishing House.
TALKE, J.
   1914   Islam in Bengal. *The Muslim World* 4(12).
TARACHAND
   1946   *Influence of Islam on Indian culture.* Allahabad: Indian Press.

Ecological Adaptation to Technology — Ritual Conflict and Leadership Change: The Santal Experience

SITAKANT MAHAPATRA

This paper is based on microstudies of the southern Santals (Mayurbhanj District in Orissa). The historical perspective is the Sanskritization process, the solidarity-emulation conflict, and the internalization of emulated traits prior to the Santal revolt of 1949. The traditional leadership is ritual-based and puristic. The modern leadership is the product of political democracy (*panchāyati raj*) and secular technology. Confrontation, sources of authority, patterns of "envy," and role differentiation show intimate linkage with the solidarity-emulation nexus. These emergent forces seem much more complex than the "rank concession syndrome" suggested in Orans' (1965) study. The ritual-based leadership often transforms itself into modern political-technological leadership and is then more successful, effective, and acceptable to both the encysted society and the encompassing greater society. Migration and industrial employment are less powerful, but the drive for the new OL script, the emphasis on nonparticipation in "mixed" functions (the Jatra Pata Enez Gira movement), and the reinterpretation of tradition, myths, and identity symbols by Guru Gomke Raghunath Murmu (particularly as reflected in his plays *Bidu-chandan* and *Kherwar Bir*, which are being translated into English) give new dimensions to the technology-ritual conflict. The experience has perhaps wider relevance: the dilemma of reconciling the cultural autonomy of tribal politics with socioeconomic integration.

Anthropologists Redfield and Singer used the concepts Great Tradition and Little Tradition in analyzing the part played by cities in the development of culture. Orans adopted the model and designated the twentieth-century growth pangs in Santal society as a search for the Great Tradition. Since a Great Tradition incorporates qualities of a systematic and well-integrated world view, a self-conscious substructure of ethical mores, and a degree of expressiveness regarding its individual excellence *vis-à-vis* neighboring communities, Orans also looked into the growth, dynamics, and distortion of these qualities in the historical process. A Great Tradition calls for a psychological proclivity for justifying the present "fall" in terms of historical decadence due to a greater community encompassing it and for a tendency to romanticize the past. Orans studied this in relation to the solidarity-emulation conflict and proposed his theory of the "rank concession syndrome." I will not go into the details of this particular thesis which is, in spite of its inadequacies, an extremely useful instrument for understanding the solidarity-emulation conflict in Santal society. Orans, however, based his study primarily on areas where migration, market economy, and industrialization were key factors in social change. He devoted special attention to a study of social change in the Jamshedpur urban area and the areas adjoining it. Among the southern Santals, however, forces of industrialization and market economy are of marginal importance.

It is the evolution of political democracy and the imposition of the three-tier system of *panchāyati raj* on the existing structure of tribal society which need to be studied for a proper appreciation of social change. The working of political democracy in a predominantly agricultural tribal community steeped in ritual and tradition has given rise to a peculiar confrontation between the "old" and the "new" leader which, in turn, has significant impact on the solidarity-emulation conflict. This paper aims at highlighting some of the more important interactions of these two forces which, it is felt, have relevance not only for the economic growth of the area, but also for the future evolution of Santal society.

The historical evolution of southern Santal society was, in some respects, significantly different from that of northern Santal society because of the enlightened Maharaja of Mayurbhanj, who made conscious attempts to foster amity and good relations between the Santals and the nontribal Hindus in what was then Mayurbhanj State. Historical records demonstrate the interest successive maharajas took in this matter. For example, during the annual Car festival (*Rath Jatra*) at Baripada, the Santals were encouraged to come and participate in the function in a big way, and a sense of involvement in the festival was always evident, generally supporting the view that Lord Jagannath was initially the god of the tribals.

Chaitra Parva [spring festival], the annual *Chhow* dance festival at Baripada, also drew Santals in large numbers. The ritualistic base of the Hindu *Chaitra Parva* and the *Chhow* dance closely resemble the Santal flower festival (*Baha Parab*). Archer (n.d.) rightly compares it to the Christian festival of Easter, since the two festivals correspond to "an exaltation in the brilliant weather and the flowering trees and the sense of sprouting life." Both celebrations coincide with the advent of spring, when the bitter winter of the hills is at an end, there is a virtual resurrection of life in nature, and the trees are full of new leaves and flowers. *Chaitra Parva*, which falls in April, has the twin aspects of spring's delicate wistfulness and the vibrant energy of the coming summer. It is the time when the *sal* trees are in blossom everywhere and the mild spring sun is fast transforming itself into the mighty Sun God roaring in the empty blue of the April sky.

The Santals have the *Pata* festival in mid-April. In Mayurbhanj and Singhbhum the *Pata* festival has essential similarity with the *Bhokta* ritual. This used to be associated with the *Uda* of the swinging-by-hook festival which has been declared now a criminal act by legislation because of the danger to human lives. It is not only the Santals: the Mundaris and Oraons of Singhbhum and Sundergarh Districts also observe during April the famous *Sarhul* festival. This is the beginning of the hunting excursions for the Mundaris and Oraons (Mahapatra 1971:2-3).

The *Bhokta* ritual of the *Chaitra Parva*, starting from the seventeenth day of *Chaitra*, was, in several interesting ways, similar to the *Pata* ritual.

The *Bhoktas* used to take to fasting like the *Patuas* before the Goddesses. These *Bhoktas* sing *Bhajans* before the Goddess and Mahadev in the last four days culminating on the *Pana Shankranti* day. They perform four different *Pata* ceremonies called *Kanta Pata* [walking or rolling on thorns], *Nian Pata* [fire-walking], *Jhula Pata* or *Ugra Tapa* [hanging, head down, on fire] and *Uda Pata* [rotating on a horizontal pole] (*Mayurbhanj Gazette* 1932).

Thus the Santals and the non-Santal Hindus participated in a single matrix of festivities.

During *Durga Puja* and *Holi* there were also many common functions and much mutual participation. The integration at the level of the masses was encouraged by the political authorities, who constantly sought to internalize the emulation of these Hindu concepts and traditions. This internalization presented no problem since the Santal community was not divided in terms of modern economic classes. The virtual nonexistence of the *nouveau riche* rendered such internalization a simple process. The traditional village leader was simultaneously responsible for maintaining his higher rank within the community, utilizing it as a bridge to the greater society and the political authorities, and also maintaining both the internal and the external solidarity of the group. Thus, right up to the merger of the state with Orissa and the Santal revolt in 1949, there was hardly any conflict between the solidarity-emulation nexus and the leadership pattern.

The merger of the state with Orissa in 1949 gave a serious jolt to this smooth relationship. The dissatisfaction and resentment of that year led to widespread agitation, which seriously threatened law and order. One of the major objectives of the agitation was noncooperation with the Dikkus, the non-Adivasis, in all possible ways. The suppression of the disturbances by force, the application of the penal provisions of the law, and the imposition of a punitive tax became the starting point for a new political "rank path." The elite in Santal society took full advantage of the resentment and sought to give a new meaning, a new dimension and urgency to the question of internal and external solidarity. There was a demand for a refund of the collective fines imposed on the tribals.

An Adivasi Cultural Association came into being in 1953 and proposed the adoption of the OL script. Among the objectives of the Association were (1) to make the Adivasis (Mundari group) literate with the help of OL script; (2) to enrich the Mundari literature by collecting old songs and traditions; (3) to write and publish books for classroom reading; (4) to encourage Adivasi songs and dances; (5) to publish and disseminate a paper on social ideas. The Association, subsequently renamed "Adivasi Socio-Educational and Cultural Association," has continued to be vocal in their efforts toward fostering recognition of the OL script and revival of the old Santal tradition. It publishes a monthly paper, *Sagen Sakam*, and insists that the Santal religion is not Hinduism but Sarana and the common language Mundari, for which the OL script suggested by Pandit Raghunath Murmu should be recognized. It is significant to note that on February 25, 1973, about ten thousand Santals came in procession to Calcutta and presented to the Chief Minister of West Bengal a memorandum asking for the recognition of OL script (*Statesman* 1973).

It is interesting that in one of the Association resolutions there was a reference to the recognition of the community headman as the authority in settling "social disputes." This is significant as a recognition of the continuing operational value of the traditional leader and the difficulty of settling disputes through the agency of the political system of *panchāyati raj*.

At this point it is worthwhile to discuss the evolution of two conflicting patterns of leadership within the Santal community, and their interaction. The traditional leader derived his authority from his hereditary position and his knowledge of folklore and the social mores. More often than not, he was illiterate. He dressed and lived like everybody else in the village, even when he possessed vast wealth. With the coming of the *panchāyati raj* in 1957, a new pattern of political leadership based on election was virtually grafted onto this traditional society. Of the three levels of the *panchāyati raj* institution, the two important levels, namely the *panchāyat* and the *panchāyat samiti*, had an unsettling effect on the traditional leadership and its relation to the community. It was no longer possible for an illiterate Santal to take up the tasks and responsibilities of this new kind of leadership, the demands of which were different. If the traditional leader was primarily concerned with social and ritual functions, the modern leader had to grapple with problems of welfare and political issues. Somewhere a road was to be improved, a school established, or a well sunk. These welfare aspirations had to be taken up and transmitted to the higher authorities. There arose the problem of articulation of the aspirations and their transmission vertically upwards.

In a traditional society articulation of modern aspirations is difficult, often distorted, and always inchoate. Their transmission is thus extremely complex. Against this background it became clear that the new leader must be one who is attuned to these stirrings of aspiration and who at the same time has access to higher authorities through his sophistication and modernity. His material culture should be akin to that of the powers that be. It is desirable that he know the language of the authorities. Thus the new leader was to derive his power from outside, and power was to be merely the economic equivalent of the benefits that were to flow into Santal society from outside. The elective principles no doubt made it necessary that the new leader have roots within the community and the necessary degree of popularity. But his primary support was from outside; and popularity, it was discovered, was a quality that could be manipulated and maintained by a flow of such benefits. A new "benefit nexus" as the primary determinant of leadership was thus established.

Three patterns emerged from this situation. First, the traditional leader *adjusted* himself to the new leader, and there was a differentiation of roles and functions, the former looking after the ritual, religious, traditional social functions, and the latter concerned with the economic, technological, modern welfare functions. The second development was a kind of *confrontation* between the old and the new leaders and their conflicting demands on the community. The third was a kind of *transformation* of the traditional leader into the modern leader. Microstudies conducted by this author in a large sampling of areas at *panchāyat* level reveal the relatively higher efficiency of this third kind of transformed leadership and its developed skill in maintaining internal solidarity while ensuring the flow of economic benefits from the political authorities. This leadership also largely frees the society from inner tensions and renders internalization of emulated traits a smooth process.

The contra-acculturative process which started in the late 1940's had two main objectives: to arrest the process of Sanskritization and complementary Westernization, and simultaneously to close the widening *social distance* between the *elite* and the *folk*. It is necessary at this stage to emphasize the point that ecological adaptation is not a static concept: it involves the dynamics of multilevel changes and their continuous interaction. Burman (1972b) has broadly categorized these changes as physical mobilization, social mobilization, and biosocial response. The low level of physical resource mobilization in the areas inhabited by the southern Santals and the consequent low level of *social capital* make the biosocial response of the masses in Santal society to the growth process, and to the leadership which is its agent, a highly ambivalent phenomenon. The common man is enamored of the benefits, which he knows can flow only by a recognized political rank path and through the new political leader. Orans (1965) has rightly referred to Santal society as being a *tradition-justifying*, rather than a *tradition-directed*, society. Moral rules in such a community are in a curious matrix with solidarity:

Though the facts of any particular issue must be decided upon the basis of evidence presented, true moral rules are felt to lie in the matrix of the traditional cultural heritage. Thus when it is a question of deciding what the rules are or ought to be, the *people* ostensibly consult the unwritten records of their tradition (Orans 1965:18)

This phenomenon, fully corroborated by the microstudies conducted by the author in the Mayurbhanj area, militates against the political rank path. The elite in Santal society, to use the formulation of Gramsci in another context, functions like an "organic intellectual." To Gramsci, such intellectuals are obsessed with their class interest. The Santal elite of the new political and technological type is actually conscious of deriving rank from the political process. There remains an unbridged gap, a margin of contradiction, between the goal orientation of this class and the goal orientation of the community as a whole.

The power of the new political elite is secular and is based on neither folklore nor folk religion. To continue in authority, however, it must derive strength from the matrix of a society steeped in ritual. Here is the essential contradiction in the new political elite's objective of maintaining the solidarity of the tribe and at the same time retaining its image as culture heroes to the masses within the tribal community. It is against this background that we must look at the role of the elite in the following three areas of activity: (1) the demand for a separate script for the language; (2) the reinterpretation of tradition, primarily in the works of Pandit Raghunath Murmu; and (3) the movement generally known as Jatra Pata Enez Gira (not to dance or participate in mixed functions with the Dikku [the nontribals]).

There is one more important difference between the traditional old rich and the modern political new rich which deserves mention. During various festivals such as *Makar, Baha*, etc., and especially at marriages, the wealthy headman was traditionally required to provide the villagers with food, *handia* [rice-beer], and other forms of pleasure. This was a kind of informal channel for the flow of wealth from rich to poor and functioned as an equilibrant of privileges. The modern political rich are neither fond of participating in social functions nor keen to spend money for such purposes. This creates a gap, a social distance, between the tribal mass and the modern elite, a cleavage between power and ethos. Though the traditional leader, with his knowledge of folklore, still represents the Santal ethos and its world view, the modern power structure is accessible to the new leader. A division within the community is thus created.

In earlier times the cultural distance between rich and poor was also minimized by the similarity of material culture. Community solidarity was not much disturbed by wealth differences. But the new leader differs from the common man in dress, habits, etc. In such a situation there is envy due to increased visible wealth difference.

The relationship of the new leader to the traditional society also tends to become impersonal and contractual, and sometimes it is difficult to adjust this to the continuous informal relationship characteristic of a traditional kinship society. In Santal society, even today, "a common body of traditional customs, common language and folklore, tradition including myths and conformation to the same pattern of social relationships are the greatest binding factors" (Kochar 1964:25).

The elite has sought to discourage participation in the festivals of nontribals. This is expressed by Shri Sonaram Soren, onetime minister in Orissa State (1954:1-4):

Historical tradition reveals that dancing in non-tribal festivals was not our custom. Our ancestors lived in the countries of Chaigal, Champagal, Bahagal, etc. and led simple, hard-working lives. The women used to paint walls with such magnificent figures that when we were driven away from those countries there was a pathetic song that ran like this: "Brothers, we have left behind those figures of musicians and dancers engaged in songs and dances painted on the walls of the houses in Champagal. What pangs, what regrets to come away leaving those treasures. . . ."
Our ancestors have given us songs and dances for all occasions beginning from birth to death and also for different festivals: The birth songs, marriage songs, death songs, *Baha* songs, *Mahmane* songs, wedding songs, *Dahar* songs, *Karam, Sohrai, Dantha* and *Dasein* songs. Besides these, there are also *lagene* songs for celebration and enjoyment on any occasion. But the ancestors never provided that Santals should dance in the festivals and celebrations of other communities. The more powerful and clever people have asked us to dance during Mahadev Puja, Car festival (*Rath Jatra*) and *Dola Purnima*, and other festivals. They have thrown up different temptations and

baits for the purpose. But we should preserve our heritage and should stop dancing in such public functions of non-tribals for ever.

This call not to dance or participate in the festivals of nontribals has, however, received slow and mixed response from the masses. The process of acculturation and assimilation has gone quite far and the masses are not as consciously aware of the need for keeping away from these nontribal functions as the elite. An elite member of the tribe once asked the local government officials to insure that the non-tribals in an urban center, Rairangpur, would not sprinkle colored water on the tribals during *Holi*. But it has been observed that the common men in the villages, where tribals and nontribals live together, have not bothered about this and have gladly participated. Perhaps this is a logical outgrowth of intercommunity dynamics; cultural symbiosis between the two units has become inescapable, and no pursuit of rank path, political or economic, can fully prevent it. To quote Sahlins (1968):

. . . a widespread recognition that cultures act as selective forces upon one another, and with it the realization that culture-contact creates complementarity, not merely similarity in structure, seems imminent.

The Santals have always looked back to a glorious historical tradition. The Santal mythology of the nineteenth century has extensive references to a mighty Santal kingdom. In different myths, such as the myth of creation and the myth of the great migration, the unity, the power, and the subsequent gradual decline of the Santal Great Tradition are stressed. These traditions, as Culshaw (1949) reported some time ago, are more intimately known and felt among the tribal masses. Among the new leaders the tradition has an academic value and is used for its utility in an intellectual formulation. Even though references are made to the myths and the traditions, they are probably not "felt in the blood" and lived by.

The Santal Rebellion of 1855–1857 was the result of the accumulation of a large number of grievances, the more important among which were the following:

(a) grasping and rapacious money lenders;
(b) personal and hereditary debt-bondage;
(c) corruption and extortion by police helping the money-lenders; and
(d) the impossibility of the Santal getting court-redress (Culshaw and Archer n.d.).

The rebellion had awakened an awareness of political power and of the pathways to political rank primarily among the northern Santals but also among the southern Santals. (The memory of this rebellion was refreshed in the 1949 revolt in Mayurbhanj.) Some Hindu customs, such as putting on the sacred thread, ritual use of sun-dried rice, oil, and vermilion, and purification with cow dung, were adopted during the rebellion. This process, as mentioned earlier, continued almost until the end of the 1940's. Roy (1912) noted the conversion of a large number of Santals to Hinduism in a village in Orissa.

Instead, the elitist culture has now moved along two different lines. First, it has attempted a codification of the Santal tradition and its reinterpretation. This cultural innovation, started by Pandit Raghunath Murmu (founder of the Sarna Dharam Semlet [Sacred Grove Religious Organization]) has far-reaching implications for the Santal community. This innovation was made immediately before the census of 1951 so that the Santals could "return their religion as Sarana." In the hands of Pandit Raghunath the concept of religion has been given a universal significance, a world view, with the purpose of teaching the people to live "peacefully with belief in the deities." In his epic play *Kherwar Bir*, the Santal equivalent of the *Mahabharat*, Pandit Raghunath emphasizes right duty and conduct, the old myth of functional division between the different Santal clans, and a charter for present independence. Much historical and archaeological material is brought up by the elite Santals to justify the historicity of the play. Pandit Raghunath's other drama, *Bidu-chandan*, seeks to reinterpret the Santal tradition and give it a world view and contemporary relevance. Along with inventing the OL script, Pandit Murmu is responsible for perhaps the most sophisticated reinterpretation of Santal mythology and tradition in a manner accessible to the new society. It is possible that, given time, this reinterpretation, which the modern political elite has sought to popularize, will catch the imagination of the rank and file.

Second, there is emphasis on the celebration of Santal festivals simultaneously in all areas, to prevent their falling on the same days as Hindu festivals. But this measure has met with limited acceptance and support from the rank and file as it takes away the advantage of the spread effect of a festival over a longer period and thus militates against the Santal pleasure principle.

The tribal languages of Orissa are oral, with no script of their own. Among them, Santali is spoken by the largest number, the Santals in Orissa, Bengal, Bihar, and Tripura. In 1932 the Reverend P. O. Bodding, the missionary lexicographer, listed more than 25,000 words in his Santali dictionary. Though no up-to-date survey is available, this author feels that the vocabulary has now doubled. Santals have an unusual feeling for adapting words from other languages. Linguists and anthropologists have referred to their "sharp sense for fine shades of meaning." The useful work of the missionaries in their field and the "new linguistic ethnocentrism" have made Santali "one of the most cultivated tribal languages" (Aiyappan 1963-1964:5).

The geographical distribution of the tribe and the consequent problem of education with Oriya, Bengali, Devanagari, and Roman scripts have highlighted the need for a single script as a unifying factor. Attempts have been made to trace references to a lost script in the folklore, though there is hardly any reliable evidence of its existence. The tribal leadership has sought to evolve a new script that would answer the sound patterns of pronunciation and the needs of writing and printing technology. The OL script introduced by Pandit Raghunath Murmu meets some of these requirements and, through Kherwal Jarpa Samity and later the Adivasi Socio-Educational and Cultural Association, official acceptance has been sought.

The movements for a separate script, for nonparticipation in Hindu festivals, and for the reinterpretation of myth and tradition have thus yet to become part of the heritage of the folk. It is in this context that the "rank concession syndrome" of Orans shows some peculiar features among Mayurbhanj Santals. "Fear and envy of the Dikku as the clever cheat and the big and new people" is very much in evidence.

But the *nouveau riche* political leader has also occasionally been misunderstood, and there have been difficulties in accepting him as a culture hero. The leader has realized that he cannot rehabilitate himself fully in the traditions of the tribe. He may even be doubtful whether the entire tradition need be retained. He finds it difficult to acquire real depth in the knowledge of folklore so popular with the common Santal. Orans (1965:129) is right when he observes:

. . . increased political power promises reward to every one of the society though it may be specially advantageous to an elite. To be achieved it requires cooperation and a solid front of opposition against competing societies.

The actual developments in the past two decades in Santal society, as in most other tribes, reveal, however, that the rewards of increased political power have benefited different strata of the tribal society differently and that the benefits are minimal for the common man. At the same time, there is a growing awareness of the death of the distributive concepts of the earlier social organization in which the riches of the traditional leader flowed liberally and voluntarily to the less privileged during social functions. That distributive channel has now become almost completely silted up. On the other hand, the observation of Orans (1965) that "pursuit of rank through economic improvement, at least within the context of an *essentially* [italics mine] market society, has the opposite effect" has limited relevance for the southern Santals. The social environment is not dominated by a market economy, and therefore the pursuit of rank through individual economic gain does not always lead to centrifugal tendencies.

The political rank path of the 1940's and 1950's has now come to a dead end. There is a growing awareness that this path has created as much cleavage as solidarity within the Santal community. The interaction of (1) internal solidarity versus flow of material benefit from outside and (2) the traditional leader versus the modern leader has unsettling effects on the entire society. The Great Tradition seems to be a long time in coming. In the meantime, the surrounding society has made systematic inroads on the vulnerable larger sections through the conferring of economic benefits such as increased road construction, educational facilities, and a general opening-up of the interior. These are perhaps inevitable concomitants of the process of economic growth.

The common man in Santal society has a tendency toward greater political-economic integration with the larger society around him, to him apparently the most effective way of bringing in economic benefits from outside. Within his own society he finds that the conflict between the new and the old leader is endemic and many-faceted. He is thus caught up in the ambivalence between the Great Tradition and the demands of socioeconomic welfare; between the traditional folklore, ritual, and myth and modern technology; and between the political *nouveau riche* and the traditional leader steeped in folklore.

This may be looked upon as part of the complex process of the adjustment between the political-economic integration of encysted societies with the greater community around them as a result of the growth process, and the preservation of cultural autonomy. The dominant ethos of ritual structure is in conflict with new developments of secular democracy and technology. The Santal finds himself helpless in this new situation. He must perhaps discover a *modus vivendi* that will take him out of this impasse. As Burman says (1972a):

The crisis of modern man has made growing numbers of tribal *elites* conscious of the fact, that there is no single great tradition to be emulated. This has led to the search for new meaning in their age-old tradition, to invest the same with the ethos of universalism and to project tribalism as an alternative great tradition.

In the years ahead the elite in Santal society must merge the "rank concession syndrome" with the new demands of cultural autonomy and the inchoate longing for economic growth and integration in the context of secular democracy. The tribal will no longer be satisfied with an academic Great Tradition while being treated as a cultural "museum specimen" to be studied by the elite from the city.

REFERENCES

AIYAPPAN, A.
  1963-1964   Tribal languages of Orissa. *Adibasi* 3:5.
ARCHER, W. G.
  n.d.   *The blue grove*. London: Allen and Unwin.
BURMAN, B. K. ROY
  1972a   "An approach to the cultural policy in respect of the tribal population of India." Paper presented at the seminar "Towards a Cultural Policy for India," organized by the Indian Institute of Advanced Study, Rashtrapati Nivas, Simla, June 5.
  1972b   "Social process in the hills of east India: an ecological perspective." Paper presented at the National Seminar on Social Change, organized by the Institute of Social and Economic Change, Bangalore (in collaboration with the Indian Council of Social Science Research and the Indian Institute of Advanced Study, Simla), November 3-7.
CULSHAW, W. J.
  1949   *The tribal heritage*. London: Lutterworth.
CULSHAW. W. J., W. G. ARCHER
  n.d.   The Santal rebellion. *Man in India* 25:4.
KOCHAR, V. K.
  1964   Attributes of social status among the Santals. *Bulletin of the Cultural Research Institute* 3 (3, 4):25.
MAHAPATRA, SITAKANT
  1971   "Chhou dance of Mayurbhanj — the tasks ahead," in *Souvenir of Chaitra Parba*. Edited by Sitakant Mahapatra. Baripada: Mayurbhanj Chhou Nrutya Pratisthan.
Mayurbhanj Gazette
  1932   *Mayurbhanj Gazette* 1:3. April.
ORANS, MARTIN
  1965   *The Santal: a tribe in search of a Great Tradition*. Detroit: Wayne State University Press.
ROY, S. C.
  1912   *The Mundas and their country*. Calcutta: Calcutta City Book Society.
SAHLINS, M. D.
  1968   "Culture and environment: the study of cultural ecology" in *Theory in anthropology*. Edited by R. A. Manners and David Kaplan, 367-373. Chicago: Aldine.
SOREN, SONARAM, *editor*
  1954   *Jatra Pata Enez Gira*. Cuttack, Orissa: Rashtrabhasa Cooperative Press.
Statesman
  1973   Article in *Statesman*. February 28.

The Santalization of the Santals

MOHAN K. GAUTAM

The Santals are a large tribe of wet rice growers who cultivate the slopes and valleys on and around the Rajmahal hills in the northeastern part of South Asia (see Figure 1). They belong to the Kolarian and the Munda linguistic families, classified under the Austroasiatic group of languages (Dalton 1872:207; de Josselin de Jong 1965:363; Grierson 1906:30; Risley 1891:224). The bulk of their population is concentrated in the Indian states of Bihar, Bengal, and Orissa; the tea plantation areas of Assam, Meghalaya, and Tripura; and the southeastern part of Nepal, the northwestern part of Bangladesh, and the southern part of Bhutan. According to the Government of India Census Survey of 1971, they number over three million people.

In the past 150 years the Santal tribe has been one of the most extensively studied groups in India (Bodding 1942; Bonnerjea 1927; Culshaw 1949; Dutta-Majumdar 1956; Hunter 1897; Man 1867; Mukherjea 1962; Orans 1965; Sherwill 1851). In spite of the mass of documentation, compilation, monographical description, administrative reports, government handbooks, gazetteers, census reports, etc., the Santals are still the focus of some interesting questions which must be answered for the objective and empirical understanding of the process of change in their multidimensional relations with ethnic and nonethnic groups.[1]

During the first half of the twentieth century most of these works

---

[1] Ethnic groups are those which live together with the Santals in more or less the same economic and ecological surroundings. In the district of Santal Pargana they are Paharia [hill-dweller], Mahli [basket maker and palanquin bearer], Maraiya [iron-smith], Mirdha [musician and leather worker], and Ghatwal [field laborer and cultivator]; and the Hinduized castes: Pal [potter and cultivator], Mandal [oilman], and Mal [cattle tender]. The nonethnic groups are the Hindu castes, such as Dhobi [washerman], Napit [barber], Bhagat [distiller and shopkeeper], Rajput, Ksatriya, Kayastha, and Brahman.

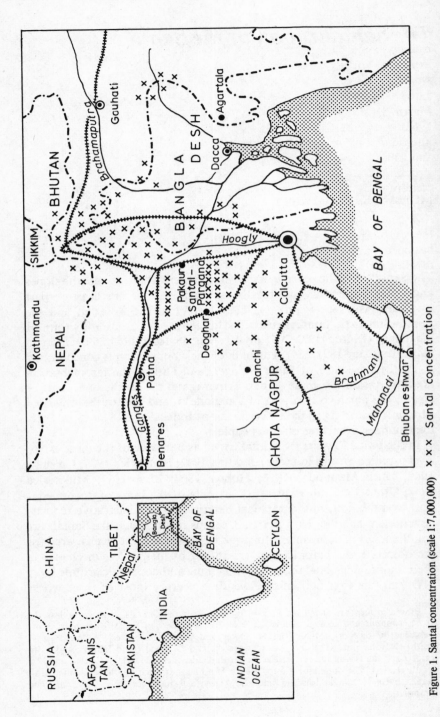

Figure 1. Santal concentration (scale 1:7,000,000) × × × Santal concentration

tried to explain the Santals descriptively. The tribe was isolated and examined with little consideration for its relations with neighbors. The expansion of anthropological research after World War II brought new working concepts, such as acculturation, folk society, folk tradition, Little Tradition, Great Tradition, Sanskritization, etc. (Foster 1953; Marriott 1969; Redfield 1956; Singer and Cohn 1968; Srinivas 1942, 1962). Here the research focused more on the Santals' relations and interdependence with their neighbors. Folk tradition, little community, and folk society, and other such concepts were aimed at analyzing the structure of the little tribal and rural communities, whereas the concepts of Great Tradition and Sanskritization tended to focus on the rural-urban continuum and the universalization of Hinduism.

A change from Little Tradition to Great Tradition was considered the result of the process of Sanskritization, which in the Santal context has been a process of accepting, adopting, or following the conventions of Hindu tradition: wearing, for instance, the *poeta* [sacred thread]; employing the services of priest and barber;[2] worshiping Hindu deities; observing rituals, feasts, and festivities; accepting ideas of pollution and purity during life crises; using *sindur* [vermilion] at marriages and following a three-generation marriage formula; observing cremation rites; and adopting Hindu names. Such practices definitely give the impression that Santals are moving toward Sanskritization and Brahmanization[3] and that they have accepted the Hindu model of superiority and caste ideology (Orans 1965).

A contrasting view is that although the Santals, like neighboring communities, have accepted some of the Hindu conventions, they are not trying to *Sanskritize* themselves. Whatever they select and assimilate is meant to strengthen the solidarity of their community. Furthermore, this acceptance is centered on the problems of land, production and distribution of available resources in relation to the neighboring groups. One might, however, ask whether or not the Santals really need the Brahmanical ideal of Sanskritization which is more suited to the Hindu castes. The question also arises as to whether or not they have lost faith and confidence in their own traditional structure and its

[2] In reality no Brahman will serve the Santals because of their impure habits, such as meat eating, use of alcohol, etc. Only the Safa Hoṛ Santals say that they are often visited by the itinerant Hindu saints, who instruct them from time to time in the ideas of purity and cleanliness. The Napits and the Dhobis serve them only during festivities and on life-crisis occasions.
[3] Sanskritization and Brahmanization are more or less the same cultural phenomenon. In practice the first is more secular in outlook, a process by which the formation of a new caste creates upward movement or social climbing in a caste hierarchy. Higher status may be attained by claiming a high-caste position and rank and practicing its eating, drinking, smoking, and sitting habits; by adherence to Hindu deities, rituals, and marriage alliances; and by adoption of names and other symbols.

values. Such an approach leads us to consider two factors which are consciously and unconsciously reflected in Santal thinking. These are (1) the Santal ideals which, revealing and guiding their thinking process, convince them that they are a separate group, unrelated to the Hindu system; and (2) the Santals' confrontation with practical day-to-day problems and dependence upon their neighbors for certain commodities.

The first factor makes it clear that the Santals do not want to embrace Hindu caste ideology[4] and object strongly to being a part of the Hindu caste system. They show dislike of the term "Santal" as it is used by the Dikkus [Hindus]. Their objection is further reflected in their strict observation of endogamy and *bitlaha* [outcasting] practices and in their using the term "Hoṛ" among themselves. For economic reasons certain transactions with neighbouring groups cannot be avoided. In fact, confronted with the practical conditions of interdependence, they avoid any possible allegiance to a single group and tend to unite against external fears. Thus, in practice, external relations do not affect their traditional thinking and living conditions but rather become a strong unifying factor.

New economic products suited to their ecological and socioritual needs are gradually adopted and integrated as a part of their material and economic culture. These new commodities are preferred because they are modern, and desired despite the fact that they are made at various places and supplied to anyone who needs and can afford them.

The term "modernity" is relative. Sometimes it is a mobilizing factor, a part of the socioeconomic change prevailing at a certain time in a certain area. In the anthropological literature the term "modernity" refers most often to the luxurious, urban, industrial, Western commodities which are found in a modern culture. Such a definition is vague and eludes concrete explanations because a modern culture never exists in isolation. In our context modernity is a state of mind, a movement, an expression, a fashion by which the present-day mind, mood, thoughts, and likings are expressed.

This state of mind has always been present, has marked the periods

---

[4] In the caste ideology, the Brahmanic model of Hindu society faces a problem of "life and death" derived from the Indian concept of "purity and pollution." Purity of life is the absolute truth, independent of this world and beyond death, in a state of *mukti*; whereas impurity is related to death, human waste, dirt, etc. This being the Hindus' thinking, it is easy to understand why most Hindus are against nonvegetarianism and the use of alcohol. Abstention keeps them away from any possible contact with death and impurity. This is the charter of caste theory. In practice, although "pure" and "impure" are kept separate in order to protect life from death, special caste specialists and groups are in fact formed, who take impurity upon themselves to free others from pollution. Hence the hierarchical enumeration of four main *varnas* [classes or colors] and a number of *jātis* [castes]. The hierarchy is based on a series of oppositions, on ritual and religious purity, high and low status, eating and drinking habits.

of and has been reflected in the economic and ecological needs of the community. Sometimes even old antique objects become a part of the movement to modernity as fashions or fads. In reality the movement does not affect traditional thinking. On the contrary, modernity stimulates efficiency, simultaneously provoking a questioning of the functional validity of old economic forces and helping to revive the traditions and unity of the community. So far anthropologists have used the concept of Sanskritization to explain the cultural phenomenon common to most Indian tribes and rural communities. The Santals have also been examined in this light (Dutta-Majumdar 1956; Orans 1965). These ideas are derived from the examples of those Santals who either live and work in the industrial-urban areas or call themselves Safa Hor [clean men] Santals and observe caste ideologies. Whatever form this cultural phenomenon has taken, it is the result of the forces of modernization, deeply rooted in reciprocal relations.

We see that modernization stimulates two types of cultural phenomenon in any given culture or geographical area in relation to socioeconomic needs:

1. There is a trend toward Sanskritization or Great Tradition, in which the cultural phenomenon works as the mechanism of social climbing in relation to other groups. By conforming to the Bihar-Bengal standard behavior of the Hindus, the community tries to imitate or take over the rules of caste ideology of the dominant caste groups and claims to be a part of it.

2. A trend toward Santalization, in which the cultural phenomenon works as a mechanism of self-restraint, can also be seen. Revivalism is based on local ethnic traditions and the ideals or idioms of a golden age,[5] a happy period in the remote past; this provides internal unity by conforming to or creating the Santal standard behavior. Santalization attacks the hierarchy of the caste ideology and eliminates the diacritical differences in the internal structure between the clans and the ethnic groups. It promotes group solidarity by accepting conventions which members of the group can share and which can gradually be nativized.

Since the concept of Sanskritization has already been discussed by so many anthropologists, I shall outline only the Santalization process and view its negative and positive aspects. This cultural phenomenon gives the Santals a sense of unity, not only of ideals but also in practice, because it is close to their own social reality. In a traditional society the conditions are often of face-to-face relations, homogeneous living

[5] In Santal context the golden age is placed back in the period of Campa. According to Santal traditions, once upon a time the Santals were living in the country of Campa, a land of seven rivers and two passes: the Cai pass and the Campa pass. It is said that in this country the Santals built many forts to insure their safety against enemies. This period of Campa is often remembered in Santal folklore as the golden age of development.

styles, mutual cooperation, and ties to a common past. Economic development moves along local lines. When Santalization works, it automatically indigenizes the local values, the Sanskritic functional norms, and consequently the content forms, molding them into a single identity.

My own data, based on fieldwork[6] in the district of Santal Pargana, suggest that although the Santals have accepted and assimilated various Brahmanic values in varying degrees, they are proceeding toward Santalization in a process parallel to that of Sanskritization. For example, when Ram Nath Murmu, a Santal teacher at Amrapara High School, was asked about his views on the extent of Hinduism and its influence upon the Santals in his village, he replied:

Hindus do not respect the Santal culture, thinking it to be backward and jungly. Those Santals who were told that they were Hindus because of their love for certain Hindu ways of living were always considered as Sudras. They were never served by the Brahmans. No Hindu caste member accepted their food as they were considered very low. In such a situation a Santal makes his mockery and is teased by his group members and in long run suffers from outcasting and mental breakdown. So when a tradition singing the songs of high ideals does not respect us and considers us outsiders why should we stick to this alien system. After all we only get problems and no betterment.

These doubts, expressed by a Santal, indicate a revival of the Santal traditions in the interests of secure feelings. The Santals' pride in their traditions and ideals is often reflected in their rituals, strict observation of tribal endogamy and clan-cum-village exogamy, adherence to the principles of patrilineality and landed interest, the practice of agnation and membership in the cult of the *Bongas*.[7] Their unity is revealed in kinship modes of expression. Whenever a modern means helps them express solidarity, they take that means and integrate it into their culture. Among the modern forces are technology, the formation of the All-India political party, elections, government development blocks, welfare departments, education, government services, public interest,

[6]   The author conducted his fieldwork in the district of Santal Pargana, in two villages near Amrapara Market and Block Center on the Dumka-Pakaur highway, at intervals: 1959-1960, 1965-1966, 1968, and 1971-1972.

[7]   Bongaism is the belief in a supernatural and impersonal power existing as a quality or attribute of objects, both animate and inanimate. The term *Bonga* is used to designate this power and quality and is considered the cause of all unseen energy. The *Bongas* are spirits. Sacrifices are offered to them in order to avert dangers. The supreme being of the Santals is *Thakur*, who is protector and giver of life. He is supposed to have created the universe, the first Santal ancestors, and the various forms of life. He is identified with the *Sing Bonga* [sungod]. On earth *Marang Buru* [the great mountain] is his assistant in charge of forests, crops, rain, and all the trees and animals that are found in the Santal ecological surroundings. His consort is *Jaher Era*, in charge of the village shrine (*Jaherthan*) and protector of villagers; she gives them welfare, health, successful marriage, fertility, etc. She is considered to be the mother earth goddess.

and transport and communication. They help bring together the scattered Santals into a single geographical unit, able to function as a unit without delay or misunderstanding. The slogan, "the unity of Santalization," is often depicted by their leaders in terms of the golden age of Campa, in contrast to the present unrest and bad conditions.

In this way modernity does not break down the Santal traditions and ideals but becomes an asset in the achievement of unity and progress in respect to local ecological and economic needs. Modernity is an ongoing, steady process resulting from exposure to the ideas of commodities, modern industry, markets, administrative systems, courts, urbanization, and the like. This situation continues because of the constant demand for economic and political progress and not because of caste principles.

After studying the case of the Santals, it would be a sweeping generalization to file them under the heading of Sanskritization. It would also be a departure from the concrete social reality, which still remains localized under particularism. As modernization continues, certain patterns are established, some of which are hostile to or compatible with the Great Tradition, and these patterns often result in conflicts and competition on the one hand and in cooperation on the other. The very fact that the Dikkus are disliked is a clear indication that change is away from Sanskritization. This dislike tends to lead to hostile relations with the high castes who, in the past, have oppressed the Santals on land issues. The relations with the lower castes are on a different level, one of friendly ties, reciprocity, mutual cooperation, and healthy competition. Most of these lower castes immigrated into the Santal area with the Santals and helped them during the Santal Rebellion of 1855. Alignment with the high castes is a different situation and is resorted to and meant only for economic transactions.

Adoption of a new type of dress, spicy foods, metalware, tiled roofs, cash crops, markets, etc., has nothing to do with Sanskritic values but much to do with modern secularization. These can be adopted by any creed, class, or group of people. Like many other neighboring castes of Hindus and Muslims, the Santals have also adopted new things often considered a part of modernity. Thus for a Santal to follow the path of caste ideology and Sanskritization would be for him to become dependent upon the caste system, not only for social recognition but also for participation in the rituals. Since the Santals would be considered very low caste, they would in fact achieve nothing. Adhering to the Santal tradition and ideals under the banner of Santalization means maintaining freedom from the caste system and keeping an independent group status.

Little Tradition and Great Tradition are interdependent and complementary and cannot be distinguished as isolated entities. Both exist in relation to the network of communication, markets, meeting places, patron-client relationships, etc., in which ideas are exchanged and protective contacts renewed in the context of reciprocity. For their economic survival, neither the Santals nor the Hindus can live apart and isolated. On the other hand, they avoid being very close to each other, carrying out their transactions with the help of intermediaries from both groups.

For example, in the district of Santal Pargana, the tribal population constitutes 90 percent of the district population. Most of the land belongs to the tribals and by law cannot be alienated. The Santals and other ethnic groups enjoy the land and its produce. The Hindus are allowed to live in the area only as contacts and as suppliers of nontribal commodities. The Hindus work as intermediaries, providing the Santals and the Paharias with special goods from outside channels through caste specialists, transport facilities, and other means. In return for their services they are allowed to stay in the area and are paid with grain and jungle produce. In reality the Dikkus are a minority and have no weight in economic and political fields. In elections the Jharkhand-Hul[8] Party generally wins the political seats.

It is clear that, in our field area, although the Hindus are rich enough to buy Santal property, they are dependent on the tribal people. They have respect and status within the Hindu caste system, but because of their meager numbers they cannot gain economic or political dominance. The Great Tradition is outnumbered by the Little Tradition. Even in economic transactions the Hindus have to exchange goods by Santali standards, speak the Santali language, and, in theory, respect Santali socioritual values. On the other hand, although the Santals dominate the economic and political fields, as a group, they feel that they are a drop in the ocean. The Great Tradition is so powerful that they cannot suppress it but need it for their economic protection. The constant supply of outside goods has now become a part of their material and economic culture, rooted in socioritual activities.

Conscious of these facts and of the need for direct contact, the Santals have even started learning specialized skills, inconceivable to them in earlier days. Consequently, there is a growing need for schools, dispensaries, political training, etc. Under Santalization, the Santal community, together with the ethnic groups, remains intact and enjoys its traditional system of living, its clans, lineages, and nuclear family, its secular and sacred village officers, and its group loyalty; it observes common-land bonds under the *manjhi* [headman], agnation, the cult of the *Bongas* and the mountains, patrilineality, village exogamy, the

---

[8] The Jharkhand-Hul political party was formed to safeguard the Santals' interests in land and their socioeconomic benefits in the state of Bihar. Literally, Jharkhand means the Chota Nagpur plateau area and Hul means rebellion.

worship of *Manjhithan* [headman's shrine] and *Jaherthan* [village shrine] by the *naeke* [religious head], and lineage sacrifices. Power and authority are diffused both in common right to land and in village activities; the power and authority of the leader to command and regulate joint control are based on mutual understanding.

This is a real world of interrelations which creates solidarity and ultimately some sort of Santal identity. It also creates mobility, political freedom, and unity of community sentiments, as expressed through kinship and marriage ties. The Santal community has no "obligations" and "claims" like those of the caste groups. Since there is no specialization like that in the caste system, the Santals depend upon their neighbors; this relationship provides a bond of economic interdependence and safeguards their right to protection from one another. These reciprocal relations are in danger only when either party migrates to another area. In reality this danger never arises, as the place left by the migrating group is soon occupied by some other group or by distant relatives. Migrations may be caused by a shortage of food or by factionalism, resulting in antagonism and hostile relations.

Santalization has helped the Santals preserve their distinctiveness and is reflected in their relations and identity. Furthermore, they have adapted borrowed traits to their own liking and their ethical cultural requirements by creating a new interpretation which fits the Santal thinking. Along with their own cultural traditions and institutions, listed above, they have Santalized non-Santal elements. Instead of having to call the Hindu priest and barber, they now have their own. The *naeke* is considered the pandit (Brahman), and the role of *Napit* [barber] is taken by the *godet* [secular-sacred messenger]. In reality, nothing is added or changed through the use of these new names. The traditional duties of these functionaries remain as they were in the past; a, new interpretation and new terms are simply added to the old ones.

Santalization also allows for social and economic mobility, as Santals need not depend upon the high castes and ultimately upon caste ideals. The forces of modernity have helped check to some extent domination and exploitation by high-caste Hindus and the caste system. With the new wave of planning departments, national extension services, development blocks, welfare services, elections, and political parties, the Santals have learned the value of government funds and protectionist welfare activities. In addition, they are becoming aware of the secularism of the Indian Constitution. As one of the Santals remarked, "Nobody should destroy any religion. [This is what] I have seen in the Constitution of India in the twenty-fifth chapter" (Orans 1965:117).

Another factor is that Hinduism does not believe in any kind of religious conversion. Binova Bhawe's remarks at a Santal Sarvodaya village are often remembered. Ramesh Soren recalled his conversation with the Sarvodaya leader:

You [the Santals] are honest people. You touch humanity and that is your religion; local variations are just related to your immediate needs. In our free India we want to help you by giving a climate in which you are protected from the outside world.

By saying this Bhawe invoked the fundamental rights provided by the Constitution regardless of caste, creed, sex, class, color, or language. Such ideas from reformers, Indian leaders, and other sympathizers have induced the Santals to reconsider their own standing in free India and to Santalize those values which are economically and ecologically functional in their own society.

The new interpretation of borrowed values fits local needs and myths. It has enabled the Santals not only to revive their traditions, but also to acquire a secular and universalized outlook. Expressions often repeated and recited by village leaders at marriage, birth, death, harvest, and other ceremonies reflect their united sentiments. It should be noted that no outsider can be recruited into the Santal community either by marriage alliances or by adoption. In adverse times all clans unite and share each other's sorrows; help is provided even by lending grain at no interest.

It can be said in conclusion that the Santals' cultural borrowing, in the form of the adoption, assimilation, or integration of alien values, does not show that they are proceeding toward Sanskritization and an embracing of the caste ideology. Rather, they are following an independent road of Santalization supplemented by the modernizing influence of progress, and they are developing their own autonomous model, with which they identify by being proud participants in this process, as, for example, is done on a political level by showing group loyalty and faith in the Jharkhand-Hul party.

To some extent modernity has affected the Santals' traditional life, but it would be wrong to presume that it has replaced traditions. For example, the Santal *gonong* [bride price] remains the same except for the inclusion of some additional cash and modern urban objects, such as synthetic dresses, factory-made shoes, watches, radios, flashlights, and bicycles. These objects are generally demanded by the parties in advance, depending on their needs. Neighboring religions such as Christianity and Hinduism have afforded the Santals greater choice in the selection of norms, which they adopt according to their needs and the needs of their ecological and geographical surroundings.

The conservative approach of Hinduism, in terms of its strict observance of eating, drinking, and smoking restrictions, has not appealed to the Santals at all. However, the caste ideology of high and low status, rank formation, purity and pollution, and dominance and suppression has led them to rethink and reconsider their status and standing in relation to their neighbors in regions where they are economically and demographically dominant. They have rediscovered their power as a local magnate group with group loyalty, a political party, the inspiring values of Bongaism that fit ecological conditions, the ritual observation of feasts and festivities, etc. As a consequence, their inclination has been toward Santalization rather than toward Sanskritization. At the same time, they have retained their interdependent relationships with ethnic and nonethnic groups, at least in the economic field, and they protect each other's interests. Present relations are on a level quite different from that of former interactions, being based on reciprocity. The cultural phenomenon of Santalization has reached a stage at which the Santals feel secure, protected, and united as a group with landed interests. Their kinship bonds are expressed in their age-old traditions, and they cherish ideals of an all-India universalization. We can see this development in Table 1, which shows that the Santals, in their present sociopolitical structure, have moved independently toward universalization on an all-India scale

Table 1. Cultural phenomena

	Santalization	Sanskritization
Ideals	Revival of tribal traditions, golden age of Campa.	Caste ideology of Brahmanism, ideals of Ramayana, Mahabharata.
	Santals (Little Tradition)	**Hindus** (Great Tradition)
Realities	Endogamous tribe, exogamous clans, lineages.	Endogamous castes, subcastes, etc.
	Against hierarchy, based on equal status; no claims, no obligations; no ranking by eating, smoking, and drinking transactions.	Hierarchy of high and low status; caste obligations, claims; ranking by eating, drinking, and smoking transactions.
	Homogeneous composition. Localized area.	Heterogeneous composition. Large area.
	Services of *naeke* and *godet* to sanctify village agnation ties for group solidarity.	Services of Brahman and barber to sanctify rituals, social status, etc.
	Oral traditions. Cult of Bongas and hills.	Written scriptures. Sanskritic gods.
	Wet rice growers, reciprocal relations with ethnic groups.	Caste specialists, patron-client relations.
	Group loyalty, agnate property, joint village landholdings.	Family, caste loyalty, private property.
	Village tribal council, tribal outcasting, exclusion of women, no adoption.	Caste council, caste outcasting, adoption, inclusion of women.
	Marriage outside the tribe unthinkable, no hypergamy.	Inter-(subcaste) marriage possible on basis of hypergamy.

almost parallel to Sanskritization. At the very basis of this development are the forces of modernity, working through the forces of change in the multidimensional relations, a change that goes on steadily in all periods of history.

REFERENCES

BODDING, P. O.
1942   *Traditions and institutions of the Santals.* Oslo: Etnografiske Museum Bulletin 6.
BONNERJEA, B.
1927   *L'ethnologie du Bengale.* Paris: P. Geuthner.
CULSHAW, W. J.
1949   *Tribal heritage.* London: Lutterworth.
DALTON, E. T.
1872   *Descriptive ethnology of Bengal.* Calcutta: Office of the Superintendent of Government Printing.
DE JOSSELIN DE JONG, P. E.
1965   "De culturen van zuid oost Azië," in *Panorama der volken,* part 2. Edited by P. van Emst. Roermond: J. J. Romen and Sons.
DUTTA-MAJUMDAR, N.
1956   *The Santals: a study in culture change.* Delhi: Manager of Publications, Government of India.
FOSTER, G.
1953   What is folk culture? *American Anthropologist* 55:1.
GRIERSON, G. A.
1906   *Linguistic survey of India,* volume four. Calcutta: Office of the Superintendent of Government Printing.
HUNTER, W. W.
1897   *Annals of rural Bengal* (fifth edition). London: Smith, Elder.
MAN, E. H.
1867   *Santhalia and the Santhals.* London: Tinsley.
MARRIOTT, M.
1969   *Village India: studies in the little community* (eighth edition). Chicago: University of Chicago Press.
MUKHERJEA, C. L.
1962   *The Santals* (second edition). Calcutta: A. Mukherjee.
ORANS, M.
1965   *The Santal: a tribe in search of a Great Tradition.* Detroit: Wayne State University Press.
REDFIELD, R.
1956   *Peasant society and culture: an anthropological approach to civilization.* Chicago: University of Chicago Press.
RISLEY, HERBERT HOPE
1891   *The tribes and castes of Bengal.* Calcutta: Bengal Secretariat Press.
SHERWILL, W.
1851   Notes upon a tour through the Raj Mahal hills. *Journal of Asiatic Society of Bengal* 8.

SINGER, M., BERNARD S. COHN, *editors*
  1968   *Structure and change in Indian society*. Chicago: Aldine.
SRINIVAS, M. N.
  1942   *Marriage and family in Mysore*. Bombay: New Book Company.
  1962   *Caste in modern India and other essays*. Bombay and New York: Asia Publishing House.

Region, Religion, and Language: Parameters of Identity in the Process of Acculturation

MAHADEV L. APTE

INTRODUCTION

Anthropological studies of the phenomenon known as acculturation or culture contact generally entail many prerequisites and subsequent analyses of its several relevant features (Beals 1953; Herskovits 1938; Redfield et al. 1936). Among the prerequisites are the ethnographies of the two or more societies which come in contact, and the duration and nature of such contact; for instance, is the contact between two societies of equal status, or is one society dominant; is the contact due to geographical contiguity or to migration, etc. Analyses may focus on such aspects as the following: (1) changes that may occur in the observable cultural traits of the populations in contact: for example, changes in clothing, diet, marriage patterns, agricultural and other occupational techniques, ceremonial behavior, family structure, child rearing, etc.; (2) attitudes of the members of each society toward such material changes: their acceptance of, or indifference or resistance to them; and (3) consistency or discrepancy between objective changes and subjective ethnic identity.

The aim of this paper is to describe briefly an extended culture contact situation resulting from the migration of one community to a different linguistic region and to analyze the ethnic identity problems faced by its members.

Although a single criterion for a distinct collective identity, such as language, may be available to the members of a minority community,

Fieldwork on which this paper is based was done in the state of Tamilnadu in south India from September 1971 to July 1972. I am grateful to the American Institute of Indian Studies for a Senior Research Fellowship which enabled me to undertake the research.

other criteria may be equally influential. Often the choice of a particular criterion or the different priorities given to various criteria is the result of socially relevant factors (Barth 1969:15) and motivations of the minority community members. In populations which are already stratified, culture contact over an extended period may develop into congruence of codes and values, if structural parallels exist by way of ascribed social status of various groups within the two populations. In such cases, change in ethnic identity from one group to its structural counterpart is conceivable.

In the South Asian region there exists a caste and/or *varṇa* structure which can be considered a special case of a stratified polyethnic system. Migrants from one region to another may therefore find it convenient to acquire the sociocultural identity of structurally parallel caste or *varṇa* groups in the dominant population in the new region.

The main thesis of this paper is that, in the South Asian context, groups with high ascribed social status, namely Brahmans, easily adapt to the regional identity because they can readily associate themselves with the Sanskritic Great Tradition[1] shared by most regions in South Asia. Similar opportunities are available to groups with low ascribed social status only if comparable groups exist in the dominant population. If, however, the structural parallels do not exist, or if a group is desirous of upward social mobility and seeks the goal of higher social ranking, then the factors emphasized in ethnic identity may be an affiliation to a broader reference group outside the new region and a continuation of religious practices emanating from the original home region. Thus the available criterion of language for the retention of a distinct identity for a whole community may be superseded by other criteria such as religion, region, or *varṇa* status.

BACKGROUND

The community under discussion is that of the Marathi-speakers (also Mahrattas) in the state of Tamilnadu in south India, which consists of about 50,000 people. Marathi, an Indo-Aryan language, is spoken by approximately forty-one million people in the state of Maharashtra on the west coast of India. Tamiḷ, the official language of the state of

---

[1] Starting with Redfield (1955), anthropologists who have worked in South Asia have generally recognized two distinct traditions. These are known as Great Tradition and Little Tradition. The former generally refers to existing Sanskritic literature consisting of religious scriptures and other works on philosophy, law, polity, literary criticism, and epistemology in general; and to the pan-Indian religious ideology and practices emanating from this literature. The latter refers to localized innovations and interpretations of the great body of Sanskritic religious and secular literature.

Tamilnadu, belongs to the Dravidian language family and is spoken by approximately thirty-seven million people.

The present-day Marathi-speakers in Tamilnadu are in most cases descendants of Marathi-speakers who immigrated approximately 200 years ago. The initial migration into Tamilnadu was due to the establishment of a small Maharashtrian principality in Tanjore District toward the end of the seventeenth century. The Maratha kings ruled Tanjore District and some of the surrounding areas for about 150 years. There were later migrations of Marathi-speakers during the nineteenth century. Although Marathi-speakers are scattered all over Tamilnadu in small numbers, they are primarily concentrated in four districts, the largest group being in the city of Madras.

There are three major caste groups among the Marathi-speakers in Tamilnadu: Deshastha Brahmans, who were closely connected with the Tanjore kings as administrators and priests; tailors, who appear to be later migrants; and Marathas,[2] who are Kshatriyas [warriors] and were the ruling caste of the Tanjore kingdom. The Brahmans, although still living in large numbers in the city of Tanjore, are now concentrated in the city of Madras. Their migration from Tanjore District to the urban center of Madras began about seventy years ago. The tailors have spread all over Tamilnadu and have sizable groups in many major cities. A large number of them live in the city of Madras. Except for a few scattered families who are related to the former Tanjore kings and still live in Tanjore City and the surrounding areas, the Marathas are mostly concentrated in the northern part of Tamilnadu and are primarily agriculturists. They also have a sizable population in the city of Madras.

LINGUISTIC PROFILE OF THE COMMUNITY

Members of the Marathi-speaking community still use their native language, but it is generally restricted to the home and to interaction with the immediate and extended family. The preferred second language is Tamil, the state language of administration. Most members of the community speak Tamil with native fluency and seem quite at home conversing with Tamil-speakers in all types of social interaction. Thus the community is clearly bilingual, although the individual members are aware that they can be identified as a separate linguistic group. The objective criterion of separate language usage is sufficient to distinguish

[2] Everywhere in India except in the state of Maharashtra, all Marathi-speakers are known as *Marathas* or *Mahrattas*, irrespective of their sociocultural background, including caste. Within Maharashtra, however, the term is used only to refer to a caste group with Kshatriya status.

the Marathi-speakers as a separate community from the rest of the Tamil population (Vreeland 1958:86) and this seems reinforced by the subjective criterion, namely the awareness of their distinct linguistic identity on the part of the Marathi-speakers. This is also substantiated by the fact that since the taking of censuses began in 1891, the number of Marathi-speakers has not altered in any substantial way.

SEPARATE GROUP IDENTITIES WITHIN THE COMMUNITY

Although the objective criterion of language exists to separate the Marathi-speakers as a community distinct from the dominant population, the separate group identities within the community seem much more influential and dominant than the common identity. These collective identities are based on caste status, socioeconomic conditions, distinct historical and sociocultural traditions, and religious ideologies. The three caste groups in the community appear isolated from each other; each has its own formal organizations, and there is very little contact and communication among them (Apte 1974). Each group seems motivated in a different direction and appears to respond differently to the existing sociocultural, political, and economic conditions. Marathas as a caste group are not relevant to this discussion. Judging by their sociocultural and historical background, however, they show characteristics similar to those of tailors rather than of Brahmans. Thus the major distinction appears to be between Brahmans and non-Brahmans. Each of these groups exhibits different trends of ethnic identity, as reflected in their attitudes and actions discussed below.

Brahmans

Brahmans as a group within the Marathi-speaking community in Tamilnadu are the most advanced in terms of education, prestige, jobs, and income. As late as the 1930's many of them owned land and had influential positions in the social structure of villages, primarily in Tanjore District. Even today many are absentee landlords and have ancestral houses and property there. Their efforts to organize themselves as a community and especially to help their group members get higher education go back to the beginning of this century. In 1912 an educational fund was established to give financial support to young Brahman boys and girls for higher education. The association has thrived through the years and now has substantial endowment funds. The majority of the Brahmans interviewed had finished school and many of them have college degrees. This educational level has been achieved not only by the younger generation but also by the previous two generations.

In terms of economic conditions, the Brahman group seems much better off than its non-Brahman counterpart. Brahmans hold the highest percentage of white-collar and professional jobs and also have a higher average income than the tailors or the Marathas. Many of them hold high administrative positions in private firms and in state and central government offices. The number of Brahmans who are engineers, doctors, lawyers, and college or university professors is also quite high in comparison to the numbers of tailors or Marathas holding such jobs. Available sources indicate that the situation was the same in the 1930's.[3] Thus it is obvious that Brahmans as a group are socio-economically more advanced than tailors.

Until recently, the Brahman group in the Tamil population enjoyed a long period as a political and cultural elite. This was due, to a considerable extent, to their religious domination of the rest of the population, to their superior position as the inheritors of the Great Tradition of Hinduism, and also to their favorable attitude toward Western education (Béteille 1969:66-67, 165; Hardgrave 1966:213). The Marathi-speaking Brahmans shared in this elite status and the advantages which accrued from it. The Marathi Brahman group has a great deal in common with its counterpart in the Tamil population, the Tamil Brahmans, with whom they share a number of rituals, religious rites, and extensive philosophical and classical literary knowledge, all part of the Great Tradition of Hinduism. They practice a number of religious restrictions similar to those followed by Tamil Brahmans, reflecting their common beliefs in pollution and purity. The divisions between Marathi Brahmans are closely linked to those between Tamil Brahmans, and are based primarily on religious and philosophical interpretations of Vedic texts. The two major religious sects among Tamil Brahmans are that of the Smarthas [worshipers of Shiva and believers in *advaita* philosophy] and that of the Shri Vaishnavas [worshipers of Vishnu] (Béteille 1969:71). The Marathi Brahmans follow the same two sects, although the majority of them appear to be Smarthas and the distinction does not exist to the same rigid degree. More Brahmans in the Marathi-speaking community in Tamilnadu know the Devanagari script than non-Brahmans, not because they read Marathi literature but because they read Sanskrit religious scriptures.[4]

---

[3] The economic inquiry undertaken by Rao and Rao (1937) included observation of family size, education, type of occupation, income, housing, and food consumption among Brahmans and non-Brahmans in the Marathi-speaking community in Madras. The conclusion of the inquiry was that Brahmans as a group were socioeconomically much better off than non-Brahmans.

[4] Both Marathi and Sanskrit are written in the Devanagari script.

In recent years the social, political, and economic domination by the Brahmans in Tamilnadu has suffered a considerable setback because of the development of non-Brahman political forces, especially those in the Dravida Munnetra Kazhagam Party which now controls the state legislature. As a result, the Brahman community generally feels discriminated against with regard to higher education and jobs in government services (Béteille 1969:164–168). The Marathi Brahmans share this feeling with the Tamiḷ Brahmans and complain about the deliberate discrimination against them and the lack of opportunities in various fields, even for qualified persons. Thus the Marathi Brahmans seem to identify themselves more with Brahmans in south India and to have little affinity with the Maharashtrians in Maharashtra.

Tailors

The tailors as a group appear to be more evenly distributed throughout Tamilnadu than the Brahmans, although they too are concentrated in large numbers in the four northern districts including Madras. They are more recent arrivals than the Brahmans. Most of them started their migration to the south with the British army camps approximately 150 years ago.

The majority of the tailors continue their traditional occupation, either in their own tailoring shops or working for others. Those who are not tailors are in related businesses, such as cloth selling or buying. The level of education among the tailors is low, and they fall into a much lower income group than the Brahmans. Very few of them hold white-collar jobs and even fewer are in any high-status professions. No caste group comparable to the Marathi tailors exists in the dominant Tamiḷ population. (Their only competitors are the Muslim tailors.)

The tailors are organized into formal associations in almost all towns in which they live in substantial numbers.[5] The goals of all tailor organizations appear primarily to be caste solidarity and high *varṇa* identity. The usual pattern of such organizations is to form a committee of active members of the community, to collect funds, and to help the community members in whatever way possible. Most of the tailors' associations in various towns own buildings specially constructed so that they can be rented out for marriages and other special ceremonies. These buildings are provided without charge to community members for religious or other functions but are rented to those outside

[5]   Tailors are concentrated in large numbers in the following cities and towns of Tamilnadu: Coimbatore, Kumbhakonam, Madurai, Salem, Tirupattur, Vellore, and Walajah Pet. There are voluntary associations of tailors in all of them.

the community. Often such buildings are the primary source of income for the associations.

The tailors seem to desire a high *varṇa* identity. Because of their traditional occupation they are included in the third category of *vaishya* of the classical fourfold *varṇa* division. They claim Kshatriya status, however, by calling themselves Bhavasara Kshatriyas. They have myths which suggest that originally the tailors were Kshatriyas [warriors]; but in order to survive during a mass destruction of the Kshatriyas by a Brahman in ancient times, they concealed their Kshatriya identity and pretended to be dyers and tailors, as advised by a goddess. They have imitated many of the religious and cultural practices of the upper *varṇa*s. Thus their efforts seem to be directed toward a broader and higher *varṇa* identity and the status associated with it. All associations of this kind in Tamilnadu are known as Bhavasara Kshatriya Associations.

The organizational pattern among the tailors in Tamilnadu is a microcosm of similar but larger-scale activities undertaken by the tailors and dyers in all parts of south, west, and north India. These groups started their organizational attempts at the national level as early as 1911, when the first all-India Conference of the Bhavasara Kshatriyas was held in Dharwar in Mysore State. Since then the tradition of holding such conferences has continued, the last one having been held in Poona, Maharashtra in December 1972. The main office of the all-India organization known as Akhil Bharatiya Bhavasara Kshatriya Mahasabha [All-India Bhavasara Kshatriya Association] is located in Bombay. Histories of the Bhavasara Kshatriyas have been written in which elaborate origin myths are told and their claims to Kshatriya status are justified. The primary emphasis of the national organization is to encourage caste organization in various parts of the country and to encourage self-help among caste members toward better socioeconomic and educational status. The prominent members of the communities in different parts of India have built temples and hostels for students and have undertaken other similar activities for the benefit of the tailor communities. A monthly caste newsletter called *Bhavasar Jyoti* is published from Poona, Maharashtra.

The religious ideology and behavior of the tailors connect them closely to their original home region of Maharashtra. Tailors are worshipers of Panduranga or Vitthal, a deity associated with an old and popular religious sect in Maharashtra, the *Vārkarī* sect (Deleury 1960). This particular sect still survives and has a large following all over Maharashtra. One of the important marks of affiliation with this sect is the semiannual pilgrimage to Pandharpur, where the oldest temple to this deity is located. From the thirteenth to the sixteenth century, a number of Marathi saints composed devotional songs in praise of the deity, and these are still popular among Marathi-speakers both within and outside Maharashtra. One of these saints, Namdev, was a tailor. He is one of the most popular saints and is said to have traveled as far north as Punjab to spread the worship of Panduranga and the philosophy of his religious sect. The tailors in Tamilnadu seem closely associated with this religious sect partly because of Namdev. In many Tamil cities and towns with a large tailor community, temples to Panduranga have been built and are usually under the control of the local community associations.[6] In many others, there exist active *bhajan* [devotional song] groups which meet every week to sing the devotional songs in praise of Panduranga composed by Namdev and his contemporaries.

Thus the tailor community appears to retain its regional religious identity which has a reference point outside Tamilnadu. At the same time the tailors are interested in upward social mobility for their whole caste group and have attempted to achieve it by claiming a higher *varṇa* status, as described earlier.

CONCLUSIONS

These rather brief descriptions of the two groups within the Marathi-speaking community in Tamilnadu clearly suggest that language, although retained by the community members in the home environment even after an absence from the homeland of more than one hundred years, does not play a significant role in creating a conscious ethnic identity for the entire community. Instead, each group appears to have a distinct focus of self-identity and emphasizes different criteria for it. The Brahmans lean toward their counterparts in the dominant population for ideological reasons and also because of common bonds at the economic, educational, and sociocultural levels. The tailors emphasize the *varṇa* identity within the framework of pan-Indian social structure, and their regional affiliation to their homeland in terms of their religious behavior. There is very little communication and interaction between Brahmans and tailors. Each group is thus self-perpetuating and uninterested in relating itself to any other status group within the minority community objectively identified as such. This conclusion is further supported by the existence of separate voluntary associations for each group, separate residential areas,[7] and separate modes of religious, occupational, and educational behavior.

[6] There are Panduranga temples in Coimbatore, Kumbhakonam, Madras, Vellore, and other cities in Tamilnadu.

[7] In the city of Madras, Brahmans are primarily concentrated in such areas as Mylapore and Triplicane. The tailors, however, are scattered through all parts including some suburban areas.

The primary *raison d'être* for these different groups thus appears to be the socially ascribed status, which determines the nature of self-identity and motivation for either assimilation into or distinctness from the dominant population of Tamilnadu. The primary parameters of identity in this culture contact situation appear to be caste, religion, and region rather than language, although language is the main objective criterion distinguishing this community from the dominant population.

REFERENCES

APTE, MAHADEV L.
1974 "Voluntary associations and problems of fusion and fission in a minority community in south India." *Journal of Voluntary Action Research* 3(1):43-48.
BARTH, F., *editor*
1969 *Ethnic groups and boundaries.* Boston: Little, Brown.
BEALS, RALPH
1953 "Acculturation," in *Anthropology today.* Edited by A. L. Kroeber, 621-41. Chicago: University of Chicago Press.
BÉTEILLE, A.
1969 *Castes: old and new.* Bombay: Asia Publishing House.
DELEURY, G. A.
1960 *The cult of Vithoba.* Poona, India: Deccan College.
HARDGRAVE, R. L.
1966 "Religion, politics, and the DMK," in *South Asian politics and religion.* Edited by Donald E. Smith, 213-234. Princeton, N. J.: Princeton University Press.
HERSKOVITS, M. J.
1938 *Acculturation: the study of culture contact.* New York: J. J. Augustin.
RAO, T. RAMCHANDRA, B. R. DHONDU RAO
1937 "South Indian Maharashtrians," in *South Indian Maharashtrians,* Silver Jubilee Souvenir. Edited by N. R. Kedari Rao. Madras: Mahratta Educational Fund.
REDFIELD, R.
1955 The social organization of tradition. *The Far Eastern Quarterly* 15(1):13-21.
REDFIELD, R., R. LINTON, M. J. HERSKOVITS
1936 Outline for the study of acculturation. *American Anthropologist,* new series 38:149-52.
VREELAND, H. H.
1958 "The concept of ethnic groups as related to whole societies," in *Report of the ninth annual round table meeting on linguistics and language study.* Edited by W. M. Austin, 81-88. Georgetown Monograph Series on Languages and Linguistics 11. Washington, D.C.: Georgetown University Press.

Identity Choice and Caste Ideology in Contemporary South India

STEVE BARNETT

What is happening to contemporary caste is the central question for Indian anthropology. Much of our research bears on caste organization and recent changes due to state capitalism and continued economic dependence, urbanization, wage labor, etc. Unfortunately, we tend to see local trends as global directions; so anthropologists have suggested that castes are now compartmentalizing traditional and modern components; that castes are being superseded by class orientations; that castes are adapting to modern conditions by mobilizing members to vote for particular political candidates; etc. Since all these trends are co-occurring, middle-range theories that purport to account for each are inadequate and misleading.

This paper will outline recent changes in one south Indian caste as an illustration of a broad approach to contemporary caste ideology. The approach focuses on identity and identity choice as the central problem in situating caste today. Since south Indians live in a world where identity choices based on caste, class, ethnicity, cultural nationalism, and race are possible, such an approach must include these within one analytic frame.

This analytic approach is a synthesis of recent anthropological work in symbolic analysis, especially that of Bateson, Dumont, Geertz, Schneider, and Lévi-Strauss, and in neo-Marxist theories of superstructure, like those of Althusser, Lefebvre, Lukács, and Sartre.[1]

[1] This list obviously includes writers who disagree with each other. Here, I am not so much concerned with that as with a selection of aspects of these approaches that does not imply full agreement with any author. I do think that potential syntheses have been hampered by partisan debate. While I will enumerate the points of the selection below, I reserve a detailed discussion for a future paper. Bateson (1972) has elaborated an approach to schizophrenia based on a theory of double binding which I extend to ideology as a whole. Dumont's (1970) notions of hierarchy and substance are basic to my

It attempts to provide an understanding of ideology that does not make self-serving distinctions between science and ideology, or explain ideology only as a cultural system, bracketing base and infrastructure relations. Given the rapid and profound changes in caste in this century, Indians can choose among a number of identities; and the relation of these choices to caste is central to understanding the operation of ideologies in everyday life. Placing ideological choice in the domain of everyday life poses most clearly questions of ideological mechanisms: how do people assert and argue over particular identity choices? Therefore the orientation of this analytic frame is, how do symbols symbolize in ideologies; what is the relation of ideology to action; how can ideologies compete; what are the interconnections between ideologies within one society; and what is the form of the relation between control over production and ideological control? Basically, we must focus on caste ideology and how changes in that ideology allowed and shaped the other ideological developments of class, cultural nationalism, etc.

I will here present a number of "starting points" and fill in their content after reviewing recent changes in a south Indian caste.[2]

1. Persons and groups act on partial understandings of their world, and these understandings are structured and altered by acts. The essential movement to praxis is the interpolation of the biological person as subject, with an identity he cannot fail to recognize. This praxis creates the need for interpretation (connecting understanding and act) and situates conflict (differing understandings, differing acts).

2. In order to act (for an act to have meaning, to make sense), a person must situate himself in terms of some construction of the world, some ideology. Or, he must be "interior" to an ideology — it must be a construction that defines the "real." And since we are talking of "reality," a person interior to a particular ideology cannot

---

understanding of south Indian culture. Geertz's (1964) paper is a basic critical foil. Schneider's (1968) concepts of substance and code for conduct enable me to make a link between an abstract understanding of south Indian ideology and everyday life. Lévi-Strauss of course has developed the most suggestive approach to abstract symbolic possibilities.

Althusser (1972, 1973) has most seriously tried to extend Marx's concepts and super-structure through an understanding of ideological fields and structures-in-dominance. Lefebvre (1971) has pointed to the crucial importance of the domain of everyday life for a Marxist appreciation of ideology. Lukács (1972) has decisively rejected the science/ideology dichotomy. Sartre (1968) has focused on the significance of the actor's position (internal, external) for analyzing ideological action.

[2]   J. Dolgin, J. Magdoff, and M. Silverman contributed to these points. This paper has also been importantly aided through discussion with P. Rabinow and P. Seitel.

consciously manipulate its most basic points. These points are accepted; they are seen by the interior person as *outside* the ideology, as part of a putative "given" (as opposed to "constructed") world. An ideology thus grounds "reality" as well as providing the range of manipulation (as styles) of that "reality." A definition of ideology should include this double distortion: that it has a "given" or "natural" ground and that its limits are "real." This definition locates the tension between ideology and history (the paradoxical replacement of ideologies which in their own terms are irreplaceable) and provides an opening for the generation of new symbolic formations.

3. At the same time a person is interior to an ideology, he is exterior to other ideologies (sex, class, race, kin, etc.) in the same society, all such ideologies constituting an ideological field. These exterior ideologies are at least partially understandable, sharing global symbols common to the whole society, but do not provide a direct frame for action. Placement (interior versus exterior) is therefore critical and moves praxis to the center of the analytical stage.

4. Since ideologies are partial understandings (or distortions, given symbolic dominance and control) yet at the same time implicated in concrete action, action both proceeds from and informs ideology. An act relates to an interior ideological position and is also an additional fact in the world, open to counterinterpretation from an external perspective: it can be seen as interior for more than one ideology. A person may shift ideological stance given the cumulative effect of new acts and persuasive counterinterpretations, so action can restructure positions of interiority and exteriority for particular persons (identity choice).

5. All symbols and meanings in an ideology or an ideological field are not restructured equally through changes in personal identity. There is some relation between kinds of action and kinds of ideological consequence. Since ideologies have form (meanings embodied in symbols are interconnected, are structured) as well as content, this form conditions the action-ideology dialectic.

6. Symbolic structure is not an abstract set of binary oppositions or taxonomic configurations or whatever, but is fundamentally tied to action. Ideologies are "structures-in-dominance"; symbols are asymmetrically related, with certain symbols in a dominant position: they inform central domains of action and can articulate basic propositions about reality. To understand symbolic meaning in ideological form, we must direct attention to symbolic dominance, the particular form of distortion. Oppositions, taxonomic relations, etc., emerge as significant as they articulate interiority and exteriority forcing choice and action. An abstract configuration of symbols can reveal possibilities for manipulation and future direction, but only if imbedded in a

discussion of dominance. This moves us toward *mechanisms* of ideological change: changes in dominance within an ideological field, quantitative change; and changes of the ideological field itself, qualitative change.

7. Symbols embody, in their range of possible meanings, meanings which specify contradictions. Such global symbols may, at the same time, be central to two or more ideologies in fundamental conflict. Here a stress on certain possibilities within a range of meanings, and a devaluation of other possibilities, defines a person's place (interiority) in an ideological field. The symbolic stress of groups controlling resources and use of resources defines an overall structure-in-dominance and an opposition to that structure. An abstract accounting of all metaphorical possibilities of meaning without regard for stressed and unstressed aspects defines the range of options within an ideological field but *not* the field itself, since it always has dominance aspects.

8. Shifts in stressed and unstressed meanings can also relate to levels of meaning, or to where a symbol's meaning is located in a particular ideological structure. ("Levels" is another word for disputes over kinds of reification.) Since there may be much overlap from one ideology to another in an ideological field, location characterizes an interior versus an exterior placement with regard to a particular ideology. Whether a symbol is seen as central or peripheral can determine one or another identity choice.

9. These starting points are directed to processual change, to the differing viewpoints and identities found in complex societies, and to the ways they interrelate. We are directed to forms of ideological struggle, to what might be called "theoretical practice."

Identity and identity choice are the central forms of ideological struggle in south India. The ideological field of caste hierarchy has been and is being replaced by a field where caste has a fundamentally altered significance and the options of ethnicity, cultural nationalism, class, and race become viable. This replacement revolves around the meanings assigned by south Indians to the symbol of blood purity: a stress on blood as embodying a caste-wide code for conduct reproduces caste hierarchy; a stress on blood as embodying natural substance opens the ideological field to other identity choices. Within particular castes, caste members can now hold widely differing views on what it means to belong to that caste; and these differences often result in verbal quarrels, factions, isolation, choice or rejection of a specific marriage partner, and physical fights. A controversial act by a caste member becomes a fact differently understood by these antagonists and is endlessly recounted, revised, and debated.

The analytic frame in points 1 to 9 is designed to help in the understanding of these struggles and to move them into ethnographic focus as generators of new ideological forms, instead of the usual ploy of using struggle and conflict to illustrate some functionalist-oriented regularity. In terms of current anthropological discussions of "idealism" and "materialism," it avoids both the idealism that divorces culture from all else and the materialism that sees culture as epiphenomena. The basic issue is the structure of ideology: anthropological idealists would have it that this structure is intelligible at the level of abstract meaning, anthropological materialists that there is no symbolic structure at all. The task of a truly radical anthropology is not to reify form or content but to follow through the implications of their connectedness.

A striking fact of south Indian life today is the range of identity choices open to people, rural and urban, rich and poor. It is possible to keep up caste appearances, deny them, stress a commonality with all "Dravidians," change the focus of caste ties from local to regional, join a union and strike against a factory owned by a man of one's own caste, or adopt racist attitudes toward lower castes, especially Adi-Dravidas. These choices relate to, but also cut across, divisions of rural/urban, class, and education. And their manifest complexity seems to defy such analytic simplifications as: modern caste is declining, modern caste is adapting to new conditions, or modern caste is compartmentalizing new and old lifeways. Theorists tend to offer replacement (caste becoming class) or additive (caste plus class) solutions without being fully aware of the "apples and pears" nature of the problem.

There are two, potentially complementary, versions of an additive solution that deserve immediate attention. One suggests "compartmentalization" (Singer 1972), the separation of conflicting domains and behaviors (e.g. home/office). The other hypothesizes the "interpenetration" of those aspects of modernity and tradition that do not directly clash and that contribute to the development of a modern state (Rudolph and Rudolph 1967).

But these solutions simplify too soon and categorize too sharply. Take the compartmentalization illustration of a Brahman businessman who eats with lower castes at the office, and who may eat meat on trips abroad, but whose wife and mother keep an orthodox kitchen at home. Rules of orthodoxy and concepts of purity are being importantly modified rather than being maintained through compartmentalization (Levenson 1968).

Take the political activities of caste associations as an example of interpenetration, of the adaptability of caste to parliamentary democracy. To what extent do regional, named groups called castes have anything to do with localized caste principles of hierarchical organization? Vote mobilization is an activity that, on the surface, seems not involved with relative purity or transactional rank and presupposes basic shifts in rank principles and purity components. To reify the category "caste" without probing the ideological organization of caste conceals the significance of recent caste change.

So these additive solutions, while initially compelling, really serve as stimulants to further speculative effort. And such effort should focus on present struggle, for identity choice seen in terms of the political and economic appeals of class alliances, cultural nationalism, and racism is a profound matter that will determine the proximate course of Indian society. (This last sentence is not what anthropologists usually think about when considering identity matters, but it is time we risked a bit more theoretically to speak to concerns of much of the world's population.)

CASTE SUBSTANTIALIZATION IN CONTEMPORARY SOUTH INDIA

Dumont (1969), not especially concerned with recent developments in India and surely no Marxist, has nonetheless put his finger on the basic change in twentieth-century caste: substantialization.

I will illustrate this discussion of ideology, identity, and recent caste change by detailing this process for an upper, non-Brahman, land-owning caste in Tamilnadu State: KoNTaikaTTi VeLaLar [also Kontaikkaṭṭi Vellālar] (hereafter KV). To begin to understand the roots of identity, we must ask what makes a person a KV. An older KV will reply, "maTi" [purity]. Purity concepts are, of course, complex, but are basically concerned with a flow of material through a person's body. This flow includes food, semen, water, and excreta. Parts of the body, such as hair and fingernails, retain purity or pollution and must be handled with caution. The person may thus be considered a kind of bag or vessel in which, through which, and around which this flow of relatively pure or polluted material occurs. An individual KV may at any one moment be more or less pure than other KVs depending on whether he has just eaten or taken a bath, is observing death impurity for a close relative, etc.

But this relatively small range of purity occurs within the purity boundaries of the KV caste as a whole. And this overarching KV purity is what makes a KV a KV. For KVs, this purity is located in a person's blood (irattam). Blood is transmitted from both parents to their children,[3] from the father through the concentrated blood that is semen

---

[3] There is evidence that for some castes blood is seen as passing from only father to children, or even from only mother to children. Correlating this with caste kinship differences (KVs emphasizing bilateral kindreds, Brahmans lineages, etc.) may prove fruitful.

and from the mother through the concentrated blood that is breast milk (or, as an occasional KV woman said, directly through uterine blood).[4] This blood purity is not fixed for life at birth but is affected by life-style (the flow of material). KVs are extremely orthodox, resembling Brahmans more than other less concerned upper non-Brahman castes, and say, for example, that eating meat lowers blood purity. Since many other actions may raise or lower blood purity, a caste-wide "code for conduct" (Schneider 1968) is enjoined by the definition of caste identity (in terms of purity) given at birth but alterable in everyday life. The traditional possibility of outcasting by the KV *panchāyat* for serious violations of the KV code for conduct institutionalizes this dual aspect of blood purity. Blood purity, as substance enjoining a code for conduct, defines what it is to be a KV: how a person becomes a KV and what he must do to remain a KV.

Within the KV caste as a whole, with members in almost all Tamil-nadu districts, there are distinct village clusters seemingly preserving the boundaries of tax-collection units in ancient Tamil kingdoms; and within most village clusters, KVs break down into ranked, noninter-marrying, bilateral kindreds (*vakaiyara*) (I use the term in Yalman's [1962] somewhat unorthodox sense). KVs say that these kindreds are ranked by life-style: lower kindreds are slightly looser about purity requirements and therefore pass on slightly lower blood purity to their children. When pushed by a persistent anthropologist, some KVs make this quantitative: there is a small range of purity for all KVs, but within this range there is still room for distinctions.

This structure — the caste as a whole, village clusters, ranked kindreds within clusters — unified by an indigenous theory of purity and conception, roughly summarizes important levels of KV identity during British rule at least until the early 1920's. Until then, caste hier-archy was intact as a structure stressing holism, interdependence of its parts, and rank corroborated through asymmetric intercaste trans-actions. Here, in Dumont's (1970) phrase, there is no "privileged level"; we cannot talk of an inviolable caste substance apart from codes for conduct that structure intercaste relations. Castes, subcastes, and kindreds emerge as plateaus which temporarily freeze the constant flow of relatively pure and polluting material in particular contexts within local wholes.

By the turn of the century things were beginning to change, and the focus of activity was the development of the south Indian cultural

---

[4] The matter is much more complex. The child is not seen as a simple unit but has com-ponents that derive from either mother or father. The question of mother's blood is tricky: does she take on her husband's blood as she becomes a part of his descent group upon marriage? These questions would require another paper and are not directly relevant to recent caste change. (See also David 1973.)

nationalist movement (M. R. Barnett 1972). Early on, south Indian cultural nationalism was anti-Brahman, reflecting in part the privileged position of Brahmans in government bureaucracy. KVs were traditionally close to Brahmans in orthodoxy and rank (just below Brahmans but above other upper non-Brahmans) and were also dominant landowners. If the non-Brahman movement was successful, KV leaders hoped their caste might assume leadership in south India along with other vegetarian VeLaLar castes. But they needed greater visibility — Brahmans were recognized throughout India but KVs were a numerically small group, known as a distinct caste only where they controlled significant village clusters. More optimistic KV leaders hoped that all six vegetarian VeLaLar castes could unite, forming a powerful bloc in what was then Madras Presidency.

In addition, Madras City emerged as a center of government, education, and small-scale indigenous industrial and entrepreneurial activities. Educated, wealthy KVs from all districts began to move to Madras City, meeting other KVs from widely separated village clusters. KVs from villages near the city also began to urbanize, taking clerical posts and working for the railroad. A very few KVs had been to England and began to question caste customs in the light of their own experiences bolstered by appeals to a transplanted utilitarian rationality.

These KV reformers saw intermarriage across village clusters and among kindreds within village clusters as basic to KV political identity and to KV advance in the urban setting; some hoped that eventually all vegetarian VeLaLars might intermarry. Intermarriage would contribute to the creation of an all-south-Indian identity and would allow educated, urban KVs to form new, advantageous alliances with other urban KVs from different village clusters. After a prolonged struggle, these reformers mustered enough votes at a late-1920's KV caste association meeting to pass a resolution endorsing interdistrict marriage. (Similar resolutions have been reported throughout India, but their significance is obscured by assumptions that widening marriage networks is an adaptive mechanism, allowing the continuation of caste forms of organization in the modern world.)

Copies of minutes of that KV caste association meeting plus recollections by participants convey the tenor of the debate over passage. Orthodox KVs were shocked at the prospect of wider alliance possibilities, arguing that a person was not simply a KV but a KV of a certain *vakaiyara* in a certain village cluster. These *vakaiyara*s were transactionally ranked; upper *vakaiyara* KVs would not, for example, take cooked food or water from lower *vakaiyara* KVs since the lower *vakaiyara* KVs were thought to be less strict in observing purity standards embodied in codes for conduct. Interdistrict or inter*vakaiyara* marriage would mean that such codes for conduct were no longer stressed since, without a transactional ranking frame, how could one know the relative purity of a KV living 400 miles away?

KV reformers countered by arguing that nowadays a KV is a KV solely by virtue of birth, because his parents were KV; since the caste *panchāyat* no longer functions to outcaste, the way a KV lived was essentially his own business as far as marriage or caste membership was concerned. These reformers invoked the Kali Yuga to justify this line of thought, suggesting that this was a general era of gathering chaos and moral laxity. Of course, they did not envisage KVs eating beef or inviting untouchables to their homes; rather, they argued for a general KV way of life (often on health, not religious, grounds), objecting to minute distinctions and the previous emphasis on subdividing the caste as a whole.

The implications of the reformers' logic are profound and ultimately confront the entire ideological field of caste hierarchy. Blood purity, including in its range of meaning heritable substance enjoining code for conduct as codefiners of KV caste identity, is now altered so that substance is stressed, code for conduct unstressed. This does not imply that KVs have no concern for how they act, only that particular acts are no longer coterminous with *being* a KV. If codes for conduct are not definers of caste identity, then the range of personal choice is broadened, including codes for conduct related to class, bourgeois Westernization, Tamil cultural nationalism, etc. Transactional caste ranking is no longer central to fixing a caste's position, since the behavior of one caste member no longer redounds to the rank of the caste as a whole. The hierarchical interdependence of castes so central to a holistic ideology is similarly challenged. Before, KVs could not perform all the tasks necessary to sustain life; they required the labor of service and untouchable castes. Now that adhering to a caste-wide code for conduct is not part of being a KV, KVs do more for themselves than before. Many KVs have "self-respect" marriages, using KV leaders to officiate at the ceremony rather than Brahman priests.

Since passage of this resolution, there have been important changes in KV kinship patterns. Rather than different levels of caste organization appearing or vanishing in different contexts, there is now a privileged level of KVs as a regional caste bloc. For rural, poorer KVs, kindred affiliation may be kept up but is desultory; alliances within a kindred may continue as a path of least resistance, but people of different kindreds regularly eat together, and it is very poor taste to talk publicly of kindred rank. The KV regional caste bloc is layered roughly into an elite at the top composed of educated, mostly urban, KVs from all districts; a mass at the bottom, usually marrying within its kindred and village cluster; and a linking group with ties in both directions. This organization is well suited to cope with increased KV demands for education, jobs, and other favors, since members of the mass can reach the elite through the linking group.

What I have described is the process of what Dumont (1969) calls the substantialization of caste. This may also be understood as the transition from caste to ethniclike regional caste blocs. "Ethniclike" because each such unit is potentially independent of other such units, defined and characterized by a heritable substance internal to the unit itself and not affected, in terms of membership in the unit, by transactions with others outside the unit. Rather than the conceptual holism of caste, we begin to see the antecedent autonomy of its component parts. In an ethniclike situation, transactional ranking no longer orders the parts of the whole, and caste interdependence is replaced by regional caste bloc independence. This qualitative change in the ideological field of caste, summarized in Table 1, is possible (it can motivate action, it makes some sense to the actors even if they do not see or accept its ramifications) to the extent that it is expressed in terms of *the* symbol of traditional caste identity: blood purity. A shift in stress from code for conduct to inviolable substance seems at once to preserve the trappings of caste and to provide a surface ideological continuity while undercutting caste ideology at its root.

Table 1. Stressed and unstressed aspects of caste and class

Caste	Class, Ethnicity
1. Hierarchy: structural logic of interdependence	1. Stratification: substantialist logic of independent units
2. Holism: sacred order (pure/impure)	2. Individualism: secular order
3. Controlled imitation	3. Imitative order: reference group behavior
4. Multiplicity of units: expansion primarily by fission at the subcaste level	4. Fewer units: expansion by fusion
5. Social order as part of nature	5. Social order as rational, distinct from nature

I emphasize the qualitativeness of this change because caste substantialization opens the way for competing and complementary identity claims. Once codes for conduct can cross caste lines, other identity possibilities arise in south Indian ideology. KV-ness, rather than providing an overriding structure for one's identity and actions, becomes one among a number of identity elements in a historical period of great flux. This crossing of caste lines allows the south Indian ideological field to be divided in any number of ways. I have already discussed KV "ethnicity" and will only add that there is strong evidence that other castes, especially other upper non-Brahman castes, have developed similar ethniclike structures. Tamil cultural nationalism (the non-Brahman movement from the Justice Party to the DK to the DMK and now, given the recent split, to the Anna DMK) suggests that all Tamils (alternatively, all south Indians) participate in the same Dravidian culture, casteless and classless in its pristine state in ancient Dravidanadu, so the argument goes, and that this culture provides an overriding and basic identity for all Tamils. M. R. Barnett and I (n.d.) have suggested that caste substantialization is an important prerequisite for the ideological appeal of Tamil cultural nationalism. If codes for conduct can cross caste lines, it becomes possible to suggest one code for conduct (Dravidian culture) for all castes, for all south Indians. In caste society, the idea of a basic commonality from upper to lower castes would have seemed absurd.

Racism, a stress on physical features to determine rank, is not a clear feature of traditional caste rank. While traditional texts do write of skin color, facial construction, body proportions, etc., these are not used actually to rank castes in particular villages or localities. One can, however, see evidence for an emerging racism in contemporary south India, although this is a sensitive matter and the data are not conclusive. South Indian racism takes the form of emphasizing supposed differences in the physiology of untouchables to account for their oppressed condition. The development of ethniclike caste blocs, and the concomitant de-emphasis of transactional ranking, has qualitatively demarcated the one group for whom transactional ranking and residential segregation have been assiduously maintained: untouchables. The poverty of untouchables, the menial work they did, and the general opprobrium in which they were held were as severe as can be imagined in caste society; but untouchables were at the bottom of a conceptual continuum that, in terms of purity, form of ranking, and holism, included all castes. Now all castes keep up asymmetric transactions with untouchables, even when they abandon them with other castes. Given this qualitative distinction, untouchables are coming to be seen as a separate "race." A survey I conducted in Madras with heads of KV households revealed that most older and rural KVs felt that untouchables were different because they *behave* differently, while most younger and urban KVs felt that untouchables were different because they *look* different (Barnett and Barnett n.d.).

Caste substantialization, seen for KVs first in a change in marriage possibilities presaging a fundamental shift in the basis of caste ideology, has consequences for diverging identities among members of the KV regional caste bloc. The shift from holism to pluralism, from transactional rank to attributional rank, from interdependence to independence, is made real for south Indians because they see it in terms of those symbols that define a person's identity. Previously, blood purity defined membership in a caste by establishing a link with caste ancestors (ultimately, those created in the KV origin myth) through heritable substance, and by establishing a code for conduct that sustained that link. A stress on blood purity as substance changes all this. Just as caste blocs can be seen as independent of other caste blocs, persons in caste blocs can see themselves as independent. Their actions are no longer subject to the scrutiny of a caste *panchāyat* with the power to outcaste. They become involved in the crosscutting, multiple identity claims of modern life: ethnicity, class, cultural nationalism, and race.

This summary of KV caste change in the twentieth century would miss the point completely if it suggested that these choices were unambiguous. Contemporary south Indian life is rather one of contention, with people putting forth competing identity claims. Members of the same family, kindred, and caste can hold basically different views of who they are, and these differences may emerge in family and public fights, verbal and physical. Identity theorists tend to see ethnic groups as monoliths espousing some ideological uniformity. Alternatively, ethnic groups can be seen as forums in which people contend, in which they feel that contending is necessary, and therefore as arenas for the presentation of diverse ideological poses.

Implicit here is a heretical view of the way symbols symbolize. Symbolic anthropologists either elide past concretely linking culture to action (much structuralist work), or fall back on some Parsonsian construction of levels. The levels approach tends to rely on external criteria ("distinctive features") to establish levels that purportedly hold throughout a society. But those distinctive features which separate levels derive from an antiseptic form of anthropological questioning; in the course of everyday life, just what a level is, what will pass for a distinctive feature, is up for grabs. It involves symbolic domination and manipulation, since different understandings of levels articulate different identity choices and these choices shape political and economic struggle. I read much current anthropology by unfreezing levels: whenever an anthropologist establishes them, I see instead a set of abstract possibilities to be fought over. The levels do not exist "out there"; "out there" is structured by power, dominance, and control: who has the power to define levels (symbolic dominance), what is the consciousness of those being oppressed by that definition, and what courses of resistance are open to them — how can they alter the definition?

So also for identity choice in south India. KVs are KVs and also workers, bosses, racists, communists, Tamil nationalists, followers of Gandhi, atheists, and pious Hindus. These possibilities can be found within families, kindreds, and neighborhoods. When disputes occur, they are over level, over the implications of being a KV and simultaneously being whatever else.

Let me illustrate with an instance from Madras City (S. Barnett 1973b). A traditionally orthodox KV refused to invite a reformist KV (a longtime Tamil nationalist who had eaten with lower castes at political meetings) to his daughter's wedding feast. When KV caste leaders heard of this, they told the orthodox KV that they would boycott the wedding meal unless he rescinded and invited the reformist.

The orthodox KV was using the traditional ploy of refusing to interdine with those of lower blood purity (in this case lower because of the reformist's particular code for conduct) to enforce his sense of what it means to be a KV. The caste leaders used the same ploy to suggest an alternate sense of KV identity, disputing the salience of the reformist's code for conduct. This is not all, for the orthodox KV was caught in a double bind: since orthodoxy in caste society is defined by a caste-wide code for conduct, when caste leaders refused to attend the wedding feast they were redefining orthodoxy itself, denying an orthodoxy pose to the father of the bride.

This revealingly simple incident revolved around levels of meaning determining KV identity. For the orthodox KV, the distinctive feature of caste membership is a code for conduct enjoined by KV blood purity. For the KV caste leaders, only ancestry counts, and that ancestry is distinct from a particular code for conduct. This was not, however, a contest of equivalent, opposing views; for, to the extent that the orthodox KV's sense of what it means to be a KV depends on caste-wide consensus, it has no standing as an individual statement of belief. Accordingly, he eventually invited the reformist KV but remained genuinely confused and a bit forlorn, understanding that his sense of KV identity was superseded, but feeling it was a "fast one," a kind of shell game (popular in Madras as one of many street-magicians' hustles).

Another incident, having to do with a possible strike in a Madras City factory where a number of KVs are employed, extends the idea of levels of meaning relating to identity choice as being up for grabs (S. Barnett fc.). During a week-long discussion on strike issues, all KV workers decided to meet to formulate a single position. The issue of that meeting, without elaborating in detail, was the relation of being a KV to being a worker. One man suggested KV workers oppose the strike: "After all, most of us own some land [village land] and have PaRaiyan [also Paraiyar] workers there so that we are bosses as well as workers. What if those PaRaiyans decided to strike?" Another countered, "It is our custom to own paddy land, but what is KV factory custom? We should lead the strike and lead other workers just as we lead other castes in the village.'' A third said, "How can we lead others if we ourselves are being commanded by the factory foremen at the same time? We are simply workers like other workers. Maybe we can use our caste to contact KVs who know the factory owner, but those KVs have nothing in common with us anyway."

Finally, someone asked, "Why are we here? If we are KVs we should have one position." Unanimity could not be reached, however, and at the end of the meeting a young KV said in disgust, "Being a KV is like being fat: you can recognize other fat people, but the only thing you have in common is eating. All we have in common is a name; either we are workers or scabs, nothing else."

What is being debated here is the centrality of KV ethnicity. Are general characteristics of KV ethnicity (landowning, links with KVs of other classes, etc.) relevant to the strike and to being a worker? Appeals to traditional prerogatives are countered with denials of relevance and, in one sense, the importance of being a KV, what it entails, is at issue.

In addition to double binding and centrality as mechanisms of ideological struggle around matters of identity, another possibility is hedging.[5] KVs in one urban neighborhood in Madras City strive to maintain transactional rank with other castes to retain their position above other upper non-Brahman castes, while at the same time denying that a caste-wide code for conduct has anything to do with being a KV. They are presenting one face to themselves (KV identity as ancestral KV substance) and another to other castes (KV identity as enjoining a code for conduct).

This hedging, presenting contradictory identities in different contexts, is really a kind of holding action and cannot be sustained in the urban setting. At a local non-Brahman temple, the priest offers *viputi* [sacred ash] to KVs before offering it to members of other castes. In 1968, some worshipers objected, asking why one caste should be privileged. The temple priest, mindful that temple donations are his basic income, went to KV leaders and suggested a compromise: KVs could get *viputi* first if they came to the temple before other castes so that no one else could see and possibly object. KVs adamantly refused, saying that the point of priority was precisely its publicity so that other castes knew KV transactional privileges. (The issue was unsettled and remained tense when I left Tamilnadu in 1969.) In this incident, a KV attempt at hedging is being challenged and could turn into a double bind for them. (The relation between hedging and double binding therefore always involves control and mobilization.)

[5] A graduate student in anthropology at Princeton first brought the philosophical literature on hedging to my attention (D'Agostino n.d.).

Once the analytic frame is understood, almost any conflict can be seen as one of identity choice, over the symbols of identity and their placement (levels) in an ideology. Let me offer one more illustration, this time a rural case (S. Barnett 1973b). In one KV village, another upper non-Brahman caste asked local untouchables to perform the same ritual service for them as they performed for any KV, offering a bribe of paddy as an inducement. The untouchables, aware that KVs still exercised important village control, refused, but since they desired the paddy, suggested that they would perform this service for *some* members of this other caste but not for *all* members. The untouchables were suggesting two levels of caste identity: for KVs, substance enjoining code for conduct, and therefore including all KVs; for the other caste, individual wealth and merit (interestingly, untouchables were willing to perform the service for important members of a number of upper castes). Members of the other caste were, of course, unhappy, since they hoped to challenge KV rank and could only do so if they *as a caste* were treated equivalently.

Untouchables hoped to play both ends against the middle by hedging, offering two criteria for caste identity in, they hoped, two arenas. But the other caste wanted to change transactional rank and so required the same criteria as those applied to KVs. They hoped to make the best of what they could get by eventually accepting the untouchables' offer and suggesting that since some caste members were being treated like KVs, all were equivalent to KVs, following the logic that the behavior and treatment of one caste member redounds to the caste as a whole. KVs ridiculed this, saying that since some were *not* treated equivalently, the caste as a whole had no claim to changed rank.[6]

These incidents point up essential features of contemporary life in south India seen in identity choices and the consequence of those choices. To understand traditional KV caste identity, we first noted their structural position, between Brahmans and other upper non-Brahmans, combining a concern for orthodoxy with local dominance (the ability to command other castes without being commanded in turn). KVs see orthodoxy as dictated by KV blood purity, a purity derived from KV ancestors and transmitted as substance, and maintained by a caste-wide code for conduct enjoined by that substance.

Given urbanization, the development of the non-Brahman movement, occupational diversification, and the introduction of Western forms of education, all given basic form by the nature of British imperialism and independent India's present political and economic structure, KV reformers persuaded the caste association to endorse

---

[6] The decision to accept the untouchables' offer was made after I left Tamilnadu, and subsequent events were reported to me by letter.

interdistrict and interkindred marriage. The rationale for and the effect of this decision were to alter the stress in the range of meaning of blood purity from code for conduct enjoined by substance to heritable substance itself. KV identity seen as this heritable, inviolable substance really changed the KV caste to a KV ethniclike regional caste bloc, a transition from caste as a holistic, interdependent, transactionally ranked hierarchy to caste blocs as substantial (in Dumont's [1969] sense), independent, attributionally ranked units in a plurality. Since codes for conduct could now cross caste lines, other identity choices could develop, most importantly those of class, ethnicity, Tamil cultural nationalism, and race.

This set of choices, corresponding to the ideological emergence of the person as antecedent and autonomous, as the agent of choice, is the focus of present-day south Indian ideological struggle. The *form* of that struggle has to do with disputes over levels, over the import and placement of one or another symbol of identity.

The form of double binding is a counterexample to the additive solution of "interpenetration." In the incident of the wedding feast, the orthodox KV attempted to push KV identity as substance enjoining code in a context where there was no agreement on what is entailed by KV substance. Since code must be caste-wide, he had no orthodox move left when caste leaders threatened not to attend the feast. Here modern and traditional elements did not so much interpenetrate as confound the orthodox KV in a situation of rapid and profound change.

The form of hedging is a counterexample to the additive solution of compartmentalization. The KVs who changed the basis of identity within the caste yet attempted to enforce urban transactional rank in *viputi* distribution were stressing *both* substance *and* code for conduct, but in different arenas. But the idea of distinct arenas (as opposed to substance enjoining code across the board) is *itself* a conceptual innovation, forced by the multiplicity of identity possibilities. The separation of arenas is open to the challenge that each arena affects the other; in the long run, KVs cannot sustain the contradiction inherent in separating and simultaneously stressing substance and code, just as, in the example of the Brahman businessman mentioned at the outset, the Brahman family cannot sustain the contradiction of simultaneously having and violating a single standard of purity.

CONCLUSION

This summary of the bases of KV caste identity and recent changes in that identity depends for its direction on the nine starting points given earlier in this paper. KV caste ideology was sufficient to order caste relations in pre-1920 villages but was inadequate to cope with twentieth-century economic and political developments. KVs were interior to this ideology: blood purity was not, in their eyes, something to be argued about or altered; it was the way the world was. That world was the ideological field of caste hierarchy. Structured by ideas of blood purity as substance enjoining a code for conduct, ideological stress was placed on holism, interdependence, and transactional rank. The foreign exposure of early KV reformers is crucial in confronting that interiority, since these KVs directly experienced alternate ideological stances. Most Europeans, especially the English, lumped all Indians together (and, as the Victorian use of "nigger" indicates, all nonwhites) in a racist ideology quite distinct from the KVs' understanding of caste hierarchy. But these same KVs also came into contact with English reformers with utilitarian underpinnings and learned biological theories of descent and biochemical approaches to the constitution of living organisms.

These contacts fundamentally altered the scope of caste hierarchy; no longer was it the only natural vision of the world, it was now one among many, and a conquered one at that. These reformers eventually challenged the particular structure-in-dominance of caste hierarchy by altering the stress on the range of meaning of blood purity (stressing an inviolable, heritable substance that does not necessarily enjoin a particular code for conduct).[7] The new stress qualitatively changed the ideological field of caste hierarchy, but not as a conscious act. KV reformers hoped to preserve caste and did not foresee KV ethnicity. KV blood purity was still "natural," as was caste hierarchy. I have summarized the effects of that change, the development of a new structure-in-dominance: ethniclike, regional caste blocs. This ethniclike structure-in-dominance, with its individualist bias, allowed ideological struggles to take form around identity choices.

South Indians now live in a world where the options of caste, ethnic, class, cultural nationalist, or racial bases of personal identity coexist. Contemporary ideological struggle is focused on either the caste ideological field versus the ethniclike ideological field, or the various ideologies of identity within the ethniclike ideological field. In this light, the incidents adumbrated above work concretely through the set of abstract possibilities that is the range of meaning of blood purity. The orthodox KV in the wedding-feast incident was interior to an ideology of caste hierarchy, while the reformer and the caste leaders were interior to an ideology of KV ethnicity. Blood purity

---

[7] Once substance is recast this way, it becomes possible for a well-educated, younger KV to say to me, "Why bother with this blood nonsense; KVs really share chromosomes — that is what makes me a KV."

was the key symbol for both ideologies but, given a different stress in each case, it specified the contradictions between them. Commensality, withheld first by the orthodox KV and then by caste leaders, pinpointed these contradictions. The orthodox KV's sense of KV identity depended on caste-wide agreement, so he was moved out of caste interiority when caste leaders expressed disagreement. The fact of commensality is open to new interpretation given another ideology (a legitimation of individual codes for conduct, eliminating transactional rank where one person's behavior has caste-wide consequences). In this alternate ideology, commensality was withheld, not because of purity danger, but as an insult. The orthodox KV's action (refusal to invite) proceeded from his sense of what it means to be a KV. The consequences of that action, counteraction by caste leaders, confounded that identity since he could no longer argue that his personal orthodoxy had caste-wide implications.

The incident over priority of *viputi* distribution illustrates the same points. Here, the significance and the arena of KV priority is interpreted differently given different positions of interiority. KVs want public distribution so all castes can understand KV rank in a caste ideological field. Other persons want *viputi* distributed on a first-come-first-served basis, given an individualistic perspective. The temple priest will give KVs *viputi* first, but privately, granting KV ethnicity but not the KV caste identity. There is no Solomon-like solution; one or another presentation of self and caste must give way.

We have just skimmed the surface of identity choice in contemporary south India as structured by the form of competing ideologies. But an elaboration of the form of ideological competition is not closed; to approach the basic question of symbolic dominance, we must expand our analysis to include those forces that, although not internal to an ideology and its problematic aspects, by that very fact shape its power to motivate and sow the seeds of its eventual replacement. Why is it that holism structures less and less action in south Indian society? Surely not because, on the analogy of chess, another ideology magically appears with superior "moves." Rather, to anticipate our answer, because one ideology expresses what it has become necessary to express: it constructs that new reality needed to reproduce a new social formation.

Starting with colonization, and perhaps earlier, given recent revisionist views of the development of factories in pre-British India, we are directed to new forms of labor outside the structure of work as ordered within caste society (generally glossed in India studies as the *jajmāni* system). This is a specific case of a general process: the transition to contractual forms of labor, and the separation of the domains of home and work. Rather than the interpretation of substance and code in caste, so that doing and being become aspects of the same structural position, substance is associated with home, and code for conduct (as a particular kind of performance: contractual) is associated with work. Or, doing and being become ideologically distinct.

Ideologically, the prior condition for the separation of substance and code as contract is a stress on individualism. In a holistic hierarchical ideology, the merging of substance and code *provides* an explanation of difference: members of a caste do what they do because they are who they are and vice versa. The whole is composed of these differentiated castes acting toward the same end. Given individualism, the merging of substance and code *prevents* an explanation of difference: if individuals are autonomous and equivalent, the merging of substance and code implies a society composed of persons all doing the same thing. Demarcating code as contract, on the other hand, allows for (creates) difference as the application of "reason" (allocating tasks, organizing functions, etc.) in society. Substance as shared by all serves to set up the possibility of different codes where difference does not, ideologically at least, immediately imply ranked distinctions.

British imperialism and Indian capitalism after political independence created the environment in which caste becomes substantialized through the introduction of a nascent individualism and the consequent separation of substance and code. Symbolic dominance is seen in the simultaneous presence of two ideologies: caste and noncaste. These ideological fields are not simply juxtaposed; rather, the caste ideological field can no longer structure and integrate basic life experiences. Once the individual becomes the basic unit of contractual codes for conduct, the individual is valorized ideologically as those contractual codes are perceived as part of the ways things are.

Further, we can only reach an understanding of symbolic dominance (as opposed to an abstract formal account of symbolic possibilities) by focusing on the problematic of an ideological field: those propositions, often unstated (that is, *supplied* by the analyst in the movement from what is stressed in one ideological field to what is unstressed in the other), that undergird actual ideological discourse. In this paper, there has been a double movement: the ideological field of holism is seen against Euro-American individualism, and then that ideological holism allows the breakdown of the individual into substance and code aspects. It is the particular relation of substance and code in the two ideological fields that allows us to speak of their respective problematics and to understand the dominance of one field over the other.

Present caste substantialization[8] develops as labor shifts from a holistic orientation to contractual forms. Contractual labor stresses the parties (persons) involved in a specific contract; ideologically, each party is an independent entity engaging in "natural intercourse" with other independent entities by contract (Marx 1971:17). As ideological struggle formed around the nature of contractual labor (glossed in the literature on "modernization" as "occupational diversification"), identity became substantialized in ethnic, in cultural nationalist, and in class terms (symbolic dominance). This processual replacement of one ideological field by another becomes at any one moment the competition of these two fields. The Marxist idea of cultural "lag" is just this overlap of ideological fields. But the overlap conceals a vector, since the ideological field of caste cannot sustain itself given ethniclike caste blocs (structure-in-dominance); or the stance of caste internality requires the related operations of double binding and hedging (the form of contradictions between fields): the orthodoxy of the orthodox KV depends on the absence of a competing ideological field. Double binding and hedging reveal the dominance of one ideological field over another — the inability of the symbols of one field to structure activity to the extent that these symbols no longer allow or justify the reproduction of present base and infrastructure relations.

Within a single ideological field, it is difficult to see vectors, for we are now talking of some projection of where a society is going, not simply its present configuration. Here, praxis is a constant reordering and reassessing of the centrality of certain symbols (recall the example of KV strikers).

What stands out in south Indian political and cultural life is the tension between class-based alliances and ethnic, racial, or cultural nationalist alliances. That non-Marxist political parties should try to blunt organization along class lines is not surprising and suggests cross-cultural comparisons. Harris (1970:12) has suggestively argued that "ambiguity in Brazilian racial identity" and the

. . . prevention of the development of racial ideology may very well be a reflex of the conditions which control the development of class confrontations. In the United States, racism and racial caste divisions have split and fragmented the lower class. In Brazil, racism and caste formation would unite the lower class (since there is a close correlation in Brazil between class and race). "Black power" in the United States lacks the revolutionary potential of the preponderant mass; "black power" in Brazil contains this potential.

[8]   Previous substantializations of caste have occurred in Indian history, especially in traditional towns, but never as a dominant factor overriding hierarchy. My guess is that present and future economic conditions alter caste ideology beyond any hierarchical recidivism.

The ambiguity built into the Brazilian calculus of racial identity is thus, speculatively at least, as intelligible as the relative precision with which blacks and whites identify each other in the United States.

In India, racial identification is redundant in the caste system, in which intercaste transactions structure relationships in particular villages and in village clusters. Further, a stress on racial identity would dichotomize the "divide, rule, and isolate" aspects of caste rank. Where regional caste blocs cross class lines, physical differentiation among these blocs is not claimed by Tamils. With the breakdown of uniform transactions among members of these blocs, it is difficult to guess a person's affiliation. Such ambiguity allows the blocs to continue while at the same time suggesting the possibility for commonality across the blocs (i.e. the development of Tamil cultural nationalism).

The ideological raciation of untouchables inhibits the revolutionary potential of the lower classes since, as in America, it fragments the lower classes. While most untouchables are lower class, they do not comprise a majority of that class, which includes members of all castes, with a skewing in favor of lower castes. If other members of the lower class come to regard untouchables as a separate race, organization along class lines is, at least temporarily, blocked.

Symbolic dominance is thus an aspect of power defined as allowing the reproduction of a particular social formation despite clear inequity and oppression (differential allocation of control and resources) within that social formation. Ideologically, this reproduction takes place through structures-in-dominance (false consciousness) which define the limits of human action within that social formation.

REFERENCES

ALTHUSSER, L.
  1972   *For Marx*. New York: Pantheon Books.
  1973   *Lenin and philosophy*. New York: Monthly Review Press.
BARNETT, M. R.
  1972   "The politics of cultural nationalism." Unpublished Ph.D. thesis, University of Chicago.
BARNETT, M. R., STEVE BARNETT
  n.d.   Contemporary peasant and postpeasant alternatives in south India: the ideas of a militant untouchable. *Annals of the New York Academy of Sciences*.
BARNETT, STEVE
  1973a "The process of withdrawal in a south Indian caste," in *Entrepreneurship and modernization of occupational cultures in South Asia*. Edited by M. Singer. Monograph and Occasional Papers Series 12. Chapel Hill, N.C.: Duke University Press.

1973b   Urban is as urban does: two incidents on one street in Madras City, south India. *Urban Anthropology* 2(2) Fall.
fc.   *Class struggles in south India.*

BATESON, G.
1972   *Steps to an ecology of mind.* New York: Chandler.

D'AGOSTINO, FRED
n.d.   "Parenthetical person: a life of Dr. Charles A. Eastman (Ohiyesa)." Unpublished M.A. thesis, Princeton University.

DAVID, KENNETH
1973   Until marriage do us part: a cultural account of Jaffna Tamil categories for kinsmen. *Man* 8(4).

DUMONT, L.
1970   *Homo hierarchicus: an essay on the caste system.* Translated by Mark Sainsbury. Chicago: University of Chicago Press.

GEERTZ, C.
1964   "Ideology as a cultural system," in *Ideology and discontent.* Edited by D. Apter. New York: Free Press.

HARRIS, MARVIN
1970   Referential ambiguity in the calculus of Brazilian "racial identity." *Southwestern Journal of Anthropology* 26(1).

LEFEBVRE, H.
1971   *Everyday life in the modern world.* New York: Harcourt-Row.

LEVENSON, JOSEPH
1968   *Confucian China and its modern fate.* Berkeley: University of California Press.

LUKÁCS, G.
1972   *History and class consciousness.* Cambridge: MIT Press.

MARX, K.
1971   *The Grundrisse.* New York: Harcourt-Row.

RUDOLPH, L., S. RUDOLPH
1967   *The modernity of tradition: political development in India.* Chicago: University of Chicago Press.

SARTRE, JEAN-PAUL
1968   *Search for a method.* New York: Random House.

SCHNEIDER, D. M.
1968   *American kinship: a cultural account.* Englewood Cliffs, N.J.: Prentice-Hall.

SINGER, M.
1972   *When a Great Tradition modernizes.* New York. Praeger.

YALMAN, N.
1962   The structure of the Sinhalese kindred: a reexamination of the Dravidian terminology. *American Anthropologist* 64(3).

PART THREE

Discussions

Symposium: Changing Identities in South Asia

Chaired by CHRISTOF von FÜRER-HAIMENDORF

Panelists (in order of presentation):

KENNETH DAVID, Michigan State University
OWEN M. LYNCH, New York University
McKIM MARRIOTT, University of Chicago
RAVINDRA S. KHARE, University of Virginia
SURAJIT C. SINHA, Anthropological Survey of India

VON FÜRER-HAIMENDORF: Ladies and gentlemen, let us begin the session organized by Professor Kenneth David which is entitled "Changing identities in South Asia." There was a preconference at Michigan State University. Most of the papers have been predigested. I would like to call on Professor David to begin his survey of the papers which have been presented. Others will then be Professor Owen Lynch, Professor Ravindra S. Khare, Professor McKim Marriott, and Professor Surajit Sinha.

DAVID: As Professor Fürer-Haimendorf said, we had a preconference at Michigan State. Our concerns at the preconference were both substantive and theoretical. The substantive concern was to ask how previously established identities in South Asia are being redefined and how emerging identities are being formulated. Our theoretical concern was to question which theoretical orientations are more suitable to deal with these changes.

Since the subtopics listed in the program of the preconference — previously established versus emerging identities — reflect several theoretical orientations of my own, I will begin my survey of the papers by giving a gloss on this dichotomy. Previously established versus emerging identities were selected in preference to traditional versus modern identities for several reasons. First, the dichotomy of traditional versus modern lacks temporal precision. In the literature, the traditional period frequently encompasses anything up to the

This symposium was convened at the IXth International Congress of Anthropological and Ethnological Sciences at the Hilton Hotel, Chicago, Illinois, December 3, 1973.

moment of fieldwork or up to the childhood of the contemporary grandparental generation. Yet in the papers here presented, the charting of different identity changes, authors choose different time cuts. For example, in Professor Joan Mencher's study of agricultural labor unions, the relevant periods are before and after the Land Reform Act and the failure of its implementation. In Professor Steve Barnett's study of identity and ideological changes in Tamilnadu, the relevant time cut is before and after the beginning of the Dravida movement. In a recent work by Professor R. S. Khare on changes in intercaste factional alliances, he calls on the periods pre- and post-zamindari abolition. Any single traditional versus modern time cut thus distorts the data on change. Second, the notion of an emerging identity — as opposed to a modern identity — is of utility in that "emerging" does not denote absolute novelty. For example, there are the two-step changes in identity among the Santal tribals, as described in the papers by Professors S. K. Mahapatra and M. K. Gautam, and among low castes, as described in the paper by Professor Rao. Whether tribals or low castes, the first step is the emulation of upper-caste life-style. The second step is the renunciation of such emulation in favor of an identity outside of Hindu ideology. These identity changes are certainly new for these particular castes and tribes. The strategy itself is quite antique, according to Professor Z. Ahmad, who also submitted a paper. He holds that lower castes have been converting to Islam for centuries. Similarly, involvement in contractual, nonlocalized intercaste relations by low-caste agricultural laborers organized into unions is new for these castes. But my own paper suggests that involvement in contractual relations by artisan and fisher castes with their clients is a structure of relations which has coexisted with the usual *jajmāni*-style relations as part of the previously established order in Jaffna, north Sri Lanka. The point is that the term "modern identities" implies a definite discontinuity with the past while the term "emerging identities" prompts the analyst to attend to structures present but not stressed in the previously established order and to discern their relevance to the changing situation. In another study, for example, I compared the responses of Sinhalese Goyigama agriculturalists with those of Sinhalese Karava fishermen with respect to the new mercantile opportunities presented by the three colonial powers. The Portuguese, the Dutch, and the British occupied Sri Lanka from the early sixteenth century until 1948. Agriculturalists, enmeshed in their *jajmāni* relations, retained their village economy until the later part of the nineteenth century. Fishermen, on the other hand, profited, first, by fighting for the Portuguese against the Kandyan kingdom, second, by running salt through the Dutch blockade to the Kandyan kingdom, and, third, by cultivating tea in the upcountry along with the British. They became a mercantile elite. Thus, variations in the previously established sociocultural order permit the charting of differences in the rate and direction of sociocultural change. I then reject the tradition versus modernity dichotomy in favor of the distinction of previously established versus emerging identities and structures because of the former dichotomy's temporal imprecision, its tendency to obscure variations in structure, and its value connotations.

What is needed to study changing identities in South Asia is an analytic scaffolding sufficiently differentiated and flexible enough to handle both the hard facts of ideas and the hard facts of resources and power. Professor Louis Dumont's notion of structure is inflexible in that it permits him to say only that a structure is either present or not present but does not change. He relegates observable political or economic changes to the secondary, encompassed sphere. Only apparently more flexible than Dumont's framework is the analytic precedent of formulating megaprocesses of change such as modernization, Westernization, and, as Professor Gautam proposes in his paper, Santalization. These megaprocesses bundle together technological, economic, political, and ideational processes.

On the other hand, the papers submitted by Professors Apte, Barnett, David, and S. K. Mahapatra do attempt to differentiate hard facts of ideas from hard facts of the use of resources and to analyze identity changes in terms of the interrelations between these aspects of purposive human action. For example, Professor Mahapatra details both the class contradictions and the ideational contradictions involved in the recent changes of Santal identity. There is a class contradiction between the emerging Santal elite and the Santal masses. Unlike the traditional chiefs, the elite fails to underplay differences in life-style between themselves and the masses. Unlike the traditional chiefs, the elite does not redistribute wealth obtained from their linking position with regional political officials and administrators. Unlike the traditional chiefs, the elite maintains impersonal, contractual relations with the masses. Professor Mahapatra then relates these contradictions to the failure of the Santal ideology innovated by the same elite. The masses have little incentive to follow a behavioral code which would unite them politically and gain political prizes which would profit the elite more than themselves. In addition to the material determinants of the failed Santal ideology, Professor Mahapatra also details ideational determinants. For example, the innovated Santal code includes non-participation in Hindu ritual. This is contrary to the preexisting Santal code which has been labeled the "pleasure principle" by several observers. In short, Mahapatra demonstrates with greater precision than previous analyses — that of Professor Martin Orans, for example — why the Santal-based Jharkhand Party failed. The religious-economic-political movement faltered due to contradictions, contradictions in the resource-control sense and in the symbolic sense. He does not restrict his analysis to changing patterns of allocations which yield new institutional forms — as does Professor Fredrik Barth in his analysis of Swat or of Darfur. He does not restrict his analysis to shifts in symbolic stress — as is mainly the case in another paper submitted to this conference, that of Professor Steve Barnett. (I understand that he intends to address the question of praxis in a further draft.) Professor Mahapatra has taken a step in bridging the analytic gap between ideational and behavior analyses of changes in identity. Rather than elaborate further on what an analytic strategy would entail, I will exercise *tapas*, restraint, and pause here.

VON FÜRER-HAIMENDORF: Thank you Professor David. Are there any comments by authors of papers discussed here? I think general comments and questions will be kept to the end. But if any author feels he wants to say a word, please do so.

S. K. MAHAPATRA: I am sorry that I could not attend the pre-Congress session of this conference at East Lansing. Having gone through the various papers included in this conference, I find that apart from the general points raised in the papers, the main issue which is being taken note of in this conference is the one raised in the excellent paper by Professor Kenneth David on the community in northern Sri Lanka. This issue is: what is the basis for understanding the dynamics of identity change in South Asia? He has very rightly quoted one of his students who said that Dumont is Dumont and Bailey is Bailey and never the twain shall meet! That is, the structuralist analysis and the behavioral analysis are both inadequate in appreciating the problems confronting identity change in the developing society. This springs from the fact that sociocultural changes on one hand and economic changes on the other hand are coming up in the growth process, particularly the economic process. He notes the presence of features in a particular field which are not just conflicts — they are really contradictions. Therefore, they cannot be resolved in simplistic analysis, either in a behavioral analysis or in a structuralist analysis. I will illustrate this by a point from my study of the Santals. The common man in the Santal community is not always opposed to the Santal elite, because he knows that it is the Santal elite who is capable of talking in a language other than Santal and therefore has access to the areas where benefits, particularly economic benefits, can flow: a road can be built, a well can be dug. The elite is his mediator to gain these benefits from the outside. But at the same time there are other factors for which the elite is held in suspicion. One, he is no longer recognized as the traditional, hereditary leader. During festivals, he no longer distributes food. The other is that among the modern professional groups among the elites, the lawyers are perhaps the most hated persons among the Santals themselves. There is a trend for them to go and see non-Santal lawyers rather than Santal lawyers on any legal matter. Given the various difficulties, language and so on, it is surprising that they want to go to a non-Santal lawyer for legal assistance. But they prefer to do that for the simple reason that the charges are much less and they feel psychologically more secure. Therefore the elite is held in great suspicion as merely an agent of the external leaders — the political-economic groups outside the Santal society. That is why the elite does not have political influence at the *panchāyat* elections. But he is a greater force during the higher-level legislative elections; because he can then operate at the level of ideology. Thank you.

VON FÜRER-HAIMENDORF: Thank you, Professor Mahapatra. If there are no more questions, we will now ask Professor Owen Lynch to speak.

LYNCH: Instead of beginning by greeting the members of the panel who attended the preconference, I want to reverse the order and greet first our distinguished colleagues of the audience, then the members of the panel, and finally the chairpersons. It has been a difficult task for us to read all of these papers which are so varied in content. All of us have tried to relate them to the main theme of the conference, that of changing identities.

In all of these papers there whispers a new wind, a *naī havā*. I find in them a new spirit of inquiry and a new willingness to look at and question our received anthropological wisdom. These papers most definitely give evidence of this *naī havā* which is blowing through Indian anthropology and social science. The question all seem to be asking is whether or not the picture of India which we anthropologists have painted over the past few decades is misleading or one-sided. Some of these papers come up with new, suggestive, or provocative answers.

What are some of the trends which these papers give some evidence of? First, a number of them make an attempt to view religion neither as a static phenomenon nor as a provider of psychological benefits preserving the status quo. On the contrary, they see religion in India as having a real force and real consequences for day-to-day life. This attempt to reinterpret religion in India tries to view it in other than the hackneyed analytical categories and theoretical constructs in which we have all been brought up. It is an attempt to ask not just how Indians believe in religion but rather how they use it for practical consequences in everyday life. It asks, how are symbols used for this life rather than for the other life? For example, Professor Aiyappan (this volume) in his paper on the Kurichiya tribals in Kerala tells how the Kurichiya migrated to Wynad District and how they "brought with them the analogues of several of their deities but modified their roles to meet their needs in Wynad." The paper tells us how these tribals came with their deities and used them to adapt to practical problems of everyday life. Another example is the paper by Professor R. S. Khare (this volume), who presents us with a very interesting analysis of prestation and prayers. He tells us, "Prayers, as part of sincere devotion, decry and aim to cut through the cobwebs of ritualism that pervade the entire Hinduism . . . and recent political trends . . . discovered here, often by chance, a strong parallel force that might be increasingly tapped in one form or another." In other words, religion itself may be increasingly tapped for developmental or political ends. Now these words from Professor Khare are, as far as I know, words from a Hindu looking at his own religion and asking a whole new set of questions about religion in India. The painful fact about all of this is that in seeking to answer these questions and in utilizing these insights nothing new will be discovered. It has been there all the time; we have just failed to look at it. Perhaps Indian social scientists failed to see it because they are so familiar with it that they take it for granted. Non-Indian social scientists have failed, perhaps, because they have not asked the right questions. Another example of this new trend is the paper by Professor L. K. Mahapatra entitled "Gods, kings, and the caste system in India," in which he describes temple organization in the city of Puri. This is a very important and concrete paper using historical evidence in reinterpreting the past and asking: how did religion operate in peoples' lives? Professor Mahapatra sees an identity between the god and the king. This is contrary to Professor Louis Dumont's theory of religion encompassing power. In this paper — which shows how real people live with religion — the reverse is true: power in the acts of men encompasses religion in real life. This paper indicates that in India there is no absolute distinction between power and religion; it speculates on the origin of the caste system's ritual organization; and finally it clearly shows that religion and temple organization were used by political powers to achieve political ends.

The second trend of the *naī havā* which appears in these papers is the attempt to go back to the rural areas and look again at social organization there. This has gotten somewhat unfashionable because once the idea of the village community as an isolated unit began to crumble, few took up the challenge in terms of actual fieldwork to analyze what is there and going on. Several suggest ideas and concepts which seem to come more directly out of Indian life. For example, to what *extent* is caste present in rural areas? Do we tend to look for it and neglect other areas of understanding which villagers have of their own society? This is a crucial question and I think there is much more than caste present. Professor Joan Mencher's paper has provided further elucidation on this question in her paper on Kerala. She finds a growing movement of class consciousness through unionization of landless agricultural laborers. This is a very important trend which points to the dynamics, and, I think, to the ever-present dynamics of Indian society, *contra* Max Weber and Louis Dumont. Similar suggestions and questions for Sri Lanka have been raised in the paper of Professor Kenneth David.

The final trend of this *naī havā* is the attempt to come to grips with identity choice. This is especially pleasing to me as it was a central concern of my own research among the Agra Jatavs. Professor Steve Barnett conceptualizes this as a process of substantialization of identity which allows all sorts of nontraditional caste actions to be done without sanction. This same kind of struggle to change and adapt to new kinds of situations is vividly documented in two papers on the Santals by Professor M. K. Gautam and Professor S. K. Mahapatra. These papers are most interesting because although they take up the same problem of Santalization among the Santals, they show how the movement and the choice of items which can be included in an identity varied from one area to another, from one group of Santals to another. Both movements were trying to solve different problems in the outside, concrete world. This trend, then, underlines the question raised in the paper of Professor Kenneth David, namely, how can ideology and action be related within one conceptual framework?

When I was in graduate school and learning something about Sanskrit poetry, the concept I had most difficulty with was *dhvani*. It was difficult for me to grasp the meanings of the suggestions and images. These papers are suggestions both implicit and explicit for new research and new ways of looking at things. It is up to us to grasp the meaning in the *dhvani* of this *naī havā*. In looking through these papers and being asked to say something about them, I was also brought back to my first lesson in Hindi, a little prayer which starts,

> *Vintī sun lo he Bhagvān*
> *Ham sab bāalak hain naadaan.*

Perhaps we must all go back to school and rethink what we know. We have to ask of India not what it has to offer by way of spiritual wisdom — there is plenty of evidence for that — but what does India have to offer by way of sociological and anthropological insight for all of us.

MARRIOTT: In his contribution to this Congress, L. P. Vidyarthi (this volume) writes that social anthropology in India should not overlook "what may be termed the 'Indianness' in its science." In parallel thought, I review some of the researches presented here with the aim of showing how they imply a distinctive South Asian ethnosociology. To develop this indigenous sociology would be to lay out a social science that agrees subjectively, that is, cognitively, with what most actors in South Asia are themselves assuming in being parts of their kind of social organization. The attempt to build a sociology on distinctive South Asian cognitions implies doubt as to whether there can be, whether there ought to be, only one universal social science. It also implies a question as to whether the world might be better served by various sociologies, each adapted cognitively to its own world region.

The anthropomorphic logo of the Congress, as well as many of its papers, may be taken as illustrating one salient feature of a possible South Asian sociology — monism — for this original ideograph is both spirit and matter, abstract and concrete, code and substance, or, to use common analogous terms of Hindu philosophy, both *puruṣa* and *prakṛti*. It is a unitary icon. South Asian thought about society may be said similarly in general to avoid dualism: it holds that everything has spirit, or code, or pattern — a kind of built-in culture. It holds also that the phenomena we call spirit, code, pattern, culture, etc., are always embodied in natural forms — in human, animal, or other material, even if subtle material, forms.

While the Congress logo can be understood as fitting a monistic South Asian ethnosociology, the dualistic and pluralistic motto of the Congress does not fit it. The Congress motto says that "mankind is one and cultures are many." A South Asian ethnosociologist could readily agree that mankind is ultimately one, having been generated through transformations of one, but would insist that cultures must therefore also have been generated out of one. All diversity, all the seeming particularity of the world has come out of the body of God, according to widespread South Asian thought, and all diversity may ultimately return to one. Through all existence, cultural behavior and biological nature, whether of groups or of single persons, must differentiate together in parallel. Culture and biology are not separate, but are aspects of each other.

Put in terms of social action, from a Western, dualistic point of view, a fundamental proposition of an ethnosociology of the South Asian region would thus be that action is inseparable from substance, that behavior is inseparable from the nature of the actor. Both are mutually immanent in each other. The way I act is and makes me what I am; conversely, what I am is and makes me act the way I act.

In any cognitive study, the way units are defined by the actors may reveal the structure of the whole cognitive system. Manisha Roy's (1975) investigation of how South Asian actors conceive of themselves is a good place to look for such definitions. As interpreted by Roy's informants, the way a Bengali woman acts is demonstrative of her nature. She does not need to wonder who she "really" is. She believes that her nature changes as she fills different roles, as she relates herself to different other persons. She may be pleased or displeased as she sees her natural action and her actional nature change, of course, but she need not question the fact of the procession of her identities as a woman. Her mind and body, her roles and self-conceptions are felt to change as one.

The Bengali woman's view of herself is very different from the self-concentrating of the American woman, according to Roy. The American woman believes that any actions she is taking may not reflect her true nature. She cannot help wondering, "What is my nature? Am I really the person who is acting in this way?" She may act differently in order to be true to her unmanifested ideal nature. She believes that she may try to change even her bodily nature to make it fit the roles in which she has decided to act. Such trials will continue to pose problems for her, because these two aspects of herself remain separable — her action and her true nature.

Some researchers in South Asia, including myself previously, have studied acts alone, apart from attention to the bodily natures of the actors. This is to apply a typically Western, or American value, that of "universalism," to borrow a term from the sociology of Talcott Parsons. Universalism means that all actors are treated as equivalent and interchangeable, either by other actors or by sociologists. "It is not who you are," most Americans believe, "but what you do that should count." Cognitively, "who you are" and "what you do" may be, and often should be, disconnected from each other. The universalistic analysis in the paper by Doranne Jacobson used acts to build up a model of the north Indian woman's relations with her kinsfolk. The analysis as originally written did not attend to the cognized nature of the actors. The woman moving from her parents' home to her husband's home was said to have "ties" in these places — ties that Jacobson expressed as a collection of emotions, economic roles, and legal rights and duties. There remained a puzzle in this analysis as to how the elements are put together, since the woman seems through some of her ties a member of three households, but wholly a member of none. The puzzle exists in the external analytic terms of economic and legal roles; it seems to be resolved in indigenous cultural terms if, as in Bengal, a woman is believed to be transformed as she acts (Inden and Nicholas 1977). There the person is evidently thought to be not a fixed, indivisible unit with roles or ties, but a changing, divisible composite of parts shared and exchanged with others (Inden 1976:44-45, 64-65).

The distinctions of gods from men, spirit from matter, code from substance, act from actor are distinctions that South Asian ethno-sociology characteristically treats as continuities or transformations. The continuity between humanity and divinity is a commonplace rather than a miracle in the thought and practice of the north Indian village researched by Susan Wadley. The paper by A. Aiyappan notes that men become gods and gods become men in south India. Its findings are a demonstration, the author suggests, of a basic monism that occurs not only at the learned and at the peasant but also at the tribal level of civilization. In daily life one constantly finds belief in such continuity. The paper by R. S. Khare similarly shows that spirit and matter are one, as I read it: words in prayers contain powers. Khare, like Wadley, finds these powers treated as forces in both moral and physical fact.

The papers by Kenneth David and L. K. Mahapatra are rich in homologous demonstrations of the inseparability of degrees of caste status from degrees of material power, according to indigenous thought. Status or rank is an outcome of what has elsewhere been called "vertical solidarity" by M. N. Srinivas and others, applying a metaphor of Durkheim's. The state of solidarity of the South Asian village community, translated into indigenous, monistic terms, is a state of substantial order. Coded substances, most notably foods, are transferred among persons and from one caste to another, establishing ordered differences. Coded substances deriving from the locality — food, water, the land itself, or even the sight of it — influence the people who live there, making them partly alike. The local community thus becomes both substantially solidary and substantially ranked through the residents' cosubsistence.

I have the impression that if he had taken the indigenous structure of Indian social thought as his object of study, rather than Dumont's dualistic theoretical view of India, which he criticizes, Owen Lynch would not have raised the complaints of idealistic and materialistic reductionism that he does raise. Idea and materiality are inseparable in the ethnosociological thought postulated here.

"Monism" may sound static, but monistic South Asian ethnosociology is not. It generates variety and change from within itself by processes of combination and exchange. From time to time it recognizes new media — that is, new substances that may be transferred about — and drops out, or pays less attention to, media that already exist. Instead of generating variation by the externally or materially forced deviance of behavior from norms, a monistic sociology can attend to different kinds of transactions and mixtures, separations of substance and transformations of substance as the processes by which variation and change are created.

Different substances and actions may be chosen for emphasis according to the needs of the situation. A person has an occupation and also has a *jāti*, but these need not coincide. A labor union's members, as in Joan Mencher's paper, may presumably share one set of coded, nonhuman substances derived from pursuing their common occupation and from following the orders of their union's leaders. Mencher does not tell us about substances. Such substantialistic interpretations are speculative, but perhaps could be investigated. The nationalists of a given region of South Asia may stress their nourishment from one territory as the source of their common substance, as many seem to have done at the time of the birth of Bangladesh. The Maharashtrians, in Mahadev Apte's paper on the Maharashtrians living in Madras, may choose *varṇa*, or *jāti*, or may choose their ancestral territorial substance as a basis of their identities, rather than the subtle but potent substance of language, which they also share with each other. The Madrasi landowners studied by Steve Barnett may well have to claim aristocracy mainly by *jāti*, that is, by blood and by seed — by original bodily substance — since their transactions in food and ideas and work are now hopelessly mixed up through varying styles of urban life. It would seem appropriate for would-be elites to make such claims of aristocracy by ancient blood. But many persons seeking to state their identities in South Asia today probably pay less heed to *jāti*, as I read the evidence, and more heed to other kinds of substances that are shared or exchanged through occupation, through education, through personal influence, through words, ideas, and so on. Still the substantial coding of solidarity endures.

Some older varieties of such changes are also evidenced in the papers of this symposium. The paper by R. S. Khare implies the use of divine substance in prayer, in the devotional (*bhaktī*) movements, to arrange old groupings in new forms. The paper by Zeyauddin Ahmad on Islam and its effects among the lower castes and higher castes of Muslims in Bihar demonstrates the separation, I believe, of Islamic brotherhoods from the order of birth (*jāti*) groups in which Muslims are also members. Muslims, like Hindus, appear to be conceived as composite persons who are born into castes but have taken other roles in Islam. These persons have added a divine message, no doubt, and this substance distinguishes them in part from their original *jāti*s.

Are there radical departures occurring from the cognitive assumptions of South Asian ethnosociology stated here? Perhaps there are, but such departures are not established, it seems to me, in any of the present papers on Hindu devotional and Islamic groups, or in those on tribal groups, although these are loci where one might expect departures. The tribals in these papers replicate the usual South Asian dynamics internally. Thus one notices in the paper by L. K. Mahapatra that while the Hill Bhuiyas are forced by Hindu kingdoms to take up a role within a larger caste division of labor, they also make their own kings among themselves. They make them by means that are very familiar to Hindu society, by simultaneous manipulation of their bodily substances and their degrees of power and rank.

The ocean fishermen of northern Sri Lanka, who may seem at first glance to be a detached, mobile, mercantile population, are found to be not really such separate groups in the lucid paper by Kenneth David. By insisting on cash transactions in the market place, rather than accepting long-term patron/client ties, these fishermen do take into delicate account that they are connected with an order based upon transactions of substance. As David says, they share the same schema of normative thought with other occupational groups, and use market tactics as do others, as a way of managing their part in that schema. The way they systematically transact with others, through symmetrical reciprocity of giving and taking, helps these fishermen to maintain precisely equivalent relations with the persons of many other castes with whom they wish to trade.

Would an ethnosociology building on assumptions of the kinds I have illustrated here — monism, substantialism, and dynamism — be a merely parochial science? Would such an ethnosociology have utility only for South Asia, while other ethnosociologies serve only the regions of their respective origins? Some such regionalization of sociologies may be realistic and desirable for the present, until the extent and nature of their variety is better known. Conscious regionalization may yield better results than the contrary pretense that basic differences in sociologies need not exist. Breadth of theory would be reduced.

I want to suggest in concluding, however, that the indigenous social thought of South Asia is in some of its abstract qualities an extremely up-to-date kind of sociology with potentially universal value. It is compatible with modern physics and biology. It is very much like communications theory. It shares much with modern linguistics. It is like sociological systems theory. It has, like all these other sciences, admirable capacities for consistency and comprehensiveness, for seriously dealing with variance as internally generated rather than as anomaly, and for dealing with the single person as a frame within which the same processes go on as between and among different persons.

I have stressed some peculiarities of a South Asian sociological view and its differences from certain peculiarities of present-day Western sociology in order to further our understanding of South Asian society. But I believe that some essentials of this South Asian ethnoscience of society may well come to be recognized as one sociology with a future metacultural world sociology. Meantime, I am certain that by forcing us to question the peculiar cultural assumptions built into the existing sociologies of Western origin, explicit awareness of the ethnosociology of South Asia can help make a better sociology for mankind.

VON FÜRER-HAIMENDORF: Thank you, Professor Marriott. Are there any comments?

MANISHA ROY (discussant): This is a footnote on Professor Marriott's observation on my paper. It will also relate to some theoretical and methodological points I have been concerned about in my own research in India and in America.

While I should thank Professor Marriott for observing rightly that I have mentioned that a Hindu woman acts because of what she is rather than distinguishing between her action and her identity, it should also be added that a Hindu woman is not a person in a static position. She is changing. She is moving like anything else in India. There is a continuity and change. This change includes lots of things which are not just substance and nature and Hindu concepts, but things such as mass media, paperback novels, movies, cheap editions of journals, and all sorts of other things that India is getting hold of either from the West or indigenously. So when you talk about the Hindu woman as a union of nature and action, you also have to remember that it is not just that. It is also changing. If it doesn't come through in my paper clearly, I must emphasize that this is very significant. When we do research as social scientists, we have to look for operational, methodological, and conceptual frames that we can use, hopefully, quite fruitfully. I have, personally, found it quite difficult to go by abstract models or empirical models. I think that something in between Dumont and Bailey is what we need. I admire them both on their own grounds. This is just a footnote to what Professor Marriott very kindly commented on my paper.

VON FÜRER-HAIMENDORF: Thank you. As we might have to break earlier than expected, perhaps we will hold comments until after the comments by Professor Khare and by Professor Surajit Sinha. There will be a further meeting of the conference tomorrow which will be chaired by Professor Tambiah. For now, I will hang on, for there is very little to do except to ask Professor Khare to be good enough to offer his comments.

KHARE: Thank you. What I intend to do here is to comment in more specific terms on a couple of papers and then proceed with more general characterizations of Indian sociology and Indian social anthropology.

I read Professor Apte's paper with great interest, particularly because I had the occasion to work with a group of Brahmans from north India. I found that some of the features he noticed for changing identities among the Brahmans with whom he had worked did not necessarily work out the same way with the Kanya-Kubja Brahmans.

The question was: where could the explanation be found for such a difference? Although it may now be a cliché when we say that certain caste characteristics are moving toward or yielding to class characteristics among these people, there is also the fact of historical differences between north and south India. The positions and situations faced by the Brahmans who migrated from Maharashtra to Tamilnadu differ from the positions and situations faced by the Brahmans who migrated from, let us say, U.P. to central India or to Bangalore. For example, among the Kanya-Kubja Brahmans, I found, as against the evidence of the Maharashtrian Brahmans, that those who were highest on the hierarchical scale tended to retain their original identity by manipulating forces of modernization rather than yielding to them quickly. On the other hand, I found that the lowest on the hierarchical scale were not given very much room for manipulation. So the phrase "identity choice" becomes almost a misnomer for them. The society surrounding them must recognize the change in their identity before it can, in fact, become a changed identity. Very often, under the traditional pattern, in a similar way, the lower castes received "negative recognition" whenever they tried to change their identity. In comparison, I found that in the middle of the hierarchical scale, there was much more leeway in which people could manipulate variables favorable to a new identity formation. Changes in identity were pursued on the analogy of a competitive game. You could recombine favorable events in various ways so that ultimately the outcome was that either you had gained economically and politically, or at least you had gained additional social recognition. Social recognition becomes quite an important motivation for changing one's identity.

The question is: why do people try to change their identity all the time even when the actual resources for bringing it about may be limited? Indians may seldom measure a change in their identity solely by economic indicators like a salary raise. Very often, they do so for the sake of advancing their social recognition. This is an important feature, and it proceeds with or without the context of caste groups.

Let me move toward some comments on Indian sociology. It seems that Indian sociology is changing its identity, and a *nai havā* has already been mentioned. Professor S. C. Malik and Mr. Ahmad produced two papers, one on the nationalist view and the other on Muslims in Bihar. Both papers raise the question about how should the past be used? I thought I should look at these papers from the viewpoint of the majority and the minority.

Formation of identity among minority groups proceeds differently than it does in majority groups. From the nationalistic point of view, all divisive tendencies, including, of course, caste, become undesirable for the majority. You always try to produce a paradigm that makes caste an oddity. But this is also true among the minorities and they also do not want caste for the same reason as the majority. Both the majority and the minority, however, agree that they need modernization. But they would like to apply modernization in different combinations and to different effects. The nationalist view of modernization is different from the common view of modernization where it merges with Westernization: the emphasis on indigenous know-how is great in the nationalist view. As compared with that, in Ahmad's paper we find it repeatedly stated that we want a proper relation to be established between Islam and modernization. Whatever problems there are between the two should be pointed out and resolved. We cannot go on without modernization, but, of course, we cannot go on without Islam. We must have both together, though we must do away with caste.

In the nationalist orientation, an increasing use of science and technology is the appropriate banner. So here we talk of science and technology replacing tradition. Emphasis is on universal application, amplification, and verification of science and technology on "proximal" problems. As compared with that, since minorities know that they can have only a limited share of the pie in this particular regard by the principle of numerical representation alone, they manipulate religious, economic, and political distinctions in such a way that they begin to set themselves apart from the majority. They seem to say that they are homogeneous from the inside but extremely distinct and unique when juxtaposed to the majority or to another minority group. This is a claim for special treatment by forging a special identity.

In such issues, the emphasis in sociological or anthropological analysis remains on the politics of counterbalance and equilibrium because it serves the national membership. Therefore, today, you hear in India that we must investigate the causes of national unity rather than disunity. When you pursue such research strategies, you value politics of counterbalance and equilibrium over politics of protest, which is held to be characteristic of minorities.

Let me briefly change to a related theme I have been looking into, as have some others, and Dr. Kenneth David's paper is a very good example of it: the question of dichotomies and dilemmas. When we study an empirical phenomenon for discovering the logical structure underlying it, the first step usually is to produce a dichotomy, or to conceive of the phenomenon in terms of a dichotomy. We have many dichotomies used in the study of cultures and societies, whether individual/whole, or pragmatism/idealism, or sentiment/relation. The more dichotomies we create, the next step — which is not unique to social sciences but is also stated very frequently in the philosophy of science — usually is the creation of dilemmas. In other words, the two extremes become bad to explore after a while. When you cannot sit very well on either of them, you want to opt for the middle course. After some research has been done, you find that even the middle course is not so comfortable. And that is what this quest for a cultural "mediator" is all about: you begin to talk of a cultural operator, a cultural moderator, and so on. But as we become more acute with our observations on cultures and societies, we come to question the utility of a mediator. What goes wrong if we keep the dichotomies up? What does it mean if we create dilemmas? How can we resolve them? Other sciences, particularly pure sciences, have told us, at least to a certain degree, that the creation of dilemmas is a very essential state in the progress of science. It seems, particularly with regard to Indian sociology and Indian anthropology, that we are engaged in creating more and more dilemmas. As we generate more dilemmas, there develops a more acute sense for resolving them. The definition of a dilemma is that either of the alternatives provided by it is uncomfortable and you perpetually try to resolve it. But this resolution usually is incomplete and this is the stage at which we stand today.

Other sciences tell us that it is at this stage that a revolution occurs. The rearrangement of the knowledge we have acquired occurs. That makes us see the dilemma in a totally different set of relationships so that it is no longer a dilemma. It is thus "resolved." When I look at Indian sociology and anthropology from the "inside" (I may be here an intellectual interloper), I can observe from the "inside" and also a bit from the "outside" and see what tendencies might be interacting. One tendency is for more particularization. This means, among other things, that we are beginning to get communications on this topic in journals, particularly like *Contributions to Indian Sociology*. Though universal sociology is fine, we must understand what Dumont has been talking about under the label "Indian sociology." Is it "Hindu sociology"? If so, what happened to "Islamic sociology"? This should also be studied with equal interest. Then, what about the subculture (and subsystem) that the Christians have produced as a social group in the last two centuries? This "sociology" should also be studied. This means more context-oriented distinctions and more dilemmatic relationships. The second stage, it seems, logically, will be to generate more dilemmas. At this particular point there will perhaps be very specific orientations made and some new interlinkages discovered, as well as certain propositions made like the one Professor Marriott today talked about: the sociology he proposes is not necessarily a parochial sociology but a very universal form of sociology.

At this point let me come back to papers. I discussed Ahmad's and S. C. Malik's papers as proposing two different strategies within the context of a nation. We can also look at the papers written earlier by Marriott and Inden, the papers written and submitted here by David and Barnett. All of them show, according to Lynch, a *naī havā*. Indians, of course, are doing the same thing but in the name of science and technology. What are they really doing? Are they doing it because it tells us something more? — which is the question Professor Lynch also asked. Are they saying something particularly new? Or is it only an adaptive strategy for replacing texts with contexts? So if the field is not open to us as it was before, we could turn more toward a textual analysis. Hopefully, this *naī havā* will not be only a *havā* but will be more substantive. It will probably bring us an inch closer to the revolution I was talking to you about.

As a concluding comment, I was a little bit uncomfortable with the distinction or the implication Professor Lynch had with regard to religion. The more we study religion dispassionately, the more we see that religion integrates with and represents very well thought systems as a whole. Religion also generates systems of thought in every society. How can you look at religion only from the point of view of action alone and not the thought implied in it? When you emphasize the thought in it, many of the particularizing things begin to fall and the thought system becomes a focal point of inquiry.

VON FÜRER-HAIMENDORF: Thank you, Professor Khare. Now Professor Surajit Sinha will talk about practical problems of social anthropological research in India, priorities, etc.

SINHA: Professor Haimendorf and friends, we have been hearing about *naī havā* from Professor Lynch and also from Professor Khare. In between, Professor Marriott brought in the concept of ethnoscience — in other words, an Indian root to anthropology. I shall speak a little bit about this *havā* business. If we look at the history of development of anthropology in India, it has primarily been a blast from outside. There are a series of *havā* which have blown into India. The Indian participation in the game has so far been in terms of catching up with the various kinds of winds which have blown in. And before they have made up their minds, another set of fads, in the form of *havā*, have come in. You have various kinds of *havā*s coming into the terrain without a genuine cumulation toward a new paradigm, as Professor Khare expects. Let me give you a small example. I will not talk so much about priorities. We had a lengthy discussion yesterday on the basis of a blueprint from the Indian Council of Social Science Research. I do not have an equivalent blueprint. If you look very briefly at the history of anthropology in the U.S.A., you find there was an endogenous involvement, first of all among the American Indians. Since the work on American Indians was very much archaeology and a little bit of ethnography, the best immediate way of recording behavior was in terms of diffusion, mapping in terms of space. After the game was more or less completed, people felt that there was more to be known about culture than by plotting on the map. Then they moved into acculturation. Then you have some kind of pattern exhaustion in acculturation studies. You bring in culture and personality and so on and so forth. In other words, *havās* were very largely generated endogenously from one set of operations which exhausted its activities nearly and began another phase when the situation demanded. Unfortunately, in India, the history of the development has been otherwise. For example, by the time you have started making an ethnographic map of distribution of cultural traits or distribution of customs, you suddenly hear that there is functionalism. So you try to catch up with that. And then you hear that it is not structural-functionalism, but structuralism and so on and so forth.

The way to get out of this cycle, to some extent, is to ask some proximal questions, not on a high level of abstraction as to what the Hindu mind should ideally be and what kinds of ethnoscience should ideally flow from it, but some very matter-of-fact questions. Look at a slum in Calcutta. Why do people just move into the slum and not come out of it? If you have such a concrete question and a number of people start putting their minds into it, then one kind of involvement in observing the behavior comes in. Similarly, I can give you another example. For the last three or four years, suddenly the leadership in India and some of the intellectuals have become aware that even the Green Revolution is not penetrating beyond a certain barrier. Of course, there are variations between regions. By and large, the western part of India has a record of greater development than the eastern half of India. Still, the record varies from area to area. The input in development, through the Community Development or the Agricultural Innovation programs, is not crossing the threshold of certain poverty lines. Maybe the line is at 20 percent or at 30 percent in certain parts of the population. How do you approach this issue, that somehow this line is not being broken by all kinds of input of resources. There, the anthropological information that we have, from the published literature that we have for the last twenty years or so, does tell us about factionalism, about the role of lineage in village solidarity, about food transactions, about ritual transactions, about elaboration in caste ranking. I find that Professor Marriott has converted himself from the interactional Western approach to anthropology to almost fall in line with, as he defines it, Hindu ethnoscience. But the problem is, where does the kind of information that we have in the existing mode of analysis and in the existing kind of concern with anthropology really address these problems in a frontal manner? It is possible that you can derive some aspects from here and there and bring them to bear on such a problem. Another way to go about it is to directly address yourself to this proximal problem and then bring in abstraction as and when it is necessary.

My own feeling is that one of the trends that will perhaps emerge in Indian anthropology — combining, perhaps, Indian sociology and anthropology — is a lot of concern with a series of proximal problems. I do not want to review these proximal problems in terms of deciding where a tube well has to be set up or things as simple or pragmatic as that. But I am sure that all our powers of abstraction could be brought to focus on some such issues which are rather burning. For example, in the course of one set of investigations, in west Bengal, we observed that the intricacies of caste ranking, with which we are very much familiar through the recent literature, divide castes in an area into many ranks, addressing themselves to a relatively simplified binary category for which you have a name in west Bengal: *bhadralok* and *chodralok*. The *bhadralok* are the upper cluster of castes and the *chodralok* are the lower cluster of castes. In spite of all the intricacies of ritual transaction, the caste system, being a fairly pervasive system of social affiliation, has to address itself to some fairly basic productive relationships. These productive relationships cannot be managed unless it is ordered in a somewhat secularized and simplified manner. In other words, along with the intricate ritual ranking, you also have a simple binary way of associating the castes in terms of operational clusters. You begin to ask these kinds of problems only when you become somewhat aware of the problems of the relatively lowly in the village situation.

It has recently been questioned that, unlike the payoff that anthropology has gotten from involvement in Africa, or in Melanesia, or among the American Indians, somehow, the anthropological involvement in South Asia has not generated important or significant ideas. I feel — and here I am talking about South Asia and not just India — I feel that Indian studies during the last twenty years have generated some very important ideas. For example, more than any other area, here we have developed a series of concepts for the comparison of civilizations on the basis of concrete observation: the ideas of Redfield, Singer, Marriott, and many others. Similarly, concerning the concepts of tradition and modernity, about which Kenneth David spoke at the beginning of this session, we do find that Indian studies have broken through this dichotomy and have pointed out the adaptability of the so-called traditional societies in dealing with emerging forces and tasks.

Similarly, I think the studies of Bailey and others have increasingly pointed out that, in spite of the importance of corporate groups, we need to study arenas, fields, and so on.

I will briefly mention the priorities for research as I see them. As

Indian anthropologists, our priority is to develop some atmosphere of accumulation. Priority cannot be spelled out in terms of details. Somehow a research and development accumulation has to be generated. How do you generate it? I have just given some examples of that. One way is to get involved in some areas of national concern which are bound to attract a number of people to think and rethink these problems. Along with this focus on problem areas, we will have to do some basic spadework. For example, India provides a tremendous area for studying the behavior of human groups at different scales: there are hunters and gatherers like the Onge of Little Andaman, there are dependent hunters and gatherers in the mainland, there are shifting cultivators, there are settled agriculturalists in villages. There has hardly been adequate measurement of the corporate groups such as caste and lineage within the village. There has been general concern that the village is not an adequate unit for study. Beyond the village, Marriott and Cohn have written that the main characteristic of networks is that it is unbounded, very loose. On the other hand, as L. K. Mahapatra's very interesting paper has shown, there is a lot to be known in terms of bounded categories like little kingdoms and chieftaincies. There has been very little study of units larger than the village but somehow bounded like chieftaincies. Another area in which lots of interesting results are likely to come is to use the mode of controlled comparison over limited areas. For example, there is a series of research projects in Surguja State, Madhya Pradesh, where a large number of tribal, two-caste groups, from the most isolated to fairly acculturated types, have been compared within Surguja State. You can compare the groups as economic systems, political systems, or whatever, but there is some control in terms of ecology or history. Similarly, work is urgently needed on Mundari-speaking groups. No meaningful comparison has yet been done on these ten or twelve distinct groups; this is likely to yield good results on the levels of structure and of processes. Similarly, numerous Gond groups, Bhotia-speaking groups, Naga groups should be studied. Whenever I meet Professor Eggan, he asks me, "Who is studying the Onge over there?" After Radcliffe-Brown, who has done it? Vijayacochari has promised to write something on the methods used by Radcliffe-Brown. But that is not enough. Where is a second ethnography of the Little Andamanese or of the nineteen or so Greater Andamanese belonging to the old nine tribal communities? Similarly, the chain of interdependence and trade between the Nicobar group of tribes. These have to be covered in the interest of the perennial concern of world anthropology.

There has been some dialogue between Professors Marriott and Lynch: both are critical of Professor Dumont but on different counts. Lynch is critical of Dumont because Dumont has some absolute ideational definition of what Indian society is; for him, the remaining details are just details. Lynch feels that the primary emphasis should be on the observation of behavior. Ideas should be inducted into the explanatory process with the primary base on behavior. Once upon a time, Marriott took such a position, but now he turns into a monist and says that you cannot make a distinction between behavior and ideas: they occur together in nature, at least in Hindu nature. But coming back to a more matter-of-fact position, which I am deliberately taking now, we were talking about forms and processes at a level of abstraction when we are talking about the tribe/caste continuum. Today, what we want to know is the social organization of the continuum, the control system of the continuum. One of the major concerns of Indian anthropology for some more time — perhaps there will be pattern exhaustion after a while — is to study the control system of all kinds of transactions, whether of symbols or activities, which have so far been left to very vague definition. With these very random observations, I would just like to stop at this point.

VON FÜRER-HAIMENDORF: Thank you, Professor Sinha. I would like now to ask for comments. Could we possibly persuade Professor Leach to come and comment on what has gone on so far?

EDMUND LEACH: I find myself in some difficulty because I have not read the papers. I have not attended the preconference. I failed to turn up.

It seems that anthropologists studying India have a great opportunity, if they haven't yet used it, in that — this point was made by Professor Sinha — the dichotomy between social anthropology and sociology — which is very strong here in the United States and is very strong in England — need not occur in India for various historical reasons. If it does not occur, I think it means that anthropologists have a great opportunity. If one takes the case in England, and I can only speak for England, the trouble with the sociologists is that they are entirely concerned with proximal problems, that is to say, things which are immediate issues, which government will support. They have lots of money, and lots of chaps to work. They do an enormous amount of work but they have no theories. They don't seem to be interested in theory and they never get anywhere with theory. And they just accumulate masses and masses of data which are thought to be relevant by the people who are financing them but don't seem to come up with anything of a general nature. The anthropologists, on the other hand, are a relatively small group. Very arrogant. Produce theories galore. Get no money — quite rightly! And yet, in a way, the theories which the sociologists use are all social anthropological theories. It's the social anthropologists who in fact have produced the theories in the past. There is this terrible divorce. In India, because the sociology that is necessary in India covers the whole field. It covers Andaman Islanders and urban squatters in Calcutta. There is no break point at which you can say, "Oh, that's stuff the sociologists should do. And that's stuff the anthropologists should do." The whole field becomes social anthropology. And you ought to get an awful lot of money out of the government for being practical, while, at the same time, you should have the opportunity to be theoretical. This is all I have to say.

VON FÜRER-HAIMENDORF: Thank you, Professor Leach. Are there any more contributions?

VIJAYACOCHARI (discussant): I am Vijayacochari, social anthropologist and medical anthropologist. I wish Dr. Roy Burman was here, for if you tell him of one theory about a particular caste or a particular ritual in Bengal or in Assam, Dr. Burman can tell you a hundred cases which do not fit that theory. Dr. Burman is in the census department. He goes around all over India. He knows many villages, castes, and communities. And he has a feel for the tremendous diversity which exists in India and which has been pointed out by Dr. Sinha briefly. The problem that we have is part of the situation. The society in India is so diverse, so different, so plural and multifarious, that Indians who are aware of those diversities are like Dr. Roy. She knows the Hindu woman so intimately that it is very difficult for her, probably, to put the Hindu woman in one category of structural description or the other, which would seem very sound and meaningful to an audience which is not so familiar. On the same account, probably, the hasty theorizations by Western anthropologists who go to India for six months and come out with fantastic theories and models do not satisfy Indian anthropologists. These do not explain the reality, the variety that Indian anthropologists are faced with. I am reminded also of the great anthropologist, Professor Nimal Kumaar Bose. The theme he frequently repeated was to forget details in a particular area. Do not get so much involved in the figures and statistics. View from a distance. Be aware of the unity in the diversity. I do not think that we yet have a theoretical basis for this. But I think that this situation of unity in diversity that we find in India is probably why we have so much of confusion and disagreement on what is being said.

VON FÜRER-HAIMENDORF: Before we go on, I would like to defend Western anthropologists, who, according to Professor Vijayacochari, go to a village only for six months and then disappear, only to come up with some fantastic views. I think that those anthropologists who have really contributed to the theory of anthropology in India, such as Dumont, Bailey, and others, have spent quite appreciable times in India. If, in the future — for at present, Americans can only go for three months on a tourist visa — they are able to spend a long period in India, I am sure they will do so. Dr. Vijayacochari may be right that they have a different view from those who are born in a society. This is inherent in the profession of anthropology, that one can understand another culture. I think if we were only looking inward into our own society, perhaps we need not take that particular profession. We could become social philosophers. I would, then, not really agree, but this is more than a chairman should perhaps say.

LAKSAMANA (discussant): I am Laksamana, Usmana University, Hyderabad, India. Throughout the session, and while going through the papers, I had the feeling that we were completely missing the point. Are we interested in a discussion between Indian anthropology and sociology on one hand and world anthropology on the other hand, or are we identifying the emerging identities in India and South Asia? If we are interested in the second, which should be our concern, then the whole discussion as to how we should evolve a social anthropology for India or a sociology for India is not so important. Incidentally, I am a sociologist who is trying to understand a little social anthropology. Therefore, I am very happy to learn that in Britain the sociologists have a lot of money at their disposal. How we wish it were the case in India! In India we don't make much of a distinction between a social anthropologist and a sociologist as far as funds are concerned. The Indian Council of Social Science Research does not make this distinction. Nonetheless, it bothers me that we did not make any specific attempt to find out what are the emerging identities in terms of certain goals that have been set by us. I don't think it is possible to divorce ourselves — if we are interested in finding out what the society is going to be after twenty, fifty, one hundred years, depending on the pace with which you are going to transform society — from the goals that have been set by the government of India on that matter or by any other government in that region. If that is the case, I think there has been no specific attempt in many of the papers here as to how this is going to affect — that means, how these goals, which are being translated into action to some extent and failing miserably sometimes, are affected by certain ethnic categories, ethnographic categories or whatever. That should have been more of the concern. For instance, whether Indian society is dualistic or nondualistic (I don't like to use the term monistic; the terms we use are *dvaita* and *advaita* — we never talk in terms of *ekata*) is of great concern for us; nonetheless, it is of greater concern whether certain ethnic categories, caste or kinship categories, have a great effect on these social processes of economic development and social transformation. For instance, India is talking in terms of a new philosophy, *garibi hatow*, which means to abolish poverty. They mean to uplift the weaker sections. But this boils down to the uplifting of the lower castes. When implementing the policies, we always confront caste categories. Many efforts have been made to classify backward classes by social scientists and administrators. Similarly, studies of the Green Revolution have shown that the underlying philosophy was one that added to the wealth of the upper-caste people in villages who are capable of manipulating the innovations to their advantage. Farmers in middle- or lower-order castes cannot take advantage of them. Thus the process of a secular modernization is being hampered by certain nonsecular forces like caste. This should have been our concern. One more question is, "Is caste dying?" The answer must deal with the question: "Is caste surviving because of its inherent strength or is it because of something else?" If we look at caste as Professor Hutton has done, with seven characteristics — occupation, importance of Brahmans, commensal taboos, marital restrictions, etc. — of these characteristics, commensal restrictions are not as rigid as they were formerly. Occupationally speaking, there has been a lot of mobility. In terms of marriage, previously separate subcastes now marry. Castes want to take advantage of the democratic process. Thus it is better to have horizontal solidarity and unification in terms of castes and subcastes and to stand in competition with other castes. Caste-ism is now prevalent; it is not the caste system. Therefore, we should address ourselves to how these ethnic categories in South Asia aid or hinder the goals set for the nations by the society as such. Social scientists cannot avoid this commitment; if they do, they will hunt after concepts for the sake of concepts and will evolve good-looking and high-sounding theories. But if these theories are not related to the social reality as it exists today in those developing societies they will be aliens. If an Indian social scientist does it, he will be alien in his own community. Likewise, he will not be any different from the Western social scientist who comes and studies them. Therefore, both Indian and Western social scientists — the latter may also be helpful since he may analyze more objectively and dispassionately — will be of great help in these developing societies by identifying the emerging identities and strengthening the forces of development. Thank you.

VON FÜRER-HAIMENDORF: Shall we let Professor Leach answer? And then we shall adjourn.

LEACH (discussant): I don't really want to answer anything. I would like to address to the Chairman a request that at our next meeting we do pick up the point that was being made. Coming as an outsider to this meeting, the theoretical issue of what you mean by identity has not been faced. You have been talking as if it were collective consciousness which was an identity, the consciousness of groups, the self-identity of groups. Now, it is by no means self-evident that groups have a self-identity. Individuals have identity. Simply in empirical terms, I would just pose this point. Groups can continue to exist even when they are leaking away very rapidly. Let me take the example of the Jewish community in Cambridge, England. The number of self-conscious members of the synagogue has increased over the years. But statistically it was quite evident that the number of persons who were ceasing to recognize themselves as Jews was also increasing. There were more Jews turning into non-Jews than there were Jews remaining Jews. And yet the community itself was in fact increasing. This whole question of what you mean by an identity in terms of persistence and change needs to be investigated somewhat in these terms, because a caste group, for example, can continue to exist even when 50 percent of it is rapidly turning into something else. Until you have explored these definitional terms, it is very difficult for the outsiders to know what you are talking about. I wonder if that could be examined in your next meeting.

VON FÜRER-HAIMENDORF: I think that this would be a very good topic to start with. Perhaps Professor Tambiah, who will be Chairman of that meeting, will start with it. We will now adjourn until tomorrow afternoon. Thank you.

REFERENCES

INDEN, RONALD B.
  1976 *Marriage and rank in Bengali culture; a history of caste and clan in middle period Bengal.* Berkeley: University of California Press.
INDEN, RONALD B., RALPH W. NICHOLAS
  1977 *Kinship in Bengali culture.* Chicago: University of Chicago Press.
ROY, MANISHA
  1975 "The concepts of 'feminity' and 'liberation' in the context of changing sex-roles: women in modern India and America," in *Being female: reproduction, power, and change.* Edited by Dana Raphael, 219–230. World Anthropology. The Hague: Mouton.

Epilogue: What Shall We Mean by Changing Identities?

KENNETH DAVID

THE JOURNEY

Near the end of the conference on Changing Identities in South Asia, which convened at the IXth International Congress of Anthropological and Ethnological Sciences, Edmund Leach quite rightly commented that the theoretical issue of what we meant by identity had not been faced; that we were talking as if identity means collective consciousness, that is, the consciousness of groups or the self-identity of groups. He then proposed that it is by no means self-evident that groups have self-identity; individuals have a self-identity. Although this point was further discussed, it was not satisfactorily resolved.

Let me make it clear that the papers collected here and the three discussions held on the topic of changing identities were not concerned with the changing self-identity of an individual nor with the very interesting social-psychological questions of consonance or dissonance between aspects of self-identity such as attributed/subjective/optative identities (Burton and Whiting 1965:612) or ideal/real/claimed/feared identities (Watson 1972). The conferees were trying to explain systems of socially shared identity categories. We debated at length the nature of the ideological, cognitive, normative, materialist, and behavioral structures in which a system of societal classification is embedded. We have no clear resolution on the question of whether to conceptualize the relation between the previously existing sociocultural structure and the

My thanks to the following persons who have commented on this work at various stages of preparation: Gregory Bateson, Abner Cohen, Maurice Godelier, Adrian Mayer, Barry Michie, Charles Morrison, David Parkin, Harry Raulet, Arthur Rubel, Joseph Spielberg, Andrew Turton, and Aram Yengoyan. Final responsibility remains with the author.

emerging sociocultural structure in South Asia as continuity and transformation or as a discontinuity. We have discussed the role of indigenous categories/nonindigenous analytic categories in this analysis and the role of indigenous/nonindigenous anthropologists in studying South Asia. These features crosscut in the several approaches that emerged in the papers and in the discussions.

As a further clarification of these contrasting approaches, I shall speak to Leach's question. To chart the area of consensus between these approaches, I shall survey previous definitions of identity and related terms and point out such pitfalls to understanding as using reified, projective, or atomistic definitions, imputing more shared consciousness to persons sharing an identity than is warranted, stressing ideational or materialist determinants out of proportion, and importing foreign analytic terms and foreign common sense where native common sense is applicable and translatable. Bridging over pitfalls is not equivalent to presenting a full-blown alternate theory.

Steps toward a theoretical framework are taken by means of a process of theoretical development that I call *cross-modeling*. In the first of these essays, "Step one," I take suggestions from various symbolic theories. In the second essay, "Step two," I take suggestions from the overlap between systems theory and structuralist Marxist theory. Having taken these theoretical choices from the spectrum of symbolic approaches now available and from the spectrum of materialist approaches at our disposal, I proceed in the third essay, "Step three," to use each chosen approach as a model to develop the opposite direction of inquiry. This process of mutual development between elements of previously developed theories may yield a direction of explanation that is less elegant but more comprehensive in dealing with the study of changing identities in posttraditional societies. In other words, this new framework is helpful to me in avoiding the above pitfalls and in paying attention to much of what is relevant in thinking about identities and changing identities.

Before starting this expedition, it seems prudent to meet the expectations of those readers who, as a British colleague said, want to hear about the "really real reality"! With full recognition that such reality is decidedly a function of one's theoretical perspective, I shall nevertheless set out a series of statements linking the shifts concerning collective identities that have been reported in the papers and the discussions collected in this volume.

This series of empirical generalizations about changing identities sketches the outlines of the changing system by tracing causal interconnections around the system and back through the position arbitrarily chosen as the starting point of the description. This series of generalizations is thus a circuitous statement intending to give equal weight to material and symbolic determinants of human action. It is nothing but a rather unified descriptive statement that nevertheless draws our attention to the fact that the analyses discussed in this volume deal with isolated arcs of an integral system of co-occurring constraints.

1. Unchecked, technology is potentially a self-promoting circuit: the more technological development, the greater the possibility of further development. Technological development has proceeded unevenly in different sectors. During the colonial period, the practice of dual economies (export production controlled mainly by colonial powers coexisting with indigenous subsistence economy [see Snodgrass 1966:4-51]) implies dual technologies. After independence, industrial sectors have grown far more than the agrarian sector, which has developed only in certain regions. Even the industrial sectors are checked, however, by government controls on the availability of raw materials (but see statement 10 below).

2. Population is a self-promoting circuit. The greater the number of people, the greater the growth of population.

3. Technology promotes the growth of population in the short run in that improved agricultural, industrial, and health-care technology increases the ability of the population to exceed the carrying capacity of the land more than birth control technology retards population growth.

4. In the long run, the combination of technological and population excesses depletes energy reserves and otherwise deteriorates the ecosystem.

5. The combination of health-care technology and population growth increases the ratio of the dependent population to the productive population: more pre- and postproductive persons in relation to productive persons.

6. Where unchecked by government controls, improved industrial technology and, in some regions, mechanized agrarian technology reduce employment opportunities, or "marginalize" a greater proportion of the productive population. In such cases, polarization between relatively advantaged identities and relatively deprived identities increases. In addition, for all sectors technology has unintended consequences, such as urban blight and a false base of production — as was recently revealed when some of the advances of the Green Revolution (tractors, fertilizers) were reduced because of the decreased availability of oil, gasoline, and petroleum-based fertilizers.

7. The combination of improved industrial and mass-communications technology (which communicates news of foreign life-styles) promotes an increase in material expectations among all identities.

8. Legislation may advantage some previously deprived identities (e.g. tenants in Kerala become small landowners) but may have the unintended consequence of further disadvantaging others (e.g. landless

laborers who previously had subsistence shares of the harvest become wage laborers with net loss of real income).

9. The above developments incite the further coordination of action by previously established identities and mobilization of action by emerging identities in competition for access to resources or power. This competition is, in part, focused on identities introduced by the British during the colonial period and vacated at independence, that is, on productive and administrative identities and on educational identities that provide recruits to the former. Such action takes several courses, depending on the preexisting structural position of the identity (its position in systems of production, power, and status, and its normative codes enjoining involvement or noninvolvement in mercantile or entrepreneurial activity).

10. Identities in a relatively adequate structural position can respond by using the political, legal, and bureaucratic processes to their advantage (see the Introduction to this volume). Khare spoke of the different potentials of high-, middle-, and low-status groups to change their identity. Higher structural position may also imply greater access to political, legal, and bureaucratic channels. Such access may short-circuit procedures (i.e. remove obstacles) that might retard the ability of advantaged identities to ameliorate their position.

11. Identities in a structural position of relative deprivation — whether of material resources, power, or status — may respond to the rising rate of expectations by attempting to redress the situation by means of normal legal, political, or bureaucratic channels. As has been reported, identities without connections to these channels may find them blocking communication of the situation of relative deprivation.

12. On the other hand, politicians and lawyers facilitate communication of unmet expectations by innovating strategies for redress of deprivation that may be incorporated into a collective strategy.

13. Conditioned by availability of resources and by the lack of class or life-style contradictions between leaders and followers in a movement, a new identity (new identity category, new codes for conduct, redefined past position, new strategies for gaining access to resources and power, etc.) and a new ideology may be constructed and collective action mobilized, perhaps in the political arena with the strategy of the politics of protest.

14. If resources are not available or contradictions are present, the previous identity will be conserved.

15. Mass-communications and transportation technology facilitate the communication of new identities or ideologies constructed in South Asia or elsewhere in the world. News of successful political protest or of revolutionary movements provides models for the construction of identities and impetus to mobilize them.

16. If these more radical strategies by deprived identities fail to redress relative disadvantage, or if connection of a relatively advantaged identity with deprived identities becomes viewed as detrimental, a system-eradicating process of revolution or separatism may occur.

17. On the other hand, with a number of identities of varying scales competing for scarce resources, the government may respond with redressive legislation and allocations and with revised bureaucratic procedures that implement them. In addition to short-term equilibrating effects, however, these actions have long-term nonequilibrating effects, such as statement 8 above, temporary relief that raises expectations without providing a firm productive base (see the Introduction to this volume, where von Fürer-Haimendorf discusses the Nagas) or further impetus to technological development.

Thus a self-promoting circuit of system-challenging shifts is completed; that is, the totality of these changes cannot necessarily be accommodated by the cognitive structure of the previous system of identities. Furthermore, several factors militate against the construction of a highly ordered new structure of identities. Identities or identity domains constructed by one collectivity are not necessarily recognized, and they may receive negative recognition, in Khare's terms (see Introduction to this volume), by other identities. Identities crosscut one another. More precisely, identity domains are not as distinctly separated. For example, Barnett reports that action taken by various *jātis* jointly as Dravidians is contradicted by class-based differences between upper-caste landowners and lower-caste laborers. Culture, unlike nature, does not necessarily abhor a vacuum. Identity structures may deteriorate without immediate construction of a new structure. For example, *jātis* may withdraw from stratifying interaction for widely different reasons, untouchables refusing to perform stigmatized labor or upper castes refusing to participate in the local political process once their power has begun to wane, for fear of losing and being dishonored. On the other hand, individuals differ widely in their ability to renounce their existing identity for another, as is witnessed by the profound dismay of the Koṇṭaikkaṭṭi Veḷḷālar gentleman caught in the double bind between two definitions of the Koṇṭaikkaṭṭi Veḷḷālar identity (see Barnett, this volume). Bateson's notion of double binding (schizophrenia being partly induced by the interpersonal communication of contradictory verbal and kinesic messages [Bateson 1972:271-278]) appears analogous to the cognitive state in which contradictory definitions of the same identity are presented to individuals.

These summary statements are not intended to do justice to all developments concerning identity changes in South Asia. This is not an exhaustive typological exercise. A typology of identity changes would be encyclopedic; for example, while some identities are constructed on more inclusive territorial distinctions, such as nations or states within nations, others are simultaneously based on more restricted territories, such as regions within states and even districts (Peter Bertocci reports "districtism" in Bangladesh); while some *jātis* are forming more inclusive identities by disregarding grades within the *jāti*, others, such as Nadars (Hardgrave 1969) or Ugrās (Srinivas 1952:220), are redefining boundaries more narrowly.

But an endless list of types would be a rather insignificant gain in knowledge. Rather, the idea is to set up a system of changes within which specific identity movements can be located. Dumont holds that the analysis of things is trivial compared with the analysis of relations between units; a structural analysis is completed when a full inventory of relations between units is done (Dumont 1970:40). This exercise, then, aims at an inventory of changing relations between changing units, an inventory that links together shifts reported separately by a number of analysts. It is certainly not a general theory of change. I have a certain distrust of such theories, for social scientists often ignore the lesson of hubris when formulating them.

An analogy may make this point more clearly. Even with a low-information system such as the breaking of a pane of glass by a rock, we are unable to predict more than that a star shape will appear in the glass. Curiously, the more we control the situation — using a ball bearing instead of a rock, projecting the bearing at a set velocity and angle, and grinding the glass to optical perfection — the *less* predictable become the results.[1] How, precisely, then, are we to predict and understand changes in a high-information system comprised of a collectivity of self-reflective beings (beings who know that they know)?

Despite all these rampant reservations, I feel I should try to draw together the series of statements into a more restricted set. The impetus for this attempt comes from Cohn's critique of the presentations by panelists at the Symposium on Changing Identities in South Asia; he remarked that after meeting for two and a half hours we had barely alluded to the radically different kinds of historical circumstances in which the people whom we take as our subjects, or the ideas which we take as our subjects, have taken place. We are all involved in a society which has been colonial and which is now becoming something else. In order to study postcolonial societies, Cohn wishes to take a position that is both historical and political.

Information from various world areas cautions us to be circumspect about the extent of intervention or "dislocation" of economic and political structures by colonials or by postcolonial national powers. For

---

[1]   Gregory Bateson, personal communication.

example, Kahn notes that the Indonesian government is unwilling to force small commodity producers into changing from a labor-intensive to a capital-intensive system of production; in contrast, "Rey and Dupré (1973) have argued that in West Africa such dislocation required direct political measures on the part of colonial governments" (Kahn 1975:145). Nor can we assume that economic intervention by colonial powers followed a monolithic, imported plan for action. It has been documented that the British East India Company established a very tentative foothold in Madras City in the early seventeenth century. Later the Company allied with and imitated the trading techniques of merchants from the interior. It was not until the end of the eighteenth century, when the Company became the functional counterpart of Vijayanagara-period overlords, thus achieving "the status of significant local leadership," that they "expanded their influence from the walled fortresses on the coast to command a considerable hinterland" (Stein 1969:198). Pursuing Cohn's suggestion for studying changing identities — defining the scope of inquiry as including the colonial experience — does not require unbridled anticolonial imperialist dogma.

What appears to be warranted is the most basic dogma of social science inquiry, that is, that analysis of human phenomena requires placing the phenomena in context. Anthropologists look askance at explanations by other social scientists who take, as a baseline for change, a stereotyped image of the imputed traditional structure ("custom-bound, rigid, and unproductive" [Hagen 1962:56]). Historians, in their turn, are dissatisfied when anthropologists' relatively more complete image of the traditional structure is described without proper time depth and without proper attention to the changing influences of national powers on the region being studied (Carroll 1975; Frykenberg 1969; Kessinger 1974).

Pursuing the topic of changing identities, then, requires attention to three historical stages:

First, the latter stages of colonial rule. During this period, different sectors of the society are differentially involved in subsistence versus mercantile activity and thus respond differently to the educational, economic, and political opportunities presented by the colonial power. Although the different sectors may be superficially united in colonially educated elites, the basis for postindependence conflict is established.

Second, the initial postindependence period when the new nation becomes constrained more directly by international political and economic policies. During this period, there is increasing competition over prizes (positions, power, resources) innovated and then vacated at independence by the colonial power. The native elite becomes crosscut by ethnic, regional, and class rivalries. These identities become exploited for political support. Collective identities, norms for conduct, ideology, and productive systems of the peasant sociocultural order deteriorate.

Third, the present period, when any sentiment of postindependence solidarity has entirely faded. During this period, there are open conflicts in response to new socioeconomic constraints. New identities are mobilized in response to biased allocations of resources. New collective identities are constructed out of the ruins (ideological, normative, and productive) of the old order. New identities emerge that just as frequently crosscut as reaffirm the "primordial ties" (Geertz 1963) of race, religion, ethnicity, and region which had been mobilized during the second period.

Having formulated this series of statements, I immediately became aware that these changes concerning emerging identities are not distinctive to South Asia. Colleagues have pointed out parallel processes occurring in a number of areas in the world. If this is so, then the more pressing is the question, "What shall we mean by identity?"

STEP ONE: THE SOCIAL CONSTRUCTION OF REALITY

The problem here is that an exhaustive analysis of identities and of change in identities requires consideration of everything in sight: ideology, cognition, codes for conduct, affect, observable patterns of behavior, ecology, demography, technology, economic and power distributions, and more. It is a dilemma to cut this problem down to size without rampant reductionism. Heeding a swami's advice that a journey of a thousand miles begins with a single step, in this section I will approach the "soft" facts of life: ideology, cognition, social categories, and codes for conduct. I will assert that these implicit and explicit dimensions of identity (later, I will call them semantic dimensions) define one another. People are simultaneously asking and leaders (constructors of an emerging identity) are trying to answer the following questions: (1) "What do we need and how are we materially (or whatever) disadvantaged?" (2) "What should we be doing?" (3) "Who are we?" (4) "Who were we?" and (5) "Why are we We?" My assertion is that each answer influences all the rest. The answers may become more coherent and more viable for dealing with the (changing) social milieu or the reverse.

There are vast differences in the definitions of *identity* in social science literature. In mainly descriptive accounts of new nations, *identity* appears as *something* in which one has a crisis when tradition breaks down. That is, it is a term that appears ubiquitously when social scientists discuss problems of modernization, just as the terms *status*, *role*, and *network* appear when they discuss societies in the ethnographic present, in an imagined steady state. Such an omnibus definition of identity, or search for identity, may direct our attention to a wide range of ills for which relief is sought, relief including economic stability, end to anomie, political unification, and so forth.

On the other hand, used narrowly, identity can be nothing more than a reification or an activity performed by any scale of collectivity of persons: "With respect to land, the Pare people are desirous of maintaining their agrarian identity. The necessity of earning cash . . . has resulted in many men going to the city to work. This in turn has provided a new base of identification, i.e. that of urban worker" (Tessler, O'Barr, and Spain 1973:313). This kind of definition would not fare well with social scientists such as Molière, Russell, Wittgenstein, or Bateson, who reject any reifying statement such as "Opium puts you to sleep because of its dormitive qualities" (Molière, *Le malade imaginaire*, my translation). That is, in both definitions, an analyst observes activity at the interface between two empirical systems — which is legitimate — but then proclaims that the activity is caused by an immanent causal structure imputed to one or the other system. To my mind, both overly broad and overly narrow definitions of identity must be rejected.

A projective definition of identity is the logical opposite of a reified definition; it is equally inadequate methodologically, insofar as such a definition simply reverses the subject-object relation. For example, Pye's definition (1962:52-53) follows the Eriksonian model:

The concept of ego identity, particularly as developed by Erik H. Erikson, can serve as a powerful intellectual tool for understanding the process of nation building in transitional societies. We can hypothesize that the struggles of large numbers of people in any society to realize their own basic sense of identity will inevitably be reflected in the spirit of the society's political life, and thus, more specifically, that those conscious and sub-conscious elements most crucial in determining the individual's identity crises must have their counterparts in the shared sentiments of the polity.

Pye recognizes the circularity of this argument when it defines a quest for identity (Pye 1962:4) or when it analyzes the solution to the collective identity crisis in terms of the projected political ideology formulated by a charismatic leader (Pye 1962:53, fn.25).

Despite this problem, Pye's treatment is of some utility. Pye is more explicit than Geertz in specifying the process of collective ratification of political identity. Geertz (1963:109) notes the political mobilization of primordial identities which stem "from the assumed 'givens' of social existence: immediate contiguity and kin connection mainly, but beyond them the givenness that stems from being born into a particular religious community, speaking a particular language, or even a dialect of a language, and following particular social practices." One assumes that these givens are derived from primary socialization of the individual. Pye notes the influence not only of primary but also of secondary socialization, that is, the individual's acquisition of skills and strategies for political participation. For Pye, the individual identity crisis occurs when the givens learned in primary socialization cannot be implemented by the methods of political participation learned in secondary socialization.

My problem with such projective statements linking individual sentiments about self-worth, self-definition, and self-recognition on the one hand, and a political ideology on the other hand, is that the collective conscious and subconscious involved are inadequately verified. As A. F. C. Wallace (1961) points out, most purposive, collective activity among humans persists despite the most diverse motivations and notions felt and thought by the persons involved in such activity. This line of thinking agrees with Leach's caution against attributing more consciousness to a collectivity than is warranted.

Another problem is to propose an atomistic (as opposed to a relational) definition of identity. Geertz uses identity on the individual level in the sense of recognition of personal significance. The search for identity is the motive "to be noticed . . . and a demand that identity be publicly acknowledged as having import, a social assertion of the self as 'being somebody in the world' " (Geertz 1963:108). He defines identity on the collective level as a "corporate sentiment of oneness" (Geertz 1963:114). Studying integration problems of new nations, he opposes two kinds of identities, primordial sentiments and civil ties, which compete for individual loyalties and organize collective competition for scarce resources and power. For Geertz, the fate of humans in transitional societies is alienation, a state of societal entropy. The institutionalization or "collective ratification" of individual identity occurs through political action. Geertz's undeniable contribution is stressing the set of potential identities (religious, territorial, linguistic, racial identities) that may be mobilized or downplayed in postcolonial political action. This procedure avoids using that procrustian rubric *ethnicity* when describing conflict or cooperation between collectivities in new nations. This procedure allows linking the study of changing collectivities with the specific ideological battles in some regions and with specific ideological attempts to avoid conflict in others (see also Marriott 1963).

For our purposes, the vision of the identity quest as a ratification of individuals' self-worth is, however, inexhaustive. We may distinguish two elements of the identity search, the first being a quest for a new and meaningful system of social differentiation and the second a favorable position for one's own unit in the system of social stratification. In other words, what is being sought is a system of identities in which one's own collectivity has, first, a recognizable position, and second, which Geertz emphasizes, a recognized position (see below, p. 505). The first element implies ordered information about a system of identities, while the second emphasizes ranking (a particular kind of ordering) and stresses a single unit rather than a system of units (compare Shils 1963:4). My position here will be to reject any definition of an identity as a thing in itself; rather, I will define identities relationally, as elements of a contrast set, as categories partitioning a domain.

Continuing now with the survey of the use of identity and related terms, the purpose is to inventory such mutually defining dimensions of a social (collective) identity as (1) the practical interests of a social identity situated in a particular structural position, (2) the role performance of the identity, i.e. expected codes for conduct, (3) the inclusion or exclusion of persons in the identity category, (4) the chosen past structural position of the identity, and (5) the ideological grounding of the above dimensions of identity. Omitting for the moment exposition of the framework relating these dimensions, I should note in advance that neither any of the dimensions nor the social practices that shape and are shaped by these dimensions are intended to be primary, that is, there is no intent of assigning any fixed starting point of analysis.

The term *interest group* covers some of the phenomena relevant to the definition of an identity. Of course, an *interest group* or a *class* implies more than the possession of common material interests or a common relation to the mode of production, more than the wielding of a certain amount of power in definable arenas of competition, more than a certain rank in a system of stratification; in short, more than certain practical interests in a given structural position. The term *interest group* implies motivated cognition, as in the Marxian theory of class consciousness. Among the many helpful statements which avoid reification concerning practical interests is Shils's suggestion (1963:4) that those who share an identity share not only ideas about their common practical interests but also a reaction against alien interests. Wriggins (1960:162) tells us that even on the small island of Sri Lanka, where communication between identities might be enhanced because networks of roads, public transportation, and communications facilities are better than elsewhere in South Asia, "the underlying familial and communal structure, and the language and education differences induce *communication within the communities rather than from one to the other!*" (emphasis added). These gaps in the communication structure may explain why "a vision of 'the public interest' encompasses not the citizenry as a whole, but only those who belong in one individual group" (Wriggins 1960:162).

Defining this dimension of identity as the practical interests of the collectivity in its structural position (as opposed to interests of other collectivities in their positions) intends to avoid both reified and deterministic statements. In this, I reject any view that all persons classifying themselves with a particular identity category share nearly identical opinions and positions on all questions of common material interests. Even Durkheim — whose reified notion of the collective unconscious may have been in Leach's mind when he cautioned us — repudiates the Spencerian and Hobbesian notions of contract based on self-interest as the microcosm of society:

There is nothing less constant than interest. Today, it unites me to you; tomorrow, it will make me your enemy. Such a cause can only give rise to transient relations and passing associations (Durkheim 1949 [1893]:203-204).

Granting that it is easy to attribute to a collectivity more cognitive sharing than is warranted, I would say that all that can be shared is a cognitive framework for perceiving, analyzing, and reacting to questions of material interests. Although a leader may formulate a precise position on interests, and although reasonably concerted action may be taken by a collectivity on the basis of such a position, it seems imprudent to assume any exact sharing by the individuals in the collectivity.

A necessary contribution to another dimension of identity, role performance — the relations among identity categories, codes for conduct, and interaction — is made by ethnoscience and symbolic interactionist approaches. Goodenough, dissatisfied with the "lumping together of different phenomena" in Linton's, Merton's, and other role theorists' definitions of status as (1) collections of rights and duties (i.e. codes for conduct), and (2) categories or kinds of persons, breaks with this precedent:

I shall consistently treat statuses as combinations of right and duty only. I shall emphasize their conceptual autonomy from social "positions" in a categorical sense by referring to the latter as social identities (Goodenough 1965:2).

His concern, which is explicitly in line with his interest in descriptive and structural linguistics, and componential analysis in particular, is aimed "at the grammatical aspect of normative behavior" (Goodenough 1965:1); hence his further definition of a social identity as "an aspect of self that makes a difference in how one's rights and duties distribute to specific others" (Goodenough 1965:3) and his argument that

... the selection of identities in composing social relationships, then, is not unlike the selection of words in composing sentences in that it must conform to syntactic principles governing (1) the arrangement of social identities with one another in identity relationships, (2) the association of identities with occasions or activities, and (3) the compatibility of identities as features of a coherent social persona (Goodenough 1965:7).

Since Goodenough is concerned with "the association of identities with occasions or activities," it would be improper to say that his is a purely "context-free" grammatical account. In using his framework in case studies of Truk, he does hold the context steady in order to clarify variations in behavior between relevant, or grammatical, identities (Doctor and Patient are grammatical identities in American culture; Doctor and Man or Doctor and Woman are not grammatical; grammatical/nongrammatical identities encode the normative constraint that the Doctor is to examine the Patient's body as if it were asexual). He does so with componential and Guttman-style analyses of the distribution of statuses (rights and duties). He then proposes that an exhaustive description would inventory all identity interrelations in all contexts of the culture. In practice, Goodenough emphasizes the proper behavior coded by identity relationships more than the contexts.

The influence of social interaction theory (e.g. Goffman or Cicourel) on Goodenough's definition of identity is marginal (Goodenough notes that he uses "the term 'persona' in much the same sense as Goffman uses the term 'character' as distinct from 'performer' " [Goodenough 1965:22, fn.12]). In contrast, Berreman's study (1972) of "Social identity and social interaction in urban India" explicitly attempts to wed social interactionist methods to those of ethnoscience:

Analysis of terminological systems is a useful — even necessary — tool, as the formal analysts have emphasized, but without behavioral, interactional, and contextual analysis it remains, as Perchonock and Werner (1969) suggest, "simply a process of description and enumeration" (Berreman 1972:580; see also 584, fn.5).

That is, the arrangement of social identity categories — the basic cognitive ordering done by ethnoscientists — is supplemented in this study by other kinds of cognitive data and social interactional data: stereotypes about identities, verbal and nonverbal indicators used to classify persons with identities, and interaction taking place on the basis of such identifications (Berreman 1972:567).

Instead of Goodenough's formal account of identity categories, Berreman's "context-sensitive" discussion of categories-in-use emphasizes situational and interactional information. He notes, for example, that the greater the structural distance separating identities, the less intense the interaction between them — the poorer is the precise knowledge about the other: such persons cannot specify the subcategories of the other's identity, do maintain sharper stereotypes, etc. It should be noted that the definition of a person as included in or excluded from the collective identity is in practice based on criteria such as these: whether a person knows and enacts the precise behaviors expected of someone in the category, and whether the person can adequately distinguish subcategories within the identity. (Persons in different cultures place different stress on this ability. My wife and I visited the Ramsbury Inn in the Cotswolds, England, in February, 1975. After the innkeeper selected a Rauzan-Segla 1962 to complement our meal, he diplomatically complimented *my* choice of wine, saying, "It is a fine wine and usually relatively dear. I had a bottle at the Brompton Grill several weeks ago at twice the price." It would not have been too difficult for him to deduce that we were visiting American academics residing in London. Visiting American academics usually live in South Kensington, Highgate, Hampstead, and other areas of London. By referring to the Brompton Grill — located several squares from our flat — he had exactly located us in South Kensington.)

There is one limitation to Berreman's "context-sensitive" discussion of categories-in-use. He stresses that the context of action influences a person's selection from the potential set of relevant categories:

[A drygoods merchant] will categorize customers only in ways relevant to the customer role, relying on stereotypes about the honesty, tight-fistedness, propensity to bargain, and buying preferences of the various social categories he encounters. . . . A teashop proprietor, on the other hand, will look at potential customers in terms of religion and major caste categories because he has to attend to his customers' notions of ritual purity and the jeopardy in which inter-dining puts them. A barber will attend to certain categories of class, religion, and region in order to assure that he can please his customers in the hair styles they prefer and expect (Berreman 1972:574).

Berreman's direction of inquiry is, then, roughly similar to Rao's discussion (this volume) of changing identities in terms of "role setting" (i.e. context), "role relationship," and "role expectation" (see the Introduction to this volume).

Berreman's position is limited, however, in that the sensitivity is uni-directional. The merchants, teashop proprietors, and barbers in the above anecdotes are being influenced by the context of action in the choice from among a set of identities they can choose to present and the choice from among the set of identities they choose to elicit from the listeners (customers). He does not discuss the opposite operation: how the chosen identity can potentially define (more technically, *index*) a context of action from among the set of potential contexts in the complex ambiguous urban situation where neither contexts nor identities are sharply defined.

Examples should clarify this point:

CASE STUDY 1: IDENTITIES AND CONTEXTS.   In an unambiguous context such as a physician's office, the context would normally be indexed by the patient's addressing the physician with the identity category, Doctor. Here, the context and the title are two social phenomena that replicate one another. Context and title are redundant, giving exactly the same information: they imply each other's existence. This is the process of indexing. In a more ambiguous context, I can, as a host, introduce a physician to another guest by saying, "This is George

Harrison. He is a doctor," or by saying "This is Doctor George Harrison." These two statements are equivalent in information (more technically, equivalent in semantic meaning). But the two statements differ in what they tell the guest about the contexts (they differ in pragmatic meaning). Although it is no new news to the host, the guest, who has heard one or the other of these messages, not only learns who the person is and what his profession is, but also learns or reaffirms, by the casualness given the physician's social identity in the introduction, how formal a party he is attending (or how stuffy the host). Contexts, then, are partially defined by the choice of identities presented.

CASE STUDY 2: IDENTITIES AND CONTEXTS. The indexical operations mutually defining social identities and contexts are useful in charting sociocultural change. In Jaffna, northern Sri Lanka, Pallar and Nalavar (untouchable) agricultural laborers previously resided in palmyrah groves. This ecological placement also reflected the prevailing technology (they would bring palmyrah thatch to the adjacent fields to be dug in as green manure) and the prevailing relations of production (they were servants to the landowners; part of their traditional subsistence remuneration was the right to residential land in the groves). In short, to someone conversant with the agricultural system of production, the categories Pallar and Nalavar indexed residence in palmyrah groves (and these other technological and productive patterns). Saying that someone lived in a palmyrah grove was tantamount to saying that the person was of either the Pallar or the Nalavar caste, and vice versa. During the twentieth century, however, some members of these castes moved out of their previous productive position and their previous place of residence. Even those who remained began to participate in a number of previously proscribed activities in various new contexts. They began innocuous intervillage competitions in volleyball (seemingly innocuous, for volleyball tournaments allowed extravillage mobilization), poetry, and drama. They began to participate in decidedly confrontational activities, such as entry into temples, teashops, and barber shops. Thus the set of social contexts which index the social identities Pallar and Nalavar have changed drastically in this century.

The point of this exercise, and the utility of defining identity categories as operating as two kinds of linguistic signs, as *symbols* with semantic meanings and as *indexes* with pragmatic meanings, is to incite systematic attention to the influence of action upon ideas and of ideas upon action.[2] Many analysts are now sensitized to the necessity of

---

[2]   These terms must be carefully defined, for I am not using them in the tradition of C. W. Morris (1935) that is currently popular among linguists and anthropologists — for example, see Greenberg (1964). Instead, I am closely following C. S. Peirce's definitions

combining symbolic and materialist analyses, but the means to do so are still being developed.

Both Goodenough and Berreman are dealing with role performance by defining the degree of predictability among identity categories, codes for conduct, and interaction. Goodenough discusses the predictability between identity categories and codes of rights and duties: when persons present grammatical identities to one another and thus establish an identity relationship, the proper code for conduct between them is predictable. Berreman finds predictability between identity categories, nonverbal indicators, and stereotypes of identities: a person who knows one of these features can predict the other two. It is not surprising that Berreman finds no certain predictability between

---

(1965), which have recently been elaborated by M. Silverstein (1974). Silverstein draws on Peirce's trichotomy of three kinds of signs: icons, indexes, and symbols: "There are three kinds of signs which are indispensable in all reasoning; the first is the diagrammatic sign or *icon*, which exhibits a similarity or analogy to the subject of discourse; the second is the *index*, which, like a pronoun demonstrative or relative, forces the attention to the particular object intended without describing it; the third [or symbol] is the general name or description which signifies its object by means of an association of ideas or habitual connection between the name and the character signified" (Peirce 1965:195).

Silverstein elaborates the Peircian trichotomy as follows:

Iconic signs imitate or duplicate some property or properties of the entities they denote. Iconic imitation is culturally defined as seen in the difference between the English and the French icons for the rooster's crow: cock-a-doodle-do versus *co-co-ri-co*. An indexical sign must occur in some spatio-temporal contiguity to the entity it can denote. These signs point out, or index, distinct factors in the sociological context of the speech act. There is a mutual implication of existence of the instance of the index and the entities indexed by it: indexical signs and factors in the context predict one another's existence. For example, the use of the French pronouns *vous/tu* index two different kinds of social relation between speaker and hearer. Symbolic signs' denotation depends neither upon physical similarity to the object denoted nor upon actual existence of the object in the speech situation: there is no dependency relation between the symbolic signifier and the entities denoted. Thus the instance of an utterance of a symbol is unpredictable from the context of the speech act: a symbol conveys new, unpredictable information. One can speak of chairs or ghosts which may or may not be present in the vicinity of the speaker.

Definition of pragmatic and semantic meanings is based on definition of indexes and symbols. Pragmatic meaning can be defined only in terms of the sets of actual uses of the indexical sign; pragmatic meaning means no more than rules of proper use, sets of contexts where their occurrence is deemed appropriate by speaker and hearer. In the utterance, "This man is wearing a cape," the demonstrative adjective *this* is an index that can be evaluated as appropriate or not depending on the spatial proximity of the speaker to the man referred to; if too distant, the index *that* would be appropriate. Pragmatic meanings are those upon which sociolinguists focus their studies, correlating, for example, speech forms with social strata. Semantic meanings, on the other hand, are definable in general sets of ("arbitrary") predicates about entities. Symbols bear a tautologous relation to the entities signified, for if the instance of a sign were correctly to denote an object, that object is assigned those predicates. Both ethnoscience and ethnosociological approaches restrict their inquiry to semantic meanings. In short, pragmatic meanings are defined by rules of use, whereas semantic meanings are defined in terms of truth propositions.

For a sociological treatment of indexicality and interpretive procedures of persons in society, see Cicourel 1973.

these three features and the fourth feature, actual interaction, and finds no consensual definition of codes for conduct — the predictability upon which Goodenough focuses. It is not surprising that Goodenough did not feel obliged to deal with indicators or stereotypes. For Berreman did research in the bustling, complex urban melting pot of Dehra Dun in north India, while Goodenough was working in a relatively isolated community, the island of Truk. Thus, the degree of predictability among identity categories, codes for conduct, and interaction is, as seen in this brief comparison, an empirical question. Exact correspondences are not assumed; rather, it is prudent only to say that persons classifying themselves with the same identity category share a cognitive code for identifying and evaluating proper role behavior.[3]

Ethnoscience/symbolic-interactionist accounts by Goodenough and Berreman contribute to our understanding of one dimension of the definition of identity, the relation between social classification and interaction. I will question, however, the adequacy of their method for dealing with another dimension, the cognitive framework for defining inclusion and exclusion of persons in identity categories.

Berreman is talking to the actor level of analysis when he discusses diacritical indicators for assigning identities to persons. He finds that certain nonverbal signs — "speech, dress and adornment, manners, life style, and physiognomy, in roughly that order" — are used by actors in this way (Berreman 1972:575). This kind of analysis helps us to understand how an actor weaves his way through social life but does not explain the structure of the categories themselves, that is, the structure of a domain of identities.

Both Berreman and Goodenough (among others) attempt the latter "by the use of contrastive analysis of terms and behaviors as prescribed by componential analysis" (Berreman 1972:568):

"A word whose meaning is the object of investigation designates some conceptual category within a set of complementary categories that partition a

---

[3] Barth rejects such an assumption in discussing the relation between ethnic identities and the sharing of "basic value orientations: the standards of morality and excellence by which performance is judged" (Barth 1969:14). For he states that: "The identification of another person as a fellow member of an ethnic group implies a sharing of criteria for evaluation and judgment. It thus entails the assumption that the two are fundamentally 'playing the same game', and this means that there is between them a potential for diversification and expansion of their social relationship to cover eventually all different sectors and domains of activity. On the other hand, a dichotomization of others as strangers, as members of another ethnic group, implies a recognition of limitations to shared understandings, differences in criteria for judgment of value and performance, and a restriction of interaction to sectors of assumed common understanding and mutual interest" (Barth 1969:15). To Barth, then, degree of shared communication and potential for interaction covary.

larger conceptual domain. . . . We learn what the category . . . is by contrasting it with the other categories" and noting the crucial differences (Goodenough 1969:331).

What has been debated between componential analysts and culture theorists such as David Schneider is how we are to approach these "crucial differences." Componential analysts use supposedly universal etic grids as their stockpile of crucial differences, for example, kin types such as father, mother, uncle, etc., based on Western theories of biogenetic substance and the transmission of substance. David Schneider's culture-theory approach (1968) and the ethnosociological analyses presented in this volume reject the imposition of alien etic grids onto the data. The structure of categories for kinsmen with this latter method is to be understood in terms of indigenous theories of natural substance, some of which have no counterpart in Western biology, for example, the nonduality of natural substance and codes for conduct (Marriott and Inden, this volume) or the transubstantiation of a woman's natural substance to that of her husband at the time of marriage (David 1973). In the ethnosociological method, these indigenous theories are the basis for understanding the crucial differences contrasting the categories that partition a domain and, thus, the structure of the categories at the cultural level of analysis (compare the actor level of analysis above).

A code for defining inclusion of persons in the category is necessarily related to other dimensions of identity. For example, verbal and nonverbal action defines membership in a category. Knowledge of the subcategories of an identity is frequently taken as a sign of membership. Knowledge of proper codes of conduct is another sign. In our conference, von Fürer-Haimendorf noted that even academically advanced, and thus potentially more sophisticated, persons were found in a survey to prefer marriage within their own caste precisely because the potential partner would not be alien but would know the daily customs and ceremonies familiar to the informant. There is a restricted distribution, as Berger and Luckman (1967) say, of social knowledge.

This leads us to another dimension of identity, the negative definition of other identities. Positive definitions, for example "a social system is a set of roles [read identities] tied together with channels of communication" (Boulding 1968:8), imply their negation: some identities have restricted channels of communication with some other identities and are indeed defined by their very difference from certain other identities. This direction of thought is of course a main thrust in the work of the sociologist Georg Simmel (see "The negative character of collective behavior," 1950), and has been applied to the changing social identity of untouchables in Agra by Lynch (1969). An example of the pervasive efficacy of negative definitions can be found in *Paradise lost*, where Milton is able to salvage the rather wooden image of the Almighty only by posing the incredibly detailed pantheon of demons. This dimension of identity is related to other dimensions. For example, it is common to think of a collective identity creating a chosen past to legitimize its present situation; but protest movements have been known not only to define a common enemy but to create an origin myth damning that enemy (see the myth about Whitey in *The autobiography of Malcolm X* [1973]).

Without implying that the list must necessarily be closed, the final dimension of identity which I will mention is a code elaborating the chosen past structural position of the collectivity: its selectively chosen historical myth or mythological history. I use *chosen* advisedly, in line with the old anthropological dictum that history is present social structure projected backwards in time. For example, Leach (1965) recounts that aspiring leaders among the Kachin of highland Burma fabricate myths and genealogies to justify their "ancient" position as chiefs. Similarly, during the 1956 Sinhalese Buddhist Nationalist movement in Ceylon (now called Sri Lanka, a testimony to the movement's success), there was much talk of the time of glory when Sinhalese kings ruled at Kandy and a "revivification of ancient, and better forgotten, Tamil-Sinhalese treacheries, atrocities, insults, and wars" (Geertz 1963:123). Giving prominence to selected events and downplaying others (Sinhalese princes did marry Tamil princesses) redefines the past.

Since reference to a past structural position is constructed in relation to other dimensions of the identity, such as the *diagnosis* of present practical interests and the *prognosis* of appropriate codes for action, a given definition of the chosen past may incite either action or inaction. The Sinhalese past was redefined in the context of the diagnosis that the English-speaking elites, and Tamils in particular, had a share of government far out of proportion to their percentage of the population; and in the context of the prognosis that this imbalance was to be drastically altered by such measures as making the Sinhalese language the sole language of government. On the contrary, the Koṇṭaikkaṭṭi Veḷḷālars of Tamilnadu did not wish to redefine their ancient heritage of being a caste so dominant that they ruled other dominant castes (Barnett 1973). In the context of the diagnosis that the balance of power in village politics was shifting against them, their prognosis was to withdraw from the political arena to avoid a public disproof of their heritage. Thus the code elaborating the chosen past structural position is a dimension of social identity, defining and being defined by other dimensions of a given identity. With this circuitous thinking about changing predictabilities between dimensions, it should be said that if perceived history is a projection backwards from present social structure, to the same extent the reverse is also true.

The above four dimensions of identity are held to be relatively *explicit* to persons. Persons in a mobilized identity, particularly a current social movement, are frequently able to state who they are, what they want, who their enemies are, what they are going to do about it. I submit that there is no exact sharing of answers to these questions but a relative coherence to all the answers, depending upon the scale of the movement, the proficiency of the leaders, the degree of unified, channeled action, etc. In other words, one way of saying that an identity has been well mobilized is to say that the above answers have been well defined, that they fit coherently together, and that they allow concerted action (if resources to implement the ideas are available).

If these four dimensions are relatively explicit to persons identifying themselves with a given collectivity, another symbolic dimension, the ideological grounding of the identity, is by no means necessarily as explicit to them. Awareness of an ideology, in my field experience, ranges from a fairly lucid statement to the more common "that-is-the-way-our-fathers-did-it" level. Because the latter is more common, I prefer to call the ideological grounding of an identity an implicit rather than an explicit kind of understanding. In a situation of radical change, leaders may take pains to broadcast the ideology in easily comprehensible form (see Nicholas 1973). Even in this case, it seems prudent to assume that followers in a movement more typically may be moved to action by evocative ideological slogans rather than able to enunciate the entire, coherent ideology. Noting that the distinction between them is relative and not absolute, I find the distinction between the implicit ideological dimension of identity and the four explicit dimensions of identity helpful in analyzing changing identities.

Despite the prolific literature on ideologies, to my mind, an ideology's function can be stated rather simply: why are we We? Individuals are not pure Machiavellian creatures, seeking only the most efficient and vigorous satisfaction of their ends. Many individuals require satisfaction of a basic skepticism: this identity (i.e. the above four dimensions) is all "man-made"; why should I throw in my lot with this particular crowd? As Barnett notes, many ideologies ground the answer to this question outside the realm of the "man-made." Existential authority and self-justification for a particular collectivity are grounded in an as-if "natural or extrahuman" realm. The Preamble to the United States Declaration of Independence reads, "We hold these truths to be self-evident, that all men *are created* equal . . .," not ". . . that we *consider* all men to be equal. . . ." The Hindu myth of the original man, Puruṣa, could similarly be paraphrased to read, "We hold these truths to be self-evident, that different kinds (*varnas*) of men *are created* unequal" (the Brahmans, Kshatriyas, Vaisyas, and Sudras being emanations from the head, shoulders, belly and feet of Puruṣa). And I submit that it is precisely because an ideology is beyond simple human verification that an ideological assertion of the form "we are We because . . ." can function to replicate an existing identity or to guide the construction of an emerging identity in response to new socioeconomic constraints (see "Step three").

In defining what we shall mean by identity, the first question is what is shared by members of such a collectivity. Following Wallace (1961), I assume that any cognitive and affective framework shared by individuals is an inexhaustive, abstract representation of the mental sets of the individuals involved, each of whom also has separate, though perhaps overlapping, sets of private meanings associated with the framework. Thus, it is no good to assume that any such cognitive framework is shared in any exact sense by the collection of individuals. It is also unacceptable to define such a cognitive framework as inhering in the individual actor. Such reification, according to Gregory Bateson (1972), is endemic in social scientific thinking: attending to an arc of a circuit instead of to the whole interconnected circuit. Against this way of thinking, Bateson argues that not only "normal" functions, such as levels of learning, but also "abnormal" functions, such as schizophrenia and cognitive dissonance (in his term, the double bind), "cease to be matters of individual psychology and become part of the ecology of ideas in systems of 'minds' whose boundaries no longer coincide with the skins of the participant individuals" (Bateson 1972:339). In answering the question of what can be shared by persons who are said to share an identity, I have tried to avoid the opposing pitfalls either of assuming shared consciousness in any exact sense or of assuming that identity inheres solipsistically in the individual.

First I would propose to define an identity category, not as a thing in itself, but relationally as a symbolic unit among other categories that partition a domain. On the cultural level of analysis, such a domain may be defined with indigenous notions. For example, the domain of kinsmen for Tamilians (for they have no domain of kinship) is defined in terms of sharing/nonsharing of natural bodily substance. On the actor level of analysis, identity domains are distinguished by both verbal and nonverbal markers (see the discussion of Berreman above).

Although this view resists the imposition of alien etic grids onto the data, the observer's perspective is not rejected wholesale. The definition of an identity within its domain can alternatively be stated in communications terminology, that is, an identity as a circuit of a wider system of communication (see the discussion of Wriggins above and Narroll's definition [1964] of ethnic identity as a field of communication).

Second, an identity is a particular kind of cultural sign. All signs mark off discontinuous, constitutive units from continuous nature. Children learn to class together ranges of phenomena, the empirical (dead men) or nonempirical (ghosts) referents of the symbol, and they learn to ignore systematically certain variations in the phenomena so classified ("These are both tables even though one has three legs and the other has four"). An identity is a distinctive kind of cultural sign because there is the possibility that the individual will class himself, rather than external objects, events, etc., into a category. An identity symbol entails the recognition of self, the epistemic subject, as a percept. An identity sign is a particular kind of cultural sign in that it operates both as a symbolic sign with semantic meanings and as an indexical sign with pragmatic meanings (see Case studies 1 and 2 above, and fn. 1).

Third, an identity category can operate as a polysemic symbol. It includes explicit ideas and beliefs for (1) defining inclusion/exclusion in the category, (2) identifying and evaluating proper role behavior of beings[4] included in the category, (3) identifying and evaluating the present structural position: resources available to and practical interests relevant to persons included in the category, (4) identifying and evaluating behavioral strategies for implementing these ideas and beliefs to produce purposive action by means of selective allocation of human and material resources, and (5) defining the past structural position, the "chosen past" image of the collectivity. It further refers to *implicit* ideological assertions which ground the above explicit understandings in a nonverifiable "natural" frame of reference. (Ideological assertions may be expected to be more explicitly known to persons in the case of a newly emerging, as opposed to a long-established, identity.)

When considering collective identities, as opposed to individual identity categories commonly called *statuses*, the exact sharing of the above kinds of understanding by persons who classify themselves in the collective category (persons interior to an identity) may be of less

---

[4] It would be more usual to refer to persons instead of beings, but such usage would exclude the possibility of nonhuman and nonverifiable beings, such as animal or demonic identities, and the possibility of identities transgressing our commonsense categories. I prefer not to build such limitations into the definition. (See discussion of Aiyappan article, Introduction, this volume; see Friedman's discussion of privileged Kachin lineages taking on descent from territorial gods, Friedman 1975:173).

import than the fact that they share more knowledge or consider themselves to share more knowledge than do persons exterior to the identity. Restated, gaps in understanding may be more important in the definition of a domain of identities (castes in a village, ethnic units in a nation) than the sharing of understanding. This consideration accords with what Berger and Luckman (1967) call the social distribution of knowledge, as opposed to Boulding's definition of social structure as "a system of roles tied together with channels of communication" (Boulding 1968:8).

Fourth, an identity category can operate as a ("polycontextual") indexical sign with pragmatic meanings. Pragmatic meanings are rules of use. That is, use of an identity category is known as either appropriate or inappropriate in (or, as Goodenough terms it, grammatical with) a given context of social action. Conversely, an ambiguous context of social action may be specified by the choice of identities presented by persons. Given this aspect of identities, changing identities can partially be described in terms of the changing set of contexts to which they are defined as appropriate. In other words, just as some analysts distinguish change from stasis by referring to "role taking" as opposed to "role playing," change may also be discussed as the innovation of "role settings" or contexts.

More needs to be said about the relations between explicit normative understandings, implicit ideological understandings, and human activity. It would be unwieldy to do so before discussing how we are to deal with the material determinants of changing identities.

STEP TWO: SOCIAL PRODUCTION IN REALITY

As I said earlier, an exhaustive analysis of identities and of changes in identities requires consideration of everything in sight. Having discussed explicit and implicit symbolic dimensions that partially constrain the activities of persons who assign themselves the same social identity, I now turn to material constraints on identities. It is indisputable that collective identities are constructed not in a vacuum but in the context of productive and political relations between humans (which yield perceptions of relative advantage or relative deprivation in practical — material, power, and status — interests) and in the context of technological and demographic relations between humans and their environment. Without understanding this material context, how can we understand why certain social identities are, as Goodenough put it, grammatical with some other identities and ungrammatical with others? These conditions are, of course, the starting point of analysis for any of the broad spectrum of interpretations of material determinants of human events.

To focus on the more edifying approaches in dealing with material determinants of changing identities, a brief review is necessary. Anthropology has come far since nineteenth-century evolutionists and diffusionists tried to explain human social systems with pseudohistorical accounts of their origins. Both empirical positivists such as Boas and Malinowski and materialists such as Marx agree that studying the totality of human social and productive relations is prior to studying the origins of customs. This rejection had a theoretical backlash: despite notable exceptions, such as Kroeber's historical studies (1940) of cycles of style, the first half of the twentieth century had a notable ahistorical bias. History — to those following the structural-functional, equilibrium view of human society — was not considered more than an inexplicable series of accidental events (Radcliffe-Brown, Nadel, Parsons).

The study of historical process reappeared in the conflict models of Gluckman and his followers. Conflict models are a limited departure from the equilibrium model: stages of temporary disequilibrium and its redress have been elaborated (Swartz, Turner, and Tuden 1966). Interest in historical processes is seen in various voluntaristic models: game theory, decision models, etc.; a "shifting emphasis from concern with social or cultural rules to an interest in adaptive strategies of human aggregates has become increasingly evident in the past 20 years" (Whitten and Whitten 1972:247). And, following the publication of the early works of Marx, a spectrum of historically oriented materialist approaches, from cultural ecology to structural Marxism, has appeared. Because the focus of the study of changing identities is societies in posttraditional, postcolonial upheavals, societies that are not likely to return in the near future to a pristine state of self-regulating equilibrium, the following discussion will be restricted to those models (voluntaristic and materialist) that do not assume such equilibrium.

The increased interest in voluntaristic decision models undoubtedly reflects the field experience of anthropologists who cannot fail to recognize — whatever their research plans — that they are dealing with societies in transition. When an analyst confronts a society in transition, decision models have a refreshing feel of reality in several senses. They focus on the process of transition and thus omit the failing of community restudy methodology, which presents two slices of time and thus describes, as Barth puts it (1967), two views of an aquarium, one containing a frog and the other containing a crab, without showing the transformation from the one to the other. Second, decision models focus as much on deviations from rules as on rules themselves. This focus intuitively captures more of social life as any person experiences it: rules are certainly only a partial account of any situation (Buchler and Nutini 1970:6). The feeling of capturing more of reality is evident, for example, in Goffman's work, which handles "both disruptive and adaptive aspects of conflict or coopera- tion within the same framework, thereby circumventing conflict versus functional arguments" (Whitten and Whitten 1972:264). Third, deci- sion models focus on human strategic choice and decision with regard to the ceaseless flux and variability of human activity. Use of the term *transaction* instead of *interaction* implies strategic exchanges and appropriations both between humans and nature and between humans. This focus is decidedly oriented to the study of change and variation and not only to continuity and firmness of expectations. To Firth, change and variation are the realm of

. . . social organization, the systematic ordering of social relations by actions of choice and decision. Here is room for variation from what has happened in apparently similar circumstances in the past. Time enters here. The situa- tion before the exercise of choice is different from that afterwards. . . . Structural forms set a precedent and provide a limitation to the range of . . . alternatives that make for variability (Firth 1951:39-40).

Decision models, then, consider institutional social forms not as givens but as the results of continuing processes of decisions adapting to various constraints:

Social form, in the sense of an overall pattern of statistical behavior, is the aggregate pattern produced by the process of social life through which eco- logic and strategic constraints channel, defeat, and reward various activities on the part of management units (Barth 1967:663).

A major difference between voluntaristic models and materialist models can be simply stated. Proponents of the latter view insist that actors cannot adequately perceive all the consequences of their sub- jectively strategic decisions. Whether considering the decisions of ad- ministrators, of local leaders vying for power by means of strategic alliances and strategic allocations of resources (Barth 1959), or of followers deciding with which of several competitive social protest movements they shall cast their lot, the materialist view holds that some properties of the system of social activities move relatively in- dependently of human intentions. This view is put formally by Godelier:

. . . the conditions for the rise, functioning and evolution of any system are twofold, some belong to the sphere of men's intentional activity, while others, of more decisive importance give expression to the unintentional prop- erties inherent in social relations, properties that do not belong to men's consciousness having neither their origin nor that basis in that sphere, and that are latent with the possibility of transforming these social relations (Godelier 1972:viii).

This point is intuitively evident if we consider that we are living in a period when, on the one hand, collective conscious representations for codes of social conduct are rapidly deteriorating, e.g. the definition of the sexual morality of women in the fifties as a matter of "good girls" vs. "bad girls" is gone; in the seventies it is not a matter of whether she does it, but only with what style. During this same period, unintentional constraints such as the ecological and demographic crises affect our lives to a greater and greater extent. By the mid-1970's, there exists in anthropology and related social sciences a broad spectrum of differing interpretations of these unintentional properties inherent in social relations that do not belong to men's consciousness.

This spectrum is notable for the tendency of different theorists to seize on different starting points of determinant causality in the analysis of human societies. A recent review article ably demonstrates that if one takes the basic Marxian diagram of categories,

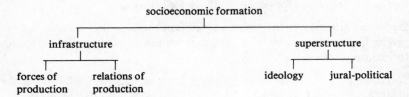

one finds proponents of every sector as entailing the locus of determinant causality: whether or not they are "monistic determinants" (Harris 1969), cultural ecologists such as Marvin Harris propose the ecological/technological/demographic forces of production as the ultimate determinant of human action and ideas. There are Marxist anthropologists, "preeminently P.-Ph. Rey, who generally maintain the dialectical unity between forces and relations of production, but who argue that in the last instance the social relations of production must be determinant" (O'Laughlin 1975:356). Still other theorists, M. Godelier and J. Friedman, "fracture the dialectic conceptually yet straddle both sides at the same time . . . by suggesting that forces and relations of production should be conceptualized as two separate structures within a functioning system" (O'Laughlin 1975:357). Yet even this last approach, which appears the least confining of the three, accepts the limitation imposed by Marx's "fundamental hypothesis of the *determinant causality*, 'in the last instance', for the replication of the social formation *by the mode or modes of production* which constitute the social formation's material and social infrastructure" (Godelier 1973:v; my translation; emphasis added).

This spectrum of contrasting interpretations of the ultimate determination of social life and the related notion of adaptive advantage, a notion common to decision models and to some versions of cultural ecology, is not intractable. To my mind, issues can be sorted out by considering a set of concepts that represent the overlap between Marxist theory, systems theory, and structuralism: *relative autonomy* of subsystems, *limits or ranges of tolerance* of subsystems and systems, *positive and negative constraints, functional compatibility* and *functional contradiction*, and the *hierarchy of constraints* within a system.

First, *relative autonomy* of a system (or a subsystem) entails that a system has relative autonomy to the extent that its properties — that is, constraints between its components — determine its breakdown point (its *limits* [Godelier 1973:214, fn.55]; the *range of tolerance* within which its components can operate [Friedman 1974:449]):

For example, Yengoyan calculated the population limit necessary to permit the functioning of marriage regulations in the Australian 8-section "Aranda" kinship. In ten local groups there must be 1070 persons equally divided between the sexes for the continuing operation of the rule that each person must marry a second-degree cross cousin, the daughter of mother's cross cousin (Godelier 1975:6).

The notion of range of tolerance is problematic. Heider (1972) notes problems of measuring limits or ranges of tolerance. Population density is a crude measure of range of tolerance, for

. . . conflict potential, energy consumption, and energy production all vary drastically across the age range of a population. The ratio of dependent, non-productive youth to independent, fully productive adults may be a crucial variable (Heider 1972:217),

and because

. . . different kinds of lands with different productive potential and different technological possibilities (extensive swidden agriculture and intensive garden agriculture in hills and valleys used by the same population) cannot be calculated as flat square land units to measure density (Heider 1972:218).

Godelier admits that limits have been adequately applied only in mathematical models of static situations. Definition of limits in situations of change is still difficult:

To think of the concept of limit is to determine the totality of relations permitted between structures of a system. It is also *to determine the totality of incompatible variations which provoke the elimination of one of the connected structures and the changing of the system.* If the first point has already been explored in part, *the second remains largely unknown* (Godelier 1973:214, fn.55; my translation; emphasis added).

Second, systems (or subsystems) are only relatively autonomous. Systems constrain and are constrained by other systems. Each system's operation either maintains related systems within their ranges of tolerance (*functional compatibility*) or drives them beyond their ranges of tolerance (*functional contradiction*):

Godelier draws from Yengoyan's demographic/kinship analysis implications for the operation of productive relations. If the demographic/kinship constraints operate/fail to operate, then there is more/less likelihood of the operation of the system of reciprocal kin exchanges including the right to hunt on another unit's territory in times of need (Bloch 1975:16).

Third, the distinction of *positive and negative constraints* aids in discerning the utility of the notion of adaptive advantage and in untangling the spectrum of differing interpretations of ultimate determination. The notion of adaptive advantage has become popular by seeming to introduce a degree of explanation for apparently bewildering and exotic social happenings such as the slaughter of pigs in New Guinea and the nonslaughter of sacred cows in India (Rappaport 1968; Harris 1966). This notion has been criticized roundly, for "as a principle of causality in general and economic performance in particular, adaptive advantage is indeterminant: stipulating grossly what is impossible but rendering suitable anything that is possible" (Sahlins 1969:29–30); "as soon as a society exists, it functions, and it is tautological to say that a variable is adaptive because it fulfills a necessary function in the total system" (Godelier 1972:xxxiv). Adaptive advantage is, of course, only one direction of deterministic statements.[5]

Godelier's and Friedman's answer to the materialist analysts'

---

[5]   An ecological model appears frequently in the study of change. It is explicitly or implicitly used by writers who cannot be titled either Marxian theorists or vulgar materialists. I find Barth's "generative" approach (1959:10) congenial in some respects with what I have been exploring here. Whereas Goodenough's componential-distributive model (1965; discussed earlier) is adequate for describing only a static system of identities and role behaviors, Barth's model clearly separates cognitive and action processes and also encourages the perception of the dynamics of changing predictability between identities and role behavior. First, there is a cognitive dynamic in situations of interethnic contact: "Because identities are signalled as well as embraced, new forms of behavior will be dichotomized: one would expect the role constraints to operate in such a way that persons would be reluctant to act in new ways from a fear that such behavior would be inappropriate for a person of their identity, and swift to classify forms of activity as associated with one or another cluster of ethnic characteristics" (Barth 1969:18).

Second, he analyzes action with an ecological perspective, analyzing "adaptive strategies," relations of "complementarity," "symbiosis," or "competition" between different ethnic identities depending on whether or not the groups exploit the same or different niches, etc. Though it seems that Barth is predominantly concerned with the ecological model, the statement quoted above is strikingly similar to a communications model or a legal model, such as Levi's notion (1948) of law as a "moveable frame of reference." Levi traces, for example, the dynamic redefinition of the American legal notion of the "inherently dangerous object" through 150 years of legal cases. The combination of two types of analysis in Barth's "generative" model appears superior to a narrow ecological model, which appears implicitly, for example, when Singer (1973) or Khare (1970) (see Introduction, this volume) write of "adaptive strategies" of modernization. While Barth's "generative" model deals separately with processes I have labeled semantic and pragmatic, the latter usage of "adaptive strategy" conflates these two processes. It may be apt, in thinking about changing identities, to focus on identity categories in terms of changing predictabilities or of changing frames of reference for identifying and evaluating behavior, material and power interests, and other shared understandings.

internecine battle over starting points of structural causality is the distinction between positive and negative constraints exerted by one subsystem on another. They hold that environmental conditions and technology used to appropriate energy from the environment (energy necessary to reproduce the material and ideological conditions of social life) can be a determinant of social forms (including social identities and the socioeconomic relations between social identities) only in the negative sense. That is, environmental and technological conditions constrain only by setting the outer limits of variability that social forms can take; these conditions do not positively constrain or determine the exact form of these identities or relations:

For example, a single ecological type, a rain forest, is occupied by all the sub-sections of the Mbuti people of Africa. Different sub-sections have made different technological/productive relations choices: there are net-hunters with larger bands and bow and arrow hunters with smaller bands. Each sector assumes the opposite size during the honey season for sociability and to relieve tensions of a fixed human collectivity (Heider 1972:215-216).

Similarly, reviewing the negative but not positive constraints imposed by ecological diversity with regard to marketing practice (and central place and location theory), Salisbury argues that studies

. . . show how social and cultural factors constrain decisions *within the potential provided by ecological diversity*. Although ecological complementarity is highly significant in the Vitaiz Strait area of New Guinea as between island communities, coastal communities, and inland communities, ecological diversity does not determine the specific form of local specialization of production, distribution by trading, motivations by "big men" to trade in order to accumulate goods for feasts that gain them prestige. Ecological diversity can only explain how social differentiation began and how resources are spatially distributed, resources, which when appropriated by humans, maintain the structure of production and distribution (Salisbury 1973:86-87).

To repeat, Godelier and Friedman reject a mechanical materialist statement of determinism: "We do not suppose that the different levels of a social formation emerge one from another" (Friedman 1975:163). Friedman proposes that there exist constraints from the ecosystem through the systems of technology and demographics to the relations of production, but stresses that "This is essentially a negative determinism, since it determines what can not occur but not what must occur" (Friedman 1975:163). This approach takes any dogmatic sting out of the phrase, *determinant in the last instance*: "If the technical conditions of production are determinant 'in the last instance' it is because the structure of the productive forces sets the outer limits on the variation and development of all the other levels" (Friedman 1975:164; cf. "restrictive determination," used in Djurfeldt and Lindberg 1975:28).

Opposed to negative constraints are positive constraints purportedly exerted by the material/social relations (Friedman 1975:164) of production (a specific form of reciprocity defined by differential control of factors of production: capital, equipment, etc.). Social relations of production are held to determine the economic rationality of the material process of production in given technoecological conditions and thus to determine (1) the use to be made of the environment under given technological conditions, (2) the division of productive labor (who labors and with what intensity of input), (3) forms of appropriation and distribution of the social product and the utilization of surplus, and (4) the socially reckoned value of the rate of surplus and the rate of profit. Social relations of production are not then a technological phenomenon. They are held to define the specific rationality of the economic system (Friedman 1974:446).

These claims for the functions of the social relations of production immediately meet a major difficulty. Marx's original hypothesis about determinant causality of one societal subsystem *vis-à-vis* other subsystems was elaborated in relation to the capitalist mode of production in Western Europe. In this mode of production, there are distinct institutional spheres, economy, polity, kinship, and so forth. In Marx's hypothesis, social relations of production are easily located in the economic sphere. In developing nations, despite the profound influence of international economic and political constraints, social relations of production have largely remained embedded in other social relations as between *jāti*s [castes] or kin. This difficulty is fully recognized by both Marxist and non-Marxist economic anthropologists. Although no one disputes that the production of the material means of human subsistence and the provisioning of societal institutions occur in every society that continues to exist, categories for analyzing these activities are tricky: it has been recognized that both the categories of orthodox economic theory and the categories of unorthodox, Marxian theory are potentially sociocentric if facilely applied to noncapitalist societies.

The answer by Balibar and others is the notion of structural causality, where "In different structures, the economy is determinant in that it determines which of the instances of the social structure occupies the dominant position" (quoted in Friedman 1975:164).

Sections of Marx are quoted to allow the interpretation that the categories in the Marxian diagram given above are only functional categories that can be filled by different contents in different societies. Then kinship or caste interrelations can be manifestly dominant in South Asian societies while, in this view, aspects of these relations maintain the determinative function of material relations of production. Material relations of production determine that kinship relations among the Mbuti, politico-religious relations among the Incas have the dominant role (Godelier 1973:43). A metaphor for the relation between determination and domination in noncapitalist societies is the event by which King John of England, in signing the Magna Carta, determined that a House of Lords would dominate the political system (compare Laclau's metaphor for capitalist society in which the economic system determines that it will be the dominant instance: his metaphor is of King Louis XIV determining that he would be his own prime minister [Laclau 1972:107]).

I pause to recapitulate the argument so far: such materialist analysts as Godelier and Friedman use the concepts of relative autonomy, limits, and negative constraints to criticize the claims of technodemographic-ecological positive determinism. Negative constraints merely influence the outer limits of variability in order that systems not drive one another beyond their limits of variability, or, put otherwise, their ranges of tolerance. These authors make three claims of positive determination in their turn: (1) Social relations of production specify the specific rationality of the economic system: use of the environment, division of labor, intensity of labor input, allocations of product, etc. (2) The mode of production specifies the form and content of other societal institutions, or, in their term, instances. Meeting the objection that Marxist categories (social relations of production, etc.) are as sociocentric as orthodox economic categories when applied to noncapitalist societies, these materialist analysts distinguish determinant structures from dominant ones. (3) The social relations of production can determine which of the social instances shall be the dominant instance in a given society. Were these three claims for positive determination demonstrated, one would agree that this theory was of immense help in understanding the unintentional determinants of human activity.

Although Godelier appears to subscribe to this view of structural causality, Friedman takes exception on the grounds of mechanical materialism, as I do. Have specific analyses demonstrated the claim that the material relations of production determine which form shall be dominant in a given society? What is delivered does not, to my mind, meet this mark. Godelier reanalyzes Turnbull's material on the Mbuti with the following steps: (1) He details principles of relations of production, that is, three constraints (dispersion of bands [minimal and maximal size and separation in space], cooperation, and fluidity or lack of closure of bands) (Godelier 1973:67). These constraints are not conscious to the Mbuti people but are stated to be a model built up in the mind of the analyst after reality (Godelier 1973:69). (2) He shows how each relation of production constraints affects the operation of every other constraint and concludes that the constraints form a system (Godelier 1973:68). (3) He intends to show that the constraints, taken together, determine the elements of the content and the form of other social forms which are compatible with these constraints and thus assure the reproduction of the Mbuti mode of production (Godelier 1973:68). He offers examples regarding territoriality, kinship terminology and marital alliances, lack of strong collective social control on the individual, lack of lineage structure, and political practices such as the avoidance of political authority and of warfare by public derision of power-seeking individuals and the buffoon-figure who obviates violence (Godelier 1973:69-73). All these social forms are held to be determined by the three constraints. For example, the Cult of the Forest prescribes the punishment of banishment for anyone who does not sing during the Molimo Festival celebrating the Forest, anyone who does not join the communal hunt, and anyone who puts his nets before those of others. Since the Forest is held to be the giver of game, harmony, cooperation, etc., not to join in its celebration is to "break cooperation and unity necessary to the band for the reproduction of its real and imaginary conditions of production" (the second constraint, Godelier 1973:67).

In reviewing this procedure, one notes a similarity between it and certain aspects of the structuralist method. The center of the analysis is exposing a system of constraints "which are determined by a social process of production and constitute the social conditions of its reproduction" (Godelier 1973:69). To find this system of constraints is to delineate "the structural causality of the economy on the society and at the same time the specific general structure of that society and the specific logic of the totality *which is never directly observable phenomena but facts which must be reconstructed by scientific thought and practice*" (Godelier 1973:69, emphasis added). This procedure then resembles Lévi-Strauss's notion that social structure is a model built up after reality in the mind of the analyst (Lévi-Strauss 1963:279). Godelier recognizes this similarity by stating that "the proof of the 'truth' of this reconstruction can only be in its capacity to explain all the observed facts and to pose new questions to the researcher of the area" (Godelier 1973:69).

The difference is that Lévi-Strauss does not propose that unconscious models determine social forms. One can then object that Godelier's system of constraints is reified as a causative agent. An analyst's model of constraints can no more "determine the elements of the content and the form of other social forms" than the word *cat* can scratch you. It is not so that the analyst's "constraints of cooperation and fluidity set limits to the development of personal authority"; public derision limits the development of a man's attempt to transform hunting prestige into personal authority (Godelier 1973:68, 72).

Granting that Godelier's account is descriptively correct, we still have to challenge a central assertion concerning the way we shall deal with unintentional properties of the socioeconomic system: that the socio-economic relations of production (or material relations of production) are shown to determine which social form is dominant in a given society. In practice, Godelier's account, based on the three constraints of dispersion, cooperation, and fluidity, is a convincing unconscious model of a wide range of permitted/proscribed reciprocities and relations concerning Mbuti production, kin, territoriality, social control, authority, and religion. In practice, there is a demonstration of "the effect, for example, of the content and of the form of Mbuti kinship relations (nonlineal), and of the social forms of authority which combine with the direct effects that the mode of production can have on all the political relations (absence of war, fluidity of affiliation of individuals to bands, etc.)" (Godelier 1973:75). This demonstration permits the first part of his theoretical conclusion: "We are here in the presence of the complex epistemological problem of the analysis of reciprocal — convergent or divergent — effects, in which all the instances combine and reciprocally limit all the other instances . . ." (Godelier 1973:75). If his conclusion is terminated at this point, we have a modest statement of a system of mutual negative determinations or constraints, each limiting the outer range of variability of the others but none positively specifying the form others will take: a statement of negative determination similar to Godelier's and Friedman's critique of the claims made by "vulgar materialists" (see "The journey") regarding positive determination by the technoecological system of other social forms. Godelier's system of constraints would then be an adequate model of the reciprocal, negative effects of social forms on one another. The conclusion does not cease at this point but continues with a claim for positive determination: ". . . on the base of their specific relation and their general articulation which is determined in the last instance by the mode of production" (Godelier 1973:75). The point is that we cannot accept this claim if we recognize Godelier's system of constraints for what it is (an adequate model of relations and reciprocities concerning production, kin, territoriality, social control, authority, and religion) and for what it is not (a reified system that cannot determine anything else).

If this argument holds, then Godelier's exercise does not aid in understanding how social relations of production determine which social form shall be dominant in a given society. We are, however, in a better situation than before in that we are acquainted with analytic tools for making a closer approximation of the material aspects of various kinds of social relations that negatively and reciprocally set the outer limits for the forms which each kind of social relation (each sub-system of relations) can take. This is certainly a gain in understanding the unintentional properties of the socioeconomic system. It is of utility for studying not only structure but also change. The uneven development of different subsystems can be studied as a system of changing constraints between subsystems, some subsystems forcing others to operate beyond their ranges of tolerance and thus changing the system.

It is at this point that I resign from the task of finding an ultimate starting point of causality in human affairs. Positive specification of social forms can only be studied as the interlock between social production in reality and the social construction of reality. This is, if I read it correctly, the point of a difficult passage in which Friedman rejects the notion that social relations of production determine which social form shall be dominant in a society. Continuing his program of rejecting mechanical material determinism, he objects that this notion over-emphasizes the material aspect (material flows) of social relations of production:

> While technological determinism is rejected, material flows, instead of being organized by social relations of production, appear as independent and determinant of those social relations. This seems an excessive attempt at reification of the material level, in the purely physical sense, as opposed to other levels of social life. The position adopted here is that *social relations are material relations if they dominate the process of material production and reproduction and that they owe their origin not to that which they dominate but to the social properties of the previous system as a whole* (Friedman 1975:164; original emphasis).

Although the discussion will be pursued in the third of these essays, where I relate the results of these first two essays, I should point out here the three claims of the italicized portion of the above quotation from Friedman. First, like other material subsystems, social relations of production constrain and are constrained by other material subsystems. Social relations of production are not just one among the others, however, for they dominate the others. That is, social relations of production operate on the relation between other material subsystems (demography, technology — the "forces of production"), either straining the relation between them or bringing them closer into adjustment one with the other. Second, such metaconstraint by the social relations of production, which marks them out as a dominant subsystem within the material order, operates not only with respect to the production of material necessities but also with respect to the reproduction of these related subsystems. Third, and here Friedman breaks with any mechanical determinism, social relations of production are not autonomous. They bear a double-interface relation with the symbolic order: (1) social relations of production negatively determine the symbolic order by setting outer limits that reciprocities may take in a given society; social relations of production reproduce the symbolic order by provisioning symbolic action that cannot provision itself; (2)

but the precise form social relations of production take is the product of a symbolic construction of reality (they owe their origin not to that which they dominate [material subsystems] but to the social properties of the previous system as a whole [the symbolic construction of reality]); thus the symbolic order, in turn, reproduces the social relations of production. Again, positive specification of social forms can only be studied as the interlock between social production in reality and the social, or symbolic, construction of reality.

By not accepting all the claims of recent sophisticated Marxist analyses (i.e. of locating the ultimate starting point of causality) and accepting the more modest program of attending to reciprocal negative constraints of subsystems on one another, I am taking a position, in this respect, that is not definitively removed from the sociological analysis of demographic and socioeconomic changes recommended and practiced by, for example, Obeyesekere in his study of the changing system of land tenure in southern Sri Lanka (Obeyesekere 1967).

There are, however, directions of the materialist program that go beyond such solid sociological studies and are able to provide a necessary corrective for the study of changing identities. Here I mean the concepts of mode of production, socioeconomic formation, and structural dominance. Rejecting both formalist and substantivist definitions of economy,

Anthropologists such as Marshall Sahlins, Jonathan Friedman, Maurice Godelier, Emmanuel Terray, etc., . . . propose to analyze and explain forms and structures of material life of societies with the aid of concepts elaborated by Marx: "mode of production" and "socioeconomic formation." By *mode of production (in a restricted sense)*, they designate the combination, which is susceptible of being reproduced, of productive forces and of social relations of production which determine the structure and the form of the process of production and distribution of material goods at the heart of a historically determined society. They suppose that such a determined mode of production (in the restricted sense) corresponds, in a relation both of compatibility and of structural causality, with various determinant forms of political, ideological, etc., relations, and designate the totality of these socioeconomic relations — analyzed in their specific articulation — by the name of *mode of production (taken this time in an expanded sense)*. For example, when one speaks of the slave mode of production of Greek cities or of antique Rome, or of the feudal mode of production in medieval France and England.

Moreover, as concrete societies are frequently organized on the base of several modes of production [in the expanded sense: KD] articulated in a specific manner, and under the domination of one or the other among them, they propose to designate such articulated totalities of modes of production with the concept of socioeconomic formation (Godelier 1973:18; my translation; emphasis added).[6]

---

[6]   There is no theoretical necessity why modes of production in a socioeconomic formation must be in such an asymmetrical relation any more than social exchanges within a society must follow only one form of reciprocity. For example, I have elsewhere shown that while such religious ranking exchanges as food exchanges between persons in dif-

The corrective value of these concepts to studies presuming to contrast "traditional structure" with "modern structure" in South Asia (or elsewhere) is evident when we note that the "traditional structure" studied by all "modern" social scientists (1) was *not* a monolithic structure but (as was said in the Introduction to this volume) a structure of ordered diversity; in my study, for example, the traditional structure was a mode of production articulating several distinguishable productive sectors (David, this volume); and (2) was a mode of production (in the expanded sense) dominated by the colonial mode of production in an encompassing socioeconomic formation; further, in the postcolonial era, modes of production of regional, ethnic, or linguistic minorities are dominated by a mode of production led by a dominant ethnic unit in the national socioeconomic formation.

For example, various studies combining anthropological and historical data have been contradicting the image of the self-sufficient village community that pretty well maintains itself whatever the regional or wider regime, and, hence, whatever the wider socioeconomic formation. When a zamindar who was superordinate over a given region in north India but subordinate to a distant king becomes a petty raja in his own right (or the reverse), there are different constraints on the village economy (Cohn 1969). Different forms and amounts of land rent in different regions of south India were imposed by the British at different periods in their attempts to fathom and to accommodate to indigenous customs, different philosophies of rulership, and different needs of the empire (Kumar 1965). Any account of the Jaffna Tamils that excludes the differences in taxation, corvée labor, constraints on local religious practice, and educational and occupational opportunities under the Portuguese, the Dutch, and the

---

ferent castes in the agricultural sector are generally asymmetrically reciprocal (a landowner gives to, but refuses to receive food from, his barber); in the artisan sector, exchanges are generally symmetrically nonreciprocal (a goldsmith neither gives to nor receives food from most other castes); in the fishing sector, exchanges are generally symmetrically reciprocal (fishermen both give and receive food with a number of castes). The same is true in the relations of reciprocity between modes of production. In the case of several adjacent ethnic units in the New Guinea highlands as studied by Meggitt, there is symmetrical reciprocity between the modes of production. There is competition for production resources, primarily land, within each ethnic unit. Alliances are made in order to gain the upper hand in the warfare between sections within each ethnic unit. Prestige of a section is important in contracting alliances. Prestige is gained by the accumulation of pigs within one ethnic unit and by the accumulation of pearl-shell necklaces within the adjacent ethnic unit. Trading, but not warring, relations exist between the two ethnic units for the accumulation of the chosen prestige commodity. Meggitt freely admits that the analysis of one ethnic unit without the other is arbitrary. Restated, the two ethnic units comprise a socioeconomic formation in which the modes of production are in symmetrical reciprocity, neither dominating the other. To repeat, there is no theoretical necessity why modes of production in a socioeconomic formation must be in a relation of dominating/dominated.

British colonials is certainly inadequate. Postindependence domination of one ethnic identity by another in new nation states is labeled neocolonialism by the minority.

This direction of inquiry intends further to specify the rationale behind the three stages I mentioned earlier in the Epilogue ("The journey"). The point is to argue for a theoretical problematic that does not radically distinguish, in some aspects, traditional from modern structure, nor colonial from postcolonial structure. Anthropologists have recently been exchanging village studies for regional studies (Beck 1973; Yalman 1971; David 1974). Although it is perhaps far more difficult to consider constraints from colonial centers of power on peripheral regions when studying India (see Djurfeldt and Lindberg 1975:47-78), my work in an isolated peninsular region in Sri Lanka, a region roughly the size of a district in India, has allowed the pursuit of this endeavor. That is, I have been tracing the constraints imposed by colonial and postcolonial national powers on the region in relation to the emergence of two competitive social protest movements. There are greater difficulties in doing the same job in India. Tom Kessinger told me of the troubles one of his students was having in carrying out a similar task because the student was working in just another district surrounded by other districts in India.

Attention to the structural dominance of one mode of production over another in a given socioeconomic formation allows the possibility of bringing back into our horizon some aspects of the voluntaristic decision models discussed earlier. While one may agree with Godelier that unintentional properties of the system of production impose constraints that do not involve intentional strategic decisions by humans, the existence of those constraints does not dispel or dismiss the existence of constraints formed by the aggregate of human decisions. Both kinds of constraints have the potential to maintain subsystems within their range of tolerance or to exceed their range of tolerance; both kinds can have unintended consequences; both can set off a new round of displacements. The following summary of a portion of my recent research illustrates (1) the interplay between constraints imposed by the dominant mode of production on the encompassed mode of production, (2) the round of individual decisions incited by these constraints, and (3) the constraints imposed by the aggregate of these decisions on the agricultural sector and the norms for conduct relevant to this sector.

CASE STUDY 3: STAGE ONE OF THE DETERIORATION OF THE JAFFNA SOCIO-ECONOMIC ORDER. In Jaffna, epidemics (occurring about every ten years and causing 8,000 to 10,000 deaths) constrained relations of agricultural production by maintaining the ratio of Veḷḷāḷar landowners to their servants at a supportable level. Two constraints from the wider socioeconomic formation — the British colonial rule — altered this demographic balance. When the British provided educational and occupational opportunities outside of Jaffna (in Colombo and Singapore), educated Veḷḷāḷar landowners emigrated from Jaffna. The emigration became significant by about the 1890's. Second, epidemic control became effective at about the same period. Census figures demonstrate an overall rise in population. Because the census did not specify caste, it can only be inferred from this data that the serving-caste population rose at a higher rate than that of the masters. Case studies document, however, that Veḷḷāḷar landowners in a number of villages were no longer able to support the traditional prerequisites of their serving castes under the previous *jajmāni*-like arrangement. The landowners voluntarily shifted their servants to various contractual arrangements — tenancy and land rental, starting in the 1920's and continuing through the 1960's. At this stage of the changing socio-economic situation in Jaffna, there was a clear contradiction between the demographic forces of production and the traditional social relations of production, resulting in a change in the latter.

CASE STUDY 4: STAGE TWO OF THE DETERIORATION OF THE JAFFNA SOCIO-ECONOMIC ORDER. By the 1960's, technological changes (introduction of petrol-driven pumps which replaced the four-man well-sweep system, and the introduction of nylon nets and motor launches and of motorized transport) reduced the dependence of small producers on wealthy landowners or fish merchants in relations of both production and distribution. On the other hand, various constraints from the wider socioeconomic formation — the nation of Ceylon — (that is, policies aimed primarily at foreign-owned industry and large-scale agriculture, such as nationalization of industry, tenants' rights legislation, and positive discrimination for the Sinhalese in education and governmental occupation) unintentionally resulted in Jaffna landowners' refraining from industrial investment and instituting self-cultivation. Thus previous servants' access to land was reduced because tenancies and land rentals were abolished. During this period, there was not only a contradiction between the technological forces of production and the relations of production but also a growing class contradiction between the landed and the landless.

In this section, I have reviewed and discussed approaches for dealing with the material determinants of human action. More particularly, the purpose has been to draw out practical suggestions for the analysis of material determinants of changing identities in South Asia.

Because we are dealing with a radically changing canvas of collective activity which responds to irreversible material constraints, equilibrium approaches will not do. Both voluntaristic and materialist (neo-Marxian) approaches reject the notion of a homeostatic, self-regulating system always tending to integration and functional compatibility. Both approaches aim to explain change as well as continuity, conflict as well as order, functional compatibility as well as compatibility of subsystems.

Recognizing the limitations of the voluntaristic model — that there are unintentional consequences of "rational" aggregate decisions and that some processes in the appropriation of energy from the environment and in the appropriation of material products of labor operate irrespective of conscious volition — I have taken suggestions from the materialist approach. Sifting through the discrepancies between claims and demonstrations, we have settled on the notion of a circuit of *reciprocal, negative determinations* between material subsystems: each subsystem sets outer limits for the range of possibilities that connected subsystems may assume. This procedure omits unwarranted deterministic statements. This relational treatment of subsystems is augmented by the notion of the relative autonomy of subsystems, meaning that the properties of a subsystem set its own breakdown limits. A number of the changes in the interconnected set of changes concerning South Asia ("The journey," statements 1-17) illustrate these notions. The notion of a hierarchy of negative constraints was also suggested as an analytic strategy that avoids mechanical materialist determinism.

Further, the notion of the socioeconomic formation in which a dominant mode of production constrains subdominant ones is seen as a corrective for the study of changing identities. Many studies of change use a "traditional structure" as a bench mark without fully attending to the fact that this structure was subdominant in the colonial socioeconomic formation. More typically in the literature, properties of the wider socioeconomic formation are assigned the status of exogenous factors affecting the pristine traditional system when *the constrained traditional system should be the bench mark for studying change.* Similarly, studies of social movements of ethnic, linguistic, or other identities in new nations do not necessarily recognize the similarities between their position in the new national socioeconomic formation and a neocolonial situation: this is clearer in Sri Lanka and Pakistan/Bangladesh than in India. By attending to dominant/subdominant modes of production in colonial and postcolonial socioeconomic formations, there is the possibility of reinserting in the analysis the influence (discussed by the voluntaristic approaches) of human decisions which, in the aggregate, may become a constraint furthering or retarding unintentional constraints to which the materialist approach gives more emphasis. The presence of one kind of constraint does not dispel or dismiss the other.

STEP THREE: THE INTERLOCK BETWEEN THE SOCIAL CONSTRUCTION OF REALITY AND SOCIAL PRODUCTION IN REALITY

I said earlier that I was renouncing the task of finding an ultimate starting point of causality in human affairs. Instead, I held that the positive specification of social forms can only be studied as the interlock between social production in reality and the social construction of reality. In this, I firmly agree with the epigraph of Godelier's volume in which the Bantu study (discussed earlier) is found:

There no longer exists a fixed point from where we can hope to seize, were it in its simple form, the configuration of knowledge, and from there, to propose to close it. It is not the attempt that is lacking, but the instrument which would permit a convincing demonstration. Neither from the side of the Subject, nor from the side of the Concept, nor from the side of Nature will we find today what is necessary to nourish and achieve a totalizing discourse. It is more worthwhile to take action and renounce an anachronistic rear combat on this point (Jean T. Desanti 1971, quoted by Godelier 1973:i; my translation; emphasis added).

Renouncing a *determined fixed point of causality* perhaps risks intellectual anomie, or, should we say, intellectual anarchy. The intellectual question for me is how to combine symbolic analysis with materialist analysis in such a way that neither is reduced to an epiphenomenon of the other. Among South Asian anthropological studies, it is not difficult to find polar explanations, each choosing different fixed points in the explanation of the totality; for some writers, ideology is held to encompass praxis, while for others, praxis encompasses ideology.

Renouncing a starting point of causality also leaves the analyst open to a charge of playing a hall-of-mirrors game in which everything reflects and constrains everything else but in which nothing is explained. This charge is quite properly leveled at some variants of systems theory. It is one of the prime aims of this set of essays to find a path between undemonstrated mechanical materialist determinism and idealist determinism on the one hand and the hall-of-mirrors effect on the other hand.

My tentative solution to this dilemma is to distinguish dominant from nondominant subsystems both in the material system and in the symbolic system. This distinction is based on the kinds of negative determination subsystems exert on one another. While all subsystems, by virtue of their "relatively autonomous" properties, set their own breakdown limits, they constrain other subsystems to operate within a certain range of variation. Dominant subsystems, in addition, operate on the relation between other subsystems: dominant subsystems function as metaconstraints, either straining or limiting the discrepancies between other subsystems. Further, distinguishing dominant from non-dominant subsystems permits the consideration of material and symbolic hierarchies of constraints. And hierarchies of constraints will be of utility in defining three kinds of change: the adjustments neces-sary for the dynamic reproduction of an established sociocultural struc-ture; liminal changes concerning nondominant subsystems that buffer the dominant subsystems from the implications of these limited changes but both retard and further the deterioration of an established socio-cultural structure; and structural changes concerning the deterioration of dominant subsystems and the construction of a revised sociocultural structure. In short, if this solution is successful, it might be possible to adopt a position without either an ultimate starting point of causality or a hall of mirrors, a position that gives equal time to symbolic and material determinants of human structure and change. The rest of this section will be spent explaining this condensed statement, using sugges-tions developed in the previous two sections.

Renouncing a determinant fixed point of causality decidedly risks political charges of one sort *and* another. In the mid-1970's, given that critics expect social scientists to be politically aware of the social import of their theoretical positions, any assignation of priority to the symbolic side of life or to the materialist side of life is, rightfully, to be taken as a political action. For example, since Marx argues that the bureaucratic institution in capitalist society is a crucial locus of political alienation and of the replication of the economic order (Avineri 1968:78), can one take it as mere coincidence that one of Weber's most detailed analyses was of the bureaucracy (Weber 1964:329–340), and that, in the name of a "value-free" sociology, Weber called this analysis an ideal-typical analysis? Can readers, however, reasonably be expected to ignore connotations of approval when the term *ideal* is used? In the mid-1970's, when a writer opts to use an equilibrium approach or to divide a socioeconomic formation into an infrastructure and a superstructure, the writer knows he or she is liable to be labeled reactionary or radical. Whether or not the label is accurate, in the context of nationalist academic politics (e.g., history textbooks in the United States have been rewritten to include the constructive participa-tion of Afro-Americans, though not yet of American Indians or Chicanos) such labels may hinder research or obscure its merits when published (see Nash 1975). In these ways and others it is not possible to divorce theoretical practice from political practice.

Faced with this double abyss (while presenting a series of seminars [David 1975] on the results of research on changing identities carried out subsequent to the ICAES conference) I used the image of the yin-yang symbol, the circle containing an s-shaped line that divides the circle into two tadpoles, interlocking head to tail. Imagine one tadpole as symbolic determinants of human activity, the other tadpole as materialist determinants of human activity, and the line, the common boundary of the two tadpoles, as observable human activity. Draw lines across the somewhat vertical axis of the line through the yin and yang areas and let the spaces between these new lines represent different contexts of activity or different stages of a historical evolution; there is more yin relevant to some contexts or stages and more yang to others, but neither is ever absent. This image implies that both symbolic and materialist constraints are always relevant to the determination of human activity and that the analyst can proceed, without fixed starting points of causality, to delineate the relatively autonomous properties of the system of symbolic constraints, the relatively autonomous properties of the system of material constraints, and the constraints operating between these systems, and, thus, to chart the relative determination of each type of constraint in different contexts of activity or at different stages of the dissolution and the reconstruction of a socioeconomic formation. It may not be apolitical to think this way, but it is of some advantage to renounce such politically tinged dichotomies as the soft and hard facts of life and to consider both symbolic and materialist determinants of human activity equally as hard facts of life.

Brave new images are all very well, but the object of the exercise is to implement them. I have set myself a task that seems hardly unique in the mid-1970's: to combine some sort of symbolic theory with some sort of materialist theory in order to understand posttraditional societal upheavals. In the last thirty years, anthropologists have had their horizons broadened by the forceful writings of an array of symbolic theorists and by a host of materialist theorists. On the one hand, the profusion of positions seems overwhelming and, to speak plainly, sometimes gives the impression of 10,000 prima donnas, each singing in his or her own key. On the other hand, this very profusion may be a blessing: one now has the opportunity to *cross-model*.

Model building has nothing to do with data. It is the borrowing of the form — the connection of the terms — of one theory in order to develop theory with respect to another domain of data (Black 1962). Cross-modeling would then be the choice of a theoretical position from the spectrum of symbolic theories, as was done in "Step one," the choice of one from the spectrum of materialist theories, done in "Step two," and the use of each theoretical position to develop and elaborate the other theoretical direction until the two directions, one hopes, dovetail, and, as one hopes even more, until the dialectic produces possibilities for explaining the question at hand: the mobilization of collective identities. The result will undoubtedly alienate theorists who choose to remain thoroughly within one or the other theoretical horizon (or problematic). This risk is preferable to the opposite alternative — of each theorist carving out a cautious niche — which had led to a baroque proliferation of microfields within our science.

The remainder of this essay, then, is no cursory outline of a general theory of human action. It is an attempt at the cross-modeling of separate developed theories into a position that is perhaps less elegant but also less reductionist than these theories.

The following pages, then, provide examples of the application of this program. Constraints operative (1) in a society dynamically reproducing itself, (2) in a society whose subsystems are unevenly developing and driving one another beyond operative limits for which accommodative, liminal changes both reflect and mask these developments and thus appear to conserve the established societal patterns, and (3) in a society in which the previous structures in dominance are contradicted and new competitive structures in dominance emerge are dealt with in turn. It should be stressed that human societies are not here considered as neatly susceptible to changes in discrete, exclusive stages; rather, the three kinds of dynamic process should be studied as cooccuring in time. Then any description of the evolution in a particular region should note, while describing stages of change, that what is meant is a stage in which one of the above kinds of change (societal reproduction is also change) appears to prevail.

Societal reproduction is change. While anthropologists' previous preoccupation with the erstwhile primitive, isolated community tended to obscure that fact, the study of posttraditional, postcolonial societies errs if it omits the dynamism, the ordered diversity, the constraints from colonial powers that are part of the "traditional structure" to be used as a bench mark for studying change. Societal reproduction is a continual process of redress of discrepancies between the various subsystems that compose the societal system. Then talking about societal reproduction is talking about the contribution of each subsystem to the limitation of discrepancies and, thus, the contribution of each to the reproduction of the totality.

Choosing an arbitrary starting point for the discussion (which in no way implies logical priority or any suggestion of ultimate causality), I want to address the constraints between dominant and nondominant material subsystems (see the discussion of Friedman in "Step two"). All material subsystems reciprocally negatively determine one another. That is, each subsystem has its relatively autonomous properties: it sets its own breakdown limits. These limits constrain all other subsystems. A kingdom cannot be built on an ecosystem of sand. A kingdom cannot be built in a lushly vegetated ecosystem if the only technology in practice is that of hunting and gathering. Relations of production are then constrained by the breakdown limits of other material subsystems.

Are relations of production, then, only one subsystem among others? Or do material relations of production dominate other material subsystems, as Friedman claims?

It is my contention that material relations of production operate on the relation between other subsystems, either straining the relation between other subsystems or bringing them closer into adjustment. The Kachin case as reported by Leach (1965) illustrates this metaconstraint. Highland Burma forest land regenerates best if left fallow for at least twelve years after one season of slash-and-burn cultivation: this is its limit. Kachins could easily allow this cycle of forest use if their demographic concentration were organized into relatively small, mobile villages. Such villages would allow highly efficient slash-and-burn technology, for villagers could rotate the use of land lying relatively near the village. This idyllic balance of subsystemic constraints does not happen, however, due to another facet of the material relations of production: the necessity to defend land from others. Then the demographic concentration is skewed into larger villages. Larger villages require cultivation of land at greater distance from the village or overuse of nearby land. Discrepancy between material subsystems is, in this case, increased by material relations of production.

There is another form of highland Burma land use. Irrigated terrace agriculture occurs on selected hill sites. Far more human labor is necessary to build and maintain terraces than to perform slash-and-burn agriculture. Fewer calories are produced per calories expended in labor. But the work done in these more densely settled hill villages need not be as intense due to another aspect of the material relations of production: these villages overlook trade routes and exact tribute from traders. Then the maladjustment between material subsystems is to some extent alleviated by the material relations of production. Although material relations of production are undoubtedly negatively determined by other material subsystems, material relations of production operate as a metaconstraint regulating the relation between other subsystems, for better or for worse. For this reason, I consider the material relations of production to be more than one material subsystem among others: it dominates other material subsystems.

The second claim made by Friedman for the social relations of production is that this subsystem is dominant because it operates not only with respect to the production of material necessities but also with regard to the reproduction in time of the material subsystems, that is, in replicating the technodemographic forces of production. When Terray (1975) analyzes the Abron kingdom of West Africa, for example, he separates the description of productive relations between aristocrats and slaves that benefit the former at any point in time from the description of features of the same productive relations that tend to reproduce the system of inequality, generation after generation. Slaves could be forced to carry on their agricultural labor and gold-mining activities even if the Abron masters did not have the policy of setting the children of these war-captive slaves free and the policy of establishing limits to the control of slaves by masters (e.g. a slave's option to bind himself to a less onerous master). The relative leniency of the Abron aristocrats (as compared with the relative harshness of the neighboring Ashanti aristocrats) is explicable as a structural feature that tended to inhibit the mobilization of second-generation slaves into slave revolts (as used to happen among the Ashanti) (Terray 1975). This feature, then, is a negative determination: it defines what cannot happen. By limiting or avoiding what would tend to destroy not only material relations of production between masters and slaves but also their technological and demographic relations, this feature of productive relations operates to reproduce not only itself but other material subsystems as well. It is thus a metaconstraint.

This metaconstraint of a dominant structure cuts both ways. Other authors have noted that the very structure that can tend to reproduce a socioeconomic system is likely to be the structure whose modification can drastically alter the entire system. This connection between structural dominance and societal reproduction/deterioration can profitably be applied to symbolic dominance as well as to material dominance.[7]

Finishing with Friedman's third claim for considering social relations of production as a dominant subsystem, social relations of production are not autonomous. They bear a double-interface relation with the symbolic order. First, social relations of production negatively determine the symbolic order by setting outer limits on the range of variation social exchanges may take and, therefore, the form that normative codes for conduct may take in a given society; and social relations reproduce the symbolic order by provisioning symbolic action that cannot provision itself. Second, the precise form social relations of production take is the product of a symbolic construction of reality.

This statement calls for a discussion, then, of the constraints between social relations of production, the dominant subsystem of the material system, on the one hand, and, on the other, the dominant and nondominant subsystems of the symbolic order: ideology and the explicit normative order.

In reviewing the discrepancy between claims and demonstration by materialist analysts regarding the positive determination of specific social forms and opting for a view that explanation of human activity

[7] This topic was explored at a symposium on Symbolic Domination, which convened at the 74th annual meeting of the American Anthropological Association, San Francisco, December 5, 1975.

requires an analysis of the interlock between social production in reality and the social construction of reality, I reserved a crucial point. Earlier, I agreed with materialist writers that the environment sets outer limits on the possibilities of social structure that can exist there. I agreed that a chosen technology further limits the range of possibilities. Now it is also necessary to specify the range of productive activity on a given technoenvironmental base that interlocks with the social construction of the situation. The lower limit of social production is not set by basic biological needs, i.e. the human subsistence level of production; it is set at a limit of productivity and efficiency necessary for the discharging of obligations and the support and reproduction of nonsubsistence activities, relations, and institutions. This lower limit has variously been designated the provisioning of society (Sahlins 1972:185) or the reproduction of the real and imaginary conditions of production (Godelier 1973:76). The Mbuti Molimo Festival produces game in excess of what the Mbuti need biologically to survive. It does not, however, produce in excess of what Mbuti bands need periodically to reproduce cooperation and to hold at bay grievances within the band, i.e. the reproduction of the real conditions of production and the explicit normative order that guides expectations and provides codes for conduct. It does not produce game in excess of what the Mbuti need periodically to reaffirm that the forest is still functioning as the provider of game, harmony, and social cooperation; such provisioning of Mbuti ideology is the reproduction of the imaginary conditions of production. Then the lower limit of social production is set by the interlock between technoenvironmental possibility and the symbolic reproduction of the social order.

The upper limit for production is not set by the technological maximum, but by the environment. The Kachins have a technology that is perfectly capable of depleting the environment. The system of tribute in Kachin *gumsa* chiefdoms requires an ever-increasing amount of production from a given territory that eventually reduces the aristocrats — the ultimate givers of tribute — to commoner status or to revolt (Friedman 1975:180–185). Environmental depletion thus sets a limit to the production of surplus necessary to reproduce the dominant forms of reciprocity in the society.

Restated, the operable range of social production lies between a lower limit of social necessity (human biological subsistence plus the provisioning and reproduction of the sociocultural order) and an upper limit of social necessity (ecological maintenance and the provisioning and reproduction of the sociocultural order). This range sets the outer limits for the forms of reciprocity (exchanges between humans and between humans and the environment) that can be designated as right and proper by socially constructed norms for conduct. The third reason for considering the social relations of production as a dominant sub-system within the material system is thus its function as a mediator between other material subsystems of production and the symbolic order, in terms both of production of material necessities and of reproduction of the sociocultural order.

Although establishing these points would require a vastly more extensive demonstration, enough has been said to hint at the possibility of distinguishing dominant from nondominant material subsystems. This position allows consideration of a hierarchy of material negative determinations between subsystems in the mode of production. And the notion of a hierarchy of constraints opens possibilities for discussing different kinds of change: limited change in which only nondominant subsystems are involved and more thorough structural change in which the dominant subsystem becomes involved (I shall return later to this problem).

The explicit normative order of social differentiation, that is, social identities, and of codes for conduct between identities is thus *negatively determined* by the conditions of production on a given technoenvironmental base. Reciprocally, human activity in social production is *negatively determined* by the explicit normative order.

This last statement must be taken as a departure from the more common Ten Commandments view of the explicit normative order. I am asserting that the normative order has no one-to-one corre-spondence with human activity. I am further asserting that the normative order does not pinpoint specific activity that must occur. I hold that it is prudent to say only that each element of the normative order, each identity category or each norm for conduct, only sets up a range of activity beyond which propriety and order are violated. The Nambudiri norm that all girls shall be married before puberty — a norm that is given great force by the belief that any father who marries off his daughter after puberty is guilty of murder for each unutilized menstruation — does not guarantee that all Nambudiri children will be legitimate within the marriage concerned, but only guarantees that every child born to a Nambudiri woman with a living husband can easily be designated as legitimate. In a novel discussion, Murphy amplifies the complex relation between normative understandings and the indexing of activity. He argues that,

Although ideas are generated by action, they are not merely a reflection of that activity or a restatement of it in symbolic and ideal form. Rather, ideas, including ones that are normative in society, may deny behavioral reality, they may reinterpret it according to other frameworks of meaning, they may simplify and distort it, or they may be in conscious conflict with social action. This does not mean that the normative system is unrelated to conduct, for ideas are the precondition of activity. *The very distortions of human images of reality are what make social life possible* (Murphy 1971:158; emphasis added).

Stifling an immediate response, i.e. the last sentence is one of "those special gems of paradoxical obfuscation for which [Murphy] is justly famous" (Schneider 1965:74; this comment was directed at another author), one finds a very special sense in Murphy's assertion. Social scientists have proposed dozens of labels to point out the discrepancy between normative understandings and activity (ideal norm vs. expected norm: Firth 1951; real norm vs. pragmatic norm: Bailey 1969:4; Cicourel 1973). Ritual can be explained as the representation of the ideal state of affairs that daily activity never approaches (Nicholas 1967). In such definitions one senses a scientific lament: we *should* be able to specify more exact correspondences between normative understandings and ongoing activity. But is this discrepancy cause for scientific lament?

Murphy responds emphatically in the negative. "Activity is sequential in time, continuous, multifaced, and non-repetitive; norms are timeless, discontinuous, repetitive, and one-dimensional . . . they are generated out of broad ranges of activity and, by virtue of the fact that they are norms, they apply to a wide spectrum of activity" (Murphy 1971:241–242). Given these differing features of norms and activity,

It is the very incongruence of our conscious models, and guides for conduct, to the phenomena of social life that makes life possible. The individual seeks security and order as a condition of his psychological functioning (cf. Leach 1965, pp. ix–xv), but society just as certainly requires tension and flexibility. The individual therefore, must be predisposed to activity, and, given the uniqueness of every social situation, he must have latitude for action. The norms provide the image of order and fitness; they bind time and activity in the mind, but they cannot be allowed to impede their flow (Murphy 1971:240).

The explicit normative order, by setting outer limits to proper behavior, thus masks and reflects reality. (This phrase, otherwise rendered as mystification, is usually applied by materialist-oriented authors to the operation of ideology.) This masking and reflecting of human activity should not be written off as a negative feature of the human condition. Rather, since it allows humans necessary flexibility in their transactions, such masking and reflecting of human activity is the contribution of the explicit normative order to reproduce the totality.

Following the materialist suggestion that subsystems have

relatively autonomous properties in addition to properties constrained by other subsystems, the next question is: what are the
self-governing properties of the explicit normative order? More
specifically with regard to the question at hand, what can be
said about the constraints within the subsystem of explicit dimensions of identity? The American poet Bob Dylan has sung that
anyone who is not busy being born is busy dying. The same appears
to be true about explicit normative dimensions of an identity. Either
dimensions of identity are dynamically reconstructing themselves or they are deteriorating, and collectivities of persons
may align themselves into a new identity.

How? Identities may be characterized as subject to what are called,
in cybernetic language, feedback constraints and predictability constraints, two "factors which determine inequality of probability" and
thus affect the pathways of change events might take (Bateson
1972:399–400). Identities are subject to feedback constraints such that
"causal interconnection can be traced around the circuit and back
through whatever position was (arbitrarily) chosen as the starting point
of the description" (Bateson 1972:404). Identities are subject to the
restraint of predictability, to the condition that information borne by
individual arcs in a communication circuit (which I have until now
called explicit dimensions of identity) is not random, but partially
replicates the information borne by other arcs (Bateson 1972:406).

It is in the continual operation of these processes that an identity
either remains a viable organizing factor in social life or does not.
First, an identity is semantically reconstructed (or not) in the mutual
accommodation of the several dimensions of the identity to one
another. The examples noted earlier (p. 461) illustrate that a dimension such as the code defining the chosen past structural position of
the identity is not constructed in a void but in relation to other
dimensions, such as the code defining the present structural position
and the practical interests (whether material, power, or status interests) to be obtained in that structural position, the code defining
inclusion of persons in the identity category, and the code defining
redressive behavior for persons in the category. Further illustration of
this point could be had by examining the history of a given changing
identity movement in which dimensions progressively elaborate or fail
mutually to define one another or by comparing the definition of
dimensions in two contemporary social movements in a region (both
movements, of course, responding to the same system of socioeconomic constraints [see Brass 1974]). In short, each explicit dimension is constructed in relation to the progressive definition or the
progressive deterioration of the other dimensions. Further, an identity
is reconstructed pragmatically (or not) depending on its adherents'

ability to predict external happenings and to guide shared understanding about real events concerning productive relations, technology, ecology, power distributions, and the like. To continue with
the Dylanesque metaphor, new information which challenges the
system for better or for worse — like anti- bodies, air pollution, or
stray cancer cells — is constantly being presented to the system of
dimensions I have called an identity. If the system can assimilate this
new information or accommodate itself to the new information, it is
busy reconstructing itself, or busy being born. If not, it is busy dying.

Continuing the review of relations between subsystems, I shall next
address relations between ideology, the explicit normative order, and
social productive activity from the viewpoint of the ideology; that is,
the constraints exerted by ideological assertions that contribute to the
reproduction of the totality. The notions of negative determination
and of masking and reflecting will again be of utility in this regard.

First, when dealing with South Asia, we are concerned with societies
heir to a historical civilization. Given the diversity of levels of texts
(see the Introduction to this volume), it is no mean methodological
task to decide, in general, which level is to be attended to as the
ideology. For the problem at hand, that of identities and changing
identities, it seems prudent to attend to a level of ideology that relates
to the masses, a level of ideology that can be demonstrated to
participate in the mobilization of collectivities of persons in social
movements.

In the paper included in this volume, I discriminated the esoteric
meanings of a symbol from its populist, exoteric meanings. Recently,
research data appeared which led me to broaden this distinction to
one of an esoteric level of ideology versus a commonsense, exoteric
level of ideology (both of which can be distinguished from explicit
normative cultural understandings, see above). The elaborate exoteric
level of ideology is well known to Asianists as the arcane writings of
the Vedas, puranas, sastras, etc. Some examples of exoteric or
commonsense propositions about reality are the segmentary structure
of natural physical substance and the transubstantiation of a woman's
physical body to that of her husband at the time of her wedding (David
1973). Such propositions deserve the title of commonsense ideology
because they are the *implicit* and elusive (in that they do not resemble
Western analytic common sense) intellectual grounding for *explicit*
normative rules, for example, rules prescribing conduct of pollution
between kinsfolk, rules of marriageable and nonmarriageable persons,
the structure of generic and specific terms for kinsfolk, etc. (David
1973; further examples of commonsense propositions are given later).
They are *common*sense in that they provide cultural orientations
about reality for persons engaged in various sectors of productive

activity and for persons of all levels of erudition or ignorance of the more esoteric ideology (David 1975). I wish to distinguish two levels of ideology: esoteric ideology and commonsense, exoteric ideology. These levels of ideology are to be distinguished from such explicit shared understandings as the dimensions of identity discussed earlier in this paper.

Next, it would seem that my distinction of implicit ideology from the explicit normative order was similar to the categories in the Marxian diagram (see above, p. 468), in which the superstructure is composed of the ideological order and the jural-political order. My problem with that diagram is that it does not express the asymmetrical constraints of the ideology with regard to the normative order. These constraints can be briefly stated as (1) the recentering of individual effect with arbitrary normative prescriptions and (2) the masking and reflecting of social productive activity from the normative order. To my mind, these constraints describe the role of ideology — as a structure-in-dominance — either in reconstructing an existing sociocultural system or in constructing a new sociocultural system from the shambles of a transitional period.

Whatever the complex discrepancy between the normative order and human activity (as noted above) one point is clear. Normatively guided behavior defines, for a given context, a range of proper conduct from a far wider range of conduct humanly possible in that context. The developmental psychologist Jean Piaget (1971) writes that persons learn the capacity for decentered thought — the ability to handle relativity of perception and of cognition (Piaget 1971; see Turner 1973:352) — necessary to interact normatively with others. Such restriction of possibilities, however, implies the potential for alienation of individual affect: norms certainly cannot please all of the people all of the time. Skepticism is not restricted to religious belief but operates with such mundane choices as classing oneself in an identity category with a particular collectivity of persons. In the present state of ferment in South Asia, persons frequently have cross-cutting identifications and must decide with which crowd they will throw in their lot. The variability of individual psyches in a collectivity cannot be accommodated by the restrictions of activity prescribed by the explicit norms for conduct.

This dilemma of discrepancy between the explicit normative order and individual affect[8] cannot be resolved by norms themselves but by

---

[8] Geertz reviews four classes of explanations of sociopsychological *strain* for which ideology purportedly provides an emotional outlet: the cathartic ("emotional tension is drained off by being displaced onto symbolic enemies"), the morale (the sustaining of "individuals and groups in the face of chronic strain, either by denying it outright or by legitimizing it in terms of higher values"), the solidarity (the effect of knitting together a

whatever form of figurative thought (religious, political, mythic) is held to provide orientations to reality. These forms of figurative thought are not empirically verifiable. They assert immanent connections between culturally defined units. They mask the above two conditions: socially constructed metaphorical thought is defined as nonmetaphorical — in short, collective figurative thought can be labeled ideology.

Figurative thought operates not only on the discrepancy between the explicit normative order and individual affect but also on the discrepancies between the explicit normative order and social productive activity. No society exists without asymmetrical appropriation, at the least between humans and the environment and between such identity categories as those of age and gender. Asymmetrical appropriation exists between more inclusive identity categories, whether lineages, castes, classes, ethnic units, or nations.

Perceptions of exploitation or of relative deprivation in a situation of asymmetrical appropriation is not automatic, however. A common ground of the various interpreters of Marx is that an ideology functions as a mode of appearances, both masking and reflecting the mode of production in a given society. Masking and reflecting of the ongoing productive system, in this view, justifies the differential control of the material resources needed for production and the differential allocation or appropriation of products. Masking and reflecting also facilitates the transmission of such differential control and authority across the generations and thus is crucial in reproducing both patterns of productive activity and the explicit normative dimensions of understandings which guide behavior between persons. As with the relation between norms and affect, ideology is viewed as operating on the relations between norms and activity.

How does it operate? Figurative forms of thought reintegrate — or should we say recenter (see Turner 1973:353) — the discrepancies between arbitrary codes for conduct with individual affect and arbitrary codes for conduct and activity. It has been suggested that central symbols in an ideology do this by

... possessing qualities which so reinforce one another that they can be distinguished only analytically: they are credible, persuasive, and authoritative. ... The credibility of an ideology derives from its demonstration of a coherence between meanings shared by a group and its new perception of

---

social group or class) and the advocacy explanation ("articulating, however partially and indistinctly, the strains that impel them, thus forcing them into the public notice") (Geertz 1973:204, 205). These explanations of the functions of ideology purport to delineate strains in the "basic personality structure" of the collectivity.

subordination and relative deprivation. . . . The persuasiveness of an ideology derives from the striking quality of its innovative symbolic formulation. . . . [that is, the innovation of] forceful metaphors that [persuade] persons to act in accord with their prescriptions. . . . If a movement seeks a positive goal, a total social, political, and economic restructuring, it does so in the face of opposition from the powers that be. . . . To overcome this fact, an ideology must be based on a higher authority (Nicholas 1973:79, 80).

Though Nicholas is discussing the role of a competitive ideology in a situation of concerted change, a social movement, the attributes he mentions — credible, persuasive, and authoritative — are just as applicable to the role of ideology in reconstructing an existing socio-cultural system. The only difference is that a long-instituted ideology that is favored and provisioned by the "powers that be" may be less explicit than a competitive ideology; such ideological assertions may appear to persons interior to the ideology as unquestionable, as common sense.

This figurative form of thought is also labeled with less charitable attributes, e.g., as "noble lies," "myths," and "derivations" by Plato, Sorel, and Pareto (Geertz 1973:200). To the positivist tradition in modern social science, ideology is an evaluative, justificatory kind of thinking whose truth value cannot be subjected to scientific affirmation: to Parsons, for example, "Deviations from social scientific objectivity are the essential criteria of an ideology"; "the problem of ideology arises where there is a discrepancy between what is believed and what can be [established as] scientifically correct" (Parsons 1959, quoted in Geertz 1973:198).

I find the jibe in these definitions of ideology strikingly similar to the lament that norms for conduct do not correspond to human activity. Perhaps the lament gains force from the situation wherein positivistic scientific thought cannot encompass ideology and frequently fails to move people to proper action, while ideology asserts that it does encompass other forms of thought and action and frequently does move people to action (whatever the propriety).

In fact, from the standpoint of pure reason the absurdity of religion [or ideology] is undeniable, and it is this very fact which gives reason for reducing all phenomena referring to such a non-empirical reality to a common denominator, and accepting that they all belong to one and the same category, the religious. This definition highlights the most specific peculiarity of the religious category. When we call it an absurdity the term is not used in a pejorative sense. The unprovable is not by definition untrue or irrelevant. On the contrary, the few truths which are humanly relevant are, without exception, believed truths, not proven ones, and this again must sound like an absurdity, as, in fact, it is. Once we accept the absurdness of the situation we are cautioned, cautioned not forthwith to reject religion as an illusion, but to concede that apparently we are up against something important. (van Baal 1971:4-5).

Whether religious, mythic, political, or whatever, figurative ideological thought is a driving force that is real in its consequences.

Ideological assertions are thus characterized as credible, persuasive, authoritative, and unverifiable by methods of positivistic social science. Geertz and Nicholas agree that ideological assertions are figurative assertions, conjoining in forceful metaphors what is otherwise disjoined (activity, normative codes, and affect). I think we can go further than these statements. A person, or a collectivity of persons, is interior to an ideology when the immanent connections established between aspects of activity, codes, and affect by means of ideological assertions are experienced as nonmetaphorical. When the United States was in the throes of a depression, many persons indeed had much more to fear than fear itself. Yet F.D.R.'s metaphor stuck. Ideological assertions are a high-risk game. For when Richard Nixon attempted to sell his metaphoric summary of the United States' disengagement from the Vietnam War with the assertion of "peace with honor," many persons found that the discrepancy between this assertion and their own judgment that the Vietnam War had indeed been hell (an alternate American ideological assertion) only increased their cynicism. The peace-with-honor metaphor was visible not only as a metaphor, but also as a very bad metaphor. Ideological assertions strike home when they sufficiently reflect reality while masking their metaphorical conjoining-of-disparates functions and thus create an aura of immanent connection.

I think we can go beyond received notions of the functions of ideology in another direction. The ideological justificatory and evaluative function is characterized in terms of displacement (damning an enemy, referring to a higher order). My fieldwork leads me to understand ideological assertions as creating immanent connections not only between this-worldly phenomena (activity, codes, and affect) and phenomena defined as otherworldly or as "natural." Immanent connections are also established *among* this-worldly phenomena, for example, a circuit of immanent connection between a temple, the village land, the people, and their activity, their crops (see Case Study 5). In such a circuit, it is difficult to assign the original point of justification. Rather, phenomena and practices that outsiders (persons exterior to the ideology) define as "otherworldly" (the "higher order"), as "natural" or as "cultural" are experienced by persons interior to the ideology as affirming and affecting one another.

Ideological assertions are not only credible, authoritative, persuasive, and unverifiable by normal scientific methods, but are also metaphors that, when experienced as nonmetaphorical, conjoin activity, codes, and affect by asserting immanent connections between the otherworldly, the natural, and the cultural. These properties of ideological assertions still do not answer how the image of a conjunction between activity, codes, and affect is maintained in the face of the frequent experience of discrepancies between activity, codes, and affect.

And here we come back to the difference between positive and negative determination. A positive deterministic statement would have it that ideology functions to justify the status quo. A negative deterministic statement would have it that ideology only functions to obviate and dispel what cannot be justified. This is done by demarcating figures and procedures for dismissing discrepancies between activity, codes, and affect. Laws in a modern nation are nothing without the metalaw that laws are to be obeyed. In the Dravidian ideology there are metafigures who operate on discrepancies between activity, codes, and affect. A swami once said that there is nothing in the world but insolvable social dilemmas (discrepancies, labeled *piraccinai* in Tamiḷ) and their solution (*samālippu*). And there are two metafigures who solve the dilemmas, the ones who are beyond the householder status: the renouncer and the man of inner virtues in the world (the *selvakku*) (see the following summary of a portion of my recent research).

CASE STUDY 5: JAFFNA COMMONSENSE IDEOLOGY AND THE REPLICATION OF THE NORMATIVE ORDER. In Jaffna, there is a coherent set of commonsense propositions concerning a circuit of immanent influences between the man who built the temple, the temple, the village land, the inhabitants, and the products of the village, some of which are returned to the temple as offerings. Building the temple defines an area of human space from what is otherwise an area occupied by malevolent spirits. The man who causes the temple to be built must be a man of inner virtues (spiritual and societal knowledge and power) as well as outer virtues (wealth, power, and prestige). His virtues are incorporated into the temple by the act of taking as the basic unit of measurement a portion of the temple donor's body and using this unit in following ṣastric proportions for building a temple. Since he is supposed to reside adjacent to the temple, there is held to be a mutual reinforcement of his virtues and those of the temple. Both his and the temple's virtues are held to radiate out to the inhabitants and the land and to affect the quality of both. All these qualities are thought to affect the quality of the products of the land, especially rice. The circuit is completed when a product of the land is both offered to the temple and consumed by the inhabitants. For better or for worse, the virtue of the village is replicated generation after generation.

In addition, the descendants of the temple donor are held to have inner virtues due to the virtue-coded particles of natural substance received from the ancestors and due to their proximity to the temple. For these reasons, they are thought to be the persons best endowed to represent the villagers in ritual (in the past, temple donors used to be *pujaris*; now they are the principal representatives of the village people, or *upayakkarars*, during ritual); these same descendants were also thought to be the best suited to settle social discord within the village in order to maintain the normative order.

This system of common sense, which includes the terms of its own replication, not only functions to maintain the normative order but also doubly masks and reflects the socioeconomic order. Differential control of productive resources and differential appropriation of the product of village labor is undercommunicated and the position of structural superiors within the village is justified. Further, the image of a self-contained village and village leadership fostered by these notions of a circuit of immanent influence undercommunicates the fact that the village leaders are themselves subordinate to regional or national powers (the Jaffna kings, the Portuguese, Dutch, and British colonials), a fact which would detract from the authority vested in the village leaders.

Both figures are held to be able to solve social dilemmas by their words alone, let alone by their ingenuity in accommodating codes to activity or in assimilating activity to codes when common people are baffled. I doubt that this function of obviating discrepancies by accommodation/assimilation is unique to the cultures of northern Sri Lanka and south India. On hearing my presentation, a student, son of a General Motors executive, remarked that these operations were exactly what his father does and that he finally understood why there exists such a mystique about executives and why they are so highly paid. Buffoons among the Mbuti both amuse and offer solutions to disputes that threaten the band. Note that I am not denying that persons refer to ideology to justify their actions; it is simply that it appears that the negative determinative function of obviating discrepancies, of setting limits to discrepancies between activity, codes, and affect is the distinctive contribution of ideology to the reproduction of the totality of the sociocultural-economic structure.

Having set the backdrop by noting relatively autonomous properties of subsystems and constraints between subsystems in the socioeconomic structure that can function to reproduce the structure, the task of discussing other kinds of change comes somewhat closer to hand. My strategy of discussing constraints between subsystems that limit discrepancies, that is, negatively determine one another, will be used in these next two sections to specify qualitatively different kinds of change.

In the literature on South Asia, many analysts use some variant of the dichotomy of positional change versus structural change (Srinivas 1966:7). Positional change involves only a socioeconomic change concerning previously existing social identities and previously existing normative codes. The categories, the normative rules of the game, and the contexts in which activity takes place do not change, but redistribution of material resources allows a previously subordinate identity to improve, through changed interactions and changed attributes, the definition of its identity *vis-à-vis* other identities. Examples are legion: a caste becomes wealthy; having become relatively more autonomous, caste members can refuse food from castes previously donors and thus remove some stigma from the definition of their identity; and they can perhaps bribe static or downwardly mobile castes to accept food from them and thus improve the definition of their collective identity. Such is positional or socioeconomic change.

Structural change is conceived of as a more radical change of distribution of material resources, change of identity categories, and change of normative codes for conduct. Structural change involves outside factors such as growth of industry, extravillage occupations, demographic displacements, radicalization by major political parties, and other factors such as those listed at the beginning of this paper. Structural change, in short, is a shorthand for socioeconomic-normative-ideological change.

In the literature, this dichotomy of positional/structural change accompanies such other dichotomies as traditional structure/modern structure, interactional/attributional definition of identities, Sanskritization/modernization or Westernization as strategies for redefining an identity, and more. Because they often rest on a premise of unilineal, irreversible evolution from the traditional to the modern, these dichotomies are oversharp. Just as there were Christians who reconverted to "pagan" religions in the centuries after Jesus of Nazareth, such caste mobility movements as the Hindustani Kayasthas imitated colonial customs (or became Westernized) in the nineteenth century and imitated Brahmanic customs (or became Sanskritized) in the twentieth, in line with different mobilization needs (Carroll 1975). No one doubts that there have been profound social, political, and economic dislocations stemming from the spread of an industrialized, capitalist/socialist mode of production. Much attention has been given to the effects on the social order when previous subordinates have the opportunity to sell their labor to nontraditional employers. It is easy to overestimate, however, the degree of dislocation. Industrial productive relations do not dispel precapitalist forms of productive relations in which peasants control some factors of production. Such was the experience, for example, of the Tata Iron and Steel Company of Jamshedpur with Santal immigrant workers; they ignore economic incentives in favor of retiring to the native village and buying land with industrial earnings (Orans 1965:83). More cases could be cited, but perhaps calling attention to reversals in expected progressions of symbolic redefinitions of collective identities and to uneven developments of coexisting modes of production is enough to indicate the existence of transitional changes not precisely caught in the net of positional and structural changes. Given the relatively autonomous properties of material and symbolic subsystems and the negative constraints between subsystems I have been outlining, it should be possible to be more precise about jostlings between *nondominant material and symbolic subsystems* that are medial or *liminal* with respect to positional and structural changes. Such changes, by masking and reflecting these developments, appear to conserve dominant material and symbolic subsystems.

What is needed is more attention to those liminal developments that are less striking in print than reports of insurrections or of untouchables being beaten with a sandal when they walk down a high-caste street carrying an umbrella. Radical confrontations are preceded by liminal changes: processes of socioeconomic-normative changes in which social identities and relations between identities are redefined, changes that, as I said earlier, tend to delay or further the deterioration of the existing totality, changes that are not only overt and publicly known changes, but also changes that, to borrow a phrase from the famous Watergate proceedings, may include covert operations.

Recalling my definition of an identity as a cultural sign that operates both as a symbol, with semantic meanings, and as an index, with pragmatic meanings (see fn.3), I will illustrate several cases of such liminal changes. These cases are related because they represent variations on the reverberations of changing material conditions (demographic, ecological, technological, and material relations of production). Those previously privileged attempt to manipulate the situation so as to avoid recognition of any decline, while those previously disadvantaged attempt to better their positions without immediately confronting previously privileged social identities in order to avoid drastic reprisals that might reverse the trend. Both variations can be finessed with either a semantic or a pragmatic redefinition of the social identities and the relations between identities involved.

Let us first consider a case of a semantic manipulation by a previously privileged identity to avoid recognition of its decline.

CASE STUDY 6: LIMINAL CHANGES. Before the impact of the constraints sketched in the first stage of the evolution of Jaffna society (see above,

pp. 479–480), Veḷḷāḷar landowners had two options regarding the allocation of productive land with different normative codes for conduct and
different implications regarding the honor of the landowner. A landowner leased some of his land to lower-ranked persons within the
Vellālar caste. This was a contractual arrangement in which three shares
of the produce were divided among the agents who provided the land,
the water, and the labor. The landowner would also act as the merchant
for any of the crop sold at a market. This relation was neutral as
concerned the honor of the landowner. On the other hand, land would
be worked by various serving castes in return for all subsistence and
ritual prerequisites. The existence of such relationships is termed an
index (*varisai*) of the master's honor (*kauravam*).

The demographic constraints noted above posed an insoluble
dilemma, or contradiction, regarding the latter form of social relations.
Landowners could no longer provide the prerequisites normatively, i.e.
the nonnegotiable right (*urimai*) of the servants; they thus voluntarily
initiated a change to contractual relations, an alternative already
present in the normative subsystem. This improvised solution
(*samālippu*) to the social dilemma (*piraccinai*) preserved the appearance
that the previous social order was still intact. Ex-serving-caste tenants
still worked the same land and occupied land owned by the landowner;
stratified ritual relations were still maintained.

At this stage, the system of common sense noted above was not
directly contradicted. Indeed, landowners were still able to implement
the system of common sense. For example, as servants became tenants
and, later, lessees at fixed land rent, case studies show that the landowners gave these people first option on the land in question because
"they are part of the land and the land is part of them; they have the
scent of the land (*man vasanai*), the touch of the land (*man totarsal*)."

This is an example of a semantic improvisation or manipulation by the
previously dominant identity. The substitution of an alternate code for
conduct between identities accommodates changes in the material
sector. This liminal change is not a pragmatic change in that the context
of productive activity remains the same. Another example of a semantic
redefinition is reported by Cohn (1955). Here, lower castes semantically
redefined their identities by adopting codes for conduct traditionally
reserved for the local dominant landowning caste; the dominant caste
did not respond by attempting violently to inhibit this imitation, as has
happened elsewhere, but by voiding that code of pure, aristocratic
conduct as the privileged code: they began to adopt Western, modern
ways of behaving as the new prestige mode. In both cases, alternate
codes for conduct were chosen in order to adjust to changes in the
material sector; these normative improvisations thus reflect these

changes while buffering or masking their implications from the prevailing ideology.

Pragmatic redefinitions of identity may operate independently or in concert with semantic redefinitions. Barnett reports the case of high-caste landowners who had ruled supremely in their village despite their small number. They recognized that they could no longer control electoral politics once their economic dominance deteriorated. Rather than risk a publicly recognizable political defeat that would clearly dishonor them, they withdrew from this context of activity (Barnett 1973).

On the other hand, upwardly mobile castes may wish to mask their rise to avoid reprisal. Having gained some economic autonomy (Case studies 3 and 4), Jaffna untouchables innovated a seemingly innocuous context of activity: intervillage volleyball competitions (Case study 2). Volleyball enhanced communications among local segments of untouchables who were previously bound in service to their masters in their various villages and who could be ordered to fight one another if the masters were quarreling. This nonconfrontational activity offended no one but prefigured the wholesale mobilization of untouchables in later violent civil rights movements such as entry into temples, tea-shops, and laundries. The volleyball strategy of gathering forces on the sly is a pragmatic redefinition of identity structurally opposite to that of the upper-caste strategy: in the lower-caste change, a context of activity is improvised; in the upper-caste situation, a context of activity is voided. Both pragmatic redefinitions mask the recognition of socio-economic changes: in the lower-caste situation, such masking furthers the deterioration of the old system, while in the upper-caste situation, the masking delays the recognition of deterioration.

These examples do not exhaust the possibilities of covert operations. A strategy popular among terrorists in the mid-1970's (whether the Irish Republican Army, the Palestine Liberation Front, or the Jewish Defense League) is to carry out such covert activities as bombings and then to broadcast the achieved deed. Such advertising attempts to gain adherents to a small unit and to influence the intervention or nonintervention of relevant powers-that-be. On the other hand, small, non-establishment elites in new nations such as the Creole of Sierra Leone maintain an elaborate hidden structure of communications to avoid recognition of their influence by the three large ethnic identities in Sierra Leone who would probably reduce them to second-class citizens (as happened to the Ibo in Nigeria and to the Tamiḷs in Sri Lanka) if their influence were known.

The term liminal, borrowed from van Gennep's theory of the stages of a rite of transition (van Gennep 1909), implies a phase of societal transition "betwixt and between," a period when a society is dynamically reconstructing and thoroughly revising its material and symbolic structures in dominance, its patterns of activity and normative construction of reality. Liminal changes are here thought of as a specific application of my program of inventorying constraints between material and symbolic subsystems that negatively determine one another, that is, *limit* discrepancies (or contradictions) between subsystems that would otherwise not allow the system to operate. Liminal changes are further thought of as an application of the notion of a hierarchy of constraints within a societal structure. For the constraints between dominant subsystems and nondominant subsystems operate differently when the structure is dynamically reproducing itself from when the structure is in transition. Regarding societal reproduction, I noted earlier that those forms of figurative thought called ideology are structurally dominant with respect to the explicit normative order. Ideological assertions constrain the normative order because they both mask and reflect material conditions and relations of production that might otherwise allow normative rules to be perceived as oppressive. Regarding liminal changes, normative improvisations can operate as a buffer for the ideology, masking and reflecting changed conditions and relations of production that would otherwise contradict the ideology and thus vitiate the ideological assertions' credibility, authority, and persuasiveness. Liminal changes are accommodations between structurally subdominant material and symbolic subsystems that buffer dominant material and symbolic subsystems from the implications of these changes.

Pursuit of the analysis of liminal changes is facilitated by the analysis of the previously established (cf. "traditional") societal structure as a structure of ordered diversity. That is, a structure in which exist a contrast set of kinds of productive relations, a contrast set of contexts of productive activity, a contrast set of identity categories, and a contrast set of normative codes for conduct between identities. Liminal changes can then be charted against such a variegated backdrop as changes medial to positional change (where no redefinition of codes or context of activity need occur) and to structural changes (where there is a thorough revision of categories, codes, contexts, and ideology). For certain semantic changes (change in the definition of the collectivity, change in normative codes for conduct) and pragmatic changes (changes in the contexts in which activity is situated) may be viewed as improvisations accommodating changing socioeconomic constraints, improvisations in which categories, codes, activities, and contexts are rematched in new combinations. These liminal changes may be pervasive and may foreshadow future overt mobilizations of social identities and overt confrontations between identities precisely because they are low-profile, even covert, operations that can appear to conserve the previously established structure, that can mask the recognition of change from the eyes of others (including ethnographers), and that can mask from the prevailing ideology the recognition of changed activities that contradict it. In sum, liminal changes are here thought of as improvisations that retard for the moment while furthering the deterioration of a previously established structure in the longer term.

Liminal changes are holding actions. Semantic and pragmatic improvisations, or liminal changes, accommodate changed material conditions and relations of production and buffer the ideology from the implications of these changes; the implication of these improvisations is that the dimensions of explicit understandings become less predictable, less redundant one with the other. The answers to "Who are we?" "What should we be doing?" "Who were we?" etc., diverge in the course of semantic and pragmatic improvisations. There is, in short, a growing discrepancy within the subsystem of normative understandings. This is important to note because the materialist line of analysis concentrates on a very similar kind of contradiction: growing antagonism within a subsystem of productive relations as between masters and servants, employers and employed. Equal time should be given to contradictions within symbolic subsystems and within material subsystems.

Holding actions cannot last forever. As the following case illustrates, improvised semantic and pragmatic solutions to discrepancies between identities, codes for conduct, contexts of activity, and activities themselves reach a point where the change is reflected and the mask appears for what it is. After the second stage of the deterioration of the prevailing socioeconomic structure (Case study 4), violent confrontations occurred over the attempted implementation of national civil rights legislation giving low castes the right to enter temples, teashops, and laundries. According to the Hindu ideology of purity/impurity, such use would render the areas polluted. If untouchables were to enter a Hindu temple, priests would have continually to perform purification ceremonies and none of the normal rites could be performed.

This dilemma was solved in various Hindu temples beginning with the Nallur Kandasamy Kovil. Whereas low castes were previously not admitted past the doors (in temple/body symbolism, past the *feet*) of the temple and high castes were previously not admitted past the outer sanctum (the *shoulders*) of the temple, the solution was to grant admission to all castes up to the flagpole (the *genitalia*) within the temple: a retreat for the high castes, an advance for the low castes.

This change was not viewed by orthodox Hindus as an improvised solution (*samālippu*) to a dilemma (*piraccinai*), but as a farce (*tamasha*). To them, proper worship could no longer occur in the temple. Similarly, at this stage, landowners no longer justified their productive decisions with reference to the ideological proposition that workers on the land are part of the land and vice versa. Faced with the options of retaining tenants of long standing and probably losing the land to these tenants or supervising cultivation themselves, hiring laborers (frequently the same former tenants), and retaining legal ownership, landowners unhesitatingly chose the latter, often at some inconvenience to those of them employed elsewhere on the island. The old ideological justification gave way to the alternate ideology of private property. In this light, Barnett's critique of Singer's notion of compartmentalization (Introduction, this volume) is open to question. Singer holds that upper-caste persons are able to maintain one code of conduct at work (disregarding dictates of purity by dining with office-mates of different castes) and another at home. Barnett retorts that the very erecting of compartments is an ideological change. He asserts that the breaking of commensal rules in the office necessarily pollutes the high-caste worker, who then pollutes the home. What appears crucial is whether or not the improvisation is viewed as mediating a discrepancy between activity and ideology. If so, then the ideology retains its function of reintegrating discrepancies among individual motivation, normative codes for conduct, and activity. If not, then its function as a symbolic structure in dominance declines and an ideological revision may occur.

It appears pointless to attempt a rigorous differentiation between a stage of liminal changes when attempts are made to conserve the image that a prevailing socioeconomic structure remains relevant, and a stage of structural changes when a new socioeconomic structure is being constructed. For during a period of ferment, some social movements aim at radical revival movements, while others aim at liminal conserving changes, while still others aim at radical structural revisions. Except in extreme situations of conquest or revolution, there is nothing comparable to the proclamation, "The King is dead, long live the King!" And the majority of social movements with which we have to deal are not this extreme.

Rather, it appears more fruitful to consider a Janus-faced double process in which, during the period when the prevailing structure is deteriorating, social movements compete not only to win a privileged place in the present but also to define the hegemony (dominance susceptible of being reproduced on the long term) of the structures they are forwarding: "The King is dying; long live whomever of these Princes accedes to the crown!" This is a competitive process both on the plane of ideology (several competitive ideologies jostle to determine which of them shall be the next societal system of common sense) and on the plane of material relations (several competitive forms of productive relations each attempt to establish hegemony). It was for this reason, for example, that I questioned Geertz's suggestion that collective identities seek to be recognized and privileged; beyond this aim is the attempt to define the domain of identities of which one's collectivity is a part. Similarly, beyond the present aim of obtaining a greater share of material resources and of strategic information necessary to dominate affairs is the aim of instituting a structure (whether by violent establishment, by legislation, or, if possible, by drawing up a national constitution) which defines for the future a reproducible mode of socioeconomic relations between identities in the domain. These are complementary aspects of the process of the construction of structures of dominance which, when established, will operate to reproduce the totatity. If so, then what is salient for the understanding of structural change in South Asia?

This is not the place to review all the material determinants of structural change concerning identities in South Asia. Colleagues specializing in other world areas have remarked that the circuit of changes listed at the beginning of this Epilogue have analogues in Latin America, Africa, Southeast Asia. There are striking similarities in the ordered diversity of the "traditional" structure in productive activity. For example, Roseberry notes that the three kinds of rent (labor rent, rent in kind, rent in cash) could all be in effect in a Mexican hacienda (Roseberry 1976:51); a Jaffna Veḷḷāḷar landowner would frequently have these three kinds of productive relations (in Tamiḷ, *kudivele*, *varam*, and *kuttikai*). During the colonial period there were similarities between South Asia and other world areas in the variations of colonial constraints on local productive activity. For example, Stavenhagen contrasts the Latin American modes of production. In the hacienda mode of production, tied laborers worked on plantations producing various crops that were distributed to regional markets. In this mode, neither the technological forces of production nor the relations of production represented much of a dislocation from the previous Aztec mode. This contrasts with mercantile, export production of monoculture plantation crops (an export economy) with a relatively free labor force (Stavenhagen 1969). The second Latin American mode resembles the African experience as well as the Ceylonese coffee- and tea-plantation experience under the British colonials. Further, during the immediate postcolonial era, there were similarities between new nations in South Asia and in other world areas in the mobilization of primordial ties — ethnic, race, linguistic, and regional identities being politically exploited in the struggle for national power vacated by the colonials. Finally, during the last few years, there have been and are similarities between South Asia and other world areas in realignments of collectives, alliances crosscutting primordial ties after one ethnic unit has assumed power in the not-so-new nation state (Sri Lanka), or the resolution of primordial ties conflict by the establishment of separate states (Bangladesh and Pakistan). Developing nations in various parts of the world are constrained by multinational corporate activity that sometimes results in what has been called the development of under-development (Poulantzas 1974; Frank 1971). To be brief, in studying structural changes concerning collective identities, the material determinants in South Asia are hardly unique.

What differs in the areas, and what makes the study of changing identities in South Asia different from the study of changing identities in Latin America or elsewhere, is the relation of the region's ideology to all these changes.

And here we come to the point of intense debate between various interpreters of South Asian societies. Certainly many material features (relative resources in the production process, relative human resources in electoral politics, relative access to strategic information, etc.) influence the success or failure of a collective identity mobilized, in part, by an ideology that limits the horizon for orientation to the more explicit dimensions of understandings discussed earlier in this paper. The key unresolved question is how potential ideologies become viewed as persuasive, credible, and pervasive by potential adherents, and thus how they become effective in at least mobilizing the collectivity.

For in the course of the 1973 ICAES conference discussions (reviewed in the Introduction to this volume), contrasting approaches were expressed. Khare's and Lynch's voluntaristic approach locates the etiology of identity changes in technological, demographic, legal, and economic processes which create material expectations, yet fail to fulfill them, and thus incite the perception of new patterns of relative dis-advantage. Thus the basic change in South Asia is the shift from a holistic, noncompetitive order in which the religious ideology pre-dominates to a segmented, competitive, politico-economic order. Identities coalesce around voting; identity mobilization is an adaptive strategy for gaining access to strategic resources and power. Other approaches stress the ideological or cognitive complement to the observed tendency to form temporary boundaries of varying sizes and ranges in political competition. In Marriott and Inden's ethnosocio-logical approach (this volume), the indigenous cognitive principle of the "nonduality of natural substance and code for conduct" is posited as underlying the structure and change of social identities. Changing frontiers of identification are examined in relation to a traditional cognitive dynamic: the propensity to recombine the *"coded dividual substances"* which define *jāti* categories. They reject the colonialist precedent of giving analytic priority to any privileged level of *jāti* [caste]. Since the form of this substantial thought remains the same, they thus assume no radical discontinuity between the previous and the emerging structure of identities in South Asia. In Barnett's ideological approach, aspects of the ethnosociological approach are combined with that of Louis Dumont (1970). Barnett explains the emerging structure of identities in terms of an ideological shift in content: the redefinition of the dominant symbols in ideology. In the previous holistic, hierarchical caste ideology, a *jāti*'s sharing of natural substance and its code for conduct are cognitively nondual. Substantialization is the ideological shift from nonduality to duality: a substantialized caste identity is defined by natural substance alone, while a wide range of previously proscribed codes for conduct are now permitted, codes which are also followed by other castes. Barnett sees this ideological shift as underlying a whole panoply of crosscutting identities now emerging in south India such as racism, ethnicity, class, and cultural nationalism. This approach thus posits a radical discontinuity between previous and present structure. Although Dumont was not present at the conference, his views on Hindu ideology were frequently referred to as a bench mark for the alternative views under discussion. His approach defines a global ideology of holism and hierarchy based on the separation and the interdependence of the pure and the impure. This ideology is held to encompass spheres of politics and economy. Therefore, recent changes in Indian political economy do not affect the global ideology. This ideology draws support from esoteric scriptural writings. There are differences of opinion as to whether the contemporary ideological scene represents a clear discontinuity from the previous ideology or continuities and transformations from that ideology, or whether the global ideology has changed at all. There are differences of opinion as to whether we should be concerned with esoteric ideology, exoteric ideology, or a version of ideology in which correspondences between various levels of ideological texts are noted. There are differences of opinion as to whether continuities of form or of content are to be stressed. There are differences of opinion as to the weight given to ideology *vis-à-vis* practical interests.

My own view at that time has changed markedly, because I returned to Sri Lanka, armed with this set of alternative approaches. The result is a final entry in this inventory of changing constraints between subsystems in a changing society. The notions of negative determination and of a hierarchy of constraints appear useful once again in thinking about the influence of ideology after the deterioration of the prevailing structure. Changes in the mode of production may proceed so far that the normative subsystem is no longer able to buffer the implications of changed productive activity from the ideology and this ideology can no longer be accepted as relevant, can no longer integrate individual affect, codes for conduct, and activity. But does a previously dominant ideology simply evaporate when its meager relevance to these aspects of reality is apparent?

To my mind, a previously dominant ideology, while not positively determining the form and content of new competitive ideologies, at least negatively determines (that is, sets limits to) how radical a departure these new ideologies may take from the previous ideology, the previous horizon for orientation. My recent studies of two social movements in Jaffna, a high-caste federalist or nationalist or separatist (depending on your viewpoint) and a low-caste mobility movement, suggest that it is an exoteric, populist system of common sense that provides the symbolic stockpile on which these two movements draw. Each movement redefines such central symbols as "sharers of natural bodily substance" (*cakōtarar*) and "the scent of the earth" (*maṉ vasaṉai*) in different was according to the collectivity to be formed, the pragmatic diagnosis of socioeconomic needs and remedies, and other shared understandings. In my view, then, it is a previously dominant exoteric ideology that sets the limits to the directions new ideologies must take if they are to integrate affect, codes for conduct, and activities, if they are to be viewed as credible, authoritative, and persuasive, and thus to mobilize collectivities of persons in an effective social identity. Restated, the previously dominant ideology sets outer limits to the form and content of emerging, competitive ideologies — each ideology attempting to provide the new horizon for orientation. At this stage, the dead ideology may be reborn in the guise of radical, competitive ideologies underlying these emerging competitive social movements.

Many changes concerning emerging identities are not particular to South Asia. Colleagues have pointed out parallel processes occurring in a number of areas in the world. What is particular about South Asia is its ideology. In this volume we have seen four contrasting versions of that ideology: is it hierarchical and holistic? particulate and dividual? substantialized and nonholistic? politico-economic, competitive, and nonholistic? none of the above? At this point, I must defer to future research for a more definitive answer as to its nature, that is, its relation to the sweeping set of changes observable in South Asia today.

REFERENCES

ALTHUSSER, L., *et al.*
   1968   *Lire le capital*, two volumes. Paris: Maspero.
AVINERI, SHLOMO
   1968   *The social and political thought of Karl Marx*. Cambridge: Cambridge University Press.
BAILEY, FREDERICK G.
   1969   *Stratagems and spoils: a social anthropology of politics*. New York: Schocken.

BARNETT, STEVE
1973   "The process of withdrawal in a south Indian caste," in *Entre-preneurship and modernization of occupational cultures in South Asia.* Edited by Milton Singer. Chapel Hill, N.C.: Duke University Press.

BARTH, FREDRIK
1959   Segmentary opposition and the theory of games: a study of Pathan organization. *Journal of the Royal Anthropological Institute* 89:5-21.
1967   On the study of social change. *American Anthropologist* 69 (6):661-669.

BARTH, FREDRIK, *editor*
1969   *Ethnic groups and boundaries: the social organization of cultural difference.* Boston: Little, Brown.

BATESON, GREGORY
1972   *Steps to an ecology of mind.* New York: Ballantine.

BECK, BRENDA E. F.
1973   *Peasant society in Koṅku.* Vancouver: University of British Columbia Press.

BERGER, PETER L., THOMAS LUCKMAN
1967   *The social construction of reality.* Garden City, N.Y.: Doubleday.

BERREMAN, GERALD D.
1972   Social identity and social interaction in urban India. *American Anthropologist* 74(3):567-586.

BLACK, MAX
1962   *Models and metaphors.* Ithaca, N.Y.: Cornell University Press.

BLOCH, MAURICE, *editor*
1975   *Marxist analyses and social anthropology.* New York: John Wiley and Sons.

BOULDING, KENNETH E.
1968   "General systems theory — skeleton of science," in *Modern systems research for the behavioral scientist.* Edited by Walter Buckley. Chicago: Aldine.

BRASS, PAUL R.
1974   *Language, religion, and politics in north India.* New York and London: Cambridge University Press.

BUCHLER, I. R., H. G. NUTINI
1970   *Game theory in the behavioral sciences.* Pittsburgh: University of Pittsburgh Press.

BURTON, ROGER V., JOHN W. M. WHITING
1965   "The absent father and cross-sex identity," in *Reader in comparative religion: an anthropological approach* (second edition). Edited by William A. Lessa and Evon Z. Vogt. New York: Harper and Row.

CARROLL, LUCY
1975   Caste, social change, and the social scientist: a note on the ahistorical approach to Indian social history. *Journal of Asian Studies* 35(1):63-84.

CICOUREL, AARON V.
1973   *Cognitive sociology: language and meaning in social interaction.* Baltimore: Penguin.

COHN, BERNARD S.
1955   "The changing status of a depressed caste," in *Village India*. Edited by McKim Marriott. Chicago: University of Chicago Press.
1969   "Structural change in Indian rural society," in *Land control and social structure in Indian history*. Edited by Robert Eric Frykenberg. Madison: University of Wisconsin Press.

DAVID, KENNETH
1973   Until marriage do us part: a cultural account of Jaffna Tamil categories for kinsmen. *Man* 8(4):521-535.
1974   Spatial organization and normative schemes in Jaffna, northern Sri Lanka. *Modern Ceylon Studies* 3(1).
1975   "The standing and the moving: the previously established and the emerging socio-cultural structure in Jaffna, northern Sri Lanka." Series of three lectures presented to the Department of Anthropology, School of Oriental and African Studies, University of London. March.

DJURFELDT, GÖRAN, STAFFAN LINDBERG
1975   *Behind poverty: the social formation in a Tamil village*. London: Curzon.

DUMONT, LOUIS
1970   *Homo hierarchicus: an essay on the caste system*. Chicago: University of Chicago Press.

DURKHEIM, EMILE
1949   [1893] *The division of labor in society*. Translated by George Simpson. Glencoe: Free Press. (Originally published as *De la division du travail social*.)

FIRTH, RAYMOND
1951   *Elements of social organization*. London: Watts.

FRANK, ANDRÉ GUNDER
1971   *Capitalism and underdevelopment in Latin America. Historical Studies of Chile and Brazil*. Harmondsworth: Penguin.

FRIEDMAN, JONATHAN
1974   Marxism, structuralism and vulgar materialism. *Man*, new series 9(3):444-469.
1975   "Tribes, states, and transformations," in *Marxist analyses and social anthropology*. Edited by Maurice Bloch, 161-202. New York: John Wiley and Sons.

FRYKENBERG, ROBERT ERIC
1969   "Introduction," in *Land control and social structure in Indian history*. Edited by Robert Eric Frykenberg. Madison: University of Wisconsin Press.

GEERTZ, CLIFFORD
1963   "The integrative revolution: primordial sentiments and civil politics in the new states," in *Old societies and new states: the quest for modernity in Asia and Africa*. Edited by Clifford Geertz. New York: Free Press.
1973   "Ideology as a cultural system," in *The interpretation of cultures: selected essays by Clifford Geertz*. New York: Basic Books.

GODELIER, MAURICE
1972   *Rationality and irrationality in economics*. Translated by Brian Pearce. New York: Monthly Review Press.
1973   *Horizon, trajets marxistes en anthropologie*. Bibliothèque d'Anthropologie. Paris: François Maspéro.

1975   "Modes of production, kinship, and demographic structures," in *Marxist analyses and social anthropology*. Edited by Maurice Bloch, 3-28. New York: John Wiley and Sons.

GOODENOUGH, WARD H.
1965   "Rethinking 'status' and 'role': toward a general model of the cultural organization of social relationships," in *The relevance of models for social anthropology*. Edited by Michael Banton. Association of Social Anthropology Monograph 1. New York: Praeger.
1969   Frontiers of cultural anthropology: social organization. *Proceedings of the American Philosophical Society* 113(5):329-335.

GREENBERG, JOSEPH H.
1964   "Linguistics and ethnology," in *Language in culture and society*. Edited by Dell Hymes. New York: Harper and Row.

HAGEN, E. E.
1962   *On the theory of social change*. Homewood, Ill.: Dorsey.

HARDGRAVE, ROBERT
1969   *The Nadars of Tamilnad: the political culture of a community in change*. Berkeley: University of California Press.

HARRIS, MARVIN
1966   The cultural ecology of India's sacred cattle. *Current Anthropology* 7(1):51-66.
1969   Monistic determinism: anti-service. *Southwestern Journal of Anthropology* 25(2):198-206.

HEIDER, KARL G.
1972   "Environment, subsistence, and society," in *Annual review of anthropology*, volume one. Edited by Bernard J. Siegel, 207-226. Palo Alto, Calif.: Annual Reviews.

KAHN, JOEL
1975   "Economic scale and the cycle of petty commodity production in west Sumatra," in *Marxist analyses and social anthropology*. Edited by Maurice Bloch, 137-160. New York: John Wiley and Sons.

KESSINGER, TOM
1974   *Vilyatpur 1848-1968: social and economic change in a north Indian village*. Berkeley: University of California Press.

KHARE, RAVINDRA S.
1970   *The changing Brahmans: associations and elites among the Kanya-Kubjas of north India*. Chicago: University of Chicago Press.

KROEBER, ALFRED LEWIS
1940   Three centuries of women's dress fashions: a quantitative analysis (with Jane Richardson). *University of California Anthropological Records*. 5(2):111-154.

KUMAR, DHARMA
1965   *Land and caste in south India*. Cambridge: Cambridge University Press.

LACLAU, ERNESTO
1972   The specificity of the political: the Poulantzas-Miliband debate. Translated by Elizabeth Nash and William Rich. *Economy and Society* 1:87-110.

LEACH, EDMUND
1965   *Political systems of highland Burma*. Boston: Beacon.

LEVI, EDWARD H.
1948   *An introduction to legal reasoning*. Chicago: University of Chicago Press.

LÉVI-STRAUSS, CLAUDE
1963   "Social structure," in *Structural anthropology*. Translated by Claire Jacobson and Brooke Grundfest Schoepf, 277-323. New York: Basic Books.

LYNCH, OWEN M.
1969   *The politics of untouchability*. New York: Columbia University Press.

MALCOLM X
1973   *The autobiography of Malcolm X*. New York: Ballantine.

MORRIS, CHARLES W.
1935   Foundations of the theory of signs. *International encyclopedia of unified science* 1(2).

MURPHY, ROBERT F.
1971   *The dialectics of social life: alarms and excursions in anthropological theory*. New York and London: Basic Books.

NARROLL, RAOUL
1964   Ethnic unit classification. *Current Anthropology* 5(4).

NASH, JUNE
1975   "Nationalism and fieldwork," in *Annual review of anthropology*, volume four. Edited by Bernard J. Siegel, 225-247. Palo Alto, Calif.: Annual Reviews.

NICHOLAS, RALPH W.
1967   Ritual hierarchy and social relations in rural Bengal. *Contributions to Indian Sociology*, new series 1.
1973   "Social and political movements," in *Annual review of anthropology*, volume two. Edited by Bernard J. Siegel, 63-84. Palo Alto, Calif.: Annual Reviews.

OBEYESEKERE, GANANATH
1967   *Land tenure in village Ceylon*. Cambridge: Cambridge University Press.

O'LAUGHLIN, BRIDGET
1975   "Marxist approaches in anthropology," in *Annual review of anthropology*, volume four. Edited by Bernard J. Siegel, 341-370. Palo Alto, Calif.: Annual Reviews.

ORANS, MARTIN
1965   *The Santal: a tribe in search of a Great Tradition*. Detroit: Wayne State University Press.

PARSONS, TALCOTT
1959   "An approach to the sociology of knowledge," in *Transactions of the fourth world congress of sociology* 25-49. Milan and Stressa.

PEIRCE, CHARLES SANDERS
1965   *Collected papers of Charles Sanders Peirce*, volume one: *Principles of Philosophy*. Cambridge: Belknap Press of Harvard University Press.

PERCHONOCK, NORMA, OSWALD WERNER
1969   Navaho systems of classification: some implications for ethnoscience. *Ethnology* 8:229-242.

PIAGET, JEAN
1971   *Structuralism*. New York: Basic Books.

POULANTZAS, NICOS
1974   Internationalisation of capitalist relations and the nation-state, *Economy and Society* 3(2):145-179.

PYE, LUCIEN W.
1962   *Politics, personality and nation building: Burma's search for identity*. New Haven and London: Yale University Press.

RAPPAPORT, ROY A.
1968   *Pigs for the ancestors: ritual in the ecology of a New Guinea people*. New Haven: Yale University Press.

REY, P.-PH., G. DUPRÉ
1973   Reflections on the pertinence of a theory of the history of exchange. *Economy and Society* 2(2)

ROSEBERRY, WILLIAM
1976   Rent, differentiation, and the development of capitalism among peasants. *American Anthropologist* 78(1):45–59.

SAHLINS, MARSHALL D.
1969   Economic anthropology and anthropological economics. *Social Sciences Information 8*.
1972   *Stone age economics*. Chicago: Aldine.

SALISBURY, RICHARD F.
1973   "Economic anthropology," in *Annual review of anthropology*, volume two. Edited by Bernard J. Siegel, 85–94. Palo Alto, Calif.: Annual Reviews.

SCHNEIDER, DAVID M.
1965   "Some muddles in the models," in *The relevance of models for social anthropology*. Association for Social Anthropology Monograph 1. London: Tavistock.
1968   *American kinship: a cultural account*. Englewood Cliffs, N.J.: Prentice-Hall.

SHILS, EDWARD
1963   "On the comparative study of the new states," in *Old societies and new states: the quest for modernity in Asia and Africa*. Edited by Clifford Geertz. New York: Free Press.

SILVERSTEIN, MICHAEL
1974   "Indexes and pragmatic meaning." Seminar delivered to the Department of Anthropology, University of Chicago. June.

SIMMEL, GEORG
1950   "The negative character of collective behavior," in *The sociology of Georg Simmel*. New York: Free Press.

SINGER, MILTON
1973   "Introduction: the modernization of occupational cultures in South Asia," in *Entrepreneurship and modernization of occupational cultures in South Asia*. Edited by Milton Singer. Chapel Hill, N.C.: Duke University Press.

SNODGRASS, DONALD R.
1966   *Ceylon: an export economy in transition*. Homewood, Ill.: Richard D. Irwin.

SRINIVAS, MYSORE N.
1952   *Religion and society among the Coorgs of south India*. Bombay: Asia Publishing House. (Second printing 1965.)
1966   *Social change in modern India*. Berkeley: University of California Press.

STAVENHAGEN, RODOLFO
1969   *Les classes sociales dans les sociétés agraires*. Paris: Anthropos.

STEIN, BURTON
1969 "Integration of the agrarian system in south India," in *Land control and social structure in Indian history*. Edited by Robert Eric Frykenberg. Madison: University of Wisconsin Press.

SWARTZ, MARC J., VICTOR W. TURNER, ARTHUR TUDEN
1966 "Introduction," in *Political anthropology*. Edited by Marc J. Swartz, Victor W. Turner and Arthur Tuden. Chicago: Aldine.

TERRAY, EMMANUAL
1975 "Classes and class consciousness in the Abron kingdom of Gyaman," in *Marxist analyses and social anthropology*. Edited by Maurice Bloch, 85–136. New York: John Wiley and Sons.

TESSLER, MARK A., WILLIAM M. O'BARR, DAVID SPAIN
1973 *Tradition and identity in changing Africa*. New York: Harper and Row.

TURNER, TERENCE
1973 Review of *Structuralism* by Jean Piaget. *American Anthropologist* 75(2):351–373.

VAN BAAL, J.
1971 *Symbols for communication: an introduction to the anthropological study of religion*. Assen: van Gorcum.

VAN GENNEP, ARNOLD
1909 *Les rites de passage. Étude systématique des rites*. Librairie Critique. Paris: Émile Nourry.

WALLACE, ANTHONY F. C.
1961 "The psychic unity of human groups," in *Studying personality cross-culturally*. Edited by Bert Kaplan. New York: Harper and Row.

WATSON, LAWRENCE C.
1972 Urbanization and identity dissonance: the Guajiro case. *American Anthropologist* 74(5).

WEBER, MAX
1964 *The theory of social and economic organization*. Translated by A. M. Henderson and Talcott Parsons. New York: Free Press.

WHITTEN, NORMAN E., DOROTHEA S. WHITTEN
1972 "Social strategies and social relationships," in *Annual review of anthropology*, volume one. Edited by Bernard J. Siegel, 247–270. Palo Alto, Calif.: Annual Reviews.

WRIGGINS, W. HOWARD
1960 *Ceylon: dilemmas of a new nation*. Princeton, N.J.: Princeton University Press.

YALMAN, NUR
1971 *Under the bo tree: studies in caste, kinship and marriage in the interior of Ceylon*. Berkeley: University of California Press.

Biographical Notes

ZEYAUDDIN AHMAD received his Ph.D. from Patna University in 1962. Currently he is Reader and Head of the Department of Sociology there. His principal research interests are the history of social thought, Indian social institutions, and social anthropology. His publications include *The social philosophy of L. T. Hobhouse* and (in Hindi) *Indian social institutions*.

AYINIPALLI AIYAPPAN (1905–), born in Kerala, was educated at Madras and the London School of Economics, London University, under Professor B. Malinowski and Sir Raymond Firth. He worked as Curator for anthropology and later as Director at the Government Museum, Madras (1929-1958); as Professor of Anthropology, Utkal University, Orissa (1958-1966); as U.G.C. Professor in the Andhra University, Andhra State; as Vice-Chancellor, Kerala University (1968-1970), and as Special Officer, Tribal Research and Training Institute, Calicut, Kerala State (1970-1972). Some publications are: *Social revolution in a Kerala village* (Asia) and *Travas and culture change* (Madras Government Press). His main interests include anthropology of the tribes of southern India and social change.

MAHADEV L. APTE (1931–) received his M.A. degrees from the Bombay and London Universities and a Ph.D. from the University of Wisconsin, Madison, Wisconsin. He taught at the University of Wisconsin and at the University of Poona, India, and has been in the Department of Anthropology at Duke University since 1965. His major research interests are sociolinguistics, South Asian languages, societies and cultures, the ethnography of humor, and acculturation and ethnicity. His publications include several articles on various aspects of linguistic diversity in India and on the society and culture in Maharashtra.

STEVE BARNETT (1941–) studied at Antioch College and the London School of Economics and Political Science, receiving his Ph.D. in Anthropology from the University of Chicago. He has taught at Roosevelt University, the University of Chicago, and New York University and is currently Bicentennial Preceptor at Princeton University. He has done extensive fieldwork in South India and the United States and is especially interested in developing marxist approaches to ideology through the study of symbolic form and action. His publications include articles on the interrelations among the concepts of caste, class, race, ethnicity, and nationalism in rural and urban south India and the United States. He is presently doing research on the Post Office in New York.

KENNETH DAVID (1943–) studied at Wesleyan University and in 1972 took his Ph.D. in Anthropology from the University of Chicago. He is now Associate Professor in the Department of Anthropology at Michigan State University. He has conducted two field studies of symbolic and social structure in Jaffna, Northern Sri Lanka, studying variations in structure in fishing, artisan, and agricultural villages. He is especially interested in symbolic and materialist approaches. His publications include articles on kinship, social stratification, and spatial structure. He is currently doing research in Jaffna, testing the implications of the contrasting approaches to identity change proposed in this volume.

MOHAN K. GAUTAM (1937–) studied Social and Cultural Anthropology at the universities of Lucknow, India (M.A., 1958) and Leiden, the Netherlands (Doctoral, 1963). He joined the Institute of Social Sciences, Agra University, in 1959 and moved to the Anthropology Department at Lucknow University in 1960, while occupying several research posts in India. Since 1962 he has been a Member of Staff of the Kern Institute, Leiden University, and is attached to the National Museum of Ethnology, Leiden. He has conducted his fieldwork among the North and Northeast Indian tribes, minority groups of South Asia, and Hindustanis in the West Indies and Surinam. His publications include works on ethnographical museology, the Santal-Munda tribes, and various village studies. He has also produced an ethnohistorical film (16 mm.) on *The Emigration of British Indians to Surinam*. Currently he is working on the Kṛṣnaite rural rituals of Brajabhūmi, the cult of the dead among the Surinamese Hindustani, the emergence of

Santal-Munda identities, and modernity and traditions reflected in modern Indian literature.

RONALD INDEN (1940–   ) received his Ph.D. from the University of Chicago in 1972 and currently teaches there in the departments of History and South Asian Languages and Civilizations. His publications include cultural and historical studies of caste, kinship, and marriage in India.

DORANNE JACOBSON (1940–   ) received her undergraduate education at the University of Michigan and the University of London, and she was awarded her Ph.D. with distinction by Columbia University in 1970. A recipient of a postdoctoral grant from the American Council of Learned Societies, she held an Ogen Mills Fellowship at the American Museum of Natural History. She has taught at the City College of New York and is currently Research Associate in the Southern Asian Institute at Columbia University. From 1965 to 1967 she conducted research on women's roles and modernization in Central India. Her publications include articles on the Navajo Indians of the American Southwest, the women of North and Central India, the seclusion of women among Hindus and Muslims, women's music, women and property rights, and modernization in village India.

R. S. KHARE (1936–   ) received his Ph.D. from the University of Lucknow in 1962, after teaching anthropology at Kanya-Kubja College, Lucknow. He was Post-Doctoral Fellow at the University of Chicago during 1963-1966. He taught anthropology at the University of Wisconsin–Green Bay and chaired the Department on Modernization Studies from 1966 until 1971, when he came to the University of Virginia as Professor of Anthropology. He has been Senior Fellow of the American Institute of Indian Studies, a Guest Fellow of the Indian Institute of Advanced Study, and a Visiting Professor at École Pratique des Hautes Études, Sorbonne, Paris, and at the Institute for Advanced Study, Princeton. His main interests are structuralism, semiotics, and South Asian social, legal, and medical organizations, and Western individualism. His publications include works on the Kanya-Kubja Brahmans and medical and legal anthropology, as well as empirical analyses of the Indian village: caste, kinship, marriage, and foods and rituals.

OWEN M. LYNCH (1931–   ) received his B.A. from Fordham University in 1956 and his Ph.D. from Columbia University in 1966. He taught at the State University of New York, Binghamton, until 1973 and is currently Charles F. Noyes Professor of Urban Anthropology at

New York University. His main interests are in urban studies and disadvantaged groups in India. He was in India from 1962 until 1964 and again from 1970 to 1971. His major publications are on the Neo-Buddhists and the Bombay squatters.

LAKSHMAN KUMAR MAHAPATRA (1929–   ) received his B.A. with honors in 1948 and his M.A. in Anthropology in 1952 from Calcutta University. In 1960 he received his Ph.D. from Hamburg University (*magna cum laude*) in Social Anthropology and Sociology. He has had teaching and research assignments at Lucknow, Gauhati, and Karnatak universities, and under the Orissa State and Indian Union (N.E.F.A.) governments before joining Utkal University, Bhubaneswar in 1964, where he became Professor in 1967. For the summer semester in 1968 he was Visiting Professor at Hamburg University. He has worked among the Hill Bhuiyan (Orissa), Oraon (Orissa and Bihar), Siddi (Karnatak), Gond (U.P.), and Dafla and Miji (Anunachal). His present research interests are: social movements and the transformation of tribal societies in India; the role of the temples and Hindu kings in the caste system; and social changes in peasant life in India. His publications include *Folklore of Orissa* (now in press at the National Book Trust of India). He is Editor of *Man in Society*, the Bulletin of the Department of Anthropology, Utkal University.

SITAKANT MAHAPATRA (1937–   ) received his B.A. with distinction from Utkal University in 1957, his M.A. from Allahabad University in 1959, and completed a course in development studies at Cambridge University (U.K.). As a Member of the Indian Administrative Service, he has worked among the Munda, Oraon, and Santal tribal communities. He has edited two anthologies of tribal poetry with critical introductions and has published several articles on the socioeconomic changes in these communities.

SUBHASH CHANDRA MALIK (1932–   ) received his M.A. in Anthropology in 1953 from the University of Delhi; his Postgraduate Diploma from the University of London, Institute of Archaeology, in 1955; and his Ph.D. from the M.S. University of Baroda in 1964. From 1956 to 1970 he taught and did research in prehistoric archaeology and anthropology at Baroda. He was associated with the University of Chicago, Department of Anthropology, with the South Asia Center and with the Oriental Institute from 1963 to 1965. From 1966 until 1968 he was a Senior Fellow at the Indian Institute of Advanced Study, Simla. In 1970, he joined the Indian Institute of Advanced Study as a Fellow and Coordinator of the Scheme on "Source book of Indian and Asian civilization." At present he continues to work on the Scheme, working on social reform, dissent, and protest movements in Indian civilization. His main interests are prehistoric archaeology, physical anthropology, and the interpretation of Indian history and civilization within a social science framework.

McKim Marriott (1924–) studied at Harvard, the University of Pennsylvania, and Stanford and in 1955 took his Ph.D. in Anthropology from the University of Chicago. He is now Professor in the Department of Anthropology and in the Social Sciences Collegiate Division at Chicago. He has conducted three field studies of culture and social organization in India, working in agricultural villages of western Uttar Pradesh over an eighteen-year span of change, and researching the history and community life of a traditional city in Maharashtra.

Joan P. Mencher (1930–) received her Ph.D. from Columbia University in 1958. Between the period of 1958 and 1960, she did postdoctoral research in India. She has taught at Lehman College and the City University Graduate Center since 1968 and is now a Professor of Anthropology at Lehman. Having studied problems of change and development in South India, she is currently engaged in research in the field of agriculture.

M. S. A. Rao (1926–) received his M.A. with distinction from the University of Mysore in 1949 and his Ph.D. from the University of Bombay in 1953. He joined the faculty of the University of Delhi in 1955 where he became Professor of Sociology in 1969. He was Visiting Lecturer at the University of London 1966–1967 and in 1972–1973 he was Visiting Professor at Syracuse, Pennsylvania, and Duke universities and Honorary Research Associate at the University of Chicago. His main interests, on which he has published several books, are urbanization, sociology and economic development, and the sociology of social movements. He has served as the Secretary of the Indian Sociological Society and as the Convenor of the Indian Council for Social Science and Research.

Surajit Sinha (1926–) received his B.Sc. (Honors) in Geology, and a M.Sc. in Anthropology from Calcutta University. A Fullbright and Smith-Mundh scholar, he received his Ph.D. in Anthropology in 1956 from Northwestern University. He has taught anthropology at the universities of Chicago, California, Duke, Visva-Bharati, and Calcutta and was Fellow at the Center for Advanced Study in the Behavioral Sciences at Stanford, 1963–1964. Presently, he is Director of the Anthropological Survey of India and President of the Indian Anthropological Society. He is editor of *Man in India* and *Journal of the Indian Anthropological Society.*

LALIT P. VIDYARTHI (1931-   ) received his doctorate from the University of Chicago and is now Professor and Chairman of the Department of Anthropology at the University of Ranchi, India. Currently (1974–1978) he is the President of the International Union of Anthropological and Ethnological Sciences and of the Xth International Congress of Anthropological and Ethnological Sciences to be held in India in 1978. Dr. Vidyarthi is the President of the Indian Anthropological Association, a Founder Member of the Indian Council of Social Sciences Research, Chairman of the Task Force on Development of Tribal Areas of the Planning Commission, and a member of the Central Council on Tribal Research, Institute of the Ministry of Home Affairs, Government of India. He is Founder Editor of *The Journal of Social Research*, *The Indian Anthropologist*, and *The Research Journal of Ranchi University*. His numerous publications include books and articles as well as many volumes which he has edited. His major fields of research are the tribal culture of India; the Andaman and Nicobar Islands; urban-industrial, political, and action anthropology; Indian civilization, the history of Indian culture, folklore, and village studies.

CHRISTOPH VON FÜRER-HAIMENDORF (1909   ) studied anthropology in Vienna and London. From 1931 till 1939 he was on the staff of the University of Vienna and in 1936–1937 he undertook fieldwork in the Naga Hills (India). From 1939 to 1949 he lived in India and carried out extensive anthropological research among the aboriginal tribes of the Deccan and Orissa. In 1944–1945, he served the Government of India as Special Officer in the North East Frontier Agency, and from 1945 to 1949 he held the joint positions of Adviser for Tribes to the Hyderabad State Government and Professor of Anthropology in Osmania University. Since 1951 he has been Professor of Asian Anthropology in the University of London and Head of the Department of Anthropology and Sociology in the School of Oriental and African Studies. For the past two decades he has mainly concentrated on research in Nepal where he conducted several field projects. His main publications range over the field of South Asian and Himalayan anthropology and also include comparative studies on morals and values. Minor publications relate to research in the Philippines.

SUSAN S. WADLEY (1943-   ) received her B.A. with distinction from Carleton College and her Ph.D. with distinction from the University of Chicago. She was an Intern in Indian Civilization at the University of

Chicago and currently is Assistant Professor of Anthropology at Syracuse University, where she is also affiliated with the South Asia Program. Her main interests are in traditions and religious beliefs in India, where she returned to do research in 1974–1975.

Index of Names

Index of Subjects